RECREATION & LEISURE

IN MODERN SOCIETY

RECREATION & LEISURE
IN MODERN SOCIETY

Fifth Edition

Richard Kraus
Temple University

Jones and Bartlett Publishers

Sudbury, Massachusetts

Boston   London   Singapore

Photo Acknowledgements

Page 12 (top) Courtesy Lewis Hartman, New York Junior Tennis Leage; (center) Frederick Charles, Manufacturers Hanover; (bottom) National Capitol Commission, Ottawa, Ontario, Canada Page 13 (top) Associated Newspapers Limited; (center) Gillinson Barnett & Partners; (bottom) Jed Williamson Page 48 (top) Courtesy Prof. Sue Durrant, University of Washington; (center) Montgomery County Recreation; (bottom) Courtesy Steve Gergick, Orlando Naval Training Center Page 49 (top) The Washington Post; (center) Courtesy Karen Sposato, Westchester County, NY, Department of Parks, Recreation, and Conservation; (bottom) Courtesy Eileen Dimes, CoreStates US PRO Cycling Championship Page 71 (top) Courtesy Paul Fogal, Pocono Adventure, Inc., Jim Thorpe, PA; (bottom) Courtesy Robert Leake, Church of Jesus Christ of Latter-Day Saints, Salt Lake City, UT Page 103 (top) Courtesy Ralph Cryder, Long Beach, CA, Department of Parks, Recreation, and Marine; (center and bottom) Texas Women's University Community Dance Center; Photographer, Allan Key, *Denton Record Chronicle* Page 125 (top) Courtesy Wendy Tank-Nielsen, Philadelphia Tennis Patrons; (middle) National Association of Police Athletic Leagues; (bottom) Boys and Girls Clubs of America, Atlanta, GA Page 163 (top, middle, and bottom) Robert Gardner and Karl Heider, *Gardens of War* (Random House, New York) and courtesy of Film Study Center, Harvard University Page 261 (top left and bottom) Courtesy Steve Sandoval, Santa Fe, NM Convention and Visitors Bureau; (top right) Calgary, Alberta, Canada, Convention and Visitors Bureau page 295 (top) Dubuque Casino Belle, Dubuque, IA; (center) Courtesy Busch Gardens, Williamsburg, VA; (bottom) Skirmish USA—Paintball in the Poconos, Jim Thorpe, PA Page 337 (top) RCH, Inc., San Francisco, CA; Photographer Bill Cogan; (center) Courtesy Professor Janet Sable, University of New Hampshire, and Northeast Passage; (bottom) South East Consortium for Special Services, Inc., Mamaroneck, NY

Recreation and Leisure in Modern Society, Fifth Edition

Library of Congress Cataloging-in-Publication Data

Kraus, Richard G.
      Recreation and leisure in modern society/Richard Kraus.—5th ed.
          p. cm.
      Includes bibliographical references and index.
      ISBN 0-7637-0604-3
      1. Recreation—North America. 2. Recreation—North America-
-History. 3. Leisure—Social aspects—North America. 4. Play—
North America--Psychological aspects. 5. Recreation—Vocational
guidance—North America. I. Title.
GV51.K7 1997
790'.097--dc20   96-1675

Printed in the United States of America
00 99 98 97   10 9 8 7 6 5 4 3 2

To Renée

Contents

EXAM #2

3
244
-136
105

11   Voluntary Nonprofit, Commercial, and Private-Membership Organizations   279

12   Specialized Agencies: *Armed Forces, Employee, Campus, and Therapeutic Recreation Service*   317

Preface

Recreation and Leisure in Modern Society has been used as a foundations text in hundreds of college and university recreation, park, and leisure-studies curricula over the past three decades. Since the publication of the first edition in 1971, immense changes have taken place in the recreational patterns of Americans and Canadians, young and old, as well as in the organized leisure-service field. This new edition reflects these changes.

In the 1960s, the primary focus of study in recreation and leisure-studies departments was on programs conducted by local government recreation and park agencies. Today, the field embraces a variety of sponsors, including nonprofit and commercial organizations and military, campus, private-membership, employee-service, and therapeutic recreation programs. In addition, the original emphasis on organized recreation as a quality-of-life service has been replaced first by a social-service approach, then an entrepreneurial, marketing-based emphasis, and most recently a benefits-based approach.

This edition of *Recreation and Leisure in Modern Society,* therefore, provides both a broad conceptual introduction to the study of recreation and leisure as societal phenomena and a detailed overview of the leisure-service system and the recreation and park profession today. While it makes extensive use of citations from the popular press, newspapers, and news magazines in order to document recreation's role in everyday life, it also incorporates findings of numerous articles and research studies drawn from a number of scholarly periodicals. These include the *Journal of Leisure Research,* the *Journal of Park and Recreation Administration,* the *Journal of Physical Education, Recreation and Dance,* the *Therapeutic Recreation Journal, Parks and Recreation, Trends, Recreation Canada, Leisure Sciences,* and *Leisure Studies.*

While the text does not contain a systematic account of the history of recreation and park development in Canada or of the present-day leisure-service system in that country, it does include numerous references to Canadian recreation and park programs. Readers seeking more information about recreation and leisure in Canada should consult books by Elsie McFarland or Mark Searle and Russell Brayley that are listed in the bibliography.

Although the structure of the text is not reflected as such in the table of contents, this book is essentially organized into four major sections, as follows.

1. Chapters 1 through 6 constitute an introduction to the field and its major concepts and include a consideration of the demographic factors that influence recreation and leisure and of the personal and social benefits to be derived from the constructive use of leisure.
2. Chapters 7 through 9 review the history of recreation and leisure in the past and provide coverage of the most recent developments in the United States through the mid-1990s.
3. Chapters 10 through 12 present an overview of the leisure-service system, including the fundamental missions and program elements of governmental agencies on three levels (federal, state, and local), nonprofit voluntary organizations, commercial and private-membership bodies, therapeutic recreation services, and other types of agencies.

4. Finally, Chapters 13 and 14 describe recreation as a field of career opportunity and professional development and summarize some of the challenges and opportunities that will face leisure-service practitioners in the decades that lie ahead.

The fifth edition has been designed to provide an interesting format for student readers by including a wealth of illustrations, provocative quotations to introduce the chapters, suggested questions for discussion at the end of each chapter, and an overall format that breaks up the text with boxed excerpts emphasizing key points. Rather than limit content to dry or narrowly academic analyses, the text includes many anecdotes and descriptions of current developments affecting leisure in real life—particularly those that have to do with racial or ethnic issues, gender-related concerns, economic and social class factors, and both positive and negative aspects of recreational involvement.

ACKNOWLEDGMENTS

The author acknowledges his debt to a number of writers who have contributed significantly to the professional literature in recreation, parks, and leisure studies. They include, among others, Lawrence Allen, M. Deborah Bialeschki, John Crompton, Daniel Dustin, Geoffrey Godbey, Thomas Goodale, Karla Henderson, James Murphy, H. Douglas Sessoms, and Peter Witt.

The author also expresses his appreciation to the professionals in public, nonprofit, commercial, therapeutic, and other agencies who have sent him useful materials. Specifically, he thanks Carl Clark of the Sunnyvale, California, Department of Parks and Recreation; James Colley and Dale Larsen of the Phoenix, Arizona, Parks, Recreation, and Library Department; Ralph Cryder of the Long Beach, California, Department of Parks, Recreation and Marine; George Fudge of the Kamloops, British Columbia, Canada, Parks and Recreation Department; John "Pat" Harden of the U.S. Bureau of Naval Personnel; Cindy Helson of the National Employee Services and Recreation Association; Joseph Johnson of the National Association of Police Athletic Leagues; Robert Leake of the Church of Jesus Christ of Latter-Day Saints; Bob McKeta of U.S. Army Recreation; Karen Sposato of the Westchester County, New York, Department of Parks, Recreation and Conservation; and Susan Wells of the Oakland County, Michigan, Parks and Recreation Commission.

Gratitude is expressed to Barbara Campbell, Diane Van Staveren, and Ingrid Mount for their expertise in shepherding *Recreation and Leisure in Modern Society* through the editing and production process.

As in the last edition, the author dedicates this book to the students he has had the pleasure of teaching at Teachers College, Columbia University; at Lehman College of the City University of New York; at Temple University in Philadelphia; and, briefly, at both the University of Utah and Cortland College of the State University of New York. With them, he looks forward eagerly to the exciting possibilities that lie ahead for the recreation, parks, and leisure field in the twenty-first century.

Richard Kraus
*Department of Sport Management
and Leisure Studies
Temple University*

one

Recreation and Leisure:
The Current Scene

And what is our mission? Recreation is a vital component of a well-planned system of intervention directed toward creating self-sufficient, responsible, involved citizens and environmental stewards and toward breaking the cycles of poverty, addiction . . . . violence, boredom [and] discrimination . . . . [It provides] citizens with positive opportunities to exercise their need for power and control [and results] in energy, excitement, enthusiasm, and an appreciation of life.[1]

INTRODUCTION

Why should recreation and leisure be regarded as significant aspects of modern life? What justification is there for a text that describes them as key elements in contemporary society— or for hundreds of college and university curricula that examine recreation and leisure theory and practice?

Certainly, many individuals regard recreation as a source of casual fun or pleasure and think of leisure as free time that provides the opportunity to relax and shed work-related responsibilities. However, as this book will show, recreation, parks, and leisure services have become an important part of government responsibility and a significant social service in modern life. Today, recreation constitutes a major force in our national and local economies and is responsible for millions of jobs within such varied fields as travel and tourism, fitness programming, popular entertainment and the arts, and professional sports.

---

[1] Mickey Fearn, "Shaping the Future of Parks and Recreation," *Parks and Recreation* (October 1994): 67–68.

Beyond its value as a form of sociability, play also provides major personal benefits in terms of meeting physical, emotional, and other important health-related needs of participants. In a broad sense, the leisure life of a nation reflects its fundamental values. The very forms of sport, entertainment, and group affiliation that people enjoy in their leisure help to shape the character and well-being of families, communities, and society at large. For these reasons, it is the purpose of this text to present a comprehensive picture of the role of recreation and leisure in modern society, including: (1) the conceptual basis; (2) the varied forms they take; (3) the social and psychological implications; (4) the network of community agencies that meet leisure needs; and (5) the development of recreation as a diversified field of professional practice.

It is important to recognize that recreation and play do not always represent positive and healthful human experiences. Instead, they may involve—in the words of an early sociological report—the potential for being both a "blessing" and a "curse."[2] Some forms of recreation may be seriously self-destructive, and outdoor play can be harmful to the natural environment. Both aspects of recreation are examined in this text, as are major shifts in American and Canadian life with respect to demographic changes, gender-related behaviors, the role of racial and ethnic minorities, and the social impact of the mass media on entertainment and other forms of popular culture.

DIFFERING VIEWS OF RECREATION AND LEISURE

The very terms *recreation* and *leisure* may convey different meanings to the public. In the story of the blind men and the elephant, one blind man leans against the elephant's leg and thinks it is a tree, while another touches the trunk and perceives it as a giant snake. We all tend to know only what we experience directly so our perceptions of recreation and leisure may vary greatly. For some, recreation means the network of public agencies that provide such facilities as parks, playgrounds, swimming pools, sports fields, and community centers in thousands of cities, towns, counties, and park districts today. They may view these facilities as an outlet for the young or a means of achieving family togetherness and positive ties between parents and children. For others, recreation may be found in a senior center or golden age club, a sheltered workshop for the mentally retarded, or a hospital for physical rehabilitation. Still others may view recreation primarily in economic terms, seeing it through the eyes of the manufacturer of sports equipment, the travel agent, or the professional sports promotor.

Environmentalists may be chiefly concerned about the impact of outdoor forms of play on our natural surroundings—the forests, mountains, rivers, and lakes that are the national heritage of Americans and Canadians.

People may regard recreation solely as an amenity that characterizes our present way of life as a fun society. For them, pleasure and amusement are the sole purposes of recreation. Carried to an extreme, leisure has become trivialized by their hedonistic search for personal release and excitement.

Without question, recreation and leisure *are* all of these things. They represent a potentially rewarding and important form of human experience and constitute a major aspect of economic development and government responsibility today. It is important to recognize that this is not a new development. Recreation and leisure are concepts that have fascinated humankind since the golden age of ancient Athens. Varied forms of play have been condemned and suppressed in some societies and highly valued and encouraged in others. Today, for the first time, there is almost universal acceptance of the value of recreation and leisure. As a consequence, government at every level in the United States and Canada has accepted responsibility for providing or assisting leisure opportunities through extensive recreation and park systems. For example, Searle and Brayley have reported that leisure expenditures by the federal government in Canada almost tripled during the 1980s and that annual recreation expenditures by Canadian families rose by 40 percent during a recent five-year period.[3]

Diversity in Participation

Often we tend to think of recreation primarily as participation in sports and games or in social activities, and to ignore other forms of play. However, recreation actually includes an extremely broad range of leisure pursuits, including travel and tourism, cultural entertainment or participation in the arts, hobbies, membership in social clubs or interest groups, nature-related activities such as camping or hunting and fishing, attendance at parties or other special events, or fitness activities.

Recreation may be enjoyed along with thousands of other participants or spectators or may be an intensely solitary experience. It may be highly strenuous and physically demanding or may be primarily a cerebral activity. It may represent a lifetime of interest and involvement or may consist of a single, isolated experience. In the past, we tended to define recreation as including only those activities that were socially constructive and highly moral in nature, and that helped to restore one for renewed work by providing physical and mental rest and refreshment. Today, we recognize that much recreation may be highly demanding or dangerous, and indeed that some forms of it—such as gambling or drinking—may be morally questionable and destructive from a physical and/or economic point of view.

Motivations for Recreational Participation

In addition to the varied forms that recreation may take, it also meets a wide range of individual needs and interests. While later chapters in this text will describe play motivations and outcomes in fuller detail, they can be summarized as follows.

Many participants take part in recreation as a form of relaxation and release from work pressures or other tensions. Often they may be passive spectators of entertainment provided by television, movies, or other forms of electronic amusement. However, other significant play motivations are based on the need to express creativity, vent hidden talents, or pursue excellence in varied forms of personal expression.

For some participants, active, competitive recreation may offer a channel for releasing hostility and aggression or for struggling against others or the environment in adventurous, high-risk pursuits. Others enjoy recreation that is highly social and provides the opportunity for making new friends or cooperating with others in group settings.

Many individuals take part in leisure activities that involve community service or that permit them to provide leadership in fraternal or religious organizations. Still others take part in activities that promote health and physical fitness as a primary goal. A steadily growing number of participants enjoy participation in the expanding world of computer-based entertainment and communication—including CD-ROMs, interactive video games, and the Internet. Others are deeply involved in forms of so-called elite culture, such as music, drama, dance, literature, and the fine arts. Exploring new environments through travel and tourism or seeking self-discovery or personality enrichment through continuing education or religious activity represent other important leisure drives.

Given these complex personal reasons for leisure involvement, it is appropriate to ask, "What factors led recreation to become such an important element in American and Canadian life? How did recreation, parks, and leisure services—as examples of managed free-time programming—emerge as a focus of national concern and professional activity in both nations?"

SOCIAL FACTORS PROMOTING THE RECREATION AND PARK MOVEMENT

The social factors that helped bring about the growth of recreation and leisure programs and services in the United States and Canada stemmed from a variety of causes. Some of these involved changes in the economic structure of society or in dramatically shifting gender values and family relationships. Others were rooted in the kinds of social expectations that emerged as we moved from an essentially rural, agrarian society—where government played a limited role—to a complex industrial, urban culture where government assumed increasingly broad functions.

Twelve of these important social trends are described briefly in the following section of this chapter and in fuller detail in later sections.

1. Increase in Discretionary Time   A key development underlying the growth of the recreation movement and our national preoccupation with leisure has been the growth of free or discretionary time in the twentieth century.

In modern, post-industrial society, nonwork time has grown markedly for many individuals. Thanks to advanced mechanical equipment and automated processes in factories, agriculture, and the service fields, productive capacity increased dramatically during the second half of the nineteenth century and the first half of the twentieth. In effect, the workweek has been cut in half since the early days of the Industrial Revolution.

In addition, more holidays and longer vacations are now taken for granted by most American and Canadian employees. With improved Social Security benefits and pension plans, as well as medical advances leading to a longer life, many employees today are assured 15 or more years of full-time leisure after retiring from work.

Finally, labor-saving devices in and around the home, such as automatic heating units, snowblowers and lawnmowers, microwave ovens, and frozen foods have simplified life's demands considerably.

Surprisingly, in the mid- and late 1980s, a number of surveys showed that this trend had been reversed and that there actually had been an increase in workweek hours for many individuals. For example, the Harris polling organization reported that a survey of 1,500 men and women in March and April 1987, indicated that their median number of leisure hours per week had declined from 26.2 in 1973 to 16.5 in 1987.[4] Similarly, some research has shown that the average workweek of Canadians increased during the 1970s and 1980s, with a significant rise in the number of persons working more than 50 hours a week.[5]

However, other research has challenged these findings. As Chapter 9 shows, the increase in work hours appears to have been selective, with certain groups in the population (such as affluent professionals or business managers) working longer hours, but with other individuals continuing to have relatively short workweeks. When other factors are taken into account, such as the increase in holidays, vacations, and early retirement and the needs of special population groups like the disabled or underemployed, it is apparent that leisure continues to present a vast opportunity to great numbers of Americans and Canadians today. Thus, we have been given a dramatic gift of free time to spend in ways of our own choosing, and numerous authorities have predicted that leisure will continue to grow steadily in the years ahead.

Moreover, increased pressures on employees stemming from a more competitive and uncertain business climate and the rapid pace of work today has led to a high degree of stress for many workers. There is growing evidence that more and more Americans and Canadians are seeking less demanding career involvements and fuller leisure opportunities.

2. Affluence and Population Growth   A second critical factor stemmed from the dramatic growth of the gross national product (GNP) and personal income in the United States and Canada.

By the mid-1980s, the U.S. Department of Commerce reported total consumer spending on recreation had climbed to almost $200 billion, with this amount rising to over $300 billion in the following decade (see table below). When one recognizes that the Commerce Department's figures do not include the hundreds of billions of dollars spent on travel and tourism, gambling, liquor, and less easily measured forms of amusement, or the operational expenses of thousands of public and private leisure-service agencies, it is apparent that total leisure spending is substantially higher then the amounts shown here.

Personal Consumption Expenditures for Recreation in Constant (1987) Dollars: 1970 to 1993
(In billions of dollars. Represents market value of purchases of goods and services by individuals and nonprofit institutions)

TYPE OF PRODUCT OR SERVICE	1970	1980	1990	1993
Total recreation expenditures	91.3	149.1	261.9	304.1
Percent of total personal consumption	5.0	6.1	8.0	8.8
Books and maps	10.5	10.2	15.3	16.6
Magazines, newspapers, and sheet music	13.2	18.4	20.9	20.4
Nondurable toys and sport supplies	9.5	17.4	28.7	32.2
Wheel goods, sports and photographic equipment	10.3	20.2	28.3	28.1
Video and audio products, computer equipment, and musical instruments	8.8	17.6	54.1	83.7
Radio and television repair	2.7	3.5	3.4	3.1
Flowers, seeds, and potted plants	4.0	5.9	9.7	10.5
Admissions to specified spectator amusements	8.2	9.9	11.5	12.5
Motion picture theaters	4.2	3.8	3.8	4.2
Legitimate theaters and opera and entertainments of nonprofit institutions	1.3	2.7	3.7	4.1
Spectator sports	2.8	3.4	4.0	4.2
Clubs and fraternal organizations except insurance	3.8	4.0	7.5	7.9
Commercial participant amusements	6.3	12.5	20.3	22.0
Parimutuel net receipts	2.8	3.6	3.2	2.9
Other	11.3	25.8	58.9	64.2

Source: *Statistical Abstract of the United States* (U.S. Department of Commerce, 1995): 253.

Linked to the growth in recreation expenditures, expanding population totals in both the United States and Canada provided a sharply expanded market for organized leisure services. The dramatically increased number of children and youth in the baby boom generation following World War II and the growth in the number of older, retired individuals in the latter decades of the twentieth century also represented significant demographic changes. The median age of Americans climbed to 31.7 years in the mid-1980s, and it was predicted that it would be over 41 years by 2033. With greater numbers of elderly and middle-aged citizens, a growing need for recreation programs designed to serve these age groups appeared.

> **M**ore citizens young and old means more people who are ready to engage in play. In the United States, for example, the population soared from 200 million in 1967 to 215 million in 1976 and 245 million in 1988. It is predicted to rise to 305 million in 2033. In Canada, population totals climbed from 19 million in 1964 to almost 23 million in 1976 and 25.8 million in 1987. Contrasting with earlier trends, the government's National Center for Health Statistics reported in 1988 that Americans had more babies in 1987 than in any year in nearly a quarter century, and that both marriage and divorce rates were the lowest in more than a decade.

Along with such age-related shifts, there was a marked increase in the number of those attending college in the United States. Just after World War II, there were about 1.6 million higher-education students enrolled; by 1990, the number had climbed to over 13 million. One of the effects of higher education is to expose students to new ideas and experiences and to broaden their interest in such leisure activities as art, music, literature, and travel. The higher one's level of education, the more likely one is to engage in a wide variety of recreational pursuits.

Another significant demographic factor affecting the provision of leisure services has been the increasing diversification of the American and Canadian populations. Instead of relatively homogeneous communities or neighborhoods composed chiefly of typical family units, today there are much greater numbers of single people, those choosing alternative lifestyles, those of more varied ethnic or national backgrounds, and other special populations. With the growth of these groups and of single-parent families headed overwhelmingly by women, the need for new kinds of recreation programs to serve such groups is clear.

3. Where People Live: Urbanization and Suburbanization   One of the key factors in the early development of the recreation movement was the growth of North America's industrial cities. As millions of immigrants came from impoverished European nations or migrated from rural regions to cities in search of better job opportunities, they tended to huddle together in crowded slum tenements. Without the natural opportunities for outdoor recreation that the countryside provided, it became obvious that leisure posed an increasingly serious problem for a heavily urbanized society.

Thanks to this dramatic growth of the cities, the recreation movement got under way in the United States and Canada. It took the form of playgrounds for children, sports fields for youths and adults, networks of parks throughout our cities, and the establishment of settlement houses, community centers, and other social-service and religious organizations to meet public leisure needs. In addition, throughout both countries, civic-minded individuals joined together to establish symphony orchestras, opera companies, art and natural history museums, and libraries.

Following World War II, there was a widespread move by millions of middle-class families away from the central cities to the suburban areas that surrounded them. The satellite communities they formed quickly established recreation and park systems—often with extensive facilities and programs. Recreation was part of the "good life" that the suburbs offered to many American and Canadian families who moved to them, and they paid taxes to support these services willingly.

Meanwhile, millions of economically disadvantaged people moved into the central cities. Often poorly educated and ill-equipped for the demands of urban living, they frequently brought with them a complex of social and economic problems as they sought to make the transition to city life. Thus, two types of local public recreation and park systems emerged: (1) the suburban agency, well-supported and serving a primarily middle-class population; and (2) big-city departments, less well-funded and often attempting to meet the leisure needs of families heavily dependent on public recreation opportunities.

More recently, recreation and park development has been seen as a key factor in promoting the revival of many larger cities, as wealthy citizens have moved into newly rehabilitated or developed residential areas (the process has become known as gentrification). Rundown waterfront or factory areas have been transformed into attractive sites for shopping, sightseeing, cultural activities, and entertainment. Recreation has been stressed as critical to making cities more livable, attracting tourists, and retaining middle-class and wealthy residents. In numerous other communities, public recreation and park departments have constructed new water-play parks, tennis complexes, creative arts centers, marinas, and other recreational facilities. Typically, in 1993, Sue Schmidt wrote in *Athletic Business:*

> Even with tightening budgets, cities are finding the money to build multifaceted indoor recreation facilities that feature everything from well-appointed weight rooms and cardiovascular areas to full-size gyms, leisure pools and family gathering areas.[6]

At the same time, facing severe economic pressures, many large cities have been forced to institute budget cuts in various community-service areas. With fewer recreation leaders and maintenance personnel, and with centers, playgrounds, and parks increasingly threatened by youthful gangs, drug dealers, and other antisocial groups, inner-city recreation opportunities for many disadvantaged city residents have been sharply reduced. The dramatic contrast between such leisure "wastelands" and the extensive, well-supported recreation programs offered in many smaller cities and more affluent suburban areas is described more fully in later chapters of this text.

4. Cultural Explosion: The Arts in Leisure   A striking aspect of the recreation movement in the post-World War II period was the so-called cultural explosion. In the 1960s and 1970s in particular, there was a remarkable surge of interest in the arts, theater-going, literature, music, dance, and museum attendance in the United States. In Canada, there was similar growth on all levels, with considerable assistance provided by Canada Council on the national scene and by numerous provincial cultural authorities.

The growth of interest in the arts has been based on a number of factors: (1) the building of numerous local community cultural centers; (2) the sponsorship of arts curricula and performing groups by many colleges and universities; (3) the increased aid given by the federal government to individual artists and performing groups through such funding programs as the National Endowment for the Arts in the United States; and (4) a marked shift in public attitudes toward arts and culture in general.

While much artistic activity has been carried on by independent cultural organizations, many programs have been sponsored by public recreation and park authorities in recent years in such cities as New York, Miami, Houston, Portland, Raleigh, Dallas, Tulsa, and Nashville. In Canada, cities like Ottawa have established arts councils that have conducted studies, provided special funding, and promoted cooperative enterprises in the fine and performing arts. In the 1980s, Bernard Conn pointed out, the National Recreation and Park Association established awards programs for the best community programs in the arts and humanities and more and more recreation and park professionals were participating in training programs designed for arts administrators.[7]

Realistically, however, it has been shown that the elite arts of classical or serious music, painting, drawing and sculpture, and opera, ballet, and modern dance tend to appeal to a relatively small segment of the population—generally those who are affluent and well educated. Dependent on such groups and on government and foundation funding assistance for support, the financial position of many major orchestras, opera and ballet companies, and museums was threatened during the 1980s and 1990s by cutbacks in private and government financial aid.

Particularly in the United States, with conservative political and religious groups opposing government subsidy of the arts through the National Endowments for the Arts and Humanities, economic pressures on major professional arts institutions have become severe.[8] At the same time, public interest in the arts and direct involvement on an amateur basis in varied forms of cultural activity have remained high throughout the United States and Canada.

5. Growth of Interest in Health, Physical Fitness, and Sport A key development during the 1970s and 1980s was the growth of public interest in exercise and physical fitness programs. With growing realization that our modern life is frequently inactive, sedentary, beset by tensions, and subject to a host of unhealthy habits including overeating, smoking, and drinking, we have developed a wave of popular concern about improving one's health, vitality, and appearance through diet and exercise.

> In 1961, it was estimated that fewer than one out of four persons 18 and older exercised on a regular basis. In 1983, *USA Today* reported that more than 100 million Americans took part in swimming, 75 million bicycled, and 35 million jogged. A year later, a Gallup poll found that 59 percent of adults reported that they exercised daily.[9]

Some authorities question whether many of the exercises that people are engaged in require sufficient energy expenditure to improve cardiopulmonary functioning—a key element in fitness activity. Beyond this, Teague argued that the widely ballyhooed growth in the number of private health clubs and employee fitness programs had not been matched by sponsorship of fitness activities in recreation and park departments and schools.[10]

Despite such reservations, it seems clear that there has been an immense wave of interest and programming by private, commercial, voluntary-agency, educational, and other sponsors in the physical fitness field. In Canada particularly, the Fitness and Amateur Sport Directorate of the federal government has carried out numerous projects involving research, public service advertising, networking among agencies, and promotion of fitness campaigns with a resultant seven-fold increase in adult physical activity.

Participation in such activities as aerobics, swimming, running and jogging, racquet sports, and similar vigorous pursuits has more than physiological effects. It also has psychological value; those who exercise regularly look and feel better. Experts have concluded that fitness is not a passing phase; the public's desire to be healthy and physically attractive is supported by a wave of continuing publicity, social values, personal vanity, and solid business sense. *Time* commented:

> The fitness boom has grown for a decade, and improving the body has become an enduring, and perhaps historically significant, national obsession.[11]

Research showed that the most successful fitness programs were likely to be those that provided an ingredient of recreational interest and satisfaction. In a study of dropouts in an employee fitness program in Canada, Wankel found that while all enrollees had physical fitness as a strong initial motivation, those who continued to be involved

> had other objectives for joining the program. These objectives of a non-health-related nature (e.g., competition, curiosity, develop recreational skills, go out with friends) were consistently rated as more important by the participants than by the dropouts.[12]

Ewert and Sutton supported these findings, pointing out that in the 1980s there was a decline in the number of specialty clubs offering primarily tennis or racquetball and of health spas focusing narrowly on weights and exercise equipment. Instead, they wrote, the demand had grown for multipurpose clubs offering a variety of fitness activities and a range of different membership levels:

> Multipurpose clubs that are successful now and will continue to be successful in the future not only offer swimming, fitness classes, racquet sports and exercise equipment but also acknowledge the social needs of their members and provide for social activities such as trips and parties.[13]

In the 1990s, reports indicated that the rate of adult participation in regular fitness activities had declined. While evidence mounted that regular, vigorous physical activity helped to prevent cardiovascular disease, cancer, and a number of other serious illnesses, the percentage of adults taking part in active exercise regimens was sharply lower than at the height of the fitness boom.[14] Similarly, there was strong evidence that children and youth in the United States were increasingly obese and in poor physical condition.[15]

At the same time, however, such recreational sports as softball, volleyball, and ice hockey are growing steadily in popularity. According to the National Federation of High School Athletic Associations, fast-pitch softball is the fastest-growing high school sport in the United States. Television coverage of beach volleyball and inclusion of that sport in the Olympics has resulted in thousands of junior and adult volleyball clubs and leagues—including many leagues sponsored by municipal recreation and park departments.[16] With the expansion of professional ice hockey, it was reported in 1995 that there were over 24,000 teams registered in U.S.A. Hockey, the Little League of ice hockey, with long waiting lists for ice rink practice time throughout the country.[17]

6. Environmental Concerns   As later chapters on the historical development of recreation and leisure will show, the establishment of public recreation programs in the United States and Canada was closely linked to the growing number of national, state, provincial, and local park systems. Outdoor recreation activities such as camping, hiking, backpacking, boating, hunting, fishing, and skiing depend heavily on parks, forests, water areas, and other natural resources that are typically operated by public recreation and park agencies. However, the concern of many Americans with the health of our outdoor resources stems from more than the need for outdoor recreation spaces. LaPage and Ranney point out that one of the most powerful sources of America's essential cultural fiber and spirit is the land itself. They write:

> The roots of this new nation and its people became the forests and rivers, the deserts and mountains, and the challenges and inspirations they presented, not the ruins of ancient civilizations most other cultures look to for ancestral continuity. Thus, America developed a different attitude and identity.[18]

For such reasons, the environmental movement has received strong support from many recreation advocates and organizations. At the same time, it is recognized that such activities as fishing and hunting are just part of a bigger scene that requires clean—and safe—air and water and wise use of the land.

Growing national concern about the need to protect the environment was buttressed by the 1962 Report of the Outdoor Recreation Resources Review Commission. During the following two decades, there was a wave of federal and state legislative action and funding support in the United States that was designed to acquire open space, to protect imperiled forests, wetlands, and scenic areas, to help endangered species flourish, and to reclaim the nation's wild rivers and trails. This movement was threatened during the early 1980s, when a new national administration in the United States sought to reduce park and open space funding, eliminate conservation programs and environmental regulations, and subject the outdoors to renewed economic exploitation. Again in the mid-1990s, the effort to open up protected wilderness areas to increased oil drilling, cattle grazing, lumbering, and other commercial uses has gained strong political support.[19]

Organizations such as the nonpartisan League of Conservation Voters, National Audubon Society, National Wildlife Federation, Wilderness Society, Sierra Club, and Nature Conservancy have been in the forefront of the continuing battle to protect the nation's natural resources. Numerous outdoor recreation organizations have joined with such groups, in both the United States and Canada, and the struggle will clearly continue as an important political issue in the years ahead.

7. Therapeutic Recreation and the Needs of Persons with Disabilities   An important aspect of the growth of the recreation movement since World War II has been the increased awareness of the leisure needs of persons with physical, mental, or social disabilities.

In both the United States and Canada, there has been a marked expansion of legislation and social welfare programs designed to improve the lives of disabled and dependent aging individuals and to open up new opportunities for them within the mainstream of community life. In the recreation movement, this trend was most strikingly illustrated by the growth of concern about children and youth with mental retardation, which began in the early 1960s under the administration of President John F. Kennedy. The Kennedy Foundation joined forces with the federal and state governments and professional organizations in physical education and recreation to provide sports opportunities for retarded individuals. This coalition initiated research, supported demonstration projects, helped prepare professional personnel, and gave rise to such major recreation ventures as the Special Olympics program.

Overall, such programs have been part of a specialized form of professional service in recreation that has been widely identified as *therapeutic recreation service.* During the last three decades, it has expanded from a narrow focus on hospitals and other residential setting to a broader concern with many different types of special populations in the community itself, in day-care centers, sheltered workshops, camps for individuals with disability, and other adapted facilities and programs.

In the United States, the Americans With Disabilities Act of 1990 symbolized and gave force to the drive to provide fuller and more equitable life opportunities to persons with disabilities and to assist them in the areas of education, career development, and social involvement. Through the efforts of such professional societies as the National Therapeutic Recreation Society and the American Therapeutic Recreation Association, the practice of recreation specialists in clinical treatment settings has become increasingly sophisticated and recognized as an important element in the care of ill and disabled persons.

8.   New Leisure Roles for Girls and Women   Another striking phenomenon of the post-World War II decades was the strong drive by girls and women in the United States and Canada toward playing a more equal role in varied aspects of community life.

The feminist movement that gathered force at this time represented a major challenge to sexist beliefs and social customs that had existed for many centuries, during which women were essentially treated as second-class citizens in marital and family life, education, careers, politics, and leisure opportunity.

Distorted and stereotyped views of women's traits and capabilities had meant that from early childhood on, they were often restricted in their play opportunities. They were barred from a variety of athletic, outdoor recreation, social, and cultural involvements—with few exceptions. Despite such discriminatory practices, a number of women had persevered in sports or adventurous outdoor pursuits, and many of the early recreation leaders who pioneered in establishing playgrounds, recreation centers, and settlement houses were women.

As the recreation and park movement expanded, men tended to dominate—particularly in administrative and policy-making roles—while women were relegated to direct leadership or programming roles at salaries far below those of their male counterparts. With the emergence of a vigorous feminist movement and antidiscrimination laws in the 1960s and 1970s, many of these inequities were corrected. Today, women are playing a far more influential role in many leisure-service agencies than in the past.

> **A**lthough public interest in women's sports continues to be considerably lower than its support for boys' and men's sports, there is growing interest in women's tennis, golf, gymnastics, track and field, and similar events on every level of competition. Participation totals in team sports such as field hockey, soccer, softball, and volleyball have continued to climb steadily. For many, increased participation in vigorous athletics and outdoor pastimes is symbolic of the need to overcome the past view of women as fragile, over-emotional, or lacking in courage and drive. Outstanding women athletes in particular have helped to create a new image of feminine strength, determination, and self-confidence, which is closely linked to women's achieving a higher degree of acceptance in formerly male-restricted fields such as the military, aviation, police and fire departments, law, and medicine.

Along with such progress, women have succeeded in breaking down the barriers to participation in a host of formerly male-restricted social, luncheon, and business clubs and semi-secret societies that have historically controlled access to the power structure and success in American and Canadian life. Accompanying these developments, a number of leading scholars have explored the special meaning of leisure in the lives of women and have spearheaded their advancement in the recreation, park, and leisure-service profession.[20]

Places for Play in Modern Society

Areas for play range from an outdoor tennis complex built by the New York Junior Tennis League in a crowded inner-city neighborhood to use of the city's Verrazano Bridge by thousands of marathoners each year. Below, Ottawa residents enjoy ice-skating each winter on the picturesque Rideau Canal.

Other settings for outdoor recreation include Hackney Marsh (top), an extensive London playfield constructed with World War II bomb rubble, and the White Mountains of New Hampshire (below) where backpackers hike along a high ridge. Many indoor aquatic complexes (center) are designed with a leisure motif, brightly lit and heavily planted, with sloping, beach-like edges.

9.   Multiculturalism in American and Canadian Life   In a related social trend, the post–World War II period brought considerable progress in meeting the leisure needs of racial and ethnic minorities, particularly those of African-American or Hispanic background. Such groups had historically been discriminated against severely in many community recreation programs—both in the South, where legal barriers sharply limited their ability to use many public facilities on an integrated basis, and in northern states, where both public and private facilities and agencies also maintained discriminatory policies.

Beginning in the 1940s in military installations and other government settings, and then elsewhere in the 1950s and 1960s, lawsuits and court decisions helped pave the way for fuller participation by racial and ethnic minorities in varied recreation settings. Civil rights legislation and federal support of many urban recreation and park programs designed to serve poverty populations, including African-Americans and other minority groups, accelerated this process. During the 1970s, there was much greater involvement by African-Americans in both college and professional sports, although special efforts to provide compensatory opportunities for minority populations received less emphasis.

One of the important priorities of public and voluntary recreation agencies has been to serve such populations and to use leisure programming as a means of promoting cooperation and understanding among different racial and ethnic groups. Gradually, this responsibility expanded to include the use of recreation programs to strengthen black "pride" and to enrich public awareness of African-American history, traditions, and contributions to national life and culture.

In the late 1980s and early 1990s, this thrust intensified, as spokespersons for various racial and ethnic minority populations—African-American, Hispanic, Asian, and American Indian groups—began to argue that the nation's educational systems and overall culture had been dominated by a Eurocentric and essentially white, Anglo-Saxon, male power elite. Rejecting the earlier melting-pot approach, in which all national and ethnic groups were pressured to assimilate within the larger culture—but in which people of color had been ignored and discriminated against—they urged a new multicultural approach in which the unique contributions of people of all backgrounds and both genders would be more fully recognized.

They pointed out that, for several decades, immigration policy in the United States had favored the entry of European immigrants—particularly those from northern or western European countries—but that in the 1960s a basic shift in national policy encouraged the entrance of people from the rest of the world. The full effects of this policy have been felt only in recent years, with immigrants arriving at the rate of more than one million a year, mostly from Asia and several Hispanic nations. A special issue of *Time* concluded in 1993:

> The impact of these new immigrants is literally remaking America. Today more than 20 million Americans were born in another country. Given that there are higher birthrates among the mostly young Third World arrivals, demographers are predicting that the U.S. before long will have to redefine just who its minorities are. In 1950, for example, 75 percent of all the minorities in the U.S. were African Americans. Hispanics now number about 24 million, and by 2010 . . . they will have surpassed blacks in number.[21]

Increasingly, the changing makeup of American society will continue to affect recreation and leisure programming in terms of having to adopt a new multicultural emphasis. At the same time, many social critics decry the thrust toward sharper self-definition on the part of various national groups. They argue that, while some individuals like Jesse Jackson now describe America as " . . . a quilt—many pieces, many colors, many sizes, all woven together by a common thread," the thread is all too fragile, with the nation's essential character and unity being torn apart by dozens of separate racial and ethnic groups that are determined to maintain their unique identities and loyalties. A vivid example of this trend is shown in Canada, which has made a strong effort to promote the cultures of its various Eskimo, Indian, and European immigrant groups, but which in the mid-1990s barely survived the effort of French-speaking eastern Canada to secede and form a new nation.

10. Commodification of Leisure: Play as an Industry   In striking contrast to the needs of the approximately 30 million Americans who live today below the poverty level, spending on recreation by the nation's middle and upper socioeconomic classes has continued to climb steadily.

Increasingly, recreation is today being described as an industry, with such multibillion dollar components as travel and tourism, commercialized sports, popular entertainment, the purchase and maintenance of family pets, toys and family entertainment centers, video games and CD-Roms, health and fitness clubs, and a host of other leisure goods and services.

For example, in the mid-1990s the cruise industry embarked on a construction boom designed to create some of the biggest passenger ships ever seen. To maintain the growth in the annual number of passengers from 1.4 million in 1980 to 5 million in 1994 and a projected 8 million by the year 2000, major cruise ship companies are now targeting greater numbers of younger and middle-class passengers, as compared to the elderly and wealthy populations served in the past. With sophisticated marketing and advertising methods, lines are now developing a variety of niche markets, including conferences and meetings, honeymoons, family cruises, and cruises built around themes like sports, music, and education.[22]

For a second major example of how play has become a commodity, it has been estimated that Americans spend approximately $50 billion a year on various forms of participant and spectator sport. Michael Ozanian comments in *Financial World* that professional sports in particular have become a way of building revenues indirectly—through cable television, the sale of team-connected merchandise, advertising, the sponsorship of sporting events of all kinds by major U.S. and Canadian corporations, and a variety of other money-making methods. Ozanian writes:

> Sports is not simply another big business. It is one of the fastest-growing industries in the U.S., and it is intertwined with virtually every aspect of the economy—from media and apparel to food and advertising . . . . Sports is everywhere accompanied by the sound of a cash register ringing incessantly.[23]

Sophisticated technology has played a key role in providing new forms of play for the American and Canadian populations. Outdoor recreation, for example, makes use of increasingly complex and expensive devices in such activities as skydiving, hang gliding, scuba diving, boating, hunting, fishing, roller-blading, skiing, and snowboarding. Computer dating provides a new form of social contact for single adults, and video games offer interactive competition or exposure to new varieties of play settings and "virtual realities." Enthusiasts may explore their leisure interests with others around the world through the Internet.

Technological advances have reshaped the offerings of theme parks, children's play and fitness centers, and other leisure settings.

Another aspect of this trend in the 1980s and 1990s was the emergence of major new leisure conglomerates, with huge corporations in the movie and television fields merging with others in book and magazine publishing, sports teams and stadium operations, music publishing, video rental chains, and resorts and tourist attractions to create multibillion dollar communications and entertainment empires. Major holdings of the Walt Disney Company, for example, include highly successful theme parks and resorts, film, television, and record companies, magazine and book publishing ventures, sports teams, and chains of retail stores. Similarly, the 1994 merger of Viacom, Blockbuster, and Paramount combined huge networks of television and radio stations, production units, and broadcasting systems with major book publishers, sports teams, stadiums, children's play centers, home video stores, and motion picture production and distribution companies.[24]

The existence of such powerful, profit-dominated business empires reinforces the reality of leisure's having become an immense industry, both nationally and with numerous international linkages. Beyond this, it makes clear the degree to which the free-time pursuits of Americans and Canadians are increasingly dominated by the business-based decisions of a few influential executives who use sophisticated marketing and advertising techniques to promote their leisure-related offerings.

11. Decline of Family and Community Values   Linked to several of the social trends just described is a marked breakdown in the quality of American and Canadian daily life, with respect to traditional family values and community interrelationships.

This deterioration has taken several forms: (1) the fragmentation of family life, with a steady increase in the number of children born out of wedlock, divorces and separations, and single-parent households; (2) the expanding problem of widespread alcohol and drug abuse, particularly among the young; (3) the increase in random and senseless violence, often on an individual basis but also linked to gang-generated conflict in cities large and small; (4) the presence of homeless people in increasing numbers, both on the streets and in parks, and under highways and viaducts, in many communities; (5) the ready acceptance of gambling as a solution to the economic problems of states and cities, along with the growing tolerance of veiled forms of prostitution and other commercially linked forms of sexual entertainment; and, finally, (6) an overall sense that the patterns of civility and human decency that should prevail in everyday life have been widely abandoned.

What do these trends have to do with recreation and leisure? First and most obviously, many of the more popular but morally questionable pursuits just described represent a search for pleasure, novelty, and excitement. Secondly, they tend to displace more traditional and constructive forms of play. Thus, they represent a major challenge to recreation managers, leaders, and program planners in public and nonprofit community leisure-service agencies, who must compete with them for the attention of participants and must struggle against their demoralizing effects on community life.

Now, a major segment of the nation's leisure sponsors—the creators and distributors of popular motion pictures and television shows, video games, books, magazines and even toys—are being blamed for having created a climate that tolerates immorality, crime, sexual and physical abuse of children, and random violence.

Beginning in the 1992 presidential campaign in the United States, attacks were leveled on the producers of television shows for undermining the nation's traditional codes of sexual behavior and parental responsibility. In the years that followed, major political figures have blamed the "cultural elite"—particularly executives and creative leaders in the communications and entertainment media—for deliberately promoting sensational themes or publicizing events, personalities, shocking crimes, and distorted relationships, which has resulted in a decline of family values and civic morality.

12. Growth of Organized Leisure-Service Field and Profession   A dramatic expansion in the number and influence of several major types of organized recreation, park, and leisure-service sponsors has also occurred over the past several decades. At the time of World War II, such organizations tended to fall under two primary headings: public recreation and park departments and voluntary, nonprofit youth-serving organizations. As Chapter 9 will show, in the years that followed a number of other forms of leisure-service sponsors gained steadily in membership and public support. Today, recreation and leisure-service providers may be classified under eight major categories. These are:

1. *Government agencies*—federal, state, and provincial agencies, and local departments of recreation and parks—that provide leisure services as a primary function, as well as hundreds of other agencies (such as those concerned with social service, education, special populations, and the armed forces) that offer or assist recreation programs as a secondary responsibility.

2. *Voluntary organizations*, which are nongovernmental, nonprofit agencies, both sectarian and nonsectarian, serving the public at large or selected elements of it with multiservice programs that often include a substantial element of recreational opportunity. Such organizations include national youth programs like the Boy Scouts and Girl Scouts and the YMCA, YWCA, and YM-YWHA.

3. *Private membership organizations*, such as golf, tennis, yacht, athletic, and country clubs, along with a wide range of service clubs and fraternal bodies, that provide recreational and social activities for their own members and in some cases assist community recreation needs as well. Under this heading are the recreation sponsors connected to residence, as in the case of swimming pools, sports or fitness complexes, or clubs attached to leisure villages, apartment or condominium units, or retirement communities.

4. *Commercial recreation enterprises*, including a great variety of privately owned, for-profit businesses, such as ski centers, bowling alleys, nightclubs, movie houses or theaters, health spas or fitness centers, dancing schools, amusement or theme parks, and other enterprises that provide leisure services.

5. *Employee recreation programs* (formerly called industrial recreation), which serve those who work for given companies or other employers by providing recreation, often as part of a total personnel benefits package, linked to other services.

6. *Armed forces recreation*, which, while it is obviously a form of government-sponsored activity, is unique in its setting and purpose. Each of the major branches of the armed forces tends to operate an extensive network of recreation facilities and programs.

7. *Campus recreation*, which includes intramural athletics or sports clubs, social activities, trip-and-travel programs, performing arts groups, entertainment, lounges, film series, and numerous other forms of recreation on college and university campuses.

8. *Therapeutic recreation services*, including any type of program designed to meet the needs of persons with physical or mental disabilities, individuals with poor health, dependent aging persons, socially deviant persons in correctional facilities or other treatment settings, and similar special groups.

The Need for Organized Leisure Services

How did these different types of recreation sponsors grow in scope and influence? First, it must be understood that most recreation does not occur as a spontaneous, self-initiated act. Instead, it represents a form of human behavior that requires some degree of stimulation, guidance, or support. Even the simplest type of childhood play tends to be initiated by older brothers or sisters, parents, or other children in the neighborhood.

Leisure activities are essentially of two types: (1) those which are initiated by individuals and carried on in their own homes or neighborhoods, usually without special assistance or instruction; and (2) those which require special facilities, equipment, or leadership, and which therefore must usually be provided by some outside agency.

The agencies that provide such sponsorship constitute the organized recreation system in modern society. It consists of many types of organizations, large and small, that offer leisure opportunities either as a primary function or as one of a number of related services or functions.

Taken all together, such organizations form a diverse and rich complex of different types of agencies and programs, meeting every sort of leisure need or interest for the public at large as well as for special populations and interest groups. Increasingly, they have been referred to as the "leisure industry." While the use of this term is widespread today and accurately reflects the entrepreneurial and marketing strategies adopted by many recreation, park, and leisure-service agencies, it does not really apply to many of the youth-serving, governmental, or therapeutic recreation programs that constitute a major segment of this field. Therefore, throughout this text, the term "leisure-service system" will be used to describe the joint efforts of the eight different types of organizations that have just been identified.

Need for Professional Leadership

Within each of these eight fields of specialization, there is a growing need for highly qualified and skilled professional leadership. Too often people assume that the task of organizing and carrying out recreation programs is a relatively simple one and that "anyone" can do it without specialized training. They do so because they realize that many youths and adults in our society do provide recreational leadership *without* such training. Volunteer leaders or coaches in the Scouting movement, Little League, hospitals, and similar organizations often help run excellent programs.

However, the professional's assignment within the organized recreation field tends to be far more complex and difficult than that of the typical volunteer leader or coach. It must involve carefully thought-out goals and objectives and often requires sophisticated planning techniques.

To pick a dramatic example, in such large-scale commercial recreation enterprises as the far-flung Disney theme park operation, including Disneyland, Disney World, and the Epcot Center, the immense investment that is at stake requires shrewd marketing and creative design approaches. Literally hundreds of millions of dollars are involved in such ventures.

Even when the scope of the program is on a lesser scale, professional management involves such varied tasks as planning and building recreation facilities that may range from golf courses to swimming complexes, supervising leadership and maintenance personnel, carrying out effective public relations campaigns, and assessing public needs and demands. Often it will require working closely with boards or commissions, advisory groups or civic officials; it may also involve effective liaison with other levels of government.

In the case of therapeutic programs that serve persons with disabilities, the recreation specialist may need an intensive knowledge of illness and its effects, medical terminology, anatomy, kinesiology, and psychopathology. Those working with the aging must have a solid understanding of geriatrics and gerontology and should be aware of the varied roles played by other community agencies that work with older populations.

On all levels, recreation professionals should be familiar with a wide range of activities and their potential values and outcomes. They should possess the skills needed for direct leadership and supervision, group dynamics, and patient or client assessment, and have the ability to carry out basic evaluation or research and write literate and meaningful reports. Underlying each of these areas of competence, there is a need for recreation professionals to be fully aware of the meaning of recreation and leisure in human society and of the history and traditions of this field.

Emerging Professional Identity

As employment in recreation, park, and leisure-service agencies and programs grew over the past several decades, it gained public recognition as a flourishing career field. Millions of men and women became employed in various specialized sectors of leisure service, with hundreds of thousands holding professional-level jobs as recreation leaders, supervisors, planners, managers, and resource specialists.

At the outset, those working in this field had very little sense of professional identity. Drawn chiefly from the teaching and physical education fields, recreation workers were typically considered as one component of the overall health, physical education, recreation, and dance spectrum. Gradually, however, the field developed a more distinct image, along with its own specialized programs of higher education and a number of sharply focused professional societies.

Emerging professionalism had a number of important aspects: (1) the identification for the first time of *recreation* as a specialized field of service, making significant contributions to society and requiring unique competencies and skills; (2) heightened visibility for the field itself and the development of channels for influencing public policy in matters related to recreation and leisure; and (3) a higher level of status for those working in the field, accompanied by the widespread acceptance of recreation as a legitimate field of social responsibility. Particularly through the efforts of national, state, and provincial societies, higher standards for practice were developed and the first steps of certification and accreditation were set in motion.

Influence of Professional Specialization

As the overall leisure-service field expanded, each of its specialized disciplines also gained strength and a sense of unique identity. Specialists also began to form their own professional societies in such areas as armed forces recreation, therapeutic recreation, campus recreation, and employee services. In some cases, they established their own certification processes and set up linkages to other professional disciplines functioning in areas related to their specializations.

> **I**t must therefore be understood that recreation leadership and management does *not* represent a single, unified field of professional practice today. Its practitioners have varying areas of responsibility and have developed specialized missions and operational strategies suited to their unique service areas.
>
> However, representatives of each of the eight types of program sponsors within the overall leisure-service field have a common concern with the provision of constructive recreation programs that meet societal needs and contribute to individual physical and mental health and positive community relationships. Increasingly, they are joining together in partnerships that share human, fiscal and other agency resources to achieve such goals. It is essential that all leisure-service practitioners seeking to be regarded as professionals recognize that they must have more than nuts-and-bolts competence in conducting program activities.
>
> In addition to such competence, recreation professionals must meet high standards of specialized training, be affiliated with appropriate professional societies, and have a rich understanding of the full range of public leisure needs and of the social challenges that face this field.

CHALLENGES FACING THE LEISURE-SERVICE FIELD

This chapter has outlined a number of the critical social trends that were responsible for the growth of recreation's popularity in modern society—and that also pose a number of serious challenges to its practitioners and planners. Leisure-service professionals must therefore be able to deal creatively with the following kinds of questions.

How can the organized recreation movement contribute to public understanding of leisure's role in daily life and to upgrading the level of the public's choices of leisure pursuits?

What role can public, voluntary, therapeutic, and other community-based agencies play in helping to reduce crime, violence, substance abuse, and other serious societal problems?

How can recreation contribute to promoting positive intercultural understanding and relationships and to enriching the lives of persons with disabilities?

How can the organized recreation movement play a meaningful role in a society that has increasingly become dominated by commercial interests—particularly conglomerates in the mass media of communication and entertainment—that place dollar profits at a higher priority than important human values?

How do the priorities of organized recreation vary according to the communities served—whether urban, rural, suburban or small town, or wealthy, middle class, or poor?

How have economic trends, including a gradual decline in the middle class, the growth of temporary and insecure forms of employment, and the increased number of workers holding two jobs, affected recreation participation?

What are the primary philosophies of recreation agencies today, including quality-of-life, marketing, human service, and benefits-driven approaches? What are the rationales supporting each of these models of service, and how can their strengths be combined in programs that will be viable in the oncoming twenty-first century?

PURPOSES OF THIS TEXT

This text is intended to provide information that will be helpful to its readers in developing personal philosophies and a broad awareness of the leisure-service field—and in answering questions not with learned-by-rote solutions, but rather through intelligent analysis, critical thinking, and problem solving.

Leisure-service professionals should have a comprehensive understanding of the full range of recreational needs, programs, strategies, and outcomes. They should have a solid foundation with respect to the behavioral and social principles underlying recreation and leisure in contemporary society. It is essential to understand that recreation, play, and leisure are not inherently good *or* evil. On the one hand, they may be boring, time-killing, superficial, or even self-degrading and destructive. On the other, they may provide the opportunity for positive growth, creative self-discovery, and the enhancement of the quality of life for *all* people.

To understand this fully and to have a sound philosophy of the goals and values of recreation and leisure in modern life, it is essential to understand recreation's history—and to be aware of its social, economic, and psychological characteristics in today's society. Should recreation be regarded chiefly as an amenity or should it be supported as a form of social therapy? What are the recreation needs of such populations as girls and women, the aging, the disadvantaged, racial minorities, persons with disabilities, or others who have not been served fully in the past? What environmental priorities should recreation and park professionals fight to support, and how can outdoor forms of play be designed to avoid destructive ecological outcomes? How can leisure-service practitioners strike a balance between entrepreneurial management approaches, which emphasize fiscal self-sufficiency, and human-service programming that responds to the issues raised in this chapter?

Recently, columnist Neal Peirce wrote:

> A quarter century from now, what will urban America be like? Ravaged wastelands? Or supportive, progressive communities with parks and kids at play?[25]

Peirce goes on to point out that low-income communities are critically undeserved—in sharp contrast to the park and recreation facilities provided in comfortable middle-class suburbs. He cites examples of a number of cities throughout the United States where crime has declined when recreation programs were expanded, and quotes Newark, New Jersey's Mayor Sharpe James: "We are going to recreate or we are going to incinerate. The choice is ours."

Throughout this text, such issues are discussed in detail. Through a vivid depiction of the field's conceptual base, history and current status, through an examination of existing agencies and programs, and through a comprehensive summary of research studies and recent reports, the reader should gain a full, in-depth understanding of the role of recreation and leisure in modern society. More than anything else, although this text promotes no single philosophical position, its purpose is to clarify the values promoted by recreation and leisure in modern society. Ultimately, these values will be responsible for the field's ability to flourish as a significant form of governmental or voluntary-agency service or as a commercial enterprise.

SUMMARY

This chapter provides an introduction to the study of recreation, park, and leisure services, seen as vital ingredients in the lives of Americans and Canadians and as growing areas of career opportunity and professional responsibility.

It outlines several of the unique characteristics of leisure involvement, such as the diverse forms of recreational involvement and play motivations shared by persons of all ages and backgrounds. It then presents several important factors or social trends that have promoted the growth of the recreation and park movement during the twentieth century. These trends range from the increase of discretionary time and growing affluence to expanded interest in the creative arts and concern about the natural environment. Emphasis is placed on the development of the organized recreation system over the past several decades, with a discussion of different types of leisure-service agencies that are responsible for facility development and activity program management.

The chapter ends by briefly describing the emergence of the recreation, park, and leisure-service profession and emphasizing the need for specialized educational preparation for those holding responsible positions in this field. It also suggests a number of critical social challenges that will face leisure-service practitioners in the years ahead; these will be discussed more fully in the chapters that follow.

Questions for Class Discussion or Essay Examinations

1. Identify and discuss at least three important social factors (example: increased affluence) that have contributed to the growth of recreation and leisure concerns over the past several decades.

2. Discuss the use of the terms "organized recreation system" and "leisure industry." What do they mean, and what are their major components? On the basis of the experiences of class members, identify and describe several examples of different types of recreation agencies.

3. This chapter summarizes the emergence of professional leadership in recreation and parks and the role of professional preparation for those working in the field. Why should men and women in responsible leisure-service positions be expected to have an understanding of the history, psychology, and sociology of recreation?

Endnotes

[2]   See J. Charlesworth, *Leisure in America: Blessing or Curse?* (Lancaster, Pa.: American Academy of Political and Social Science, 1964).

[3]   Mark Searle and Russell Brayley, *Leisure Services in Canada: An Introduction* (State College, Pa.: Venture, 1993): 2.

[4]   Louis Harris, *Inside America* (New York: Vintage, Random House, 1987): 20.

[5]   Russell and Brayley, *op. cit.,* 1.

[6]   Sue Schmid, "Cities on the Move," *Athletic Business* (October 1993): 28.

[7]   Bernard Conn, "Arts in the Mainstream," *Parks and Recreation* (June 1988): 26–27.

[8]   Stephen Salisbury, "Financial Support for the Arts Plunges," *Philadelphia Inquirer* (6 December 1993): A-1.

9   "Keeping in Shape—Everybody's Doing It," *U.S. News and World Report* (13 August 1984): 24.

10   Michael Teague, "Vigorous Physical Activity for Adults—A Descriptive Epidemiology," *Journal of Physical Education, Recreation and Dance—Leisure Today* (April 1988): 47–49.

11   "America Shapes Up," *Time* (2 November 1981): 95.

12   Leonard Wankel, "Personal and Situational Factors Affecting Exercise Involvement: The Importance of Enjoyment," *Research Quarterly for Exercise and Sport* (Vol. 56 no. 3 1985): 281.

13   Alan Ewert and William Sutton, "Leisure Sports and the Changing American Life Style," *Journal of Physical Education, Recreation and Dance—Leisure Today* (April 1988): 12.

14   John Robinson and Geoffrey Godbey, "Has Fitness Participation Declined?" *American Demographics* (September 1993): 36–38.

15   "Study Finds a Soaring Rate of Obesity in U.S. Children," Associated Press (7 October 1995).

16   Joanne Kaldi, "Volleyball: This Fast-Growing Sport Serves Up Fun and Profit," *Parks and Recreation* (April 1995): 55–57.

17   Debra West, "Young Hockey Players Bring New Ice Age, Prompting Need for More Rinks," *New York Times* (31 July 1995): B-5.

18   W. F. LaPage and S. R. Ranney, "America's Wilderness: The Heart and Soul of Culture," *Parks and Recreation* (July 1988): 24.

19   John Cushman, Jr., "Forest Service Is Rethinking Its Mission," *New York Times* (24 April 1994): 22.

20   See, for example, Karla Henderson, M. Deborah Bialeschki, Susan Shaw and Valeria Freysinger, *Both Gains and Gaps: Feminist Perspectives on Women's Leisure* (State College, Pennsylvania: Venture Publishing, 1996).

21   "America's Immigrant Challenge," *Time* (Special Issue, Fall 1993): 3.

22   Edwin McDowell, "Cruise Lines Betting That Business Will Be Better," *New York Times* (15 June 1994): D-1.

23   Michael Ozanian, "Following the Money," *Financial World* (14 February 1995): 30.

24   Thomas McCarroll, "A Blockbuster Deal for Beavis and Butthead," *Time* (17 January 1994): 41.

25   Neal Peirce, "We Are Going to Recreate or Incarcerate," *Philadelphia Inquirer* (15 September 1994): 31.

Basic Concepts of Play, Leisure, and Recreation

It appears that recreation experience is much more than a casual, inconsequential time filler. Recreation is a cluster of human experiences of great range and subtlety. Among them are some fleeting impressions that fit the popular stereotype—pleasurable for the moment and soon gone. But we have found when people are asked to recount their most memorable recreation experiences [they often recall]. . . events of extraordinary personal meaning. These experiences are so significant that they are often a part of the personal identity of the individual and so memorable they last a lifetime. . . . In these narratives, largely unreported and often unanticipated, we find the recreation experience as a major source of self-discovery.[1]

INTRODUCTION

Any consideration of the broad field of recreation and leisure should begin with a clarification of terms and concepts. The words *play, leisure,* and *recreation* are frequently used interchangeably. However, while related, they have distinctly different meanings, and it is important for students and practitioners in this field to understand their varied implications and the differences among them.

---

[1] David Gray and Hilmi Ibrahim, "The Recreation Experience: A Source of Self-Discovery," *Journal of Physical Education, Recreation and Dance—Leisure Today* (October 1985): 8.

The rationale for stressing such conceptual understanding is clear-cut. Just as a doctor must know chemistry, anatomy, kinesiology, and other underlying sciences in order to practice medicine effectively, so the recreation and park professional must understand the meaning of leisure and its motivations and satisfactions if he or she is to provide effective recreation programs and services.

Similarly, the leisure scholar should not withdraw from the real world of leisure programming and participation by focusing only on abstract or theoretical models of free-time behavior. Instead, the scholar should become familiar with the profession of recreation service and should contribute to its effective performance. This chapter presents an analysis of play, leisure, and recreation, showing how they have been regarded by philosophers and social critics in the past and how their meanings have evolved in the present day.

A PRELIMINARY LOOK AT CONCEPTS

Of the three terms examined in this chapter, *play* is probably the oldest and most widely discussed. While it has often been described as a childish form of activity, not worthy of serious thought, leading psychologists and anthropologists today agree that play is an essential element in healthy human development. Found in all human societies and throughout the animal world as well, play involves basic drives and makes an important contribution to psychological well-being.

Leisure has been the concern of philosophers and other writers since the days of ancient Greece. At one point, it served chiefly to identify the upper classes in society, since it was regarded as their unique possession. More recently, leisure has been defined by economists and sociologists simply as non-work time. It is also regarded as a way of life marked by a sense of freedom and independent choice, and as the individual's opportunity for achieving self-actualization.

Recreation, while sharing some common elements with play, differs from it in the sense that it encompasses many types of experiences that are not at all playlike, such as reading, attending cultural events, or other intellectually based hobbies. In the past, recreation was regarded chiefly as a pleasurable and relaxing activity that served to restore and refresh individuals so that they might return to their work with new energy. Today it is understood to be a much more complex phenomenon, with meanings that extend far beyond simply taking part in activity.

These three terms are defined and fully discussed in this chapter, as they have evolved throughout history. In each case, a number of past or contemporary theories underlying the concept are presented, with a synthesis of the most relevant views at the end of the each section.

THE MEANING OF PLAY

The world *play* is derived from the Anglo-Saxon *plega,* meaning a game or sport, skirmish, fight, or battle. This is related to the Latin *plaga,* meaning a blow, stroke, or thrust. It is illustrated in the idea of striking or stroking instrument or playing a game by striking a ball. Other languages have words derived from a common root (such as the German *spielen* and the Dutch *spelen*) whose meanings include the playing of games, sports, and musical instruments. *Webster's New International Dictionary* offers several definitions of the noun *play*. Primary meanings include:

> a brisk handling, using, or plying; as, the play of a sword; any exercise or series of actions intended for diversion; a particular amusement; a game; a sport.[2]

Other dictionary meanings of play include stage exhibitions or dramatic presentations; any form of amusement or frolic; the act of carrying on a game; a way of acting or proceeding, often with the implication of deception or trickiness; or action or movement, as in the play of life. Play is traditionally thought of as a child's activity, in contrast to recreation, which is usually described as an adult activity. De Grazia expresses this view, saying:

> Play is what children do, frolic and sport. . . . Adults play too, though their games are less muscular and more intricate. Play has a special relation to leisure. . . . When adults play, as they do, of course, they play for recreation.[3]

Linked to this view is the idea that play is not serious or in earnest, in contrast with work, which is considered purposeful and productive. Some authors point out that in societies with a strong streak of puritanism, play is therefore denigrated and seen as markedly inferior to work.[4] Despite such limited views of play's significance, however, throughout history scholars, philosophers, and educators have been intrigued by its meaning and have assigned it an important place in communal life and education.

Historical Perspectives

In ancient Greece, play was assigned a valuable role in the lives of children, based on the writings of Plato and Aristotle. The Athenians placed great value on developing qualities of honor, loyalty, and beauty and other elements of productive citizenship in children. For them, play was an integral element of education and was considered a means of positive character development and teaching the values of Greek society. Torkildsen writes:

> Play to the Greeks was associated with childhood. Yet the citizenship of adult life and the appreciation of aesthetics, music, art, athletics, drama and poetry might be seen as the products of play. . . . [Moreover] the Greek citizen was bound to social commitment. There was a belief in universal personality/character which was held to be true of all noble persons. Hence life's activities were structured to fulfill this ideal. Play, then, was a means of integrating children into Greek culture.[5]

Later, as the Catholic Church gained dominance among the developing nations of western Europe, play came to be regarded as a social threat. The body was thought to detract from more spiritual or work-oriented values, and every effort was made to curb the pleasurable forms of play that had been popular in the Greek and Roman eras. During the Protestant Reformation, as Chapter 7 will show, varied play pursuits were widely condemned by leading theologians.

Gradually, however, educators and philosophers like Froebel, Rousseau, and Schiller came to the defense of play as an important aspect of childhood education. For example, Froebel wrote of play as the highest expression of human development in childhood:

> Play is the purest, most spiritual activity of man at this stage. . . . A child that plays thoroughly, with self-active determination, perseveringly until physical fatigue forbids, will surely be a thorough, determined man, capable of self-sacrifice for the promotion of the welfare of himself and others.[6]

EARLY THEORIES OF PLAY

In the nineteenth and early twentieth century, a number of influential scholars evolved comprehensive theories of play—explaining how it had developed and its role in human society and personal development.

Surplus-Energy Theory

The English philosopher Herbert Spencer, in his mid-nineteenth century work *Principles of Psychology,* advanced the view that play was primarily motivated by the need to burn up excess energy. He was influenced by the earlier writings of Friedrich von Schiller, who had suggested that when animals or birds were fully fed and had no other survival needs, they vented their exuberant energy in a variety of aimless and pleasurable forms of play. Spencer saw play among children as an imitation of adult activities; the sport of boys, such as chasing, wrestling, and taking one another prisoner, involved "predatory instincts." Even the games of skill practiced by adults were seen as involving the same motivation—satisfaction in getting the better of an antagonist.

Recreation Theory

An early explanation of play that was regarded as the converse of the Schiller-Spencer view was developed by Moritz Lazarus, a German philosopher, who argued that rather than serving to *burn up* excess energy, the purpose of play was to *conserve* or *restore* it. In other words, when one is exhausted through toil, play recharges one's energy for renewed work. Lazarus distinguished between physical and mental energy, pointing out that when the brain is "tired" (provided that it is not overtired), a change of activity, particularly in the form of physical exercise, will restore one's nervous energy. To illustrate, the desk worker who plays tennis after a long day's work simultaneously discharges surplus physical energy and restores mental energy. This theory was directed primarily at adults, who were seen as requiring recreation in order to be restored for further work. Lazarus felt that children were most inclined to play when they had an excess of physical and mental energy, and thus did not really use play for recreative purposes.

Instinct-Practice Theory

A more elaborate explanation of play was put forward by Karl Groos, a professor of philosophy at Basel, who wrote two major texts—one in 1896 on the play of animals and another in 1899 on the play of humans.

Groos argued that play helped animals survive by enabling them to practice and perfect the skills they would need in adult life. He concluded that the more adaptable and intelligent a species was, the more it needed a period of protected infancy and childhood for essential learning to take place. Thus among humans there was a lengthy early period during which children engaged in varied activities to perfect skills before they really needed them.

Groos saw play as a single, generalized instinct. In practice, it took four major forms: (1) fighting play, including contests, hunting play, and mental and physical competition; (2) love play and courtship activities; (3) imitative or dramatic play; and (4) social play. While it was necessary to distinguish between play and work, he conceded that work might include an element of play.

Modern ethologists who have systematically studied the behavior of animals and birds in interaction with each other and with their environment have identified varied forms of play that appear to illustrate the instinct-practice theory. For example, much play among young animals, particularly primates, involves aggressive teasing and mock battles. Such play represents a ritualized form of combat, in which the combatants practice their fighting skills and learn to interact with each other in establishing a "pecking order." In a special *National Geographic* feature on the play of animals, Stuart Brown wrote:

> New and exciting studies of the brain, evolution, and ethology, or animal behavior, suggest that play may be as important to life—for us and for other animals—as sleeping and dreaming. Play is key to an individual's development and to its social relationships and status. . . . Conversely, if young are prevented from playing or maltreated so that their play is abnormal, their development may also be abnormal.[7]

Anthropologists who have observed preindustrial tribal societies point out that "playing house" is often a form of rehearsal for adult roles. In some African rural villages, it may involve both technical and social skills, as boys and girls build and thatch small houses and make various tools and utensils. Often the play forms are gender-related: boys typically make axes, spears, shields, slings, bows, and arrows, or build miniature cattle kraals, while girls make pottery for cooking real or imaginary food or perhaps weave mats or baskets of plaited grass.

Catharsis Theory

The catharsis theory is based on the view that play—particularly competitive, active play—serves as a safety valve for the expression of bottled-up emotions. Among the ancient Greeks, Aristotle saw drama as a means of purging oneself of hostile or aggressive emotions; by vicarious sharing in the staged experience, onlookers purified themselves of harmful feelings. A number of early twentieth-century writers expanded this theory. Harvey Carr, an American psychologist, wrote:

> Catharsis . . . implies the idea of purging or draining of that energy which has *anti-social possibilities*. . . The value of football, boxing, and other physical contests in relieving the pugnacious tendencies of boys is readily apparent as examples. Without the numberless well-organized set forms of play possessed by society which give a harmless outlet to the mischievous and unapplied energy of the young the task of the teacher and parent would be appalling.[8]

Coupled with the surplus-energy theory, the catharsis theory suggested a vital necessity for active play to help children and youth burn up excess energy and provide a socially acceptable channel for aggressive or hostile emotions and drives. Among other modern social scientists, Konrad Lorenz wrote extensively on aggression and pointed out that it was probably in ritualized fighting that sport had its origin. He concluded that the major value of sport today lies in providing a healthy safety valve for dangerous forms of aggression.[9]

Recapitulation Theory

A theory of play widely discussed at the turn of the twentieth century was the so-called recapitulation theory advanced by G. Stanley Hall, a prominent American professor of psychology and pedagogy. Hall's dual interest in evolutionary theory and education led him to study children's behavior with scientific rigor; for the first time a serious scientist concerned himself with the kinds of dolls children preferred and their building of sand castles.

Through play, children were thought to be re-enacting the lives of their ancestors, engaging in activities—like fishing, canoeing, hunting, or camping—that were vital to the species eons ago. Play was seen as "the purest expression of heredity. . . . not doing things to be useful later on, but . . . rehearsing racial history." Hall developed a "culture-epoch" analogy that showed how children traveled in their play through successive periods of human history, such as the *animal* stage, the *savage* stage, the *nomad* stage, and ultimately the *tribal* stage of development. To each of these he attached typical forms of children's play found at that stage of maturation.

Hall's theory was obviously more applicable to a primitive, preindustrial society in which village customs were handed down faithfully and in which many games and sports replicated earlier customs and traditions than to a modern, urban culture heavily dependent on newly developed technological games, toys, and entertainment.

TWENTIETH-CENTURY CONCEPTS OF PLAY

During the first three decades of the twentieth century, a number of psychologists and educators examined play, particularly as a developmental and learning experience for children.

Self-Expression Theory

Two leading physical educators, Elmer Mitchell and Bernard Mason, saw play primarily as a result of the need for self-expression. Humans were regarded as active, dynamic beings with the need to find outlets for their energies, use their abilities, and express their personalities. The specific types of activity that an individual engaged in were, according to Mitchell and Mason, influenced by such factors as physiological and anatomical structure, physical fitness level, environment, and family and social background.[10]

In addition to these elements, the "self-expression" theory also suggested that certain universal wishes of humankind were influential in shaping play attitudes and habits. These included: (1) the wish for new experience; (2) the wish for participation in a group enterprise; (3) the wish for security; (4) the wish for response and recognition from others; and (5) the wish for the aesthetic.

Mitchell and Mason's analysis avoided the pitfalls of earlier theories by explaining the varied forms that play takes among different individuals of all ages. Because their theory of play incorporated a variety of motivations and psychological theories that had gained influence in the early part of the twentieth century, it was accepted by many educators and recreation professionals in the United States and Canada.

Play as a Social Necessity

Joseph Lee, who is widely regarded as the father of the play movement in America and who promoted the establishment of numerous playgrounds and recreation centers, was instrumental in the public acceptance of play as an important force in child development and community life.

> **L**ee believed that play contributed to the wholesome development of personal character because it involved lessons of discipline, sacrifice, and morality. He saw it as more than mere pleasurable pastime, but rather as a serious element in the lives of children and—along with his contemporary pioneer, Luther Halsey Gulick—he considered it a vital element in community life. This view extended itself to a literal application of play as a means of preparing children for the adult work world. Wayne Stormann points out that play was considered a useful form of manual training because it coordinated bodily functions, promoted health, and prepared children for the "indoor confinement," first of schools and then of factory life. Quoting Goodman, he points out that on most playgrounds there were activities specifically designed to socialize children toward their future roles as wage earners, including raffia work, woodworking, and *sloyd,* a Swedish-designed system of toolwork and manual training. He continues:
>
> > Even those activities that were not specifically preparations for factory work were ruled by the major regulator of factory life, the clock. In accommodating the organized play movement to industry, the idea was to use play and sport as a way of socializing people to efficiency, sacrifice, and self-control.[11]

Typologies of Play Activity

In the twentieth century, more and more social and behavioral scientists began to examine play empirically. One such investigator, the French sociologist, Roger Caillois, examined the play experience itself by classifying the games and play activities that were characteristic of various cultures and identifying their apparent functions and values. Caillois established four major types of play and game activity: agon, alea, mimicry, and ilinx.

Agon refers to activities that are competitive and in which the equality of the participants' chances of winning is artificially created. Winners are determined through such qualities as speed, endurance, strength, memory, skills, and ingenuity. Agonistic games may be played by individuals or teams; they presuppose sustained attention, training and discipline, perseverance, limits, and rules. Clearly, most modern games and sports, including many card and table games involving skill, are examples of agon.

Alea includes those games or contests over whose outcome the contestant has no control; winning is the result of fate rather than the skill of the player. Games of dice, roulette, and baccarat, as well as lotteries, are examples of alea.

Mimicry is based on the acceptance of illusions or imaginary universes. It includes a class of games in which players make believe, or make others believe, that they are other than themselves. For children, Caillois writes:

> The aim is to imitate adults. . . . This explains the success of the toy weapons and miniatures which copy the tools, engines, arms and machines used by adults. The little girl plays her mother's role as cook, laundress and ironer. The boy makes believe he is a soldier, musketeer, policeman, pirate, cowboy, Martian, etc.[12]

Clearly, this analysis reflects a pattern of sex stereotyping in children's play that has been sharply challenged in recent years. On the adult level, mimicry is found in theatrical presentations or games involving simulation and role playing. Caillois saw a strong relationship between agon and mimicry in contests such as boxing or wrestling and football, tennis, or polo games, which are

> intrinsic spectacles, with costumes, solemn overtures, appropriate liturgy and regulated procedures. . . . In a word, these are dramas whose vicissitudes keep the public breathless, and lead to denouements which exalt some and depress others. The nature of these spectacles remains that of an *agon,* but their outward aspect is of an exhibition.[13]

Ilinx consists of play activities based on the pursuit of vertigo or dizziness. Historically, ilinx was found in primitive religious dances or other rituals that induced the trancelike state necessary for worship. Today it may be seen in children's games that lead to dizziness by whirling rapidly, and in the use of swings and seesaws. Among adults, ilinx may be achieved through certain dances involving rapid turns or through such amusement park rides as rollercoasters.

Contrasting Styles of Play   Caillois also suggested two extremes of play behavior. The first of these, which he calls *paidia,* involves exuberance, freedom, and uncontrolled and spontaneous gaiety. The second, *ludus,* is characterized by rules and conventions and represents calculated and contrived activity. Each of the four forms of play may be conducted at either extreme of *paidia* or *ludus* or at some point on a continuum between the two. Caillois's analysis provides a rich historical perspective on play activity, showing how many play artifacts and activities—such as masks, kites, tops, and balls, as well as songs, games, and dances—are the cultural residue of past "magical" beliefs and rites that have lost their original potency and are now carried on as play as a matter of tradition and custom.

Anthropological Analysis of Play

Other social scientists have focused on the functions of play within different human societies. In tribal cultures, they have found it to be a form of behavior that is connected to many aspects of daily life and linked to major events and ceremonies. One authority, Edward Norbeck, points out that play, defined as "voluntary, pleasurable behavior that is separated in time from other activities and that has a quality of make-believe," is found among many living creatures and throughout the entire class of mammals. However, of all forms of life, Norbeck says, the human is the "supreme player."

Play behavior is commonly found at rites of birth, coming of age, marriage, and death and burial—indeed, all of our important social events tend to be incorporated into social observances that include a rich element of play. Norbeck concludes that play is both a biological and a sociocultural phenomenon; he feels that it has significance in many areas, often in those involving important social problems.[14]

Communal Functions

Play has been assigned an important communal role throughout human history, in addition to the pleasure it may provide for individual participants. For example, all cultures have rituals involving music, dance, and dramatic play. Sometimes based on religious belief, they may also serve as healing rites or as celebrations of historic events. Such customs serve to reinforce the ties that bind members of the tribe or other social group together, and to transmit traditional beliefs and values from generation to generation.

Numerous anthropologists have documented such forms of communal play in societies. Bronislaw Malinowski describes varied rituals as a unique blending of both practical and mystical beliefs and customs, intended to deal with forces of nature that cannot otherwise be combated or controlled. Such rituals are kept strictly apart from work:

> Every magical ceremony has its distinctive name, its appropriate time, and its place in the scheme of work, and it stands out of the ordinary course of activities. . . . Work is always tabooed on such occasions, many of which are uniquely playlike.[15]

Food is frequently a part of ceremonies of a religious character or at harvest celebrations, seasonal feasts, or the return of successful hunters or fishermen. Malinowski points out that there are many occurrences of collective play in areas of life not dominated by religion. He writes:

> Collective work in the gardens, as I have seen it in Melanesia, when men became carried away with emulation and zest for work, singing rhythmic songs, uttering shouts of joy and slogans of competitive challenge, is full of this "collective effervescence.". . . A battle, a sailing regatta, one of the big tribal gatherings for trading purposes, a . . . corroboree, a village brawl, are all from the social as well as from the psychological point of view, essentially examples of crowd effervescence.[16]

Another anthropologist, Felix Keesing, has identified several distinctly different functions of play in tribal societies. These include: (1) pleasurable, or hedonistic, effects; (2) relaxing or energy-restorative functions; (3) integrative effects, which develop stability and cohesion among both individuals and groups in the society; (4) therapeutic or sublimative functions, which channel off conflicts, aggressions, and hostilities; (5) creative opportunities for innovation and self-expression; (6) communicative functions, which assist learning and habit formation among both children and adults; and (7) symbolic values, in expressing cultural values and beliefs.[17]

Keesing observes that in some cases the same activity may readily be adapted to new uses and needs, while retained in its original form for traditional purposes. The ceremonies of American Indians are frequently used in one form for tourist exhibitions and in another quite different form as part of traditional religious practice.

The Play Element in Culture

Probably the most far-reaching and influential theory of play as a cultural phenomenon was advanced by the Dutch social historian, Johan Huizinga, in his provocative work *Homo Ludens* (Man the Player).

Huizinga presents the thesis that play pervades all of life. He sees it as having certain characteristics: it is a voluntary activity, marked by freedom and never imposed by physical necessity or moral duty. It stands outside the realm of satisfying physiological needs and appetites. It is separate from ordinary life both in its location and its duration, being "played out" within special time periods and in such special places as the arena, the card table, the stage, and the tennis court. Play is controlled, says Huizinga, by special sets of rules, and it demands absolute order. It is also marked by uncertainty and tension. Finally, it is not concerned with good or evil, although it has its own ethical value in that its rules must be obeyed.

In Huizinga's view, play reveals itself chiefly in two kinds of activity—contests *for* something and representations *of* something. He regards it as an important civilizing influence

in human society and cites as an example the society of ancient Greece, which was perme-
ated with play forms. He traces historically the origins of many social institutions as ritualized forms of play activity. For example, the element of play was initially dominant in the
evolution of judicial processes. Law consisted of a pure contest between competing individuals or groups. It was not a matter of being right or wrong; instead, trials were conducted through the use of oracles, contests of chance that determined one's fate, trials of
strength or resistance to torture, and verbal contests. Huizinga suggests that the same principle applies to many other cultural institutions:

> In myth and ritual the great instinctive forces of civilized life have their origin: law and order, commerce
> and profit, craft and art, poetry, wisdom and science. All are rooted in the primeval soil of play.[18]

While Huizinga's view may seem extreme, it may be illustrated by examining two aspects
of contemporary life: war and the business world.

War as Play   Although we tend to regard play as nonserious, it may obviously be carried
on for stakes as important as life or death. High-risk sports such as hang gliding or extremely
violent spectator sports are the most obvious examples of this. Indeed, Huizinga points out that
war itself developed historically as a kind of game. The elements of competing national armies
(teams), stratagems and deception, elaborate codes for prisoners, hostages and noncombatants,
permissible weapons, and honorable behavior all support the idea of war as a game on a giant
scale. Until recently, armies went off to fight in a spirit of national celebration. Even today in
some primitive cultures warfare is practiced as a game and carried on under strict limitations
rather than as a serious attempt to wipe out or actually conquer one's opponents. Likewise, the
origins of much modern play are inextricably bound up with warfare. Many sports, for example,
once represented military skills. Hunting, horsemanship, archery, fencing, and shooting are
recreational activities once essential to warfare.

To illustrate the point, a military historian describes the "derring-do" spirit in which soldiers in an earlier era approached battle—as an occasion for valor and sheer fun. Young men,
Farwell writes, relished the subsidized irresponsibility of commissioned service in which they
could do what they liked best: riding, hunting, drinking, making friends, seeing the world,
and showing initiative and courage. One future British field marshal wrote to his aunt during
the Crimean War, "Man shooting is the finest sport of all." Others describe war as life's greatest experience: "Indescribably exciting, filled with the thunder of cannon, the clash of steel,
clatter of horse's hooves and blare of the trumpet."[19]

Play in the Business World   Huizinga's thesis may also be illustrated in the world
of business, as in the takeover battles waged recently among giant corporations. The "investment game" is an obvious form of gambling for many participants. Beyond this, much business practice—including the development of new technology, advertising strategy, personnel
"raids," and even the pervasive practice of company spying—suggests that business is often
approached as an exciting game.

The modern industrial leader (as revealed in a study of 250 top executives in leading
American companies) likes to take calculated risks and is fascinated by new techniques. This
person views a career in terms of options and possibilities as if it were a huge game. Such a
person's character may reveal a number of contradictions: at once cooperative and competitive, detached and playful, but also compulsively driven to succeed; a team player or a

hopeful superstar; a team leader or a rebel against bureaucratic regulations; a "jungle fighter" or a loyal company member. Maccoby writes:

> Unlike other business types, the leader is energized to compete not because he wants to build an empire, not for riches, but rather for fame, glory, the exhilaration of running his team and of gaining victories. His main goal is to be known as a winner, and his deepest fear is to be labeled a loser.[20]

Huizinga concludes that within contemporary civilization, play is slowly declining. In sports, for example, games have been raised "to such a pitch of technical organization and scientific thoroughness that the real play spirit is threatened with extinction." It has become too serious a business. He suggests that in many other areas of life—such as warfare, contemporary politics, and international law—the old play rules are no longer respected and that culture therefore suffers.

PSYCHOLOGICAL ANALYSIS OF PLAY

Over the past several decades, numerous authorities in the fields of psychology and psychoanalysis have examined play and its role in personality development, learning theory, mental health, and related areas.

Play in Personality Development

A respected child psychologist, Lawrence K. Frank, points out that play is important to the psychological and emotional development of children. He writes:

> Play, as we are beginning to understand, is the way the child learns what no one can teach him. It is the way he explores and orients himself to the actual world of space and time, of things, animals, structures, and people. Through play he learns to live in our symbolic world of meaning and values, of progressive striving for deferred goals, at the same time exploring and experimenting and learning in his own individual way. Through play the child practices and rehearses endlessly the complicated and subtle patterns of human living and communication which he must master if he is to become a participating adult in our social life.[21]

Jerome Bruner, a leading authority on cognitive growth and the educational process, and past president of the American Psychological Association, reinforces this view, pointing out that even apparently casual play expressions are structured and governed by rules and contribute significantly to childhood learning. Bruner writes:

> We have come a long way since Piaget's brilliant observation that play helps the child assimilate experience to his personal schema of the world, and more research on play is under way. We now know that play is serious business, indeed, the principal business of childhood. It is the vehicle of improvisation and combination, the first carrier of rule systems through which a world of cultural restraint replaces the operation of childish impulse.[22]

Jean Piaget theorized that in the process of intellectual development, the child moves through several different phases, including the *sensory-motor* phase, the *pre-operational* phase, the *concrete operations* phase, and the *formal operations* phase. Within each phase, appropriate play activities provide skills that need to be mastered as children move away from their own ego-centered play to involve others, adapt to real situations, and learn game structures and rules.[23]

In other research on the linkage between play and personal development, psychologist J. Nina Lieberman determined that the quality of playfulness was closely associated with originality and creativity in such areas as science, music, writing, and painting.[24]

Psychoanalytical Perspectives on Play

Sigmund Freud, the father of modern psychoanalysis, had a number of distinctive views regarding the meaning and purpose of play. Freud saw play as a medium through which children are able to gain control and competence and to resolve conflicts that occur in their lives. He felt that children are frequently overwhelmed by their life circumstances, which may be confusing, complex, and unpleasant. Through play, they are able to reexperience threatening events, and so to control and master them. In this sense, play and dreams serve a therapeutic function for children.

In general, Freud felt that play represented the child's way of dealing with reality—in effect, by playing with it, making it more acceptable, and exerting mastery over it. He wrote:

> Might we not say that every child at play behaves like a creative writer, in that he creates a world of his own, or, rather rearranges the things of his world in a new way which pleases him? It would be wrong to think he does not take his play seriously; on the contrary he takes his play very seriously and he expends large amounts of emotion on it. *The opposite of play is not what is serious but what is real.*[25]

Ellis sums up the Freudian position by suggesting that children unconsciously add elements from their environment to their fantasies, thus combining both reality and unreality in play. In contrast, adults are more inhibited in their outward, visible play and feel constrained to behave realistically; they tend to rely on fantasy, which is hidden, to explore and play with reality. The distinguished psychoanalyst, Bruno Bettelheim, writes that Freud assigned play a broader role than this, regarding it as the "means by which the child accomplishes his first great cultural and psychological achievements; through play he expresses himself."[26]

A number of Freud's other theories, such as the "pleasure principle" and the "death wish," have also been seen as having strong implications for the analysis of play. The Freudian view of play influenced many psychotherapists and educators in their approach to childhood education and treatment programs. Bettelheim, Erik Erikson, and Anna Freud, Freud's daughter, all experimented with the use of play in treating disturbed children. Erikson, for example, saw play as

> a function of the ego, an attempt to bring into synchronization the bodily and social processes of which one is a part . . . the emphasis [being placed] on the ego's need to master the various areas of life.[27]

Erikson describes play as a way of testing fate and causality and a means of breaking away from sharply defined social reality and the confinement of time and space. In working with disturbed children, Erikson comments that "to play it out" is the most natural self-healing measure childhood affords.

Play as Creative Exploration

Other contemporary theories of play emphasize its role in creative exploration and problem solving. Studies of arousal, excitement, and curiosity have led to two related theories of play: the *stimulus-arousal* and *competence-effectance* theories.

Stimulus-Arousal

This approach is based on the observation that both humans and animals constantly seek stimuli of various kinds, both to gain knowledge and to satisfy a need for excitement, risk, surprise, and pleasure. For example, Ellis sums up the work of Berlyne, a leading investigator of the stimulus-arousal process, who showed that

> humor, and its overt behavioral concomitants, smiling and laughter, are created by variables such as novelty, surprise, incongruity, ambiguity, complexity, all of which possess arousal potential. Humor is a cognitive process whereby a sequence of stimuli or ideas are strung together in such a way as to generate an expectation which is shattered or a conflict which is suddenly resolved surprisingly. . . .
>
> That subclass of stimulus-seeking behaviors that are humorous and engender smiles and laughter is generally referred to as fun, and explains the frequent occurrence of the words *fun, positive affect,* and *pleasure* in definitions of the word *play.*. . . . Fun has arousal potential.[28]

However, the expectation that play is always light, enjoyable, pleasant, or humorous can be misleading. Often, play activities can be frustrating, boring, unpleasant, or even physically painful—particularly when they lead to addiction (as in the case of drug, alcohol, or gambling abuse) and subsequent ill-health or economic losses.

Arousal-seeking play may often be centered about experiences that are *not* overtly pleasant or safe, such as high-risk, outdoor adventure pastimes. A professor of psychology at Johns Hopkins University, Marvin Zuckerman, discovered that many individuals rate high on a "sensation-seeking" scale. Such men and women abhor monotony and boredom, are eager to try risky sports and outdoor pursuits, and have varied and exciting sexual partners and involvements. Even in their jobs, such sensation seekers welcome challenge and excitement; they tend to experiment with drugs and are frequently involved in hedonistic activities.

In the past, wars, public executions, orgiastic feasts, or even the danger inherent in daily living in a primitive and risky environment meant that people were subjected to many forms of exciting stimuli. In the modern world, with life much safer and more secure, people often suffer from boredom, with the need to search for new, nonvicarious sources of excitement and novel experience. Zuckerman writes:

> "Boredom" is the term we use to describe the negative feeling produced by lack of change in the environment. When we are bored, we may be inclined to indulge in risky adventures, artistic creation, adulterous sex, alcohol, drugs, and sometimes even aggression. I call this demand for stimulation and varied experience "sensation seeking." It is one of man's primary needs, and the source of much of our creativity as well as much of our discontent and destructiveness.[29]

The essential point of this theory is that play often serves not to *reduce* drives and tensions but instead to *create* and *satisfy* them, and thereby the player achieves a sense of arousal and emotional release.

Competence-Effectance

A closely related theory holds that much play is motivated by the need of the player to test the environment, solve problems, and gain a sense of mastery and accomplishment. Typically, it involves experimentation or information-seeking behavior in which the player—whether human or animal—observes the environment, tests or manipulates it, and observes the outcome.

Beyond this, the player seeks to develop *competence,* defined as the ability to interact effectively with the environment. Often this is achieved through repetition of the same action even when it has been mastered. The term *effectance* refers to the player's need to be able to master the environment and, even when uncertainty about it has been resolved, to produce desired effects in it. R. W. White argues that the knowledge-seeking motivation in itself is not a sufficient explanation for behavior which continues after the novelty of a new situation has been experienced. Instead, the feeling of mastery, which leads to a sense of personal effectiveness and accomplishment, is often responsible for the repetition of certain play behaviors.[30]

Cziksentmihalyi's "Flow" Principle　　Related to this is Mihaly Cziksentmihalyi's view of play as process in which ideally the player's skills are pitched at the challenge level of the tasks. If the task is too simple, it may become boring and lacking in appeal. If it is too difficult, it may produce anxiety and frustration, and the player may discontinue activity or change the approach to it so it becomes more satisfying.

Beyond this idea, Cziksentmihalyi suggests that there is a unique element in true play, which he identifies as a sense of flow. This is the sensation players feel when they are totally involved with the activity. It involves a feeling of harmony and full immersion in play; at a peak level, players might tend to lose their sense of time and their surroundings and even to experience an altered state of being. Such flow, he argues, could be found in some work situations, but it is much more commonly experienced in play such as games or sports.[31]

Play Defined

It is difficult to arrive at a single definition of play because it takes so many forms and appears in so many contexts. However, a general definition would describe it as a form of human or animal activity or behavioral style that is self-motivated and carried on for intrinsic, rather than external, purposes. It is generally pleasurable and is often marked by elements of competition, humor, creative exploration and problem-solving, and mimicry or role-playing. It appears most frequently in leisure activities, but may be part of work. It is typically marked by freedom and lack of structure, but may involve rules and prescribed actions, as in sports and games.

THE MEANING OF LEISURE: SIX VIEWS

Over the past several decades, the statement has frequently been made that one of the most crucial challenges of the present day is the need to come to grips with the "new leisure." What exactly is leisure?

Etymologically, the English world *leisure* seems to be derived from the Latin *licere,* meaning "to be permitted" or "to be free." From *licere* came the French *loisir,* meaning "free time," and such English words as *license* (originally meaning immunity from public obligation) and *liberty.* These words are all related; they suggest free choice and the absence of compulsion.

The early Greek word *scole* or *skole* meant "leisure." It led to the latin *scola* and the English *school* or *scholar*—thus implying a close connection between leisure and education. The word *scole* also referred to places where scholarly discussions were held. One such place was a grove next to the temple of Apollo Lykos, which became known as the *lyceum.* From this came the French *lycée,* meaning "school"—again implying a bond between leisure and education.

Leisure has been given six interpretations. These are: (1) the *classical* view of leisure, as found in the writings of Sebastian de Grazia and Josef Pieper; (2) the view of leisure as a *social class* attribute; (3) the concept of leisure as *free* or *discretionary time;* (4) the idea of leisure as *activity* that is carried on in free time; (5) the more recent interpretation of leisure as a *state of being* marked by perceived freedom; and (6) leisure as a form of *spiritual involvement* or *expression.*

The Classical View of Leisure

Aristotle regarded leisure as "a state of being in which activity is performed for its own sake." It was sharply contrasted with work or purposeful action, involving instead such pursuits as art, political debate, philosophical discussion, and learning in general. The Athenians saw work as ignoble; to them it was boring and monotonous. A common Greek word for work is *ascholia,* meaning the absence of leisure—whereas we do the opposite, defining leisure as the absence of work. Simpson and Yoshioka distill five basic principles from Aristotle's writings regarding the functions of leisure in society:

> (1) Leisure is activity, the basis of culture, and the source of the good life; (2) Leisure includes music, art, community involvement, physical fitness and contemplation; (3) Moderation is a prerequisite for leisure and for a good life; (4) Peace is a prerequisite for leisure, and a nation trained for war is ill-prepared for peace and for leisure; and (5) People must be taught the proper use of leisure, and this education is the responsibility of the state.[32]

For the Athenians particularly, leisure was the highest value of life, and work the lowest. Since the upper classes were not required to work, they were free to engage in intellectual, cultural, and artistic activity. Leisure represented an ideal state of freedom and the opportunity for spiritual and intellectual enlightenment. Within modern philosophies of leisure that have descended from this classical Athenian view, leisure is still seen as occurring only in time that is not devoted to work. However, it is considered far more than just a temporary release from work used to restore one for more work. Instead, according to Pieper,

> leisure does not exist for the sake of work—however much strength it may give a man to work; the point of leisure is not to be a restorative, a pick-me-up, whether mental or physical. . . . Leisure, like contemplation, is of a higher order than the active life. . . . [it involves] the capacity to soar in active celebration, to overstep the boundaries of the workaday world and reach out to superhuman, life-giving existential forces that refresh and renew us before we turn back to our daily work.[33]

Pieper goes on to say that leisure does not represent mere idleness; indeed, this is the very opposite of leisure. And de Grazia stresses the view that free time is not necessarily leisure; anybody can have free time, but not everybody can have leisure. "It is an ideal, a state of being, a condition of man, which few desire and fewer achieve." Both authors agree that leisure involves a spiritual and mental attitude, a state of inward calm, contemplation, serenity, and openness.

How meaningful is this classical view of leisure today? It has two flaws. First, it is linked to the idea of an aristocratic class structure based on the availability of slave labor. When Aristotle wrote in his *Treatise on Politics* that "it is of course generally understood that in a well-ordered state, the citizens should have leisure and not have to provide for their daily needs," he meant that leisure was given to a comparatively few patricians and made possible through the strenuous labor of the many.

In modern society, leisure cannot be a privilege reserved for the few; instead, it must be widely available to all. It must exist side by side with work that is respected in our society, and it should have a meaningful relationship to work. Moreover, the classical view of leisure imposes an extremely narrow definition on this concept. De Grazia specifically rejects the modern concept of recreation, seeing it as an inappropriate use of leisure. Recreation, he says, is purposeful and intended to restore one for further work; therefore, it cannot be considered part of leisure.

The implication is that leisure should be calm, quiet, contemplative and unhurried, as implied by the word *leisurely*. Obviously, this concept would not apply to those uses of leisure today that are dynamic, active, and demanding or that may have a degree of extrinsic purpose about them.

Leisure as a Symbol of Social Class

The view of leisure as closely related to social class stemmed from the work of Thorstein Veblen, a leading American sociologist of the late nineteenth century. Veblen showed how, throughout history, ruling classes emerged that identified themselves sharply through the possession and use of leisure. In his major work, *The Theory of the Leisure Class*, he pointed out that in Europe—during the feudal and Renaissance periods and finally during the industrial age—the possession and visible use of leisure became the hallmark of the upper class.

Veblen attacked the "idle rich"; he saw leisure as a complete way of life for the privileged class, regarding them as exploiters who lived on the toil of others. He coined the phrase "conspicuous consumption" to describe their way of life throughout history:

> The . . . gentleman of leisure . . . consumes freely and of the best, in food, drink, narcotics, shelter, services, ornaments, apparel, weapons and accoutrement. . . . He must cultivate his tastes . . . he becomes a connoisseur . . . and the demands made upon the gentleman in this direction therefore tend to change his life of leisure into a more or less arduous application to the business of . . . conspicuous leisure and conspicuous consumption.[34]

To maintain their status, Veblen wrote, members of the leisure class—from the feudal nobleman to the self-made millionaire industrialist—had to give valuable presents and expensive feasts and entertainments to impress society. Chiefly through Veblen's influence, the concept of the leisure class came into being. His analysis is not as applicable to contemporary life as it was to the time when it was written, since the working classes today tend to have far *more* free time than industrial managers, business executives, and professionals. Veblen's contempt for leisure as belonging only to the "idle rich" no longer applies with full force, both because of this greater working-class leisure and because of the involvement of the present generation of our most wealthy and influential families (such as the Rockefellers, Harrimans, and Kennedys) in finance and public life. With the exception of a small group of "jet setters," the class he criticized no longer exists.

To some degree, however, Veblen's analysis is still relevant. The wealthy or privileged class in modern society—although its members may not have an immense amount of free time—continues to engage in a wide variety of expensive and prestigious leisure activities. They tend to travel widely, entertain, patronize the arts, and engage in exclusive and high-status pastimes. Although rarely called the "leisure class" today, this group continues to define itself through its use of leisure.

Leisure as Unobligated Time

The most common approach to leisure is to regard it as unobligated or discretionary time. In a number of sociological references, this concept of leisure is clearly stated. The *Dictionary of Sociology* offers the following definition:

> Leisure is the free time after the practical necessities of life have been attended to. . . . Conceptions of leisure vary from the arithmetic one of time devoted to work, sleep, and other necessities, subtracted from 24 hours—which gives the surplus time—to the general notion of leisure as the time which one uses as he pleases.[35]

This view of leisure sees it essentially as time that is free from work or from such work-related responsibilities as travel, study, or social involvements based on work. It also excludes time devoted to essential life-maintenance activities, such as sleep, eating, or personal care. Its most important characteristic is that it lacks a sense of obligation or compulsion. This approach to defining leisure is most popular among economists or sociologists who are particularly concerned with trends in the economic and industrial life of the nation.

While this appears to be convenient and largely a matter of arithmetic (subtracting work and other obligated tasks from the 24 hours that are available each day and coming out with a block of time that can be called leisure), it has some built-in complexities. For example, is it possible to say that *any* time is totally free of obligation or compulsion or that any form of leisure activity is totally without some extrinsic purpose?

Semi-Leisure and Free Time   Joffre Dumazedier, a leading French sociologist, comments that if leisure is governed in part by commercial, utilitarian, or ideological concerns or purposes, it is no longer wholly leisure. He suggests that activities in which there is a degree of such obligation or purpose be regarded as semi-leisure. Semi-leisure occurs when the world of work and of primary obligations partially overlaps with the world of leisure.[36]

For example, some uses of free time that are not clearly work or paid for as work may contribute to success at work. A person may read books or articles related to work, attend evening classes that contribute to work competence, invite guests to a party because of work associations, or join a country club because of its value in establishing business contacts or promoting sales. Within community life, those nonwork occupations that have a degree of obligation about them—such as serving on a school board or as an unpaid member of a town council—may also be viewed as part of a person's civic responsibility. In terms of time, energy, or degree of commitment, it would be difficult to distinguish such activities from work.

The strict view of leisure as time that lacks *any* obligation or compulsion is suspect. If one chooses to raise dogs as a hobby or to play an instrument in an orchestra, one begins to assume a system of routines, schedules, and commitments to others. De Grazia suggests that none of these semi-leisure activities should be regarded as true leisure. He points out that the approximately eight hours left over each day after work and sleep are typically devoted to such activities as

> shopping, grooming, chores, transportation, voting, making love, helping children with homework, reading the newspaper, getting the roof repaired, trying to locate the doctor, going to church, visiting relatives, and so on. Do all these activities rightly belong to free time?[37]

Leisure as Activity

A fourth common understanding of leisure is that it is activity in which people engage during their free time. For example, the International Study Group on Leisure and Social Science defines it thus:

> Leisure consists of a number of occupations in which the individual may indulge of his own free will—either to rest, to amuse himself, to add to his knowledge and improve his skills disinterestedly and to increase his voluntary participation in the life of the community after discharging his professional, family, and social duties.[38]

Similarly, Dumazedier defines leisure in these terms:

> Leisure is activity—apart from the obligations of work, family and society—to which the individual turns at will, for either relaxation, diversion, or broadening his knowledge and his spontaneous social participation, the free exercise of his creative capacity.[39]

An American sociologist, Bennett Berger, echoes this concept by pointing out that the sociology of leisure during the 1950s and 1960s consisted of "little more than a reporting of survey data on what selected samples of individuals do with the time in which they are not working, and the correlation of these data with conventional demographic variables."

Obviously, this concept of leisure is closely linked to the idea of recreation, since it involves the way in which free time is used. Early writers on recreation stressed the importance of activity; for example, Jay B. Nash urged that the recreative act be thought of as an active, "doing" experience. Recuperation through play, he wrote, is not wholly relegated to inertia—doing nothing—but is gained through action. Activity, involving a wide variety of responses to internal or external stimuli, is fundamental to the best use of leisure. Certainly, for many individuals, Nash's view of leisure is too confining. They would consider relatively passive activities, such as reading a book, going to a museum, watching a film, or even dozing in a hammock or daydreaming, to be appropriate leisure pursuits—along with forms of active play.

Leisure as a State of Being

This fifth concept of leisure places the emphasis on the perceived freedom of the activity and on the role of leisure involvement in helping the individual achieve personal fulfillment and self-enrichment. Neulinger writes:

> To leisure means to be engaged in an activity performed for its own sake, to do something which gives one pleasure and satisfaction, which involves one to the very core of one's being. To leisure means to be oneself, to express one's talents, one's capacities, one's potentials.[40]

This concept of leisure implies a lifestyle which is *holistic,* in the sense that one's view of life is not sharply fragmented into a number of spheres such as family activities, religion, work, and free time. Instead, all such involvements are seen as part of a whole in which the individual explores his or her capabilities, develops enriching experiences with others, and seeks "self-actualization" in the sense of being creative, involved, expressive, and fully alive.

The idea of leisure as a state of being places great emphasis on the need for perceived freedom. Recognizing the fact that some constraints always exist, Godbey defines leisure in the following way:

> Leisure is living in relative freedom from the external compulsive forces of one's culture and physical environment so as to be able to act from internal compulsion in ways which are personally pleasing and intuitively worthwhile.[41]

Perceived Freedom in Leisure

The word "leisurely" has always implied behavior that is relaxed, easygoing, and unpressured. In an essay written while on vacation on the Maine coast, the columnist Ellen Goodman tells how she takes her wristwatch off, sheds her city wardrobe, and gradually frees herself of the time pressures of her workaday life:

> Like most people in the Western world, I have grown up in the artificial environment of modern society. It's a place dominated by external timekeepers, calendars, schedules, clocks. Our lives are subdivided into fiscal years, academic years, weekdays, weekends, deadlines. We are taught that there is a time to get up, a time to go to work, a time to eat. We set the clock by a single standard.[42]

Gradually, the columnist slips into a true state of leisure, with her daily life in Casco Bay becoming ordered by the coastal tides—nature's reminder—rather than the artificial alarm clock. Eventually, she knows that she is on vacation when she forgets which day of the week it is. As the vacation nears its end, Goodman tries to postpone the tasks that await her at home, longing to sink for just a few more hours into a state of timelessness and ease in her rope hammock.

Such contemporary leisure theorists stress the need for the true leisure experience to yield a sense of total freedom and absence from compulsion of any kind. Realistically, however, there are many situations in which individuals are pressured to participate or in which the activity's structure diminishes his or her sense of freedom and intrinsic motivation.

For example, Chick and Roberts describe the phenomenon of "anti-leisure" in game playing. By this, they mean that the rules and strategic elements of games as well as the social context in which they are played may be so confining or pressureful that the resulting experience is not at all a leisurely one.[43] Illustrating this anti-leisure phenomenon are recent studies that show a high proportion of children and youth who drop out of sports participation do so because of coaching pressures and the high priority placed on playing to win.

Beyond this, many individuals become so caught up in the leisure activities they pursue that their daily lives are dominated by them. Mark Jury tells the story of a Philadelphian enrolled in a Moto-Cross seminar at Pocono International Raceway. He was in a hurry to carry out his prescribed exercise because his wife would soon finish showing their cats in a competition at a nearby resort, and the two of them would then be driving back to Philadelphia to watch their daughter compete in a baton-twirling contest. The man explained that he would return to the Poconos the next day for the American Motorcycle

> Association qualifying race—but would have to hurry back to Philadelphia again for a monthly bridge game.
> "What do you do in your spare time?" joked one of the cyclists.
> "I work," replied the man.[44]

Too often, such individuals tend to be dominated by a consumer mentality, in which they engage in a host of games, hobbies, social pursuits, or other activities as part of a crowded, hectic lifestyle. Psychiatrist Erich Fromm suggested in *The Sane Society* that people today suffer from a lack of autonomy and self-direction in leisure and recreation, as in other areas of their lives. As consumers, they are manipulated and sold products that they do not really need or understand. Marketing techniques in the twentieth century have created a receptive orientation—in which the aim is to "drink in," to have something new all the time, to be a passive, alienated recipient of leisure goods that are thrust upon one. Fromm writes of the consumer:

> He does not participate actively, he wants to "take in" all there is to be had, and to have as much as possible of pleasure, culture and what not. Actually, he is not free to enjoy "his" leisure; his leisure-time consumption is determined by industry, as are the commodities he buys; his taste is manipulated, he wants to see and to hear what he is conditioned to want to see and to hear; entertainment is an industry like any other, the customer is made to buy fun as he is made to buy dresses and shoes. The value of the fun is determined by its success on the market, not by anything which could be measured in human terms.[45]

Fromm calls this a "push-button" mentality in which dependence on mechanical devices excludes the possibility of truly meaningful experiences. The tourist who is constantly occupied with taking pictures sees nothing at all, and does nothing except through the intermediary of the camera. Upon returning home, "the outcome of his 'pleasure' trip is a collection of snapshots, which are the substitute for an experience which he could have had, but did not have." Certainly, such experiences negate the view of leisure as a meaningful and self-enriching form of personal growth.

Leisure as Spiritual Expression

A sixth way of conceptualizing leisure today sees it in terms of its contribution to spiritual expression or religious values. For example, during the early decades of the twentieth century, play and recreation were often referred to as uplifting or holy kinds of human experiences. In a systematic study of the professional literature of this period, Charles Sylvester found numerous references to God, Christ, divine ends, or other terms that suggested a clear linkage between leisure and religion.[46]

Writing from a Judeo-Christian perspective, Paul Heintzman and Glen Van Andel point out that both work and leisure have traditionally been viewed as parts of a God-ordained whole in which work and play complement each other, with the Sabbath serving as a time for both worship and leisure. Leisure, they argue, is seen as a theological virtue through the Christian doctrines of creation, rest, worship and celebration, freedom, and grace. They continue:

> From the new age paradigm, the leisure experience is characterized by a mystical or spiritual feeling of being connected with oneself, with all else, and a sense of oneness with the universe. [It may also] facilitate spiritual experiences as "extreme states of consciousness" which may be similar to "peak" experiences of self-actualization or "flow" experiences.[47]

John Hultsman points out that our tendency is to think about leisure within the context of Western philosophical thought and social values. However, he writes, in the modern industrial world, marked as it is by such influences as urbanization, bureaucratization, and commodification, it becomes difficult to experience true leisure. We have become slaves to our technology and to the frenetic, busy, and pressured way of life that it imposes. However, in such non-Western philosophies or religious systems of belief as Confucianism, Hinduism, Zen Buddhism, and Taoism, leisure may be viewed within an entirely different framework. In such settings, life itself tends to be more serene and harmonious, simple rather than complex, and natural rather than contrived.

The various facets of existence—play, education, work, and social and family relations—are not compartmentalized, but rather are part of a seamless whole in a truly integrated lifestyle. Hultsman cites the example of a rural community in Tepoztlan, Mexico, in which the daily experiences of peasant families

> . . . exist in a natural, integrated and harmonious fashion very much in keeping with the notion of the lived experience of leisure. Tepoztlan knows what life is for, because every move it makes contributes to a legitimate function of living.[48]

Leisure Seen in Relationship to Work

While it is generally accepted that, by definition, leisure does not exist *during* work, it nonetheless may have a connection with work. Two theories that present alternative views of this relationship are the "compensatory" and "spillover" theories.

Compensatory Theory of Leisure   According to this theory, leisure stems from and is influenced by work, in the sense that leisure is used to compensate for the strains or demands of work. For example, if work is extremely boring and repetitive, or involves a great deal of stress or physical exertion, leisure may be used to provide a contrast in the individual's daily life. Burch writes:

> The compensatory hypothesis suggests that whenever the individual is given the opportunity to avoid his regular routine, he will seek a directly opposite activity.[49]

To illustrate: the clerical worker, bound to a desk and kept indoors during the working day, might choose to take part in hunting, fishing, or hiking during leisure hours—in direct contrast to the work environment.

Spillover Theory of Leisure   This theory suggests that leisure becomes an extension of work. This is the reverse of the compensatory theory. Either the individual is so exhausted by work that leisure hours are treated passively and negatively or work is so enjoyed that it affects leisure positively. In the first case, Wilensky suggests that the exhausted assembly-line worker may develop a

> spillover routine in which alienation from work becomes alienation from life; the mental stultification produced by his labor permeates his leisure.[50]

More positively, the worker may enjoy work so much that its basic themes are repeated in leisure pastimes. For example, the truck driver who enjoys long hours of highway driving may also have a hobby of riding motorcycles or restoring and exhibiting antique cars. The commercial artist in an advertising agency may do watercolor painting during vacations. Another example of spillover leisure was seen in a recent newspaper photograph that depicted members of the Philadelphia Eagles football team—highly paid professional athletes—competing against each other in a game of electronic football. Daily throughout the season's tough final stretch, in the team's locker room, they

> . . . pit their skills against each other on a 16-inch color screen, whooping, gloating, laughing, cheering, teasing, and tormenting each other like the teenagers the game is designed to amuse. . . hands feverishly pumping the hand-held controls.[51]

Distinguishing between work and nonwork may also be complex. The same activity may be carried on by an individual with the only distinction between work and nonwork being whether the person in receiving pay for participation, along with the differences of motivation that may result from this. This is critical to the idea of defining one's time as free or obligated. Kelly, for example, has suggested a typology of leisure in relation to work. Within his framework, four types of leisure appear: (1) *unconditional leisure*—activity independent of work influence and freely chosen as an end in itself; (2) *coordinated leisure*—activity similar to work in form or content (such as a work activity carried on at home as a hobby), but not required by the job; (3) *complementary leisure*—activity independent of work in its form and content but in which the need to take part is influenced by one's work, as in the case of a business manager involved in the work of community organizations because he or she is expected to be; and (4) *recuperative* or *preparatory* leisure nonwork activity related to work by its form or purpose.[52]

In some job settings, as in an office where employees gather around a coffee machine or where individuals "surf" the Internet to explore subjects not connected with work, there may be a rapid shift between work and nonwork. Beyond this, the very idea of free time as defined on page 40 poses some problems. Max Kaplan has identified several different kinds of free time that have appeared in modern society. These include: (a) the permanent, voluntary leisure of the wealthy, who need not work if they choose not to; (b) the involuntary leisure of the unemployed, whether permanent or temporary; (c) the scheduled, voluntary leisure of the employed who are on holidays or vacation; (d) the temporary or permanent leisure of the ill or disabled; and (e) the continuing leisure of retired persons.[53] Obviously, free time may vary greatly in its amounts and implications for each of these groups.

Issue of Leisure's Quality

Some believe that free time is not to be considered leisure unless it is spent or used in the pursuit of significant and worthwhile experiences. Lee writes, for example, that

> leisure is the occasion for the development of broader and deeper perspective, and for renewing the body, mind and spirit. . . . Leisure provides the occasion for learning and freedom for growth and expression, for rest and restoration, for rediscovering life in its entirety.[54]

If one accepts the premise that only free time spent in desirable or self-enriching ways is really leisure, a philosophical question arises. Is there some universally acceptable set of values that can be used to determine what is a desirable use of free time—particularly when individuals are likely to differ so greatly in what they regard as desirable? Certainly the answer is not to be found in community custom or law, as the following excerpt from a news article on "victimless" crime indicates:

> In Connecticut, it is legal to bet on jai alai and dog races, but not on tennis matches or track meets. It is all right in New Jersey to purchase a three-digit "number" from the state's computerized "Pick-It," but not

from a runner on the street. Las Vegas-type betting became legal in New York City last week, but only for religious and charitable organizations. New Yorkers may drink at home at any hour, but not at a neighborhood tavern from four to eight o'clock in the morning. In New York State, certain sexual activity is legally permissible for married couples but illegal for unmarried people.[55]

Obviously, there are difficulties in classifying leisure solely as time spent in the pursuit of desirable and socially constructive ends. It would be more realistic to conclude that leisure represents *all* free time and that it provides the basis for freedom of choice. Then within it, one may engage in a wide range of activities—including some that are negative and destructive and others that are positive, self-enhancing, and constructive for the community as a whole.

Leisure Defined

Recognizing that each of the six concepts of leisure just presented stems from a different perspective, a general definition that embraces several of the key points follows:

Leisure is that portion of an individual's time that is not directly devoted to work or work-connected responsibilities or to other obligated forms of maintenance or self-care. Leisure implies freedom and choice and is customarily used in a variety of ways, but chiefly to meet one's personal needs for reflection, self-enrichment, relaxation, or pleasure. While it usually involves some form of participation in a voluntarily chosen activity, it may also be regarded as a holistic state of being or even a spiritual experience.

THE MEANING OF RECREATION

In a sense, recreation represents a fusion between play and leisure, and is therefore presented as the third of the important concepts that provide the framework for this overall field of study.

The term itself stems from the Latin word *recreatio*, meaning that which refreshes or restores. Historically, recreation was often regarded as a period of light and restful activity, voluntarily chosen, that permits one to regain energy after heavy work and to return to work renewed. This view is essentially the same as the recreation theory of play described earlier. Even in the modern era, this point of view is often expressed. De Grazia writes:

> *Recreation* is activity that rests men from work, often by giving them a change (distraction, diversion) and restores (re-creates) them for work. When adults play—as they do, of course, with persons, things and symbols—they play for recreation. Like the Romans, our own conception of leisure is mainly recreative.[56]

This point of view lacks acceptability today for two reasons. First, as most work in modern society becomes less demanding, many people are becoming more fully engaged, both physically and mentally, in their recreation than in their work. Thus, the notion that recreation should be light and relaxing is far too limiting. Second, the definition of recreation as primarily intended to restore one for work does not cover the case of persons who have *no* work, but who certainly need recreation to make their lives meaningful.

In contrast to work, which is often thought of as tedious, unpleasant, and obligatory, recreation has traditionally been thought of as light, pleasant, and revitalizing. However, this contrast too should be rethought. A modern, holistic view of work and recreation would be that *both* have the potential for being pleasant, rewarding, and creative and that *both* may represent serious forms of personal involvement and deep commitment.

CONTEMPORARY DEFINITIONS

Most modern definitions of recreation fit into one of three categories: (1) recreation has been seen as an activity carried on under certain conditions or with certain motivations; (2) recreation has been viewed as a process or state of being—something that happens within the person while engaging in certain kinds of activity, with a given set of expectations; and (3) recreation has been perceived as a social institution, a body of knowledge, or a professional field.

Recreation as Activity or Experience

Most definitions, particularly those advanced by authors within the field, treat recreation as a form of activity or experience. Thus, Neumeyer and Neumeyer write that recreation is

> any activity pursued during leisure, either individual or collective, that is free and pleasureful, having its own immediate appeal, not impelled by a delayed reward beyond itself or by any immediate necessity.[57]

A second definition, offered by Hutchinson, includes the element of social acceptability:

> Recreation is a worthwhile, socially accepted leisure experience that provides immediate and inherent satisfaction to the individual who voluntarily participates in an activity.[58]

Traditional Views   Other definitions offered over the past several decades have included the following elements:

1. Recreation is widely regarded as *activity* (including physical, mental, social, or emotional involvement) as contrasted with sheer *idleness* or complete *rest*.
2. Recreation may include an extremely wide range of activities, such as sports, games, crafts, performing arts, fine arts, music, dramatics, travel, hobbies, and social activities. They may be engaged in by individuals or by groups, and may involve single or episodic participation or sustained and frequent involvement throughout one's lifetime.
3. The choice of activity or involvement is voluntary, free of compulsion or obligation.
4. Recreation is prompted by internal motivation and the desire to achieve personal satisfaction, rather than by extrinsic goals or rewards.
5. Recreation is dependent on a state of mind or attitude; it is not so much *what* one does as the reason for doing it, and the way the individual *feels* about the activity, that makes it recreation.
6. Although the primary motivation for taking part in recreation is usually pleasure-seeking, it may also be meeting intellectual, physical, or social needs. In some cases, rather than provide "fun" of a light or trivial nature, recreation may involve a serious degree of commitment and self-discipline and may yield frustration or even pain.

Challenges to Past Assumptions   One might logically challenge a number of these assumptions. First, although recreation *is* widely regarded as activity rather than complete idleness or rest, it may range from the most physically challenging pursuits to those with much milder demands. Watching television, listening to a symphony orchestra, reading a book, or playing chess are all forms of recreation.

Ideally, all such activities, when pursued for pleasure or other significant personal values, should be viewed as recreation. However, often they are not. For example, Thomas Kando

Leisure Pursuits Today

Among the leisure pursuits of today are a vast range of hobbies, sports and games, cultural activities, and outdoor programs. Illustrating these pursuits are women athletes at Washington State University (top), older women share gardening hobby which is sponsored by Montgomery County Recreation Department in Maryland (center), and men and boys in a track meet held at the Orlando Naval Training Center (bottom).

Large-scale activities are illustrated by hundreds of adults competing in a bridge tournament in Washington, D. C. (top), or corporate sponsored community recreation events such as the annual CoreStates bike race in Philadelphia (bottom). Small scale events are readily available like the traditional sack race in a playday sponsored by the Westchester County Recreation, Parks, and Conservation Department in New York (center).

suggests that intellectual pursuits should not really be thought of as forms of recreation. Recreation, he writes:

> frequently refers to sports and outdoor activities and almost never refers to activities that are intellectually strenuous. . . . Unlike the leisure ideal, recreation. . . describes activities that are generally not edifying.[59]

This is an unfortunately narrow point of view, both in its theoretical base and its practical implications. There is no reason that intellectual, artistic, or other culturally significant activities should *not* be considered legitimate forms of recreation. Many public recreation and park departments provide extensive courses, workshops, and performance series in the arts. Often they sponsor or cosponsor ballet, opera, or other musical organizations and events, and numerous recreation agencies operate arts centers. Clearly, such pursuits belong within the domain of recreation.

Similarly, other individuals may have serious scholarly or scientific interests or hobbies; for them, such pursuits clearly are a form of recreation.

Voluntary Participation

While it is generally accepted that recreation participation should be voluntary and carried out without any degree of pressure or compulsion, often this is not the case. We tend to be influenced by others, as in the case of the youngster whose parents urge him to join a Little League team, or the gymnast or figure skater who is encouraged in the thought that he or she might become a professional performer.

Although ideally recreation is thought of as being free of compulsion or obligation, once one has entered into an activity—such as joining a company bowling league or playing with a chamber music group—one accepts a set of obligations to the other members of the team or group. Thus, recreation cannot be entirely free and spontaneous and, in fact, assumes some of the characteristics of work in the sense of having schedules, commitments, and responsibilities.

A clear example of involuntary recreation might be found in treatment centers where patients may be strongly urged or even pressured to take part in activities. Under such circumstances, should participation in an activity truly be regarded as recreation?

Motives for Participation

Definitions of recreation generally have stressed that it should be conducted for personal enjoyment or pleasure—ideally of an immediate nature. However, many worthwhile activities take time to master before they yield the fullest degree of satisfaction. Some complex activities may cause frustration and even mental anguish—as in the case of the golf addict who is desperately unhappy because of poor putting or driving. In such cases it is not so much that the participant receives immediate pleasure as that he or she is absorbed and challenged by the activity; pleasure will probably grow as the individual's skill improves.

What of the view that recreation must be carried on for its own sake and without extrinsic goals or purposes? It is essential to recognize that human beings *are* usually goal-oriented, purposeful creatures. Murphy and Williams have identified different recreational behaviors that suggest the kinds of motives people may have when they engage in activity. They include:

> *Socializing behaviors*—activities such as dancing, dating, going to parties, or visiting friends, in which people relate to one another in informal and unstereotyped ways.
>
> *Associative behaviors*—activities in which people group together because of common interests such as car clubs, stamp-, coin-, or gem-collecting groups, or similar hobbies.
>
> *Competitive behaviors*—activities including all of the popular sports and games, but also competition in the performing arts or in outdoor activities in which individuals compete against the environment or even against their own limitations.
>
> *Risk-taking behaviors*—an increasingly popular form of participation in which the stakes are often physical injury or possible death.
>
> *Exploratory behaviors*—in a sense, all recreation involves some degree of exploration; in this context, it refers to such activities as travel and sightseeing, hiking, scuba diving, spelunking, and other pursuits that open up new environments to the participant.
>
> *Vicarious experience*—much modern recreation consists of reading, watching television or movies, viewing art, listening to music, or attending spectator sports events.
>
> *Sensory stimulation*—behaviors that involve primarily pleasure and the stimulation of the senses include drinking, drug use, sexual activity, and such visual experiences as light shows and rock concerts, which may blend different kinds of stimuli.
>
> *Physical expression*—many activities, such as running, swimming, dancing, and yoga, may involve physical expression without emphasizing competition against others.[60]
>
> To these one might add such categories as *artistically creative* experiences or pursuits that are of an *intellectual* nature, such as writing or taking part in group discussions. One might also ask whether activities that involve *volunteer service* to others, or *spiritual involvement* in a religious program, should be considered recreation.

Recreation as an Emotional State

Recognizing that different people may have many different motives for taking part in recreation, Gray and Greben suggest that it should not be thought of simply as a form of activity. Instead, they argue that recreation should be perceived as the *outcome* of participation—a "peak experience in self-satisfaction" that comes from successful participation in any sort of enterprise. They write:

> Recreation is an emotional condition within an individual human being that flows from a feeling of well-being and self-satisfaction. It is characterized by feelings of mastery, achievement, exhilaration, acceptance, success, personal worth, and pleasure. It reinforces a positive self-image. Recreation is a response to aesthetic experience, achievement of personal goals, or positive feedback from others. It is independent of activity, leisure, or social acceptance.[61]

Elliott Avedon supports this position, commenting that many activities, including those with survival or utilitarian value, may have recreational value for participants. This is so, he suggests, because the values we ascribe to any activity are not inherent within the activity, but stem from our own thinking and past experience. Following this idea, he describes recreation as

> an internal psychic phenomenon, and. . . a different, individualized experience for each of us. That which we collectively label "recreation" is the result of a social convention, and is really only an approximation, because the experience is different for each of us.[62]

Depth of Involvement   The degree to which many individuals become deeply committed emotionally to their recreational interests may be illustrated within the realms of sports and popular entertainment. So fervently do many Americans and Canadians root for popular sports teams and stars that sports have increasingly been referred to as a form of folk religion. One professor of religious studies comments:

> For growing numbers of Americans, sport religion has become a more appropriate expression of personal religiosity than Christianity, Judaism or any of the traditional religions [as illustrated in] terms that athletes and sportwriters regularly use: *faith, ritual, ultimate, dedicated, sacrifice, peace, commitment, spirit.*[63]

The glorification of leading athletes as folk idols and the national preoccupation with such major events as the Stanley Cup, the World Series, or the Super Bowl both demonstrate the degree to which sports—as a popular form of recreation—captures the emotional commitment of millions of Americans and Canadians today.

Similarly, the popular fascination with leading entertainment figures makes the same point. We have made legends and deities out of a few great performers. The brilliant rock-and-roll entertainer, Elvis Presley, died at the age of 42 as an overweight, drug-dependent, and burned-out saloon singer. Nonetheless, million of fans maintain shrines to him, collect his albums and memorabilia, and make pilgrimages to Graceland, his Tennessee home. The anniversary of his death is marked by a solemn Death Week each August, with candlelit processionals and prayers. Elvis is believed to be able to heal the ill, emotionally troubled, or physically disabled; for many, he has become a religion in his own right.[64]

Social Acceptability

Another question arises with respect to defining recreation. Should activity that is often widely disapproved, such as drug use, be regarded as a form of recreation? One school of thought maintains that *any* form of voluntarily chosen, pleasurable, leisure-time activity should be regarded as recreation. This view seems to be supported by those behavioral scientists and writers in recent years who have begun to refer to "recreational sex" or "recreational drug use."

Other writers take the opposite view—that recreation must be wholesome for the individual and for society and must serve to recreate the participant physically, psychologically, spiritually, or mentally. Some even argue that recreation should be clearly distinguished from mere amusement, time-filling, or negative forms of play. Rojek characterizes this approach to defining recreation and leisure as an element in "moral regulation" theory, in which different noneconomic societal institutions are used to control and "civilize" the behavior of the working classes.[65]

Whether or not one accepts this position, it is important to recognize that all publicly financed programs must have significant goals and objectives in order to deserve and obtain support. It therefore becomes necessary to make an important distinction. Recreation, as such, may not imply social acceptability or a set of socially oriented goals or values. When, however, it is provided as a form of community-based service, supported by taxes or voluntary contributions, it must be attuned to prevailing social values and must be aimed at achieving desirable and constructive results.

The task of determining exactly what is socially acceptable or morally desirable is a complex one, particularly in a heterogeneous society with many different religious groups and with laws that may vary greatly from state to state or even county to county.

Standards of appropriate sexual behavior have grown increasingly permissive during the past three decades. Does this mean that what was *not* recreation in 1967 has *become* recreation in 1997? Our attitudes toward other leisure pursuits are equally ambiguous from a moral perspective. Certain forms of gambling have traditionally been morally or legally disapproved. Compulsive gambling is seen as an illness, and the law prohibits private gambling games, the "numbers" game, and similar pastimes. Yet, we legalize gambling, and many of our states depend heavily for income on licensed casinos or state lotteries. Similarly, many churches sponsor bingo games, a form of gambling. Is one form of gambling recreation because it is countenanced, and another not?

Apart from the obvious point that it is difficult to make such distinctions, it should be stressed that recreation is carried on within a social context. It must respond to social needs and expectations and it is influenced by prevailing social attitudes and values. Indeed, although we tend to think of recreation as a form of *personal* involvement or experience, it must also be defined as a *social* institution.

Recreation as a Social Institution

Increasingly, recreation has become identified as a significant institution in the modern community, involving a form of collective behavior carried on within specific social structures. It has numerous traditions, values, channels of communication, formal relationships, and other institutional aspects.

Once chiefly the responsibility of the family, the church, or other local social bodies, recreation has now become the responsibility of a number of major agencies in our society. These may include public, voluntary, or commercial organizations that operate parks, beaches, zoos, aquariums, stadiums, or sports facilities. Recreational activities may also be provided by organizations such as hospitals, schools, correctional institutions, and branches of the armed forces. Clearly, recreation has emerged as a significant social institution, complete with its own national and international organizations and an extensive network of programs of professional preparation in colleges and universities. Increasingly, recreation is widely referred to as a *business* or *industry,* involving a cluster of major profit-seeking categories of leisure-related enterprises.

Recreation Defined

Acknowledging these contrasting views of the meaning of recreation, the following definition of the term is offered. Recreation consists of human activities or experiences that occur in leisure time. Usually, they are voluntarily chosen for intrinsic purposes and are pleasurable, although they may involve a degree of compulsion, extrinsic purpose, and discomfort, or even pain or danger. Recreation may also be regarded as the emotional state resulting from participation or as a social institution, a professional career field, or a business. When provided as part of organized community or voluntary-agency programs, recreation should be socially constructive and morally acceptable in terms of prevailing community standards and values.

RELATIONSHIPS AMONG PLAY, LEISURE, AND RECREATION

Obviously, the three terms discussed in this chapter are closely interrelated. Leisure, for example, provides an opportunity to carry on both play and recreation. Much of our free time in modern society is taken up by recreation, although leisure may also include such activities as continuing education, religious practice, or community service, which are not usually thought of as forms of recreation.

In turn, it should be understood that although play and recreation tend to overlap, they are not identical. *Play* is not so much an activity as a form of behavior—marked stylistically by teasing, competition, exploration, or make-believe. Play can occur during work or leisure, whereas recreation takes place only during leisure.

Recreation obviously includes many forms of play, but it also may involve distinctly nonplaylike activities such as traveling, reading, going to museums, and other cultural or intellectual activities. As a final distinction, recreation is often thought of as goal-oriented and constructive activity, particularly when it is community-sponsored. Play, on the other hand, may or may not be goal-oriented and ranges from the most richly creative and self-enhancing behavior to the most negative and self-destructive behavior. Play is an important concern of parents and child-development experts, including educators, psychologists, and anthropologists.

Leisure is a subject of scholarly study for many economists and sociologists; it also has come increasingly under the scrutiny of psychologists and social psychologists. However, to the public at large, leisure tends to be a somewhat abstract or remote concept. Although many academic departments and some community agencies use the term leisure in their titles, it lacks a sense of urgency or strong appeal as a public issue or focus of government action.

While recreation is generally perceived in a positive and optimistic way, leisure tends to evoke two kinds of reactions. On the one hand, it may be seen as providing the opportunity for pleasure and self-enrichment and for contributing to a society's cultural development, an important thread in the social fabric. On the other hand, leisure has been feared because nations that have used it poorly in the past have grown soft and decadent and have lost their vitality and sense of purpose.

Of the three terms, *recreation* is at once the most understandable and significant for most persons. It is easily recognizable as an area of personal activity and social responsibility, and its values are readily apparent for all age groups and special populations as well. For these reasons, it will be given primary emphasis in the chapters that follow, particularly in terms of program sponsorship and professional identity.

The themes that have just been introduced will be explored more fully throughout this text, as the historical development of recreation and play and the evolution of the present-day leisure-service system are described. Throughout, issues related to the social implications of recreation and leisure and to the role of recreation and park professionals will be fully discussed, along with the challenges that will face practitioners in the field as we approach the year 2000 and the twenty-first century that lies ahead.

SUMMARY

Play, recreation, and leisure represent important basic concepts that are essential aspects of the overall field of organized leisure services. They have been explored by philosophers, psychologists, historians, educators, and sociologists from ancient Greek civilizations to the present.

Play may best be understood as a form of activity or behavior that is generally nonpurposeful in terms of having serious intended outcomes, but that is an important element in the healthy growth of children and in other societal functions. The chapter presents various theories of play, ranging from the classical views of Herbert Spencer and Karl Groos to more contemporary concepts that link play to Freudian theory or to exploratory drives of human personality.

Six concepts of leisure are presented which depict it as the possession of the upper classes or aristocrats through history, as free time or activity, as a state of being, and as a form of spiritual expression. Recreation is also explored from different perspectives, with a key issue being whether it must be morally constructive or socially approved to be considered recreation. The role of recreation as an important contemporary social institution and force in economic life is also discussed.

Questions for Class Discussion or Essay Examinations

1. This chapter presents several perspectives on play, including a review of traditional definitions of play, its role as a social ritual in community life, and its contribution to personality development. Which of these do you find most interesting and useful? Why?

2. Recreation has been simply defined as socially desirable activity carried on voluntarily in free time for purposes of fun or pleasure. Critically analyze this definition. For example, must activity always be considered socially desirable in order to be regarded as recreation? Is recreation always pleasurable? Is it always carried on voluntarily? What elements would you add to this definition to make it more meaningful?

3. The chapter presents two contrasting views of leisure—one as the slow-paced, relaxed, or contemplative use of free time, and the other as active participation in a wide range of often challenging or demanding activities. Which of these do you believe is the more accurate picture of leisure today?

4. Discuss the contrasting meanings of play, leisure, and recreation, and show how they overlap and differ from each other in their separate meanings. Which of the three do you feel is the more useful term as far as public understanding of this field is concerned?

Endnotes

2   *Webster's New International Dictionary* (Springfield, Mass.: G. and C. Merriam Co., 1954).

3   Sebastian de Grazia, *Of Time, Work and Leisure* (New York: Doubleday-Anchor, 1962): 233.

4   M. J. Ellis, *Why People Play* (Englewood Cliffs, N. J.: Prentice-Hall, 1973): 11.

5   George Torkildsen, *Leisure and Recreation Management* (London: E. and F. N. Spon, 1992): 48–49.

6   Friedrich Froebel, cited in Torkildsen: 50.

7   Stuart Brown, "Animals at Play," *National Geographic* (December 1994): 8.

[8] Harvey Carr, "The Survival Values of Play," quoted in Harvey C. Lehman and Paul A. Witty, *The Psychology of Play Activities* (New York: A. S. Barnes, 1927): 19.

[9] Konrad Lorenz, *On Aggression* (New York: Harcourt, Brace and World, 1963).

[10] The original source of this theory was W. P. Bowen and Elmer D. Mitchell, *The Theory of Organized Play* (New York: A. S. Barnes, 1923).

[11] C. Goodman, cited in Wayne Stormann, "The Recreation Profession, Capital and Democracy," *Leisure Sciences* (Vol. 15 No. 1 1993): 51.

[12] Roger Caillois, *Man, Play and Games* (London: Thames and Hudson, 1961): 21.

[13] *Ibid.*, 22.

[14] Edward Norbeck, "Man at Play," in *Play: A Natural History Magazine Special Supplement* (December 1971): 53.

[15] Bronislaw Malinowski, *Magic. Science and Religion* (New York: Doubleday-Anchor, 1955): 29.

[16] *Ibid.*, 42.

[17] Felix Keesing, "Recreative Behavior and Culture Change," *Papers of the Fifth Congress of Anthropological and Ethnological Sciences* (1959): 130–131.

[18] Johan Huizinga, *Homo Ludens: A Study of the Play Element in Culture* (Boston: Beacon Press, 1944, 1960): 5.

[19] Eugen Weber review of *Eminent Victorian Soldiers: Seekers of Glory* by Byron Farwell, in *New York Times Book Review* (16 June 1985): 13.

[20] Michael Maccoby, *The Gamesman: The New Corporate Leaders* (New York: Simon and Schuster, 1977): 100.

[21] Lawrence K. Frank, quoted in Ruth Hartley and Robert Goldenson, *The Complete Book of Children's Play* (New York: Thomas Y. Crowell, 1963): 43.

[22] Jerome Bruner, "Child Development: Play Is Serious Business," *Psychology Today* (January 1975): 83.

[23] For a full discussion of Piaget's view of play, see Susanna Millar, *The Psychology of Play* (Baltimore: Penguin Books, 1968): 55.

[24] J. Nina Lieberman, *Playfulness: Its Relationship to Imagination and Creativity* (New York: Academic Press, 1977).

[25] Sigmund Freud, quoted in M. J. Ellis, *op. cit.*, 60.

[26] Bruno Bettelheim, "The Importance of Play," *Atlantic Monthly* (March 1987): 35.

[27] Erik Erikson, *Childhood and Society* (New York: W. W. Norton, 1950): 184.

[28] Ellis, *op. cit.*, 99–100.

[29] Marvin Zuckerman, "The Search for High Sensation," *Psychology Today* (December 1978): 38.

[30] R. W. White, "Motivation Reconsidered: The Concept of Competence," *Psychological Review* 66 (1959): 297–333.

[31] See Mihaly Cziksentmihalyi, *Beyond Boredom and Anxiety* (San Francisco: Jossey Bass, 1975) and (with S. Bennett) "An Exploratory Model of Play," *American Anthropologist* 73 (1971): 45–58.

[32] Steven Simpson and Carlton Yoshioka, "Aristotelian View of Leisure: An Outdoor Recreation Perspective," *Leisure Studies* 11 (1992): 219–231.

[33] Josef Pieper, *Leisure, the Basis of Culture* (New York: Mentor-Omega, 1952, 1963): 43.

[34] Thorstein Veblen, *The Theory of the Leisure Class* (New York: Viking, 1899, 1918): 73.

[35] See Martin H. Neumeyer and Esther Neumeyer, *Leisure and Recreation* (New York: Ronald Press, 1958): 19.

[36] Joffre Dumazedier, *Toward a Society of Leisure* (New York: Free Press, 1962): 250.

[37]   De Grazia, *op. cit.*, 59.

[38]   See Isobel Cosgrove and Richard Jackson, *The Geography of Recreation and Leisure* (London: Hutchinson University Library, 1972): 13.

[39]   Dumazedier, *op. cit.*, 16–17.

[40]   John Neulinger, *The Psychology of Leisure* (Springfield, Ill.: Charles C. Thomas, 1974): xi.

[41]   Geoffrey Godbey, *Leisure in Your Life: An Exploration* (Philadelphia: W. B. Saunders, 1981): 10.

[42]   Ellen Goodman, "That Time of Year to Forget the Time," *Philadelphia Inquirer* (22 August 1987): 9-A.

[43]   Garry Chick and John Roberts, "Anti-Leisure in Game Play," *Leisure Sciences* (Vol. 11 No. 1, 1989): 73–84.

[44]   Mark Jury, *Playtime! Americans at Leisure* (New York: Harcourt Brace Jovanovich, 1977): 76.

[45]   Erich Fromm, *The Sane Society* (New York: Fawcett, 1955): 124.

[46]   Charles Sylvester, "The Ethics of Play, Leisure and Recreation in the Twentieth Century, 1900–1965," *Leisure Sciences* 9(1987): 173–188.

[47]   Paul Heintzman and Glen Van Andel, "Leisure and Spirituality," *Parks and Recreation* (March 1995): 22, 24.

[48]   John Hultsman, "Spelling Leisure," *Leisure Studies* (Vol. 14 1995): 87–101.

[49]   W. R. Burch, Jr., "The Social Circles of Leisure: Competing Explanations," *Journal of Leisure Research* 1 (1969): 125–147.

[50]   Harold Wilensky, "Work, Careers, and Social Integration," *International Social Sciences Journal* 12 (1960): 543–560.

[51]   Mark Bowden, "Timeout: What Do Eagles Do for Fun? They Play Electronic Football," *Philadelphia Inquirer* (20 December 1991): C-1.

[52]   John R. Kelly, "Work and Leisure: A Simplified Paradigm," *Journal of Leisure Research* 4 (1972): 50–62.

[53]   For a fuller discussion, see Max Kaplan, *Leisure Theory and Policy* (New York: John Wiley and Sons, 1975): Ch. 4.

[54]   Robert Lee, *Religion and Leisure in America* (Nashville: Abingdon Press, 1964): 34.

[55]   "Rethinking Victimless Crimes," *New York Times* (6 February 1977): E-5.

[56]   De Grazia, *op. cit.*, 233.

[57]   Neumeyer and Neumeyer, *op. cit.*, 22.

[58]   John Hutchinson, *Principles of Recreation* (New York: Ronald Press, 1951): 2.

[59]   Thomas Kando, *Leisure and Popular Culture in Transition* (St. Louis: Mosby, 1975): 28.

[60]   James Murphy, *et. al.*, *Leisure Service Delivery System: A Modern Perspective* (Philadelphia: Lea and Febiger, 1973): 73–76.

[61]   David Gray and Seymour Greben, "Future Perspectives," *Parks and Recreation* (July 1974): 49.

[62]   Elliott Avedon, *Therapeutic Recreation: An Applied Behavioral Science Approach* (Englewood Cliffs, N.J.: Prentice-Hall, 1974): 46.

[63]   Charles Prebish, in R. Chandler, "Are Sports Becoming America's New Folk Religion?" *Philadelphia Inquirer* (3 January 1987): 1-C.

[64]   Ron Rosenbaum, "Among the Believers," *New York Times Magazine* (24 September 1995): 50–57.

[65]   Chris Rojek, *Capitalism and Leisure Theory* (London: Tavistock, 1985): 42.

Personal Leisure Perspectives: *Motivations, Values, Constraints*

To a large degree, to experience leisure with the characteristics of perceived freedom, competence, self-determination, satisfaction, and perceived quality of life is to experience a subjective state of health. In this sense, the development of a broad repertoire of leisure skills to facilitate rich, meaningful experiences provides the foundation for extending such holistic quality experiences to all of life.

Personal initiative, choice, meaningful involvement, and enjoyable, supportive social networks—key aspects for leisure—also have important implications for well-being. In the more extreme subjective view, distinctions between leisure and health disappear. Leisure is no longer restricted to discretionary time, but the high quality personal experience of leisure becomes synonymous with a state of personal health and well-being.[1]

---

[1] Leonard Wankel, "Health and Leisure: Inextricably Linked," *Journal of Physical Education, Recreation and Dance* (April 1994): 29–30.

INTRODUCTION

Recreation, play, and leisure may be viewed from several perspectives including: (1) leisure as a personal, individual experience; (2) leisure as a community-based form of opportunity or human service; and (3) leisure in terms of the broader society, involving elements shared by all groups as well as those in separate subcultural groups. This chapter is concerned with the first of these perspectives. It examines recreation and leisure as a personal, individual phenomenon, identifying the motivations that drive varied forms of leisure involvement, the values and outcomes of such experiences, and the constraints and barriers that often limit personal recreational experiences. Throughout, it documents the degree to which leisure may be used as a vehicle for improving the quality of life and achieving significant physical, emotional, social, intellectual, and spiritual benefits. In so doing, it identifies the kinds of motivations that underlie recreational participation, showing how they differ according to the given demographic variables of participants or the nature of different leisure pursuits.

In the second section of the chapter, the positive outcomes of personal recreational involvement that have been demonstrated through systematic research are summarized. In the concluding section, a number of the barriers that prevent a full range of leisure involvement for many individuals are discussed. The essential purpose of the chapter is to show how the somewhat theoretical concepts presented in Chapter 2 are translated in real life—with recreation, play, and leisure providing meaningful experiences for those of all ages, genders, and varied backgrounds.

MOTIVATIONS FOR RECREATIONAL PARTICIPATION

People have varied reasons for taking part in recreational activities. Through the years, a number of researchers have identified the motivations expressed by different groups of subjects—extending beyond the obvious search for fun or pleasure, relaxation, or escape that most would name as reasons for taking part in play.

Obviously, any activity in which people of all ages and backgrounds engage must be influenced by a range of possible needs and desires, as well as by family or other environmental circumstances. Typically, a person's choice of recreation experiences is likely to be affected by his or her educational background, physical and emotional health, economic status, and similar factors. Basic personality also clearly influences leisure choices and behaviors. Outgoing, enthusiastic, and sociable people are likely to engage in a wide variety of active games, sports, and group pastimes. Others more introverted or intellectually grounded may choose to be involved in quieter, less group-oriented activities, possibly of a cultural nature. Some children welcome challenge, risk, and adventure, while others are more cautious and conservative in their play.

As the personality becomes more fully defined, a person will adopt certain roles in harmony with his or her overall personality and chosen lifestyle. Kaplan points out that there are *many* roles that we each play on "the stage of life": as father, husband, worker, congregant, American, Kiwanian, Republican, friend, golfer; and so forth.[2]

Leisure is an important element in this model. Different roles express various aspects of a person, and a person's roles within leisure contribute to or stem from other roles—as athlete in school, club leader in church, trip-organizer on the job, volunteer in a hospital, or stagehand in an amateur theater program. Often, the activities themselves change from one stage of life to the next, in the wake of physical and emotional changes. Godbey writes:

> Many leisure activities which did not interest you as a child are now important to you (as an adult). It is sometimes difficult for us to understand the pleasure that those in different stages of the life cycle derive from certain leisure activities. During the journey from birth to death the activities which we find pleasurable, what we do voluntarily, and the economic and social constraints on our free time, health, and work roles are in a state of change, and these changes affect our leisure attitudes and behavior.[3]

General Motivational Factors

Through the years, a number of researchers have studied the reasons that people give for taking part in recreation as a generalized experience. For example, in 1980, Rick Crandall summarized a list of 17 motivational factors identified by a cross section of American adults as reasons for taking part in varied forms of leisure activity. They included such motivations as: enjoying nature and escaping civilization; escaping from routine and responsibility; physical exercise and health-related benefits; social contact and companionship; creativity and aesthetic expression; gaining a sense of power and influence; altruism and being of service to others; excitement or thrill-seeking; enrichment of one's personality or self-actualization; and escaping boredom.[4]

Personal Influences on Leisure Motivations

Depending on the life stage of the individual, different kinds of recreational motivations may prevail. For example, systematic studies of the reasons why children engage in competitive sports programs have yielded the following kinds of ranked responses: (1) to have fun; (2) to improve my skills; (3) to stay in shape; (4) to do something I am good at; and (5) for the excitement of competition.[5]

In studies of the recreational motivations of adults, Kelly found that these included such elements as the need for rest and relaxation, excitement, self-expression, enjoying companionship, or to escape the pressure from one's spouse.[6]

In contrast, a comprehensive analysis of the psychological needs of elderly individuals that are met through recreational involvement yielded the following eight areas of value:

1. *Self-expression*, involving creative use of talents, and the satisfaction and recognition derived from this;

2. *Companionship*, involving playful and supportive relationships with others;

3. *Power*, based on the need to be in control of social situations;

4. *Compensation*, involving the need for new or unusual experiences beyond the daily routine;

5. *Security*, based on safe and familiar pursuits;

6. *Service*, assisting others or providing volunteer efforts;

7. *Intellectual* and *aesthetic stimulation* through creative or cultural pastimes; and

8. *Self-sufficiency*, based on the need to be able to spend time alone comfortably.[7]

Gender obviously has a powerful impact on leisure needs and choices. In an extensive study of several thousand adult women in the province of Ontario, Canada, researchers Bolla, Dawson, and Harrington identified the basic meanings of leisure for women and described their subjective experiences reported during leisure involvement. These included such elements as the feeling of competence, security, or playfulness and the expression of serenity, femininity, or assertiveness. Clearly, such factors were closely tied to their motivations for taking part in leisure pursuits.[8]

Motivations Linked to Major Activity Areas

The reasons for taking part in recreational activities also tend to be influenced by the nature of the activities themselves. In some cases, participation may be linked to a set of specific personal benefits. For example, Clough, Shepherd, and Maughan examined a sample of recreational long-distance runners and found that these marathoners had motivations linked to such underlying needs as health, challenge, and personal well-being. They listed the following kinds of benefits to be gained from running: (1) it keeps me fit: (2) it keeps me healthy; (3) it provides me with a physical challenge; (4) it gives me a sense of achievement; (5) it helps me relax; (6) it gives me more energy in my other activities; and (7) it increases my self-discipline.[9]

Often, leisure motivations extend beyond such direct needs or benefits and include complex areas of interpersonal relationships or emotional growth. For example, in a study of the motivations of people involved in international travel and vacations, Fisher and Price identified such categories as kinship, new people, escape, and coping. (See table on the next page.)

Other studies of travel and tourism indicate that people travel to meet personal needs to enrich their lives, relax, escape routine, or learn about different environments. Research in tourism suggests that there are four distinct purposes of vacation travel:

(1) Educational, cultural, and historical, involving cultural awareness and enrichment; (2) sightseeing, which focuses on spectacular, beautiful, or unusual scenery or natural phenomena; (3) relaxation and hedonism, which emphasize simple pleasure as a focus of travel; and (4) adventure, in which the tourist seeks out experiences that provide a challenge and often a physical risk.[10]

Still other research has identified the major purposes of an individual taking part in wilderness recreation, such as extended hiking and camping, backpacking, rock climbing or similar pursuits to include such elements as responding to the splendor of nature, resting and relaxation, enjoying adventure, challenge, and contact with others, escaping the pressures of modern, urban life, or living in simple and natural ways. Simon Priest examined the function of privacy as part of camping in the Canadian wilderness and identified such personal needs and values as:

Personal autonomy—the need to avoid being manipulated or dominated by others; to safeguard one's individuality;

Emotional release—providing for respite from the psychological tensions and stresses of everyday life; and

Intimacy—being part of a small social unit, achieving a close personal relationship with others involved in the wilderness experience.[11]

Often, leisure motivations are shaped by the interplay of both participants and activities at different levels of skill, experience, or difficulty. For example, Williams, Schreyer, and Knopf

Pleasure Travel and Vacation Motivations and Outcomes[12]

I wanted this vacation to. . .

Kinship
- . . . allow me as much time as possible with friends or family
- . . . surround me with people that are significant to me
- . . . be a social event with people that are important to me

During this vacation I wanted to. . .

New people
- . . . meet many new people
- . . . make new friends
- . . . interact with people different from myself

During this vacation I planned to. . .

Escape
- . . . forget about everything else
- . . . get so involved [that I] take my mind off [my daily life]

During this vacation I wanted to. . .

Coping
- . . . evaluate a stressful situation [objectively]
- . . . try to see the positive side of some negative aspect of my life
- . . . develop a plan of action for some aspect of my life

examined the multidimensional nature of river floating, as experienced by several types of participants:

Novices—persons making their first river trip;

Beginners—persons with a small amount of experience on a few rivers;

Locals—persons with a considerable amount of experience on the river being sampled, but limited experience elsewhere;

Collectors—persons who have floated many rivers, but with limited experience on any one river;

Visitors—persons with considerable river-running experience elsewhere, but little experience on the "sample" river; and

Veterans—persons with considerable experience on the "sample" river and on other rivers.[13]

Overall motivations for river floating as an outdoor recreation experience included such categories as escape, challenge, action, autonomy, self-awareness, learning activity, and interest in nature. However, these motivations varied considerably according to the experience background of those studied. For example, less experienced participants rated escape as a primary motivation, while more advanced floaters rated challenge or learning activity as primary goals.

Similarly, in a study of adult recreational groups, Scott and Godbey analyzed the differences between social and serious contract bridge players in terms of the purposes, styles, and social settings of participation.[14] In a study of community orchestra members in the Delaware Valley, Susana Juniu distinguished between amateur players, who saw their playing as an intrinsically motivated leisure activity, and more advanced professional players, who regarded music as an extrinsically motivated, worklike activity.[15]

OTHER MOTIVATIONAL AREAS

Beyond the examples cited, a number of other motivational factors underlie leisure participation today. Some of these include *social* and *affiliation* needs, the search for *excitement* and *physical challenge, hedonistic urges,* and even *nostalgia,* as a motivation of middle-aged or elderly persons.

Social and Affiliation Drives

The need to be part of a social group and to have friends who provide companionship, support, and intimacy is at the heart of much recreational involvement. It helps to explain why people join sororities, fraternities, or other social clubs, senior citizen centers, tour groups, or other settings where new acquaintances and potential friends may be met. It is an underlying element in sports in terms of the friendships and bonds that are formed among team members. It accounts for young people, in particular, going to bars, clubs, dances, and similar social events. It is one of the appeals of youth membership organizations, such as Boys and Girls Clubs, YMCAs and YWCAs, or religious-connected groups.

At some levels, the social motivation may be the basis for commercially sponsored ventures, such as singles cruises, resort hotel packages or weekends, computer dating services, and telephone conversation services. It may also be linked to volunteer participation, membership in political or environmental action groups, or similar leisure involvements—along with the social values of such activities.

Excitement and Challenge Motivations

A great deal of recreational involvement today is based on the need for excitement and challenge, particularly in such outdoor recreation activities as skiing, mountain climbing, or hang gliding, or in active, highly competitive individual or team sports.

Risk recreation and outdoor adventure pursuits have become increasingly popular program elements, and they serve the needs of individuals who have a strong sensation-seeking drive. For many people, such urges are met through spectatorship—by watching action-oriented movies or television shows—or in the form of video games based on high-speed chase or conflict. For others, ballooning, skydiving, para-sailing, amateur stock car racing, or scuba diving satisfy risk-related motivations.

While varied forms of deviant social behavior, such as gang fighting, vandalism, or other types of juvenile crime, are not commonly thought of as leisure pursuits, the reality is that they often are prompted by the same need for thrills, excitement, and challenge that other, more respectable recreation pursuits satisfy.[16]

Hedonistic Motivations

Similarly, many leisure pursuits today are based on the desire for pleasure of a sensual nature. These include a wide range of activities, such as gambling, drug or alcohol use, or direct or indirect sexual involvement, that are essentially hedonistic.

Such motivations are part of the normal range of leisure behavior for many individuals in modern society and, in fact, have existed in many cultures throughout history. While they have been condemned or prohibited in some societies, and while laws still exist in most North American communities to control gambling, drinking, drug use, or commercialized sex, public participation and spending on these activities continues to be high. A number of research studies have examined the linkage between substance abuse and leisure values and behaviors, and others have analyzed gambling and sexual activities as recreationally oriented pursuits.

In general, programs of higher education that prepare students for careers in recreation, parks, and leisure services do not deal with such marginal aspects of leisure behavior. However, since they are elements of leisure behavior that compete with other forms of recreational involvement and influence public leisure values and choices, it is essential to understand their role.

Nostalgia-Based Motivations

While it is not commonly thought of as a significant influence on recreational participation, nostalgia, in the sense of a need to recapture or relive the past, affects a number of significant leisure pursuits. A striking example may be found in the sports camps that have been formed to permit mostly middle-aged professional men or business executives to play basketball or baseball with former professional stars. Organizations like Sports Dreams, Inc., have sponsored week-long training camps in Arizona and other states where men who played on school, college, or amateur sports teams decades before are given the chance to be coached by and to play with ex-big-leaguers in a fantasy week setting. For example, in a camp featuring the 1969 Chicago Cubs

> . . . any Cub-smitten manchild was offered a trip to Scottsdale, Arizona, for a week of the kind of training the big leaguers get, a chance to mingle with the holdover heroes of '69 and be coached by them [and finally] to play against the aging Chicago stars at Scottsdale Stadium, where the team had trained in '69.[17]

In another example of nostalgia underlying leisure involvement, many older men and women attend band concerts and rock-and-roll events where they are able to relive the dance and music crazes of past decades. Such parties attract fans from the sixties and seventies, who enjoy the Latin-American, rock, disco, or other popular music of the past, and revive memories of their youth—often with the graying performers of the earlier era. One woman comments:

> It was the pre-drug era, the pre-war era. . . . Wow, back then, when I used to get in that convertible and listen to [a popular disk jockey] we didn't worry about the war, or AIDS. It was a happy-go-lucky time.[18]

Still another example of efforts to recapture the past in leisure activities may be found in the dozens of groups that are fascinated by ancient history, that replay medieval court rites, tournaments, or festivals, or that wear Revolutionary War or Civil War uniforms and re-enact century-old battles.

PERSONAL VALUES OF RECREATIONAL INVOLVEMENT

We now turn to an examination of the positive values of recreational involvement, as demonstrated by systematic research studies. In describing the major areas of human development, behavioral scientists use such terms as *cognitive* (referring to mental or intellectual development), *affective* (relating to emotional or feeling states), and *psychomotor* (meaning the broad area of motor learning and performance). Because these terms are somewhat narrow in their application, this chapter will instead use the more familiar terms *physical, emotional, social,* and *mental* development, together with a fifth category, *spiritual* experience. These are all closely related to each other and should be treated under the single heading of personality development. However, to focus more sharply on each aspect of recreation's contribution to personal well-being, this chapter will discuss them separately.

Physical Values and Outcomes

Active recreational pursuits such as sports and games, dance, and even such moderate forms of exercise as walking or gardening have significant positive effects on physical development and health. The value of such activities obviously will vary according to the age and developmental needs of the participants. For children and youth, the major need is to promote healthy structural growth, fitness, and endurance, and the acquisition of physical qualities and skills. It is essential that children learn the importance of fitness and develop habits of participation in physical recreation that will serve them in later life. This is particularly important in an era of electronic gadgets, labor-saving devices, and readily available transportation, all of which save time and physical effort but encourage a sedentary way of life.

The physical fitness of American children became a matter of serious national concern when the Kraus-Weber tests after World War II showed the fitness of American boys and girls to be much lower than that of children in other nations. Expanded programs of physical education and community sports for youth helped American schoolchildren to improve their fitness levels at this point. In the 1960s and 1970s, many schools shifted their elementary school physical education programs from calisthenics and team games, which are less likely to be carried on in adult life, to lifetime recreational pursuits and fitness activities. In some schools, children learned to test their own fitness levels and to work on individual or small-group activities.

Despite such efforts, however, it became apparent in the 1980s that American youth were *not* fit. "It's the best kept secret in America today," commented the chairman of the President's Council on Physical Fitness and Sport. "It's a disgrace." Based on national surveys of 19,000 children between the ages of 6 and 17, the Council reported that 40 percent of boys and 70 percent of girls were unable to do more than a single pull-up, and fitness experts generally agreed that athletic ability had sagged steadily over the past two decades. An article in *Time* magazine reported:

Other studies echo the litany of laxity; in the past two decades the prevalence of obesity increased from 18 percent to 27 percent among children ages six to eleven and from 16 percent to 22 percent among those ages twelve to 17; 40 percent of youngsters ages five to eight have elevated blood-pressure or blood-cholesterol levels or do not exercise at all; any of these factors probably increases their risk of developing heart disease. . . . Warns Dr. Kenneth Cooper, founder of Dallas' Aerobics Center: "What's happening to our kids now will reap adverse effects in ten to 15 years."[19]

Recognizing that the picture is less promising among America's children and youth than among its adults, what are the *specific* benefits of vigorous recreation activity for all age groups? These have been clearly documented in such areas of concern as obesity and cardiovascular health.

Control of Obesity

Scientists agree that physical activity plays a major role in weight control. Obesity among American adults has grown steadily and is now a serious health problem in this country. Per capita energy consumption has decreased as much as 10 percent over the past 50 years because of the use of automobiles and other mechanical devices and the popularity of television and spectator sports. A study carried out at Pennsylvania State University confirmed that male business executives have more body fat than most Americans because they work too hard and exercise too little. A group of 250 middle-aged executives had an average 22 percent body fat per participant, compared with an average of 12 to 15 percent body fat for the average American male, and only 4 to 5 percent body fat for athletes in rigorous training programs.[20]

Numerous medical studies have documented the serious impact of obesity on people of all ages. According to research reported in 1992 by the U.S. Department of Agriculture Nutrition Research Center, overweight teenagers are more likely to suffer from such illnesses as heart disease, colon cancer, arthritis, and gout than are other adolescents, through their life span.[21] By the age of 45 they begin to die at a higher-than-usual rate, and when they reach their 70s their risk of death is twice that of those who were normal size as teenagers. In recent years, the problem has become increasingly severe. In 1995, results from a long-term study conducted by the federal Centers for Disease Control and Prevention show that the number of Americans who are seriously overweight

> . . . after holding steady for 20 years at about a quarter of the population, jumped to one-third in the 1980s, an increase of more than 30 percent [with] some 58 million people in the U.S. weighing at least 20 percent more than their ideal body weight [which puts] them at increased risk for diabetes, hypertension, heart disease, stroke, arthritis and some forms of cancer.[22]

Apart from the psychological, sociological, and other factors that tend to promote obesity, one critical cause has to do with the sedentary lifestyle of many Americans. Regular, vigorous exercise is a key element in maintaining healthy body weight. For example, experts have calculated the exact number of calories burned per hour by various types of activities, such as handball, running, swimming, jogging, tennis, or cycling. Jogging at the rate of 12 minutes per mile will burn up between 480 and 600 calories per hour for a 158-pound adult. Running for one hour at a pace of 7.5 miles per hour will burn up 800 calories. In contrast, watching television uses only 80 calories per hour—just 15 more than sleeping.

Preserving Cardiovascular Health

Of all fitness-related aspects of active recreation, maintaining cardiovascular health has represented the highest priority. Until recently, Americans were known to have more coronary attacks than the people of any other nation, with heart and circulatory system diseases claiming nearly a million lives each year. The continuing rise in the number of such deaths is believed to have been partly caused by the fact that more people are escaping such illnesses as pneumonia or tuberculosis and living to the age when degenerative vascular disease becomes more of a threat. Doctors have also noted, however, an alarming increase of mortality from cardiovascular illness among comparatively young adults, especially males.

In the early 1990s, heart attack was identified as the leading cause of death in the United States, killing about 500,000 people a year. In 1992, a report by the American Heart Association classified physical inactivity as a major risk factor for heart disease, with a sedentary lifestyle being every bit as bad for one's heart as smoking, high cholesterol, or high blood pressure. Supporting this report, the director of epidemiology at the Institute for Aerobics Research in Dallas stated that 20 to 30 percent of Americans engage in so little physical activity that they are at especially high risk for developing the clogged arteries that lead to heart attacks. Federal health habit surveys found that only one-third of American adults exercise or play sports regularly. Even among teenagers, only 37 percent do some sort of sustained and vigorous physical activity three times a week.[23]

On the basis of long-term population studies, authorities have generally recommended that a minimum of three half-hour periods of vigorous aerobic exercise with pulse-rate targets keyed to one's age is necessary to have a desired cardiovascular impact. However, recent research involving thousands of men and women indicates that even moderate forms of exercise, including such activities as walking, stair-climbing, gardening or housework, have a beneficial long-term effect on one's health. While high-intensity, pulse-pounding workouts yield the most dramatic benefits, more modest forms of exercise do yield significant benefits.

Beyond these findings, other research has demonstrated that regular exercise reduces the incidence of diabetes, colon cancer among men and breast and uterine cancer among women, stress and hypertension, strokes, osteoporosis, and other serious illnesses.[24]

Need for Recreation Motivation

However, exercise alone, in the form of solitary aerobic activity or body conditioning, is not likely to become a long-term health measure if it lacks sociability or recreational atmosphere. Summerfield and Priest point out that more than half of all adults exercise intermittently and that, of those who start an exercise program, less than half will still be exercising six months later. They write:

> For many adults, exercise is no longer as pleasurable as it was when they were children. To some, exercise has become another form of work that is structured (5 minutes of warm-up; 36 sit-ups; 15 minutes of peak work) and monitored (target heart rates every 5 minutes).[25]

Wankel found, in a study of adult fitness programs in a Canadian industrial setting, that the key factors associated with people continuing to engage regularly in group exercise had to do with the need for sociability, competition, and developing recreational skills. Thus, the most effective fitness activities are likely to be those with enjoyable recreational elements.[26]

Similarly, Rod Dishman, professor of exercise science at the University of Georgia, points out that the habit of exercise has both physical and psychological components. Dishman writes:

> The social side of exercise—the shared experience of activity—is one of the main reasons people keep on doing it. Many people who exercise regularly mention the lasting friendships they've made in aerobics classes, on jogging trails, tennis courts or elsewhere. When the social support goes, the exercise regimen often slips.[27]

As a consequence, many colleges and universities, YMCAs and YWCAs, and company recreation programs designed to serve employees have initiated fitness centers and programs in order to promote active play and conditioning activities within a recreational framework. In both the United States and Canada, federal authorities have joined together with professional societies and educational agencies to stimulate public interest and involvement in physical fitness and sports.

In Canada, for example, in the late 1970s and 1980s, Fitness Canada, a program section of the Fitness and Amateur Sport Directorate of the federal government, sponsored extensive research and promotional efforts to encourage Canadians to become more physically active. A private, independent, and nonprofit communications company was established to spearhead this effort through public service advertising and a host of co-sponsored special events and campaigns. Blake Ferris and co-authors write:

> In addition, through the efforts of provincial and territorial governments, national agencies in health, physical education, recreation and sport, dynamic and successful programs have emerged to focus on most segments of the population such as youth, seniors, employees and the disabled.[28]

At the same time, it is important to recognize that vigorous outdoor recreation, sport, or exercise regimens can be overdone from a health and safety perspective. Obviously, such activities as downhill skiing, scuba diving, mountain climbing or hang gliding involve a substantial risk of serious injury, and even such an innocuous pastime as in-line skating—which some estimates indicate has become the fastest-growing sport in the United States—results in thousands of injuries each year.

Furthermore, obsessive devotion to exercise may often represent a sign of emotional difficulty including marital conflict, social withdrawal, or other forms of unhealthy escape. Boone suggests a number of warning signs of over-exercise: frequent colds and sore throats; painful and/or stiff muscles and joints; or when the element of fun in physical recreation and sport is lost or there is an exaggerated emphasis on improving performance skill, distance, or time.[29]

Emotional Values and Outcomes

What are the specific ways in which recreation contributes to emotional well-being? Millions of people who function within a presumable normal range of behavior tend to suffer from tension, boredom, stress, frustration, and an inability to use their leisure in satisfying ways. Mental depression afflicts an estimated 35 million people in the United States. The feeling of engagement and control over one's life that may be achieved in leisure is critical to sound mental health. Iso-Ahola and Weissinger point out that many psychologists base their treatment on this principle—seeking to help patients develop freedom and control in their lives, as well as the kind of engagement with others in leisure that contributes to psychological well-being.[30]

Relaxation and Escape

Going beyond these broad categories of leisure benefits, Chubb and Chubb have suggested that one of the most important psychological benefits of recreation is relaxation. Some people obtain this through physical activity, others from reading or other mental pastimes, and still others by dozing, daydreaming, or taking it easy. Relaxation, they write:

> provides a respite from life's worries and pressures, relieves feelings of tension and fatigue, and restores mental efficiency. Most people need it after a day's work, following an emotionally disturbing experience, or part way through a long period of involvement in one task.[31]

They comment also that one of the emotional benefits of recreation is that it provides a valuable means of escaping from one's problems. For growing numbers of people,

> recreation is important because it offers temporary relief from unpleasant realities in their personal lives that they find difficult or impossible to bear. By immersing themselves in the make-believe world of books, magazines, games, music, sports, motion pictures, television, bars, or discotheques, or by losing themselves in daydreaming, they escape from their problems.[32]

Obviously, great numbers of individuals find escape from the unpleasant realities of life through liquor or the use of drugs. However, these forms of escape in leisure are temporary and invariably cause greater problems for the alcoholic or addict, especially in health, work, and family life. Other kinds of leisure experiences offer escape without such undesirable consequences.

Overcoming Loneliness

Another important contribution of recreation to mental health consists of its role in providing social contact, friendship, or intimacy with others. Peplau describes loneliness as a widespread phenomenon: typically, as many as three-quarters of all college students report being lonely during their first term away from home. Loneliness can have unpleasant and even life-threatening consequences and often is directly linked to alcoholism, physical illness, or suicide.[33] Harry Stack Sullivan, a leading psychotherapist, commented that loneliness is an intense, unpleasant experience that can happen to an individual at any point in the life cycle. Sullivan stated, "Man is a gregarious animal with a need for contact with others. When this need is unfulfilled, it is expressed in loneliness. When action is taken to avoid or relieve loneliness, there is enhancement of self-esteem."[34]

In a poll taken by *Psychology Today,* loneliness was the most frequently mentioned personal problem, with 38 percent of female and 43 percent of male readers saying they often felt lonely. Jeffrey Young points out:

> We know that severe loneliness can lead to a variety of problems . . . (including serious health risks). There are also psychological consequences. People who are chronically lonely are often less productive in their work lives. They feel that life is less satisfying and are prone to psychiatric disorders such as depression and anxiety.[35]

The value of recreation in overcoming problems of loneliness is obvious. Most leisure activities are carried on in groups, and sociability is a key outcome of many recreational involvements. For example, the 1981 Canada Fitness Survey found that 24 percent of respondents rated companionship as a very important motivation for recreation participation, with this figure increasing to 34 percent among older adults.

Linked to its value in overcoming loneliness is the important role of recreation in overcoming boredom. Mounir Ragheb, for example, has conducted research showing that leisure satisfaction ranks significantly higher than other social or psychological variables in helping individuals to reduce or control boredom in their lives.[36]

Stress Management

A closely related value of recreation is its usefulness in stress reduction. A leading authority on stress, Dr. Hans Selye, defines it as the overall response of the body to any extreme demand made upon it, which might include threats, physical illness, job pressures, and environmental extremes—or even such life changes as marriage, divorce, vacations, or taking a new job. Increasing amounts of stress in modern life have resulted in many individuals suffering from migraine or tension headaches, allergies, ulcers and ulcerative colitis, hypertension, and a number of psychosomatic illnesses, as well as accident proneness.

Once it was thought that the best approach to stress was rest and avoidance of all pressures, but today there is an awareness that some degree of stress is desirable and healthful. Cleaver and Eisenhart point out that physical activity can play a significant role in stress reduction. Typically, people work off anger, frustration, and indignation by taking long walks or engaging in some kind of physical activity such as chopping wood. Physical exertion, which consumes the sugar and fats that have poured into the bloodstream, reduces the stress reaction through the process of *syntropy*. All of the body's systems—the working muscles, heart, hormones, metabolic reactions and the responsiveness of the central nervous system—are strengthened through stimulation. Following periods of extended exertion, the body systems slow, bringing on a feeling of deep relaxation. Attaining this relaxed state is essential to lessening the stress reaction.[37]

> Indeed, for many individuals, strenuous physical activity does more than reduce tension; it may actually promote a state of elation or euphoria. So-called "runner's high" results from the appearance of chemicals called endorphins which are produced by the brain and pituitary gland following prolonged exercise. Endorphins help the body control pain and produce a strong sense of well-being. High-risk activities such as rock climbing, mountaineering, white-water canoeing, hang gliding, or wilderness backpacking may literally provide a sense of emotional release and an improved outlook, which helps to overcome tension in daily life. A former foreign correspondent, Steve Lohr, writes:
>
> > . . . when I can grab an hour here or there for a workout, I do . . . three or four times a week. Why do I keep doing it? Mainly because I like the way it feels, soaked in sweat, heart pounding, lungs heaving, muscles straining, blood pumped into every capillary. I liked the feeling as an 8-year-old, and I still do.[38]

Under conditions of extreme stress, different forms of recreation may help individuals maintain a degree of emotional balance. Sportwriter George Vecsey cites the example of Allied prisoners of war in a German prison camp, Stalag Luft III, where sports such as rugby, basketball, and even modified golf helped them keep sane.[39]

PLAY AS EMOTIONAL RELEASE

Another important benefit of leisure activity is that it can provide strong feelings of pleasure and satisfaction and can serve as an outlet for discharging certain emotional drives which, if repressed, might produce emotional distress or even mental illness.

The role of pleasure is increasingly recognized as a vital factor in emotional well-being. Researchers like Walter Podilchak have begun to analyze the simple concept of fun—defined as intense pleasure and enjoyment and an important dimension of social interactional leisure.[40] Similarly, R. Bruce Hull and Sean Michael have examined the nature of mood, with its impacts on human cognition, behavior, health, and general well-being, as it is experienced

Risk Recreation

Organized outdoor recreation activities often include challenging forms of adventurous play—as in white water rafting offered by the Pocono Adventure Co. in Pennsylvania (top) or kayaking and camping in Utah (center). Far more dangerous (bottom) is the leap by a 12-year-old from one high tenement rooftop to another in a Bronx neighborhood.

in recreation.[41] And, in a review of studies on the "anatomy of joy," Natalie Angier reports that scientists are finding that sensations like optimism, curiosity, and rapture—as opposed to puritan condemnation of pleasure—

> . . . not only make life worth living, but also make life last longer. They think that euphoria unrelated to any ingested substance is good for the body, that laughter is protective against the corrosive impact of stress, and that joyful people outlived their bilious, whining counterparts.[42]

As additional evidence that fun and enjoyment have direct, positive health benefits, scientists have recently confirmed that even minor or casual experiences like taking part in social activities, or leisure involvement in fishing or jogging, have a measurable reinforcing effect on the human immune system.[43]

The direct satisfaction that comes from playing a game well, sharing a good time with others, or enjoying a fine play or social occasion is obviously a desirable feature of leisure activity. Beyond this, many people have a strong need to express violent feelings of hostility or aggression, and these can be released by competing strenuously with others in socially acceptable forms of play.

In modern society where we no longer face the kinds of dangers that threatened our ancestors, we tend to seek out ways of competing, meeting challenges, and testing ourselves against such artificial risks as dangerous outdoor pursuits. Major team sports, particularly the more violent ones like football or ice hockey, boxing, or automobile racing, meet this need—either directly for participants or vicariously for spectators. Numerous examples can be cited of how people discharge their feelings of hostility and aggression in leisure activities. When aggression is worked out in supervised and acceptable forms of play, it is obviously less destructive than when it is expressed in delinquent behavior, arson, or the like.

Self-Actualization

Linked to the issue of emotional well-being is *self-actualization,* a term that became popular in the 1970s chiefly through the writings of Abraham Maslow, who stressed the need for individuals to achieve their fullest degree of creative potential. Maslow developed a convincing theory of human motivation in which he identified a number of important human needs, arranging them in a hierarchy. As each of the basic needs is met in turn, a person is able to move ahead to meet more advanced needs and drives. Maslow's theory includes the following ascending levels of need:

Physiological needs: food, rest, exercise, shelter, protection from the elements, and other basic survival needs

Safety needs: self-protection needs on a secondary level—protection against danger, threats, or other forms of deprivation

Social needs: needs for group associations, acceptance by one's fellows, giving and receiving affection and friendship

Ego needs: needs for enhanced status, a sense of achievement, self-esteem, confidence, and recognition by others

Self-actualization needs: needs for being creative, and realizing one's maximum potential in a variety of life spheres[44]

Obviously, play and recreation can be important elements in satisfying at least the last three, highest levels of need in Maslow's hierarchy. In his writing, Maslow stressed the need for individuals to be more spontaneous and creative and to find fulfillment in a variety of expressive activities—both work and play. From the 1950s on, Maslow promoted the view that psychology, instead of studying the mentally ill, should study the healthiest and most productive people—those he called the "self-actualizers." Turning to historical examples, he found that self-actualizers were

> more autonomous, spontaneous, democratic, altruistic and esthetically sensitive. They also seemed more open to transcendent experiences, accepting of themselves and others, and possessed of genial rather than cruel humor.[45]

Healthy Balance of Work and Play

For most people, emotional well-being is greatly strengthened if they are able to maintain a healthy balance of work and recreation in their lives. Today, we recognize that there can be *too much* commitment to work, resulting in the exclusion of other interests and personal involvements that help to maintain mental health.

Alexander Reid Martin, a psychiatrist who served for 12 years as chairman of the American Psychiatric Association's Committee on Leisure Time and Its Uses, wrote extensively on the problem of leisure in relation to mental health today. Martin pointed out that the Protestant work ethic and the overemphasis on work values in our society made it extremely difficult for many people to use their leisure in self-fulfilling and satisfying ways. In his professional practice, he found many highly successful people who could justify their lives only through work and material accomplishment and who felt intensely guilty about play and leisure. Often they suffered from what Martin called "weekend neurosis," and it was not uncommon for them to have severe psychological upsets while on vacation.[46]

Workaholism   The tendency to place excessive emphasis on work, at the expense of other avenues of expression, has been popularly termed "workaholism." For some people, work is an obsession and they are unable to find other kinds of pleasurable release. For those who find their work a deep source of personal satisfaction and commitment, this may not be an altogether undesirable phenomenon.

A psychologist who has done an intensive analysis of the life patterns of workaholics, Marilyn Machlowitz, comments that they are neither good nor bad—simply "frustrated or fulfilled."[47] Some such people enjoy a life committed to high-pressure, demanding, and rewarding work, particularly if it is creative and challenging. On the other hand, Machlowitz notes, many other workaholics appear to be rigid and terrified of unstructured time—"burnt-out drones who drive subordinates crazy with incessant demands."

For those executives who fear that "letting go" in leisure is likely to hinder their career advancement, it is helpful to know that a study of Ivy League college graduates has shown that the most successful professionals and company executives tend to be those who enjoy hobbies, sports, and vacations and who have varied and interesting leisure-time activities.

The condition of many workaholics who feel guilty about enjoying recreation and leisure may have serious medical implications. A team of cardiologists at the Mount Zion Hospital and Medical Center in San Francisco concluded that much heart disease is caused by an emotional component that produces "Type-A behavior," described as follows:

> The Type-A man [is] ambitious, competitive, impatient and aggressive; he is involved in an incessant struggle against time and/or other people. His sense of *time urgency* is perhaps his most predominant trait. Almost always punctual, he is greatly annoyed *if kept waiting*. . . . The Type-A man does not usually spare the time to indulge in hobbies; or when he does, he prefers competitive games or gambling. [He] generally strives frantically for things worth *having* (a beautiful home, a better job, a bigger bank balance) at the expense of things worth *being* (well-read, knowledgeable about art, appreciative of nature).[48]

Epidemiological studies led the San Francisco research team to conclude that the creative use of leisure can be more important than diet or exercise in preventing heart attacks.

Leading authorities on business management and personnel practices now stress the need for business executives to find outside pleasures that open up, diversify, and enrich their lives. The guilt that successful people too often have about play must be assuaged, and they must be helped to realize that, with a more balanced style of life, they are likely to be more productive in the long run—and much happier in the present.

Summing up, many studies have established a positive relationship between leisure involvement and life satisfaction and psychological well-being, particularly among older adults. For example, Dupuis and Smale have found that participation in such activities as walking and swimming, crafts and hobbies, visiting friends, or taking part in social clubs is positively linked to a sense of well-being and negatively related to depression.[49]

Numerous other studies carried out with special populations have reinforced these findings. For example, Rawson and McIntosh found that therapeutic camping programs that stressed such elements as positive reinforcement, peer group recognition, frequent episodes of personal success, and the expression of approval and affection resulted in dramatic gains in self-esteem among children who were socially or culturally deprived or who had severe behavior problems.[50]

SOCIAL VALUES OF RECREATION

A third important area in which recreation promotes favorable personal development involves healthy socialization. Many adults today find their primary social contacts and interpersonal relationships not in their work lives, but in voluntary group associations during leisure hours.

Clearly, different types of recreation groups and programs impose a set of social norms, roles, and relationships that participants must learn to accept—and that contribute to their own social development. Even in the relatively free environment of outdoor recreation, where people hike, camp, or explore the wilderness in ways of their own choosing, interaction among participants is a key element in the experience. In a study of social order in forest recreation settings conducted for the U. S. Forest Service, John Heywood explored such factors as crowding and conforming behavior in wilderness areas, vandalism and conflict among campers, environmental elements, and managerial strategies.[51]

For children, play groups offer a realistic training ground for developing both cooperative and competitive skills. The youngster who is part of a group in an after-school center, summer camp, or teenage social club is testing his or her social role and preparing for involvement in the adult world. Through group participation, children learn to interact with others, to accept group rules and wishes, and, when necessary, to subordinate their own views or desires to those of the group. They learn to give and take, to assume leadership or follow the leadership of others, and to work effectively as part of a team.

Sport and Social Development

One form of play that has been widely assumed to have a positive effect on participants is sport. Wilderson and Dodder comment that sport is an institution that reflects the cultural ethos of a society and helps socialize its participants into accepting normative value patterns. Sport has been credited with producing or reinforcing such qualities as

> emotional maturity, moral values, self-reliance, self-sacrifice, effective citizenry, respect for authority, democratic ideals, mental health, academic success, competitive spirit, manliness and, of course, Godliness.[52]

Similarly, Frey and Massengale point out that the values associated with school sports are those widely accepted in American society. They include striving for excellence, achievement, humility, loyalty, self-control, respect for authority, self-discipline, hard work, and deferred gratification. However, these authors contend that the structure of modern school sports at all levels no longer permits the inculcation of these values:

> Goal displacement has taken place. Building character and enhancing education have been replaced as guiding values by the desire for profit, power, prestige, notoriety, visibility, community support, and organizational survival. Modern school sports . . . profess the goals and values of a participatory or amateur model [but] operate under the structure of commercial enterprise.[53]

What are some of the specific expectations of sport as a form of socialization? The former president of Purdue University has stated:

> College football breeds discipline and leadership. . . . Competitive team sports keep us strong and vigorous. . . . I find no convincing evidence that leadership can be taught. It is something that can only be learned by facing successfully its demand on the individual's total capability.[54]

One of the most important elements of sport is the rigorous training process, which requires dedication not just to a sport, but to a way of life. A leading college long-distance runner describes running as a character-building experience in which the daily workouts become more enjoyable and valuable than the weekly competition:

> The essence of the enterprise lies in the daily workout. It is the workout that regulates the runner's whole life—his eating habits, his social schedule and his academic future . . . the distance runner enjoys the daily routine of workouts more than the weekly ordeal of competition. The lust for victory is too often overemphasized as the motive to run.[55]

However, Wilderson and Dodder point out that sport has also been credited with less desirable socializing effects by reinforcing such social values as conformity, dehumanization, authoritarianism, and the need to win at all costs.

Realistically, the benefits of sports participation depend heavily on the circumstances under which games are played. Truly amateur sports competition may foster positive and unselfish values, while commercialized, high-pressure sports in big-time universities may be responsible for fostering a host of hypocritical and manipulative practices. Such traits as the ability to play by the rules, show good sportsmanship, and win or lose gracefully are often given little support in such institutions.

One of the most frequently expressed justifications of sport as a form of social development is that it provides a medium through which children and youth learn to compete, thus supposedly becoming equipped to survive in a tough, "dog-eat-dog"adult world. Yet there is evidence that our national emphasis on competition and glorification of winning as an all-consuming goal has serious undesirable effects on character. Increasingly, the goal of building competitive fervor through sport is being challenged.

Opposing Views on Competition and Cooperation

A major theme of much criticism of competitive youth sports is that they tend to eliminate the spontaneity and sense of fun that should be present in children's play, and instead foster unacceptable values such as the desire to win at all costs. Lundquist writes:

> In competitive sport the opponent is the enemy and obstacle in the way of victory. . . . In the continuous use of terminology such as the "long bomb," "war," and "blitz," the references of gaining territory and more yardage than your opponents, the whole relationship to combat is all too obvious.[56]

Studies of the behavior of American children have shown that ten-year-olds repeatedly failed to earn rewards for which they strove, because they were too highly competitive and were unable to assist others in problem-solving games that required cooperation. In other situations, overcompetitiveness caused children to sacrifice their own rewards in order to reduce the rewards of their peers. In contrast, ten-year-old children in rural Mexico found it easy to cooperate with each other and to win the prizes that eluded their American counterparts.[57] Iso-Ahola argues that in large-scale organized youth sports programs, the pleasure of matching one's skills against one's peers is diminished by extrinsic rewards and sanctions, such as trophies and authoritarian coaching. Often the outcome of the game is made so important for youngsters by the pressure of their coaches and parents that a high level of frustration and tension results.

By way of contrast, Iso-Ahola concludes that cooperation is superior to competition in many respects:

> In general, competition impairs while cooperation facilitates interpersonal relationships. It has been shown that cooperation encourages mutual liking and concern and is . . . positively related to such qualities as social adjustment, open-mindedness, and acceptance of differences. By contrast, competition appears to increase anxiety and the desire for individual rewards. . . . to reduce self-assurance, the desire to talk to others, to share information, and to work together.[58]

There have been a number of events illustrating how the need to win, carried to the extreme, may cause people to lose sight of the proper goals of sport. Two episodes in 1986 and 1987 occurred when promising athletes, faced with defeat or failure, deliberately injured themselves. An outstanding North Carolina State distance runner, who had set the collegiate record in the women's 10,000-meter race, was hospitalized with a serious spinal injury. She had deliberately leaped from a bridge after having to drop out of an NCAA outdoor track-and-field championship event. Similarly, a Tennessee high school football player was paralyzed from the chest down when, frustrated by a close loss in a state championship playoff game, he charged head first into a brick wall outside the locker room, breaking his neck and severing his spinal cord. A number of youth coaches' associations and groups of parents in both the United States and Canada have striven to develop new and more sensible values with respect to winning and losing.

Play and Social Mobility

Recreation is also believed to lead to improved social mobility for children and youth by opening up new horizons of awareness—even to lead directly to career opportunities. Again, sport provides a valuable example. The point has frequently been made that high school sports too often discourage emphasis on scholarship and divert school resources and student energies from the goal of academic excellence. Outstanding high school graduating seniors may find it almost impossible to get academic scholarships, while star halfbacks who can barely read or write find dozens of coaches beating at their doors with attractive offers for full scholarships and more.

On the other hand, sociological studies of midwestern high school boys have shown that, on all social class levels, athletes performed on a higher level academically than nonathletes and that proportionally more athletes than nonathletes were motivated to attend college. Almost five times as many nonathletes as athletes dropped out of high school; in general, participation in student activity programs seems to be closely related to the school's holding power and provides constructive outlets for students' social and psychological needs.

John Loy points out four important values of sports that can contribute to upward mobility: (1) early participation may develop skills that permit direct entry into professional sports; (2) sports participation may promote educational achievement by providing scholarships and strengthening the student's motivation to remain in school; (3) it may lead to occupational sponsorship or assistance or to the kinds of contacts that assist later career development; and (4) it may lead to the development of attitudes and behavior patterns valued in the larger occupational world.[59]

In general, however, the odds against youthful athletes gaining college scholarships or, beyond that, moving into the professional ranks, are daunting. In the mid-1990s, Thomas writes:

Of the 400,000 high school seniors who play football or basketball, only about 20,000 will be signed by the 1,000 colleges affiliated with the National Collegiate Athletic Association. Some 5,000 will play for the 400 colleges in the National Association of Independent Athletics and 3,000 for the 500 members of the National Junior College Athletic Association.

What's more, while virtually all two-year and four-year colleges offer varsity athletics, no more than 300 routinely grant full athletic scholarships. . . .[60]

For those talented athletes who do play on varsity college teams, the odds against making it to the professional ranks are proportionately far greater. However, for those who do complete their college degrees, this obviously represents a major step up the socioeconomic career ladder, and sports participation may also have involved making positive contacts within the business or professional world that can help to promote future success.

Viewed more broadly, recreation provides an early form of exposure and training ground for *all* sorts of career directions for children and youth. Early experience in arts and crafts may lead to an occupational interest in construction, design, commercial art, carpentry, and similar career possibilities. Children with scientific or mathematical hobbies may gradually sharpen their interests through school and college study and ultimately make science, mathematics, or computer work their lifelong occupation. Similarly, many other forms of recreational involvement help young people to become aware of their own skills and talents and of the careers that these might lead to.

In community life as well, recreational involvement tends to be seen as an avenue to status and success. William F. Whyte, in a 1955 study of slum youth, found two social groupings. One group, which he called the "corner boys," was content to hang around on street corners; this group had low occupational goals. The other group, which he called the "college boys," was much more ambitious and upwardly mobile. Whyte found that the "college boys" realized that certain kinds of affiliations and social behavior would help them in getting ahead. Correctly perceiving the neighborhood settlement house as representative of middle-class, goal-oriented values, they tended to join and become active in its clubs and programs.[61]

Particularly in inner-city settings, youth organizations like the Boys and Girls Clubs or the Police Athletic League provide rounded experiences for disadvantaged children that help them broaden their interests, gain a sense of accomplishment, and set new and more ambitious goals for their lives. One such Puerto Rican youth who had been a student of the author's, Ricardo Carreras, described his experience at the Tompkins Square Boys' Club in New York City. He entered almost all of the activities available in the center and excelled in basketball, judo, and boxing; competed at the Cultural Olympics in Mexico; received a scholarship to attend the Outward Bound School in Marble, Colorado; climbed a mountain, took part in a marathon, won a leadership and citizenship award; and, through dozens of other experiences and trips, gained the sense that he had great potential—and that he could do anything he set his mind to.

In the business world itself, participation in such sports as tennis, squash, sailing, hunting, or especially golf may represent a key factor in becoming part of the old-boy network that occupies executive offices in major corporations. Writing on executive "fun and games," N. R. Kleinfield points out that shared recreational pursuits breed an atmosphere of intimacy that can further corporate goals or lead to deal-making:

> The world of business and the world of sport enjoy an inescapable symbiosis. When they are not trapped in a whirl of conferences or making phone calls from the corporate jet, many top executives are likely to be off blasting ducks out of the sky, or swatting a golf ball 300 yards down the fairway. . . . [Some] indulge in swimming and tennis, usually at their own weekend hideaways. And golf is a favorite, for women executives as well as the men. . . . [Others] play polo and race sailboats and go hunting in rugged, out-of-the-way places. Macho-competitive is the operative state, and the equal-opportunity strictures of the office are generally left far behind.[62]

Socialization in "Singles" Groups

Another important socialization function of leisure has to do with the role of recreation groups in helping both men and women make new friends—either for simple companionship or possibly for fuller relationships that might include marriage. In the past, most courtship was initiated through family ties and acquaintances, the church, work, or neighborhood associations. Today, increasing numbers of people tend to rely on such settings as bars and clubs, health and fitness spas, political action groups, singles cruises or hotel weekends, or such mechanisms as dating services or singles listings in magazines.

In the mid-1990s, nearly 73 million or 39 percent of American adults over 18 were unmarried—either divorced, widowed, or never married—far more than the 38 million unmarried persons in 1970. These individuals are increasingly joining singles groups of similar people in order to share their hobbies and to explore potential companionships. These niche or special interest groups often assist their members in meeting each other through newsletters and mailings of personal biographies. Murray Dubin writes:

> The niches are filling fast and their members are more often women than men. Hikers. Classical music fans. Farmers. Film aficionados. Herpes sufferers. Graduates of prestigious colleges. Gay men's covered-dish groups. Bridge players. Sailors. Book lovers. Jews. Christians. Gourmets. Fat folks. Scuba divers.[63]

Another type of leisure-linked organization that facilitates social contact is the club or business designed to help single travelers find compatible companions and avoid the expensive fees that are charged as single supplements for occupying a hotel room or cruise ship cabin alone. Typically, such groups use computerized listings to match travel partners.

In numerous other ways, recreation helps to promote the social lives of individuals at all age levels and in varied types of settings. Several of these areas of personal value also have important community-related benefits and are described in Chapter 6.

INTELLECTUAL VALUES OF RECREATION

Of all the personal benefits of play and recreation, probably the least widely recognized are those involving intellectual or cognitive development. Play is typically thought of as physical activity rather than mental—and has by definition been considered a nonserious form of involvement. How then could it contribute to intellectual growth?

Researchers have slowly come to realize that physical recreation tends to improve personal motivation and make mental and cognitive performance more effective. Numerous studies, for example, have documented the effects of specific types of physical exercise or play on the development of young children. For example, one study comparing four-year-olds who had been exposed to swimming after their second month of life to others who had been involved in swimming after their 28th month found that the "swimming babies" were better adjusted, more independent, and better able to make decisions. Through various types of observation it was determined that they had a better ability to cope with new and strange situations. Beyond this:

> Early swimmers in nearly all sub-tests of the administered intelligence tests (Wechsler PreSchool, Primary Scale of Intelligence—WPPSI, and Hamburg-Wechsler Intelligence Test for Children—HAWIK) showed higher intelligence . . . than did the [later-entry children].[64]

Other research studies have shown a strong relationship between physical fitness and academic performance. While a number of these studies have focused on formal instructional programs, others have utilized less structured experimental elements. Several studies have shown that playfulness as a personal quality is closely linked to creative and inventive thinking among children. Bruner cites one study in which three- to five-year-olds were encouraged to play with a specially designed "supertoy" that permitted a wide variety of possible uses; the children were then rated on their degree of inventiveness, as nonexplorers, explorers, and inventive explorers. Four years later, the experimenter rated the children on a number of personality tests, including one for creativity:

> The more inventive and exploratory the children had been in their previous play with the supertoy, the higher their originality scores were four years later. In general, the nonexploring boys viewed themselves as unadventurous and inactive, and their parents and teachers felt they lacked curiosity. The nonexploratory and unplayful girls turned out to be rather unforthcoming in social interactions, as well as more tense than their more playful comrades.[65]

Play as a Way of Learning

In the past, play was viewed as a frivolous activity, and children were discouraged from playing in order to devote fuller effort to serious learning activities. Today, we recognize that play does contribute to cognitive growth, and indeed may provide a uniquely effective way of learning. How does this happen?

The leading psychologist in the field of child development over the past several decades was the late Jean Piaget, professor at the University of Geneva and director of the *Institut Rousseau*. Piaget suggested that there are two basic processes to all mental development—*assimilation* and *accommodation*. Assimilation is the process of taking in, as in the case of receiving information in the form of visual or auditory stimuli. Accommodation is the process of adjusting to external circumstances and stimuli. In Piaget's theory, play is specially related to assimilation, the process of mentally digesting new and different situations and experiences. Anything important that has happened is reproduced in play; it is a means of assimilating and consolidating the child's emotional experiences.[66]

Another leading authority on cognitive development has been Jerome Bruner, formerly director of Harvard University's Center for Cognitive Studies and later professor of psychology at Oxford University. Bruner's analysis suggests that cognitive development in children has three broad stages. In the first, which he calls the "preoperational" stage, the child's mental task consists chiefly of establishing relationships between experiences and their results and of learning how to understand and represent the external world through symbols established through simple generalizations. The second stage, that of "concrete operations," involves the child's learning to gather data about the environment and to understand and be able to predict its operations within his own mind, rather than through trial and error. In the third stage, "formal operations," the child's ability becomes based on hypothetical propositions and understandings of relationships, rather than on immediate experiences and observation. Play serves as a valuable environment for such learning to take place.

Bruner stresses the need to establish the child's sense of autonomy as well as encourage intense involvement if the fullest degree of learning is to occur. He urges that children be freed from the immediate controls of environmental rewards and punishments, the need to gain parental or teacher approval, and the need to avoid failure. Learning should be approached as the discovery of ideas, rather than as learning "about" something. In an article, Bruner summarized the results of a study of the effects of play on the problem-solving abilities of three- to five-year-olds. This study focused on a basic principle of learning—that in approaching complex tasks, too much motivation can interfere with learning by placing pressure on the learners and creating a state of anxiety and frustration:

> By deemphasizing the importance of the goal, play may serve to reduce excessive drive and thus enable young animals and children to learn more easily the skills they will need when they are older.[67]

Games and Cognitive Development

Games provide a vivid demonstration of the role of play in the intellectual development of children. Anthropologists and psychologists have long examined the relationship of games to child-rearing practices in tribal societies. For example, games of physical skill predominate in societies that stress achievement and success as important life goals. Strategic games that simulate war and combat are found chiefly in tribes with complicated social and political structures. Games of chance reflect tribal religious practices and beliefs. In one series of studies, Sutton-Smith and Gump explored the role of children's games in more advanced cultures. They concluded that games provided children with "action-based social relationships," giving them the opportunity to assume a variety of roles and status positions and providing gratification and psychological release.[68]

There has been a marked increase in the use of games specially devised to teach fundamental concepts, provide information, and encourage strategic behavior. James Coleman, a leading authority on adolescent development, has written on the value of playing games as a learning experience:

> Recently, educators have begun devising games for high school and pre-high school students that simulate complex activities in a society. One of the ways that simulation and games were first combined was in war games. Many of the oldest parlor games (chess and checkers, for example) were developed as war simulations long ago, and today armies use games to develop logistic and strategic skills. From war games developed the idea of management games, a simulation of management decision-making which is used in many business schools and firms to train future executives by putting them in situations they will confront in their jobs.[69]

Games also have been used to help children learn simple scientific, mathematical, and linguistic concepts. One firm provides game kits and visual aids that use playlike approaches to teach number relationships and mathematical symbols; puzzle boxes and equation games are just two of these approaches. Other games deal with civics, government, history and political science, banking, international trade, geometry, and physics.

Over the past two decades, video games have been shown to contribute to learning. In the early 1980s, the U.S. Army explored the use of video games such as *Battlezone,* made by the Atari Corporation, to train soldiers for real-life combat. In another example of the link between games and real-life learning, the McDonnell-Douglas Corporation, the nation's leading defense contractor, joined with a California company that created the popular video games *Donkey Kong* and *Space Shuttle* to develop a sophisticated speech-recognition system for aircraft communication.[70]

Strikingly, games may sometimes provide the catalyst for individuals from disadvantaged backgrounds with limited environmental stimuli that would nurture intellectual or academic growth to discover their own talents and learning potential. For example, in a number of inner-city schools with student populations composed chiefly of minority racial groups from impoverished homes, outstanding chess teams have developed that have competed successfully against teams representing schools from much wealthier communities. Similarly, the student debating team at Science High in Newark, New Jersey, has been state debating champion 12 times and is one of the few urban public school teams on the national debating circuit. It is the only team competing nationally that is composed entirely of African-American and Hispanic students.[71]

On another level, a reporter for *Forbes* magazine points out that business executives frequently enjoy high-level competitive play in games such as contract bridge, chess, or backgammon, and that they value competence in these pastimes in the people they employ. Investment advisors in particular recognize the risk-taking elements involved in such games and the need for strategic flair in taking calculated risks. Whether the game is poker, gin rummy, bridge, backgammon, or chess, the skills involved are all equally important in business. They include, Ross writes:

. . . discipline, memory, coolness under pressure, psychological insightfulness, a readiness to stick to a strategy even when it produces losing streaks in the short run, and rapid and intuitive calculation of probabilities—of spotting opportunities and balancing risks against rewards.[72]

Diversified Values of Recreation   In still other ways, recreation experiences may contribute to the cognitive development of children and youth by promoting creative learning and conceptual growth. Such hobbies as reading, art, music, drama, and nature study all provide learning experiences that may add to a child's fund of knowledge and experience and that develop problem-solving, communication, and other important personal skills.

Even some outdoor experiences may be designed for exploring complex environments in depth, with the kinds of exposure and involvement that could never be achieved in a typical classroom. Outward Bound, which has traditionally taught self-discovery and cooperation through backpacking and risk-taking in wilderness settings, has ventured into the urban "wilderness" of New York City. In pilot programs, groups of "explorers" who were stripped of their credit cards, workday identities, and almost all of their money explored the city by foot, subway, and occasionally rowboat and canoe. They explored deteriorating neighborhoods, camped on the city's sandy fringes, collected artifacts, interviewed residents, and took part in projects to rehabilitate housing for the homeless. Through these experiences, participants came to understand the city, with its startling contrast of great wealth and poverty, and to appreciate its strengths and weaknesses.

Summing up research in this field, Roggenbuck, Loomis, and Dagostino conclude that a number of studies have demonstrated that considerable gains are made in factual knowledge, memory, and other related areas of personal growth through leisure involvements.[73] Even very social or physical forms of play appear to be associated with superior academic performance, as shown in the following report on the link between secondary school student activities and academic performance.

◊ **E**vidence that leisure-time activities are linked to academic performance is found in a 1986 report of the U.S. Department of Education. In a study of 30,000 high school sophomores and 28,000 seniors, the researchers found that "the more activities students were involved in, the higher they ranked" on such measures as grades and test scores. Only 10 percent of the students who participated in four or more activities—such as varsity athletics, cheerleading, debate or drama, band activities, chorus or dance, hobby clubs, or similar groups—had grade point averages of less than 2.0, as opposed to 30 percent of all students.

In a study of the relationship between leisure activity, motivation, and academic performance among secondary school students in the San Francisco Bay area, David Bergin confirmed that school experiences tended to generate interests leading to leisure involvements out of school and a higher level of intellectual motivation overall.[74]

SPIRITUAL VALUES OF RECREATION AND LEISURE

A final area in which recreation and leisure make a vital contribution to the healthy growth and well-being of human beings is within the spiritual realm. The term *spiritual* is commonly taken to be synonymous with religion, but here it means a capacity for exhibiting humanity's higher nature—a sense of moral values, compassion, and respect for other humans and for the earth itself. It is linked to the development of one's inner feelings, a sense of order and purpose in life, and a commitment to care for others and to behave responsibly in all aspects of one's existence.

How does recreation contribute in this respect? Pieper and others have suggested that in their leisure hours, humans are able to express their fullest and best selves. Leisure can be a time for contemplation, for consideration of ultimate values, for disinterested activity. This means that people can come together simply as people, sharing interests and exploring pleasure, commitment, personal growth, beauty, nature, and other such aspects of life.

Often, in leisure people may make commitments to serve their neighbors or their society—through serving on boards or community committees, by volunteering their time in community agencies, by being Big Brothers or Big Sisters, by working to improve the environment, or in other civic roles. Through travel, they get a sense of the range of human experience. In the wilderness, they see the great beauty and complexity of nature, and whether they attribute it to God or not, they must come away with a fuller awareness of and respect for life.

In part, the use of outdoor settings for organized recreation experiences is based on the view of the natural world as "God's great temple" that has often been expressed in literature on the outdoors. Such settings often provide places for wilderness retreats, Bible study, or other religiously oriented programs. The Zen Buddhist view that sees God in every aspect of nature, and in the relationships of human beings with the natural world, underlies this concept. For men and women who accept the challenge of being alone in the natural world, even in perilous circumstances, the experience may often be a highly religious one.

Peter Matthiessen, a famous novelist, naturalist, and outdoor adventurer, has often written in close-to-mythological terms of the challenge of solitary travel, being confronted by the forces of the natural world at sea:

. . . one reason I like boats so much is that you have to pare everything down to the bare necessities, and there you are, the captain of a little boat, without a shelter, without a past, without future hopes.[75]

Spiritual contacts with nature need not be limited to distant or wilderness settings. Even in the crowded, often hostile world of the urban ghetto, people may find such experiences, as in the case of tenement dwellers who keep pigeon coops on their rooftops. In Harlem, for example, where a special breed of rock doves that are accustomed to living and nesting on cliffs have learned to adapt themselves to urban heights, many hobbyists maintain lofts to train the pigeons that soar in brilliant flights far above the city. John Miller writes of two young men who sent their flock high into the dark blue sky—far beyond his vision—soon to have it return with a bird that had been passing over Harlem to some far-off destination. The stranger, an all-black, red-eyed pigeon, so wild and innocent that it marched lockstep with the others through the trapdoor and into the screened loft, was retrieved by one of the men who

. . . held up this catch, grinning. Once again, I felt in the company of fishermen. This time they had cast their birds high into the May sky and netted an exotic creature such as neither of them had ever seen before.

I felt as if they had taken me on an expedition to some wide ocean when all the while I had been standing less than a mile from my Manhattan apartment.[76]

While varied forms of recreation provide a setting for spiritual experience and enrichment, it is ultimately *within* the individual that the growth takes place. Learning to be a decent human being, sharing the joys and challenges of creative, competitive, and cooperative pastimes with others, discovering one's talents and meaningful roles in life—all of these elements help to make recreation a spiritual experience.

The ultimate point is that human values—good and bad—are expressed through play. Leisure may be spent in a self-centered, hedonistic search for pleasure through alcohol, drugs, or similar pursuits, or it may contribute deeply to one's health, vigor, and morale. Godbey comments that, just as leisure is the product of culture, so it also influences and shapes culture, Summarizing Pieper's view that leisure is the basis of culture in the Western world, he cites Pieper's definition of culture as:

the quintessence of all the natural goods of the world and of those gifts and qualities which, while belonging to man, lie beyond the immediate sphere of his needs and wants. All that is good in this sense, all man's gifts and faculties are not necessarily useful in a practical way; though there is no denying that they belong to a truly human life.[77]

Nash's Leisure "Pyramid"

In this sense, culture is not possible without leisure, and at the heart of it is a celebration of the divine or, as Godbey puts it, "a receptiveness to religious experience in the broadest sense of the word." Jay B. Nash illustrates this view in his book, *Philosophy of Recreation and Leisure,* by organizing the types of leisure activities according to a pyramid-like model.[78]

At the very lowest level, the base of the pyramid, are acts performed against society, such as delinquency or crime, and acts that do injury to one's self, such as alcoholism or obsessive gambling. At the next level are passive or noncreative activities, ways of seeking escape from monotony, killing time, or consistently relying on entertainment for amusement. Above this level are the kinds of active pastimes in which most people engage frequently—such as games, sports, hobbies, or social activities—all quite positive in Nash's view.

> At the very highest level, the peak of the pyramid, are those activities in which the person is most fully involved, emotionally, physically, and intellectually, and in which the person finds deep creative satisfaction as an inventor, artist, or performer. Here too we have a view of leisure as a form of spiritual experience through which the individual transcends the everyday self and reaches for new heights of personal growth and achievement.

RECREATION AS AN INTEGRATIVE EXPERIENCE: HOLISTIC WELLNESS

Thus far this chapter has examined the important personal values of recreation and leisure involvement from five different perspectives: physical, emotional, social, intellectual, and spiritual. It is essential to recognize that these are *not* distinctly separate components of human development, but are instead closely interrelated from a *holistic* perspective.

This principle may be illustrated broadly through the wellness concept of personal health or more narrowly through the recently developed idea of emotional intelligence.

Wellness Concept of Health

Traditionally, health has been conceptualized as the absence of disease or, more positively, as the quality of personal physical fitness. Increasingly, however, the modern view of wellness holds that a variety of physical, emotional, social, and other factors underlie health in the fullest sense—and that these varied factors help to support and strengthen each other. McDowell writes that true wellness is a holistic state of being that is closely linked to one's leisure life:

> Because each individual is unique, [his or her] quality of wellness will be unique. Wellness and leisure wellness *is* a holistic concept, both a goal and a process. The broad field of wellness looks at one's nutritional awareness, physical fitness, stress management, environmental sensitivity, and level of self-responsibility. These areas find essential meaning when also viewed [in terms of] one's leisurestyle, workstyle, familystyle, even spiritualstyle.[79]

He goes on to say that leisure values, the breadth and depth of one's leisure interests, and the degree to which one uses leisure with purpose and joy are all part of holistic wellness. As indicated earlier, numerous research studies have confirmed that active and satisfying leisure experiences throughout one's life span contribute significantly to emotional and physical well-being and to successful aging. Such findings are reinforced by a growing body of evidence confirming the linkage of emotional, physical, and intellectual well-being. The concept of psychosomatic illness, in which an emotional state affects physical health, has long been accepted by medical authorities. Increasingly today, scientists are exploring the role of such mind-body techniques as meditation, yoga, guided imagery, and relaxation in combatting disease.

Within this framework, positive leisure experiences may make an important contribution to wellness through their role in stress management, building positive interpersonal relationships, overcoming loneliness and isolation, providing healthy physical outlets, reinforcing a sense of personal worth and competence, and reducing the overdependence on work that is pervasive in modern life. The very experience of leisure is described by Mihaly Csikszentmihalyi as the state of "flow," in which:

Alienation gives way to involvement, enjoyment replaces boredom, helplessness turns into a feeling of control, and psychic energy works to reinforce the sense of self, instead of being lost in the service of external goals.[80]

Emotional Intelligence

A second illustration of the linkage of qualities that were formerly thought of as distinctly separate aspects of human personality is found in the newly coined term of emotional intelligence. This concept suggests that the traditional view of intelligence, as a purely intellectual quality or as a key factor in academic or professional success is far too narrow. Instead, recent studies of effective performers in high-tech work settings indicate that the most successful team members are not those with the highest IQs, the most impressive academic credentials, or the best scores on achievement tests.

Those who excelled at times of crisis or innovation, Goleman writes, were the individuals who exhibited rapport, empathy, cooperation, persuasion, and the ability to build consensus among co-workers. He continues:

The new term for these traits is emotional intelligence, which in addition to the social graces, includes the ability to read one's own feelings, to control one's own impulses and anger, to calm oneself down and to maintain resolve and hope in the face of setbacks.[81]

Recently publicized by a number of leading psychological authorities, the concept of emotional intelligence seems likely to enter the national conversation to influence our fundamental views of personality, the requirements for success in the business or professional world, and the kinds of qualities that make for happiness and security in one's personal life.

The potential of youth-serving agencies for incorporating goals related to developing higher levels of emotional intelligence seems clear. Throughout social activities, club programs, sports, outdoor recreation, and leadership development projects, this approach would appear to be a rewarding new direction for organized leisure-service leadership. That many recreation agencies are already achieving such values is illustrated in a research report by McCormick, White, and McGuire, which documented the effectiveness of summer camp programs for children with mental retardation in such areas as: (1) improving consideration for others; (2) developing ability to work in groups; (3) improving social skills; (4) improving communication skills; (5) developing feelings of success through participation in activities; (6) improving sense of personal worth; and (7) improving decision-making and problem-solving skills.[82]

LEISURE CONSTRAINTS: BARRIERS TO PARTICIPATION

Having explored recreational motivations and the positive outcomes of leisure involvement, this chapter finishes with an overview of the factors that tend to inhibit or limit participation in recreational activities. It is obviously important to understand not only why people engage in leisure pursuits and what they gain from them, but also why they do not take advantage of such opportunities. McGuire and O'Leary identify a number of questions that researchers have asked about leisure constraints. These include the following:

Is the delivery of leisure services adequate, or do gaps in service create constraints for potential participants?

What other constraints affect participation?

Which constraints are most appropriately coped with by practitioners and which are beyond their influence?

Are any subgroups of the population at a particular disadvantage with regard to their access to leisure services because of specific constraints on participation?

What strategies can be developed to alleviate the effects of constraints on participation?[83]

McGuire and O'Leary then suggest a number of major constraints that limit participation in general, such as lack of free time, interest, money, facilities, or recreational skills. In each case, they suggest a number of strategies that might be used to reduce the constraints and promote participation, such as increased publicity or leisure education, flexible program scheduling, reduced fees or sliding-fee scales, and more accessible facility locations.

Beyond these general constraints, a number of other types of barriers exist with respect to different categories of potential program participants. For example, individuals with physical disabilities have historically been barred from many recreation facilities because of limited access arrangements, poorly designed lavatories, or other architectural barriers. In addition to being reluctant to deal with such physical or environmental factors, many persons with disabilities do not engage in available recreation programs because of a lack of skills, a sense of social disapproval or rejection by others, overprotectiveness on the part of family members, or simply laziness and the "couch potato syndrome," which is encouraged by the ease of simply watching television for many hours each day.

Other Barriers

In a study of park attendance in the Greater Cleveland area, Scott and Munson found that income was the best single predictor of perceived constraints to park visitation. Individuals with low income, they write:

> . . . reported that their use of parks was limited by fear of crime, lack of companionship, poor health, transportation problems, and costs. A disproportionate number also stated they might use parks more if they are made safer [and] . . . costs associated with going to parks are reduced, and they are provided assistance in the care of children and other family members.[84]

In a similar study of the constraints on leisure involvement by older adults, Mannell and Zuzanek identified a number of inhibiting factors that were widely shared by the elderly. Among familiar reasons such as lack of interest, skill, or time, many elderly do not engage in leisure activities because of poor health, fear of crime, lack of a companion to share recreation activities, limited transportation, and an ambivalent attitude toward organization-sponsored programs.[85]

Linked to the problem of constraints on leisure involvement is the question of why people drop out of organized recreation programs. A number of studies, for example, have explored the reasons why so many children quit organized sports leagues or clubs by the age of 12. Apart from noting such reasons as not having fun or too much emphasis on winning (see page 76), Gina Kolata suggests in the *New York Times Good Health Magazine* that far too often children are overscheduled with team practices, games, and meets.[86]

An equally important reason why many children burn out on organized sports is that they are introduced to them before they are ready, in both physical and psychological terms. Many physical educators and medical authorities suggest that children should not be learning basic sports skills until the age of 9 or 10 rather than competing actively in full gear in tackle football, as 7-year-olds do in Pop Warner League, the nation's largest organized football league. As a result, millions of children who begin sports with a burst of optimism and enthusiasm quit within a few years—discouraged and with an active distaste for competitive athletics.

Such studies suggest that numerous personal and social factors are involved in the process of selecting and taking part in recreational activities. These factors include such elements as the participants' age, gender, and ethnicity, which are discussed in Chapters 4 and 5 of this text.

SUMMARY

Beyond the familiar motivations of seeking fun, pleasure, or relaxation, people engage in leisure pursuits for a host of different reasons. Recreational motivations include personal goals such as the need for companionship, escape from stress or the boredom of daily routine, and the search for challenge, a sense of personal accomplishment, physical fitness, or emotional release. In addition to being based on widely shared motivations, leisure involvement is also influenced by the age, gender, race, or other characteristics of participants, as well as by the unique nature of the play activities themselves.

The outcomes of recreational involvement may be classified under five major headings: physical, emotional, social, intellectual, and spiritual. This chapter summarizes the findings of a number of formal research studies that document the values of recreational experience and cite evidence derived from anecdotal accounts of the personal outcomes of recreation. While the outcomes are separately described, the text stresses that each type of outcome is closely integrated with the others, as part of a holistic view of personality.

The chapter concludes with an overview of some of the constraints or barriers that limit personal participation in recreation, including those based on financial factors, physical or mental disability, a lack of skill or confidence, or a fear of rejection by others. These elements are discussed at fuller length in later chapters dealing with the needs of different recreation participants.

Questions for Class Discussion or Essay Examinations

1. The physical benefits of exercise have been well documented. Vigorous use of exercise machines and treadmills, running, swimming, and bicycling all contribute greatly to cardiovascular health. Why is it desirable to approach such activities as recreation, rather than prescribed exercise carried on for fitness purposes alone? In addition to cardiovascular benefits, what other important health outcomes have been identified?

2. The chapter describes some of the specific contributions of recreation to emotional or mental health. What are they? On the basis of your own experience, can you describe some of the positive emotional outcomes resulting from recreational involvement?

3. We generally regard sports as a valuable means of achieving positive personal development, including encouraging elements of socialization and promoting self-discipline, team loyalty, acceptance of rules, and good sportsmanship. How valid are these expectations? What are some of the less desirable aspects of sport that have been discussed in recent years?

Endnotes

[2]   Max Kaplan, *Leisure: Lifestyle and Lifespan* (Philadelphia: W. B. Saunders, 1979): 4.

[3]   Geoffrey Godbey, *Leisure in Your Life: An Exploration* (Philadelphia: W. B. Saunders, 1981): 167.

[4]   Rick Crandall, "Motivations for Leisure," *Journal of Leisure Research* (Vol. 12 No. 1 1980): 45–54.

5   M. Ewing and V. Seefeldt, *American Youth and Sports Participation* (North Palm Beach, Fla: Athletic Footwear Association and Michigan State University, 1991).

6   John Kelly, "Leisure Styles and Choices in Three Environments," *Pacific Sociological Review* 21 (1978): 178–208.

7   H. E. Tinsley, J. D. Teaff, and S. Colbs, *The Need Satisfying Properties of Leisure Activities for the Elderly* (Southern Illinois University and Andrus Foundation Report, n.d.): 2–3.

8   Pat Bolla, Don Dawson, and Maureen Harrington, "Women and Leisure: A Study of Meanings, Experiences and Constraints," *Recreation Canada* (Vol. 51 No. 3 1993): 223–226.

9   Peter Clough, John Shepherd, and Ronald Maughan, "Motives for Participation in Recreational Running," *Journal of Leisure Research* (Vol. 21 No. 4 1989): 305.

10   Richard Kraus, *Leisure in a Changing America: Multicultural Perspectives* (New York: Macmillan College Publishing, 1994): 221.

11   Simon Priest et al., "Functions of Privacy in Canadian Wilderness," *Journal of Applied Recreation Research* (Vol. 17 No. 3 1992): 234–254.

12   Robert Fisher and Linda Price, "International Pleasure Travel Motivations and Post-Vacation Cultural Attitude Change," *Journal of Leisure Research* (Vol. 23 No. 3 1991): 200.

13   Daniel Williams, Richard Schreyer, and Richard Knopf, "The Effect of the Experience Use History on the Multidimensional Structure of Motivations to Participate in Leisure Activities," *Journal of Leisure Research* (Vol. 22 No. 1 1990): 36–54.

14   David Scott and Geoffrey Godbey, "An Analysis of Adult Play Groups: Social vs. Serious Participation in Contract Bridge," *Leisure Sciences* (Vol. 14 1992): 46–47.

15   Susana Juniv, "Leisure or Work? Amateur and Professional Musicians' Perception of Rehearsal and Performance," *Abstracts of Leisure Research Symposium* (San Jose, Cal.: National Recreation and Park Congress, 1993): 79.

16   J. Katz., *Seductions of Crime: Moral and Sensual Attractions of Doing Evil* (New York: Basic Books, 1988).

17   "The Boys of Winter," *Time* (7 February 1988): 66.

18   David Preston, "Reliving Dance Craze of the '60s" *Philadelphia Inquirer* (20 January 1992): B-1.

19   "Getting an F for Flabby," *Time* (26 January 1987): 64.

20   "Male Execs: Too Much Fat, Too Little Exercise," *Philadelphia Inquirer* (24 July 1980): 5–B.

21   Daniel Haney, "Overweight Teens, Poor Health Linked," Associated Press (5 November 1992).

22   Philip Elmer-Dewitt, "Fitness in America," *Time* Cover Story (16 January 1995): 60–65.

23   See Lauran Neergaard, "Sofa Still Mightier Than Gym," Associated Press (7 November 1993).

24   Vic Sussman, "No Pain and Lots of Gain," *U.S. News and World Report* (4 May 1992): 86–88.

25   Liane Summerfield and Laurie Priest, "Using Play as Motivation for Exercise," *Journal of Physical Education, Recreation and Dance—Leisure Today* (October 1987): 24.

26   Leonard Wankel, "Personal and Situational Factors Affecting Exercise Involvement: The Importance of Enjoyment," *Research Quarterly for Exercise and Sport* (3rd Quarter 1985): 275–282.

27   See *New York Times Magazine* (2 October 1994): 69.

28   Blake Ferris, Russ Kisby, Cora Lynn Craig, and Fernand Landry, "Fitness Promotion and Research in Canada," *Journal of Physical Education, Recreation and Dance* (September 1987): 26.

29   Tommy Boone, "Obsessive Signs of Exercise—Some Reflections," *Journal of Physical Education, Recreation and Dance* (September 1990): 45.

30   Seppo E. Iso-Ahola and Ellen Weissinger, "Leisure and Well-Being: Is There a Connection?" *Parks and Recreation* (June 1984): 40–44.

[31] Michael Chubb and Holly Chubb, *One Third of Our Time: An Introduction to Recreation Behavior and Resources* (New York: John Wiley and Sons, 1981): 51.

[32] *Ibid.*, 325.

[33] Letitia Peplau, *Loneliness: A Sourcebook of Current Theory, Research and Therapy* (New York: John Wiley, 1982).

[34] Harry Stack Sullivan, cited in Linda C. Copel, "Loneliness: A Conceptual Model," *Journal of Psychosocial Nursing* (Vol. 16 No. 1 1988): 14.

[35] Jeffrey Young, "Loneliness May Create Serious Health Risk," *U.S. News and World Report* (1984, n.d.).

[36] Mounir Ragheb, "The Contributions of Leisure Participation, Leisure Satisfaction, and a Set of Social Psychological Variables to Boredom," *National Recreation and Park Association Research Symposium Abstracts* (1990): 42.

[37] Vickie Cleaver and Henry Eisenhart, "Stress Reduction Through Effective Use of Leisure," *Journal of Physical Education, Recreation and Dance* (October 1982): 33–34.

[38] Steve Lohr, "An Exercise High That Lasts," *New York Times Magazine* (2 October 1994): 67.

[39] George Vecsey, "When POW's Kept Sane with Golf's Help," *New York Times* (16 April 1995): 2–S.

[40] Walter Podilchak, "Establishing the Fun in Leisure," *Leisure Sciences* 13 (1991): 123–124.

[41] R. B. Hull IV and Sean Michael, "Nature-Based Recreation, Mood Change and Stress Restoration," *Leisure Sciences* 17 (1995): 1–14.

[42] Natalie Angier, "The Anatomy of Joy," *New York Times Good Health Magazine* (26 April 1992): 50.

[43] Daniel Goleman, "Seeking Out Small Pleasure Keeps Immune System Stronger," *New York Times* (11 May 1994): C–11.

[44] Abraham Maslow, "A Theory of Psychological Motivation," *Psychological Review* (July 1943): 370–396.

[45] See Edward Hoffman, *The Right to Be Human: A Biography of Abraham Maslow* (New York: Jeremy P. Tarcher/St. Martin's Press, 1988).

[46] Alexander Reid Martin, "Leisure and Our Inner Resources," *Parks and Recreation* (March 1975): 10–a.

[47] "The Work Junkies," *Newsweek* (8 October 1979): 87.

[48] Nancy Mayer, "Leisure—or a Coronary," *Travel and Leisure* (December-January 1972): 36.

[49] Sherry Dupuis and Bryan Smale, "An Examination of the Relationships Between Leisure Activity Participation, Psychological Well-Being, and Depression Among Older Adults," *Abstracts of Leisure Research Symposium* (1993): 26.

[50] Harve Rawson and David McIntosh, "The Effects of Therapeutic Camping on the Self-Esteem of Children with Severe Behavior Problems," *Therapeutic Recreation Journal* (Fourth Quarter, 1991): 39–49.

[51] John Heywood, "Social Order in Forest Recreation Settings," Ohio State University School of Natural Resources, *Report for U.S. Forest Service* (1992).

[52] Martha Wilderson and Richard Dodder, "What Does Sport Do for People?" *Journal of Physical Education, Recreation and Dance* (February 1979): 50–51.

[53] James Frey and John Massengale, "American School Sports Enhancing Social Values Through Restructuring," *Journal of Physical Education, Recreation and Dance* (August 1988): 40.

[54] Frederick Lawson Hovde, quoted in the *Miami Herald* (6 December 1967).

[55] "Happiness for a Distance Runner," *New York Times* (11 August 1968): S–6.

[56] Al Lundquist, "Is It Just the Winning That Counts?" *Recreation Canada* (April 1973): 40.

[57] Linden Nelson and Spencer Kagen, "Competition: The Star-Spangled Scramble," *Psychology Today* (September 1972): 53–56.

58 Seppo Iso-Ahola, "Who's Turning Children's Play Into Work?," *Parks and Recreation* (June 1980): 51.

59 John W. Loy, "The Study of Sport and Social Mobility," *Symposium Presentation at University of Wisconsin* (Novermber 1968).

60 Robert Thomas, Jr., "You Want to Play, Not Pay? Listen Up," *New York Times Education Life* (8 January 1995): 23.

61 William F. Whyte, *Street Corner Society* (Chicago: University of Chicago Press, 1955): 98–104.

62 N. R. Kleinfield, "Executive Fun and Games," *New York Times Business World* (8 June 1986): 1.

63 Murray Dubin, "Shared Passions," *Philadelphia Inquirer* (9 July 1995): K–1.

64 Liselott Diem, "Early Motor Stimulation and Personal Development," *Journal of Physical Education, Recreation and Dance* (November-December 1982): 27.

65 Jerome S. Bruner, "Child Development: Play Is Serious Business," *Psychology Today* (January 1975): 83.

66 See Susanna Millar, *The Psychology of Play* (Baltimore: Penguin Books, 1968): 55.

67 Bruner, *op. cit.,* 82.

68 Brian Sutton-Smith and Paul Gump, "Games and Status Experience," *Recreation* (April 1955): 172.

69 James Coleman, "Learning Through Games," *National Education Association Journal* (January 1967): 69.

70 John Schneidawind, "It Is No Longer Kid Stuff: Video-Toy Creator Teams with Defense Contractor," Knight-Ridder News Service (14 July 1987).

71 As another example, a debating team composed solely of African-American, Hispanic and Asian-American students at City College of New York competes successfully against top college teams nationally and internationally.

72 Philip Ross, "They Play to Win," *Forbes* (13 March 1995): 162.

73 Joseph Roggenbuck, Ross Loomis, and Jerry Dagostino, "The Learning Benefits of Leisure," *Journal of Leisure Research* (Vol. 22 No. 2 1990): 112–124.

74 "Link Found Between High School Activities and Good Grades," Associated Press (20 December 1986).

75 Pico Iyer, "Laureate of the Wild," *New York Times* (11 January 1993): 44.

76 John Miller, "Bird Men of Harlem," *New York Times Magazine* (19 November 1989): 48–49.

77 Geoffrey Godbey, *Leisure in Your Life, op. cit.,* 123–124.

78 Jay B. Nash, *Philosophy of Recreation and Leisure* (Dubuque, Iowa: Wm. C. Brown, 1960): 89.

79 C. Forrest McDowell, "Leisure: Integrating a Wellness Consciousness," in Bob Riley, John Shank, and Sharon Nichols, eds., *Therapeutic Recreation: A Holistic Approach* (Durham, N.H.: New England Therapeutic Recreation Consortium, 1987): 22.

80 Carol Tavris, in review of Mihaly Csikszentmihalyi, *Flow: The Psychology of Optimal Experience,* in *New York Times Book Review* (18 March 1990): 7.

81 Daniel Goleman, "The Decline of the Nice-Guy Quotient," *New York Times* (10 September 1995): 6–E.

82 Bryan McCormick, Charles White, and Francis McGuire, "Parents' Perceptions of Benefits of Summer Camp for Campers with Mental Retardation," *Therapeutic Recreation Journal* (Third Quarter 1992): 27–37.

83 Francis McGuire and Joseph O'Leary, "The Implications of Leisure Constraint Research for the Delivery of Leisure Services," *Journal of Park and Recreation Administration* (Summer 1992): 31–40.

84 David Scott and Wayne Munson, "Perceived Constraints to Park Usage Among Individuals with Low Incomes," *Journal of Park and Recreation Administration* (Vol. 12 No. 4 1994): 79–86.

85 Roger Mannell and Jiri Zuzanek, "The Nature and Variability of Leisure Constraints in Daily Life: The Case of the Physically Active Leisure of Older Adults," *Leisure Sciences* (Vol. 13 No. 4, 1991): 337–351.

86 Gina Kolata, "A Parents' Guide to Kids' Sports," *New York Times Good Health Magazine* (26 April 1992): 12–15.

Life Span and
Family Influences
on Leisure

Without question . . . early adolescence is one of life's trickiest transitions. Kids can seem simultaneously childlike and adult [and] in a troubled, media-saturated society, they deal ever earlier with tough issues like sex, drugs, divorce and gun violence. But a growing body of research brings a surprising new view of early adolescence: it is a crucial period in human development, equaled only by infancy. In the years between 10 and 14, kids search for the roles and values that will guide them all their lives. . . . Yet, early adolescence remains the least understood and "most neglected phase of the life span from conception to senescence."[1]

[A] study [conducted by the American Board of Family Practice] found that large majorities of Americans agreed that mid-life is associated with a search for meaning, compassion, purposeful contributions and positive growth. In middle age, the people surveyed said, they are likely to become closer to their spouses, children or friends (89 percent); assist an adult child with financial needs (89 percent); enjoy an active and fulfilling sex life (86 percent); participate regularly in religious activities (79 percent); and care for a frail parent (79 percent).[2]

---

[1] Joseph Shapiro, "Science and Society: Teenage Wasteland," *U.S. News & World Report* (23 October 1995): 84.

[2] Jim Detjen, "Study Finds Midlife Isn't Crisis Time," *Philadelphia Inquirer* (23 January 1990): 6–A.

INTRODUCTION

The leisure values and behavior patterns of Americans and Canadians are influenced by several demographic factors, including age, gender, and ethnic or racial identity. In contemporary society, these characteristics—along with other influences such as place of residence, socioeconomic status, family circumstances, and degree of ability or disability —help shape the kinds of leisure pursuits that people are attracted to and the extent to which they are provided by the organized leisure-service system. This chapter focuses primarily on the impact of one's age and family circumstances on leisure values, choices, and patterns of recreational participation. Gender and racial or ethnic identity are discussed in Chapter 5.

INFLUENCE OF AGE ON RECREATION PROGRAMMING

The impact of one's age on recreational values and patterns of participation has been analyzed in a number of recreation and leisure-service programming textbooks. Typically, key stages of the life span are identified, together with details of the growth process and developmental tasks to be accomplished at each stage.

Apart from differences of individual personalities within each age bracket, there is also the reality that developments in modern technology, economic and social trends, and shifts in family relationships have been responsible for major changes in age-related norms of human behavior. Our patterns of birth and parenthood have been radically altered by innovative technology in medical practice. We now have the potential for mothers to give birth to their own daughters' babies through the surgical implant of fertilized ova. Similarly, men can now father babies for many years after their own deaths.

Today, children are exposed to the realities of life and mature physically at a much earlier point than in the past. At the same time, paradoxically, they have a longer period of adolescence and schooling before entering the adult workforce. Adults now tend to marry later and have fewer children. Older people have a much longer period of retirement, and a significantly greater number of elderly persons live active and adventurous leisure lives today than in the past.

To fully understand the impact of societal trends on public involvement in recreation, park, and leisure-service programs, it is helpful to examine each major age group in turn.

PLAY IN THE LIVES OF CHILDREN

Childhood is the age group that includes children from early infancy through the pre-teen years.Throughout this period, play satisfies important developmental needs in children— often helping to establish values and behavior patterns that will continue throughout a lifetime. Psychologists have examined the role of play at each stage of life, beginning with infancy and moving through the preschool period, middle and late childhood, and adolescence.

Susanna Millar points out that children typically move through several stages: (1) solitary play, carried on without others nearby; (2) parallel play, in which children play side by side without meaningful interplay; (3) associative play, in which children share a common game or group enterprise but concentrate on their own individual efforts rather

> than group activity; and (4) cooperative play, beginning at about age three, in which children actually join together in games, informal dramatics, or constructive projects. By the age of six or seven, children tend to be involved in loosely organized play groups, leading to much more tightly structured and organized groups in the so-called gang age between eight and twelve.[3]
>
> Throughout this process, the child's personality is developing. Youngsters learn how to cooperate and compete, to quarrel and make up, to gain and lose friends, to obey and disobey rules. Taking turns, respecting others' property rights, accepting group values—all of these are important elements in the play experience of children. Thus, play provides a medium through which children can develop inner psychological strengths and methods of self-control.

The important role of play in child development is illustrated by Lynn Barnett, who summarizes a number of the values and outcomes of constructive forms of leisure activity for children. These include play's demonstrated contribution to cognitive development, including problem solving and creative thinking, based on its flexible or experimental nature, which helps the child's transition from concrete experiences to abstract thought processes.[4]

Typically, we tend to think of childhood as a happy time, picturing it in literature or other forms of entertainment as a period of innocence—marked by a warm nostalgic glow. Television shows of the 1950s, for example, generally idealized the American family in terms of love, support, and security. Within this context, family play was presented as an experience that all could share, one with elements of companionship, humor, and self-discovery. Over the past three decades, however, a number of major changes have taken place that have radically changed the lives of children in terms of their family and neighborhood environments, the community services provided to meet their needs, and the commercial forces that entertain them and shape their personal values and view of the world.

Decline of the Family Structure

A major problem facing the American family involves the steadily growing divorce and separation rate, as well as the spiraling number of out-of-wedlock births and increasing employment of women in both one-parent and two-parent households. In the late 1970s, *U.S. News & World Report* concluded that the American family, buffeted on all sides over the past 20 years, would continue in ferment during the 1980s. The movement of mothers from home to job, the high divorce rate, and a low birth rate would persist; growing numbers of children would have to be cared for outside the home. By 1985, 20 years after he wrote a highly controversial report on African-American families, Senator Daniel Moynihan renewed his call for a national family policy to preserve the traditional American family. And in 1988, despite evidence that the divorce rate was declining and marriage was regaining a degree of stability in American society, an authoritative report concluded that family erosion had continued over the past decade. Based on government statistics, researchers concluded that

> increasing out-of-wedlock births, continuing growth in the number of female-headed families and a rising number of children living in deprivation are among "deeply troubling" changes in the American family structure. . . . The so-called traditional American family is no longer dominant. . . . Just 10 percent of American households are now made up of a breadwinner-husband, homemaker-wife and children.[5]

By the mid-1990s, it was apparent that the "Ozzie and Harriet" or "Leave It to Beaver" family of the past had been effectively eclipsed. In 1995, the Census Bureau's annual analysis of households reported that the number of single parents raising children had risen dramatically since 1970. It found:

> While 51 percent of kids still live with both biological parents, the other 32 million are being raised with a single parent, step-parents, half-siblings or grandparents seated across the dinner table. . . . More kids than ever—27 percent—are being raised by a lone parent, twice as many as in 1970. And for the first time in history, those children are almost as likely to be living with a *never*-married parent as with a divorced one. Fifty-four percent of all kids under six now live in families in which the sole parent or both parents work.[6]

In homes where both parents or a single parent works, children are frequently left without supervision for much of the day. Left with only a door key, these "latchkey" youngsters are twice as likely to abuse alcohol, tobacco, or marijuana as children with parental supervision, according to a Southern California study of nearly 5,000 middle-school students.

Economic Status of Family

A second key influence in the 1980s and 1990s has been the family's economic status. Today, children of affluent parents have a wealth of toys (now a $17.5 billion industry), games, sports, equipment and uniforms, computers, and other play-related goods—along with special classes in music, ballet, martial arts, and gymnastics and frequent visits to video-game arcades, miniature golf centers, skating rinks, and other family play facilities.

In contrast, children in economically disadvantaged households—predominantly in urban ghettos or rural slums—tend to have few resources for constructive play. In the early 1990s, the National Commission on Children reported that there was ample evidence that the poverty rates for children had risen sharply over the past three decades. In 1955, over 11 million children lived in families whose income was below the federal poverty line. Research showed that United States youth were among the worst off in a study of children in 18 industrialized nations. Strikingly, for the first time there was evidence that the problem was beginning to affect suburban areas as well as urban neighborhoods. A Tufts University report showed that the proportion of children living in suburban settings whose family income fell below the poverty line had risen by 76 percent, compared to 56 percent in inner cities and 36 percent in rural areas.[7]

Nevertheless, the problem of inadequate recreational opportunities for the poor remains most severe in America's inner cities. Poor children have fewer toys, games, books, or trips to the zoo or beach; they seldom have access to special classes, vacation day camps—or even well-equipped and staffed playgrounds, recreation centers, or pools in communities where such facilities have been vandalized or dominated by drug dealers or youthful gangs.

At the same time, youngsters in such settings often are subject to pathologies that are made worse by poverty, such as alcoholism, drug abuse, violence, and other negative forces. Lacking the ability to provide for safe, supervised play after school or during vacation periods, many working parents in inner-city slums must choose between the enforced boredom of locking children in their apartments during free hours or days or "street roulette"—the sometimes fatal dangers of outside play.

Influence of Commercial Media: Violence and Sex

A third important influence on the lives of children today stems from the overwhelming barrage of violence and sex-laden stimuli contained in the movies, television shows, video games, and music that saturate their environment.

In the early 1980s, Marie Winn documented what she termed "the loss of childhood" of America's children, based on hundreds of interviews with children in the upper elementary grades. She comments that within an amazingly short span of time, society's most fundamental attitudes toward children have been transformed. Where parents once felt obliged to shelter their children from life's vicissitudes, she writes, today many parents believe that children must be exposed early to adult experiences and life's realities in order to survive in an increasingly uncontrollable world. She continues:

> The Age of Protection has ended. An Age of Preparation has set in. And children have suffered a loss. As they are integrated at a young age in the adult world, in every way their lives have become more difficult, more confusing—in short, more like adult lives.[8]

Outside the confines of a stable family structure with good parental supervision, children are surrounded by a permissive, highly charged sexual atmosphere in terms of readily available pornographic literature and X-rated cable television movies. Younger and younger children are able to acquire alcohol, marijuana, or other drugs. Their sense of humanity is undermined by increasingly realistic video games that feature sex and gore, vampires and demons—or contain such scenes as ripping out an opponent's heart in *Mortal Kombat* or drilling holes in scantily clad teenage girls in *Night Trap*.

A number of psychologists today agree that many modern children show an attachment disorder—a lack of the love and empathy that is normally fostered within a caring family setting. Mike Capuzzo concludes:

> The most severe critics contend that we have dehumanized a generation, desensitized the young to violence. . . . The latest FBI statistics show a rising tide of juvenile violence. From 1983 to 1992, the number of children 18 and under arrested for major crimes—murder, rape, robbery, assault and arson—rose 16 percent . . . with slayings by children doubling over the past 15 years.[9]

Physical Fitness of Youth

The physical fitness of children has steadily deteriorated largely because of their heavy dependence on mass media for entertainment and reliance on physically passive forms of play. A 1993 report by the American Alliance for Health, Physical Education and Recreation sums up statistics showing that today's students are less fit—and more overweight—than children in previous generations. Similarly, findings of the National Center for Health Statistics showed in 1995 that the proportion of American children who are overweight has more than doubled over the last three decades. Such reports confirm that a critical task facing both the educational and leisure-services systems of the United States in the years ahead is to encourage and provide more opportunities for active play of all kinds for children and youth.

Overall Pattern of Neglect

To complete this picture of negative social trends affecting children today, Roger Rosenblatt points out that in the early 1990s, an estimated three million children suffering from abuse or neglect were reported to public social service agencies.

> Approximately half a million children are in foster care or similar substitute homes, an increase of 250,000 since 1986. About 14 million live in poverty. About 100,000 children are homeless [and current welfare reform legislation] ending guaranteed assistance to poor families, should add significantly to the number of children in need.[10]

He points out that since 1988, American teenage boys are more likely to die from gunshot wounds than from all natural causes combined. For teenage girls, studies of pregnancy in Seattle and Chicago show that two-thirds of these young women reported having been sexually abused. Rosenblatt concludes that the difference between past and present abuses is that today's children are not assaulted by one or two destructive forces; they are assaulted by everything, all at once.

While the picture that has just been drawn may seem to be overwhelmingly negative, it represents a realistic summary of the societal forces affecting millions of American and Canadian children today.

Within this framework, the role of organized recreation agencies and programs would appear to be clear. The role must be to provide healthy and constructive forms of leisure involvement for children that will act as positive forces to counter the destructive aspects of today's culture. From a physical, emotional, and social perspective, it will be essential for recreation programs to involve greater numbers of children and youth, particularly those from broken families or in poverty-ridden settings who suffer from the highest degree of risk in terms of the likelihood of their reaching adulthood safely and enjoying a happy and fulfilling life.

RECREATION IN THE LIVES OF ADOLESCENTS

Psychologists who have done extensive research into the lives of adolescents, document a significant relationship between their recreational habits and their emotional and social development. Early studies found that the self-image of teenagers was closely related to their involvement in school activities. High school students with a high degree of self-esteem tended to take part in team sports, musical groups, publications, outdoor recreation, and social activities. Those with a low degree of self-esteem were much less involved.

In study of high school subcultures, researchers have identified three distinct groups of adolescents: (1) the "fun" subculture, similar to the collegiate world of football, fraternities, sororities, dates, cars, and drinking; (2) the "academic" subculture of serious students who work hard, get the best grades, and are career-oriented; and (3) the "delinquent" subculture, which rebels against the whole school enterprise and is associated with "negativism, hedonism and violence."[11] For each of these groups, the school's extracurricular activities meet different kinds of needs and can be used to promote positive school involvement for teenagers.

Another study, by Kleiber, Larson, and Csikszentmihalyi, examines the ways in which high school students use their time for "productive" (school and work-oriented), "maintenance" (related to personal care and daily living needs), and "leisure" (socializing, sports, television, and similar activities) involvement. They focused on leisure activities that combined the fun element with the need for exertion and effort, which they referred to as transitional activities. Commenting that many adolescents tend to be bored and disinterested in purposeful and productive activities and have not learned to find enjoyment in the demands and challenges placed on them by the adult world, they concluded:

> The transitional activities would appear to provide a bridge. They offer the experience of freedom and intrinsic motivation within highly structured systems of participation, systems that require discipline and engage the adolescent in a world of symbols and knowledge outside the self . . . [and] the enjoyment found within this category of leisure—whether it takes the form of sports, learning a musical instrument, carrying out a 4-H project, or something similar—lays a groundwork for experiencing enjoyment in more obligatory adult activities.[12]

Negative Trends in Adolescent Leisure Pursuits

Linda Caldwell points out that a national study of over 46,000 sixth through twelfth grade students identified both positive influences in adolescents' lives and countervailing influences, which included

> . . . such things as being alone at home, hedonistic values, television overexposure, drinking parties, physical and sexual abuse, and social isolation. In each grade . . . the *majority* of students report at least two out of ten countervailing influences.[13]

Caldwell summarizes research findings showing that high-risk behavior that potentially limits the future psychological, physical, or economic well-being of students is prevalent. Twenty at-risk indicators, including frequent alcohol use or "binge" drinking, tobacco use, illegal drug use, sexual involvement, depression/suicide, or other forms of antisocial or deviant behavior, were examined. She cites specific findings:

> Thirty-one percent of all students in grades nine to 12 reported drinking six or more drinks at one time in the last 30 days or binge drinking (one or more times a week in the past two weeks); 25 percent reported frequent depression and/or attempted suicide. Of all 12th graders, 60 percent were sexually active, and 53 percent of those did not use contraceptives. . . . [In a] typical high school, 40 percent of all students in grades nine to 12 were at risk in *three or more* of eight at-risk areas.[14]

In 1992, the Surgeon General of the United States emphasized the link between youthful drinking and teen suicides, drowning and vehicle deaths, the commission of serious crimes including rape, and other youth problems. A 1995 study by the Parents Resource Institute for Drug Education showed a significant increase in the use of marijuana, cocaine, LSD, inhalants, and other illicit substances among eighth graders, and a similar rise in the drinking of beer and wine coolers by children in the sixth to eighth grades.[15]

Teenage gambling has been growing steadily since the legalization of casino gambling, state lotteries, riverboat games, and similar forms of play over the past two decades. Pam Belluck writes:

> Teenagers are gambling everywhere: in schools, on ball fields, at racetracks, in casinos . . . [one California authority] estimates that there are seven million teenagers—one in four nationwide—gambling today and that more than one million of them are at risk of becoming compulsive gamblers.[16]

In terms of sexual activity, during the 1970s and 1980s it became apparent that the attitudes and behavior of American youth had become much more permissive toward premarital and extramarital sexual involvement—and indeed that the prevailing view of sex had become a recreational one.

In 1993, the International Planned Parenthood Federation reported that the United States had the highest rate of teen pregnancies among Western developed nations, with a total of more than 600,000 unintended pregnancies a year.[17] Other reports show that the percentage of sexually active teenage girls who have several partners has risen sharply, with a growing number of girls under the age of 14 reporting sexual involvement.

Cases such as that of the "Spur Posse," the heavily publicized group of teenage boys in Lakewood, California, who competed against each other in keeping score of their sexual conquests, confirm that America has become transformed into an increasingly predatory society in sexual terms—with the serious danger that great numbers of adolescents will become victims of AIDS in the years ahead.[18]

A final major area of concern is the growing involvement of adolescents in thrill-seeking, high-risk activity, that is linked to random acts of violence and gang-related criminal behavior. Numerous shocking newspaper accounts have depicted teen gangs committing brutal assaults and rapes, risking and often losing their lives in daredevil stunts, and justifying their behavior as a response to boredom. In cities large and small, violent activities by teenage gangs within the schools are having a devastating effect on school academic programs. A study of 700 communities by the National League of Cities concludes that

> The academic challenges are being made more difficult by the disturbing presence and growing fear of crime and violence in our schools . . . Reports of attacks, shootings, searches for weapons, gang activity and other incidents have created fear, anxiety and uncertainty about what happens when children go to school each day.[19]

Causes of Adolescent Problems

The problems discussed in the previous section do not apply to all adolescents. Millions of school-age youth are leading secure, purposeful, and happy lives. However, the problems are so widespread and severe that they pose a critical threat to society's well-being. A number of causes have been suggested as explanations for the growing difficulties of teenagers today with respect to substance abuse, promiscuous sexual activity, compulsive gambling, and violent and delinquent behavior.

Influence of Mass Media   As was the case with younger children, there is widespread concern about the influence of movies, television, mass media, and music on the values and behavior of teenagers. First, there is the conviction that excessive television watching may have serious outcomes. The thousands of hours that children and youth spend in passive contemplation of the screen during their formative years are hours "stolen" from the time needed to learn to relate to others and gain usable and enjoyable skills of active participation. It is believed that intensive exposure to television stifles creative imagination and encourages a passive outlook toward life.

Beyond this, there is mounting evidence that television actually encourages violent and criminal youth behavior. As early as 1969, the National Commission on the Causes and Prevention of Violence concluded that violence on television had to be reduced because it encouraged imitation and strengthened "a distorted, pathological view of society." Studies have repeatedly documented lowered inhibitions of aggressive behavior after exposure to violence on television, and there have been numerous examples of crimes committed shortly after similar crimes were shown on television. Reports in the *Journal of the American Medical Association* and other authoritative sources have concluded that the once popular "catharsis" theory holding that TV violence offers a harmless outlet for natural hostilities and aggressions does not hold up.[20]

Boredom and the Need for Excitement   Since the last decades of the nineteenth century, the perceived need to provide positive recreation programs and facilities for children and youth has been based on the belief that constructive free-time alternatives not only keep youngsters off the street, but also help prevent the kinds of delinquent play that otherwise might result from boredom. Again and again, adolescents apprehended for criminal activity use the excuse that they were bored, that there was nothing else to do, or that their delinquent actions were a form of fun.

> **I**t is increasingly recognized that many forms of deviant, delinquent, and high-risk behavior represent forms of play that are intended to bring thrills, excitement, and challenge to otherwise empty and boring lives. Brenda Robertson argues that these activities are not meaningless or incomprehensible; instead, they are pursued for fun and pleasure and, although disapproved of by adult society, represent an understandable form of individual or group expression. She writes:
>
>> A study of gangs in California revealed that the pursuit of pleasure, often through activities such as surfing, parties, sex, and drugs, is one main reason for the cohesiveness of gangs. Many of these gang members were middle-class adolescents who found reinforcement for their counter-culture attitudes through association with others within the gang. . . . Participation in such activities as theft, drug abuse, vandalism, and assault has recently been found to be motivated in some cases by the same factors as those traditionally associated with positive forms of leisure.[21]

Challenges Facing the "Fast Forward" Generation

Even without such factors, there is the reality that adolescents of today are growing up in a turbulent, unpredictable, and often insecure world. Examining a high school senior class of 1993, Tanya Barrientos wrote:

> . . . there is a new generation inside this and all high schools across the nation. It's the Fast Forward generation. Raised on CNN, DOS and MTV. Schooled in limits by recession, AIDS and ozone holes.

Hardened to parents' divorces. Impatient with unfulfilled ideals. A generation both enraged about the mess its elders have made and pragmatically determined to deal with it. These are the babies of the Boomers, a new set of rebels with no cause but survival.[22]

Barrientos describes the lives of the new generation of teenagers who have learned to live with "mix-and-match" families, a bewildering array of stepfathers and stepmothers, half-brothers and step-sisters, and single parents' live-in lovers. Challenged as they are by mass layoffs by huge corporations, assaults on the limits of public sexuality, and often by hostile race relations, it is understandable that their lives are often chaotic and confused.

At the same time, a recent report by the Carnegie Council on Adolescent Development suggests that the period between the ages of 10 and 14 is the least understood and "most neglected phase of the life span from conception to senescence." Young teens' mental and physical growth is accelerated, with puberty coming two years earlier than it did a century ago. It is argued by feminists that, because schools and society favor boys, adolescent girls seriously suffer from a lack of self-esteem. It has been documented that adolescent girls can be vulnerable to depression, eating disorders, and other addictions. Yet boys make up 85 percent of special-education students with such diagnoses as learning-disabled or behavior-disordered. They get lower grades and more punishment, commit suicide at a higher rate, and get into far more problems of delinquency than do girls.[23]

Given such problems, it is ironic that more than half of all adolescents will spend at least part of their lives in a single-parent family, and that the total time that American children spend with their parents has decreased by at least one-third over the past 30 years. The Carnegie Council report concludes that the United States is neglecting its 19 million adolescents

... to such an extent that half of them may be irrevocably damaging their chances for productive and healthy futures. Early adolescents are being abandoned by their governments, communities, schools and parents just when they most need guidance and support. They are in danger of becoming lifelong casualties of drug and alcohol abuse, violence, suicide, AIDS, teen pregnancy and failed education.[24]

Within this frightening picture of America as a dismissive and preoccupied parent, a country trying to wish away the troubles of its teenagers, the obvious role for organized leisure services is to provide a measure of healthy personal growth opportunities and supportive adult relationships in the lives of adolescents.

ADULT LEISURE NEEDS AND INVOLVEMENTS

The adult population in modern society, defined as those in their late teens to their early or mid-60s, may logically be subdivided into several age brackets or lifestyle patterns. These include, among others, young single adults (those who attend college and those who do not), those who remain single throughout their lives, adults who marry and raise families, adults in their middle years, and elderly adults.

Continuity in Leisure Interests

A number of research studies have examined the relationship between recreational interests developed during childhood or adolescence and those enjoyed during later adult life. Scott and Willits, for example, in a longitudinal study, gathered data from 1,298 subjects during their high school years and compared it to information taken from the same group in their early 50s. They found that, despite the 37-year time interval, there was a significant degree of continuity in the recreational pursuits of those studied. For all types of leisure activities analyzed (socializing pastimes, intellectual pursuits, memberships in clubs, creative and artistic hobbies, and sports activities), adult participation was positively related to earlier adolescent involvement. Scott and Willits comment:

> Moreover, for the sample as a whole, adolescent participation was more predictive of adult involvement in socializing and formal organizations than the subjects' health rating, education, or income. Similarly, among the women in the sample, adolescent participation in sports and creative/artistic activities was more strongly related to adult involvement than the control variables.[25]

Refuting the assumption that participation in active forms of play declines through the years of adulthood, Rodney Warnick summarizes research statistics showing that both 25-to-34-year-olds and 35-to-44-year-olds maintained higher rates of participation in a variety of outdoor recreational pursuits than did younger adults aged 18 to 24. He writes:

> [P]articipation rates were higher for 24- to 34-year-olds than for 18- to 24-year-olds in such activities as bicycling, swimming, fresh water fishing, salt water fishing, hiking, cross-country skiing, health club membership. . . . This trend carried over to the . . . middle-aged adult segment in activities such as salt water fishing, health club membership, and travel. . . . These changes appear to have occurred in the 1980s. In fact, for probably the first time, evidence now exists that participation rates are higher among older adults, particularly the middle-aged adults, than young adults in a wide variety of activities.[26]

Young Single Adults

This population, extending from late teens to early or mid-30s, has expanded over the past two decades. In the mid-1970s, *Newsweek* commented that there were 48 million single adults over the age of 21 in the United States. In the past, the term "single" usually meant a lonely person, a "loser" whose solitary status was a temporary sidetrack on the way to happy matrimony. But, in the decade of the "Me Generation," with its emphasis on narcissistic pleasure and self-fulfillment, singlehood came to be regarded as a happy ending in itself—or at least an enjoyable prolonged phase of postadolescence. While marriage was still the statistical norm, *Newsweek* concluded, "within just eight years, singlehood has emerged as an intensely ritualized—and newly respectable—style of American life."[27]

The findings of a 1980 Study of American Families, an 18-year intergenerational study of several hundred American families, showed that both young people and their parents had begun to see the single life as a legitimate alternative to marriage. When this trend became obvious, a vast number of singles-only institutions sprang up to meet the needs of this newly recognized population with an estimated $40 billion of annual spending power. Singles apartment complexes, bars, weekends at resort hotels, "ex-married" clubs, rap groups at local churches, cruises, and a variety of other leisure programs or services emerged—including computer dating services and other techniques for helping singles to find each other.

For young single adults, recreation provides the opportunity for establishing positive group and one-to-one relationships with others. Godbey points out that this stage of life is a time for young men and women to develop fuller identification with social institutions,

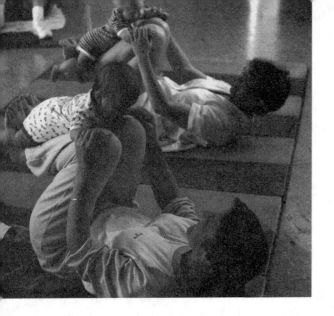

Recreation Through the Life Span
Play begins at an early age, as in this "Mommy and Me" mother-infant movement class (top) sponsored by the Long Beach Department of Parks, Recreation, and Marine in California. Young children enjoy creative dance (center) and older women perform in a tap dance routine (bottom) at the Texas Women's University Community Dance Center in Denton, Texas.

including work and other organizations, as well as a commitment to appropriate personal goals.[28] Whether single or married, young adults require a healthy range of opportunities for leisure in order to maintain a balance of work and play, needed outlets for emotional release, and a sense of challenge and accomplishment in the nonwork areas of their lives.

Young Adults Attending College

As a subgroup of the young adult population, college students are usually strongly influenced in their choice of leisure activities by their status as students. Students living at home are likely to have relatively little free time, often holding jobs and traveling back and forth to school, and they often find much of their recreation with friends in their neighborhoods. Students living on college campuses generally take part in social or religious clubs, athletic events, fraternity or sorority parties, college union programs, entertainment, or cultural activities.

Many young college students regard their first experience in living away from home for a sustained period of time as an opportunity to engage in hedonistic forms of play without parental supervision. For students who were part of a drinking culture during their earlier adolescent years, college life represents an opportunity for increased drinking—at this point with the approval of a peer culture that accepts liquor as a valued part of campus life.

A 1994 research report by the Harvard School of Public Health confirms the heavy incidence of binge drinking—with 44 percent of all students consuming five drinks in a row and female students consuming four drinks in a row in the two weeks before the survey conducted at 140 representative colleges around the United States.[29] Typically, students living in fraternity or sorority houses drank three times as much as the average student. Of all groups on campus, white males were reported to drink the most, and African-American females the least.

Among adults generally, the use of illicit drugs has persisted. In 1960 there were fewer than 30,000 arrests for drug offenses; by 1990, the total had soared beyond one million, with more individuals being incarcerated for drug offenses than for *all* violent crimes—with most violent crimes being committed by substance abusers.[30] Although government reports have claimed a significant decline in drug abuse, the range of intoxicants has increased, with heroin becoming increasingly popular among many professionals and other middle-class users. As an indication of the degree to which substance abuse is an adult problem today, 98 percent of Americans who die from illegal drug use are over the age of 20.[31]

Despite the serious problems attached to alcohol and drug abuse, the majority of young adults are able to use their leisure time in positive and constructive ways. Particularly for those who have finished school and are financially independent, travel, participation in sports or fitness clubs, social clubs or forms of popular entertainment, and involvement in hobbies and creative activities enrich the lives of young single persons—both in colleges and in community settings.

Married Adults and Family Recreation

While millions of men and women have joined the trend toward a continuing single lifestyle, a majority of young American and Canadian adults today accept marriage and family life as a preferred option. Leisure behavior is markedly affected when people marry and have children. Social activities tend to center around the neighborhood in which the couple lives, and the home itself becomes a recreation center for parent and child activities. The family takes part in social programs sponsored by religious agencies, civic and neighborhood associations, or PTAs. As children move into organized community programs, parents begin to use their leisure time for volunteer service as adult leaders for Scout groups, teachers in cooperative nursery schools, Little League coaches and managers, or in similar ways.

In a review of the literature on family leisure and recreation programming, Susan Shaw points out that shared leisure experiences are an important part of life for many people in contemporary society. She writes:

> Home-based activities and family-oriented activities outside the home are the most common forms of leisure activity, and there is some evidence that families are now spending more time together than they did in the past. Moreover, research has consistently shown that family time and family leisure are highly valued.[32]

Research by Orthner and Mancini confirms the value of shared recreation involvement in contributing to family satisfaction, interaction, and stability.[33] Other studies by Madrigal, Havitz, and Howard illustrate the importance of specific recreational experiences (i.e, family vacations) in enhancing marital relationships, although vacation-taking styles may vary considerably according to whether marriages are traditional or contemporary in terms of the roles of the male and female partners.[34]

Valeria Freysinger has shown that leisure involvement is especially significant for divorced parents today as they seek to maintain positive and affectionate parental roles with their children.[35]

Leisure Limitations   The group in this age bracket that is most deprived of leisure consists of single mothers who often must work, raise a family under difficult economic and emotional circumstances, and still try at the same time to find needed social outlets and recreational opportunities for themselves. A limited number of municipal and school recreation agencies provide day-care or after-school programs to assist such single parents; in addition, some commercial and voluntary recreation agencies sponsor baby-sitting services in order to permit mothers of young children to take part in their programs during the day.

Although the number of working mothers has increased dramatically, there continue to be many mothers of young children who have homemaking as their major responsibility. For them, many municipal recreation and park departments, Ys, and similar organizations sponsor clubs, fitness programs, classes, or other types of recreational activities during the day while children are at school. Recreation departments and adult education programs also provide evening classes in hobbies, sports, cultural activities, or other forms of continuing education.

Middle Adult Years

This age group, which includes individuals ranging from the mid-30s through the 50s, consists heavily of so-called baby boomers—people born during the population surge after World War II, or, more particularly, from 1946 to 1964. Paul Light comments that the baby boomers were remarkably homogeneous in terms of the widely accepted social values prevailing in their early childhoods. However, in the following turbulent period of social change, the members of this young generation shifted abruptly from the values of their parents and grandparents. Light writes:

> They may love their parents, but when it comes time to talk about politics, marriage, drugs, or sex, the baby boomers respectfully disagree. From questions on the government's role in creating jobs, religion in the schools, war and peace, political trust, and race, to questions on AIDS, homosexuality, drugs, pornography, and women's rights, the baby boomers maintain their distance from their parents and grandparents.[36]

While baby boomers share a number of common values, D. Quinn Mills suggests that they fall into a number of distinctly different categories in terms of their self-images. These include the following:

Pleasure-seekers—those who strive to enjoy life

Competitors—those who are business- and profession-obsessed

Trapped—those who are in difficult situations at home or at work and cannot free themselves

Contented—those who are generally satisfied with their lives

"Get Highs"—those who are heavily involved in alcohol or drug use or even in spiritual experiences and commitments.[37]

Mills also concludes that baby boomers show immense diversity in their lifestyles as well. Some are devoted to their families; others remain unattached. Some "boomers" are sports-minded or wilderness-oriented, while others are committed to the arts, hobbies, or literary pursuits. Growing numbers of this age group have begun to place a high value on the creative satisfaction found in work or devote a fuller portion of their time to family and personal involvements.

Effect of Family Changes For parents in the middle adult years, patterns of leisure involvement begin to change as children become more independent. Many nonworking mothers in particular, who have devoted much time and energy to the family's needs, begin to find these demands less pressing. They have more available time, as well as a need to find a different meaning and fulfillment in life through new interests and challenges.

At this point, many middle-aged adults shift their leisure pursuits away from family centered activities and develop their own interests. Although men and women in their middle years tend to become less physically active, it is highly desirable that the sports, games, and outdoor recreational pastimes carried on at a younger age be continued if medically feasible. Medical authorities have stressed the importance of regular exercise in maintaining cardiovascular fitness, relieving nervous tension and anxiety, and contributing generally to good health for mature adults. With the growing awareness of the true capability of older men and women, there has been a wave of participation by those approaching retirement (and after) in jogging, running, and other active sports and outdoor pursuits.

There is increasing evidence that, for many middle-aged Americans, this period of life does not involve radical change or emotional turmoil. Rejecting the idea that midlife is a time when "men chuck their wives and begin driving fancy sports cars," a 1990 study of the American Board of Family Practice concluded that for most individuals it represents a search for meaning in one's life, compassion, purposeful contributions, and positive growth.

Similarly, Gail Sheehy, in her 1995 book, *New Passages: Mapping Your Life Across Time*, suggests that middle age has been extended to a much later point in the life span, and that Americans can now look forward to what she calls the "Flourishing Forties," the "Flaming Fifties," and the "Age of Integrity" in their 60s.[38] Another social researcher, Lydia Bronte, suggests that middle age today covers the period from roughly age 50 to age 75—with many individuals reaching their peak of creativity and achievement well into their 70s and 80s.[39]

Numerous research studies have documented the importance of recreation and leisure during the middle and later years of life. Valeria Freysinger found that leisure had various connotations; it provides: (1) an agent for change and an opportunity for exerting personal choice and freedom; (2) an opportunity for relaxation, enjoyment, and rejuvenation; (3) a means of affiliation and interaction with others; (4) an area for self-expression and gaining feelings of mastery and accomplishment; and (5) a time for maintenance of friendships and affirming family values.[40]

RECREATION AND THE ELDERLY

Recreation and leisure have assumed a high priority in the lives of most elderly persons, but particularly for the majority of individuals in their late 60s and beyond who have retired from full-time jobs. Without work to fill their time, and often with the loss of husbands, wives, or friends, such persons find it necessary to develop new interests and often to establish new relationships. Loneliness can be devastating to the aging. One study showed for example, that the mortality rate rose dramatically for older men who had been widowed.

The lives of elderly persons have changed dramatically over the past three or four decades. Not only can they expect to live much longer, but their living circumstances are likely to be radically different from those of past generations in terms of familial roles, social activities, economic factors, and other important conditions. Even the patterns of retirement have been transformed. Backman and Backman write:

> Not only is the population aging, but the age at which people retire is declining, thus extending the number of years in retirement. Labor force data show us that retirement age has declined between four and five years for men and women from the 1950s to the 1980s. As more of the population ages, this means more people are reaching the age of retirement sooner and living longer.[41]

It is now popular to assert that elderly persons are far more active, vigorous, economically secure, and happy than we had assumed in the past. With improved financial support and pension plans, a much higher percentage of older persons are relatively well-to-do and able to enjoy a far longer period of retirement. Research has shown that many elderly individuals continue to enjoy sexual relations and to maintain active and creative lives well into their 70s and 80s.

Negative Views of Aging

In the recent past, a number of highly negative views of the elderly were widely held in American society. Aging persons were seen as helpless, poor, suffering from illness or severe disability, lonely, and sexless. In the late 1970s, a 25-year-old gerontology student transformed herself into an "old" woman by putting splints on her knees so that she walked haltingly and by wearing clouded contact lenses and layers of latex that mirrored the natural wrinkles of an 80-year-old. She wanted to find out how older persons were treated on the streets of a major city, and she did. Repeatedly, she was ignored or cursed for her awkwardness, shortchanged by shopkeepers, robbed by boys, and treated harshly by many others—with little respect shown for her "age."[42]

In recent years, our view of the aging process has changed dramatically. We used to think of the aging process as "an inexorable slide into illness, impotence and immobility." It was recognized that the extended family—in which older people once lived with their children and grandchildren, maintaining significant relationships—had all but disappeared. More and more communities have developed in which there are few older persons, just as there are many sections of older cities in which there are large numbers of the elderly—often living alone in residential hotels, in SROs (single-room-occupancy units), or in institutions for aging persons. Many older persons tend to withdraw from meaningful contact and involvement with others. One group of sociologists explained this phenomenon by a theory of disengagement, viewing withdrawal from social interaction as a normal process of aging. The "disengagement" theorists held that gradual withdrawal from meaningful human contacts and involvement was a necessary and inevitable process preceding death which the aging chose for themselves, and which others should accept. This theory has generally been rejected, and most authorities today believe that older people do not withdraw by choice, but because of a feeling of exclusion.

Yet, in many ways, a new complex of problems or changing life circumstances now affect the lives of the elderly. These include such factors as changed family structures, growing numbers of persons who become single in their later years, and new economic trends causing financial insecurity.

Changes in Family Structure   In the past, it was common for several generations of family members to live together. Older persons continued not only to receive the affection and support of their children and grandchildren, but also to play meaningful roles in family life. With the shift toward living in urban and suburban apartments and small one-family homes, increasing numbers of elderly persons must now live separately; often they become isolated, ill, and unable to care for themselves—and wind up prematurely in long-term care facilities. A vivid example of this trend is found in the growing incidence of "granny dumping." This phenomenon involves elderly abandonment—family members leaving their aged parents or grandparents in wheelchairs in front of hospital emergency rooms or nursing homes, and quickly disappearing.

A second shift in the family structure is found in the growing number of cases where elderly grandparents are forced to take responsibility for young children because their own children—the parents—are alcoholic, drug dependent, or otherwise unable to maintain a stable household. In other cases, people who are themselves middle-aged must care for much older, infirm parents, as well as the younger family members who are dependent on them. Furthermore, 1995 report by the American Association of Retired Persons confirmed that growing numbers of the elderly are living in nontraditional households, with nonrelatives, siblings, or other companions.[43]

Increase in Elderly Singles   As part of this picture, census reports and legal writers have noted the recent growth in the number of older couples—including couples that have been married for 30 or 40 years—obtaining divorces. Seen as a reflection of the growing acceptance of divorce by younger persons, as well as of changing state laws and the lengthening of the typical life span, this trend has resulted in hundreds of thousands of older men and women suddenly shifting to single lifestyles.[44] The problems of adjustment that they face are mirrored in the circumstances of elderly persons who are widowed. If such groups are combined with the millions of individuals who never married or who divorced at an earlier point, it has been predicted that the number of older people living alone in the United States—about three-quarters of them women—will increase from 8.5 million in the late 1980s to over 13 million in the year 2020.[45]

Effect of Economic Trends   Compounding such difficulties, many individuals in their preretirement years who had relatively well-paid and supposedly secure jobs during the late 1980s and early 1990s were released or forced to retire as a result of the major downsizing policies of large corporations at that time. With reduced incomes, many have been forced to continue working long past the point at which they had hoped to retire.

Positive Changes for Elderly Persons

Even though these negative trends must be acknowledged, the reality still is that most older persons are living longer, happier, and healthier lives than in the past.

Indeed, there is striking new evidence that the very old are enjoying remarkably good health in comparison to other age groups. Natalie Angier points out that the average annual Medicare bill for people who live to be quite elderly—that is, into their late 80s and 90s—is significantly lower than that for those who die sooner. Part of the reason, she writes, is that very elderly persons tend to be relatively robust. Cancer and heart disease, the two chief killers for retired persons in the younger age brackets, tend not to affect the very old, and Alzheimer's disease also attacks slightly younger men and women.

There is also evidence that aging need not be accompanied by mental deterioration. Although some losses in memory or other aspects of mental performance do commonly occur, studies have shown that from 20 to 30 percent of people in their 80s who volunteer for cognitive testing perform as well as volunteers in their 30s and 40s, who are presumably at the peak of mental performance.

With improved medical care, people are not just living longer, healthier lives, but are living them differently. Particularly in the so-called retirement states of New Mexico, Arizona, Nevada, and Florida, with fast growing populations of elderly men and women, they are engaging in active sports, volunteering, going back to school, and developing new networks of friends and relationships. Within this changing setting, recreation and leisure authorities have two primary tasks: (1) to make leisure activities vital and meaningful pursuits for the elderly, so that they do not view them simply as "rocking-chair" time-wasters, without the appeal, social status, or value of real work; and (2) to reach and serve the substantial numbers of elderly persons who do *not* have the financial resources and resolve to engage in leisure activities, or who *do* have physical or mental disabilities that limit their involvement.

Specific Contributions of Recreation and Leisure

As Chapter 3 points out (see page 60), recreational involvement meets a number of important physical, emotional, and social needs of elderly persons. Numerous studies have shown that regular physical exercise has immense health-related value for older persons within a range of specific benefits that include preventing heart disease, stroke, cancer, osteoporosis, and diabetes; assisting in weight reduction; improving immunity against common infections; reducing arthritic symptoms; countering depression; and even helping to improve memory and the quality of the older individual's sleep.[46]

In terms of social benefits, one of the key problems affecting the elderly is that they tend to become isolated and lose a sense of playing a significant role in family life or in the community at large. One of the most useful leisure activities for the elderly therefore involves community service and volunteerism. In fact, volunteerism is frequently conceptualized as a satisfactory substitute for paid work for older persons.

Elderly persons gain an important sense of recognition and self-worth through volunteerism. It provides a structure in their lives in terms of regular time commitments and offers social contacts that often lead to friendship and other group involvement.

Another important leisure pursuit for the elderly consists of continuing education—either on a fairly casual basis with classes or workshops in nearby after-school or community center programs or on a more formal basis in noncredit courses taken through Elderhostel or other college-sponsored programs.

Many leisure activities of older persons are relatively simple close-to-home pursuits, such as reading for pleasure, talking on the telephone, gardening or raising plants, watching television, socializing with friends and family, and carrying on individual hobbies. Other activities may be more active and demanding, such as sports, outdoor recreation, fitness classes, and dancing. These may be enjoyed with people of all ages, or in special senior citizens groups, golden age clubs, or retirement communities.

As an example of the latter, Sun City, one of the largest retirement communities in the United States, operates a network of recreation centers that house sports, arts and crafts, hobbies, and other pursuits, with over 140 chartered special-interest clubs and tennis, golf, swimming, and other facilities for outdoor play. Similarly, California's Laguna Hills retirement community offers its members over 45 different activities including aerobics, art, billiards, bocce, bowling, calligraphy, and cards, as well as stamp collecting, swimming, table tennis, a therapy pool, weaving, and woodworking.

SUMMARY

Age and family status represent key factors that affect the recreational needs and interests of individuals throughout life. Human development experts have outlined a sequence of age groupings extending from infancy through old age, and recreational authorities have developed guidelines for program planning for each group based on the developmental characteristics at each stage.

Today, changes in family life and social environment have altered traditional models of development with significant implications for recreation programmers. The chapter points out that children today grow up much earlier and are subjected to influences that they would have been shielded from in the past. Youth in affluent families often have lavish recreational goods and abundant opportunities for structured play, while children in poverty settings frequently lack recreation facilities or programs. This pattern continues into adolescence, which is marked today by higher rates of teenage drinking and drug abuse, irresponsible sexual activity, and varied forms of delinquency or antisocial play.

The chapter also discusses adult life, pointing out that while a higher percentage of individuals remain or become single than in the past, the majority tend to marry and raise families, with much of their recreation centering around the home and family unit. For the middle-aged and elderly, who represent a steadily increasing proportion of the population, many of the negative stereotypes of the past no longer apply. People today live longer and tend to be more independent and active in the varied forms of recreation that promote their overall well-being and life satisfaction.

Questions for Class Discussion or Essay Examinations

1. Select one of the following age groups: children, teens, or adults. What are their special needs for recreation in modern society, and what barriers or problems do they face in the appropriate choice of satisfying leisure activity? If you wish, you may deal with a subgroup of the overall category, such as "young single adults."

2. The elderly make up a rapidly growing segment of the American and Canadian populations. How have we traditionally thought of the aging process and of the role of older persons in community life? What new views have developed in recent years? What are the implications of these changes for recreation practitioners working with elderly persons?

3. The family structure has been radically altered in the United States and Canada since World War II. What are some of the changes that have occurred, and what are their effects on family needs for recreation programs and services?

Endnotes

3   Susanna Millar, *The Psychology of Play* (Baltimore, Md.: Penguin, 1968): 178–184.

4   Lynn Barnett, "Developmental Benefits of Play for Children," *Journal of Leisure Research* (Vol. 22 No. 2 1990): 138–153.

5   Elizabeth Mehren, "Study: U.S. Family Continuing Its Downward Slide," *Philadelphia Inquirer* (21 July 1988): 14-A.

6   "Changing Families," *U.S. News & World Report* (2 January 1995): 111.

7   Anne Thompson, "Suburban Children Now Poorer," Associated Press (28 September 1994).

8   Marie Winn, "The Loss of Childhood," *New York Times Magazine* (8 May 1983): 18.

9   Mike Capuzzo, "The End of Innocence," *Philadelphia Inquirer* (14 November 1993): G-1.

10   Roger Rosenblatt, "The Society That Pretends to Love Children," *New York Times Magazine* (6 October 1995): 60.

11   For a fuller discussion, see Jere Cohen, "High School Subcultures and the Adult World," *Adolescence* (Fall 1979): 491–501.

12   Douglas Kleiber, Reed Larson, and Mihaly Csikszentmihalyi, "The Experience of Leisure in Adolescence," *Journal of Leisure Research* (Vol. 18 No. 3 1986): 175.

13   Linds Caldwell, "Research Update: On Adolescents and Leisure Activities," *Parks and Recreation* (March 1993): 19.

14   *Ibid.*

15   Jennifer Weiner and William Macklin, "Getting Hooked," *Philadelphia Inquirer* (12 November 1995): H-1.

16   Pam Belluck, "Starting Too Young, Getting in Too Deep," *Philadelphia Inquirer* (16 August 1992): A-1.

17   Marie McCullogh, "Wave of Teen Pregnancies Reported," *Reuters* (30 May 1993).

18   Jill Smolowe, "Sex with a Scorecard," *Time* (5 April 1993): 41.

19   John Woestendick, "Survey Finds Rise in School Violence," *Philadelphia Inquirer* (2 November 1994): A-3.

[20]   See "Kids and T.V. Violence," in *Changing Times*, March 1976.

[21]   Brenda Robertson, "Leisure in the Lives of Male Adolescents Who Engage in Delinquent Activity for Excitement," *Journal of Park and Recreation Administration* (Vol. 12 No. 4 1994): 37.

[22]   Tanya Barrientos, "'93 Class Looks Anxiously Ahead: The Fast Forward Generation," *Philadelphia Inquirer* (21 March 1993): A-1.

[23]   Joseph Shapiro, *op. cit.*

[24]   Peter Applebome, "Study Says Society Fails 19 Million Youths," *New York Times* (12 October 1995): A-14. See also "Generation Excluded," *Time* (25 October 1995): 86.

[25]   David Scott and Fern Willits, "Adolescent and Adult Leisure Patterns: A 37-Year Follow-Up Study," *Leisure Sciences* 11 (1989): 323-335.

[26]   Rodney Warnick, "Recreation and Leisure Participation Patterns Among the Adult Middle-Aged Market from 1975 to 1984," *Journal of Physical Education, Recreation and Dance* (October 1987): 49.

[27]   "Games Singles Play," *Newsweek* (16 July 1973): 52.

[28]   Geoffrey Godbey, *Leisure in Your Life: An Exploration* (State College, Pa.: Venture Publishing, 1985): 170.

[29]   "The Disruptions of Campus Drunkenness," *U.S. News & World Report* (19 December 1994): 12.

[30]   Joseph Califano, Jr., "It's Drugs, Stupid," *New York Times* (29 January 1995): 40.

[31]   Mike Males, "It's the Adults, Stupid," *New York Times* (9 September 1995): 19.

[32]   Susan Shaw, "Family Leisure and Leisure Services," *Parks and Recreation* (December 1992): 13.

[33]   Dennis Orthner and Jay Mancini, "Leisure Impacts on Family Interaction and Cohesion," *Journal of Leisure Research* (Vol. 22 No. 2 1990): 125–137.

[34]   Robert Madrigal, Mark Havitz, and Dennis Howard, "Married Couples' Involvement with Family Vacations," *Leisure Sciences* 14 (1992): 287–301.

[35]   Valeria Freysinger, "Leisure with Children: What It Means to Mothers and Fathers," *Abstracts of NRPA Research Symposium* (San Jose, Cal.: 1993).

[36]   Paul Light, *Baby Boomers* (New York: W. W. Norton and Co., 1988): 28.

[37]   D. Quinn Mills, *Not Like Our Parents: How the Baby Boom Generation Is Changing America* (New York: William Morrow and Co., 1987): 16–17.

[38]   Gail Sheehy, *New Passages: Mapping Your Life Across Time* (New York: Random House, 1995).

[39]   Lydia Bronte, *The Longevity Factor: The New Reality of Long Careers and How It Leads to Richer Lives* (New York: HarperCollins, 1993).

[40]   Valeria Freysinger, "Dialectics of Leisure and Development for Men and Women in Mid-Life: An Interpretive Study," *Journal of Leisure Research* (Vol. 27 No. 1 1995): 61–84.

[41]   Sheila Backman and Kenneth Backman, "The Role of Park and Recreation Services Retiree Relocation Decisions," *Trends* (Fall 1993): 19.

[42]   Robert Stock, "Senior Class: Wrong-Headed Views Persist About the Old," *New York Times* (1 June 1995): C-8.

[43]   "Retirement Trends," *New York Times Magazine* (17 September 1995): 24.

[44]   Murray Dubin, "Over 60—and Splitting Up," *Philadelphia Inquirer* (17 November 1993): G-1.

[45]   Barbara Wilhite, Kathleen Sheldon, and Nancy Jekubovich-Fenton, "Leisure in Daily Life: Older Widows Living Alone," *Journal of Park and Recreation Administration* (Vol. 12 No. 4 1994): 64.

[46]   "Personal Health: More of the Elderly Seek the Benefits of Exercise," *New York Times* (4 October 1995): C-11.

Gender, Race, and Ethnic Influences on Recreation and Leisure

The history of Western civilization is that of a male-dominated, that is, sexist, society in which women have generally been dominated by males and have been systematically exploited. This institutionalized sexism is usually referred to as being "patriarchal." Like racism, it is not simply a matter of values and ideologies, but is a thoroughgoing institutionalization of roles, expectations, resources, opportunities, rewards, and, most important, the power of self-determination.[1]

Much of the research examining the influence of ethnicity on recreation participation has attempted to explain participation rates and patterns of minorities relative to the larger society. . . utilizing two possible explanations: *marginality* and *ethnicity*. The marginality hypothesis explains under-participation as the influence of factors such as low socio-economic status, lack of access to desired facilities, and discrimination. The ethnicity explanation holds that under-participation is the result of subcultural differences in values and expectations based on the history and traditions of a given racial or ethnic group.[2]

---

[1] John Kelly, *Leisure* (Boston: Allyn and Bacon, 1996): 80.

[2] Deborah Carr and Daniel Williams, "Understanding the Role of Ethnicity in Outdoor Recreation Experiences," *Journal of Leisure Research* (Vol. 25 No. 1 1993): 22–23.

INTRODUCTION

As we examine the influences on recreation and leisure in contemporary society, it is evident that in addition to age and family status, a number of other demographic factors play an important role. Citizens of any nation share, to a degree, the values and traditions of the larger society. However, beyond such overall cultural influences, people are also members of other subcultural groups that affect their values and life styles. James Murphy and his co-authors have described many of the subcultural groups in American life. They include the following:

Subcultures of gender and marital status: single, married, widowed, and divorced groups, as well as heterosexual, homosexual, and bisexual lifestyles, all constitute different subcultures;

Subcultures of racial origin or ethnic identity: different ethnic or racial groups represent an important force in affecting leisure values and behavior, along with religious affiliations that can be linked to ethnic identity;

Subcultures of wealth and poverty: one's socioeconomic status, ranging from wealth to extreme poverty—in both urban and rural settings, clearly affects one's recreational potential;

Subcultures of place: neighborhoods, towns and cities, and provinces and regions affect attitudes and behaviors, partly through climate and partly through major differences in opportunities for recreational participation.[3]

This chapter examines two of the most important of these elements, beginning with gender as a key force that shapes leisure values and involvement today and concluding with an analysis of the role of race and ethnicity in this area.

GENDER'S INFLUENCE ON RECREATION AND LEISURE

A distinction must be made between the two terms *sex* and *gender*. Although they are often used interchangeably, social scientists have generally accepted the principle that the term sex should be used to identify one's biological or physical classification in terms of the structure and functions that are possessed by one sex or the other. In contrast, the word gender is used to describe a broad range of characteristics, roles, or behaviors that society usually attaches to males and females. Stated simply, the words male and female apply to one's sex, while the words masculine and feminine are descriptive adjectives applying to gender traits.

Throughout history, distinctions between males and females have been made that extend beyond the procreative functions. These distinctions encompass family or marital roles, educational status, career opportunities, political influences, and all other aspects of daily life. In some societies, women have held considerable power, for example, women worshipped as gods or where they headed nations. For the most part, however, women have been subordinate to men in many societies.

This chapter will illustrate the inferior status of women in the area of recreational opportunity. Throughout America's history, women have been barred from many opportunities in sports that were freely open to men. For the past several decades, one of the key efforts of the feminist movement has been to make a greater diversity of leisure experiences available for girls and women.

Traditionally, men and boys have been encouraged to participate in physically active, challenging, and competitive activities conforming to the image of masculinity in society at large.

In contrast, girls and women have been expected to take part in a range of domestic pursuits centered around the home or in essentially aesthetic or decorative activities that are relatively quiet or passive in nature.

Among younger children, play has served to reinforce gender-related stereotypes. Little boys were given toy guns or cowboy outfits and encouraged to play-act in stereotypically masculine roles—like doctors, firefighters, or airline pilots. Girls were given dolls or play equipment designed to encourage stereotypically feminine roles, like caring for babies, cooking, and sewing, or dramatic play as nurses or airline hostesses. Only after the resurgence of the feminist movement following World War II did we begin to question these roles and assumptions and challenge such sexist uses of play in childhood.

At other age levels as well, research has shown that recreation has been influenced by gender-role orientation. For example, in an analysis of adolescents in a midwestern community, Hollingshead contrasted the degree of control that families exerted over teenage girls and the freedom enjoyed by adolescent boys during the early 1940s.[4] In addition, Havighurst reported in 1957 that middle-aged women preferred socializing and reading in their leisure time, while their male counterparts were more involved in sports and outdoor pursuits like fishing and hunting.[5]

During the decades after World War II, this pattern began to break down. Research by Rosenberg and Sutton-Smith in 1960 found that females were beginning to be attracted to traditionally male play activities.[6] In the 1970s, research began to examine the influence on one's leisure choices by the *degree* of masculine or feminine personality traits. Gentry and Doering found, for example, that many androgynous individuals, who had mixed masculine and feminine orientations, also had a high degree of participation in across-the-board leisure activities.[7]

Recreation Program Planning Differences

Throughout the development of organized recreation and park programs in the United States and Canada, agency planners typically responded to prevailing societal attitudes regarding appropriate leisure activities for the sexes by developing community recreation programs that supported the traditional stereotypes.

Foster Rhea Dulles points out that during the early decades of this century, leadership roles and activities assigned to girls and women, as well as the expectations regarding their ability to work well in groups, reflected past perceptions of women as weak and inferior in skills, lacking drive, confidence, and the ability to compete and persevere.[8] Victorian-like prudery and misconceptions about physical capability and health needs also limited programming for girls and women.

Discrimination based on gender was most vividly demonstrated in the field of athletics at this time. Bill Gilbert and Nancy Williamson documented in 1973 the widespread prejudice against females in sport in the United States:

> There is no sharper example of discrimination today than that which operates against girls and women who take part in competitive sports, wish to take part, or might wish to if society did not scorn such endeavors. No matter what her age, education, race, talent, residence or riches, the female's right to play is severely restricted. The funds, facilities, coaching, rewards and honors allotted women are grossly inferior to those granted men. In many places absolutely no support is given to women's athletics, and females are barred by law, regulation, tradition or the hostility of males from sharing athletic resources and pleasures.[9]

IMPACT OF FEMINIST MOVEMENT

A number of important social trends were responsible for bringing about major changes with respect to women's roles in recreation and leisure. First, there was the evolving independence of women in terms of family status and work-related roles. With the dramatic increase in divorce, millions of women became single parents and heads of households. Following their counterparts of World War II, who enlisted in the armed forces and worked in war plants by the millions, this new generation of women was determined to assume greater responsibilities. They wanted to break through the accepted patterns of gender-related discrimination that limited their employment in the past. The feminist movement, which in earlier periods of American history resulted in women obtaining fuller legal and political rights, was revived with a stronger thrust toward obtaining equality with men in a wide range of societal roles. This movement led to the creation of militant women's organizations and support groups and was responsible for legislation and court decisions that broke down the walls of gender discrimination in the 1970s and 1980s.

Differences between Males and Females

Linked to the feminists' social-action objectives were their efforts to overcome the overall subordination of women in society. This had been based in part on the assumption that there were major, genetically based differences between the sexes that justified the limitations placed on the lives of women. In terms of actual differences between males and females, it had been popularly accepted that women were the "weaker" and essentially inferior sex. Even when the new science of intelligence tests revealed clear superiority among girls, researchers kept tinkering with the tests until they confirmed the old stereotypes. Such beliefs, for the most part, have been effectively rejected. During the period of ideologically fervent 1970s feminist scholarship, it was argued that

> apart from the obvious dimorphism of human beings, there were *no* real differences between the sexes—that seeming disparities in mental abilities, emotional makeup, attitudes, and even many physical skills were merely the product of centuries of male domination and male-dominated interpretation.[10]

Further, it was held that the unmistakable differences between men and women—that women become pregnant and men have the strongest shoulders—were no longer critical in the modern era when the neighborhood drugstore or clinic offer freedom from fertility and every American fingertip can control horsepower in the hundreds. However, scientists continue to explore the fine points of how men and women really differ from each other in physiology and psychology, and the subtle ways in which society influences both. Research in a dozen disciplines, ranging from neurology, endocrinology, and sports medicine to psychology, anthropology, and sociology, is confirming that there are major differences between the sexes apart from their anatomy and reproductive functions.

Ethologists who observe the social behavior of primates note distinctly different patterns of male and female behavior, with males being far more adventurous, aggressively playful, and risk-taking while females stay closer to home and are more cautious, domestic, and nurturing. Such observations suggest that gender-based differences are largely caused by inherited genetic factors.

On the other hand, numerous researchers today suggest that the different capabilities of girls and boys in such fields as mathematics and the sciences are the result of parental or teacher conditioning—where boys are usually favored in these areas and where girls are usually discouraged, with a consequent effect on their confidence and self-esteem. When even young children show contrasting play interests, with little boys enjoying trucks and fire engines and little girls choosing dolls and domestic hobbies, it is argued that they are responding to unspoken, but nonetheless powerful, adult "messages" about appropriate behavior. Katha Pollitt suggests that many feminist women who complain about their sons' passion for sports would not think of discouraging them from participating:

> Could it be that even sports-resistant moms see athletics as part of manliness? That if their sons wanted to spend the weekend writing in their diaries, or reading, or baking, they'd find it disturbing? Too antisocial? Too lonely? Too gay?[11]

Thus, even parents who decry gender-based discrimination may unconsciously reinforce traditional stereotypes in their own children. At the same time, it is apparent that we *are* steadily moving toward a society in which gender-based barriers are breaking down in terms of family life, education, careers, and the world of recreation and leisure.

Emphasis on Sports and Physical Recreation

Recreation and leisure help the feminist movement achieve key goals today. This is particularly true in sports and outdoor recreation, in which relatively few girls and women had been encouraged to participate in the past. Historically, M. Deborah Bialeschki writes, the

> domination of sport by men and their exclusion of women had been one among many forms of male control of women's bodies. This control had been ideological in the form of cultural denigration of women's athletic ability and the myth of female frailty. . . . Through sports and fitness, many women gain a sense of self-definition and self-determination, for learning the lesson "I can." Facing a challenge heightens a woman's sense of vitality and the awareness of her individuality. . . . [At the same time] by applying the principles of strength, cooperation, and solidarity learned through physical recreation activities to other social constructs, women may transform politics, business, the family, as well as physical recreation, into less oppressive social constructs.[12]

Women have increasingly become engaged in a wide range of individual and team sports, achieving a higher participation rate in secondary school and college competitive programs. As professional athletes or international competitors in such sports as tennis, golf, gymnastics, and skiing, they have been successful. Beyond this, many highly skilled women have achieved success as race-car drivers, horse-racing jockeys, dog-sled racers, and triathletes. These changes have occurred not only in schools and colleges and at professional levels of sports participation, but also in many community-based programs. In part, this has occurred because of challenges to the exclusion of females from programs that have historically been restricted to male participants.

For example, in baseball programs for children and youth, girls were not permitted to join Little League until 1974. At that time, thanks to civil rights suits throughout the United States (including some supported by the National Organization for Women), Little League changed its charter to incorporate girls. However, at the same time, it organized a softball league. Although softball is not legally restricted to girls, few boys join this program. And, although some girls do play hardball, they are extremely rare. Thus, segregation by gender continues on a voluntary basis, although it is legally possible to cross the line.

In some cases, public recreation and park authorities have been forced to take action to eliminate sex-based discrimination in sports. In Philadelphia, for example, in 1985 the Fairmount Park Commission revoked the ballfield permits of a community sports association that sponsored several baseball leagues with hundreds of youth participants, because they refused to let a single girl play hardball in her local league. In the same year, in Canada, a 12-year-old Toronto girl's effort to play on an all-boy hockey team in a city league governed by the provincial Ontario Hockey Association led to a trial before the Ontario Supreme Court. Backed by the Canadian women's movement and several prominent players and officials in the National Hockey League, her campaign led to a repeal of the section of the Ontario Human Rights Code that allowed discrimination by sex in athletics.

Other Areas of Progress

In numerous other areas of public life, barriers against girls and women have been broken down in recent years. An interesting example has been the effort to open up exclusive private clubs in many of the nation's cities to female membership. While, nominally, these are social groups that should have the right to restrict their membership, they are also places where influential people meet to do business and where exclusively male memberships mean that women are placed at a marked career disadvantage. *Time* magazine reports:

> amid the antique rugs and deep leather chairs, the clubs do furnish a setting for the exertions of professional life: back slapping, ego massage and one "contact" sport—making business connections. . . . Meal tabs and annual dues that can run into the thousands of dollars are often picked up by a member's employer. . . .[13]

In less prestigious businessmen's clubs, luncheon clubs, service groups, and other formerly gender-segregated organizations, barriers have similarly been removed through court decisions or state legislation.

> **I**n terms of employment, growing numbers of women in the 1970s and 1980s rose to executive positions in major public recreation and park agencies and nonprofit organizations. In the late 1980s, after protracted legal challenges, the Boy Scouts of America agreed to let women become scoutmasters and hold all other leadership positions—a long-resisted policy change. And in May 1995, California's Disneyland adopted a comprehensive unisex "casting" approach for all of its rides:
>
> > In the last month, women have begun taking guests on the circuitous Jungle Cruise, past water-squirting elephants and stalking tigers, where only male guides had ventured before. And next month, men will begin relating the same fables as their female counterparts on the [sedate] Storybook Land ride. Park officials say they are considering inviting women to work in some of the Magic Kingdom's other male bastions—train locomotives, Main Street omnibus, and the steamboat. It may take as long as a year, they say, but it *will* happen.[14]

At the same time, some of the entertainment-oriented activities that portrayed women as sex objects have been removed or modified in recent years. After years of commercial success, the Playboy bunnies gradually went out of style, and the Atlantic City Miss America

Pageant, which began as a bathing beauty contest, now requires its contestants to demonstrate performing talents and to speak out on a significant social issue or platform.

Constraints on Women's Leisure

Another limitation on women's enjoyment of leisure stems from their work responsibilities. Firestone and Shelton summarize research showing that, for the most part, women in the paid labor force remain responsible for household labor, with men's contribution to household tasks being relatively unresponsive to shifts in their wives' labor force participation. They write:

> Even when employed full time, women are more likely to be responsible for household and child care. Whether the result of socialization, wage discrimination, or different aptitudes, the result is a "double day" that comes at the expense of other activities.[15]

In a similar vein, Harrington and Dawson conducted a study of over 1,500 adult females in Ontario, Canada, in three categories: those employed full-time, those employed part-time, and homemakers not employed outside the home. Homemakers in particular felt they lacked needed leisure skills and confidence, had weak self images and leisure concepts, and tended to agree that certain leisure activities were clearly "only for men." Of the entire group, part-time workers reported the highest levels of feelings of serenity, playfulness, and femininity in their leisure, and they also had fewer perceived constraints on their enjoyment of leisure.[16]

A final constraint shared by all women consists of the threat of sexual harassment or rape in recreation situations where they are isolated—as in entering or leaving buildings late at night, jogging, hiking, or engaging in other outdoor or wilderness pursuits. Numerous reports in the 1990s confirm the danger of such settings for women and make it clear that the statistics of harassment and sexual attacks continue to threaten all women today.

MEN AND LEISURE

Although most of the professional literature and research studies dealing with gender in recreation and leisure focuses on past discrimination against girls and women and the efforts made to strengthen their opportunities today, it is essential to examine the changing role of males in this area as well. Generally, men have been portrayed as the dominant sex within most areas of community life, and have been seen as responsible for denying women access to a full range of leisure pursuits and professional advancement. However, it would be misleading to assume that men's lives are invariably richer and more satisfying than those of women.

Andrew Kimbrell points out that, in addition to having a markedly shorter life span than women, men have four times the suicide rate, three times the alcoholism rate, and substantially higher rates of drug dependency and imprisonment than their female counterparts. Kimbrell continues:

> Men are also a large part of the growing crisis in the American family. . . . Men are increasingly isolated from their families by the pressures of work and the circumstances of divorce. In a recent poll, 72 percent of employed male respondents agreed that they are "torn by conflict" between their jobs and the desire to be with their families.[17]

> Rather than view them as the invariably favored sex, we should perhaps note that many men lead relatively powerless, subservient lives in the factory or office, and that they are pressured by the fictional depiction of daring "macho" men in the mass media of entertainment to embrace an unrealistic and unrewarding masculine lifestyle.

Realistically, many men find it difficult to have close friends who provide support, as women do. Often, they are constrained by the inability to feel or show emotion, as is illustrated in the episode of a Minnesota sales engineer who was laid off from a new position after only six weeks on the job, and only two days after his wife announced that she wanted a divorce. When his co-workers at the elevator company agreed to take a pay cut so that he could be rehired, he made it a point to shake everybody's hand on his first day back, saying gratefully that

> [their generosity] was a personal high. It shows an incredible amount of heart. If I wasn't a man, I'd be emotional about the whole thing.[18]

Many men are now making a strenuous effort to come to grips with their need to share with others, to get a better sense of their masculine identities, and to become warmer, more expressive individuals. Robert Bly's book, *Iron John*, has encouraged men to join drumming groups and wilderness retreats where they explore their past relationships with their fathers and their own roles as fathers and providers. Tens of thousands of men in the mid-1990s have been filling huge stadiums for meetings sponsored by a Denver-based organization called Promise Keepers, which offers religious revival, inspirational pep talk, and spiritual support.

The "Million Man March," held in Washington, D.C., in the fall of 1995, stressed similar themes of responsibility, brotherhood, and commitment to family values for African-American men.

As part of a manifesto for the new politics of masculinity, men are being urged to press for changes in the workplace—flexible hours, job-sharing, part-time work, and home-based job assignments—that will permit them to devote more time and energy to their families and to their own creative and social interests. In contrast to the findings of Firestone and Shelton cited earlier, some recent studies show that more men *are* beginning to take on child-care responsibilities, for reasons ranging from rising day-care costs to the growth in the number of working women and joblessness among males.

Implications for Leisure

What are the implications of these trends in masculine identity and lifestyle values for recreation and leisure? In the first place, many boys and men who formerly felt pressured to be involved heavily in sports, both as participants and as spectators, may now feel free *not* to conform to this traditional masculine image. Further, growing numbers of males are increasingly likely to take part in domestic functions or hobbies, the creative arts, or other leisure pursuits that in the past might have raised questions about their degree of "maleness."

This new freedom to engage in leisure pursuits once considered inappropriate for men also extends to attitudes toward women. Increasingly, many parents are becoming sensitive to the way they permit their sons to behave toward girls. Too often, Myriam Miedzian writes, parents of boys tolerate language and behavior that demean girls:

> Parents allow their sons to watch entertainment and play video games that treat women as sex objects created to fulfill the sexual needs of men, and that focus on male power and dominance and the use of violent means to achieve those ends.[19]

At the same time, many males are rebelling against the notion that all men are "evil" oppressors. Male "bashing," Lance Morrow writes, has become a popular pastime, with men viewed as sexual oppressors, business cheats, and political phonies. Popular culture, in the form of movies, television sitcoms, video games, and sensational talk shows, perpetuates and exaggerates this image and inflames hostility between the sexes.

Men are resisting this distorted image of their character and, within the broad range of recreation and leisure pursuits, are exploring healthier areas of personal expression and masculine identity. Some men are even beginning to argue that *they* are being oppressed, as in the case of the Title IX lawsuits filed by male student-athletes at Drake University and the University of Illinois. They claim that men are now being subjected to reverse sex discrimination in college athletic programs.

HOMOSEXUALITY AND LEISURE

Closely linked to any consideration of the role of gender in determining one's leisure choices and behavior must be an awareness of a substantial and increasingly visible group that pursues alternative sexual lifestyles—gays, lesbians, and bisexuals, as they are usually referred to in the popular press.

In the past, throughout much of the Western world, homosexuality was condemned by religious and civil authorities. Until recently, it was categorized as a form of mental illness by the psychiatric establishment and as a crime subject to prosecution by law enforcement agencies. Being identified as gay or lesbian meant that one was barred from employment in many occupational fields. Thus, most homosexuals hid their identity in the "closet." Despite this background, scholars point out that there was a pattern of gays and lesbians sharing a social life in dance halls, night-clubs and resorts, living in specific neighborhoods of large cities, and often clustering in artistic or creative occupations throughout much of the early 20th century.

David Greenberg describes the social life of many homosexuals in this period, particularly during the 1920s:

> Far from being hidden, its existence was well known. Gay gathering spots were listed in guidebooks, and huge numbers of spectators attended well-publicized drag balls in Harlem and Midtown venues . . . . [There were] speakeasies featuring female impersonators and other gay-oriented entertainment that drew both gay and straight audiences who prided themselves on their sophistication. Popular songs, films, plays and novels gave increasing visibility to gay life.[20]

However, during the 1930s and 1940s, a backlash developed against gay forms of entertainment, with state assemblies barring the performance of plays dealing with sexual "degeneracy" and Hollywood agreeing not to depict homosexuality in movies. State liquor authorities closed many bars that catered to gay personnel, arrests for homosexual solicitation rose dramatically, and in the 1950s, gay government employees lost their jobs because it was assumed that they could be easily blackmailed into spying for other countries on the basis of their hidden identities.

In the 1960s and 1970s, the effect of the Stonewall riot in New York City (a mass protest against police persecution of gays), the impact of the counterculture movement with its emphasis on sexual freedom, and the militant action of other gender or racial minorities all converged to help homosexuals gain a greater measure of public acceptance.

Growing Acceptance

With research into the causes of homosexuality—including new evidence suggesting that it has a genetic or biological base—the psychiatric profession withdrew its classification of homosexuality as a form of mental illness. Beyond this, homosexuality began to gain visibility on the national scene.

Numerous universities began to employ openly homosexual faculty members, to institute courses and curricula in gay, lesbian, and bisexual studies, and to approve student organizations that sponsored publications, events, and other programs that were homosexual-oriented.

Gay and lesbian community centers were established in a number of cities to promote homosexual causes and concerns. School curricula and textbooks were adopted that provided information about homosexuality, gay and lesbian families, and related issues of prejudice and discrimination.

Gay and lesbian lifestyle issues began to appear more positively in popular culture with homosexual-related themes in books, theater, dance, and fine arts events. Many gay rights groups began to openly take part in public events and celebrations from which they had been barred in the past.

However, on a number of other levels, gay liberation remained a highly contentious issue, as conservative religious and political factions resisted the increasing acceptance of homosexuals in public life.

Continuing Resistance to Homosexual Acceptance

In some cases, state legislation or local initiatives have been approved that would nullify civil rights laws or policies giving homosexuals the same freedom from discrimination as women, racial minorities, the aging, or those with a disability. On the national level in the United States, efforts to pass a federal antidiscrimination bill were abandoned in the face of the conservative Congressional tide of the mid-1990s.

In a number of public school systems, strong opposition was mounted to the adoption of textbooks providing favorable descriptions of gay or lesbian families. In other cases, teachers were dismissed for distributing novels in literature classes that depicted homosexual characters sympathetically and boards of education have banned gay and lesbian clubs in school systems.

In the armed forces there has been an ongoing struggle between those who seek to eliminate the Pentagon's ban against homosexual men and women serving in the military, and those who remain opposed to this proposed policy change.

A number of religious denominations, including the Presbyterian Church, the Southern Baptist Convention, and the United Methodist Church, have debated issues relating to the ordination of homosexual members of the clergy, same-sex marriages, or their overall stance with respect to homosexuality. The Catholic Church in particular has been vigorous in its resistance to any lessening of its opposition to homosexuality—calling it an objective "disorder" and comparing it to mental illness.[21]

Implications for Leisure Policy

How have these trends affected recreation and leisure-service organizations designed to serve the full range of community members? In the past, most public and nonprofit organizations did not deal with such issues or simply accepted gay or lesbian participants as part of their total membership without recognizing or making a point of their sexual orientation. In some cases, however, they have openly refused to employ homosexual staff members in leadership roles with young people or to permit gay or lesbian individuals to continue as program members.

In one such case, a Superior Court judge in New Jersey ruled against a gay Eagle Scout and assistant scoutmaster who brought a discrimination suit against the Boy Scouts of America for expelling him. The judge found

that the state's Law Against Discrimination, which was amended in 1991 to cover "affectional or sexual orientation," did not apply to the distinctly "private" Boy Scouts. . . .

In his decision [the judge] equated homosexuality with sodomy, which was illegal in New Jersey until 1979, and noted that "all religions deem the act of sodomy a serious moral wrong." As such, homosexuality was incompatible with the Boy Scouts, which he called a "moral organization."[22]

In contrast, a number of recreation, park, and leisure-service educators have vigorously promoted the idea of enriched recreation services for gay and lesbian youth. Pointing out that there are an estimated 7.2 million such individuals in the United States who are often stigmatized and isolated because of their identity, Arnold Grossman suggests that many of these young people are at risk for dropping out—or being forced out—of school, losing their homes, abusing alcohol and drugs, getting AIDS, or committing suicide. Grossman continues:

Cultural, ethnic and familial support disappear[s] in the face of homosexuality, leaving gay and lesbian youth to experience prejudice, discrimination, and violence. Until there is acceptance of such youth by mainstream institutions, there is the need for special services . . . .[23]

In an example of such special services, a nonprofit agency, the Lavender Youth Recreation and Information Center (LYRIC), and the San Francisco Recreation and Park Department have joined together to promote comprehensive recreation and social activities for gay, lesbian, and bisexual youth in a safe and positive social environment.[24] Preliminary studies of gay and lesbian youth suggest that leisure may have special meaning for such individuals because of the link to issues of sexual identity, accessibility, and safety.[25]

Programs in Other Settings

Beyond services provided by public or nonprofit organizations, the gay and lesbian community itself has established leisure-linked organizations by forming recreation clubs, sports leagues, outdoor recreation associations, and other groups that have functioned on local, state, national, and even international levels. Examples include the Gay Olympic Games, which have involved several thousand participants from 19 countries in 17 different sports. To illustrate, Brenda Pitts conducted a study of over 130 organizations providing organized sports or outdoor recreation for primarily gay and lesbian participants. She found that these groups offered a total of 57 different activities, including camping, bicycling, backpacking, snow skiing, volleyball, swimming, cruises, bowling, sailing, travel, running, mountaineering, and tennis.[26] In addition, there are literally thousands of gay-oriented resorts, travel services, tours, events, cruises, and other tourist attractions serving this market today.

As an example of this trend, the Greater Miami Convention and Visitors Bureau and other Dade County, Florida, tourist and resort associations are now making a concerted attempt to woo the nation's gay and lesbian travel market. Over the 1995 Memorial Day weekend, Miami Beach treated 17 journalists from the European gay press to an all-expense-paid, four-day tour of Dade County in the hope that these nicely treated junketeers would then promote tourism in Florida by European gays and lesbians.[27]

While it seems probable that a substantial segment of American society will continue to resist social advances for homosexuals in the years ahead, it is also probable that growing numbers of recreation and leisure-service agencies will recognize the need to serve this population more effectively as part of their social mandate to meet the leisure needs of the nation's overall population.

INFLUENCE OF RACE AND ETHNICITY

In addition to the factors of age and gender, a third major demographic element is of key importance in determining leisure values and behaviors. A succession of past research studies show that recreational involvement is heavily influenced by one's racial or ethnic identity. The provision of public, nonprofit, and other forms of recreation facilities and programs is also affected by these demographic factors, and the broader fields of popular culture—including the sports and entertainment worlds—continue to reflect their impact.

How does it happen that a nation that prides itself on its democratic origins and its professed ideology of equality continues to be divided by issues of race and ethnicity? In actuality, although the ideal of the melting pot has expressed the hope that the United States would blend the unique talents of the immigrants from many lands into a single multigifted creature—the "American"—this has never really happened. Instead, the nation's history reveals a long record of both official and unofficial racial oppression against people of color, as well as widespread prejudice against immigrants from less-favored European nations.

Meaning of Race and Ethnicity

Before examining the actual influence of race and ethnicity on recreation and leisure, it is helpful to clarify the meaning of the two terms. Although they are often used interchangeably, social scientists do distinguish between them. Race has been defined as follows:

> A race is considered to be a statistical aggregate of people who share a composite of genetically transmitted *physical* traits, such as skin pigmentation, head form, facial features, stature, and the color, distribution and texture of body hair . . . . Estimates of racial types range from three—Caucasoid, Mongoloid, and Negroid—to thirty or more.[28]

Recreation Programs Serving Inner-City Youth

Many organizations that serve youth involve minority-group youngsters in typically middle-class pursuits, as in this Philadelphia tennis clinic (top) founded by the late Arthur Ashe or golf programs (center) sponsored by the Police Athletic League in Tuscaloosa, Alabama. The Boys and Girls Clubs of America offer useful life-skills computer classes to club members (bottom).

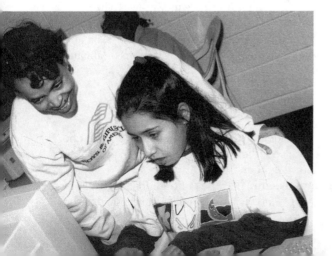

In contrast, ethnicity involves having a unique social and cultural heritage that is passed on from one generation to another. Ethnic groups are often identified by patterns of language, family life, religion, recreation, and other customs or traits that distinguish them from other groups.

It is important to recognize that the systems used to classify people into different racial categories, and even the concept of race itself, have been under attack. At a 1995 meeting of the American Association for the Advancement of Science, biological anthropologists argued that race is no longer a valid way of distinguishing among people, and that instead it is

ethnicity

> a social construct derived mainly from perceptions conditioned by events of recorded history, and it has no basic biological reality.[29]

A recent statement by the American Association of Physical Anthropologists, which is intended to provide a guideline for UNESCO and other international organizations in dealing with racism around the globe, states in part that:

> Pure races in the sense of genetically homogeneous populations do not exist in the human species, nor is there evidence that they have ever existed in the past history of the human family.
>   Hereditary potentials for overall intelligence and cultural development do not appear to differ among modern human populations, and there is no hereditary justification for considering one population superior to another.[30]

Realistically, of course, we tend to follow the principle of racial identity in daily life, in government policies, and in a wide range of popularly held stereotypes about different racial or ethnic groups. Yet even here there is a growing challenge to the traditional classifications used to identify people.

> **I**ncreasingly, the U.S. Census Bureau is confounded by the difficulty of classifying multiracial people who represent a blend of two or more family origins. The limited categories of "white," "black," "Asian and Pacific Islanders," and "American Indian or Alaskan native" used in the census cannot begin to convey the differences among different groups of Pacific Islanders or the immense number of markedly different Asian-Americans. The broad category of Hispanic-Americans or Latinos may consist of individuals from the Spanish mainland, those of mixed African, Spanish, and Indian backgrounds, or others from dozens of different geographical and cultural groups.

Within any particular population group, sizable segments of people may prefer to be identified by different labels. Typically, 44.2 percent of Americans of African origin prefer to be called "black" while 28.1 percent prefer African-American, 12.1 percent Afro-American, and only 3.3 percent Negro and 1.1 percent colored.[31] Similar variations of preferred labeling exist within other major racial and ethnic groups.

Implications for Recreation and Leisure

Despite the limitations of racial or ethnicity-based identification and its meaning in scientific terms, the reality is that the public continues to accept the concept of race and to apply it in terms of popular stereotypes about one group or the other.

This is particularly significant for recreation and leisure because our traditional patterns of facility development and program planning were essentially based on the assumption that the public being served was predominantly a white, middle-class population familiar with the literature, traditions, and customs that came to America from the British Isles.

Now, for the first time, we are seeing the rapid growth of non-European populations in the United States as a consequence of recent immigration and birthrate trends. In a number of major cities throughout the country, nonwhites now outnumber those of European background, with the percentage of African-American, Hispanic-American, and Asian-American children in the schools representing sizable majorities in some cases.

If this population trend continues, it is predicted that Hispanics will become the dominant minority in the United States, with major political, social, and economic implications. Similarly, the number of Asian-Americans has grown from 3.5 million in 1980 to over 7.2 million in 1990 and is expected to climb steadily in the decades ahead. In 1990, a *Time* cover story, entitled "Beyond the Melting Pot," made it clear that the rapidly approaching twenty-first century would see racial and ethnic groups in the United States outnumbering whites for the first time, with the "browning of America" transforming every aspect of society.

Research into Minority-Group Recreation Patterns

Since the 1920s, a number of researchers in psychology, sociology, urban studies, and, more recently, recreation, park, and leisure studies have carried out systematic examinations of the leisure-related patterns of racial and ethnic minority-group members.

As far back as 1927, Lehman and Witty compared the play activities of African-American and white elementary and secondary school children and came to the conclusion that African-American youngsters participated much more actively in social forms of play than their Caucasian counterparts.[32] In the 1950s, a striking analysis of the leisure pursuits of middle-class African-Americans was carried out by E. Franklin Frazier. He found that many of the pleasure-seeking activities of the black bourgeoisie were influenced by their feelings of insecurity and inferiority in American society and by their effort to escape from the oppressive circumstances of their lives.[33] Other studies at this time by the Wharton School of Finance and the Outdoor Recreation Resources Review Commission found that there were marked differences between African-American and white families with respect to spending on varied forms of entertainment and involvement in outdoor recreation.[34]

In the 1970s and 1980s, a wave of research studies examined the recreation patterns of African-Americans, Mexican-Americans, Asian-Americans, and other minority group members. Stamps and Stamps, for example, reviewed 17 different studies that analyzed African-Americans' use of leisure in terms of urban-suburban, regional, and social class variables, and compared them to the involvement of whites.[35] In 1992, Dwyer and Gobster reported on several other research studies by Washburn, Klobus-Edwards, Dwyer, and Hutchinson, which showed generally lower recreational participation by African-Americans in dispersed outdoor activities like camping and hiking, and a higher level of involvement in active, social, and urban-oriented activities.[36]

Similarly, Floyd, Gramann, and Saenz looked at the influence of ethnic acculturation on the use of public outdoor recreation and park areas by Mexican-Americans in a number of Arizona counties.[37] Allison and Geiger studied the leisure involvements of elderly Chinese-American residents in a southwestern city, finding that their pursuits met a number of their educational, cultural, and personal development needs.[38]

Focus on Ethnic-Related Differences and Constraints

Beyond measuring the differences between or among various racial and ethnic groups in their leisure involvements, researchers have sought to develop a theoretical framework that would explain the reasons for the differences. The most prominent models used to explain such differences as "underparticipation" in varied leisure activities by African-Americans are the *marginality* and *ethnicity* hypotheses. Floyd, Shinew, McGuire, and Noe explain the marginality model in terms of the limited economic resources of and historical patterns of discrimination against African-Americans. Stated differently, they write:

> . . . by occupying a subordinate class position, minorities have had limited access to society's major institutions which negatively affects life-chances and lifestyles, and which is reflected in reduced participation in certain types of activities.[39]

Applied to a specific form of recreation, travel and tourism, the marginality hypothesis is illustrated by the centuries-long discrimination against African-Americans and by the relatively lower economic resources of many African-American families.

The ethnicity hypothesis essentially says that different racial groups are influenced in their leisure choices by different norms, values, and socialization processes. In the case of African-Americans, these might include a range of recreational pursuits that were influenced by African-American history and cultural development, including activities in the realm of music, dance, or traditional games that stem from African heritage, slavery days, or the era of Reconstruction in the rural South.

In general, both models may serve as partial explanations of the distinctive behaviors of racial and ethnic minority populations—combined with continuing factors of social exclusion and self-segregation.

Continuing Examples of Discrimination

Well into the 1990s, a major chain of health and fitness clubs covertly sought to exclude or discourage African-American members, believing that their presence would have a negative effect on white club members.[40] Major restaurant chains have similarly discriminated against black patrons or potential employees, as revealed in recent major court cases and settlements. Private-membership golf clubs have systematically excluded African-American or other minority group members, until forced to accept them by public pressures relating to the sponsorship of major tournaments.

In the realm of professional and college sports, there is strong evidence that, despite the success of African-American athletes in the major team sports of basketball, baseball, and football, they have been disproportionately excluded from the coaching or management positions in these sports.[41] In the early and mid-1990s, many sports commentators and athletes spoke out against such discrimination, and leaders from the baseball, football, and basketball players' unions formed a coalition with the heads of the NAACP, National Urban League, and Southern Christian Leadership Conference to eliminate racist practices in professional sports.

Self-Segregation and Comfort Levels

A key thrust of the civil rights movement in the period from the 1950s through the 1970s was to break down barriers to full participation in society and to forge positive links between different ethnic and racial groups. In contrast, the period of the 1980s and 1990s has been marked by growing racial hostility and patterns of self-segregation.

On many college campuses, minority group students tend to band together in social activities, housing choices, and other areas in which there would be the potential for friendly contact and improved intergroup relations. While this might appear to be simply a matter of preferring to be with friends of one's own background, there has been increased evidence on many college campuses of a growing racial "divide"—with marked friction between African-American, white, and other racial or ethnic group minority students.

Steven Philipp examined this issue in a study comparing African-American and European-American participation in a range of leisure activities. Although the two groups of survey respondents had similar socioeconomic characteristics—in terms of household size, median income, educational background, and gender—there were statistically significant differences in the ratings of "appeal" and "comfort" that they assigned to different activities. Philipp concludes that continuing discriminatory practices in such areas as housing, employment, and education extend also to many recreation and park settings. He continues:

> Viewed from this position, nearly all of the activities in the investigation that showed significantly lower African-American appeal or comfort were located outside of the study area, in public settings located in other areas of the city or beyond: mountains, beaches, zoos, festivals, restaurants, museums, picnic areas, snow skiing resorts, and country clubs. Conversely, all the leisure activities that showed significantly higher African-American appeal or comfort were found in the study neighborhoods . . . . The lower levels of appeal or comfort may be associated with perceptions of present or historic patterns of discrimination and feeling unwelcome in these leisure areas.[42]

Supporting this view and giving credence to the marginality theory of racial behavior, a study by P. C. West found that African-American residents tended to use Detroit city parks more than whites, and that whites from Detroit used parks in the wider tricounty regional area more than African-Americans.[43] Poorer access to transportation and feelings of being unwelcome or unsafe in the regional parks because of interracial prejudice were the apparent reasons for the failure of the African-American residents to use the broader park system.

Implications for Recreation and Park Managers

What are the implications of these findings for professional leisure-service managers? First, recreation and park managers must make a greater effort to recognize and respond to the special needs and interests of all racial and ethnic minority populations—including the considerable number of individuals who have come to North America from European countries. The new emphasis on multicultural approaches to the teaching of literature, art, music, history, and the other social sciences that have been widely adopted in many school systems should be reflected in recreation and leisure-service programming as well.

To accomplish this, it will be necessary to have a dialogue with representatives of different racial or ethnic groups, through informal consultation and diverse representation on advisory councils and committees—and by achieving a greater balance on all levels of agency staffing. While various legislative acts in the United States, including the Civil Rights Act of 1991, are intended to prevent overt job discrimination based on race, color, religion, sex, national origin, or disability, it will be necessary for agency heads to go beyond mandated guidelines to achieve more representative staff balance.

Beyond this, efforts should be made to make programs truly multicultural. Certainly, Western culture has been dramatically enriched by the contributions of African-Americans, Hispanics, and Asian-Americans, with leading performers from these groups being featured within the realms of motion pictures, television, music, dance, and the theater.

Many public recreation and park departments sponsor courses, workshops, performance series, and other events that present African-American or other minority group artists or that recount the history and contributions of different races or ethnic groups. Such programs serve to enrich the general public's understanding of the nation's total multicultural heritage, and to help members of minority groups gain an understanding of their own background, which is often a higher degree of pride in their own traditions.

Such attention to the special cultural interests and needs of different ethnic and racial groups must be applied to members of newer immigrant groups as well. In some cases, Sessoms and Orthner write:

> . . . many of these new immigrants wish to maintain their culture, not become assimilated as Americans. They want their children to play soccer, not football; they prefer to speak their native tongue, not to have to communicate in English; they would like to make America a mosaic, not a melting pot. Their sense of culture and cultural priorities are different; they wish to maintain their values, their way of life, and they are often unaware of our systems and approaches to service.[44]

This reality poses a problem for leisure-service program managers in that providing exclusionary attention to the needs and backgrounds of members of different minority groups runs the risk of helping to create a totally fragmented society—with a loss of the nation's uniquely American cultural identity and set of common values.

This priority is particularly important in the face of the growing hostility and racial antagonism within the larger society and, in some cases, between members of different ethnic minorities—such as the conflicts between African-American and Hispanic or Asian-American residents in different regions of the nation.

Whatever the origins of the conflicts, it is essential that recreation and leisure-service managers plan programs that will contribute to intergroup understanding and favorable relations. This may be done through community celebrations, holidays, ethnic and folk festivals, friendly sports competition, and a host of other program activities. It is also essential that leisure-service managers continue to strive to overcome the long-standing patterns of prejudice and racial discord that linger in many communities today. For example, in 1995 the placement of a statue honoring Arthur Ashe, a great African-American tennis champion, known in his later years as a successful author and leading humanitarian, led to an abrasive racial controversy in Richmond, Virginia. The plan was not only to place the statue of Ashe on Richmond's Monument Avenue, a boulevard that the National Park Service has called the "South's grandest commemorative precinct dedicated to the heroes of the Lost Cause," but to place it close to statues of five leading Confederate statesmen or military heroes. Both blacks and whites objected raucously to this controversial decision.[45]

In other cities, conflicts over the assignment of staff personnel on ethnic grounds or the use of publicly owned facilities by sports groups that do not serve diverse racial populations have also proven to be inflammatory.[46]

A FINAL CONCERN

No discussion of racial and ethnic influences on leisure would be complete without recognizing that the majority population in the United States and Canada still consists of whites of European ancestry.

Historically, many individuals from the same European background have tended to band together in sports or gymnastic societies or in folklore groups, sometimes in connection with churches that continue to stress the particular national language and customs to second- or third-generation members of their congregations. Often, public recreation and park departments may assist such groups by providing facilities for their meetings or sponsoring large festivals that showcase their traditional arts.

In some regions or cities, members of a particular national group may still tend to cluster in certain neighborhoods, where the stores, churches, or other community-service organizations continue to meet their specialized needs.

Although the issue of bilingual instruction in public schools has been made controversial in some cities—particularly with reference to Hispanic-Americans—recent research confirms that the majority of citizens of Spanish descent speak and read English and are determined to be absorbed within the majority culture. Richard Brookhiser summarizes some surprising results from a private survey of Hispanic opinion in the United States:

> The Latino National Political Survey found that the very labels "Hispanic" and "Latino" are rejected by those on whom they are pasted. Americans of Latin-American origin think of themselves as urban Americans, Mexican Americans or Puerto Ricans whenever they think in ethnic terms. Mostly they think of joining the American mainstream . . . Hispanics are going the way of the Germans [who have been thoroughly assimilated]. By 2050, burritos will be as all-American as Budweiser.[47]

A final concern for recreation and leisure authorities must be white Americans who are increasingly falling into the category of the economically disadvantaged. Although racial and ethnic minority populations—particularly those who are nonwhite—have tended to fall disproportionately into the lower socioeconomic brackets, with the crime, welfare, substance abuse, educational, and other statistical imbalances traditionally associated with poverty, the majority of poor Americans are of European descent.

There is increasing evidence that, with changing economic conditions, more and more white Americans are slipping from the middle socioeconomic group into the lower income brackets, with higher statistics of children being born out of wedlock, unemployment, and similar problems. The term "underclass" has generally been applied to urban or rural members of racial or ethnic minorities who have remained in poverty through successive generations. Today, it is increasingly being applied to whites. Charles Murray writes:

> The [growing] white underclass will begin to show its face in isolated ways. Look for certain schools in the white neighborhoods to get a reputation as being unteachable, with large numbers of disruptive students and indifferent parents. Talk to the police; listen for stories about white neighborhoods where the incidence of domestic disputes and casual violence has been shooting up. Look for white neighborhoods with high concentrations of drug activity and large numbers of men who have dropped out of the labor force.[48]

This trend has major implications for the providers of recreation and leisure services who have increasingly come to rely on revenue sources such as program fees and charges—which, by and large, can be paid only by reasonably affluent community residents. It suggests that large numbers of whites, along with members of other racial and ethnic minorities, will constitute an economically disadvantaged class in the years ahead, and that recreation and park managers will need to develop program strategies to serve such individuals. In an era in which recreation has become increasingly commodified, this priority will represent a serious challenge.

SUMMARY

Major influences on recreation and leisure in contemporary society are the demographic factors of gender and race. This chapter defines these terms and shows how they have affected recreational participation in the past and continue to do so today.

As the chapter notes, women and girls have historically been denied many of the leisure opportunities open to men and boys. However, the feminist movement has succeeded in urging colleges, school systems, and community recreation agencies to provide more support to female participants in a wide range of sports and physical activities. This also helps women to develop positive self-images and feelings of empowerment. In addition, many women have overcome barriers to professional advancement in various types of agencies in the leisure-service field. Women are also being admitted to business and social groups that had excluded females in the past.

The status of males with respect to recreation and leisure is also discussed. In the past, many men were pressured to adopt stereotypical "macho" roles in leisure activities. Today, they are being encouraged to play a more open, sensitive, and creative role in their recreational pursuits, as well as in domestic life and their relationships.

The issue of homosexuality is dealt with as well. The chapter points out that although much progress has been made in terms of acceptance, many organizations continue to resist gays and lesbians in professional roles. In turn, homosexuals have developed a wide range of recreational groups and are beginning to be courted as patrons by different sectors of the commercial recreation fields.

A second major section of the chapter deals with race and ethnicity. America's history of racial and ethnic discrimination is reviewed, along with the progress that has been made in serving minority populations and in developing a multicultural approach to recreation programming. Recent research examining the differences among various racial and ethnic groups in terms of leisure interests and values is examined, along with the theories that have been offered to explain these differences. In an era of increasing hostility on many levels, it is essential that organized recreation service contribute to positive intergroup relations in community life.

Questions for Class Discussion or Essay Examinations

1. How have women's roles with respect to recreation and leisure differed from those of men, in terms of societal attitudes and constraints, throughout history? How have they changed from the past? As a class, have male and female students analyze and compare their gender-related patterns of leisure interests and involvement.

2. Why is the area of sport and active physical recreation particularly important to girls and women from a feminist perspective? What has been the impact of legislation, court cases, and similar factors in terms of programming policies and other leisure-related areas?

3. Although there is still significant resistance to considering homosexuals as a minority population comparable to women or racial minorities, there has been major progress in terms of their legal standing and status in community life. What issues do you perceive as critical in terms of involving gays and lesbians as identifiable groups in community recreation programs—and what policies would you support in this area?

4. The United States has traditionally regarded itself as a leading example of democracy. With respect to racial prejudice and discrimination, has this actually been the case? Specifically, how have racial or ethnic minorities been treated in terms of recreation and leisure? What progress has been made recently—and what problems continue to exist?

5. In terms of the general cultural scene, members of different racial and ethnic minorities have gained prominence in recent years in film, television, and other artistic or literary areas. What images are generally presented?

Endnotes

[3] James Murphy, E. William Niepoth, Lynn Jamieson, and John Williams, *Leisure Systems: Critical Concepts and Applications* (Champaign, Ill: Sagamore Publishing, 1991).

[4] August Hollingshead, *Elmtown's Youth: The Impact of Social Class on Adolescence* (New York: Wiley, 1949):157.

[5] Robert Havighurst, "The Leisure Activities of the Middle-Aged," *American Journal of Sociology* (1957): 157–162.

[6] B. Rosenberg and Brian Sutton-Smith, "A Revised Conception of Masculine-Feminine Differences in Play Activities," *Journal of Genetic Psychology* (1960): 165–170.

[7] James Gentry and Mildred Doering, "Sex Role Orientation in Leisure," *Journal of Leisure Research* 2 (1979): 102–105.

[8] Foster Rhea Dulles, *A History of Recreation: America Learns to Play* (New York: Appleton-Century-Crofts, 1965): 96.

[9] Bill Gilbert and Nancy Williamson, "Sport Is Unfair to Women," *Sports Illustrated* (28 May 1973): 85.

[10] "Men vs. Women," *U.S. News & World Report* (8 August 1988): 50.

[11] Katha Pollitt, "Why Boys Don't Play with Dolls," *New York Times Magazine* (8 October 1995): 46.

[12] M. Deborah Bialeschki, "The Feminist Movement and Women's Participation in Physical Recreation," *Journal of Physical Education, Recreation and Dance* (January 1990): 45–47.

[13] "Storming the Last Male Bastion," *Time* (4 July 1988): 43.

[14] Chris Woodyard, "Magic Kingdom Is Going Unisex," *New York Times* (13 May 1995): C-1.

[15] Juanita Firestone and Beth Anne Shelton, "A Comparison of Women's and Men's Leisure Time: Subtle Effects of the Double Day," *Leisure Sciences* (January–February 1994): 45.

[16] Maureen Harrington and Don Dawson, "Who Has It Best? Women's Labor Force Participation, Perceptions of Leisure, and Constraints to Enjoyment of Leisure," *Journal of Leisure Research* (Vol. 27 No.1 1995): 4–24.

[17] Andrew Kimbrell, "A Time for Men to Pull Together," *Utne Reader* (May–June 1991): 66. See also Andrew Kimbrell, *The Masculine Mystique: The Politics of Masculinity* (New York: Ballantine Books, 1995).

[18]   Ann Merrill, "A Very Down Week . . . ," *Minneapolis Star-Tribune* (11 October 1994): 1-D.

[19]   Myriam Miedzian, "Nothing's Changed in the Way We Raise Our Sons," Letter to *New York Times* (21 July 1994): A-22.

[20]   David Greenberg, "Boys and Boys Together," review of George Chauncey, *Gay New York* (New York: Basic Books, 1994), in *New York Times* (26 June 1994): 14.

[21]   Laura Stepp, "Vatican Supports Gay Bias," *New York Times* (8 July 1992): A-3.

[22]   Chris Conway, "Scornful Judge Rejects Gay Scout's Bias Claim," *Philadelphia Inquirer* (10 November 1995): B-1.

[23]   Arnold Grossman, "Until There Is Acceptance," *Journal of Physical Education, Recreation and Dance—Leisure Today* (April 1995): 47.

[24]   "San Francisco to Offer Recreation Programming for Gay, Lesbian Youth," *Dateline: NRPA* (July 1994): 2.

[25]   Beth Kivel, "Lesbian and Gay Youth and Leisure: Implications for Practitioners and Researchers," *Journal of Park and Recreation Administration* (Vol. 12 No. 4 1994): 15–28.

[26]   Brenda Pitts, "Beyond the Bars: The Development of Leisure Activity Management in the Lesbian and Gay Population in America," *Leisure Information Quarterly* (Vol. 15 No. 3 1988–1989).

[27]   Tammerlin Drummond, "Not in Kansas Any More," *Time* (25 September 1995): 54–55.

[28]   P. Rose, *They and We: Racial and Ethnic Relations in the United States,* (New York: Random House, 1964): 7–8.

[29]   Robert Hotz, "Scientists Say Race Has No Basis in Biology," *Los Angeles Times* (20 February 1995): A-2.

[30]   Boyce Rensberger, "Human Variation Is More Than Skin Deep, But Is Not Linked to Race," *Washington Post* (16 November 1994): H-1.

[31]   "People Labels," *U.S. News & World Report* (20 November 1995): 38.

[32]   Harvey Lehman and Paul Witty, *The Psychology of Play Activities* (New York: A. S. Barnes, 1927): 161.

[33]   E. Franklin Frazier, *Black Bourgeoisie* (New York: Collier Books, 1957, 1962): 169.

[34]   "Outdoor Recreation for America," *Report to the President and Congress by the Outdoor Recreation Resources Review Commission* (Washington, D.C.: Government Printing Office, 1962): 28.

[35]   S. M. Stamps and M. B. Stamps, "Race, Class and Leisure Activities of Urban Residents," *Journal of Leisure Research* (Vol. 17 No. 1 1985): 40–55.

[36]   J. Dwyer and P. Gobster, "Recreation Opportunity and Cultural Diversity," *Parks and Recreation* (September 1992): 22–31.

[37]   Myron Floyd, James Gramann, and Rogelio Saenz, "Effects of Acculturation and Structural Assimilation in Resource-Based Recreation: The Case of Mexican-Americans," *Journal of Leisure Research* (Vol. 25 No. 1 1993): 6–21.

[38]   Maria Allison and Charles Geiger, "Nature of Leisure Activities Among the Chinese-American Elderly," *Leisure Sciences* 15 (1993): 309–319.

[39]   Myron Floyd, Kimberly Shinew, Francis McGuire, and Francis Noe, "Race, Class and Leisure Activity Preferences: Marginality and Ethnicity Revisited," *Journal of Leisure Research* (Vol. 26 No. 2 1994): 159.

[40]   Public Notice of U.S. Department of Justice and U.S. Health, Inc., *Philadelphia Inquirer* (20 May 1989): 4-A. See also Carolyn Skorneck, "A Program to Remedy Bias," Associated Press (3 January 1992).

[41]   Glen Macnow, "Progress Slow for Blacks in NFL," *Philadelphia Inquirer* (14 January 1992): 3-D.

[42]   Steven Philipp, "Race and Leisure Constraints," *Leisure Sciences* 17 (1995): 109–120.

[43]   P. C. West, "Urban Regional Parks and Black Minorities: Subculture, Marginality, and Interracial Relations in Park Use in the Detroit Metropolitan Area," *Leisure Sciences* 11 (1989): 11–28.

44 H. Douglas Sessoms and Dennis Orthner, "Parks and Recreation and Our Growing Invisible Populations," *Parks and Recreation* (August 1992): 63.

45 For a full account of Ashe's career and confrontation with racial prejudice, see Arthur Ashe, *Days of Grace: A Memoir* (New York: Alfred Knopf, 1993).

46 Amy Rosenberg and Gwen Knapp, "High and Dry Above a Tide of Diversity," *Philadelphia Inquirer* (27 March 1994): A-1.

47 Richard Brookhiser, "The Melting Pot Is Still Simmering," *Time* (1 March 1993): 72.

48 Charles Murray, "The Emerging White Underclass," *Philadelphia Inquirer* (15 November 1993): A-15.

Social Functions of
Community Recreation

At an October 24th [1994] press conference in Washington, D.C., the National Recreation and Park Association released a new study giving evidence that a collective answer for many serious social issues, including juvenile crime, can be found in local park and recreation departments.

The study, "Beyond Fun and Games: Emerging Roles of Public Recreation," illustrates recreation-based programs that are successful at reducing crime, improving health and quality of life, and creating safer communities. In addition, the recreation programs profiled in the study are. . . replicable for other communities around the country. "This study reveals the broad range of public programs, services and resources that make recreation an essential human service," said R. Dean Tice, NRPA executive director.[1]

INTRODUCTION

As Chapter 2 shows, past definitions of recreation suggested that it served to restore participants' energy for renewed work while being carried out without extrinsic purpose. Today, it is quite clear that this is no longer the case. Contemporary recreation programs and services—whether sponsored by public, nonprofit, educational, therapeutic, or other types of agencies—are goal-oriented and intended to achieve constructive outcomes for both participants and the community at large.

---

[1] R. Dean Tice, "Beyond Fun and Games," *Dateline: NRPA* (December 1994): 1.

These outcomes range from improving the quality of life for all community residents and reducing antisocial and destructive uses of leisure, to promoting the arts, serving special populations, and protecting the environment. This chapter outlines the societal benefits of organized recreation service in detail and provides a strong rationale for supporting recreation as an essential community function.

NEW EMPHASIS ON COMMUNITY BENEFITS

Thus far in this text, recreation and leisure have been described conceptually as important aspects of human experience. We now examine their contribution to community well-being on a broader scale. The term "community" is used here to mean a significant clustering of people who have a common bond, such as the residents of a city, town, or neighborhood. It may also refer to other aggregations of people, such as the employees of a company or those who live and work on an armed forces base.

Until recently, there was little concerted effort to identify the values and outcomes of community recreation. However, beginning with the period of fiscal austerity that affected many units of government and nonprofit social agencies during the 1980s, it became necessary to document the positive benefits derived from organized recreation programs and services in order to secure support for them.

Over the last several years, a number of major reports have been issued that present the demonstrated outcomes of organized recreation. One report by the Parks and Recreation Federation of Ontario, Canada, and several cooperating Canadian organizations concluded that the benefits of community recreation fell under four major headings: personal, social, economic, and environmental. Under social benefits, for example, this report summarized research findings documenting the contributions of organized recreation services in the following categories:

> Building strong communities; reducing alienation, loneliness and antisocial behaviors; promoting ethnic and cultural harmony; building strong families; providing for community involvement and shared management and ownership of resources; creating quality-of-life opportunities for people with a disability and disadvantaged individuals; providing foundations for community pride; and complementing protective services for latchkey children.[2]

In another detailed text in the early 1990s, Driver, Brown, and Peterson outlined the overall benefits of organized recreation services, with an emphasis on recreation and park functions.[3] Similarly, a major study supported by the National Institute on Disability and Rehabilitation Research of the U.S. Department of Education summarized hundreds of research reports showing the benefits of therapeutic recreation—chiefly in a medical or rehabilitative context.[4] And, in the mid-1990s, a task force affiliated with the National Recreation and Park Association initiated a systematic analysis of the social functions of community recreation in dealing with major community needs—including problems involving ethnic or racial relations, the environment, disability, family life, and poverty.[5]

RECREATION'S CONTRIBUTION TO COMMUNITY LIFE

This chapter outlines 11 major areas of recreation's contribution to community life, providing documentation both from formal research studies and from anecdotal or qualitative evidence. In a number of cases, the functions about to be described are similar to those presented in Chapter 3 as personal outcomes of recreation. However, in this context, they apply to broader community needs or to the lives of major groups in the population.

FUNCTION NO. I   Enriching the Quality of Life

PURPOSE   to enrich the quality of life in the community setting by providing pleasurable and constructive leisure opportunities for residents of all ages, backgrounds, and socioeconomic classes.

Recreation's most obvious value is the opportunity that it provides for fun, relaxation, and pleasure through active participation in sports and games, social events, cultural pursuits, and a host of hobbies and leisure involvements. Throughout all of society—particularly in larger cities, which often tend to be impersonal and cold—people need meaningful ways to make contact with each other in direct, open, and friendly situations. Janet MacLean has written:

> In a . . . hurried, noise-bombarded, harried, compacted, technological society, the opportunity for identity, positive self-image, social interaction, creative expression, and even the intellectual or physical stimuli to maintain physical and mental health may come in exciting leisure opportunities or not at all.[6]

One very specific contribution of recreation to the quality of life lies in its value in overcoming stress. Pollster Louis Harris found in a national survey that 89 percent of American adults reported experiencing high levels of stress, with almost 60 percent feeling great stress at least once or twice a week. Strategies found to be effective for controlling stress were physical activities that discharged tension or social situations that were relaxing. Other means of reducing stress, Harris noted, were pursuing hobbies, playing or listening to music, exercise, and other satisfying recreational experiences.[7]

Parks provide a vivid illustration of the social value of leisure. During the warmer months of the year, they provide outdoor living spaces that are used by people of all ages and backgrounds. In swimming pools, zoos, playgrounds, nature centers, and sports facilities, community residents enjoy vigorous and sociable forms of group recreation. In community centers, children and adults can join clubs and special interest groups, take courses in a variety of enriching hobbies or self-development skills, and find both relaxation and challenge. Thus, in many ways, organized leisure service contributes significantly to the overall quality and enjoyment of community life.

A number of research studies have examined the degree to which recreation and leisure contribute to residents' satisfaction with community life. Lawrence Allen, for example, demonstrated their importance by citing evidence to show that, out of seven dimensions of community life, recreation was the best predictor of overall satisfaction among residents surveyed.[8] In a later study, Jeffres and Dobos summarized the findings of three surveys of demographically diverse residents in a midwestern metropolitan area. They found that while individuals' assessments of the quality of life and leisure opportunities varied according to their environmental circumstances and awareness of community recreation resources, leisure values generally were significantly and positively related to perceptions of the quality of life in the area.[9]

FUNCTION NO. 2   Contributing to Personal Development

PURPOSE   to contribute to a person's healthy physical, social, emotional, intellectual, and spiritual development, as well as to family cohesion and well-being.

As earlier chapters in this text illustrate, recreation does far more than simply provide fun or pleasure for participants. It also makes an important contribution to their growth and development at each stage of life. While we often tend to focus on such obvious goals as improving physical fitness or social adjustment, recreation participation also can help people to reach their full potential as integrated human beings. For example, psychologists point out that many individuals have vivid memories of sports experiences in their childhood. Such experiences often play a key role in developing positive self-concepts and, beyond this, help to strengthen the bonds between parents and their children. In addition to providing benefits for children, they may also contribute to the parent's own sense of well-being and mental health.[10] Recreation promotes healthy growth with joy, enthusiasm, and a sense of intense commitment and pleasure that reinforces learning and involvement. And society benefits when children and youth have experiences that promote their physical health, social competence, emotional well-being, and intellectual growth, and when family "togetherness" is promoted.

Varied types of community-sponsored recreation programs provide a rich setting in which children and youth are able to explore and confirm their personal values, experience positive peer relationships, discover their talents, and achieve other important personal benefits. Writing in the *New York Times*, Roger Rosenblatt expresses the concern that many young people today are growing up in a "moral vacuum." He describes the "character education" movement that is striving to fill this gap: a number of boards of education have developed programs designed to inculcate positive core values that relate to such issues as self-respect and responsibility, loyalty, self-discipline, good citizenship, stereotyping and prejudice, and family values.[11]

Similarly, there is growing interest in the emerging concept of "emotional intelligence," as described in Chapter 3. This quality differs from the possession of purely verbal, mathematical, or intellectual skills in that it deals with one's ability to live life in an intelligent and sensitive way—making wise choices, exhibiting zeal and persistence, maintaining self-control, and responding to others with empathy and support.[12]

Camp Fire Boys and Girls, for example, states that its fundamental purpose is to provide, through a program of informal education (which includes camping, recreation, and service projects), opportunities for youth to realize their potential and to function effectively as caring, self-directed individuals, responsible to themselves and to others. It continues:

> To achieve this purpose, Camp Fire works with individuals, communities and society as a whole to encourage the development and preservation of spiritual and ethical values; the realization of the dignity and worth of each individual; and the elimination of human barriers which prejudge individuals. . . .[13]

Similarly, the Girl Scouts of America strives to help young girls grow up in a healthy and positive way, able to face the stresses and challenges that threaten all children and youth today. Many of its program activities promote self-knowledge, creative thinking and problem-solving, feelings of self-worth, skills in relating to people, and other important areas of personal growth. Illustrative of its mission with respect to the emotional and social development of its members is the Contemporary Issues Series of leadership manuals published by the Girl Scouts. The series contains such titles as:

Tune In to Well-Being, Say No to Drugs: Substance Abuse

Staying Safe: Preventing Child Abuse

Girls Are Great: Growing Up Female

Into the World of Today and Tomorrow: Leading Girls to Mathematics, Science and Technology

Reaching Out: Preventing Youth Suicide

Caring and Coping: Facing Family Crises
Decisions for Your Life: Preventing Teenage Pregnancy
Valuing Differences: Pluralism[14]

How effective are such programs? While it is difficult to demonstrate their effectiveness through rigorous experimental research studies, there is a wealth of information regarding the positive benefits of membership in youth organizations. A 1994 report by the Boy Scouts of America is particularly convincing in this regard. Summarizing the results of three surveys conducted by Louis Harris Associates of several thousand men and boys, including present and former adult Scout leaders and non-leaders as well as boy members and non-members, the report found that there was powerful evidence of the value of scouting. Overall, the study compared the values, standards, and life experiences of men and boys of different ages, racial and ethnic backgrounds, and geographic locations. It found that, within a national pattern of declining ethical and moral standards in such areas as cheating, shoplifting, carrying a gun to school, drinking and using drugs, and similar activities, both former and present scouts reported higher standards for personal behavior than did non-scouts. In terms of social and environmental responsibility, relationships with co-workers and colleagues, and a host of other family- and work-related functions, those with extended scouting backgrounds ranked far higher than others.[15]

FUNCTION NO. 3   Making the Community a More Attractive Place to Live

PURPOSE   to improve the physical environment and make the community a more attractive place to live by providing a network of parks and open spaces, incorporating leisure attractions in the redesign and rehabilitation of run-down urban areas, and fostering positive environmental attitudes and policies.

In local governments, the recreation function is closely linked to the management of parks and other open spaces, historical sites, and cultural facilities. Together, they help to make cities and towns more physically appealing as places to live. In the post–World War II decades, it was recognized that many of our cities had deteriorated greatly. Gradually, we have come to realize that we can no longer permit our urban centers to be congested by cars, poisoned by smog, cut off from natural vistas, and scarred by the random disposal of industrial debris, ugly signs, auto junkyards, decaying railroad yards, and burned-out slum tenements. It is essential to protect and grace rivers with trees, shaded walkways, boating facilities, and cafes; to eliminate auto traffic in selected areas by creating pedestrian shopping centers; and to provide increased numbers of malls, playgrounds, and sitting areas that furnish opportunities for both passive and active uses of leisure.

In a number of American cities, once-abandoned freight yards, wharves, waterfront ports, or junk-filled streams winding through inner-city slums have been dramatically transformed into new, attractive open plazas and park-like settings. Frequently with the help of the business community, these eyesores have been rebuilt into condominium housing, offices, up-scale shopping centers, marinas for boating or waterfront play, and outdoor amphitheaters for various forms of entertainment throughout the year. Run-down architectural masterpieces have been restored, and older ethnic neighborhoods have been preserved while adding restaurants, art galleries, and other cultural activities that appeal to tourists. In some cases, cities have been farsighted enough not to have to reclaim their waterfronts. Chicago, for example, thanks to a series of turn-of-the-century lawsuits initiated by A. Montgomery Ward—a leading businessman who was also a strong conservationist—never had to reclaim its priceless lakefront from rotting wharves and warehouses:

> It has preserved the area as practically a 20-some-mile-long park lined with smooth, paved bicycle and jogging paths, marinas, parks, picnic grounds, barbecue pits and beaches whose fair-weather scenes, smells, and patrons provide revealing insights into the ethnic mix of the Midwest's capital. . . . Sport fishing is coming back on [Lake Michigan]. And boating never left. Few cities can rival Chicago's view on summer Sundays when the yellow sun burns brightly on the azure lake, dotted by hundreds of brightly colored sails and pleasure craft on comfortable cruises and in regular regattas.[16]

Beyond recreation's role in helping to maintain and improve the environment in the central cities themselves, it also is a key player in helping to reclaim or protect natural areas within the larger framework of surrounding county or metropolitan regions. Environmental planners and park authorities are collaborating in many communities on remodeling abandoned railway corridors and establishing greenways to permit outdoor play or environmental education, provide hiking trails, or protect historic sites.[17]

Yet, realistically, much outdoor play tends to result in damage to the environment through threats to wildlife, erosion of natural areas, or pollution of streams and lakes. More environmentally sensitive policies and enforcement efforts can help to prevent recreational activities that harm natural settings. Today, many recreation planners are taking environmental concerns into account as they design new facilities that protect and enhance natural vistas and meet practical leisure-related needs.

FUNCTION NO. 4   Preventing Antisocial Uses of Leisure

PURPOSE   to prevent or reduce antisocial or destructive uses of leisure, such as delinquency or substance abuse, by providing challenging programs that offer young people constructive and enjoyable recreational opportunities linked to other needed services.

As Chapter 8 will show, one of the major objectives of the early recreation movement in the United States and Canada was to help prevent or reduce juvenile delinquency. Indeed, during the last decades of the nineteenth century and for much of the first half of the twentieth century, it was widely accepted that vigorous group activities were helpful in burning up the excess energy of youth, diverting their aggressive or antisocial drives, and "keeping them off the streets" and sheltered from exposure to criminal influences.

In the United States, there was widespread support for playgrounds, community centers, and other recreation programs for city youth by the police, juvenile court judges, and other youth authorities (see page 205). A number of sociologists pointed out that much delinquent behavior on the part of younger children stemmed from the search for excitement, risk-taking, and the need to impress their peers. It was argued that, if other, more challenging forms of constructive play could be offered to youngsters at this stage, it would be possible to divert them from more serious involvement in criminal activities.

On the other hand, some investigators identified play as one of the ways in which delinquency becomes established as a way of life. Tannenbaum located the beginning of the alienation of gang youth from societal controls and values in the random play activities of youngsters.

> In the very beginning, the definition of the situation by the young delinquent may be in the form of play, adventure, excitement, interest, mischief, fun. Breaking windows, annoying people . . . playing truant—all are forms of play, adventure, excitement.[19]

Other investigators pointed out that much juvenile crime was committed for "the hell of it"—apart from considerations of gain or profit. Gradually, however, social workers and other experts on juvenile crime sought other explanations for youth delinquency. One school of sociologists developed psychological theories that emphasized the impact of the child's personality: children from broken homes with unstable, high-impulse behavior patterns, with a need for excitement, and with poor tolerance for delayed gratification were seen as delinquent-prone types. Other behavioral scientists held that juvenile delinquency was a cultural problem whose real roots were in the society itself. They cited research showing that delinquency was highest in poor neighborhoods marked by slum housing, ineffective schools, the lack of desirable adult role models, and limited opportunities for social advancement. Some sociologists argued that the antisocial behavior of juvenile gangs represented hostility toward accepted middle-class values and the substitution of lower-class norms, such as respect for toughness, masculinity, and physical prowess. Others developed typologies of gang behavior, such as fighting, criminal, and retreatist gangs.[20]

Increasingly, sociologists began to conclude that juvenile crime was almost always committed for utilitarian gain and that to view it as a form of negative play was no longer realistic. Short and Strodbeck wrote:

> Weapons and the intent of gang conflict are more lethal, and "kicks" more addicting. Theoretically, delinquency is seen as rooted less in community tradition and "fun," and more in frustration and protest or in the serious business of preparing for manhood as conceived by the gang members, including the "mysterious and powerful underworlds of organized crime."[21]

Beyond this, in many so-called ghetto areas, membership in a gang becomes a form of survival and a means of protecting oneself against extortion and random violence. Particularly in the barrios of southwestern cities, gang membership involves strong ties of loyalty and brotherhood that may continue through the years of adolescence and become strengthened through stays in correctional youth centers and later criminal activity and prison sentences.

Despite such motivations for gang affiliation, it is also true that a considerable amount of juvenile delinquency is carried out in a spirit of excitement and challenge and in response to what young lawbreakers describe as "boredom—nothing to do" (see page 100). While it may be hard to conceive of mugging, savage gang attacks, or rape as forms of play, they certainly involve risk and a spirit of adventure that might otherwise be found in various forms of thrill-seeking outdoor recreation.

Riemer points out, however, that social scientists generally have consistently ignored the idea of deviant behavior as being as form of fun. They have been unwilling to treat juvenile delinquency or other forms of deviant youth behavior as activity carried on for hedonistic, pleasure-seeking reasons:

> Rather than incorporate this simple, yet potentially useful dimension into our understanding of deviance phenomena, sociologists have continued to be preoccupied with elaborating the more . . . psychological and sociological explanations.[22]

It is important to recognize that deviant behavior is now found across all socioeconomic class lines. Only a portion of today's delinquents are lower-class urban youth involved in gangs. A considerable amount of crime is carried on by teenagers, often of middle- or upper-class backgrounds, in well-to-do suburbs. There has been an increase in amateur shoplifting, auto theft, and vandalism by such youth. Thrill-seeking and joyriding are cited as the primary reasons for car theft by juveniles, and vandalism is obviously motivated by reasons other than economic gain. In addition to such forms of delinquent behavior, many other acts reveal a search for excitement on the part of modern teenagers. Drag-racing or pranks involving desperate risks (like playing "chicken" and risking head-on collisions on highways or in tunnels) are examples of such thrill-seeking stunts. Indeed, one study found that the highest rate of illegal drug use is among families with over $50,000 in annual income; typically, many teenagers in such families are bored and searching for "kicks."

Linkage Between Recreation and Delinquency

While it is difficult to prove the specific benefits of organized recreation services for at-risk youth through experimental research, a number of other studies have demonstrated positive outcomes.

In an extensive study of the relationship between sports and delinquency, Donnelly noted several research reports that demonstrate the value of athletic participation. One such study, involving several midwestern high schools, found that only 7 percent of the boys who had participated for at least a full year in an interscholastic sport had been apprehended for delinquent behavior, compared with 17 percent of nonathletes.[23] It seems likely that many of the elements of sports competition, including the physical risk, excitement and emotional highs, may satisfy the impulses that among nonathletic teenagers are channeled into delinquent behavior.

M. S. Searle documented the effects of youth sports programs in reducing juvenile delinquency in towns in northern Manitoba, Canada, as compared to communities that had not undertaken such programs.[24] Kelly and Baer found that juvenile delinquents who had taken part in Outward Bound programs had a substantially lower rate of recidivism than young offenders who had not been involved in such experiences.[25] Similarly, John Crompton has described a three-year study of several English cities that linked sports and other leisure pursuits with counseling and other probationary or social services for high-risk juvenile offenders. The final report of the British Sports Council, which evaluated the project, concluded that its overall impact was positive, although British confidentiality laws limited the ability to publish actual recidivism rates.[26]

It is unlikely that recreation programs can be effective in working with hard-core juvenile gang members or individuals who are seriously antisocial and committed to a criminal lifestyle. Such individuals tend to avoid involvement in organized youth service agencies and shun the rules and disciplined behavior required in youth clubs and sports. However, many other adolescents who are at risk because of conflict-ridden or dysfunctional home and neighborhood environments *can* find organized recreation a rewarding alternative to the lures of street gang activity.

It should be stressed that, for purposes of reducing delinquency, recreation must be part of a total effort to restructure the environment and values of at-risk youth. This restructuring should include provision of such services as substance abuse treatment, job training and vocational assistance, health and family services, legal assistance and gang-directed projects, family programs, and improved housing and educational services. Often, recreation can serve as a "threshold" activity that encourages young people to enter youth agencies or social programs, where the first contacts are made that may lead to a fuller range of involvement.

Numerous cities in the United States and Canada have undertaken programs that link recreation and park activities with other community services. For example, the Dallas, Texas, Park and Recreation Department sponsors an aggressive gang intervention program that reaches out to at-risk youth with varied services.[27] The Chicago Housing Authority initiated a highly successful Midnight Basketball League designed to serve older youth and young adults by providing exciting league play during the hours of the night when much criminal activity takes place. A number of other cities have begun similar programs, as have county recreation agencies in such places as Prince Georges County, Maryland.[28]

Probably the leading example of such at-risk youth programs is to be found in Phoenix, Arizona, where the public Parks, Recreation and Library Department has sought special funding from a variety of sources to sponsor the following innovative services:

1. Several new teen centers in high-impact crime neighborhoods or public housing projects;

2. Numerous special interest clubs to serve adolescents, along with talent shows, sports leagues, dances, tournaments, adventure trips, and similar recreation programs;

3. Employment assistance through a Teens-n-Training Project partially funded through the Job Training Partnership Act and including the provision of occupational skills, counseling, and job development services;

4. Cultural enrichment activities promoting multicultural awareness, with an emphasis on African-American and Hispanic themes;

5. Teen leadership forums, councils, and peer mentorship programs; and

6. An extensive Juvenile Curfew Program, in which the public recreation agency works with police and other authorities to counsel hundreds of youthful curfew violators.[29]

Increasingly, recreation is being recognized as an essential ingredient in curbing juvenile crime and violence. In July 1994, for example, *Time* reported that Denver, Colorado, was

> . . . determined to head off a reprise of last year, when a string of vicious youth crimes unhinged the city's calm. The upshot is an activities budget of $6 million, twice the amount allotted a year ago. Recreation programs—from swimming and camping to video production—have grown from 900 last year to 1,300 this summer.[30]

On a national scale, Schultz, Crompton, and Witt confirm that a majority of the public recreation and park agencies responding to a recent survey indicated that they had developed special programs targeted toward at-risk children and youth. Such programs frequently involve collaborative efforts with the business community, foundations, voluntary agencies, school districts, and law enforcement agencies. It should be noted that 72 percent of the public agencies providing such programs emphasizing prevention initiated them after 1989—illustrating growing governmental awareness of the problems of at-risk youth and the role of recreation in meeting their needs.[31]

FUNCTION NO. 5   Improving Intergroup and Intergenerational Relations

PURPOSE   to help improve intergroup relations among community residents of different racial, ethnic, or religious backgrounds, and among different generational groups, through shared recreational and cultural experiences.

As Chapter 5 points out, racial and ethnic identity plays an important role in shaping the leisure-related values and behavior patterns of community residents throughout the United

States and Canada. Clearly this presents a challenge to recreation and park professionals in terms of the need to provide program opportunities suited to the tastes and traditions of different racial and ethnic groups, while at the same time maintaining a core of shared values and interests.

A related concern involves the need to use recreation as a means of overcoming the hostility and tension that have been building in many communities due to economic competition, negative stereotyping of minority populations, and other social factors that promote bigotry such as the growing use of the Internet to incite prejudice.[32] In the late 1980s, there was considerable evidence that racism was on the rise in American society, with numerous incidents of violence and the revival of hate organizations in different regions of the country. An overwhelming 92 percent of blacks and 87 percent of whites polled by *Time* magazine in 1987 agreed that racial prejudice was still widespread in the United States. *Time* concluded:

> Though racism has ancient origins, it must be taught anew to each child, and the best way to teach it is through ignorance. "Separation of racial groups breeds fear and misunderstanding," says William Taylor of the Center for National Policy Review.[33]

Hatemongering groups on college campuses have promoted both racial and religious bigotry, and a number of riots and instances of arson directed at businesses in minority neighborhoods have testified to the increase of ethnic-based hostility. While other factors— including housing, education, political representation, and job opportunity—are critical to any solution of this problem, recreation continues to be one of the avenues in which conscious efforts may be made to improve intergroup understanding and build positive contacts.

The arts in particular represent a major area of opportunity for sharing cultural traditions and increasing the self-knowledge and pride of different racial and ethnic populations. As an example, the Recreation Department of Prince George's County, Maryland, regularly features performances by choral groups, storytellers, theater companies, and dance and music groups, as well as workshops, festivals, arts and crafts fairs, and similar activities that illustrate the history, traditions, and cultural contributions of African-American and other minority groups.

Karlis and Dawson have examined the role of recreation in helping members of different national groups to maintain their ethnic identity in Canada. In a study of participation in Greek cultural affairs in the city of Ottawa, for example, they analyzed the role of the Hellenic Community Association in serving both newly arrived Greek immigrants and those of an earlier generation who have undergone a process of cultural transition. They comment:

> A primary function of ethnic community organizations is to enhance the degree of "communityness;" that is, to remain cohesive using the processes of community development in order to preserve ethnicity. . . . To attain this objective, many ethnic community organizations, engage, consciously or otherwise, in a process of community development through recreation and leisure incorporating elements of the wider society within traditions of their particular ethnic culture.[34]

In some cases, leisure-service agencies and programs may focus on problems of intergroup hostility and prejudice through meetings, staff training programs, workshops, and similar efforts. Organizations like the YWCA have focused on the elimination of prejudice and discrimination as a key program goal, and in some cases youth camping programs have been established to promote intercultural friendship and understanding. In one such camp, the "Seeds of Peace" camp in Wayne, Maine, hundreds of Arab and Israeli boys and girls designated by their respective governments have come together for several summers to share cultural traditions and begin to build respect and friendship—with marked success.[35]

Intergenerational Programs

A related function of a growing number of leisure-service agencies involves the need to improve relationships between members of different generations—particularly between adolescents and the elderly. Research has shown that, in many cases, older citizens attending senior centers and golden age clubs are fearful of teenage youth and seek to avoid them because of repeated instances of harassment or attacks. Recognizing this problem, some agencies are establishing Intergenerational (IG) initiatives; these have been described by Marcia Cram as:

> . . . programs and exchanges that purposefully bring together old and young in ongoing planned activities designed to achieve the development of new relationships as well as specified program goals.[36]

Programs have been designed and carried out by recreation agencies in which members of one age group assist members of the other. Examples include elderly persons helping children and youth with reading and writing skills and offering support to latchkey children, and teenagers helping homebound elderly persons with household chores and providing respite aid for caregivers of persons with disabilities. Cram writes:

> Research conducted in a variety of areas demonstrates the value of IG programs in impacting social skill improvements of older adults, altering attitudes of youth towards older adults and of older adults toward youth, improving students' grades, reducing truancy, and improving high school retention rates.[37]

FUNCTION NO. 6   Strengthening Neighborhood and Community Ties

PURPOSE   to strengthen neighborhood and community life by involving residents in volunteer projects or service programs and events to enhance civic pride and morale.

An important tenet of the early recreation movement was that shared recreational experiences helped to strengthen neighborhood and community ties by giving residents of all backgrounds a sense of belonging and common purpose; helping them to maintain social traditions and cultural ties, and enabling them to join together in volunteer service roles. For example, in many Canadian cities during the early decades of the twentieth century, community-based organizations initiated the development of after-school centers and community recreation programs. In Edmonton, Alberta, ten volunteer community leagues were established that organized and conducted recreational, cultural, and educational programs within their geographical areas.

By the late 1980s, there were 139 individual community leagues in Edmonton, sustained by thousands of volunteers; approximately one-third of the city's population of 600,000 was actively involved in supporting their community leagues and participating in local programs. In many other Canadian and U.S. cities, parents' leagues sponsor youth sports activities, using public sports fields or indoor gymnasiums to schedule instructional or competitive programs year-round. Often they raise funds to rehabilitate or maintain facilities, purchase needed equipment, hire referees, or support such programs in other ways.

For the ordinary community resident, involvement in recreation programs often provides a means of developing a sense of acceptance and identity. Many communities sponsor neighborhood block parties or community festivals as a means of getting to know each other better and strengthening their feelings of unity, as well as for fund-raising purposes. Sometimes such events are even sponsored by the police. For example, a Police Open House and Community Day sponsored in North Philadelphia combined entertainment such as puppet shows, police wagon rides, children's games, and displays of police, fire, and National Guard equipment, with the obvious purpose of building favorable relations between the police and local community residents.

In the same city, residents in depressed neighborhoods have joined together to revive and rebuild drug-ridden, trash-filled, vandalized, and graffiti-covered recreation centers in cooperation with the Philadelphia Recreation Department—building a sense of civic responsibility and community pride. In Madison, Wisconsin, elderly volunteers recruited and trained through the Dane County Retired Senior Volunteer Program collect and repair used bicycles for distribution to low-income children. In cities like Eugene, Oregon, Seattle, New York and Los Angeles, thousands of volunteers contribute their efforts to diversified projects by serving as program aides, administrative assistants, event planners, and in numerous other roles.[38]

In a more formal way, citizens can assist recreation and park programs by serving on legally established boards and commissions or on district or neighborhood advisory councils. A *Parks and Recreation* editorial points out that citizen leaders, whether they serve as elected or appointed officials, and whether they are policymakers or advisors, have great influence in improving and expanding recreation and park programs, facilities, and services.

> Concerned citizens . . . can forward programs that will serve the leisure needs of the people; they can support those efforts designed to improve and expand the recreation and park profession as an enhancement of public service: and they can shape the parks and recreation program as an integral part of the community.[39]

Unselfish involvement in such civic-betterment activities is particularly important today, when many Americans see the signs of a spreading social and moral breakdown around them. As later chapters will show, growing individualism and privatization in modern society have weakened the bonds that provided support for many citizens in the past.

At such a time, it is critical that every means be explored to develop a true sense of community, of sharing and mutual support in neighborhood life. Clearly, volunteerism and the kinds of projects just described do help to promote such values and positive interactions among community residents.

FUNCTION NO. 7   Meeting the Needs of Special Populations

PURPOSE   to serve special populations like those with physical or mental disabilities, both through therapeutic recreation service in treatment settings and through community-based programs serving individuals with a broad range of disabilities.

While all people need diversified recreational opportunity, those with disabilities find it especially difficult to meet these needs in constructive and varied ways, partly because their physical or mental impairments limit their participation and partly because of society's reluctance to help them engage in activity to their full potential. Yet, recreation is of even greater importance to many disabled persons. A study published by the federal government's General Accounting Office in the late 1980s revealed that although an estimated 10 to 15 percent of the nation's 2.7 million disabled workers were capable of paid employment, less than 1 percent of those who receive job training actually go back to work. This report, which illustrates the difficulty that the Social Security Administration has had in rehabilitating disabled workers, makes it clear that great numbers of disabled individuals do *not* work and have overwhelming amounts of free time—and thus have a critical need for appropriate leisure programming.[40]

In the past, many recreation and park departments barred disabled persons from their programs claiming that to serve the disabled would require specialized leadership that their agencies could not afford to provide. The stigma that society attached to disability often caused administrators to fear that the presence of blind, retarded, or orthopedically disabled participants would be distasteful to the public at large, who might then cease to use the facilities. Sometimes parents or relatives sheltered the disabled excessively, and often the disabled person's lack of skill or fear of rejection by others limited his or her recreational participation.[41]

Today, a number of factors have combined to make this function an increasingly important one for recreation, park, and leisure-service agencies. First, public agencies have been barred by law, through Title II of the Americans With Disabilities Act of 1990, from refusing to provide disabled individuals with equal opportunities to participate in or benefit from their programs simply because of their disabilities.[42] Secondly, while the initial thrust of therapeutic recreation was to use leisure-based programs as a treatment tool in hospitals or rehabilitation settings, today an equally important goal is to provide adequate recreational opportunities to disabled persons living in the community. The emphasis has essentially been shifted toward "mainstreaming" or integrating such individuals into programs with nondisabled persons. Jane Broida sums up the present-day thrust:

> Inclusions, partnerships, and transitional services. These aren't just fads or catchy buzzwords. They are trends of the 1990s—and perhaps the 21st century—for the provision of community therapeutic recreation services. While specialized programs—those planned specifically for individuals with disabilities—will continue to fulfill the recreation needs for many people, there is a growing demand from many others for inclusive recreation opportunities [involving] participation of all individuals in activities, facilities and resources without restriction.[43]

To coordinate the various types of agencies that serve people with disabilities, some communities have formed special committees or task forces to promote or sponsor leisure-service programs. Often representatives of wheelchair sports associations, local branches of the Easter Seal Society, service clubs, fraternal organizations, the Boy Scouts and Girl Scouts, and similar organizations are members of such bodies.

Throughout this process, it is essential that disabled persons themselves be involved in determining needs and in planning programs, so that they are no longer kept in a dependent or subordinate role but are empowered to take a degree of control over their own lives.

A final major trend of the 1990s has been to extend the range of therapeutic recreation services to a number of social disabilities, rather than limiting programs to the traditional roster of physical and mental illnesses or impairments. Therapeutic recreation specialists have been joining with those in the broader field of community recreation to initiate expanded programs to serve those with problems of substance abuse, unemployment, homelessness, physical or sexual abuse, HIV-AIDS, and similar categories of disability.

FUNCTION NO. 8   Maintaining Economic Health and Community Stability

PURPOSE   to maintain the economic health and stability of communities by acting as a catalyst for business development and a source of community or regional income and employment and by keeping neighborhoods desirable places to live.

Recreation has become a major focus of business investment and an essential element in the total national economy. Some cities have set out deliberately to transform themselves into centers of entertainment and sports. San Jose, California, for example, has built a huge new downtown arena that has housed circuses, ice shows, concerts, amateur and professional sports (including the city's professional ice hockey team, the San Jose Sharks), tractor pulls, and numerous expositions. It is now moving ahead on the development of varied arts institutions, including a symphony, opera company, civic light opera company, repertory theater, and art, technology, and children's museums—all designed to breathe new life and appeal into a formerly dull and charmless city.[44] In other cases, cities depend on a single major recreational event, carried on year after year, to stimulate economic activity. For example, the Calgary Stampede in Canada, held each July for ten days

> is big business, drawing almost two million visitors annually to a raucous party that turns the entire city into a western theme park featuring rodeo events, chuckwagon racing, a huge agricultural fair and even Las Vegas-style casinos and star-studded performances.[45]

Numerous states report that recreation, when defined to include tourism, represents one of their key industries. A 1982 study of the Commonwealth of Pennsylvania showed that annual spending on recreation was responsible for $11.8 billion in revenue, with employment in all types of recreation-related positions estimated at over 415,000 jobs. Similarly, in the early 1990s, it was found that visitors to park and conservation districts and forest preserves in Illinois accounted for about $3.1 billion in revenue and created 7,000 jobs—apart from all other forms of recreational and tourist activity.[46]

For many American Indian tribes, tourism, gambling casinos, and outdoor recreation have proven to be important economic assets. Programs administered by tribal governments on about 56 million acres of Indian land from Maine to California and from Florida to Alaska help to meet the growing demand for outdoor recreation experiences, including hunting, hiking, horseback riding, biking, and such winter sports as snowmobiling.

> Tribal fish, wildlife and other natural resources support millions of recreational use days annually. Indian pow-wows, fiestas, fairs and religious ceremonies—many featuring traditional dancing, dress and foods—draw additional millions of visitors, including many from foreign countries. Indian museums, cultural centers, heritage displays, and arts and crafts shops are popular attractions.[47]

Economists and environmental planners have stressed the value of sustainable rural tourism, which does not destroy the environment and can continue to function indefinitely, in comparison to lumbering, mining, or similar commercial uses of the wilderness, which exploit natural resources for temporary economic benefit but leave them in a ravaged state. Increasingly, as Steven Burr and Jeffrey Walsh point out, tourism is being used

> as an economic development strategy for stabilizing, diversifying and improving the local economies of struggling rural communities. [In addition, planning economic development strategies helps residents become] more oriented toward meeting the general needs and concerns of the entire community . . . and function effectively as an interactive community.[48]

Evidence shows that the public, private, and commercial leisure attractions and services of cities contribute to their appeal, not only to visitors and tourists but also to potential residents and companies that are seeking to relocate. Taken altogether, it is clear that recreation represents a major economic asset on national, state, and local levels—although the actual dollar impact of specific activities, such as fairs, festivals, and other programs, may sometimes be unclear or exaggerated.[49] This is particularly true for casino gambling, in which the claims of economic benefits often do not take into account the hidden costs of gambling to the host communities.

FUNCTION NO. 9 Enriching Community Cultural Life

PURPOSE to enrich cultural life by promoting fine and performing arts, special events, and cultural programs and by supporting historic sites, folk heritage customs, and community arts institutions.

It is generally recognized that the arts provide a vital ingredient in the culture of nations. Through the continued performance and appreciation of the great works of the past, in the areas of symphonic and choral music, opera, ballet, theater, painting, and sculpture, or through contemporary ventures in newer forms of expression, such as modern dance or experimental art forms, people of every age and background gain a sense of beauty and human creativity. Although America generally lagged far behind Europe in its support for the arts, after World War II public interest and participation increased dramatically.

During the 1970s and 1980s, many public recreation and park departments assumed fuller responsibility for sponsoring or assisting programs in the arts. Such cities as Indianapolis, Seattle, Detroit, and Los Angeles began to offer extensive arts programs—including directly sponsoring music, dance, and theater performances, maintaining fine arts centers, assisting independent arts organizations, and sponsoring arts festivals and summer workshops. Barry Mangum describes the diversified cultural arts activities of the Maryland–National Capital Park and Planning Commission in Prince George's County, Maryland. This outstanding park system owns and operates two large full-time cultural arts facilities, with several galleries, a master workshop series in fine arts, a playhouse for the performing arts, and a fully equipped concert hall. Mangum writes:

> The . . . Commission's Arts Division strives to meet the needs of 700,000 residents by working with the County's cultural communities to provide the public with quality art experiences. Services offered to individual artists, performers and County-based dance, music, theater and visual arts groups include securing performing and exhibiting opportunities; financial assistance . . . ; and informational clearinghouse on County arts activities . . . . The Arts Division awards limited honoraria to provide groups with soloists, judges, and specialists for specific programs.[50]

However, in the late 1980s and early 1990s, the performing and fine arts fields began to suffer a dramatic decline in support. With tighter municipal and educational budgets, many communities reduced the financial support they had given to music, dance, and theater companies, while boards of education eliminated classes and performances in the arts.

At the same time, conservative political leaders and religious factions joined together to attack the National Endowment for the Arts, which had been responsible for funding both major arts institutions and tiny, grass-roots companies and performers throughout the United States. With a declining level of support from foundations, corporations, and private funding as well, many orchestras and other performing companies have been forced to cut back on their seasons or slash the pay and employment schedules of performers and staff members.

Within this overall picture, increasing concern has been raised about another aspect of the arts—the "popular culture," provided by the mass media of entertainment and communication. There is a growing consensus that television, movies, and much rock and rap music is contributing to a national climate that encourages crime and immorality. Elizabeth Kolbert writes:

> Americans have a starkly negative view of popular culture, and blame television more than any other factor for teen-age sex and violence . . . . These are among the findings of a *New York Times* poll [in August 1995] examining Americans' attitudes about the influence of popular culture. The results of the poll

suggest that Americans are deeply ambivalent about their own diversions. Although the average adult in the United States watches television for more than four hours a day, a little more than half of the adults polled could not think of a single good thing to say about television or about movies or popular music. Instead, nine out of ten mentioned too much sex, violence and vulgar language . . . bias and just plain stupidity.[51]

Such dissatisfaction with many of the aspects of popular culture makes it all the more imperative that community agencies, both public and nonprofit, play a stronger role in presenting programs in the arts that improve the level of popular taste and provide an opportunity for direct personal expression through music, dance, theater, and arts and crafts.

One such program is found in Vero Beach, Florida, where a major Center for the Arts has been established in the city's Riverside Park. Backed by extensive community support, successful fund-raising activities, and cooperation from hundreds of volunteers and civic groups, this Center's primary goal is to provide opportunity for the public's cultural enrichment, through:

Exhibition of the highest accomplishments of all cultures in the visual arts, with an emphasis on American art and Florida artists in particular;

Explorations in the humanities through programs of lectures and seminars by eminent scholars and cultural leaders and offerings in the musical, cinematic, and dramatic arts by recognized artists and performers;

Professional studio and classroom instruction in the arts for students of all ages; and

The collection, preservation and presentation of important art with emphasis on American art and Florida artists in particular.[52]

As evidence that growing numbers of Americans are taking advantage of such opportunities to become more directly involved in varied forms of cultural expression, the table below shows the increase in participation rates over a 12-year period.

FUNCTION NO. 10   Promoting Health and Safety

PURPOSE   to promote community heath and safety by offering needed services and programs, including leadership training and certification courses and supervision or regulation of high-risk activities.

Percentage of Americans Engaging in Amateur Creative Activities at Least Occasionally

ACTIVITY	1975	1987
Take photographs	19%	51%
Do needlepoint or weaving	39	41
Play a musical instrument	18	30
Paint, draw, or etch	22	27
Write stories or poems	13	24
Do ballet or modern dance	9	23
Sing in a choral group	11	22
Do folk or ethnic dance	5	15
Make pottery or ceramics	8	14
Sculpt	5	8

Source: National Research Center for the Arts, March 1990.

A little recognized but extremely important value of community recreation is its role in promoting public health and safety. As shown in Chapter 3, its most obvious value is the effect that its varied programs of sports and other physical activities have in promoting fitness. A wealth of recent recent studies have shown the value of systematic exercise in combating cardiovascular disease, obesity, and even some forms of cancer. There is striking evidence that athletically active women cut their risk of breast and uterine cancer in half, and risk of diabetes by two-thirds; another study shows that exercise reduces the risk of colon cancer.[53]

Increasing recognition is being given to recreation's role as a health-related field of service. A special issue of *Leisure Today* in April 1994 was devoted to the theme of "Enabling Healthy Lives Through Leisure," and a number of Canadian communities have developed cooperative programs to promote active lifestyles with input from recreation and park agencies, business, environmental and educational bodies, and various health and social-service organizations.[54] Similarly the supervision by public departments of organized sports leagues, ice skating, sledding, or other carefully directed activities helps to prevent many injuries and deaths. Many departments offer courses in boating skills, riflery, camping, or even—in Vancouver—a driving skills program for young children that has a miniature car facility complete with traffic lights, intersections, and police officers.

In terms of popular activities like swimming, which remains a leading cause of accidents for children, hundreds of thousands of youngsters ages three to five receive water safety and skills instruction today. In addition to discussing the role of public recreation and park departments in this area, K. Johnston, L. Bruya, and S. Langendorfer describe the work of numerous nonprofit organizations:

> Over the past decade, numerous preschool aquatic programs have emerged. The YMCA of the U.S.A. organized the Y Skippers in 1987, the American Red Cross established the Infant and Preschool Aquatics Program (IPAP) in 1988; the American Swimming Coaches Association started their Swim American preschool program in 1987; and most recently, the National Safety Council published the Learn to Swim program, which is endorsed by the National Recreation and Park Association, in 1993.[55]

In numerous other ways, public, private, and nonprofit agencies are working to reduce the injuries and deaths that frequently result from high-risk recreational activities. For example, many state commissions today regulate the use of boats—requiring that children or adults operating them have boating safety certificates—govern the use of jet skis, and maintain strict controls by prohibiting the use of alcohol while boating. Twenty-seven states have skiing safety acts that define skiers' and ski area operators' responsibilities on the slopes. Commercial companies and business associations provide safety education and guidelines along with training programs in such areas as scuba diving, roller-blading, skate-boarding, and other popular forms of outdoor play.

Organized recreation programs also help to divert or channel the drive that many young people in particular have for extremely dangerous forms of unsupervised or informal play into controlled or supervised programs. While the formal recreation system in the community can never fully satisfy these urges to dare and risk, it can and often does provide physically demanding and exciting alternatives in which the danger of serious accidents is much lower.

FUNCTION NO. 11   Providing Outlets for Ritual, Ceremony, and Aggressive Drives

PURPOSE   to meet the needs of residents for ritual, ceremony and celebration and to provide a release for tension and aggression by channeling such impulses into socially acceptable pursuits.

A final goal for community recreation is less obvious, but equally important. A unique function of recreation in modern society is to meet the need for ritual and ceremony. In past ages, people enjoyed a succession of year-round holidays and communal celebrations. Some of these survive in modern communities in the form of fairs and carnivals, which combine historical displays and various forms of entertainment, sports, and contests. Often, to acknowledge a national hero or a major national achievement, we celebrate with great tickertape parades. Major holidays, political events, and sports victories are also marked by celebrations and rituals. Modern industrialized societies have a need for displays marked by music, parades, dancing, costumes, and huge cheering throngs. In the United States, Independence Day provides an occasion for such rituals; it remains an example of what John Adams called for in July 1776:

> It ought to be commemorated as the day of deliverance, by solemn acts of devotion to God Almighty. It ought to be solemnized with pomp and parade, with shows, games and sports, guns, bells, bonfires and illuminations, from one end of this continent to the other, from this time forward, forever more.[56]

Sport as Ritual   The leading modern-day example of the need for rituals in which people join in mass demonstrations is popular sports. A number of social scientists have suggested that sporting events have become America's new folk religion, with millions of enthusiasts avidly following their favorite teams and stars through the different championship seasons of the year.

The urge to participate in mass ceremonies and rituals is also demonstrated in college sports events. These events, particularly football, present marching bands, drill teams, dancing, banners, huge crowds, mascots, parades before "bowl" games, bonfire pep rallies, and similar ceremonial aspects.

Community Celebrations   Numerous other examples of community celebrations, in which crowds gather together for religious, patriotic, entertainment, or other purposes, may be cited. Sometimes it may be in a spirit of fun—to break a "record," as in the March 1988, Calle Ocho Open House Festival in Miami, Florida. The world's greatest conga line was organized, with 120,000 dancers. Sometimes it occurs annually, as in Mardi Gras or similar celebrations, or when a city greets its returning professional team after winning a national sports championship. Often events of this kind have a major economic impact. The number of Mardi Gras revelers in New Orleans in a recent year was one million visitors, who spent an estimated $660 million. The three largest New Orleans "krewes" (private clubs that sponsor parades) had a combined number of 110 floats, 90 bands, and 3,500 float riders in their parades. Originally part of the religious celebration of the Lenten season, today Mardi Gras is chiefly a time for extravagant balls, parades, and uninhibited celebrating.

Often, as in Latin American and certain European carnivals at the time of Lent, the emphasis seems to be on breaking down the distinctions of class and status and temporarily abandoning the year-round code of seriousness, hard work, social restraints, and formality. It has been said that even a machine must have a little play if it is not to break down; the same axiom applies to people, both as individuals and as a society.

Release of Aggressive Drives

A related function of recreation in modern society has to do with its potential for releasing hostile and violent drives in socially acceptable ways—essentially the "catharsis" theory described earlier in this text. Over the past three decades, concern about growing violence has increased throughout the world, but particularly in the United States, which ranks especially high among the industrial nations of the world in criminal violence. Also alarming is the American Medical Association's conclusion in a 1995 report that sexual assault and family violence are devastating the nation's physical and emotional well-being. It stated that:

> . . . domestic violence, child physical abuse and neglect, child sexual abuse and mistreatment of the elderly—were widespread. Each year [were] in the United States, two million to four million women are battered, 1,500 women are killed by intimate partners, 1.8 million elderly people are mistreated and 1.7 million reports of child abuse are filed.[57]

It should be noted, however, that the tendency toward violence is found throughout the world and has existed throughout history. For prehistoric people, life was an incessant battle against the hostile Pleistocene environment—against other mammals for food and against other humans for shelter, a water hole, or a hunting range. Violence was necessary and socially approved. John Fischer writes:

> Success in the battle was the basic status symbol. The best fighters were feted in victory celebrations, heaped with honors and plunder . . . the weak and timid, on the other hand, were scorned . . . and in many societies cowardice was punished by death. For nearly all of human history, then, the aggressive impulse—so deeply embedded in our genes—had no trouble in finding an outlet.[58]

In modern society, however, we have banned many outlets for pugnacity that were once available on the frontier or in rough-and-ready occupations. In a nation of city dwellers, the traditional testing ground of people against the savage elements has all but disappeared. Life itself has become easier and safer, and warfare no longer provides a regular outlet for the primitive instinct for violence as it once did. We have shown remarkable ingenuity in inventing fashionable surrogates for violence, including such strenuous and risky sports as skiing, skin diving, surfing, mountain climbing, and sailing. These activities, however, are available chiefly to the well-to-do; they are too expensive for the poor and too remote from their way of life. Ultimately, Fischer concludes, many of the poor turn to crimes of violence, largely because of the need to vent aggressive impulses fanned by boredom, frustration, and anger.

Such scientists as Konrad Lorenz and Robert Ardrey have explored the historical roots of aggression and territoriality, and they suggest that such urges apparently arise from an inherited, atavistic behavior pattern stemming from humankind's primitive past. Obviously, the need is to control or channel them—both through education that will lead to providing understanding and mastery of the tendency toward violence and through acceptable outlets for such behavior.

Unfortunately, exactly the opposite kind of education is taking place in our society today, as various forms of popular culture—movies, television, music, and video games—have combined to make the taboo against murder less powerful. A former Army psychologist, Lieutenant Colonel Dave Grossman, argues that, in the past, there was a strong natural disinclination among most people to the direct taking of human life, an in-built taboo against intraspecies destruction. To overcome this, he writes, Vietnam War training techniques sought to make killing of the enemy a conditioned reflex by simulating actual battle experience, with the circular targets previously used being replaced by "pop-up" human figures that fell down when the trainee scored a hit. Today, Grossman suggests, an "epidemic, a virus of violence" has been unleashed in America by popular forms of entertainment:

> His theory is that video games and violence on television [and] in the movies have had some of the same effect on young people [as the Vietnam War training methods]. There are popular video games, he points

out, "where you actually hold a weapon in your hand and fire it at human-shaped targets on the screen." Combined with the rise of gangs and their leaders to replace the nonexistent family, the media violence has . . . substantially lowered the barriers that once existed to taking another's life.[59]

The challenge to the organized recreation movement is to offer other types of experiences that provide the same kinds of rewards or satisfactions as riots or other acts of gratuitous violence, but without their devastating social consequences. It must be recognized that this is a complex process. The easy assumption that competitive team sports provide an automatic safety valve for anger and aggression is not always valid. Under some circumstances, sports may simply provoke greater hostility and violent explosions if the participants' needs are not met. This suggests that we need to explore a wide range of pursuits—including many hazardous and active outdoor recreation activities—particularly in providing programs for those who are most violence-prone.

Need for a Coherent Philosophy of Service

This chapter has presented 11 major areas of social concern in which community recreation may satisfy important needs, constituting a strong justification for providing socially oriented recreation programs and facilities. However, if such programs and facilities are not based on a sound philosophy of service, they may not achieve the desired ends. Chapter 14 discusses a number of issues or problems facing this field today and suggests guidelines for developing a coherent philosophy for solving these issues.

SUMMARY

Far from simply providing casual or superficial amusement, organized recreation services help to satisfy a number of significant community needs, including the following:

1. *Quality of Life.* Constructive and enjoyable leisure for people of all ages and backgrounds contributes significantly to their quality of life and satisfaction with their communities.
2. *Personal Development.* As described in Chapter 3, organized recreation promotes healthy personal development in physical, emotional, social, intellectual, and spiritual terms—thus contributing to overall community well-being.
3. *Environmental Attractiveness.* Recreation and park agencies maintain parks, nature reserves, riverfronts, and other natural areas and may assist in rehabilitating or sponsoring historic and cultural settings.
4. *Combating Juvenile Delinquency.* As an important element in the community's educational, social, and other services for youth, organized recreation assists in preventing or reducing delinquency and other deviant forms of play.
5. *Improving Intergroup Relations.* Recreation serves as a useful tool in promoting ethnic or racial pride and intergroup understanding and cooperation. It also assists in positive intergenerational programming.
6. *Strengthening Community Ties.* Volunteerism and taking part in neighborhood efforts to improve the community environment, assistance programs for children or disabled persons, and similar involvements help to build civic togetherness.

7. *Needs of Special Populations.* In both treatment settings and in the community at large, therapeutic recreation service promotes mainstreaming and independence for persons with physical, mental, or social disabilities.

8. *Maintaining Economic Health.* As a growing form of business enterprise, recreation employs millions of people today. By helping to attract tourists, industries that are relocating, or new residents, it also provides income and promotes community stability.

9. *Enriching Cultural Life.* Many public and nonprofit leisure-service agencies today assist or sponsor programming in the various artistic and cultural fields, strengthening this important dimension of community life.

10. *Promoting Health and Safety.* Increasingly, recreation is recognized as a health-related discipline by helping individuals to maintain sound lifestyles and by helping to promote safety in outdoor recreation and other risk-related leisure pursuits.

11. *Providing Outlets for Ritual, Celebration, and Aggression.* Sports, fine arts, major community celebrations, and similar programs help to channel individuals' needs for competition, aggression, ritual, and celebration in socially acceptable ways.

Questions for Class Discussion or Essay Examinations

1. This chapter presents 11 different areas in which recreation, parks and leisure services contribute to community life. If you had to present a positive argument for establishing or expanding a community recreation and park department, which of these areas would you emphasize, and why?

2. Prevention of juvenile delinquency has been a long-standing purpose of many public and voluntary leisure-service agencies. Recognizing that there is limited research evidence to support the effectiveness of recreation in this area, could you sum up the evidence that exists, search for other research findings, and make a logical case for recreation's anti-delinquency role?

3. Explain and discuss the importance of community recreation within one of the following areas: (a) economic contribution; (2) health-related benefits; (3) promoting the cultural arts; or (4) improving intergroup relations among residents of different socioeconomic, racial, or cultural backgrounds.

Endnotes

[2]   Parks and Recreation Federation of Ontario, Canada, *The Benefits of Parks and Recreation,* summarized in *Programmers Information Network* (National Recreation and Park Association, Vol. 4 No. 4, 1993): 1.

[3]   B. L. Driver, Perry Brown, and George Peterson, eds., *Benefits of Leisure* (State College, Pa.: Venture, 1991).

[4]   Catherine Coyle, W. W. Kinney, and John Shank, *Effect of Therapeutic Recreation and Leisure Lifestyle on Rehabilitation Outcomes and on the Physical and Psychological Health of Individuals with Physical Disability* (Philadelphia, Pa.: Temple University and U.S. Department of Education, Office of Special Education and Rehabilitative Services, 1993).

[5]   "New Study Reveals Recreation, Parks' Impact on Serious Social Issues," *Dateline*: NRPA (December 1994): 1–2.

[6]   Janet MacLean, "Leisure and the Quality of Life," in Timothy Craig, ed., *The Humanistic and Mental Health Aspects of Sports, Exercise and Recreation* (Chicago: American Medical Association, 1975): 73–74.

7 Louis Harris, *Inside America* (New York: Vintage, 1887): 8–10.

8 Lawrence Allen, "Benefits of Leisure Attributes to Community Satisfaction," *Journal of Leisure Research* 22 (1990): 183–196.

9 Leo Jeffres and Jean Dobos, "Perception of Leisure Opportunities and the Quality of Life in a Metropolitan Area," *Journal of Leisure Research* 25 (1993): 209–217.

10 "Assessing Bond Between Fathers and Their Children," *Philadelphia Inquirer* (17 January 1988): 5-J.

11 Roger Rosenblatt, "Teaching Johnny to Be Good," *New York Times Magazine* (20 April 1995): 36–41.

12 Daniel Goleman, *Emotional Intelligence* (New York: Bantam Books, 1995).

13 *The Fire We Light Is the Fire Within* (Kansas City, Mo.: Camp Fire Boys and Girls Program Brochure, 1995).

14 *Contemporary Issues: Reaching Out* (New York: Girl Scouts of the U.S.A. Program Brochure, 1992).

15 *The Values of Men and Boys in America* (New York: Louis Harris Associates and Boy Scouts of America Research Report, 1994).

16 "The Midwest's Brawny Capital," *New York Times* (5 May 1985): X-14.

17 Lynn Iles and Katherine Wiele, "The Benefits of Rail-Trails and Greenways," *Recreation Canada* 51 (No. 3 1993): 25–27.

18 Peter Donnelly, "Athletes and Juvenile Delinquents: A Comparative Analysis Based on a Review of the Literature," *Adolescence* (Summer 1981): 415.

19 Frank Tannenbaum, *Crime and the Community* (New York: Columbia University Press, 1938): 17–20.

20 See James Short, Jr., and Fred Strodtbeck, *Group Process and Gang Delinquency* (New York: The Free Press, 1960): 20–130, 161–186.

21 *Ibid.,* 77.

22 Jeffrey Riemer, "Deviance as Fun," *Adolescence* (Spring 1981): 39.

23 Donnelly, *op. cit.,* 415–431.

24 M. S. Searle, *Synthesis of the Research Literature on the Benefits of Recreation: A Technical Report* (Winnipeg, Manitoba: University of Manitoba, 1989).

25 See Stacey McKay, "Research Findings Related to the Potential of Recreation in Delinquency Prevention," *Trends* (Vol. 30 No. 4 1993): 27.

26 John Crompton, "Rescuing Young Offenders with Recreation Programs," *Trends* (Vol. 30 No. 4 1993): 23–26.

27 Pamela Robinson-Young, "Recreation's Role in Gang Intervention," *Parks and Recreation* (March 1992): 54–56.

28 For a description of an extensive youth basketball program, see Frank Martin, "Bringing Basketball to At-Risk Kids," *Parks and Recreation* (March 1992): 50–53.

29 "Recreation Fights Crime," *Parks and Recreation* (March 1994): 45. See also *City Streets—At Risk Youth Division* (Phoenix, Ariz.: Department of Parks, Recreation and Library Report, 1994).

30 Jill Smolowe, "Out of the Line of Fire," *Time* (25 July 1994): 25.

31 Lorina Schultz, John Crompton, and Peter Witt, "A National Profile of the Status of Public Recreation Services for At-Risk Children and Youth," *Journal of Park and Recreation Administration* (Fall 1995): 1–25.

32 Richard Chesnoff, "Hatemongering on the Data Highway," *U.S. News & World Report* (8 August 1994): 52.

33 "Racism on the Rise," *Time* (2 February 1987): 20.

34 George Karlis and Don Dawson, "Ethnic Maintenance and Recreation: A Case Study," *Journal of Applied Recreation Research* (Vol. 15 No. 2 1990): 85–99.

35 Sara Rimer, "A Camp Sows the Seeds of Peace," *New York Times* (3 September 1995): 16.

36 Marcia Cram, "Building Bridges Across Generations: NRPA's Intergenerational Initiative," *Parks and Recreation* (March 1995): 94–98.

37 *Ibid.*

38 Lawrence Allen, *Philadelphia Recreation Volunteerism Project: Final Report* (Philadelphia: Temple University and American Academy for Park and Recreation Administration, May 1986).

39 L. W. Gahan, "Citizen Involvement," *Parks and Recreation* (July 1982): 24.

40 "Study: Few Disabled Go Back to Job," *Philadelphia Inquirer* (23 February 1988): 7-B.

41 See Richard Kraus and John Shank, *Therapeutic Recreation Service: Principles and Practices* (Dubuque, Iowa: Wm. C. Brown, 1992): 50–55.

42 James Kozlowski, "ADA Requires Integration, Prohibits Stereotyped Segregation of Disabled," *Parks and Recreation* (October 1994): 26.

43 Jane Kaufman Broida, "Community Options for All Individuals," *Parks and Recreation* (May 1995): 55–59.

44 Jane Gross, "Big League Ambition Transforms San Jose," *New York Times* (6 May 1994): A-16.

45 Suzanne Carmichael, "What's Doing in Calgary?" *New York Times* (18 June 1995): 10-XX.

46 Michael Kanters and M. R. Botkin, "The Economic Impact of Public Leisure Services in Illinois," *Journal of Park and Recreation Administration* (Fall 1992): 1–15.

47 Gary Rankel, "Few Know Extent of Outdoor Recreation in Indian Country," *Recreation Executive Report* (October 1994): 1–16.

48 Steven Burr and Jeffrey Walsh, "A Hidden Value of Sustainable Rural Tourism Development," *Trends* (Vol. 31 No. 1 1994): 9–13.

49 Doug Turco and Craig Kelsey, "Measuring the Economics of Special Events," *Parks and Recreation* (December 1993): 33–34.

50 Barry Mangum, "Giant Step Forward for the Arts in Leisure," *Parks and Recreation* (July 1982): 30.

51 Elizabeth Kolbert, "America's Despair of Popular Culture," *New York Times* (20 August 1995): H-23.

52 *Center for the Arts: Annual Report,* Vero Beach, Fla. (1993–1994): 1.

53 Vic Sussman, "No Pain and Lots of Gain," *U.S. News & World Report* (4 May 1992): 86–88.

54 Randy Swedburg and Bill Izso, "Active Living, Promoting Healthy Lifestyle," *Journal of Physical Education, Recreation and Dance* (April 1994): 32.

55 K. Johnston, L. Bruya, and S. Langendorfer, "Ready to Paddle," *Parks and Recreation* (February 1994): 50.

56 Excerpt from a letter from John Adams to Abigail Adams, speaking of July 2, 1776, the day the Continental Congress passed a resolution calling for the independence of the American colonies.

57 "Doctor Group Says Violence Imperils Nation," *New York Times* (Reuters, 7 November 1995): A-21.

58 John Fischer, "Substitutes for Violence," *Harper's Magazine* (January 1966): 16.

59 Richard Bernstein, review of Dave Grossman, *On Killing: The Cost of Learning to Kill in War and Society* (New York: Little Brown, 1995), in *New York Times* (13 October 1995): C-33.

Early History of
Recreation and Leisure

In the year A.D. 80 the Colosseum opened with what must stand as quite the longest and most disgusting mass binge in history. According to Suetonius, various sorts of large-scale slaughter, both of animals and of men, were appreciatively watched by the Emperor Titus and a packed audience for 100 days. All of this was considered highly laudable, an extra-special celebration of the state, duly enhanced by the presence of Roman senators, court officials, priests, vestal virgins, and sacred effigies of the gods. The Emperor Titus was quite happily footing the enormous bill just as he and his father, the imperial Vespasian, had already footed the bill for building this vast arena. Such payments were the privilege of power; the new arena was officially the gift of the Emperor to the Roman people and would ensure his fame forever.[1]

INTRODUCTION

Having examined the concepts of recreation, play, and leisure, and having learned about their meanings for people of different ages, genders, and racial identities, as well as their varied social functions, we now turn to an examination of recreation's past. To provide a meaningful background for the study of recreation and leisure in modern society, it is helpful to have a clear understanding of its role in the past. To some, history may appear to be dry, boring, or meaningless, especially if it is taught with an emphasis on simply memorizing dates and

---

[1] John Pearson, *Arena: The Story of the Colosseum* (New York: McGraw-Hill, 1973): 7.

names of rulers or battles. Such an approach, dealing with the bare skeleton of events, lacks vitality and human interest.

Instead, history should be presented as a rich panorama of humanity's past existence. It should provide a tapestry of people, places, events, and social forces—showing the role of religion, education, and government and the customs and values of different cultures, their arts, sports, and pastimes. By becoming familiar with earlier historical epochs, we are better able to understand and deal effectively with the present. As the philosopher George Santayana said, "Those who cannot remember the past are condemned to repeat it."

This chapter therefore reviews the early history of recreation and leisure, beginning with the era of prehistory (before the written word was used) and extending to the period just before the Industrial Revolution in Europe and America.

THE PLAY OF EARLY SOCIETIES

One would expect a chronological study to begin by examining the play of prehistoric peoples during the Paleolithic and Neolithic epochs. However, relatively little is known about the nature of leisure and play in these early periods.

We have tended to focus on what have been called existing "primitive" societies as a means of speculating on what life may have been like for prehistoric human groups. The term "primitive" has often been applied to present-day or recently observed tribal societies in North or Central America, the Pacific Islands, Africa, or other regions of the world that have not developed in terms of written language or technological systems. It should not be implied that these groups were or are inferior to other societies. Indeed, they often have highly complex social structures, religious practices, art forms, or ways of surviving in natural environments. However, because the word primitive may have negative connotations, it is preferable to refer to such societies as "tribal, pretechnological" cultures.

Attitudes Toward Work and Leisure

Tribal people do not make the same sharp distinction between work and leisure that we in more technologically advanced societies do. While we set aside different periods of time for work and relaxation, a tribal, pretechnological society has no such precise separations. Instead, work is customarily done when it is available or necessary, and it is often infused with rites and customs that lend it variety and pleasure.

In such tribal societies, work tends to be varied and creative, rather than being a narrow, specialized task demanding a sharply defined skill, as in modern industry. Work is often accompanied by ritual that is regarded as essential to the success of the planting or harvesting or to the building or hunting expedition. The ritual may involve prayer, sacrifice, dance, or feasting, which thus becomes part of the world of work.

Origins of Games and Sports

In tribal societies, play may have many sources. Popular games are often vestiges of warfare—now practiced as a form of sport. Occasionally play activities depict historical events, transportation practices, or the use of household or farming implements. When an activity is no longer useful in its original form (such as archery for hunting or warfare), it may become a form of sport. Often, the origin is religious ritual. P. C. McIntosh writes:

> The Tailteen Games in Ireland, wrestling among the Aztecs, the team game of Tlachtli played by Maya people in Central America, and ju-jitsu practiced by the Samurai Warriors of Japan, all had religious significance. In Britain, too, the early history of some games of football suggests that fertility rites were involved.[2]

Among North American Indians, games were sometimes so seriously regarded that captains of losing teams were sacrificed; sports were a modified form of warfare, as in the lacrosse games of the Choctaw and Cherokee Indians. These contests often involved as many as a thousand young braves and continued for hours over considerable distances, resulting in numerous injuries and deaths. It is believed that they were a means not only of testing warriors in battlelike situations but of keeping their fighting spirits high. Indeed, lacrosse was known as the "little brother of war."

In many tribal societies, there is a division of the community into halves, each usually marked by distinctive totems (generally a sacred bird or animal) that dictate a complicated system of obligations, taboos, and customs between the tribal halves. There tends to be a constant sequence of contests and rivalry between the two groups, and, at the same time, a process of constant help and assistance. Together, the two groups perform a series of precisely designed ceremonies; often the games played as part of such ceremonies symbolize a continuing struggle between good and evil or life and death.

The game of *tlachtli*, which was widely practiced in Central America centuries ago, is an example of such a contest. Tlachtli courts were about 200 feet long and 30 feet wide and were situated near temples. A stone ring was fixed about halfway up the wall at either end. The players struck a rubber ball with their knees or hips, the purpose being to drive it through one of the rings. Michael Lemonick writes that the ball game among the Mayans was both ritual and recreation:

> Spectators gambled on the competition's outcome. The solid rubber ball, which may have symbolized the sun or the moon, was kept in constant motion in the air, mimicking planetary movements. The players may also have attempted to reenact the battles they had won. Human sacrifice frequently provided the grisly finale of a game: either the defeated players were decapitated and their heads possibly used as balls, or they were tortured to death when the winners trussed up their bodies into human spheres and bounced them down pyramid steps.[3]

Some tribes that continue the traditions of their ancient ancestors often practice dangerous and painful sports. For example, at the Arctic Winter Games in recent years, Eskimo contestants have competed not only in such conventional sports as cross-country skiing, ice hockey, or figure skating, but also in unusual games peculiar to their culture. These include contests like kicking a sealskin ball dangling from a pole, precision whip-flicking, and bouncing on a walrus hide. Other games include traditional forms of what could best be described as "self-torture" endurance contests, such as the "knuckle hop" (hopping a distance on toes and knuckles), "arm pulls," "finger pulls," and "ear pulls," all involving high levels of pain and designed to help members of the tribe learn to bear the privations of their daily struggle for existence in the Arctic.

A vivid example of the linkage of sport and warfare in tribal societies is found in the Willigiman–Wallalua and Wittaia tribes of New Guinea. Every week or so, these two neighboring mountain peoples, who have the same language, dress, and customs, arrange a formal battle at one of their traditional fighting grounds. As described by anthropologists who observed the tribes during the 1960s, these frays seem more like a dangerous field sport than true war:

> Each battle lasts but a single day, always stops before nightfall (because of the danger of ghosts) or if it begins to rain (no one wants to get his hair or ornaments wet). The men are very accurate with their weapons—they have all played war games since they were small boys—but they are equally adept at dodging, and hence are rarely hit by anything.[4]

In addition to arranged contests, however, the two New Guinea tribes (who, despite their cultural similarities, regard each other with hatred) also practice sneak raids, during which they mercilessly slaughter men, women, and children. Victories are celebrated by *etais,* or victory dances, and are part of an unending cycle of fighting, death, mourning, and revenge. The fighting continues but not for the usual reasons for waging war. The Willigiman–Wallalua and the Wittaia do not capture territory, goods, or prisoners, nor do they ever try to annihilate their enemies and thus end the warfare. They fight because they "enthusiastically enjoy it, because it is to them a vital function of the complete man, and because they feel they must satisfy the ghosts of slain companions."

This fascination with warfare dominates the play of young children in these tribes. Robert Gardner and Karl Heider point out that because of the demands of their harsh life, the children cannot afford to lose time growing up. When boys are four or five, they join older boys in a variety of games that help to prepare them for the formal warfare organized by their elders. The play of girls is different:

> . . . not as free as the boys, they spend less time at play; at a very early age their energy is channeled into the purposeful pursuits of female life. Long before boys begin to behave like men, girls are little women—planting, cultivating, cooking and doing a great variety of other more complicated tasks. . . . Still, while they are children they are not without some childish pleasures. Occasionally they even compete with their male contemporaries and are more than able to hold their own, playing at war with little cane spears and short grass darts.[5]

Other Play Functions   On the North American continent, play has had similar functions among Indian tribes, helping to equip the young for adult life. Indian boys practiced warriors' skills and were taught to survive unarmed and unclothed in the wilderness. Girls were taught the household crafts expected of mature women. Through dancing, singing, and storytelling, both sexes learned of the history and religion of their cultures. Among such southwestern American Indian tribes as the Navajo, Zuni, or Hopi, shamans or medicine men practiced healing rites that made use of chanting, storytelling, dancing, sacred "kachina" dolls, and elaborate, multicolored sand paintings. Varied forms of dance have also been used by American Indians and African tribes to intercede with the gods for good fortune in planting and harvesting crops, hunting and fishing expeditions, and warfare.

In such societies, games and sports sometimes served in more specialized roles. Huizinga points out that ritualized verbal contests were often part of judicial proceedings among North American Indians and Eskimos. Among the rice farmers of the Ifugao country in the Philippines, wrestling was used to settle cases of disputed ricefield boundaries. John Loy and Gerald Kenyon write:

> The reasoning behind this practice was that the ancestral spirits of the contestants knew which party was in the right, just where the true boundary was, and would see to it that he who was right would win. In spite of this expressed faith in supernatural intervention, the Ifugao were sufficiently practical to insist that

Early Sports and Games

New Guinea mountain tribes engage in warfare as a form of violent team sport (top), warriors dance to celebrate a victory (center), and games of childhood are used to practice warlike skills.

the wrestlers be approximately evenly matched. Owners of adjacent fields could do the actual wrestling, or might choose champions to represent them.[6]

RECREATION AND LEISURE IN PRE-CHRISTIAN CIVILIZATIONS

As prehistoric societies advanced, they developed specialization of functions. Humans learned to domesticate plants and animals, which permitted them to shift from a nomadic existence based on hunting and food-gathering to a largely stationary way of life based on grazing animals and planting crops.

There have been many conflicting theories regarding the amount of time for leisure in early societies. Garry Chick describes the view of Franz Boas, an American anthropologist, that as economies progressed from hunting and gathering to a more complex agricultural culture and more specialized economic roles, the amount of free time grew— essentially that "economic surplus" created abundance and leisure. However, Chick points out that later evidence shows that hunting, gathering, and simple farming tended to be more reliable sources of food and to provide more free time than the complex agricultural economies. In effect, Chick concludes, contrary to traditional theories, "the more primitive the society, the more leisured its way of life."[7]

Ultimately, ruling classes developed, along with soldiers, craftsmen, peasants, and slaves. As villages and cities came into being and large estates were tilled (often with complex water storage and irrigation systems) and harvested by lower-class workers, upper-class societies gained power, wealth, and leisure. Thus, in the landed aristocracy of the first civilizations that developed in the Middle East during the five millennia before the Christian era, we find for the first time in history a leisure class.

Ancient Egypt

The Egyptian culture was a rich and diversified one; it achieved an advanced knowledge of astronomy, architecture, engineering, agriculture, and construction. The Egyptians had a varied class structure, with a powerful nobility, priesthood, and military class and lesser classes of workers, artisans, peasants, and slaves. This civilization, which lasted from about 5000 B.C. well into the Roman era, was richly recorded in paintings, statuary, and hieroglyphic records.

The ancient Egyptians led a colorful and pleasant life; it is said of them that their energies were directed to the arts of living and the arts of dying. They engaged in many sports as part of education and recreation, including wrestling, gymnastic exercises, lifting and swinging weights, and ball games. Bullfighting was a popular spectacle, and at least at its inception was religiously motivated. Music, drama, and dance were forms of religious worship as well as social entertainment. The Egyptians had complex orchestras that included various stringed and percussive instruments. Groups of female performers were attached to temples, and the royal houses had troupes of entertainers who performed on sacred or social occasions. Slaves were often taught both dancing and music, and in the later dynasties developed into a class of professional performers who provided entertainment for the nobility.

The diversions of peasants and field laborers were few and inexpensive. They assembled in the "house of beer," which was probably the equivalent of a modern bar or saloon, and apparently were much given to drunkenness.

Egyptian children played with toy dolls, boats, marbles, tops, and balls. Such adult games as chess, checkers, backgammon, and other table games also originated during this period.

Ancient Assyria and Babylonia

The land known as the "fertile crescent" between two great rivers, the Tigris and the Euphrates, was ruled by two powerful empires, Assyria in the north and Babylon in the south. These kingdoms were in power for approximately 26 centuries, from about 2900 B.C. until the invasion by Alexander the Great in 330 B.C. Like the ancient Egyptians, the Assyrians and Babylonians had many popular recreation activities, such as boxing, wrestling, archery, and a variety of table games.

In addition to watching dancing, listening to music, and giving banquets, Assyrians were also devoted to hunting; the nobles of Assyria went lion hunting in chariots and on foot, using spears. The chase was a daily occupation, recorded for history in numerous reliefs, sculptures, and inscriptions. C. W. Ceram writes that as early as the ninth century B.C.

> The Assyrians had animal parks, "paradises," as they called them, precursors of our zoological gardens. Within their large confines were kept freely roaming lions and herds of gazelles. They arranged battues— that is, hunts, in which the animals were driven by beaters and hunted with nets.[8]

These early parks were primarily spectacular sites for royal hunting parties, but also provided settings for feasts, assemblies, and royal gatherings. On the estates of other monarchs during the ninth and tenth centuries B.C. were vineyards, fishponds, and the famed hanging gardens of Babylon.

Ancient Israel

Among the ancient Israelites, music and dancing were performed for ritual purposes as well as for social activities and celebrations. The early Hebrews distinguished dances of a sacred or holy character from those that resembled pagan ceremonies. While there are no wall reliefs or paintings to tell of dance as performed by the ancient Hebrews, there are abundant references to this practice in the Old Testament. Dance was highly respected and was particularly used on occasions of celebration and triumph:

> And David danced before the Lord with all his might.   (2 Samuel 6:14)

> Let them praise his name in the dance: let them sing praises unto him with the timbrel and harp.
> (Psalms 149:3)

As evidence that the ancient Hebrews must have danced on every possible occasion, both in daily life and for special ceremonies, is the fact that Biblical Hebrew has no less than 12 verbs to express the act of dancing. At the same time, the ancient Jews disapproved of certain forms of worldly or sacrilegious dance. For example, they condemned dancing around the golden calf as a form of idolatry that reflected the influence of the Egyptian religion (which worshipped the bull Apis as a major deity).

Like other pre-Christian societies, the ancient Hebrews also engaged in hunting, fishing, wrestling, and the use of such weapons as the sword and javelin for both recreational and defensive purposes. As for leisure itself, their major contribution was to set aside the seventh day—the Sabbath—as a time for people to rest from work and to worship their creator.

Recreation and Leisure in Ancient Greece

In the city–states of ancient Greece, particularly in Athens during the so-called Golden Age of Pericles from about 500 to 400 B.C., humankind reached a new peak of philosophical and cultural development. The Athenians took great interest in the arts, in learning, and in athletics. These pursuits were generally restricted to the wellborn, aristocratic noblemen, who had full rights of citizenship including voting and participation in affairs of state. Craftsmen, farmers, and tradespeople were also citizens, but had limited rights and less prestige. Labor was performed by slaves and foreigners, who outnumbered citizens by as much as two or three to one.

The amenities of life were generally restricted to the most wealthy and powerful citizens, who represented the Athenian ideal of the balanced man—a combined soldier, athlete, artist, statesman, and philosopher. This ideal was furthered though education and the various religious festivals, which occupied about 70 days of the year. The arts of music, poetry, theater, gymnastics, and athletic competition were combined in these sacred competitions.

Sports appear to have been part of daily life and to have occurred mainly when there were mass gatherings of people, such as the assembly of an army for war or the wedding or funeral of some great chieftain. There were also bardic or musical events, offering contests on the harp and flute, poetry, and theatrical presentations. Physical prowess was celebrated in sculpture and poetry, and strength and beauty were seen as gifts of the gods.

From earliest childhood, Athenian citizens engaged in varied athletic and cultural activities. Young children enjoyed toys, dolls, carts, skip ropes, kites, and seesaws. When boys reached the age of seven, they were enrolled in schools in which gymnastics and music were primary elements. They were intensively instructed in running and leaping, wrestling, throwing the javelin and discus, dancing (taught as a form of military drill), boxing, swimming, and ball games.

Athletics gradually became an important part of Athenian political life. James Thompson points out that political leaders provided athletic grounds for the masses and subsidized participation by the poor, who could not afford to attend festival celebrations. He concludes:

> Official games were developed, expanded, and maintained as important actions of democratic Athens. . . . Moreover, imperialistic Athens foisted her athletic interests on her colonies and tribute-paying states.[9]

Greek Philosophy of Recreation and Leisure   The Athenian philosophers believed strongly in the unity of mind and body and in the strong relationship of all forms of human qualities and skills. They felt that play activity was essential to the healthy physical and social growth of children.

Plato believed that education should be compulsory and that it should provide natural modes of amusement for children:

> Education should begin with the right direction of children's sports. The plays of childhood have a great deal to do with the maintenance or nonmaintenance of laws.[10]

Music and dance were also considered essential for the full development of youth. Plato urged that all children be instructed in the performing arts and tested with frequent contests. These arts were to be consecrated to the gods, since the gods themselves were musicians and dancers. Both gymnastics and music were directed toward a total cultivation of the body and the emotions as the foundation upon which to build a sound intellectual and physical life. Pericles wrote:

> We cultivate the mind without loss of manliness; whereas our adversaries from early youth are always undergoing laborious exercises which are to make them brave, we live at ease and yet are equally willing to face the perils which they face. We have our regular games to provide our weary spirits many relaxations from toil.[11]

The Athenian philosophers recognized the need for leisure and recreation, although they regarded the two differently. Aristotle commented that it was necessary to work to defend the state in order to secure leisure, and made a distinction between leisure and amusement:

> Nature requires that we should be able, not only to work well, but to use leisure well; for, as I must repeat once again, the first principle of all action is leisure. Both are required, but leisure is better than occupation and its end; and therefore the question must be asked, what ought we to do when at leisure? . . . we should introduce amusements only at suitable times, and they should be our medicines, for the emotion which they create in the soul is a relaxation, and from the pleasure we obtain rest. But leisure of itself gives pleasure and happiness and enjoyment of life, which are experienced not by the busy man, but by those who have leisure.[12]

Changes in the Greek Approach to Leisure   The ancient Greeks developed the art of town planning and customarily made extensive provisions for parks and gardens, open-air theaters and gymnasiums, baths, exercise grounds, and stadiums. During the time of Plato, the gymnasium and the park were closely connected in beautiful natural settings, often including indoor halls, gardens, and buildings for musical performances. Early Athens had many public baths and some public parks, which later gave way to privately owned estates.

A gradual transition occurred in the Greek approach to leisure and play. At first, all citizens were expected to participate in sports and games, and the Olympic games were restricted to free-born Greeks only. Gradually, however, the religious and cultural functions of the Olympic games and other festivals were weakened by athletic specialization and commercialism. In time, sports and other forms of activity such as drama, singing, and dance were performed only by highly skilled specialists (drawn from the lower classes, or even slaves) who trained or perfected their skills throughout the year to appear before huge crowds of admiring spectators.

Recreation and Leisure in Ancient Rome

Like the Greek city–states, the Roman republic during its early development was a vigorous and manly state. The Roman citizen, although he belonged to a privileged class, was constantly ready to defend his society and fight in its wars. He willingly participated in sports and gymnastics, which kept his body strong and his spirit courageous. Numerous games held in connection with the worship of various Roman gods later developed into annual festivals. Such games were carefully supervised by the priesthood and were supported by public funds, frequently at great cost. The most important of the Roman games were those that celebrated military triumphs, which were usually held in honor of the god Jupiter, the head of the Roman pantheon.

Like the early Greeks, young Roman children had toy carts, houses, dolls, hobbyhorses, stilts, and tops, and engaged in many sports and games. Young boys were taught various sports and exercises such as running and jumping, sword and spear play, wrestling, swimming, and horseback riding. The Romans, however, had a different concept of leisure than the Greeks. Although the Latin words for "leisure" and "business" are *otium* and *negotium,* suggesting the same view of leisure as a positive value (with work defined negatively as a lack of leisure), the Romans supported play for utilitarian rather than aesthetic or spiritual reasons. The Romans were much less interested than the Athenians in varied forms of cultural activity. Although they had many performing companies, usually composed of Greek and southern Italian slaves, the Romans themselves did not actively participate in the theater. As for dance, after a brief period beginning at about 200 B.C. when it was fashionable for Roman patricians to dance, they began to disapprove of dance for men. Cicero wrote that

> no man, one may almost say, ever dances when sober, unless perhaps he be a madman; nor in solitude, nor in a moderate and sober party; dancing is the last companion of prolonged feasting, of luxurious situation, and of many refinements.[13]

Even more than the Greeks, the Romans were systematic planners and builders. Their towns generally included provisions for baths, open-air theaters, amphitheaters, forums for public assemblies, stadiums, and sometimes parks and gardens. They developed buildings for gymnastic sports, modeled after the Greek *palaestra* and including wrestling rooms, conversation areas for philosophers, and colonnades where games might be held in winter despite bad weather. Wealthier Romans often had private villas, many with large gardens and hunting preserves.

As the empire grew more powerful, the simple agricultural democracy of the early years, in which all male Romans were citizens and free men, shifted to an urban life with sharply divided classes. There were four social levels: the *senators,* who were the richest, holding most of the land and power; the *curiae,* who owned more than 25 acres of land and were officeholders or tax collectors; the *plebs,* or free common people, who owned small properties or were tradesmen or artisans; and the *coloni,* who were lower-class tenants of the land.

The society became marked by the wealth and profiteering of businessmen and speculators, with the cooperation of the rulers and governing officials. In time, a huge urban population of plebs lived in semi-idleness, since most of the work was done by coloni and slaves brought to Rome. Gradually it became necessary for the Roman emperors and senate to amuse and entertain the plebs; they did so with doles of grain and with public games—thus the slogan "bread and circuses."

As early as the reign of the Emperor Claudius in the first century A.D., there were 159 public holidays during the year, 93 of which were devoted to games at public expense, including many new festivals in honor of national heroes and foreign victories. By 354 A.D., there were 200 public holidays each year, including 175 days of games. Even on working days, the labor began at daybreak and ended shortly after noon during much of the year.

As leisure increased and the necessity for military service and other forms of physical effort declined for the Roman citizen, he began to do fewer things for himself. The normal practice was for him to be entertained or to follow a daily routine of exercise, bathing, and eating. The Roman baths became popular social and athletic clubs, but were not exclusive; gradually public baths were established throughout Rome. By the fourth century A.D., there were over 856 baths in Rome which could accommodate over 60,000 people at once, either free of charge or for a nominal fee.

Roman citizens were no longer as active in sports as they had once been. They now sought to be amused and to entertain their guests with paid acrobats, musicians, dancers, and other artists. Athletes now performed as members of a specialized profession with unions, coaches, and training schools and with conditions of service accepted and approved by the emperor himself.

During the reign of Julius Caesar, there was considerable social turmoil, with the mob and urban riots being used by conspirators as instruments in a violent battle to control the state. John Pearson writes that Caesar blunted these attempts

> . . . by channeling the emotions of the masses into his shows. Their success showed that with careful staging public games could form the perfect surrogate for politics. . . . [Later, the Emperor Augustus] had immense resources to devote to this one purpose, and constructed the facade of Empire round these great popular events. In the process he developed extraordinary techniques of mass participation in his shows—ritual, religion, mass hysteria. . . . Augustus was at liberty to choose from the whole Roman repertoire of races, athletic contests, mock battles, combats to the death. He used them all, but in his reign the greatest spectacle of all was chariot-racing.[14]

Chariot racing in Rome was carried on in the Circus Maximus, which held over 250,000 spectators, who were organized into four parties—each distinguished by a color—that cheered for the four factions of chariot-racing teams. The factions, or *familia quadrigaria*, were well funded with elaborate facilities and star charioteers who gained immense public fame. Taking the place of a mass cult, racing diverted the rivalry to sport, rather than political battles among different groups of Roman citizens.

Corruption of Entertainment   Gradually, the focus on the traditional sports of running, throwing, and jumping gave way to an emphasis on human combat—first boxing and wrestling and then displays of cruelty in which gladiators fought to the death for the entertainment of mass audiences. By the time of Emperor Tiberius (14–37 A.D.), competitive sport in the Roman Empire had become completely commercialized. To maintain political popularity and placate the bored masses, the emperors and the senate provided great parades, circuses, and feasts. The Roman games featured contests that were fought to the death between gladiators using various weapons, on foot, on horseback, or in chariots. Even sea battles were fought in artificially constructed lakes in the Roman arenas. Imported wild beasts, such as tigers and elephants, were pitted against each other or against human antagonists. The scale of these bloody entertainments was tremendous. The Colosseum held 60,000 spectators, and other amphitheaters held audiences that sometimes totaled half the adult population of their cities.

Under the reign of Caligula and Nero, the persecution of Christians became particularly prevalent and unrelenting. Tacitus wrote that many Christians

> were dressed in the skins of wild beasts, and exposed to be torn to pieces by dogs in the public games, were crucified, or condemned to be burnt; and at nightfall serve in place of lamps to light the darkness, Nero's own gardens being used for the purpose.[15]

Both animals and humans were maimed and butchered in cruel and horrible ways. Spectacles were often lewd and obscene, leading to a mass debauchery, corruption, and perversion of the human spirit. It was for these reasons that the term "Roman holiday" came to mean a wild and corrupt celebration.

Decline of Rome   During the third and fourth centuries, the Roman Empire began to crumble. Some historians have concluded that a major reason for the downfall of Rome was its inability to deal with mass leisure; its citizens grew physically weak and spiritually corrupt. Although they were great engineers, builders, soldiers, and administrators, the ancient Romans did not have the coherent philosophy of life of the Athenians. When faced by the challenge of excess wealth, luxury, and time, they responded as a nation by yielding to corruption and losing the simple virtues that had made them strong.

EARLY CHRISTIAN ERA: DARK AND MIDDLE AGES

Under attack by successive waves of northern European tribes, the Roman Empire finally collapsed. For a period of several centuries, Europe was overrun with warring tribes and shifting alliances. The organized power of Rome, which had built roads, extended commerce, and provided civil order, was at an end. Gradually the Catholic church emerged to provide a form of universal citizenship within Europe.

Having suffered under the brutal persecutions of the Romans, the early Christians condemned all that their pagan oppressors had stood for—especially their hedonistic way of life. Indeed, the early church fathers believed in a fanatical asceticism which in the Byzantine, or Eastern, Empire was marked by the Anchorite movement—with its idea of salvation through masochistic self-deprivation.

Even in western Europe, early Catholic church leaders condemned Roman practices as displaying the essential depravity of human nature. In this setting, all forms of pleasure were seen as evil. Margaret H'Doubler points out that sharp distinctions were made between the "here" and the "hereafter" and between good and evil, mind and body, spirituality and carnality:

> the paramount consideration of all living was to save the soul. Consequently, the body was looked upon as a hindrance. To exalt the soul, the body was ignored, punished, and bruised. Anything that expressed the livelier feelings of instinctive human nature or in any way suggested former pagan ways and ideals of living, was banished.[16]

Many aspects of Roman life were forbidden during the Dark and Middle Ages. The stadiums, amphitheaters, and baths that had characterized Roman life were destroyed. The Council of Elvira ruled that the rite of baptism could not be extended to those connected with the stage, and in 398 A.D. the Council of Carthage excommunicated those who attended the theater on holy days. The great spectacles and organized shows of imperial Rome were at an end. The Roman emphasis on leisure was replaced by a Christian emphasis on work. The influential Benedictine order in particular insisted on the dignity of labor. Their rule read, "Idleness is the great enemy of the soul. Therefore, monks should always be occupied either in manual labor or in sacred readings."

It would be a mistake, however, to assume that the Catholic church eliminated all forms of play. Many early Catholic religious practices were based on the rituals of earlier faiths. Priests built churches on existing shrines or temple sites, set Christian holy days according to the dates of pagan festivals, and used such elements of pagan worship as bells, candles, incense, singing, and dancing.

Pastimes in the Middle Ages

Despite disapproval from the church, many forms of play continued during the Middle Ages, Medieval society was marked by rigid class stratification; below the nobility and clergy were the peasants, who were divided into such ranks as freemen, villeins, serfs, and slaves.

Life in the Middle Ages, even for the feudal nobility, was crude and harsh. Manors and castles were little more than stone fortresses—crowded, dark, and damp. Knights were responsible for fighting in the service of their rulers; between wars, their favorite pastimes were hunting and hawking. Hunting was considered the loftiest pursuit to which the nobility could devote themselves. The eighth century French emperor Charlemagne, was a great hunting enthusiast. Although most of his career was spent in waging war, he

> never missed an opportunity of hunting: so much so that it might be said that he rested himself by galloping through the forests. He was on those occasions not only followed by a large number of huntsmen and attendants of his household, but . . . by his wife and daughters . . . and surrounded by a numerous and elegant court who vied with each other in displaying their skill and courage in attacking the fiercest animals.[17]

Hunting skill was considered a virtue of medieval rulers and noblemen. The sport was thought to be helpful in keeping hunters from the sin of idleness (a vigorous and tiring sport, it was also believed to prevent sensual temptation). Hunting also served as a useful preparation for war. In a later era, the Italian Machiavelli pointed out that since the main concern of the prince must be war, he must never cease thinking of it. In times of peace, thoughts of war should be directed to the sport of hunting.

Other pastimes during the Middle Ages were various types of games and gambling, music and dance, sports, and jousting. The games played in castles and medieval manors included early forms of chess, checkers, backgammon, and dice. Gambling was popular, although forbidden by both ecclesiastical and royal authority. "Dice shall not be made in the kingdom," said one law of 1256, and "those who are discovered using them, and frequenting taverns and bad places, will be looked upon as suspicious characters." Other table games were forbidden from time to time; the Council of Paris in 1212 even condemned chess.

Often there was an attempt to suppress youthful play, which tended to explode into periodic violence or hooliganism. In medieval England, for example, schoolboys in twelfth century London arranged different games at holiday times but were ordered not to take part in football because it usually degenerated into an unorganized rough-and-tumble battle. J. J. Bagley writes that, in many cathedral-sponsored schools, young students would celebrate various religious holidays by sacreligious parodies of church services—often with boys playing the parts of bishops and other senior clergy and mocking the church.[18]

As the chaos of the Dark Ages yielded to greater order and regularity, life became more stable. Travel in reasonable safety became possible, and by the eleventh century commerce was widespread. The custom of jousting emerged within the medieval courts, stemming from the tradition that only the nobility fought on horseback; common men fought on foot. Thus the term chivalry (from the French *cheval*, meaning horse) came into being. By the dawn of the twelfth century, the code of chivalry was developed, having originated in the profession of arms among feudal courtiers.

At the outset, tournaments were martial combat between great numbers of knights; violent and dangerous, they were often condemned by the church. Gradually the tournaments became more stylized and came to represent a form of war game. (The tournament was a contest between teams, and the joust was a trial of skill between two individual knights.) An elaborate code of laws and regulations was drawn up for the combat, and no one below the rank of esquire was permitted to engage in tournaments or jousting.

Games of the Common People   Meanwhile, what of the life of the peasantry during the Middle Ages? Edward Hulme suggests that life was not all work for the lower classes. There were village feasts and sports, practical joking, throwing weights, cockfighting, bull-baiting, and other lively games. "Ball games and wrestling, in which men of one village were pitted against men of another, sometimes resulted in bloodshed."[19]

There was sometimes dancing on the green and, on holidays, there were miracle and morality plays (forms of popular religious drama and pageantry). However, peasants usually went to bed at dark, reading was a rare accomplishment, and there was much drinking and crude brawling. For peasants, hunting was more a means of obtaining food than a sport. Although the nobility usually rode through the hedges and trampled the fields of the peasantry, peasants were not allowed to defend their crops against such forays or even against wild animals. If peasants were caught poaching, they were often maimed or hanged as punishment.

Typically, certain games were classified as rich men's sports and others as poor men's sports; sometimes a distinction was also made between urban and rural sports. As life in the Middle Ages became somewhat easier, a number of pastimes emerged. Many modern sports were developed at this time in rudimentary form.

Archery was popular and encouraged by English kings during the fourteenth and fifteenth centuries because of its military value. Every Englishman was commanded to have a bow of his own height, and targets were set up in every town; inhabitants were required to shoot on all feast days or be fined.

The people of the Middle Ages had an insatiable love of sightseeing and would travel great distances to see entertainments. There was no religious event, parish fair, municipal feast, or military parade that did not bring great crowds of people. When the kings of France assembled their principal retainers once or twice a year, they distributed food and liquor among the common people and provided military displays, court ceremonies, and entertainment by jugglers, tumblers, and minstrels.

An illustration of the extent to which popular recreation expanded during the Middle Ages is found in the famous painting of children's games by the Flemish artist, Pieter Breughel. This painting depicts more than 90 forms of children's play, including marbles, stilts, sledding, bowling, skating, blindman's bluff, piggyback, leapfrog, follow-the-leader, archery, tug-of-war, doll play, and dozens of others, many of which have lasted to the present day.

THE RENAISSANCE

Historians generally view the first half of the Middle Ages in Europe (roughly from 400 to 1000 A.D.) as the Dark Ages, and the next 400 to 500 years as *le haut Moyen Age* or high Middle Age. The Renaissance is said to have begun in Italy about 1350 A.D., in France about 1450, and in England about 1500. It marked a transition between the medieval world and the modern age. The term "renaissance" means rebirth, and describes the revived interest in the scholarship, philosophy, and arts of ancient Greece and Rome that developed at this time. More broadly, it also represented a new freedom of thought and expression, a more rational and scientific view of life, and the expansion of commerce and travel in European life.

As the major European nations stabilized during this period under solidly established monarchies, power shifted from the church to the kings and their noblemen. In Italy and France, particularly, the nobility became patrons of great painters, sculptors, musicians, dancers, and dramatists. These artists were no longer dominated by the ideals and values of the Catholic church, but were free to serve secular goals. A great wave of music and literature swept through the courts of Europe, aided by the development of printing. Dance and theater became more complex and elaborate, and increasingly lavish entertainments and spectacles were presented in the courts of Italy and France.

The dance in particular was an important adjunct to court life in all of the palaces of the Renaissance. Queen Elizabeth of England was said to have selected her Lord Chancellor not because of his special knowledge in the law, but because he wore "green bows on his shoes and danced the Pavane to perfection." As the Renaissance continued, music, dance, theater, and opera all became professionalized; throughout Europe, opera houses, theaters, and ballet companies were founded under royal sanction and subsidy.

In sixteenth century England, Henry VIII tried to restrict the playing of tennis to noblemen and property owners, but it nevertheless became a popular sport among all classes; football, however, was seen chiefly as a lower-class sport. In contrast, Peter McIntosh points out that one of the most popular pastimes of the Italian nobility during the fourteenth and fifteenth centuries was football, known as *calcio*. Regulations in Florence stipulated that only those of high social class might play, such as "honorable soldiers, gentlemen, lords, and princes" and that "rapscallions, artificers, servants and low-born fellows" might not take part.

Play as Education

Varied forms of play became part of the education of the youth of the nobility at this time. The French essayist, Michel de Montaigne, in discussing the education of children, wrote:

> Our very exercises and recreations, running, wrestling, music, dancing, hunting, riding, and fencing will prove to be a good part of our study. . . . It is not a soul, it is not a body, that we are training up; it is a man, and we ought not to divide him into two parts.[20]

The Athenian philosophy which had supported play as an important form of education was given fuller emphasis during the Renaissance by such educators and writers as Francois Rabelais, John Locke, and Jean Jacques Rousseau.

In early sixteenth century France, Rabelais advanced a number of revolutionary theories on education, emphasizing the need for physical exercises and games as well as singing, dancing, modeling and painting, nature study, and manual training. His account of the education of Gargantua describes play as an exercise for mind and body.

Locke, an Englishman who lived from 1632 to 1704, was also concerned with play as a medium of learning. He recommended that children make their own playthings and felt that games could contribute significantly to character development if they were properly supervised and directed. "All the plays and diversions of children," he wrote, "should be directed toward good and useful habits." Locke distinguished between the play of children and recreation for older youth and adults. "Recreation," he said, "is not being idle . . . but easing the wearied part by change of business."

Another French philosopher, Rousseau (1712–1778), was also a great theorist of experimental education. His revolutionary text *Émile* advocated full freedom of physical activity, rather than constraint. Rousseau suggested that mankind should return to a state of nature marked by simplicity and freedom. He urged that children play freely in a variety of activities. Defending his theories, Rousseau wrote:

> You are troubled at seeing him [Émile] spend his early years in doing nothing. What! Is it nothing to be happy? Is it nothing to skip, to play, to run about all day long? Never in his life will he be so busy as now.[21]

Rousseau also believed that play contributed to character training, and that children should be given activities that would satisfy their needs in each stage of their development. Sports and games were valuable in preventing idleness and antisocial activity. Rousseau was one of the first to suggest that sport be used for political and nationalistic ends. Asked to prepare a proposal on education for the reconstituted government of Poland, in 1773 he published *Considerations on the Government of Poland,* in which he suggested that games were to make children's "hearts glow and create a deep love for the fatherland and its laws."

INFLUENCE OF THE PROTESTANT REFORMATION

The Reformation was a religious movement of the 1500s which resulted in the establishment of a number of Protestant sects whose leaders broke away from Roman Catholicism. It was part of a broader stream that included economic, social, and political currents. In part it represented the influence of the growing middle classes, who allied with the nobility in the emerging nations of Europe to challenge the power of the church.

The new Protestant sects tended to be more solemn and austere than the Catholic church. Calvin established an autocratic system of government in Geneva in 1541 that was directed by a group of Presbyters, morally upright men who controlled the social and cultural life of the community to the smallest detail. They ruthlessly suppressed heretics and burned dissenters at the stake. Norman Miller and Duane Robinson describe the unbending Puritanism in Geneva:

> "Purity of conduct" was insisted upon, which meant the forbidding of gambling, card playing, dancing, wearing of finery, singing of gay songs, feasting, drinking and the like. There were to be no more festivals, no more theaters, no more ribaldry, no more light and disrespectful poetry or display. Works of art and musical instruments were removed from the churches. [22]

Throughout Europe there was an aura of grim dedication to work and a determination to enforce old codes against play and idleness. A German schoolmaster named Franke wrote at the beginning of the eighteenth century:

> Play must be forbidden in any and all of its forms. The children shall be instructed in this matter in such ways as to show them, through the presentation of religious principles, the wastefulness and folly of all play. They shall be led to see that play will distract their hearts and minds from God, the eternal good, and will work nothing but harm to their spiritual lives. Their true joy and hearty devotion should be given to their blessed and holy savior, and not to earthly things, for the reward of those who seek earthly things is tears and sorrow.[23]

Puritanism in England

The English Puritans waged a constant battle to limit or condemn sports and other forms of entertainment during the period from the sixteenth to the eighteenth century. Maintaining strict observation of the Sabbath was a particular issue.

Anglican clergy during the Elizabethan period bitterly attacked stage plays, church festival gatherings, dancing, gambling, bowling, and other "devilish pastimes" like hawking and hunting, holding fairs and markets, and reading "lascivious and wanton books."

James I, however, recognized that the prohibition of harmless amusements like dancing, archery, and the decorating of maypoles caused public anger. In 1618 he issued a *Declaration on Lawful Sports,* in which he asked, "When shall the common people have leave to exercise, if not upon the Sundayes and holy daies, seeing they must apply their labour and win their living in all working daies?" James stressed the military value of sport and the danger of an increase in drinking and other vices as substitute activities if sport were denied to people.

During the Civil War and the Commonwealth period in England, there were strict laws to repress Sunday trade and pastimes. Peter Fryer comments that by the closing decades of the eighteenth century, people in England were forced to take their Sunday pleasures by stealth:

> The hallmark of the English Sunday was hypocrisy. Many who would not walk in the fields for pleasure, where their wickedness would be seen . . . did not scruple to drink all day in private alehouses.[24]

Growing Interest in Science   A significant trend among many gentlemen of leisure during the seventeenth and eighteenth centuries in England was a growing interest in scientific theory and experimentation. Puritan belief emphasized the value of work, diligence, and practical accomplishments. Rejecting the Aristotelian view of science as elitist, contemplative, and not concerned with practical outcomes, many amateur scientists in their leisure began to conduct experiments that were directed to purposeful outcomes. They were, in Charles Sylvester's words:

> . . . "lovers of science" who conducted experiments in their leisure as a way to know and serve God . . . devout and dutiful men who delighted in a leisure pursuit well suited to their interests and abilities and that harmonized with Puritan doctrine.[25]

Their common interest in freely pursued scientific investigations (including studies in the natural and physical sciences) and the collection of antiquities led a number of these individuals to form a club to discuss science in an atmosphere free from the "tumult" of religion and politics. It became the Royal Society, the leading scientific academy in the Western world.

DEVELOPMENT OF PARKS AND RECREATION AREAS

During the Middle Ages, the need to enclose cities within protective walls necessitated building within a compact area that left little space for public gardens or sports areas. As the walled city became more difficult to defend after the invention of gunpowder and cannon, residents began to move out of the central city. Satellite communities developed around the city, but usually with little definite planning.

As the Renaissance period began, European town planning became characterized by wide avenues, long approaches, handsome buildings, and similar monumental features. The nobility decorated their estates with elaborate gardens, some of which were open to public use, as in Italy at the end of the thirteenth century. There were walks and public squares, often decorated with statuary. In some cases, religious brotherhoods built clubhouses, gardens, and shooting stands for archery practice that were used by townspeople for recreation and amusement.

> **T**hree major types of large parks came into existence during the late Renaissance. The first were royal hunting preserves or parks, some of which have become famous public parks today, such as the four-thousand-acre Prater in Vienna and the Tiergarten in Berlin. Second were the ornate and formal garden parks designed according to the so-called French style of landscape architecture. Third were the English garden parks, which strove to produce naturalistic landscape effects. This became the prevailing style in most European cities. In England, there were beginning efforts at city planning during the eighteenth century. Business and residential streets were paved and street names posted. Since it was believed that overcrowding led to disease (in the seventeenth century, London had suffered from recurrent attacks of the plague), an effort was made to convert open squares into gardens and to create more small parks. Deaths from contagious disease declined during each successive decade of the eighteenth century, and this improvement was believed to have been due to increased cleanliness and ventilation within the city.

Use of Private Estates

From 1500 to the latter part of the eighteenth century, the European nobility developed increasingly lavish private grounds. These often included topiary work (trees and shrubbery clipped in fantastic shapes), aviaries, fishponds, summer houses, water displays, outdoor theaters, hunting grounds and menageries, and facilities for outdoor games. During this period, such famed gardens as the Tuileries and the Luxembourg in Paris as well as Versailles were established by the French royalty; similar gardens and private estates were found all over Europe.

Following the early Italian example, it became the custom to open these private parks and gardens to the public. At first they were opened only on special occasions or by caprice; some might be kept open for a time and then suddenly closed at the whim of the owner. In London the great parks were the property of the Crown, and in the eighteenth century they were opened to the public. When Queen Caroline had a fancy to close Kensington Gardens, she asked her advisor, Lord Walpole, what it might cost to do so; he gave the significant reply, "Only three crowns."

Popular Diversions in England

Great outdoor gardens were established to provide entertainment and relaxation. Vauxhall, a pleasure resort founded during the reign of Charles II, was a densely wooded area with walks and bowers, lighting displays, water mills, fireworks, artificial caves and grottoes, entertainment, eating places, and tea gardens. The park was supported by the growing class of merchants and tradesmen and its admission charge and distance from London helped to "exclude the rabble."

Other pleasure resorts open to the public during the eighteenth century featured music, singing, tea, and coffee. They were considered to be helpful in raising moral standards; even the caustic critic Dr. Johnson declared, "I am a great friend to public amusements; for they keep people from vice."

Following the Restoration period in England, Hyde Park and St. James Park became fashionable centers for promenading by the upper classes during the early afternoon. Varied amusements were provided in the parks—wrestling matches, races, military displays, fireworks, and illuminations on special occasions. Aristocrats, merchants, and tradesmen all rode, drove carriages, and strolled in the parks. Horse racing, lotteries, and other forms of gambling became the vogue.

Among the lower classes, tastes in entertainment varied according to whether one lived in the country or city. Countrymen continued to engage vigorously in such sports as football, cricket, wrestling, or "cudgel playing," and to enjoy traditional country or Morris dancing and the singing of old folk songs.

RECREATION IN FRANCE

France provides another example of the growth of recreational opportunity during the Renaissance. For the wealthy in the eighteenth century, Paris was a "city of pleasure carried to a high pitch." They had the opportunity for leisurely play all week long—playing and receiving visits, dining, and passing evenings at gaming, at the theater, ballet, or opera, or at clubs. In contrast, the working classes had only Sundays and fête days, or holidays, for their amusements. La Croix points out, however, that these represented a third of the whole year; in addition to those holidays decreed by the state, many other special celebrations had been either authorized or tolerated by the Catholic church. Many economists and men of affairs argued that the ecclesiastic authorities should be called upon to reduce the number. Voltaire wrote in 1756:

> Twenty fête days too many in the country condemn to inactivity and expose to dissipation twenty times a year ten millions of workingmen, each of whom would earn five pence a day, and this gives a total of 180 million livres . . . lost to the state in the course of a twelve-month. This painful fact is beyond all doubt.[26]

Concerns About Leisure

Within the larger cities in France, many places of commercial amusement sprang up. Cafes provided meeting places to chat, read newspapers, and play dominoes, chess, checkers, or billiards. The Marquis de Mirabeau was one of many who complained about the growing use of such establishments:

> The lower order of working men frequent the *guinguinettes*, licensed places of dissipation, which, it is rumored, the authorities tolerate because of taxes levied on them. They all go home tipsy and are unfit for work the next day. Employers of labour will tell you that their men work half time on Saturday and on Monday sleep off the effects of their dissipation; they are not up to much on Tuesday, and if there should happen to be a saint's-day in the middle of the week they do not see anything of them the other four days.[27]

People made frequent excursions to the country, where they enjoyed dancing or bathing in outdoor pavilions. In winter a great crowd would enjoy sliding on the ice of the frozen Seine. The chief amusement of Parisians of all classes and ages was the promenade, which the wealthy enjoyed every day and the lower classes on Sundays and holy days. For these, they visited the great parks, the Luxembourg and Tuileries Gardens, and other such areas.

There were many public festivals on occasions of royal marriages, coronations, or other times of celebration, when free wine and food were provided for the public and as many as a hundred illuminated boats cruised up and down the Seine as their bands played. Dancing continued throughout the year, with the lower classes visiting commercial dance halls or outdoor pavilions and the upper classes giving private balls for guests. The theater enjoyed a great vogue in eighteenth century Paris; many of the production expenses were paid by the Crown. By the 1770s, all the chief cities in the provinces had theaters comparable to those in Paris, and there were many strolling companies that visited smaller towns.

RECREATION IN AMERICA: THE COLONIAL PERIOD

We now cross the Atlantic to examine the development of recreation and leisure in the early American colonies. First, it needs to be recognized that when English and other settlers came to the New World, they did not entirely divorce themselves from the customs and values of the countries they had left. Commerce was ongoing, governors and military personnel traveled back and forth, and newspapers, magazines, and books were exchanged regularly. Thus, there was a constant interchange of ideas and social trends; one historian has summed it up by saying that an Atlantic civilization existed which embraced both sides of the great ocean. Michael Kraus writes:

> What came from the New World . . . was embedded . . . in the pattern of European life. The revolutions of the sixteenth and seventeenth centuries—political, scientific, religious and commercial—make for a remarkable fertility of speculation and social reorientation. . . . The era of democratization was thus well begun, and this, truly, was in large measure the creation of the Atlantic civilization.[28]

Despite this linkage, the North American settlements represented a unique and harsh environment for most Europeans who arrived during the period of early colonization. The first need of seventeenth century colonists was for survival. They had to plant crops, clear forests, build shelters, and in some cases defend themselves against attack by hostile Indians. More than half of the colonists who arrived on the Mayflower did not survive the first harsh winter near Plymouth. In such a setting, work was all-important; there was little time, money, or energy to support amusements or public entertainment. Without a nobility possessing the wealth, leisure, and inclination to patronize the arts, there was little opportunity for music, theater, or dance to flourish. But the most important hindrance to the development of recreation was the religious attitude.

Restrictions in New England

The Puritan settlers of New England came to the New World to establish a society based on a strict Calvinist interpretation of the Bible. Although the work ethic had not originated with the Puritans, they adopted it enthusiastically. Idleness was detested as the "devil's workshop," and a number of colonies passed laws binding "any rougs, vagabonds, sturdy beggards, masterless men or other notorious offenders" over to compulsory work or imprisonment.

Puritan magistrates attempted to maintain curbs on amusements long after the practical reasons for such prohibitions had disappeared. Early court records show many cases of young people being fined, confined to the stocks, or publicly whipped for such "violations" as drunkeness, idleness, gambling, dancing, or participating in other forms of "lascivious" behavior. Yet, despite these restrictions, many forms of play continued. Alice Earle writes of football being played by boys in Boston's streets and lanes, and points out that although playing cards (the "devil's picture-books") were intensely hated by the Puritans, they were abundantly imported from England and openly on sale.[29]

There were strict ordinances against gambling, drama, nonreligious music, and dancing—particularly dancing between men and women. Dancing in taverns and maypole dancing were especially condemned; Governor Endicott of the Massachusetts Bay Colony cut down the maypole at Merry Mount, grimly warning the revelers against this "pagan" practice. The theater was completely prohibited in several colonies during the seventeenth century. A number of New England colonies banned dice, cards, quoits, bowls, ninepins, and similar pastimes in "house, yard or garden." There was especially strong enforcement of the Sabbath laws; Sunday work, travel, or recreation, even "unnecessary and unseasonable walking in the streets and fields," was prohibited. Merrymaking on religious holidays such as Christmas or Easter was banned.

Leisure in the Southern Colonies

A number of the southern colonies had similar restrictions during the early years of settlement. The laws of Virginia, for example, forbade Sunday amusements and made imprisonment the penalty for failure to attend church services. Sabbath-day dancing, fiddling, hunting, fishing, and cardplaying were strictly banned. Gradually, however, these stern restrictions declined in the southern colonies. There the upper classes had both wealth and leisure from their large estates and plantations, on which the labor was performed by indentured servants and slaves. Many of them had ties with the landed gentry in England and shared their tastes for aristocratic amusements. As southern settlers of this social class became established, plantation life became marked by lavish entertainment and hospitality. Holiday, weddings, family reunions, and even funerals were observed by lavish feasting, dancing parties, and music.[30] Hunting and fishing were especially popular, as was gambling. Card games of all types, lotteries, roulette tables, and dice were common. Jane Carson writes:

> Gambling was not considered an evil in itself; it became a vice only when "inordinate" pursuit of the amusement led one to neglect his business or lose more money than he could afford. Professional gamesters were condemned for cheating if caught red-handed, but controlled "deceit" was only a mark of the skillful player. In Virginia, as in England, gaming was a gentleman's privilege, forbidden by law to those who were supposed to be working: apprentices, artificers, fishermen, husbandmen, laborers, mariners, servants of all kinds.[31]

Such "unlawful games" as bear-baiting, bull-baiting, bowling, cards, cockfighting, quoits, dice, football, ninepins, and tennis were usually forbidden to workingmen, servants, apprentices, and students. Yet it is clear that they enjoyed these forbidden activities frequently. By the close of the eighteenth century, a French visitor, the Marquis de Chastellux, observed:

> The indolence and dissipation of the middling and lower classes of white inhabitants of Virginia, are such as to give pain to every reflecting mind. Horse racing, cock fighting, and boxing matches are standing amusements, for which they neglect all business.[32]

Decline of Religious Controls

Despite the stern sermons of New England ministers and the severe penalties for infractions of the established moral code, it was clear that play became gradually tolerated in the colonies. In terms of gambling, the lottery was introduced during the early 1700s and quickly gained the sanction and participation of the most esteemed citizens. Towns and states used lotteries to increase their revenue and to build canals, turnpikes, and bridges. This "acceptable" form of gambling helped to endow leading colleges and academies, and even Congregational, Baptist, and Episcopal churches had lotteries "for promoting public worship and the advancement of religion."

In the realm of sexual behavior, the practice of bundling was widely accepted. A fairly open invitation to premarital sexual activity, bundling permitted engaged couples to sleep together through the night, separated by a low wooden board. Despite the supposedly rigorous religious principles in New England, there is much evidence that

> among New Englanders of all social classes in the early part of the eighteenth century . . . fornication if followed by marriage, no matter how long delayed, was considered a venial sin, if sin at all.[33]

Even in the area of drinking, the climate began to change despite the very strong opposition of the Puritan magistrates in New England. Under Puritan law, drunkards were subject to fine and imprisonment in the stocks, and sellers were forbidden to provide them with any liquor thereafter. A frequent drunkard, according to Earle, was punished by having a large *D* made of "Redd Cloth" hung around his neck or sewn on his clothing, and he lost the right to vote. Yet, by the early part of the eighteenth century, taverns were widely established throughout New England, providing places where gentlemen might "enjoy their bowl and bottle with satisfaction" and engage in billiards, cards, skittles, and other games. Drinking soon became widespread throughout the colonies. Charles Andrews writes:

> The colonists were heavy drinkers and . . . consumed liquors of every variety in enormous quantities on all important occasions—baptisms, weddings, funerals, barn raisings, church raisings, house raisings, ship launchings, ordinations . . . at meeting of commissions and committees, and in taverns, clubs, and private houses.[34]

Gradually, restrictions against play were relaxed in New England and elsewhere. Recreation became more acceptable when amusements could be attached to work, and thus country fairs and market days became occasions for merrymaking. Social gatherings with music, games, and dancing were held in conjunction with such work projects as house raisings, sheepshearing, logrolling, or cornhusking bees. Many social pastimes were linked to other civic occasions such as elections or training days for local militia. On training days in Boston, over a thousand men would gather on the Boston Common to drill and practice marksmanship, after which they celebrated at nearby taverns.

Even in the sports of the woods and waters, Puritans could find acceptable diversion justified by necessity. The wolf, then among the most hated and destructive of all wild animals, was a "proper prey." Countrymen caught wolves in pits, log pens, and traps, or on mackerel hooks dipped in tallow and baited by dead carcasses. Groups of hunters encircled wooded areas, beating the woods and swamps as they tightened the circle, driving the wolves before them; after catching them, they often put them to death cruelly.

As in England, fascination with such spectacles was not limited to the torture of animals. Earle writes that diversion was also furnished to the colonists by the punishment of criminals of all sorts. Offenders were not only whipped and set in the stocks, cage, or pillory, but were hung with "much parade before the eyes of the people, as a visible token of the punishment of evil living." Executions were very widely publicized, and great crowds came to observe them. When a group of pirates were hanged in Boston in 1704, several hundred boats and canoes covered the river to watch the spectacle.

By the mid-1700s, the stern necessity of hard work for survival had lessened, and religious antagonism toward amusements had also declined. However, the Sunday laws continued in many settlements, and there was still a strong undercurrent of disapproval of play. Certain religious groups refused to relax their firm opposition to all forms of play. The Methodist Episcopal church in the late eighteenth century revealed its distrust of idleness and the temptations of play in its statement of policy:

> We prohibit *play* in the strongest terms. . . . The students shall rise at five o-clock . . . summer and winter. . . . Their recreation shall be gardening, walking, riding, and bathing, without doors, and the carpenter's, joiner's, cabinet-maker's, or turner's business within doors. . . . The students shall be indulged with nothing which the world calls play. Let this rule be observed with the strictest nicety; for those who play when they are young, will play when they are old.[35]

Parks and Conservation in the Colonial Era

Compared with the nations of Europe, the early American colonies showed little concern for developing parks. With land so plentiful around the isolated settlements along the eastern seaboard, there seemed to be little need for such planning. Even in the earliest colonies, however, particularly in New England, a number of towns and villages established "commons" or "greens," used chiefly for pasturing cattle and sheep but also for military drills, market days, and fairs. Similar open areas were established in towns settled by the Spanish in the South and Southwest, in the form of plazas and large squares in the center of towns or adjacent to principal churches.

Beautiful village greens established during the colonial period still exist throughout Massachusetts, Connecticut, Vermont, and New Hampshire. In the design of new cities, the colonists began to give attention to the need for preserving or establishing parks and open spaces. Among the first cities in which such plans were made were Philadelphia, Savannah, and Washington, D.C.

The description in a plan drafted for the city of Philadelphia in 1682 by William Penn's Surveyor-General reveals a conscious effort to provide public parks.

> The city, as the model shows, consists of a large Front-street on each river, and a High-street near the middle, from river to river, of one hundred feet broad, and a Broad-street, in the middle of the city from side to side, of the like breadth. In the center of the city, is a square of ten acres; at each angle to build houses for public affairs. There is also in each quarter of the city a square of eight acres, to be for the like used.[36]

The plans developed in 1773 by General Oglethorpe for Savannah, then the principal city of Georgia, made even more extensive provision for public open space and greenery. Oglethorpe spared many large forest trees when the site for the town was cleared, and his land-grant scheme permitted each freeholder, in addition to his own plot of land within the town, five rural acres for a garden and orchard. Besides the common and the public gardens covering 10 acres of rolling land near the river, Savannah had 24 other small squares and open spaces. By comparison, the majority of colonial communities made very limited provision for parks or open recreation areas.

Early Conservation Efforts

Almost from the earliest days of settlement, there was concern for the conservation of forests and open land. As early as 1626 in the Plymouth Colony, the cutting of trees without official consent was prohibited by law. The Massachusetts Bay Colony passed the Great Ponds Act in

1641, which set aside 2,000 bodies of water, each over 10 acres in size, for such public uses as "fishing and fowling." The courts supported this conservation of land for recreational use. Pennsylvania law in 1681 required that for every five acres of forest land that were cleared, one was to be left untouched. Other laws prohibiting setting woods on fire or cutting certain types of trees were enacted long before the Revolution.

As early as the late seventeenth century, Massachusetts and Connecticut defined hunting seasons and established rules for hunting certain types of game. Although originally a means of obtaining food, hunting rapidly became a sport in the colonies. Andrews writes:

> The woods and waters offered endless opportunity in summer for fishing and in winter for such time-honored pursuits as hunting, fowling, trapping, and fishing through the ice. John Rowe of Boston was a famous and untiring fisherman; thousands of other enthusiasts played the part of colonial Isaak Waltons; and there was a fishing club on the Schuylkill as early as 1732.[37]

What appeared to be an inexhaustible supply of wildlife began to disappear with the advance of settlements and the destruction of the forests. Wildfowl in particular were ruthlessly hunted, especially in New England, and "so unlicensed had the destruction of the heath hen become in New York that in 1708 the province determined to protect its game by providing for a closed season."[38] Thus, before the Revolution, the colonists had shown a concern for the establishment of parks and urban open spaces and for the conservation of forests and wildlife.

SUMMARY

This chapter shows the long history of recreation, play, and leisure by discussing their roles during the ancient civilizations of Assyria, Babylonia, and Egypt, then in the Greek and Roman eras and, finally during the Middle Ages, the Renaissance, and the pre-Revolutionary period in the North American colonies.

Religion and social class were major factors that influenced recreational involvement in terms of either prohibiting certain forms of activity or assigning them to one class or another. Leisure, seen as an aristocratic devotion to knowledge, the arts, athletics, philosophy, and contemplation in ancient Athens, took a different form in Rome where it became a political instrument devoted to perpetuating the rule of the Roman emperors by entertaining and placating the common people.

During the Dark and Middle Ages, the Catholic church placed a strong value on work and worship and sought to prohibit forms of play that had descended from pagan sources. However, such activities as sports and games, music, dance, the theater, and gambling persisted, even under the stern condemnation of the new Protestant sects that gained influence during the period of the Reformation. At this time, class distinctions in terms of appropriate forms of play became clearly evident in England, France, and other European nations. However, the value of play as a form of childhood education was championed in the writings of numerous educators and philosophers of that era.

In the pre-Revolutionary American colonies, New England Puritans were very strict in their condemnation of most recreational pursuits. After an initial conservative period, however, play and varied social pursuits flourished in the plantations of the southern colonies, which had been settled by members of the English gentry who used slaves and indentured servants to make their own leisure possible. By the end of the eighteenth century, a more relaxed attitude toward play was widely evident with the increased appearance of sports and games, horse racing and gambling, dancing and music, taverns, and holiday and civic celebrations.

In Europe, royal estates and gardens had begun to be opened to the public and were, in time, transformed into famous parks. In the New World, however, with the exception of village greens in New England towns and a few cities that made planning provisions for parks, there were few outdoor areas designated for public leisure use. However, as early as the seventeenth century, conservation efforts were made to protect wildlife and forest areas.

Questions for Class Discussion or Essay Examinations

1. One way to understand what play may have been like during the early, prehistoric period of human development is to look at the rituals, sports, and other customs or forms of play in more recently observed tribal cultures. On the basis of such observations, what kinds of play do you believe early peoples engaged in?

2. Contrast the attitudes toward sports and other uses of leisure that were found in ancient Greece with those found in the Roman Empire. How did their philosophies differ, and how did the Roman philosophy lead to a weakening of that powerful nation? Could you draw a parallel between the approach to leisure and entertainment in ancient Rome and that in the present-day United States?

3. Trace the development of religious attitudes and policies regarding leisure and play from the Dark and Middle Ages, through the Renaissance and Reformation periods, to the colonial era in seventeenth and eighteenth century North America. What differences were there in their approach to recreation between the northern and southern colonies at this time?

Endnotes

2   P. C. McIntosh, *Sport in Society* (London: C. A. Watts, 1963): 4.

3   Michael Lemonick, "Secrets of the Maya," *Time* (9 August 1993): 48.

4   "The Ancient World of a War-Torn Tribe," *Life* (28 December 1972): 73.

5   Robert Gardner and Karl Heider, *Gardens of War: Life and Death in the New Guinea Stone Age* (New York: Random House, 1968): 63.

6   John Loy, Jr., and Gerald Kenyon, *Sport, Culture, and Society* (New York: Macmillan, 1969): 92.

7   Garry Chick, "Leisure, Labor and the Complexity of Culture: An Anthropological Perspective," *Journal of Leisure Research* 3 (1986): 154–168.

8   C. W. Ceram, *Gods, Graves and Scholars,* quoted in Charles Doell and Charles Fitzgerald, *A Brief History of Parks and Recreation in the United States* (Chicago: The Athletic Institute, 1954): 7.

9   James Thompson, "Political and Athletic Interaction in Athens During the Sixth and Fifth Centuries B.C.," *Research Quarterly for Exercise and Sport* 3 (1988): 183–190.

10   Plato, *The Laws*, translated by R. G. Bury (Cambridge: Harvard University Press, 1926, 1961): 23.

11   Pericles, quoted in Allen Sapora and Elmer Mitchell, *The Theory of Play and Recreation* (New York: Ronald Press, 1961): 18.

12   Aristotle, quoted in Robert Ulich, *History of Educational Thought* (New York: American Book Co., 1950): 17.

13   See Lincoln Kirstein, *Dance: A Short History of Classical Theatrical Dancing* (New York: G. P. Putnam, 1935): 7.

14   Pearson, *op. cit.,* 41.

15   Kirstein, *op. cit.,* 57.

16   Margaret H'Doubler, *Dance: A Creative Art Experience* (New York: F. S. Crofts, 1940): 13.

17   Paul La Croix, *France in the Middle Ages: Customs, Classes, Conditions* (New York: Frederick Ungar, 1963): 179.

18   J. J. Bagley, *Life in Medieval England* (London: B. T. Batsford, 1960): 96.

19   Edward M. Hulme, *The Middle Ages* (New York: Holt, 1938): 604.

20   Fred Leonard, *A Guide to the History of Physical Education* (Philadelphia: Lea and Febiger, 1928): 55.

21   See Walter Wood, *Children's Play and Its Place in Education* (London: Kegan Paul, Trench, and Trubner, 1913): 48.

22   Norman Miller and Duane Robinson, *The Leisure Age* (Belmont, Cal.: Wadsworth, 1963): 66.

23   See Harvey Lehman and Paul Witty, *The Psychology of Play Activities* (New York: A. S. Barnes, 1927): 1.

24   See Peter Fryer, *Mrs. Grundy: Studies in English Prudery* (London: House and Maxwell, 1964): 106.

25   Charles Sylvester, "Leisure, Science and Religion in 17th Century England," *Leisure Sciences* (Vol. 16 No. 1, January-March 1994): 9.

26   La Croix, *op. cit.,* 346.

27   *Ibid.*

28   Michael Kraus, *The Atlantic Civilization—18th Century Origins* (Ithaca, N.Y.: Cornell University Press and American Historical Association, 1949): 3.

29   Alice Morse Earle, *Customs and Fashions in Old New England* (Rutland, Vt.: Charles E. Tuttle, 1893, 1975): 239.

30   Foster Rhea Dulles, *A History of Recreation: America Learns to Play* (New York: Appleton–Century–Crofts, 1965): 57.

31   Jane Carson, *Colonial Americans at Play* (Charlottesville, Va.: University Press of Virginia, 1965): 53.

32   Dulles, *op. cit.,* 35.

33   James Truslow Adams, *Provincial Society, 1690–1763* (New York: Macmillan, 1973): 159.

34   Charles Andrews, *Colonial Folkways* (New Haven, Conn.: Yale University Press, 1919): 104.

35   *The Doctrines and Discipline of the Methodist Episcopal Church in America* (Philadelphia: Parry Hall, 1782): 68.

36   Thomas Holme, quoted in Doell and Fitzgerald, *op. cit.,* 24.

37   Andrews, *op. cit.,* 113.

38   *Ibid.*

Leisure Comes of Age: Industrial Revolution and Early Twentieth Century

By building a park [Prospect Park] arguably superior even to the newly completed Central Park, Brooklyn's city fathers hoped to lure affluent residents and increase the tax base.

So how marvelous that these hard-headed goals perfectly coincided with prevailing progressive ideology. Parks were seen as specks of sanity in sinister, dehumanizing cities. America might have been teeming with new immigrants, torn by new technologies and dominated by robber barons, but this was at heart an agrarian nation. There was also the thought that parks might act as a civilizing influence on the foreign hordes, perhaps making them less prone to riot.

Using designs owing much to the picturesque tradition of English landscape design, they used heavy equipment to contrive bucolic settings in emphatically non-rural areas. . . . From the beginning, Prospect Park fulfilled its joyful purpose. Sepia photographs showed Sunday-only gentry and a flock of sheep crowded on the Long Meadow. There was a wind-powered carousel on the lake, a penful of deer in the woods. Traditions coalesced: fishing contests, ice carnivals, Maypole dancing.[1]

---

[1] Douglas Martin, "The Country in the City: A Great Notion Lives on in Brooklyn's Prospect Park," *New York Times* (27 May 1990): 6-E.

INTRODUCTION

During the nineteenth century, tremendous social change took place in both Europe and America. It was a period of growing democratization, advancement of scientific knowledge, and huge waves of immigration from Europe to the New World. More than any other factor, the Industrial Revolution changed the way people lived, and it also had a major effect on popular patterns of recreation and leisure. By the early decades of the twentieth century, leisure was more freely available to all, and a widespread recreation movement had begun in the United States and Canada.

NINETEENTH CENTURY INDUSTRIAL REVOLUTION

The Industrial Revolution extended from the late eighteenth through the twentieth century. Science and capital combined to increase production, as businessmen invested in the industrial expansion made possible by newly invented machines. Industry moved from homes and small workshops to new mills and factories with mechanical power. The invention of such devices as the spinning jenny, the water frame, the weaving machine, and the steam engine— during the 1760s, drastically altered production methods and increased output.

The locomotive, the steamboat, and the telegraph gave rise to greater world trade, exploration, and colonization. Networks of canals, rapidly expanded railroad lines, the completion of the transatlantic cable, and the scientific study of navigation made a vast expansion of industry possible and created a totally new way of life.

Urbanization

Throughout the Western world, there was a steady shift of the population from rural areas to urban centers. Because factory wages were usually higher than those in domestic industry or agriculture, great numbers of people moved to the cities to work. Millions of European peasant families immigrated because of crop failures, expulsion from their land, religious or social discrimination, or political unrest. The American population increased rapidly. When Andrew Jackson became President in 1829, about 12.5 million people lived in the United States. By 1850 the total had reached 23 million, and a decade later America's population was 31 million. In the large cities, the proportion of foreign born was quite high: 45 percent of New York City's population in 1850 was foreign born, mostly Irish and German.

About 85 percent of the population in 1850 was still rural, living in areas of less than 2,500 population. However, as more and more people moved into factory towns and large cities along the eastern seaboard or around the Great Lakes, the United States became an urban civilization.

Expansion of Slums   Rural townspeople and foreign immigrants moved into the congested tenement areas of growing cities, living in quarters that were inadequate for decent family life. Often a family lived crowded in a single room under unsanitary and unsafe conditions. The new urban slums were marked by congestion and disease; their residents were oppressed by low wages and recurrent unemployment and by monotonous and prolonged labor, including the use of young children in mills, mines and factories and at piecework tasks at home.

The Availability of Leisure

The trend in manual occupations in Europe from the late Middle Ages to 1800 was toward longer working hours. With industrialization, the average working day in both France and England climbed from 12 hours in about 1700 to a 14- to 18-hour day in 1800. By 1850, the average workweek in French cities was about 70 hours. In addition, the number of holidays provided during the year was sharply reduced.

The peak of working hours appears to have been reached during the first half of the nineteenth century. Gradually, pressure by trade unions and industrial legislation improved the situation. In England, for example, factory acts during the first 40 years of the nineteenth century removed the youngest children from factories and limited the working hours of others. The hours of labor were limited by law to 10 per day in 1847; a 9-hour day was won by contract for most workers between 1869 and 1873. By 1919, the 8-hour day had been formally adopted in nearly all European countries.

Acceptance of the Protestant Work Ethic

The Puritan ideal, which glorified work and condemned leisure and play, became even stronger as a consequence of the Industrial Revolution. In the United States, dedication to work became a hallmark of American life. As industrialization became more widespread, there was a renewed emphasis on the importance of "honest toil" and a strong antagonism expressed against play. Religious leaders supported the 10- or 14-hour workday as part of the "wholesome discipline of factory life."

Work became the basis for a person's self-justification, and the capitalist system was believed to rest on the moral and religious justification that the Reformation had given to work. Americans became more consciously dedicated to the Protestant work ethic than Europeans had ever been; their single-minded dedication to work was noted by many foreign visitors.

Not just in America, but throughout the Western world, life was seen as a sober business. The British philosopher and historian Thomas Carlyle expressed the spirit of his times in such statements as: "All work, even cotton-spinning, is noble; work is alone noble . . . a life of ease is not for any man, nor for any god," and "Even in the meanest sorts of labor, the whole soul of a man is composed into a kind of real harmony the instant he sets himself to work." John Ruskin, the English critic, wrote, "Life without industry is guilt," and "When men are rightly occupied, their amusement grows out of their work."

In the United States and Great Britain, there were recurrent efforts to prohibit various forms of popular play. Gary Cross points out that the English gentry in the late 1700s abandoned support for traditional sports and that, in the 1810s, the British Society for the Suppression of Vice pressed local magistrates to prosecute drunks, bear baiters, Sabbath breakers, and other offenders. He continues:

Throughout Britain in the 1840s, new professionalized police forces drove the young playing pitch-and-toss from the streets and even exterminated the ancient sport of pigeon-flying. Rural traditions in 1800 of up to 13 days of games, dancing, and drinking at Whitsuntide were reduced to a single Bank Holiday by the 1870s.[2]

Work was considered the source of social and moral values, and therefore the proper concern of the church which renewed its attack upon most forms of play. The church condemned many commercial amusements as "the door to all the sins of iniquity." As late as 1844, Henry Ward Beecher, a leading minister, savagely attacked the stage, the concert hall, and the circus, charging that anyone who pandered to the public taste for commercial entertainment was a moral assassin.

GROWTH OF POPULAR PARTICIPATION IN RECREATION

Despite such efforts, which were fueled by a religious revival before the Civil War, the first half of the nineteenth century saw a gradual expansion of popular amusements in the United States. Foster Rhea Dulles writes:

> The first half of the nineteenth century witnessed the growth of the theater as entertainment reaching out to all classes of people. It saw the beginnings of variety, minstrel shows, and the circus; the establishment of amusement parks, public dance-halls, concert saloons and beer-gardens; a revival of horse-racing and the rise of other popular sports. By the Civil War the nation was in the midst of these far-reaching changes in the recreational scene.[3]

The theater, which had been banned during the American Revolution, gradually gained popularity in cities along the eastern seaboard and in the south. Large theaters were built to accommodate audiences of as many as 4,000 people. Performances were usually by touring players who joined local stock companies throughout the country in presenting serious drama as well as lighthearted entertainment, which later became burlesque and vaudeville. By the 1830s, about 30 traveling shows were regularly touring the country, with menageries and bands of acrobats and jugglers. Ultimately the latter added riding and tumbling acts and developed into circuses.

Another popular form of stage entertainment, especially during the 1840s and 1850s but continuing after the Civil War, was the minstrel show. Combining music, singing, dancing, and "blackface" comedy routines in which plantation blacks were caricatured by white performers in burnt-cork makeup, minstrels conveyed a distorted image of blacks in American folklore.

Drinking also remained a popular pastime. At this time, the majority of American men were taverngoers. Printed street directories of American cities listed tavernkeepers in staggering numbers. J. Larkin writes that as the nation's most popular centers of male sociability:

> . . . . taverns were often the scene of excited gaming and vicious fights and always of hard drinking, heavy smoking, and an enormous amount of alcohol-stimulated talk. . . . Taverns accommodated women as travelers, but their barroom clienteles were almost exclusively male. Apart from the dockside dives frequented by prostitutes, or the liquor-selling groceries of poor city neighborhoods, women rarely drank in public.[4]

Working class districts presented particular problems of social control—marked as they were by frequent battles between different racial or ethnic factions and by rioting during the holidays. Susan Davis points out that, even in the pre-Revolutionary period, Quaker authorities in Philadelphia had tried to eliminate festive Christmas customs, such as wearing disguises, drumbeating, firing guns, noisemaking, drinking, and feasting. Now, during the first half of the nineteenth century, the city was torn at such times by rioting gangs of men and boys, mob attacks on blacks, firemen's riots, arson, and huge crowds in major streets and squares.[5]

Growing Interest in Sport

A number of sports gained their first strong impetus during the early nineteenth century. Americans had enjoyed watching amateur wrestling matches, foot races, shooting events, and horse races during colonial days and along the frontier. In the early 1800s, professional promotion of sports events began as well.

Professionalism in Sports   Crowds as large as 50,000 drawn from all ranks of society attended highly publicized boating regattas, and five- and ten-mile races of professional runners during the 1820s. The first sports promoters were owners of resorts or of commercial transportation facilities such as stagecoach lines, ferries, and, later, trolleys and railroads. These new sports impresarios initially made their profits from transportation fares and accommodations for spectators; later, they erected grandstands and charged admission.

Horse racing flourished; both running and trotting races attracted crowds as large as 100,000 spectators. Prize fighting also gained popularity as a professional contest. It began as a brutal, bare-knuckled sport that was often prohibited by legal authorities; but by the time of the Civil War, gloves were used and rules established, and boxing exhibitions were becoming accepted. Baseball was enjoyed as a casual diversion in the towns of New England through the early decades of the nineteenth century (in the form of "rounders" or "town-ball"), and amateur teams, often organized by occupation (merchants and clerks, or shipwrights and mechanics), were playing on the commons of large eastern cities by the mid-1850s.

Racial and Ethnic Influences on Leisure

Throughout the period before the Civil War, slaves living on southern plantations had relatively few opportunities for leisure or recreation. Particularly for black field hands, work hours were long and oppressive; however, Sundays were free of work and could be spent fishing, hunting, socializing, or pursuing other leisure pursuits, as well as religious worship. In describing the slave community in the antebellum South, John Blassingame points out that house slaves were sometimes permitted to organize balls and parties. On most plantations, work was suspended for a short time after crops were raised in the fall or during the Christmas season. Some plantation owners arranged feasts for their slaves and even permitted them to visit neighboring plantations at such times.[6]

At the same time, southern planters sought to prevent their slaves from using drums or horns that might be used to signal rebellions such as those which had occurred during the 1700s in South Carolina and Georgia; they also tried to stamp out other aspects of African culture that many slaves continued to practice. Blassingame comments that, however oppressive plantation life was, slaves managed to create a number of unique cultural forms that lightened their burden and helped to maintain morale in an area of life free from the control of their masters:

> Among the elements of slave culture were: an emotional religion [that combined Christian elements with earlier African rites], folk songs and tales, dances, and superstitions. His thoughts, values, ideals and behavior were all greatly influenced by these processes. . . . the more they were immune from the control of whites, the more the slave gained in personal autonomy and positive self-concepts.[7]

Similarly, the large numbers of European immigrants who came to the United States during the nineteenth century tended initially to practice their own folk customs, games, sports, and traditions in separate ethnic groupings—until, with succeeding generations, they gradually blended into the overall American pattern of leisure pursuits.

CHANGING ATTITUDES TOWARD PLAY

The Civil War was a stimulus to recreational involvement for several reasons. One was the spreading of interests as men from different areas of the country learned each other's games and sports. Army life offered more free time than life at home, and there was no puritanical influence to prevent play. Men on both sides of the war engaged in a wide variety of recreational pursuits. Soldiers actively participated in combative sports (boxing and wrestling), cockfighting, fencing matches, boating and fishing, horseback riding, team sports, and other pursuits like tenpins, gymnastics, card playing, and table games (checkers, chess, dominoes).

During the last half of the nineteenth century, the Industrial Revolution was flourishing with factories, expansion of urban areas, and railroads criss-crossing the country. Free public education had become a reality in most regions of the country, and health care and life expectancy were improving. As the industrial labor force began to organize into craft unions, working conditions improved, levels of pay increased, and the hours of work were cut back. Children, who had worked long, hard hours in factories, mines, and big-city sweatshops, were freed of this burden through child labor legislation.

Gradually, the climate grew more receptive toward play and leisure. Although the work ethic was still widely accepted and there was almost no public provision for recreation, leisure was about to expand sharply. The strong disapproval of play that had characterized the colonial period began to disappear.

By the 1880s and 1890s church leaders recognized that religion could no longer arbitrarily condemn all play and offered "sanctified amusement and recreation" as alternatives to undesirable play. Many churches made provisions for libraries, gymnasiums, and assembly rooms.

A number of leading mid-nineteenth century preachers began to argue that physical prowess and sanctity were compatible. Henry Ward Beecher drew a line between "harmful" amusements and those that contributed to well-being, saying, "Don't be tempted to give up a wholesome air-bath, a good walk, or a skate or ride every day (as) it will pay you back . . . by freshness, elasticity, and clearness of mind." For the first time, Americans took a hard look at themselves and were not pleased with what they saw. Oliver Wendell Holmes argued that widespread participation in sports would create a physically fit citizenry.

The growth of popular amusements, such as music, vaudeville, theater, and dance that had characterized the first half of the century became even more pronounced. Popular hobbies such as photography caught on and were frequently linked to new outdoor recreation pursuits. Sports was probably the largest single area of expanded leisure participation, with increasing interest being shown in tennis, archery, bowling, skating, bicycling, and team games like baseball, basketball, and football.

Athletic and outdoor pastimes steadily became more socially acceptable. Skating became a vogue in the 1850s, and rowing and sailing also grew popular, especially for the upper social classes.

The Role of Sports

In Europe, sports had been seen as an important means of achieving physical fitness and national morale since the late eighteenth century. J. F. Jahn had envisioned a national sporting movement that would regenerate the German people after their crushing defeats in the Napoleonic Wars. During the early decades of the nineteenth century, Jahn's *turnen* (system of gymnastics) spread rapidly throughout Germany, where it had strong military and political support. Soon his ideas were adopted in other countries throughout Europe.

In England, the development of recreational sports was strongly influenced by social class. The British aristocracy greatly enjoyed golf and tennis in addition to such traditional field sports as hunting, shooting, and angling. Only the land-owning aristocracy were permitted to hunt on horseback; the game laws prohibited buying or selling game and as late as 1816 threatened heavy penalties for poachers. The lower ranks of society participated in a number of popular sports, including athletic competitions at country fairs that featured a "mob" form of football.

Team sports gradually gained approval in the fashionable English public (actually private, or preparatory) schools. Earlier schoolmasters had opposed them because of their origins. P. C. McIntosh writes:

> Headmasters were hostile to sport. Dr. Keats at Eton tried to prevent cricket against Harrow; the headmaster at Westminster tried to prevent rowing races with Eton, and Dr. Butler, headmaster of Shrewsbury, thought that football was "only fit for butcher boys."[8]

Despite such lack of support, however, students organized their own interscholastic sports competitions. Gradually rugby football spread, and then cricket and organized boating matches. In time, leading headmasters began to believe that sports improved discipline and contributed to "valuable social qualities and manly virtues."

The Muscular Christianity movement—so named because of the support given to it by leading church figures and because sports and physical activity were thought to build morality and good character—had its greatest influence in schools and colleges, which began to initiate programs of physical education and athletic competition. In addition, the newly founded Young Men's Christian Association based its program on active physical recreation.

College Sports   In America, colleges initiated their first competitive sports programs. In colonial New England, youthful students had engaged in many pastimes, with some tolerated by college authorities and others prohibited. The first college clubs had been founded as early as 1717, and social clubs were in full swing by the 1780s and 1790s. By the early nineteenth century, most American colleges had more or less officially recognized clubs and their social activities. The founding of social fraternities in the 1840s and the building of college gymnasiums in the 1860s added to the social life and physical recreation of students.

Intercollegiate sports competition in rowing, baseball, track, and football was organized. The first known intercollegiate football game was between Princeton and Rutgers in 1869; interest spread rapidly, and by the late 1880s college football games were attracting as many as 40,000 spectators.

Baseball   It was baseball, however, that drew the greatest public interest. The National Baseball League was formed during the 1870s, and the modern professional game and its system of major and minor leagues had begun. Baseball also thrived as an amateur sport for millions of persons in other settings: colleges, high schools, YMCAs, and community life.

Amateur Sports   Track and field events were widely promoted by amateur athletic clubs, some of which, like the New York Athletic Club, had many influential members who formed the

Amateur Athletic Union and developed rules to govern amateur sports competition. Gymnastic instruction and games were sponsored by the German *turnvereins,* the Czech *sokols,* and the YMCA, which had established some 260 large gymnasiums around the country by the 1880s and was a leader in sports activities.

Other Activities   Other popular pastimes included croquet, archery, lawn tennis, and roller-skating, which became so popular that skating rinks were built to accommodate thousands of skaters and spectators. Women began to participate in recreational pastimes, enjoying gymnastics, dance, and other athletics in school and college physical education programs. Bicycling was introduced in the 1870s, and within a few years hundreds of thousands of people had become enthusiasts. During the last decades of the nineteenth century, there was a growing vogue for outdoor activities. Americans began to enjoy hiking and mountain climbing, fishing and hunting, camping in national forests and state parks, and nature photography.

During the late 1800s, a number of economic factors also combined to promote sports interest. With rising wages and a shorter workweek, many workers began to take part in organized sports on newly developed sports fields in city parks. Cheap train service carried players and fans to games, and newspapers publicized major sporting events to build circulation. With the invention of the incandescent light bulb, sports fields and indoor gymnasiums began scheduling evening games and matches, including professional prizefights, wrestling matches, and pedestrian contests, which were popular at the time.

GROWTH OF COMMERCIAL AMUSEMENTS

Particularly in larger cities, new forms of commercial amusement sprang up or expanded during the nineteenth century. The theater, in its various forms, was more popular than ever. Dime museums, dance halls, shooting galleries, bowling alleys, billiard parlors, beer gardens, and saloons provided a new world of entertainment for pay. In addition to these, many cities had "red light districts" where houses of prostitution flourished. Drinking, gambling, and commercial vice gradually became serious social problems, particularly when protected by a tacit alliance between criminal figures and big-city political machines.

Amusement parks grew on the outskirts of cities and towns, often established by new rapid transit companies offering reduced-fare rides to the parks in gaily decorated trolley cars. Amusement parks featured such varied attractions as parachute jumps, open-air theaters, band concerts, professional bicycle races, freak shows, games of chance, and shooting galleries. Roller coasters, fun houses, and midget-car tracks also became popular.

Reduction in Work Hours

Throughout this period, there was steady pressure to reduce the workweek, both through industry–labor negotiation and legislation. Benjamin Hunnicutt points out that the effort to obtain shorter work hours was a critical issue in reform politics in the United States throughout the nineteenth century and up until the period of the Great Depression:

> It was an issue for the idealistic antebellum (pre-Civil War) reformers. It had a prominent place in the Populists' Omaha platform and the Bull Moose platform, and appeared in both the Democratic and Republican platforms as late as 1932.[9]

The eight-hour day had been a union objective for many years in the United States, paralleling efforts to reduce the workweek in other countries. In 1868, Congress established the eight-hour day by law for mechanics and laborers employed by or under contracts with the federal government. Following the 1868 law, labor unions made a concerted effort to obtain the eight-hour day in other areas, and in 1890 began to achieve success. The carpenters' union, for example, established shorter hours for its members in 137 cities, affecting about 50,000 carpenters as well as persons in other building trades and craft unions.

Overall, the average workweek declined from 69.7 hours per week for all industries (including agriculture) in 1860 to 61.7 hours in 1890, and to 54.9 hours in 1910.[10] As a consequence, during the last half of the nineteenth century, concerns about increases in free time began to appear—including fears about the dangers of certain forms of play and the broader question of what the potential role of leisure might be in the coming century.

Concerns About Leisure

Intellectual and political leaders raised searching questions. The English author Lord Lytton commented, "The social civilization of a people is always and infallibly indicated by the intellectual character of its amusements." In 1876, Horace Greeley, a leading American journalist, observed that although there were teachers for every art, science, and "elegy", there were no "professors of play." He asked, "Who will teach us incessant workers how to achieve leisure and enjoy it?" And, in 1880, President James Garfield declared in a speech at Lake Chautauqua, "We may divide the whole struggle of the human race into two chapters: first, the fight to get leisure; and then the second fight of civilization—what shall we do with our leisure when we get it."

This new concern was an inevitable consequence of the Industrial Revolution. Americans now lived in greater numbers in large cities, where the traditional social activities of the past and the opportunity for casual play were no longer available. They had increasing amounts of free time and could afford to pay for recreation. There was a need for organized recreation programs that would provide wholesome and enriching leisure experiences for all classes.

Work and Leisure in Socialist Doctrine

At another level entirely, support was given to leisure as a potentially vital force in changing and enriching the life of working people in Europe. For example, Karl Marx viewed work, religion, and the power of the state as closely linked elements of a vast repressive structure—the capitalist system. In Marx's view, leisure time for the "privileged" class was produced by converting the lifetime of the working masses into labor time.[11] Marx concluded that, as a consequence of this laissez-faire capitalism, under which employers were free to determine all aspects of working conditions, the workers were forced to spend long hours at toil—often in dangerous or unhealthy conditions. They were poorly educated, had little meaningful family life or culture, and had no voice in affairs of government or in determining social policy. Marx theorized that if workers were freed for a substantial portion of their time, they could use this new leisure to become more fully educated, to gain in culture, become more involved in civic affairs, and free themselves of the repressive controls of the capitalist system.

Many trade unions in Europe fought to gain free time. Increased leisure was seen as the worker's right, and unions not only fought for it, but also sponsored educational programs, sports, and other cultural activities to fill the free time constructively for their members.

THE BEGINNING RECREATION MOVEMENT

The term *recreation movement* is used here to describe forms of leisure activity that are provided in an organized way by social agencies, either governmental or voluntary, with the intent of achieving desirable social outcomes. Four major streams of development had their roots in the nineteenth century: (1) the adult education movement; (2) the development of a national, state, and municipal parks network; (3) the development of national voluntary organizations and settlement houses; and (4) the playground movement in cities and towns.

The Adult Education Movement

During the early nineteenth century, there was considerable civic concern for improving intellectual cultivation and providing continuing education for adults. Again, this was found in other nations as well; in France, workers' societies were determined to gain shorter workdays and more leisure time for adult study and cultural activities, and they pressed vigorously for the development of popular lectures, adult education courses, and municipal libraries.

In the United States, there was a growing conviction that leisure, properly used, could contribute to the idealistic liberal values that were part of the American intellectual heritage. As early as the founding of the republic, such leaders as Thomas Jefferson and John Adams had envisioned the growth of a rich democratic culture. Adams is said to have written of his children's and America's future:

> I must study Politicks and War that my sons may have liberty to study Mathematicks and Philosophy. My sons ought to study Mathematicks and Philosophy, Geography, Natural History, Naval Architecture, Navigation, Commerce and Agriculture, in order to give their Children a right to study Painting, Poetry, Musick, Architecture, Statuary, Tapestry and Porcelaine.[12]

One of the means of achieving this dream took the form of the Lyceum movement, a national organization with more than 900 local chapters. Its program consisted chiefly of lectures, readings, and other educational events reflecting the view that all citizens should be educated in order to participate knowledgeably in affairs of government.

The Lyceum movement was widely promoted by such organizations as Chautauqua, which sponsored both a lecture circuit and a leading summer camp program in upstate New York for adults and families, with varied cultural activities, sports, lectures, and other educational features. While the professed purpose of Chautauqua was education, it actually provided substantial entertainment and amusement to its audiences as well. By the twentieth century, circuit Chautauquas were formed, in a fusion of the Lyceum movement and independent Chautauquas, to provide educational programs, culture, and entertainment. Carole Hanson describes the later program:

> A circuit was composed of a group of towns or villages, more or less adjacent, pledged to receive an associated company of performers or "talent," as it was commonly referred to, through a designated number of days.[13]

A closely related development was the expansion of reading as a recreational experience, which was furthered by the widespread growth of free public libraries. This development was linked to the adoption of compulsory universal education and to the increasing need for better-educated workers in the nation's industrial system. As an example of the growing interest in cultural activity, the arts and crafts movement found its largest following in the United States in the beginning of the twentieth century. Between 1896 and 1915, thousands of organized groups were established throughout the country to bring artists and patrons together, sponsor exhibits and publications, and promote the teaching of art in the schools. National organizations like the National League of Handicraft and the National Society of Craftsmen were established, and cities like Minneapolis and Detroit erected impressive buildings to house classes and workshops in such activities.

The Development of National, State, and Municipal Parks

Concern for preservation of the natural heritage of the United States in an era of increasing industrialization and despoilment of natural resources began in the nineteenth century. The first conservation action was in 1864, when Congress set aside an extensive area of wilderness primarily for public recreational use, consisting of the Yosemite Valley and the Mariposa Grove of Big Trees in California. This later became a national park. The first designated national park was Yellowstone, founded in 1872. In 1892 the Sierra Club was founded by John Muir, a leading Scottish-born conservationist who, along with Theodore Roosevelt, encouraged national interest in the outdoors and ultimately the establishment of the National Park Service.

All such developments did not lend themselves immediately to an emphasis on recreation. The primary purpose of the national parks at the outset was to preserve the nation's natural heritage and wildlife. Similarly, C. Frank Brockman writes that the current interest in recreational use of national forest lands was not typical in the initial years of the forest conservation movement in the United States:

> Early foresters could not envisage the great public interest in the recreational values of the national forests . . . of the present day. . . . Consequently, although a few forestry leaders began calling attention to growing public interest in and use of national forests for outdoor recreation about 1910, official U.S. Forest Service recognition of recreation as a valid part of national forest management did not develop for more than a decade.[14]

State Parks   As federal park development continued, state authorities became concerned with the preservation of their forest areas and wildlife. As early as 1867, Michigan and Wisconsin established fact-finding committees to explore the problem of forest conservation; their example was followed shortly by Maine and other eastern states. Within two decades, several states had established forestry commissions. Between 1864 and 1900, the first state parks were established, as were a number of state forest preserves and historic parks.

Municipal Parks   Until this time, North America had lagged far behind Europe in the development of municipal parks, partly because America had no aristocracy with large cultivated estates, hunting grounds, and elaborate gardens that they could turn over to the public. The first major park to be developed in an American city was Central Park in New York; its design and the philosophy on which it was based strongly influenced other large cities during the latter half of the nineteenth century.

There had long been a need for open space in New York City. During the first 30 years of the nineteenth century, plans were made for several open squares to total about 450 acres, but these were not carried out completely. By the early 1850s, the entire amount of public open space in Manhattan totaled only 117 acres. Pressure mounted among the citizens of the city for a major park that would provide relief from stone and concrete. The poet William Cullen Bryant wrote:

> Commerce is devouring inch by inch the coast of the island, and if we would rescue any part of it for health and recreation it must be done now. All large cities have their extensive public grounds and gardens, Madrid and Mexico [City] their Alamedas, London its Regent's Park, Paris its Champs Elysées, and Vienna its Prater.[15]

There was concern about the reckless and haphazard course of urban growth in the nineteenth century, which had been guided almost exclusively by narrow commercial interests. Reformers were disturbed not only by the obvious "social failures"—the growing number of criminals, prostitutes, alcoholics and insane—but also by the effects of the relentless commercial environment on the culture of cities. Large public parks came to be seen as "necessary institutions of democratic recreation and indispensable antidotes to urban anomie."

When the public will could no longer be denied, legislation was passed in 1856 to establish a park in New York City. Construction of the 843-acre site began in 1857. Central Park, designed by landscape architects Frederick Law Olmsted and Calvert Vaux, was completely man-made: "Every foot of the park's surface, every tree and bush, as well as every arch, roadway and walk, has been fixed where it is with a purpose." The dominant need was to provide, within the densely populated heart of an immense metropolis, "refreshment of the mind and nerves" for city dwellers through the provision of greenery and scenic vistas. The park was to be heavily wooded and to have the appearance of rural scenery, with roadways screened from the eyes of park users wherever possible. Recreational pursuits permitted in the park included walking, pleasure driving, ice skating in the winter, and boating—but not organized or structured sports.

Before Central Park was built, people expressed concern about the behavior of those who would use it. The *New York Herald* declared in 1858 that it would be nothing but a "great beargarden for the lower denizens of the city." Olmsted established strict rules for the park's use, however, saying, "A large part of the people of New York are ignorant of a park. . . . They will need to be trained to the proper use of it, to be restrained in the abuse of it." As executive head of the park, he hired special police to enforce an extensive code of regulations, including restrictions against walking on the grass, turning domestic animals loose, or damaging the landscape or wildlife in any way.[16]

County Park Systems   In later years, planning began for what was to become the nation's first county park system in Essex County, New Jersey. Bordering the crowded industrial city of Newark, it was outlined in a comprehensive proposal in 1894 that promised that the entire cost of the park project would be realized through tax revenues from increased property values. Set in motion in the following year, the Essex County park system proved to be a great success and set a model to be followed by hundreds of other county and special district park agencies throughout the United States and Canada in the early 1900s.

Establishment of Voluntary Organizations

During the nineteenth century, a number of voluntary (privately sponsored, nonprofit) organizations were founded that played an important role in providing recreation services, chiefly for children and youth. One such body was the Young Men's Christian Association, founded in Boston in 1851 and followed by the Young Women's Christian Association 15 years later. At first, the Y provided fellowship between youth and adults for religious purposes. It gradually enlarged its program, however, to include gymnastics, sports, and other recreational and social activities.

Another type of voluntary agency that offered significant leisure programs was the settlement house—neighborhood centers established in the slum sections in the East and Midwest. Among the first were University Settlement, founded in New York City in 1886, and Hull House, founded in Chicago in 1889. Their staffs sought to help poor people, particularly immigrants, adjust to modern urban life by providing services concerned with education, family life, and community improvement. Many of the early settlement house workers saw recreation as a major need. A pioneer social worker, Jane Addams, urged that recreation be provided as a safety valve for slum conditions, saying:

> It is as if our cities had not yet developed a sense of responsibility to the life and the streets, and continually forget that recreation is stronger than vice and that recreation alone can stifle the lust for vice.[17]

Numerous other national or local nonprofit youth organizations were founded during the early decades of the twentieth century, many of them based on British models (see page 208). They were particularly important in providing a setting in which children of immigrant families might become acclimated to American values, customs, and lifestyles.

The Playground Movement

To understand the need for playgrounds in cities and towns, it is necessary to know the living conditions of poor people during the latter decades of the nineteenth century. The wave of urbanization that had begun earlier had now reached its peak. The urban population more than doubled—from 14 to 30 million—between 1880 and 1900 alone. By the century's end, there were 28 cities with over 100,000 residents because of the recent waves of migration. A leading example was New York, where nearly five out of every six of the city's 1.5 million residents lived in tenements in 1891. Social reformers of the period described these buildings as crowded, with dark hallways, filthy cellars, and inadequate cooking and bathroom facilities. In neighborhoods populated by poor immigrants, there was a tremendous amount of crime, gambling, gang violence, and prostitution.

Local leaders, in cooperation with such outspoken social reformers as Jacob Riis, Walter Vrooman, and Louise DeKoven Bowen, created a public awareness of the need for improved recreational opportunities in the cities. They welded public-spirited citizens, clergymen, educators, and newspaper editorial writers into a force that ultimately compelled action from civic officials and gave rise to the playground movement.

Boston Sand Garden—A Beginning   Within poor working class neighborhoods, there were few safe places where children might play. The first such facility—and the one which is generally regarded as a landmark in the development of the recreation movement in the United States—was the Boston Sand Garden. Linda Oliva points out that the city of Boston had been the arena for many important developments in the park and recreation movement in the United States. The Boston Common, established in 1634, has generally been regarded as the first municipal park; a 48-acre area of green rolling hills and shady trees, it is located in the heart of the city. Boston was also the site of the first public gardens with the establishment of an outstanding Botanic Garden in 1838.

The famous Boston Sand Garden was the first playground in the country designed specifically for children. A group of public-spirited citizens had a pile of sand placed behind the Parmenter Street Chapel in a working class district. Young children in the neighborhood came to play in the sand with wooden shovels. Supervision was voluntary at first, but by 1887 when ten such centers were opened, women were employed to supervise the children. Two years later, the city of Boston began to contribute funds to support the sand gardens. So it was that citizens, on a voluntary basis, began to provide play opportunities for young children.[18]

New York's First Playgrounds   In the nation's largest city, Walter Vrooman, founder of the New York Society for Parks and Playgrounds, directed the public's attention to the fact that in 1890 there were 350,000 children without a single public playground of their own. Although the city now had almost 6,000 acres of parkland, none of it was set aside specifically for children. Civic leaders pointed out that children of working parents lacked supervision and were permitted to grow up subject to various temptations. Vrooman wrote that such children

> are driven from their crowded homes in the morning . . . are chased from the streets by the police when they attempt to play, and beaten with the broom handle of the janitor's wife when found in the hallway, or on the stairs. No wonder they learn to chew and smoke tobacco before they can read, and take a fiendish delight in breaking windows, in petty thievery, and in gambling their pennies.[19]

Gradually, the pressure mounted. Two small model playgrounds were established in poor areas of the city in 1889 and 1891 by the newly formed New York Society for Parks and Playgrounds, with support from private donors. A second new organization, the Outdoor Recreation League, opened a more ambitious playground called Seward Park in June 1893. League members raised substantial sums to pay for maintenance and leadership, and for costs that might accrue to the city through accident damage suits; however, the city government itself also assumed some of the financial responsibility for Seward Park.

In the years that followed, New York moved rapidly to develop a network of playgrounds that were administered and paid for by the city. All schools constructed after this time were required to have open-air playgrounds. In July 1897, the first recreation piers were opened and became an immediate success; by 1902 there were seven such piers jutting out into the rivers surrounding Manhattan Island, providing new places to play and bathe.

The period between 1880 and 1900 was of critical importance to the development of urban recreation and park programs. More than 80 cities initiated park systems; a lesser number established "sand gardens," and, shortly after, playgrounds. Illinois passed a law permitting the establishment of local park districts in which two or more municipalities might join together to operate park systems.

EFFECT OF RACIAL AND ETHNIC DISCRIMINATION

Throughout this period, public and nonprofit youth-serving organizations often discriminated against members of racial or ethnic minorities. As late as the 1930s and 1940s, prejudice against those perceived as lower-class "undesirables" or those from less-favored European nations was evidenced in some organizations.[20] Such practices reflected widespread attitudes of snobbery, as well as the nativist political agitation of the nineteenth century that opposed the flow of immigration from Europe, preached hatred against Catholics and Jews, and barred citizens of color from mainstream American life.

Prejudice Against Minorities

Generally, the most severe discrimination was leveled against African-Americans who, though no longer slaves, were kept in a position of economic servitude through the practice of sharecropping and were without civil, political, or judicial rights in the southern and border states. However, there was an extreme degree of prejudice against Mexican-Americans and other Hispanics of mixed racial origins. For example, Anglo settlers in Texas regarded Mexicans as savage "heathens" who had historically practiced human sacrifice, and saw them as a decadent and inferior people. Most prejudice was expressed in racial terms; Tejanos (Texans of mixed Spanish, Indian, and sometimes African origin) were considered to be lazy, dirty, and illiterate "greasers." One traveler wrote of the Mexicans of Brownsville, Texas, in the 1860s that they were "mere pilferers, scavengers and vagabonds."[21]

A popular journal, the *Southern Review,* expressed the dominant feeling of many white Americans at this time with respect to "mongrelism"—the term often applied to mixing among different racial groups.[22] In time, intermarriage between whites and blacks or American Indians was defined as "miscegenation" and forbidden by law through much of the country.

There was also widespread prejudice expressed against Asian-Americans, mostly Chinese nationals who began to arrive in California in the mid-1800s and who worked on the transcontinental railroad. As the number of Asians grew, so did xenophobia. Americans viewed them as heathens who could not readily be assimilated within the nation's essentially Anglo-Saxon framework, and condemned them as unsanitary, immoral, and criminal. Based on such prejudice, Chinese were often the victims of mob violence, particularly at times of national depression, and were barred from entry into the United States by the Oriental Exclusion Acts of 1882 and 1902.

Similar views were frequently expressed against Americans of African origin, who were increasingly barred from social contact, economic opportunity, or recreational involvement with whites by a wave of state legislation and local ordinances in the late nineteenth century and the early years of the twentieth. As a result of these laws and the segregated nature of most communities at this time, citizens of color were extremely limited in their use of organized recreation and park facilities and programs.

RECREATION AND PARKS: EARLY TWENTIETH CENTURY

For the majority of Americans, however, the beginning of the twentieth century was an exciting period marked by growing economic and recreational opportunity. By 1900, 14 cities had made provisions for supervised play facilities. Among the leading cities were Boston, Providence, Philadelphia, Pittsburgh, Baltimore, Chicago, Milwaukee, Cleveland, Denver, and Minneapolis. In Canada, there was a similar thrust, although it relied more heavily on voluntary community associations.

At the same time, municipal parks became well established throughout the United States. In addition to the urban parks mentioned earlier, the first metropolitan park system was established by Boston in 1892. In the West, San Francisco and Sacramento, California, as well as Salt Lake City, Utah, were among the first to incorporate large open spaces in town planning before 1900. The New England Association of Park Superintendents, the predecessor of the American Institute of Park Executives, was established in 1898 to bring together park superintendents and promote their professional concerns.

An early historian of the recreation movement, Clarence Rainwater, identified nine important transitions that took place in the playground movement during its early period, and that led to the emergence of a broader and more widely accepted recreation movement. These involved a shift:

1. From provision for small children only to services for all age groups.
2. From operation of facilities only during the summer to operation throughout the year.
3. From outdoor equipment and activities only to those that could be enjoyed year-round.
4. From an emphasis on serving only congested urban districts to serving both urban and rural communities.
5. From philanthropic support by private citizens to public support and control.
6. From free play and casually organized events to directed play with leadership and carefully scheduled programs.
7. From a simple range of activities, chiefly games and sports, to a more complex offering, including manual, physical, aesthetic, social, and civic projects.
8. From the provision of facilities to the definition of standards for the use of leisure time.
9. From the satisfaction of individual interests to meeting group and community needs.[23]

Growth of Public Recreation and Park Agencies

Gradually, the concept that city governments should provide recreation facilities, programs, and services became widely accepted. By 1906, 41 cities were sponsoring public recreation programs, and by 1920, 465. More and more states passed laws authorizing local governments to operate recreation programs, and between 1925 and 1935 the number of municipal recreation buildings quadrupled.

Park departments also expanded rapidly in the United States during this time. From 1892 to 1902, the number of cities possessing parks grew from 100 to 800, and by 1926 the figure was 1,680. George Butler comments that, during the 1920s:

> the number and variety of recreation facilities increased by leaps and bounds. Playgrounds, golf courses, swimming pools, bathing beaches, picnic areas, winter sports facilities, and game fields were constructed in unprecedented numbers. Municipal park acreage expanded during the latter half of the decade more than in any other period of equal length.[24]

Municipalities were also discovering new ways to add parks. Many acquired areas outside their city limits, while others required that new real estate subdivision plans include the dedication of space for recreation. Some cities acquired major park properties through gifts. The pattern that began to develop was one of placing a network of small, intensively used playgrounds throughout the cities, particularly in neighborhoods of working class families, and placing larger parks in outlying areas.

Chicago: A Leading Example   Of the major cities that initiated park systems at this early stage, Chicago was outstanding. It was one of the first cities to develop a network of neighborhood recreation parks, passing a $5 million bond issue in 1903 to acquire and develop recreation parks (ranging in size from 7 to 300 acres) in crowded neighborhoods in the southern part of the city. Ten of these parks, combining excellent outdoor sports facilities with fieldhouses that included gymnasiums, clubrooms, shower and locker rooms, and branches of the public library, were opened in 1905. They set a new standard for American cities, particularly because the first convention sponsored by the new Playground Association of America was held in Chicago in 1907. President Theodore Roosevelt called the creation of the South Park playgrounds and centers "the most notable civic achievement of any American city."

Federal Park Expansion

As President, Theodore Roosevelt, a dedicated outdoorsman, encouraged the acquisition of numerous new areas for the federal park system, including many new forest preserves, historic and scientific sites, and wildlife refuges. Thanks in part to his assistance and support, the Reclamation Act of 1902, which authorized reservoir-building irrigation systems in the West, was passed, along with the Antiquities Act of 1906, which designated the first national monuments. Establishment of the U.S. Forest Service in 1905 and of the National Park Service 11 years later helped place many of the scattered forests, parks, and other sites under more clearly defined policies for acquisition, development, and use.

EMERGENCE OF THE RECREATION MOVEMENT: THREE PIONEERS

As the recreation field developed during the first three decades of the twentieth century, several men and women emerged as influential advocates of play and recreation. Three of the most effective were Joseph Lee, Luther Halsey Gulick, and Jane Addams.

Joseph Lee

Regarded as the "father" of the playground movement, Joseph Lee was a lawyer and philanthropist who came from a wealthy New England family. Born in 1862, he took part in a survey of play opportunities conducted by the Family Welfare Society of Boston in 1882. Shocked to see boys arrested for playing in the streets, he organized a playground for them in an open lot, which he helped supervise. In 1898, Lee helped create a model playground on

Columbus Avenue in Boston that included a play area for small children, a boys' section, a sports field, and individual gardens.

Lee's influence soon expanded; he was in great demand as a speaker and writer on playgrounds and served as vice-president for public recreation of the American Civic Association. President of the Playground Association of America for 27 years, he was also the president and leading lecturer of the National Recreation School, a one-year program for carefully selected college graduates.

Lee's view of play was idealistic and purposeful. In *Play in Education,* he outlined a set of major play instincts that he believed all children shared and that governed the specific nature of play activities. He believed that play forms had to be taught and that this process required capable leadership. Lee did not make a sharp distinction between work and play, but saw them as closely related expressions of the impulse to achieve, to explore, to excel, and to master. "True work is the highest form of play; but it is always the play element in work that is the most important." Lee stressed that play was not carried on in pursuit of pleasure; indeed, in somewhat puritanical fashion, he condemned such a motive:

> Pleasure results from play . . . but it is not the play motive. It is extraneous, a by-product; it does not in any way account for the play attitude or the direction of the play instincts. In play, the motive of the act is the doing of it. . . . The man who goes out to have a good time is usually disappointed. The one who goes out to play the game, and does play it for all it is worth, is never wholly so.[25]

Lee stressed that play might involve pain, sacrifice, and fatigue, and for these reasons it helped to "drill" the child in the service of ideals and a dedicated way of life. His moralistic view of play was illustrated in his reference to recreation as a means of combating "excessive youth preoccupation with sex."

Luther Halsey Gulick

Another leading figure in the early recreation movement was Luther Halsey Gulick. A physician by training, he developed a special interest in physical education and recreation. He also had a strong religious orientation, as did many of the early play leaders. Beginning in 1887, Dr. Gulick headed the first summer school of "special training for gymnasium instructors" at the School for Christian Workers (now Springfield College) in Massachusetts. He was active in the YMCAs in Canada and the United States, was the first president of the Camp Fire Girls, and was instrumental in the establishment of the Playground Association of America in 1906. Gulick lectured extensively on the significance of play and recreation and taught a course in the psychology of play as early as 1899. He also vigorously promoted expanded recreation programs for girls and women.

Gulick distinguished play from recreation. Gulick defined play as "doing that which we want to do, without reference primarily to any ulterior end, but simply for the joy of the process." But, he went on to say, play is not less serious than work:

> The boy who is playing football with intensity needs recreation as much as does the inventor who is working intensely at his invention. Play can be more exhausting than work, because one can play much harder than one can work. No one would dream of pushing a boy in school as hard as he pushes himself in a football game. If there is any difference of intensity between play and work, the difference is in favor of play. Play is the result of desire; for that reason it is often carried on with more vigor than work.[26]

Gulick also pressed forcefully for recognition of the important role of recreation and leisure in contemporary life. He believed that the bulk of modern crime, as well as antisocial or "degenerative" behavior throughout history, resulted from "wrong play and recreation."

Making the point that the "playground is cheaper than the reformatory," Gulick urged that as much support be given to providing suitable play activities for children as was given to funding public schools.

Jane Addams

Jane Addams is the social work pioneer who established Hull House in Chicago. Her interest in the needs of children and youth, and in the lives of immigrant families and the poor in America's great cities, led her to develop outstanding programs of educational, social, and recreational activities. Beyond this, she was a leading feminist pioneer and so active a reformer that she was known as "the most dangerous woman in America."

Mary Duncan points out that Jane Addams, along with a number of other recreation and park leaders in the late nineteenth and early twentieth centuries, was part of a wider radical reform movement in America's cities. Joining with muckraking editors, writers, ministers, and other social activists, they

continually fought city hall, organized labor strikes, marched in the street, gave public speeches, and wrote award-winning articles deploring the living conditions of the poor. The issues and problems they faced were well defined: slavery, the aftermath of the Civil War, thousands of new immigrants, slums, child labor, disease, the suffrage movement, World War I, and a rapidly industrializing nation.[27]

Duncan comments that, in facing these problems, Addams and her fellow reformers were not

meek and mild, easily intimidated or swayed by local politicians. They worked in, around, and with the political system. The political battles they fought gave them the skills needed in order to establish the park, playground and recreation services we enjoy today.[28]

Addams was instrumental in forming a Juvenile Protective Association which met at Hull House; this body pressed for social centers, recreation rooms, public gardens, and bathing beaches that could be pleasurable and safe. Karla Henderson comments:

Addams encouraged youthful energy and the creative possibilities of channeling it. In looking at juvenile court records, she realized that youths broke laws in search of adventure, and self-expression. Jane Addams directed Hull House to provide opportunities for adventure and expression through a structured public program.[29]

Contrasting Roles of Recreation Pioneers

Although Lee, Gulick, and Addams were described as muckraking radicals, it is clear that they also were individuals who worked through the major societal institutions of government and voluntary agencies. Addams, for example, helped to found the Playground Association of America, encouraged the Chicago School Board's involvement in playground and recreational sports programs, and supported the early development of the Chicago Parks District. Indeed, these early recreation pioneers often walked a tightrope between their desire on the one hand to promote individuality, to give youth the opportunity for creative development, and to overcome old barriers of prejudice and class distinction and the need on the other hand to maintain order and control and to indoctrinate youth with traditional social goals. Dominick Cavallo writes that the first play organizers sought to achieve a balance between such conflicting values as:

social order over individual freedom, cooperation between groups instead of competition between individuals, and pre-approved goals rather than individual aspirations.[30]

While these three fought to help the downtrodden and illiterate immigrant families living in crowded urban slums, they were also using recreation to maintain the status quo and enforce traditional values. Play was seen as a means of "Americanizing" foreigners and perpetuating and protecting the traditional small-town, moralistic, white Anglo-Saxon heritage that had dominated national culture over the past century. Recreation would be used as a way of repressing the "overwhelming temptation of illicit and soul-destroying pleasures." For example, Addams felt that commercial recreation—particularly theatrical entertainment—was blatantly vulgar, addictive, and led to vicious excitement and family break-up.

At the same time, writers again began to make the connection between religion and recreation, play, and leisure that was briefly described in Chapter 2 (see page 43). In an analysis of twentieth century literature, Charles Sylvester found numerous references to play as "a means for joyfully celebrating God," "a means of preparation for the religious life," or "a divinely placed means for revitalization and preparation for the higher tasks of spiritual development." Similarly, leisure was viewed as "an end and a means for divine contemplation" and as a way of achieving "spiritual fulfillment."[31]

EMERGING NEW LIFESTYLES

However, such views of recreation, play, and leisure were not shared by the entire population. The early twentieth century was a time when the traditional Victorian mentality that had been taught and enforced by the home, school, and church was being challenged. For the first time, many young women took jobs in business and industry in cities throughout the country. With relative freedom from disapproving, stern parental authority, and with money to spend, they frequented commercial dance halls, boat rides, drinking saloons, social clubs, and other sources of popular entertainment. Kathy Peiss describes the new freedom for working class youth in general:

> they fled the tenements for the streets, dance halls, and theaters, generally bypassing their fathers' saloons and lodges. Adolescents formed social clubs, organized entertainments, and patronized new commercial amusements, shaping, in effect, a working-class youth culture expressed through leisure activity.[32]

Part of what appealed to young people were the playgrounds, parks, public beaches, and picnic grounds. However, often these were considered too tame and unexciting, and more and more young people became attracted to commercial forms of entertainment involving liquor, dancing, and sex that were viewed by the establishment as immoral and dangerous. Increasingly, organized recreation programs were promoted by churches, law enforcement agencies, and civic associations in an attempt to resist the new, hedonistic forms of play. They sought to promote traditional, idealistic activities, such as youth sports, music, games, crafts, and dramatic activities, as a way to repress the urge for more "sinful" behavior.

PUBLIC CONCERNS ABOUT THE USE OF LEISURE

President Herbert Hoover addressed a White House Conference on Child Health and Protection in 1930, stating:

> In the last half century we have herded 50 million more human beings into towns and cities where the whole setting is new to the race. . . . Perhaps the widest range of difficulties with which we are dealing in the betterment of children grows out of this crowding into cities. Problems of sanitation and public health

loom in every direction. Delinquency increases with congestion. Overcrowding produces disease and contagion. The child's natural play space is taken from him. . . . Architectural wizardry and artistic skills are transforming cities into wonderlands of beauty, but we must also preserve in them for our children the yet more beautiful art of living.[33]

To some degree, the support for public recreation was based on the fear that without public programs and facilities adult leisure would be used unwisely. Many industrial leaders and civic officials believed that the growth of leisure for the working classes represented a dangerous trend; when unemployment increased they expressed concern about what idle men would do with their time. Similarly, when the eight-hour workday laws first came under discussion, temperance societies prepared for increased drunkenness, and social reformers held international conferences on the worker's spare time and ways to use it constructively.

The major concern, however, was for children and youth in the large cities and their need for healthful and safe places to play. Indeed, much "juvenile delinquency" arose from children being arrested for playing on city streets. Gulick wrote:

Playing baseball on the streets of New York is forbidden by a city ordinance. Yet every day during the spring a large proportion of the boys brought before the judge of Children's Court are there for the crime of playing ball. The black-robed judge questions them from behind a high desk; a big policemen stands near to give testimony. The boys are in the position of lawbreakers, yet most of them are decent, respectable boys, frequently very young and much frightened.[34]

Educators and law enforcement officials believed that the best solution to juvenile delinquency was to provide play facilities for city children. A Philadelphia judge commented:

The public playground is the greatest deterrent of juvenile delinquency and lawlessness among children. It stands for body and character building, and produces better children, homes, morals and citizens. On the score of public economy alone, the playground is a necessity.[35]

Authorities during this period reported reduced rates of juvenile delinquency in slum areas where playgrounds had been established. A probation officer of the juvenile court in Milwaukee described "a very noticeable dropping off of boys coming before the court" and a disappearance of "dangerous gangs," concluding that playgrounds and social centers were "saviors" for American youth. Typically, the judge of the juvenile department of the Orange County Court in Anaheim, California, noted that after

the opening of supervised playgrounds in the public park in the summer of 1924, juvenile delinquency decreased. During the first six months of 1925, it was 70 percent less than for the same period in 1924.[36]

Concern About Commercial Amusements

At this time, there was also fear that unregulated and unsupervised places of commercial amusement posed a serious threat to children and youth. Commercially sponsored forms of entertainment and recreation had grown rapidly during the early twentieth century. George Counts pointed out that prior to the rise of industrial civilization, recreation had been primarily a function of the family and the neighborhood. As cities grew, however, neighborhoods often lost their character and traditional functions, and families were no longer as self-sufficient as they had been.

Business enterprise was quick to grasp the opportunity for material gain presented by the breakdown. . . . Commercial recreation has provided for the American people a bewildering variety of cheap forms of amusement; dance halls, houses of prostitution, speakeasies, pool and billiard rooms, vaudeville performances, burlesque shows, amusement parks, and many others.[37]

In major cities such as Milwaukee, Detroit, Kansas City, and San Francisco, extensive recreation surveys scrutinized the nature of commercial amusements, the extent and kind of their patronage, and their character. There was much concern about movies and stage performances, with frequent charges that they were immoral and led to the sexual corruption of youth.

A high percentage of privately operated dance halls had attached saloons that were freely patronized by young girls. Dancing seemed to be only a secondary consideration. Pickups occurred regularly, often of young girls who had come to cities from the nation's farms and small towns with a presumed degree of innocence; so-called "white slavers," who trapped or recruited girls and women into prostitution, appeared to ply their trade with little interference. Dance halls were often attached to disreputable rooming houses, and girls in their early and middle teens were easily recruited into prostitution. As an example, Louise Bowen describes the practice of having excursion boats cross Lake Michigan from Chicago with as many as 5,000 persons on board at a time. These boats carried many unsupervised young teenagers; although they were billed as daytime outings, they often did not return until the early morning hours. She writes:

> The Juvenile Protective Association . . . discovered that the boats . . . were violating many laws. Gambling machines and devices of every sort were run openly upon the boats; liquor was sold to minors, while staterooms were rented over and over again during the night. These boats were largely patronized by young people who . . . became drunk and engaged in orgies.[38]

The same studies that examined commercial amusements also surveyed the socially approved forms of recreation. They found that in many cities the schools were closed in the evening and throughout the summer, that libraries closed at night and on weekends, that churches closed for the summer, and that publicly provided forms of recreation were at a minimum. Jane Addams concluded that the city had "turned over the provision for public recreation to the most evil-minded and the most unscrupulous members of the community."

Gradually, pressure mounted for more effective control of places of public amusement. In city after city, permits were required for operating dance halls, pool parlors, and bowling alleys, and for the sale of liquor. Regulations concerning the admission of minors, gambling, closing hours, and the proper ventilation and sanitation of such places were all rigidly specified and enforced.

Fear of "Spectatoritis"

There was also a fear that Americans were moving away from the traditional active ways of using their leisure to pursuits in which they were passive spectators. Richard Edwards commented that instead of believing in the wholesome love of play, Americans now had a love of being "played upon." It had become wholly outdated to make one's own fun.[39]

Many shared Edwards' view of the "fan," whom he described as a "flabby creature symbolic of a multitude, a parasite upon the play of others, the least athletic of all men, never playing himself at anything, a spectacle hunter, not a sportsman." There was fear that with growing professionalism, America was moving toward a jaded sensationalism that would ultimately lead to the "Roman amphitheater and the Spanish bullfight."

EMERGING MASS CULTURE

Such complaints and fears were the inevitable reaction of civic leaders to what they perceived to be a threat to traditional morality and values. There was a great need to control places of amusement that attracted children and youth and exposed them to liquor, illicit sex and entrapment in prostitution rings, and other criminal activity.

However, to regard all commercial recreation sponsors as evil-minded and unscrupulous and to see all forms of spectator entertainment as threats to American society was obviously narrow-minded and biased. Today, we recognize that a wealth of desirable recreational pursuits are offered by profit-oriented businesses, and we accept spectator entertainment as one aspect of a rounded leisure-time experience. The reality is that America in the early decades of the twentieth century was undergoing massive changes in response to changing economic and social conditions. These included the emergence of new middle class and working class people who had the time and money to spend on leisure, as well as a steady infusion of varied ethnic peoples who contributed new ideas and values to American society.

Part of the change involved a growing rejection of authoritarian family structures and church-dominated social values, as well as a readiness to accept new kinds of roles for young people and women. All of these influences resulted in a new mass culture that emerged during the new century. John Kasson writes:

> At the turn of the century this culture was still in the process of formation and not fully incorporated into the life of society as a whole. Its purest expression at this time lay in the realm of commercial amusements, which were creating symbols of the new cultural order.[40]

Kasson goes on to point out that nineteenth century America was governed by a coherent set of values—highly Victorian in nature and directed by a self-conscious elite group of ministers, educators, and reformers drawn chiefly from the Protestant middle class of the urban Northeast. These apostles of culture preached the values of character, moral integrity, self-control, sobriety, and industriousness. They believed that leisure should be spent in ways that were edifying and that had moral and social utility. They founded museums, art galleries, libraries, and symphony orchestras, and they lent moral sanction to the recreation and park movement. However, they were unable to exert a significant influence on the growing masses of urban working classes and new immigrant groups.

As a single example of the new craze for excitement and freedom in leisure, a host of amusement parks were developed close to various cities around the country. Typically, they put together a mélange of popular attractions, including bathing facilities, band pavilions, dance halls, vaudeville theaters, sideshows, circus attractions, freak displays, food and drink counters, and daredevil rides of every description. They were loud, garish, and risqué—but they appealed to the masses and they epitomized the explosion of thrill-seeking pastimes that began to dominate America's new mass culture.

MAJOR FORCES PROMOTING ORGANIZED RECREATION SERVICES

At the same time that mass culture was providing new kinds of pastimes that challenged traditional community values and standards, the forces that sought to guide the American public in what they regarded as constructive uses of leisure were becoming active.

Settlement Houses and Community Centers

From the very beginning, the directors of the settlement houses and community centers that were established in larger cities during the 1880s and 1890s were vitally interested in play and recreation. Jane Addams was responsible for opening the first independent playground in Chicago in a vacant lot adjoining Hull House, and equipping it with swings, seesaws, slides, and sand bins. At Hull House itself, music, dance, and drama were all part of the total program. The settlement house movement expanded rapidly during the first decades of the twentieth century. Well into the 1930s, these agencies regarded recreation services as one of their primary functions. Social group work and recreation were seen as closely related forms of professional service. It was only in the late 1930s and the 1940s that group work became more heavily concerned with the task of dealing with social problems—including family and individual needs—and less concerned with providing recreation.

Growth of Voluntary Organizations

In the opening decades of the twentieth century, a number of important youth-serving, non-profit organizations were formed, either on a local basis or through nationally organized movements or federations. The National Association of Boys' Clubs was founded in 1906, the Boy Scouts and the Camp Fire Girls in 1910, and the Girl Scouts in 1912. Major civic clubs and community service groups such as the Rotary Club, Kiwanis, and the Lions Club were also founded between 1910 and 1917.

By the end of the 1920s, these organizations had become widely established in American life and were serving substantial numbers of young people. One of every seven boys in the appropriate age group in the United States was a Scout. The YMCA and YWCA had more than 1.5 million members in 1926. Although these and many similar organizations were meeting important recreational and social needs of American youth and adults, it was apparent that a strong national voice was needed to provide coherent leadership to the growing recreation movement in America.

Playground Association of America

In the early 1900s, leading recreation directors called for a conference to promote public awareness of and effective practices in the field of leisure services. Under the leadership of Luther Halsey Gulick, representatives of park, recreation, and school boards throughout the United States met in Washington, D.C., in April 1906. Unanimously agreeing upon the need for a national organization, the conference members drew up a constitution and selected Gulick as the first president of the Playground Association of America. The organization had President Theodore Roosevelt's strong support.

A basic purpose of the Playground Association was to develop informational and promotional services to assist people of all ages in using leisure time constructively. Field workers traveled from city to city, meeting with public officials and citizens' groups and helping in the development of playgrounds and recreation programs. In order to promote professional training, the association developed *The Normal Course in Play*, a curriculum plan of courses on play leadership on several levels. In keeping with its broadening emphasis, the organization changed its name in 1911 to the Playground and Recreation Association of America, and in 1926 to the National Recreation Association. It sought to provide the public with a broader concept of recreation and leisure, and to promote recreation as an area of government responsibility. Charles Hartsoe writes:

> through these transitional changes, the association has played a major role in helping shape recreation and park policies and programs in communities across the nation. The organization has attracted the personal interest and involvement of several presidents, as well as key public figures, countless citizens, and professional leaders.[41]

Recreation Programs in World War I

The nation's rapid mobilization during World War I revealed that communities adjacent to army and navy stations and training camps needed more adequate programs of recreation. The Council of National Defense and the War Department Commission on Training Camp Activities asked the Playground and Recreation Association to assist in the creation of a national organization to provide wartime community recreation programs. The association established the War Camp Community Service, which utilized the recreation resources of several hundred communities near military camps to provide wholesome recreation activities for both military personnel and civilians.

At its peak, WCCS employed a national staff of approximately 3,000 paid workers who organized programs in 755 cities with the help of more than 500,000 volunteers. At other military bases in the United States and Europe, organizations like the Young Men's Christian Association sponsored canteens and other morale-boosting services. At the conclusion of the war, community recreation programs began to expand in number. Butler writes:

> The people who saw during the war what community singing, pageants, athletic meets, and neighborhood parties could mean in community life insisted that means be devised for continuing them. . . . Social, civic, and religious agencies had acquired common interest in community recreation and a sense of responsibility for providing it.[42]

ROLE OF THE SCHOOLS

As indicated earlier, a number of urban school boards had initiated after-school and vacation play programs as early as the 1890s. This trend continued in the twentieth century. Playground programs were begun in Rochester, New York, in 1907; in Milwaukee, Wisconsin, in 1911; and in Los Angeles, California, in 1914. These pioneering efforts were strongly supported by the National Education Association, which recommended that public school buildings be used for community recreation and social activities. The report of the fiftieth annual meeting of the NEA in 1912 included a number of major presentations concerned with the school's role in leisure programming. For example, one statement pointed out that

> much of the millions of dollars invested in our school systems is wasted owing to the fact that, outside of school, children form wrong habits due to unwholesome play conditions, and develop traits of character which make much of their school training useless. [Today] many communities are trying to find out and to plan systematically for their recreational needs.[43]

In addition to playgrounds, other facilities of the schools that could be useful for recreational purposes were assembly rooms and gymnasiums, swimming pools, music and arts rooms, and outdoor areas for sports and gardening. Education for the "worthy use of leisure" became one of the major objectives of modern education, as stated in the famous bulletin, "Cardinal Principles of Secondary Education," issued by the Commission on the Reorganization of Secondary School Education of the National Education Association:

> Aside from the immediate discharge of these specific duties [home membership, vocation, and citizenship], every individual should have a margin of time for the cultivation of personal and social interests. This leisure, if worthily used, will recreate his powers and enlarge and enrich life, thereby making him better able to meet his responsibilities. The unworthy use of leisure impairs health, disrupts home life, lessens vocational efficiency and destroys civic-mindedness. . . . In view of these considerations, education for the worthy use of leisure is of increasing importance as an objective.[44]

Support by Prominent Educators

The school's role in providing leisure education and recreation programs was supported by leading educators and psychologists, who recognized the value of play in child development. Psychologist John Watson wrote:

> In short, play is the principal instrument of growth. It is safe to conclude that, without play, there would be no normal adult cognitive life; without play, no healthful development of affective life; without play, no full development of the power of the will.[45]

John Dewey, the leading American philosopher, was influential in the development of modern educational practices. His view of education was that it was most effective when based on activity that challenged all of one's faculties—physical, creative, and intellectual.

Dewey believed that children should be introduced to the idea and the experience of more formal work through play:

> The idea that the need [for play] can be suppressed, is absolutely fallacious, and the Puritan tradition which disallows the need has entailed an enormous crop of evils. If education does not afford opportunity for wholesome recreation . . . the suppressed instincts find all sorts of illicit outlets. . . . Education has no more serious responsibility than making adequate provision for enjoyment of recreative leisure; not only for the fact of immediate health but still more, if possible, for the fact of its lasting effect upon habits of mind.[46]

With such support, public opinion encouraged the expansion of organized playground and public recreation programs in American communities. Between 1910 and 1930, thousands of school systems established extensive programs of extracurricular activities, particularly in sports, publications, hobbies, and social- and academic-related fields. And, in 1919, the first college curriculum in recreation was established at Virginia Commonwealth University.

PUBLIC RECREATION DURING THE 1920s

The period following World War I was marked by the increase of public involvement in all types of recreational activities. With the production of low-cost automobiles and the construction of better highways, people became more mobile and traveled widely in search of recreation. Camping, sightseeing, and varied forms of outdoor play became popular family pursuits. Huge stadiums were built to house major sports teams and accommodate exciting entertainment events. Radios, phonographs, and motion pictures became virtual crazes, as did numerous other hobbies and special interests. During the so-called "Jazz Age" of the 1920s, nightclubs and speakeasies (illegal drinking places) flourished, new forms of popular music and dance appeared, and conservative sexual values were widely discarded.

Outdoor Recreation Developments

The role of the federal and state governments in promoting outdoor recreation was enlarged by the establishment of the National Park Service in 1916 and an accelerated pattern of acquisition and development of outdoor areas by the U.S. Forest Service. In 1921, Stephen Mather, Director of the National Park Service, called for a National Conference on State Parks. This meeting made it clear that the Park Service was primarily to acquire and administer areas of national significance; it led to the recommendation that state governments take more responsibility for acquiring sites of lesser interest or value.

Park administrators began to give active recreation a higher priority in park design and operation. The founding of the American Association of Zoological Parks and Aquariums in 1924 was an indication that specialized recreational uses of parks were becoming widespread in American communities.

This trend was promoted by a National Conference on Outdoor Recreation, called by President Calvin Coolidge in May 1924 and attended by several hundred representatives of 128 national organizations. One of their recommendations was that the American Institute of Park Executives and the Playground and Recreation Association jointly create a handbook on parks; in response, L. H. Weir wrote the two-volume *Manual on Parks*. In 1926, the National Recreation School for graduate training in recreation was established. It continued until 1935, under the sponsorship of the National Recreation Association, graduating a total of 300 students, many of whom became leading administrators in cities throughout the United States.

The play movement gradually became thought of as the recreation movement, and began to embrace other agencies and forms of service rather than simply playgrounds for children. It spread to suburbs and small towns; the construction of recreation facilities became a government function, with substantial support from tax funds. Leadership shifted from volunteer or part-time supervisors to full-time, paid leaders and administrators, who came to regard themselves as specialists within a unique field of public service.

The End of Shorter Hours

At the same time that the recreation movement continued to gain impetus, a reverse trend took place as the movement to shorten the workweek and provide workers with more free time gradually slackened. Benjamin Hunnicutt points out that the most dramatic increase in free time occurred in the period between 1901 and 1921, when the average workweek dropped from 58.4 hours to 48.4 hours, a decline never before or since equalled.[47]

Since the mid-nineteenth century, shorter hours and higher wages had been a campaign issue for progressive politicians. Union pressure, legislation, and court decisions achieved the eight-hour day in jobs under federal contracts, sections of the railroad industry, and certain hazardous occupations. The policy was supported by the findings of scientific management experts like Fredrick Taylor, who argued that workers' efficiency declined significantly after eight hours. It also responded to a trend in other industrialized nations, such as France, Germany, Italy and Belgium, to approve legal restriction of working time, based on the 8-hour day or 48-hour workweek. At the International Labor Conference of 1924, held in Geneva, Switzerland, this standard was adopted in a draft recommendation that emphasized the necessity of more free time to meet health, family, and cultural needs.

In the movement to shorten the workweek, the hours gained were thought of as free time, rather than leisure. Indeed, many Americans thought of leisure as Thorstein Veblen had used the term: as a "disreputable waste of energy or dissipation in idleness, useless and unconscionable in the face of the need for more production."[48] However, the term "leisure" became more widely used and was given a new dignity. No longer was it justified solely as a health- or safety-related concern, or as needed time for recuperation from toil. Instead, as Hunnicutt points out, labor leaders viewed leisure as

a form of industrial wealth that promised great things . . . "a dawn of a new era" . . . and a "revolution in living" for workers who could at last have enough time for the "finer things in life in a democratic culture."[49]

New problems began to arise in the American economy though as overproduction and "economic maturity" left the nation with an excess of goods and services. Many leading businessmen and economists began to promote a "New Gospel of Consumption" during the 1920s. They argued that the way to stimulate the economy was not to provide more leisure, but to increase productivity and public spending on a broad range of consumer goods. A debate ensued. It was argued that to continue to add free time by reducing the workweek would result in reduced production and consumption and limit investment opportunities. E.H. Gary of U.S. Steel responded to Henry Ford's support of the five-day workweek in 1926 by saying that the shortened workweek was impractical and would endanger competition with European nations. In the light of such fears and pressures, the shorter-hours movement lost its impetus.

IMPACT OF THE GREAT DEPRESSION

Following the flourishing 1920s, the Great Depression of the 1930s mired the United States—as it did much of the industrial world—in a period of almost total despair. The Depression resulted in mass unemployment and involuntary idleness for American workers. By the end of 1932, an estimated 15 million people, nearly one-third of the labor force, were unemployed. Banks crashed, home and farm mortgages were foreclosed, and breadlines appeared everywhere. The nation was at its lowest ebb.

Federal Recreation Projects

As part of a broader plan to combat the effects of the Depression, the federal government soon instituted a number of emergency work programs related to recreation. Richard Knapp points out that the Federal Emergency Relief Administration, established early in 1933, financed construction of recreation facilities such as parks and swimming pools and hired recreation leaders from the relief rolls. A second agency, the Civil Works Administration, was given the task of finding jobs for 4 million people in 30 days! Among other tasks, this agency built or improved 3,500 playgrounds and athletic fields in a few months.

Both the National Youth Administration and the Civilian Conservation Corps carried out numerous work projects involving the construction of recreational facilities. During the five years from 1932 to 1937, the federal government spent an estimated $1.5 billion developing camps, buildings, picnic grounds, trails, swimming pools, and other facilities. The Civilian Conservation Corps helped to establish state park systems in a number of states that had no organized park programs before 1933. According to Knapp, projects under the Works Progress Administration spanned the nation and built or improved 12,700 playgrounds, 8,500 gymnasiums or recreation buildings, 750 swimming pools, 1,000 ice skating rinks, and 64 ski jumps.

These programs initiated under President Franklin D. Roosevelt's New Deal had a beneficial effect on the development of the recreation and park movement throughout the United States: they made it clear that leisure was an important responsibility of government.

Special Programs for Youth   An interesting development at this time was the emergence of "cellar clubs" in large cities. These were youth-organized social and recreation groups that sprang up spontaneously in low-income neighborhoods and were often based on ethnic and racial ties. The clubs met in vacant stores, cellars, or building lofts, where young people were free from adult supervision and interference. The memberships of cellar clubs consisted of between 20 and 100 boys and young men, usually ranging in age from about 16 to well past 25. In New York City alone, there were 6,000 clubs by 1940.

The federal government was concerned about this trend. In large cities, federations of clubs were formed to establish rules for their behavior and operation. Settlement houses worked with club members, and the Youth Service Division of the WPA assigned many youth leaders to work with unaffiliated cellar clubs in an effort to end much of the petty racketeering and other forms of delinquency and to help them achieve the status of youth agencies.

In addition, a number of cities established "play street" programs. Although such operations, which set aside streets for play in congested areas (by blocking off traffic and providing equipment and leadership), had been in existence for some years, they received a new emphasis during the Depression.

At one time, about 49,000 persons were employed by the Recreation Division of the Works Progress Administration, and, as late as 1940, 60,000 out-of-school youth between the ages of 18 and 24 were employed in National Youth Administration projects providing leisure services. The WPA provided leadership for varied recreation activities in local communities, including direct operation of 15,000 community centers and assistance to 8,000 more. Supervision was provided for parks, playgrounds, athletic fields, beaches, and swimming pools. Community social events were organized, and classes were formed in dance, crafts, drama, music, and social studies. Knapp writes:

> Recreation under WPA auspices was . . . immensely popular at the local level. In the first year operations similar to normal community recreation functioned not only in many of the 1,159 cities with permanent public recreation programs but in 1,045 additional towns where the WPA provided the only organized recreation.[50]

By 1939, an estimated five million people, excluding spectators, were participating in the programs of the WPA's Recreation Division each week. Many of the employees of this program later found permanent employment in local recreation agencies.

Another major emphasis was cultural programs. The Federal Art Project operated many community art centers, with a total attendance of 2.5 million in a single year. The Federal Music Project, which sponsored thousands of musical performances, had more than 100 federal symphony and concert orchestras, and more than 160,000 in its classes. The Federal

Theater Project, with drama companies operating in 20 states, gave a monthly average of 2,800 performances, reaching millions of Americans who had never been exposed to the creative arts. Altogether, the federal arts programs gave employment to more than 30,000 writers, artists, musicians, dancers, actors, and directors.

Sharpened Awareness of Leisure Needs

The Depression helped to stimulate national concern about problems of leisure and recreational opportunity. For example, a number of studies in the 1930s revealed a serious lack of recreation programs for young people, especially blacks, girls, and rural youth.

In the early 1930s, the National Education Association carried out a major study of leisure education in the nation's school systems and issued a report, *The New Leisure Challenges the Schools,* which urged the educational establishment to take more responsibility for this function and for enlarging the school's role in community recreation.[51] Shortly thereafter, the National Recreation Association examined the public recreation and park programs in a number of major European nations and published a detailed report that included implications for American policy-makers.[52]

The American Association for the Study of Group Work studied the overall problem and in 1939 published an important report, *Leisure: A National Issue.* Written by Eduard Lindeman, a leading social work administrator who had played a key role in government during the Depression, the report stated that the "leisure of the American people constitutes a central and crucial problem of social policy." Lindeman believed that the relation of leisure to social policy was clearly evident in those totalitarian European states that during the 1920s and 1930s had embraced leisure as an integral part of their programs:

> In Germany, the latest and most extreme of these new autocracies, leisure is organized primarily for the purpose of propaganda, of sustaining an attitude of loyalty toward the state, and of keeping the time of the people. . . fully occupied in. . . mass activities. Recreation in totalitarian nations is merely another form of subservience to the state, a planned form of action which follows the usual pattern of regimentation.[53]

Lindeman urged that, in the American democracy, recreation should meet the true needs of the people. Pointing out that American workers were gaining a vast national reservoir of leisure estimated at 390 billion hours per year, he suggested that the new leisure should be characterized by free choice and a minimum of restraint. He urged, however, that if leisure were not to become "idleness, waste, or opportunity for sheer mischief," a national plan for leisure had to be developed, including the widespread preparation of professionally trained recreation leaders:

> I have no doubt that a distinct profession of recreation leadership is now coming into being. Indeed, it is my expectation that this newer occupation will enlist recruits at an accelerated rate of speed and that within the next quarter century there will be a demand for at least one hundred thousand trained recreation professionals. Some of these will be concerned with problems of administration and planning; others will work in research; others will be engaged in developing newer forms of facilities; some will be supervisors, recreation teachers and trained specialists.[54]

Before Lindeman's urgent recommendations for formulating a national policy for leisure could be acted upon, however, the nation underwent another major crisis that was even more dangerous to its existence than the Great Depression—World War II.

A NATION AT WAR

World War II, in which the United States became fully involved on December 7, 1941, compelled the immediate mobilization of every aspect of national life: manpower, education, industry, and a variety of social services and programs.

The Special Services Division of the U.S. Army provided recreation facilities and programs on military bases throughout the world, making use of approximately 12,000 officers, even more enlisted personnel, and many volunteers. About 1,500 officers were involved in the Welfare and Recreation Section of the Bureau of Naval Personnel, and expanded programs were offered by the Recreation Service of the Marine Corps. These departments were assisted by the United Service Organizations (USO), which was formed in 1941 and consisted of the joint military effort of six agencies: the Jewish Welfare Board, the Salvation Army, Catholic Community Services, the YMCA, the YWCA, and the National Travelers Aid. The USO functioned in the continental United States and outside of camps and in clubs, hostels, and lounges throughout the western hemisphere. The American National Red Cross established approximately 750 clubs in wartime theaters of operations throughout the world and about 250 mobile entertainment units, staffed by more than 4,000 leaders. Its military hospitals overseas and in the United States involved more than 1,500 recreation workers as well.

In American communities, many programs had to be curtailed during World War II because of the manpower shortage and travel restrictions. However, recreation and park departments instituted special new programs to assist the war effort, and the National Recreation Association established a new field service to help communities near military bases and training camps organize special programs for members of the armed forces.

Many municipal directors extended their facilities and services to local war plants and changed their schedules to provide programs around the clock. Because of the rapid increase in industrial recreation programs, the National Industrial Recreation Association (now known as the National Employee Services and Recreation Association) was formed in 1941 to assist in such efforts. Also, the Federal Security Agency's Office of Community War Services established a new Recreation Division to assist programs on the community level. This division helped set up 300 new community programs throughout the country, including numerous child-care and recreation centers, many of which continued after the war as tax-supported community recreation programs. The Women's Bureau of the U.S. Department of Labor developed guidelines for recreation and housing for women war workers, based on their needs in moving from their home environments into suddenly expanded or greatly congested areas.

By the end of World War II, great numbers of servicemen and servicewomen had participated in varied recreation programs and services and thus had gained a new appreciation for this field. Many people had been trained in recreation leadership (more than 40,000 people were in the Special Services Division of the U.S. Army alone) and were ready to return to civilian life as professionals in this field.

AMERICA AT MID-CENTURY

The United States in the late 1940s was about to embark on a period of tremendous expansion in population, economy, and involvement in a tremendous range of recreational pursuits.

Given the optimistic spirit of a nation that had survived a grave crisis and the pent-up demand for consumer goods and services, leisure provided a channel for the nation's search for happiness and pleasure and was closely tied to the widespread migration of young urban families to new suburban neighborhoods. Curiously, though, it was at this time that the long struggle to increase the nation's free time by further reducing the workweek came to a full halt.

Hunnicutt points out that, during the Great Depression, some businessmen temporarily abandoned their resistance to shorter hours, accepting them as a solution to unemployment; it was better to institute a shorter workweek than to lay off workers. While attempts were made to legislate a 30-hour workweek, these failed. However, by 1937, union agreements for a 35- or 36-hour week were the rule in five major American manufacturing industries, and a number of others had union agreements for workweeks ranging from 30 to 36 hours—including building construction, newspaper publishing, hat manufacturing, the rubber industry, and West Coast longshoring.

However, during the late 1930s, the Roosevelt administration characterized the shorter-hour movement as regressive, and

> the 30 hour bills as a clever ruse to disguise the tragedy of unemployment. Such legislation would not cure unemployment; it would simply "redistribute the misery." According to Roosevelt and his advisors, unemployment was unemployment. It had to be cured by full recovery and reliable economic growth.[55]

At this time, the Roosevelt administration committed the federal government to assuring American workers the 40-hour workweek as the reasonable standard through the Fair Labor Standards Act. During World War II, with an extreme shortage of manpower because of military demands, and with a tremendous need for production of war material, women found jobs replacing men in factories and service industries. Work hours were extended dramatically, along with double and even round-the-clock shifts. At war's end, they stabilized at 40 hours and remained in that neighborhood for more than four decades. For the most part, the labor movement turned its attention instead to higher wages, collective bargaining rights, and fringe benefits.

Despite this development, as Chapter 9 will show, the decades following World War II brought unparalleled expansion in recreation and leisure for the United States and Canada.

SUMMARY

This chapter covers almost two centuries of American history—from the time of the American Revolution to the mid-twentieth century. It traces the influence of the Industrial Revolution, which brought millions of immigrants from Europe to America where they lived in crowded tenements in large cities or in factory towns. It also led to increased attempts to impose the stern strictures of the Protestant work ethic on the nation's population.

By the middle of the nineteenth century, however, religious opposition to varied forms of play and entertainment began to decline. Sports became more popular and accepted and, after reaching a high point at mid-century, work hours began to decline. Four major roots of what was ultimately to become the recreation and park movement appeared: (1) the establishment of city parks, beginning with New York's Central Park, and the later growth of county, state, and national parks; (2) the growing interest in adult education and cultural development; (3) the appearance of playgrounds for children, sponsored first as charitable efforts and shortly after by city governments and the public schools; and (4) the development of a number of nonprofit, youth-serving organizations that spread throughout the country.

After 1900, each of these elements flourished as the playground movement grew and ultimately joined forces with the parks movement in merged agencies, professional societies, and programs of higher education. Popular culture gained momentum during the "Jazz Age" of the 1920s, with college and professional sports, motion pictures and radio, new forms of dance and music, and a host of other crazes capturing the public's interest. While the Great Depression of the 1930s had a tragic impact on many families, the efforts of the federal government to build recreation facilities and leisure services to provide jobs and a morale boost for the public at large meant that the Depression was a powerful positive force for the recreation movement in general.

By the early 1940s, organized recreation service was firmly established in American life, and both government officials and social critics began to raise searching questions about its future role in postwar society.

Questions for Class Discussion or Essay Examinations

1. In the second half of the 19th century, the roots of what was to become the modern recreation and park movement appeared. What were these roots (i.e., the adult education or Lyceum movement), and how did they relate to the broad social needs of Americans?

2. Three important pioneers of the early recreation movement in the United States were Lee, Gulick, and Addams. Summarize some of the key points of their philosophies and their contributions to the playground and recreation developments in the pre-World War I era. Describe the conflict between the traditional Victorian values and code of morality and the emerging popular culture, especially during the 1920s.

3. Trace the expanding role of government in terms of sponsoring recreation and park programs during the first half of the 20th century, with emphasis on federal policies in wartime and during the Depression of the 1930s. What were some of the growing concerns about leisure during this period?

Endnotes

[2]   Gary Cross, *Social History of Leisure Since 1600* (State College, Pa.: Venture Publishing, 1990): 64.

[3]   Foster Rhea Dulles, *A History of Recreation: America Learns to Play* (New York: Appleton–Century–Crofts, 1965): 98–99.

[4]   J. Larkin, "The Secret Life of a Developing Country (Ours)," *American Heritage* (September–October 1988): 60.

[5]   Susan Davis, *Parades and Power: Street Theatre in Nineteenth Century Philadelphia* (Philadelphia: Temple University Press, 1986): 39.

[6]   John Blassingame, *The Slave Community: Plantation Life in the Antebellum South* (New York: Oxford University Press, 1972): 42.

[7]   *Ibid.*

[8]   P. C. McIntosh, *Sport in Society* (London: C. A. Watts, 1963): 65.

[9]   Benjamin Hunnicutt, "The End of Shorter Hours," *Labor History* 3 (1984): 373–374.

[10]   Sebastian de Grazia, *Of Time, Work and Leisure* (New York: Doubleday–Anchor, 1962): 441.

[11]   Hugh Cunningham, *Leisure and the Industrial Revolution* (London: Croom Helm, 1980): 20.

[12]   John Adams to Abigail Adams, May 1780, *Adams Family Correspondence III* (Cambridge, Mass.: Harvard University Press, 1973): 342.

[13]   Carole Hanson, "Circuit Chautauqua, 1904–1938: An Influence for Leisure Activity and Community Sociability" (Paper presented at National Recreation and Park Congress, Dallas, Tex., October 1985).

[14]   C. Frank Brockman, *Recreational Use of Wild Lands* (New York: McGraw–Hill, 1959): 67–70.

[15]   Quoted in Henry Hope Reed and Sophia Duckworth, *Central Park: A History and a Guide* (New York: Clarkson N. Potter, 1967): 3.

[16]   Michael Chubb and Holly R. Chubb, *One Third of Our Time? An Introduction to Recreation Behavior and Resources* (New York: Wiley, 1981): 25.

[17]   Jane Addams, *The Playground* (March 1910): 24.

[18]   Linda Oliva, "A Boston Sand Garden Kicks Off the Playground Movement," *Parks and Recreation* (August 1985): 36–37.

[19]   Walter Vrooman, "Playgrounds for Children," *The Arena* (July 1894): 286.

[20]   See, for example, August Hollingshead, *Elmtown's Youth: The Impact of Social Class on Adolescence* (New York: Wiley, 1949).

[21]   Arnoldo De Leon, *They Called Them Greasers* (Austin, Tex.: University of Texas Press, 1983): 15.

[22]   *Ibid.*, 22.

[23]   Cited in Martin H. Neumeyer and Esther Neumeyer, *Leisure and Recreation* (New York: Ronald Press, 1958): 73.

[24]   George D. Butler, *Introduction to Community Recreation* (New York: McGraw–Hill, 1976): 78.

[25]   Joseph Lee, *Play in Education* (New York: Macmillan, 1915, 1929): 255.

[26]   Luther H. Gulick, *A Philosophy of Play* (New York: Scribner, 1920): 125.

[27]   Mary Duncan, "Back to Our Radical Roots," in Thomas Goodale and Peter Witt, eds., *Recreation and Leisure: Issues in an Era of Change* (State College, Pa.: Venture Publishing, 1980): 287–295.

[28]   *Ibid.*

[29]   Karla Henderson, "Jane Addams: Leisure Services Pioneer," *Journal of Physical Education, Recreation and Dance* (February 1982): 43.

[30]   Dominick Cavallo, cited in review of his book, *Muscles and Morals: Organized Playgrounds and Urban Reform,* by Jerry Dickason, *Journal of Leisure Research* (Vol. 15 No. 1 1983): 86.

[31]   Charles Sylvester, "The Ethics of Play, Leisure and Recreation in the Twentieth Century, 1900–1983," *Leisure Sciences* 9 (1987): 173–186.

[32]   Kathy Peiss, *Cheap Amusements: Working Women and Leisure in Turn-of-the-Century New York* (Philadelphia: Temple University Press, 1986): 57.

[33]   Herbert Hoover, quoted in James Rogers, "The Child and Play," *Report on White House Conference on Child Health and Protection* (1932): 27.

[34]   Gulick, *op. cit.,* 3.

[35]   See Walter Wood, *Children's Play and Its Place in Education* (London: Kegan Paul, Trench, Trubner, 1913): 197.

[36]   Rogers, *op. cit.* 36.

[37]   George Counts, *Social Foundations of Education,* Report of the Commission on the Social Studies (1934): 300.

38   Louise DeKoven Bowen, *Safeguards for City Youth: At Work and at Play* (New York: Macmillan, 1914): 38.

39   Richard Edwards, *Popular Amusements* (New York: Association Press, 1915): 134.

40   John Kasson, *Amusing the Millions: Coney Island at the Turn of the Century* (New York: Hill and Wang, 1978): 3–4.

41   Charles E. Hartsoe, "From Playgrounds to Public Policy," *Parks and Recreation* (August 1985): 48.

42   Butler, *op. cit.*, 76–77.

43   *Proceedings and Addresses of the Fiftieth Annual Meeting of the National Education Association* (July 1912): 233–234.

44   *Cardinal Principles of Secondary Education: Report of the Commission on the Reorganization of Secondary School Education* (Washington, D.C.: National Education Association, 1918): 10.

45   John B. Watson, *Psychology from the Standpoint of a Behaviorist* (Philadelphia: J. B. Lippincott, 1924): 439–440.

46   John Dewey, *Democracy and Education* (New York: Macmillan, 1921): 241.

47   Benjamin Hunnicutt, "Historical Attitudes Toward the Increase of Free Time in the Twentieth Century: Time for Work, for Leisure, or Unemployment," *Loisir et Societe* 3 (1980): 196.

48   *Ibid.*, 199.

49   *Ibid.*, 201.

50   Richard Knapp, "Play for America: The New Deal and the NRA," *Parks and Recreation* (July 1973): 23.

51   Eugene Lies, *The New Leisure Challenges the Schools* (Washington, D.C.: Report of National Education Association, 1933).

52   Lebert H. Weir, *Europe at Play: A Study of Recreation and Leisure Time* (New York: A. S. Barnes and National Recreation Association, 1937).

53   Eduard Lindeman, *Leisure: A National Issue* (New York: American Association for the Study of Group Work, 1939): 32.

54   *Ibid.*

55   Benjamin Hunnicutt, "The End of Shorter Hours," *Labor History* 3 (1984): 402.

Recreation and Leisure
in the Modern Era

Organized recreation and park services [during the post–World War II years] were part of this explosion. Following the war, hundreds of towns and cities constructed community centers, swimming pools, playgrounds, and athletic facilities as "living war memorials." Tax-supported public recreation systems increased in number, and states gave greater attention to their responsibility in organizing recreation and youth services. Hospitals established therapeutic recreation services, universities created degree programs in parks and recreation, and tourism became a major industry. Americans were on the go, seeking their pleasure and enjoying their new found leisure.[1]

INTRODUCTION

From the end of World War II to the mid-1990s, recreation, park, and leisure services evolved from a relatively minor area of government responsibility and nonprofit agency or business function to an enormous complex enterprise.

This chapter chronicles the expansion and diversification of the recreation movement, seen against the broader background of social and economic change in the nation. In addition to describing the growth of government-sponsored programs and professional development during this period, the chapter presents a number of trends in leisure services that were affected by environmental, demographic, and other shifts occurring during the 1960s, 1970s, and 1980s. It concludes with a discussion of the conflict between marketing-oriented

---

[1] H. Douglas Sessoms and Karla Henderson, *Introduction to Leisure Services* (State College, Pa.: Venture Publishing, 1994): 53.

and human service goals in this field, the "time famine" affecting many Americans, and the growing concern about social and family values at century's end.

POST–WORLD WAR II EXPECTATIONS

Immediately after World War II, expectations for the growth of leisure in the United States were high. In the 1950s and 1960s, it was predicted that leisure—usually defined as non-work or discretionary time—would expand dramatically and have an increasing influence on the lives of Americans in the years ahead.

Think tanks like the Rand Corporation or the Hudson Institute, and special planning bodies like the National Commission on Technology, envisioned futurist scenarios with such alternatives as lowering the retirement age to 38, reducing the workweek to 22 hours a week, or extending paid vacations to as many as 25 weeks a year. Other authorities predicted that the three-day or four-day workweek, which some companies had been experimenting with, would soon be widespread.[2]

It was also assumed that leisure would become an increasingly important source of personal values and life satisfaction for many Americans. There was widespread agreement that the work ethic was declining sharply, with work in the industrial era having become more and more specialized, routine, and unfulfilling. Leisure was seen as having immense potential, and writers and educators like David Gray and Seymour Greben suggested that it offered new possibilities for confronting such social problems as human misery and suffering, health and fitness concerns, environmental and energy problems, and worker dissatisfaction.[3]

The 1950s and 1960s were a period of striking social change, including struggles to overcome racial and sexual discrimination, poverty, and environmental pollution. Shifts in American values and lifestyles were dramatic. From a widespread reliance on the work ethic and an acceptance of traditional moral and patriotic values, many young people in particular turned to a new set of highly individualistic personal values, resisting the Vietnam War, and challenging the importance of work and other "establishment" beliefs. The institution of marriage and family-centered ways of life were threatened by a steadily rising rate of marital breakup and divorce, along with a popular swing toward alternative lifestyles, a recreational view of sex, and fuller acceptance of homosexuality. Gambling, pornography, and drug abuse became rampant, and crime—particularly that related to illegal drug trafficking or juvenile gangs in the nation's cities—became far more violent and widespread.

In the late 1970s and 1980s, there was a pronounced shift toward more conservative moral views and government policies. From the economic boom of the postwar decades, the nation shifted to a period of economic constriction caused by inflation, energy shortages, and the competition of foreign manufacturers. In the mid- and late 1980s, the nation's economy revived, with growing employment figures and a generally optimistic national outlook, although a critical foreign trade imbalance and the skyrocketing national debt continued to cause great concern. In the 1990s massive company downsizing and job layoffs helped create an atmosphere of widespread insecurity and economic tension.

EXPANSION OF RECREATION AND LEISURE

Through it all, recreation and leisure witnessed an immense growth in participation. There was a steady increase in sports, the arts, hobbies, outdoor recreation, and fitness programs, along with a parallel expansion of home-based entertainment through the use of stereo, television, videocassette recorders, and other electronic equipment.

Government recreation and park agencies dramatically expanded their budgets, personnel, facilities, and programs until the mid-1970s. Then, many federal, state, and local agencies were forced by funding cuts to cut back or freeze budgets. At the same time, the recreation and park profession continued to grow in numbers and public visibility. Pre-professional curricula were established in many colleges and universities during the 1960s and 1970s, and several national organizations, including the National Recreation Association, the American Recreation Society, and the American Institute of Park Executives, merged to form the National Recreation and Park Association—a stronger and more unified voice for the park and recreation field overall.

Influence of National Affluence

An important factor in the growth of recreational participation was the national affluence of the postwar years. The gross national product rose from $211 billion in 1945 to over a trillion dollars annually in 1971. In the late 1950s, it was reported that Americans were spending $30 billion a year on leisure—a sum that seemed huge then but was just one-tenth of what it was to become in the 1980s. In *Leisure in a Changing America: Multicultural Perspectives,* this author states:

> Involvement in varied forms of recreation exploded during this period. Visits to national forests increased by 474 percent between 1947 and 1963, and to national parks by 302 percent during the same period. Overseas pleasure travel increased by 440 percent and attendance at sports and cultural events also grew rapidly. Sales of golf equipment increased by 188 percent, of tennis equipment by 148 percent, and use of bowling lanes by 258 percent. Hunting and fishing, horse-racing attendance, and copies of paperback books sold all gained dramatically and—most strikingly—the number of families with television sets grew by 3500 percent over this 16-year period.[4]

Effect of Demographic Changes: Suburbanization and Urban Crises

In the years immediately after World War II, which had disrupted the lives of millions of servicemen and women, great numbers of young couples married. Within a few years, many of these new families with young children moved from the central cities to new homes in surrounding suburban areas. In these suburban communities, recreation for growing families became an important concern. Most suburbs were quick to establish new recreation and park departments, hire personnel, and develop programs and facilities to serve all age groups—often in concert with local school districts.

At the same time, the population within the inner cities changed dramatically. With the rapid mechanization of agriculture in the South and the abandonment of the sharecropper system, millions of southern blacks moved to the cities and industrialized areas of the Northeast, the Midwest, and the West in search of jobs and better opportunities. Growing numbers of Hispanic immigrants surged into the cities from the Caribbean islands and Central America. Generally, these new residents were accustomed to rural living and had limited job skills; they posed serious problems of health, housing, welfare, and social control for the cities.

TRENDS IN PROGRAM SPONSORSHIP

As a result of such population shifts and changes in lifestyle, a number of trends in recreation program functions and in the role to be played by government emerged. These included: (1) programs aimed at improving physical fitness; (2) emphasis on environmental concerns; (3) activities and services designed to meet special age-group needs; (4) recreation for persons with disabilities; (5) increasing programming in the arts; (6) services for the economically and socially disadvantaged; and (7) programs concerned with the needs of racial and ethnic minorities.

Physical Fitness Emphasis

Beginning in the 1950s, there was a strong emphasis on the need to develop and maintain the physical fitness of youth. In both World Wars, a disappointingly high percentage of male draftees and enlistees had been rejected by the armed forces for physical reasons. Then, after World War II, comparative studies such as the Kraus-Weber tests showed that American youth were less fit than the youth of several other nations. This led schools to strengthen their programs of physical fitness, and many public recreational departments expanded their leisure activities to include fitness classes, conditioning, jogging, and sports for all ages.

Concern with fitness remained at a plateau until the mid-1970s, when it emerged as a major national preoccupation. The interest in health and wellness (defining health not merely as the absence of disease, but as vigorous well-being in many spheres of life) spread rapidly during this period.

Health spas began to appear all over the country, providing exercise facilities with heavy equipment like Nautilus or Universal gym machines, as well as racquetball and squash courts, jogging tracks, pools, saunas, and other specialty areas—frequently in combination with consultants who prescribed exercise and nutritional programs. This emphasis on physical fitness has continued into the present, although, as pointed out later, there is some evidence that the rate of involvement has declined (see page 239).

Environmental Concerns

A key concern of the recreation field has been the environment. In the postwar period, it became evident that there was a critical need to preserve and rehabilitate the nation's land, water, and wildlife resources. We had permitted the great rivers and lakes to be polluted by waste, forests to be ruthlessly razed by lumbering interests, and wildlife to be ravaged by over-hunting or lack of adequate breeding areas or by chemical poisons and invasion of their environments. Greater and greater demands had been placed on our natural resource bank, with open space shrinking at an unprecedented rate.

In the late 1950s, President Dwight Eisenhower and the Congress formed the Outdoor Recreation Resources Review Commission to investigate this problem. The result was a landmark, heavily documented report in 1962 that helped to promote a wave of environmental efforts by federal, state, and municipal governments. The Federal Water Pollution Control Administration divided the nation into 20 major river basins and promoted regional sewage treatment programs in those areas. The Water Quality Act of 1965, the Clean Water Restoration Act of 1966, the Solid Waste Disposal Act of 1965, the Highway Beautification Act of 1965, and the Mining Reclamation Act of 1968 all committed the United States to a sustained program of conservation and protection of its natural resources. Another major piece of legislation was the Wilderness Act of 1964, which gave Congress the authority to declare certain unspoiled lands permanently off-limits to human occupation and development. John Daniel writes:

> Thus was born the National Wilderness Preservation System, which did the national park system one better. Wilderness allows no roads or vehicles—you enter on your own two feet, as explorers and settlers once entered the greater wilderness that was North America.[5]

Many states and cities embarked on new programs of land acquisition and beautification, and developed environmental plans designed to reduce air and water pollution. Nonprofit organizations like the American Land Trust, The Nature Conservancy, and the Trust for Public Lands took over properties encompassing hundreds of thousands of acres—many of them donated by large corporations—for preservation or transfer to public agencies for recreational use. Such programs were accompanied by efforts within federal agencies like the National Park Service, the Forest Service, the Fish and Wildlife Service, and the Bureau of Land Management to meet public needs for outdoor recreation.

The environmental progress of the 1960s and 1970s was, however, soon to be halted. In the early 1980s, federal expenditures for parks and environmental programs were sharply reduced, the rate of land acquisition was cut back, and government policies regulating the use of wild lands for mining, timber cutting, grazing, oil drilling, and similar commercial activities were dramatically relaxed. Outdoor recreation and park enthusiasts and conservation organizations engaged in a continuing battle with Secretary of the Interior James Watt, and to a lesser degree with his successors, to protect the nation's parks and forests from encroachment and neglect.

As this struggle continued in the mid-1990s, it became evident to some that outdoor recreation enthusiasts—although generally regarding themselves as allies of the environmental movement—can often constitute a serious threat to the wilderness through the use of off-road vehicles, crowding of wilderness sites, and poor waste disposal methods. Recreation and park educators have begun to preach the need for an effective "environmental ethic" to govern our management of the nation's outdoor resources.[6]

Meeting Age-Group Needs

In addition to the demographic trends cited earlier, three other important changes in the nation's population that gathered force in the postwar decades were: (1) the dramatic rise in the birth rate, with millions of children and youth flooding the schools and community recreation centers; (2) the lengthening of the population's life span, resulting in a growing proportion of elderly persons in society; and (3) the increasing incidence of marital breakup and divorce and of children born out of wedlock, leading to a huge number of single-parent households.

In response to these trends, thousands of governmental and nonprofit organizations expanded their programs for children and youth, and numerous youth sports leagues like Little League, Biddy Basketball, and American Legion Football recruited millions of participants. At the other end of the age range, public and nonprofit organizations developed golden age clubs or senior centers, often with funding from the federal government through the Administration on Aging. Various types of special leisure programs and volunteer projects for elderly persons were established, and "leisure villages" and retirement communities offering extensive recreation opportunities for older persons became popular. With the development of university curricula in gerontology, recreation and leisure practitioners began to develop specialties in this area, and extensive research into the linkage of aging and leisure was conducted.

The high divorce rate and growing number of single-parent households confirmed the need for recreation programs to provide day-care services for children of working parents and to meet other leisure-related needs. Religious organizations in particular are stressing family-oriented programming today in an effort to strengthen marital bonds and improve parent-child relationships.

Special Recreation for Persons with Disabilities

An area of increased emphasis in the postwar era was the provision of special services for persons with physical and mental disabilities. As in the environmental field, this trend was strengthened by federal legislation (see page 335). Various government agencies concerned with rehabilitation were expanded to meet the needs of individuals with disabilities, especially the large numbers of returning veterans who sought to be integrated into community life.

The federal government sharply increased its aid to special education. In recreation, assistance was given to programs serving children, youth, and adults with developmental disability. Beginning in the mid-1960s, there was an increased emphasis on developing social and recreational programs for aging persons in both institutional and community settings. Overall, the specialized field of what came to be known as therapeutic recreation service expanded steadily in this period.

With the establishment of the National Therapeutic Recreation Society in the mid-1960s and the American Therapeutic Recreation Association in the 1980s, professionalization in therapeutic recreation service developed rapidly. The establishment of curriculum guidelines for courses in professional preparation, the setting of program standards, and the development of registration and certification plans all served to make this field a significant specialized area within the broad leisure-service field.

As awareness grew of the needs of persons with disability who live in the community and are not part of active treatment programs—a majority of this overall population—support also increased for the providing of leisure programs in noninstitutional settings. Initially, such recreation offerings were regarded as "special recreation" and were not considered to be part of the scope of therapeutic recreation service as a professional discipline. However, over the last 20 years, community programming for disabled persons has become a recognized component in this field, and growing numbers of public and nonprofit leisure-service agencies today accept it as a high-priority function.

Increased Interest in the Arts

Following World War II, the United States embarked on an expansion of cultural centers, museums, and art centers. In part this represented a natural follow-up to the stimulus that had been given to art, theater, music, and dance by emergency federal programs during the Great Depression. Another element, however, was that Americans had now come to respect and enjoy the arts—as spectators and participants.

Through the 1970s and early 1980s, community arts activities continued to flourish, with the assistance of federal funding through the National Endowment for the Arts, which helped to support state arts units, choreographers and composers, and individual performers and companies. In the mid- and late 1980s, some decline in attendance at music, drama, and dance events was noted, possibly due to declining federal support and to the increasing public interest in home-based video entertainment. To meet this challenge, many cultural organizations in the fine and performing arts, as well as many museums, libraries and similar institutions, have developed new methods of fund-raising by diversifying their offerings and marketing them to a broader community audience. As an example, art, natural history, and science museums today offer lectures, tours, classes, films, innovative displays, special fund-raising dinners, and other events designed to attract a wide spectrum of patrons.

Many arts organizations have also been confronted by the hard reality that numerous school systems throughout the United States have been forced by tightened budgets to reduce their programs in the arts—not filling teacher specialist positions, relaxing curriculum requirements, and cutting back on support for performing music, dance, or theater groups. Recognizing that this trend threatens to decimate future audiences for the arts, many cultural institutions have created innovative educational programs in cooperation with the public schools. As a single example, the New York Philharmonic

> . . . is in the second year of a "partnership" with five public schools in Manhattan. Under this program, orchestra members and other symphony representatives work with students, parents and teachers; classroom curriculums are designed by the Philharmonic; performances are held in schools, and students attend Philharmonic concerts. Its education programs in other schools and with families have also grown significantly. [Similar efforts to promote arts education have been designed] for public schools in Chicago and Detroit, as well as for the San Francisco Symphony and other arts organizations.[7]

Recreation's Antipoverty Role

An important development of the 1960s was the expanded role given to recreation as an important element in President Lyndon Johnson's "war on poverty." Initially, the nation's concern about the economically and socially disadvantaged had been aroused by a widely read book on poverty in America by Michael Harrington—published in 1962 at a time of great prosperity for most citizens.[8]

During the 1930s and 1940s, a number of federal housing programs had provided funding to support small parks, playgrounds, or centers in public housing projects. Now, a new wave of legislation, such as the Economic Opportunity Act of 1964, the Housing and Urban Development Act of 1964, and the Model Cities program approved in 1967 provided assistance for locally directed recreation programs to be conducted by disadvantaged citizens themselves, in depressed urban neighborhoods. Other federal programs, such as the Job Corps, VISTA (Volunteers in Service to America), and the Neighborhood Youth Corps, also included recreation-related components.

Recreation as such was not usually the prime thrust in such federal antipoverty efforts. The Economic Opportunity Act, for example, was designed to strengthen and expand services in the fields of "education and training, provision of jobs, youth opportunities, family units, better living conditions, and better housing." However, it was considered that recreation contributed significantly to these goals by providing constructive leisure outlets, the opportunity for job training and placement, and a sense of empowerment for poor residents.

Linkage of Antipoverty and Race-Related Programming

In the mid-1960s, destructive riots erupted in a number of major American cities, with a shattering loss of life and housing. Occurring chiefly in ghetto neighborhoods where blacks and Hispanics lived, these riots stemmed from a number of causes. Later research disclosed that among the causes were increasing frustration over continuing job and educational discrimination, unheeded protests against the justice system and poor community services, *and* inadequate recreation and park programs and facilities for minority groups.

In a number of cases, riots began as a protest by African-Americans against police who were turning off hydrants that afforded children and youth a measure of summer relief on steaming city streets—where no swimming pool was accessible. In other cases, they stemmed from the overall lack of parks, playgrounds, or other recreation facilities in inner city neighborhoods, as compared to wealthier sections. Yet it was also recognized that to a great degree the situations were aggravated by the frustration, anger, and boredom felt by boys and men who were unemployed and had little to do but mill about in the streets or taverns.

In a sense, there was a curiously playlike aspect to much of the rioting, according to numerous reports. In 1967, a policeman commented bitterly about Puerto Rican rioters in New York City's East Harlem district: "they're like kids. They get a big kick out of the riots. It's like a carnival to them." And, in the same disturbance, a Puerto Rican antipoverty official commented, "It wasn't a gang effort but a series of unrelated incidents—kids in it for the fun of it." In Newark, New Jersey, during the tremendously destructive 1967 conflagration, Governor Hughes said after inspecting the district that he had found the "holiday atmosphere" among the looters most repelling. The Governor and the Mayor of Newark drove through the core of the riot area and "watched helplessly as men, women and children almost gaily raided wrecked stores." During the 1967 Puerto Rican riot, a passing nun remarked, "They were doing it out of sport, you know, not maliciously. They were laughing like: 'Isn't this great fun, getting something for free.'"[9]

Riots of this type appeared to serve a widely shared need for excitement, abandon, and release. They are real, as television is not. They fulfill the same function as high-risk outdoor recreational pursuits or competitive contact sports.

In an effort to "cool" the hot summers and prevent further rioting, many of the antipoverty programs of the mid- and late 1960s placed their emphasis on serving minority groups in urban slums. Hundreds of millions of dollars were granted each year to local governments and to organizations of "indigenous" residents to provide enriched recreation services aimed particularly at youth. These included sports and social activities, cultural pursuits, job-training and tutorial programs, and trips and similar recreation activities.

On a national scale, Job Corps, VISTA, Neighborhood Youth Corps, and an aggregate of special projects known as Community Action Programs continued into the 1970s, but were gradually terminated in the years that followed. While hundreds of thousands of inner-city residents were employed during this period under CETA (the federal Comprehensive Employment and Training Act), this too ended in the 1980s as the threat of urban rioting on a large scale lessened. A variety of community development "block" grants continued to be offered and were sometimes used for recreation and park purposes.

COUNTERCULTURE: YOUTH IN REBELLION

Paralleling the period of the urban riots, what came to be known as the counterculture made its appearance in America. The term "counterculture," as John Kelly points out, is generally applied to a movement that develops in opposition to an established and dominant culture—

and it manifests itself in language, symbols, and behavior. He suggests that countercultures may be of many types:

> Some have been highly political with their opposition to war, racism, sexism, and educational authoritarianism. Others have withdrawn from the political scene to concentrate on self-development and inner awareness. Some have been based on a religious ideology and still others have rejected religion. . . . Some movements have been ascetic and others have stressed sensuality and sexuality.[10]

The counterculture movement in the United States during the 1960s was part of a larger youth movement that challenged the political, economic, and educational establishments in a number of other nations around the world. Here, it symbolized the rebellion of young people against parental authority and the curricular and social controls of schools and colleges. Much of it stemmed from mass protests against the Vietnam War as students initiated strikes and takeovers of administrative offices in a number of universities.

Rock music and lyrics that challenged traditional values became popular, and many young people joined "hippie" communes or fled to neighborhoods like Haight-Ashbury in San Francisco or the East Village in New York City, where they experimented with drugs and a variety of alternative lifestyles. Traditional family values declined as even many adults accepted a freer sexual code of behavior, living together out of wedlock and accepting the view that marriage and having children were not essential for happiness.

Rejection of the Work Ethic

A significant aspect of the counterculture movement was its rejection of work as the be-all and end-all of one's life—and of the widely accepted goal of "making it" in the business or professional world.

As Chapter 8 has shown, a deep-rooted belief in the value of hard work, which was linked to an essentially conservative, industrious, and moralistic view of life, had long been a fundamental tenet of American society. Workers, for the most part, tended to be loyal to their companies, fellow employees, and the task itself—although labor-management conflict sometimes found expression in pitched battles between company heads and union organizers in a number of industries.

However, since World War II, there had been a retreat from the stern precepts of the Protestant work ethic. As establishment values and monetary success were undermined in the thinking of young people during the counterculture period, leisure satisfactions assumed new importance. Writers urged new, holistic approaches to the use of free time that would integrate varied aspects of human personality and lead to the self-actualization spoken of by Maslow and other psychologists. Although recreation was perceived as a legitimate area of human expression, many critics attacked the highly competitive approach to sports that had dominated society, urging instead a low-pressure, noncompetitive "New Games" approach in which all could take part and all might win.

By 1981, a poll by the Louis Harris survey organization found that:

78 percent of all working Americans feel that "people take less pride in their work than they did 10 years ago."

73 percent believe that "the motivation to work hard is not as strong today as it was a decade ago."

69 percent feel that our workmanship is worse than it was.

63 percent simply believe that "most people do not work as hard today as they did 10 years ago."[11]

Similarly, many workers showed interest in reducing work time and making work hours more flexible. There was growing use of part-time and part-year work assignments, as well as job-sharing and experimentation with three-day and four-day workweeks. Fred Best, a research associate with the National Manpower Commission, found that many workers expressed a willingness to exchange income for more free time, although there appeared to be resistance to the idea of extended free time in the form of long vacations.[12]

DRIVES FOR EQUALITY BY DISADVANTAGED GROUPS

Another important aspect of the counterculture movement was that it provided a climate within which various populations in American society that had historically been disadvantaged were encouraged to press vigorously for fuller social and economic rights.

Racial and Ethnic Minorities

For racial and ethnic minorities there was a strong thrust during the 1960s and 1970s toward demanding fuller recreational service in terms of facilities and organized programs. In response, many public recreation and park departments not only upgraded these traditional elements, but also began to provide mobile recreation units that would enter impacted neighborhoods with cultural, social, and other special services. Building on projects that had been initiated during the "war on poverty" and the period of urban riots, many departments initiated classes, workshops, festivals, and holiday celebrations designed to promote ethnic pride and intercultural appreciation. In many urban areas, this effort extended to programming that reflected the customs, traditions, and leisure pursuits of national groups of European background.

Through legislation, Supreme Court decisions, other judicial orders, and voluntary compliance, public, nonprofit, and commercial facilities were gradually desegregated through the 1970s and 1980s. Major youth and adult social membership organizations like the Boy Scouts and Girl Scouts and the YMCA and YWCA, which had tended to maintain segregated units for racial minorities or to not serve them at all, opened up their memberships and in some cases identified racial justice as a high-priority mission for the years ahead. Efforts were made to recruit more minority group members into professional recreation and park positions, and in many cities African-American staff members in particular were advanced to upper-level management positions.

In terms of the broader culture, as college and professional sports were desegregated in the 1940s and 1950s, minority group members went on to achieve remarkable success in the three most popular team sports—basketball, football, and baseball. Within the mass media of entertainment, black and Hispanic actors, singers, musicians, and comedians became outstanding stars in movies, television, and the recording industry. The formerly limited or stereotyped treatment of minorities—as in the "Amos and Andy" radio show and the roles given comic movie actor Stepin Fetchit—gave way to a full range of themes and representations.[13]

Women

Earlier chapters in this text have described the historic subordination of women. In the 1960s and 1970s, feminist groups mobilized themselves to attack two major areas of gender-based discrimination in recreation and leisure: (1) employment practices and (2) provision of program activities.

Employment of Women   Numerous studies showed that women tended to secure fewer high-level administrative positions and were paid lower salaries than men in recreation and park departments throughout the United States. In 1977, Diana Dunn summarized the findings of a national two-year study:

> Some might assume that women's participation in the recreation profession has increased over the last three quarters of a century, but a glance at the record shows otherwise. In local recreation and parks, where 95 percent of (public) recreation professionals are employed, women have moved from a majority to a minority, and are trending toward extinction.[14]

Similarly, William Theobald carried out an exhaustive study documenting the situation in Canada. He found:

> There were almost 2.5 males to each female full-time recreation staff member in the cities investigated. The higher the level of responsibility, the fewer the number of females. . . . Females on an average received $1,300 less than males when entering the recreation profession. . . . the male to female salary ratio increased in each salary level.[15]

However, in response to equal opportunity laws and other pressures, governmental recreation and park departments and other agencies began to hire women in greater numbers than in the past. Several states hired their first women park rangers, naturalists, and park superintendents, and in a number of cities women were appointed as directors of the recreation and park departments. While men still tend to be favored in positions dealing with maintenance and the operation of special facilities, women have been successful in moving into many other types of administrative and supervisory roles.

Participation by Women   A fundamental principle in community recreation has been that all persons should be given an equal opportunity, regardless of sex, religion, race, or other personal factors. However, in the postwar decades, it became evident that this principle had not been applied toward participation of girls and women in public recreation programs in either the United States or Canada. To document the preferential treatment given to males as participants in public and nonprofit agency recreation programs, Michael Heit and Don Malpass studied program differentiation by gender in the Sport and Fitness Division of the Ontario, Canada, Ministry of Culture and Recreation. Their findings clearly documented the unequal provision of programs for females.[16]

In the United States, similar investigations, when combined with pressure from women's groups, legislation like Title IX of the Education Amendment Act of 1972, and lawsuits directed at colleges, school boards, and various community recreation agencies, led to significant changes in public recreation programming. As a result, girls and women today have a far greater range of sport and physical recreation opportunities than they did in the past.

Nevertheless, there continued to be an imbalance in the program offerings provided by nonprofit youth-serving organizations, which had historically been supported more generously for activities serving boys than for activities serving girls. As a consequence, some organizations that formerly served only girls, like the Girls Clubs of America and Camp Fire Girls, have either merged with their male counterparts or have broadened their membership to include both boys and girls.

Gays and Lesbians

A third group of persons who traditionally have been disadvantaged in American society consists of homosexuals. During the counterculture era, they began to mobilize themselves as an economic and political force. In the 1960s and 1970s many gay and lesbian groups began to organize and promote their recreational and social activities openly on college campuses and in community life. In a number of cities, they had to fight through the courts for the right to take part in community celebrations, parades, and other civic events. In the 1980s and 1990s, with heavily attended Gay Games—athletic events featuring thousands of homosexual participants—and with gay and lesbian themes becoming commonplace in the movies, at the theater, and on television, this population began to achieve a much higher degree of acceptance within the sphere of leisure activity.

In other cases, when they have sought to enter homosexual groups as such in big-city St. Patrick's Day Parades, or when they held a huge gay festival at Florida's Walt Disney World, a number of conservative Christian organizations protested vigorously.[17] In retaliation, when rural Cobb County, Georgia, passed a resolution condemning the gay lifestyle as incompatible with its values, gay groups and their allies pressured the International Olympic Committee to withdraw some of its featured events from the county after they had already been scheduled to take place there as part of the 1996 Olympics.

As Chapter 5 points out, the need to serve gays and lesbians in public recreation and park programs has just begun to be considered, while in nonprofit, youth-service organizations—particularly those with religious sponsorship or assistance—it represents a highly controversial, even explosive, issue.

The Elderly in Community Life

Although the counterculture was primarily a youth movement in the United States and abroad, it also prompted many middle-aged and older persons to examine their value systems and their status in community life.

The elderly at this time represented a fourth group of disadvantaged persons in the sense that they were generally regarded and treated as powerless individuals, who were both physically and economically vulnerable. However, under the leadership of such growing organizations as the American Association of Retired Persons and the much smaller Gray Panthers, elderly persons began to mobilize and exert political clout in order to obtain improved benefits. With support from various federal programs, including the

Administration on Aging, senior citizens' groups and golden age clubs around the United States began to offer diversified programs of health care, social services, nutrition, housing and transportation assistance and recreation.

Consequently, the popular image of elderly persons as fragile, dependent, and sexless individuals began to disappear and be replaced by a vision of old age as a time for vigorous, active participation in a host of recreational pursuits that prolonged life and yielded important physical and emotional benefits. Today, many states and communities sponsor sports leagues and fitness programs for elderly persons, along with educational, social, counseling, political awareness, and other services.

With population forecasts in the 1990s showing that older individuals will constitute a larger section of the population, service to the elderly will clearly represent a high-priority goal for all types of recreation sponsors in the future.

Programming for Persons with Disabilities

Although significant progress had been made following World War II, both treatment-centered and community-based programming for persons with disabilities received a major impetus during the counterculture. Like other disadvantaged groups that had essentially been powerless, persons with disabilities began to act as their own advocates, demanding their rights and opportunities.

As Chapter 12 will show, such groups as the hearing-impaired have pressured vigorously for the appointment of agency heads or educational administrators from their own ranks. Disabled persons in general have mobilized themselves as a political force in order to promote positive legislation and increased community services for those with physical, mental, or social disabilities. At the same time that therapeutic recreation specialists have begun to include a broader range of disabilities within their scope of service, numerous organizations have gone one step farther and promoted such innovative programming as theater arts for physically disabled individuals, skiing for those with visual disabilities, and a full range of sports and track-and-field events for the mobility-impaired.[18]

ERA OF AUSTERITY AND FISCAL CUTBACKS

Despite this general picture of positive progress, the recreation, parks, and leisure-service field faced a serious threat in the 1970s and 1980s as mounting costs of government led to tax protests and funding cutbacks in states and cities across the United States.

As early as the mid-1970s, a number of older industrial cities in the nations's "rust belt" began to suffer from increased energy costs, welfare and crime problems, and expenses linked to rising infrastructure maintenance problems. Along with some suburban school districts confronted by skyrocketing enrollments and limited tax bases, such communities experienced budget deficits and the need to freeze expenditures. At the same time, as John Crompton and Brian McGregor point out, a series of opinion polls showed that there had been a significant decline in the public's confidence in government. They write:

> There was a growing perception that governments wasted money, taxes were too high, government employees were highly paid and lazy, welfare services were fraudulently consumed, and that many services were non-essential or inefficiently provided. A sizable proportion of the electorate believed that taxes could be cut without endangering "basic" or "essential" services.[19]

In 1976, a tax limitation law was passed in New Jersey, and in 1978 California's much more radical Proposition 13 sharply reduced local property tax rates and assessment increases. A "tax revolt" soon spread rapidly across the United States. By the end of 1979, statutory provisions had been approved in 36 states that either reduced property, income, or sales taxes or put other types of spending limits in place. Austerity budgets had to be adopted in many communities, counties, and other governmental units. Typically, Proposition 13 resulted in major funding cutbacks for parks, libraries, recreation, social services, and street sweeping and maintenance, while police and fire departments tended to be protected against cuts. A survey of 183 California park and recreation agencies found that city, county, and special district operational expenditures declined by 11.6 percent and per capita expenditures by 18.2 percent, in constant dollar terms, between fiscal years 1977–1978 and 1981–1982. At the same time, the amount of developed park land and the number of recreation facilities grew by over 10 percent, posing a severe challenge for local public agencies.[20]

Expanding Use of Revenue Sources

Many local recreation and park agencies adopted the policy of instituting or raising fees and charges for participation in programs, for use of the facilities, for rental of equipment, and for other types of involvement in a wide range of leisure activities and services. In the past, it had generally been the practice to provide all basic play opportunities, particularly for children and youth, without charge and to impose fees only for classes with special expenses or for admission to facilities such as skating rinks, swimming pools, golf courses, or tennis courts—often with arrangements made for annual permits at modest cost.

The revenues gained from such sources usually amounted to no more than five or ten percent of a department's operating budget. However, Crompton and McGregor found that between 1964–1965 and 1990–1991 there was, in real dollar terms, a 259 percent increase in the self-generated revenues of local public recreation and park agencies. In a study of 372 local public leisure-service agencies in Illinois, the average self-generated income of responding departments was found to be 32.7 percent of total department operating expenses by the late 1980s. What this meant was that more and more public departments either were imposing new charges on programs like day camps, sports league registration, classes, or outings, or were raising the level of existing fees—often to the point where substantial numbers of families could not afford to pay them.

Despite such concerns, many local recreation and park agencies began to place increasing reliance on self-generated funding, not only as a means of survival but also as a way to provide a wide range of attractive programs and facilities and ensure the quality in program offerings. As an added bonus, administrators found that their ability to gather their own revenues raised their status among civic officials and improved their public image.

Acceptance of Marketing Orientation   Directly linked to this trend was the widespread acceptance of an entrepreneurial, marketing-oriented approach to recreation and park programming and administration. It was argued by both educators and practitioners that it was necessary to be aggressive in seeking out new program opportunities and creative in responding to fiscal challenges—rather than relying on past, and often outmoded, formulas or policies.

References were being made to recreation as an "industry" in both the popular and the professional literature. Typically, in 1986, the *American Association for Leisure and Recreation Reporter* stated:

> The recreation industry is a mosaic of thousands of businesses interwoven, directly or subtly, into the American economy. The scope of the recreation industry stretches far beyond what many people immediately perceive. In addition to the large recreation businesses that immediately come to mind—such as Coleman, Winnebago and Disney—there are also tens of thousands of small businesses which contribute to satisfying the demand for recreation and tourism opportunities in this country.[21]

In other professional publications, it was argued that managers of recreation and park programs, directors of nonprofit youth organizations, and operators of commercial play facilities were all essentially in the same "business"—that of meeting the public's leisure needs and interests. *Trends*, published by the National Recreation and Park Association and the National Park Service, agreed:

> Managed recreation is a profession that provides services to consumers of all demographic stripes and shades. Under this designation, a public park superintendent is in the same business as a resort owner . . . a theme park operator and the fitness directors of a YMCA.[22]

It was often argued that in order to compete effectively public recreation agencies had to adopt the philosophy and businesslike methods of successful companies. This meant that at every stage of agency operations—from assessing potential target populations and planning programs to pricing, publicizing, and distributing services—sophisticated methods of analysis and businesslike approaches to attracting and satisfying "customers" were to be used.

This trend was not unique to leisure-service agencies. Throughout American society, all professions and all forms of social service or artistic performance have been compelled to be far more innovative and marketing-oriented in serving the public. Doctors and lawyers now advertise their services freely and form nationwide multimillion dollar chains, while symphony orchestras and art museums sponsor entertainment and social events, offer film series and classes, and sell memorabilia in order to make money. Local hospitals in some cases operate catering and laundry services as a separate business.

Even religion has become entrepreneurial, with churches or denominations sponsoring television evangelism programs or networks, camps and resorts, and the sale of books, records, and video products. Some churches today offer user-friendly, drive-in 22-minute services in suburban shopping malls, and a number of huge "mega-churches" present professionally designed services that are almost indistinguishable from popular rock-and-roll concerts.

As an example of religion-based enterprise, Protestant televangelist Pat Robertson presides over a financial empire with annual revenues of $140 million. It includes both nonprofit educational and charitable institutions and such enterprises as a jet-chartering service, a hotel and travel agency, a Hollywood production company, television and radio channels and stations, and at one point a company called Kalo-Vita, which sold "Sea of Galilee" mud masks and a vitamin drink called American Whey.[23]

Privatization of Recreation and Park Operations

As a second type of response to the era of austerity that began in the 1980s, many recreation, park, and leisure-service agencies resorted to privatization—subcontracting or developing concession arrangements with private organizations—to carry out functions that they could not themselves fulfill as economically or efficiently.

This has become a major thrust in American life as the role of government has been challenged. Many cities now rely on private businesses to construct or maintain facilities, provide food and health services, or manage a variety of other formerly public functions. In a number of cases, prisons and correctional institutions are managed by for-profit companies under contract with public authorities, and several cities have experimented with assigning private organizations the responsibility for running all or part of their school systems.

As for recreation and parks, numerous public departments have contracted with private businesses to operate golf courses, tennis complexes, marinas, and other facilities under contractual agreements that govern the standards they must meet and the rates they may impose. Particularly in the construction of massive new facilities such as sports stadiums and arenas, similar arrangements have been made with commercial developers or businesses for private funding of all or part of construction expenses, with long-term leases being granted to owners of major sports teams.

Clearly, such privatization strategies represent a means by which public departments can shed responsibility for programs or facilities that they cannot operate efficiently. At the same time, they present a basic question about the fundamental responsibility of public leisure-service agencies in contemporary community life—an issue that is discussed more fully in Chapter 14.

Accepting Funding Cuts

The third response of many recreation and park agencies has been to cut back on maintenance and recreation programming, particularly in older cities where there are substantial numbers of residents below the poverty line who are unable to pay fees for recreational involvement. In 1978, the National Urban Recreation Study reported that hiring freezes and staff cutbacks had taken place in a majority of urban park and recreation departments during the preceding five years. Two years later, a study of U.S. cities having over 150,000 in population found that a majority of the responding recreation and park departments had experienced major cutbacks over the preceding decade (see table below).

Percentage of Respondents Reporting Effects of Budget Cut[24]

	1971	1979
Manpower freeze on new hiring	41	59
Personnel discharged because of budget cuts	4	35
Significant programs eliminated	29	35
Bond issues rejected or facilities development halted	29	25
Facilities maintenance reduced or eliminated*	X	44

*Asked as a new question in 1979; X means no data available.

Even when annual budgets showed an increase, the increases were generally below the rate of inflation and the cost-of-living increases for city employees. In many departments, the staff reductions were severe; in one large eastern city, 80 percent of the supervisors had been fired, the entire maintenance system had been disbanded, and all facilities were temporarily closed. In other cities, playground programs at elementary schools were eliminated; operating hours at recreation centers were reduced; swimming pools had shorter seasons; and special events were canceled.

In their 1994 report, Crompton and McGregor found that self-generated revenues of recreation and park departments had been able to compensate for budget cuts in tax-supported funding only to a limited degree. They remark:

> The data for the most recent three years [in the late 1980s] suggest that much of the potential for significant increases in self-generated revenue may have been exhausted, and future aggregate increases from this source are likely to be relatively modest.[25]

Some reports suggest that many municipal and county recreation and park agencies have weathered the financial crisis that followed the tax revolt and have reached a point of relative stability. A study of small-town public recreation departments in several western and midwestern states by Ellen Weissinger and William Murphy found that, while these departments had experienced somewhat similar cutbacks to those reported in larger cities, they have generally avoided drastic reductions in staff and programs.[26] In some of the hard-hit communities, neighborhood residents have successfully mobilized to take up the slack and have even provided new programming, particularly for children and youth, with the help of public agencies and local businesses.

However, the reality is that in many larger cities, which have the greatest number of poor families—and are marked by high welfare statistics, school dropouts, drug and alcohol abuse, youth gangs, and random violence—recreation and park programs today offer only the most minimal opportunities. The facilities that are provided are often vandalized and covered with graffiti, staff members are threatened, and overall agency operations are extremely limited.

Beyond this, Jack Foley and Veda Ward point out that in the most severely disadvantaged communities, such as South Los Angeles, nonprofit sports groups like Little League, Pony League, AAU swimming, and gymnastic and track clubs (which use public facilities but rely on volunteer leaders and membership fees) do not exist. There is also no commercial recreation in the form of movie theaters, malls, skating rinks, or bowling alleys. They continue:

> Boys and Girls Clubs, YMCAs and YWCAs, Scouts, and so forth, which rely on business and community support, are under-represented and financed in poor communities. A market equity policy (one gets all the recreation one can buy) [has] created a separate, unequal and regressive City of Los Angeles recreation system. Many city parks [in wealthier neighborhoods] raise from $50,000 to $250,000 annually from user fees and donations for state-of-the-art services, while recreation centers in South Los Angeles exist on small city subsidies and what money they can squeeze out of the parents of poor children.[27]

EXPANSION OF OTHER RECREATION PROGRAMS

In sharp contrast with this negative picture, other forms of recreation services have flourished over the past three decades. Today, the largest single component of leisure services is the diversified field of commercial recreation businesses. Travel and tourism, fitness spas, professional sports and sports equipment, the manufacture and sale of hobbies, toys and games, and the various forms of popular entertainment represent only part of this major sphere of leisure involvement.

The impressive increase in consumer spending on primarily commercial forms of recreation participation is illustrated in its rise from \$91.3 billion in 1970 to \$304.1 billion in 1993, in constant (inflation-adjusted) dollars.[28] According to Thomas Blaine and Golam Muhammad, the U.S. Department of Commerce reports show that, over the last four decades, an increasing share of the U.S. consumer's budget has gone toward recreation-related goods and services.[29]

Similarly, most of the other areas of specialized recreation programming, such as therapeutic recreation, employee services, campus recreation, and private-membership and residential leisure services, have expanded steadily. In each case, these fields have sharpened their own identities and public images by developing professional societies or business associations, sponsoring national and regional conferences, publishing newsletters and magazines, and in some cases establishing continuing education and certification programs.

Implications for Professional Education

As Chapter 13 will further demonstrate, the period from the 1960s through the mid-1990s saw a major expansion of professional education in the field of recreation, parks, and leisure services. After the merger of several different professional and service societies into the National Recreation and Park Association in the mid-1960s, hundreds of colleges and universities initiated new or expanded curricula in recreation and park programming and management.

Initially, all of these programs in higher education focused on preparing individuals for positions that were available in public recreation and park agencies in municipal, county, and special district governments. With the development of professional registration, certification, and accreditation procedures (see pages 360–368), a number of specialized areas of professional preparation were identified. Although these principally continued to relate to public recreation and park employment on supervisory or management levels, separate specializations in resource management, programming, and therapeutic recreation did emerge. In addition, some colleges offered major concentrations in such areas as employee services, armed forces recreation, and youth-service agencies.

Today, each of the major components of the leisure-service system to be described in the chapters that follow represents a major focus of professional education and potential employment for those choosing recreation and leisure as a career field. In some cases, they continue to be within the sphere of general recreation, park, and leisure services and to fit appropriately within the activities of the National Recreation and Park Association and its special branches. In other cases, they are represented more directly by other professional bodies, such as the National Employee Services and Recreation Association (NESRA), which serves those working in company personnel units, and the National Intramural and Recreation Sports Association (NIRSA), which meets the needs of individuals working in college and school sports and physical recreation programs. In still other cases, such as the fields of travel and tourism, theme park management, or fitness spas, there are numerous specialized professional and business associations that have very little connection to the recreation, parks, and leisure-service field, either as an academic discipline or as an area of social concern.

OTHER CHALLENGES: TIME CONSTRAINTS AND SOCIAL VALUES

Two significant challenges to recreation and leisure agencies and professionals have emerged in the 1980s and 1990s. These are:

1. the reported trend toward increased work and lessened leisure time; and
2. the deterioration in social and family values that has led to a significant decline in the quality of life in many American communities.

Growing "Time Famine"

As this chapter points out, a leading cause of the growth of the recreation movement throughout this century was the increase in free time—stemming from the shortened work-week, expanded vacations and holidays, longer periods of retirement, and greater use of labor-saving devices. The expectation in the 1950s was that this trend would be accelerated by the increased use of automation, and that this would lead to much more leisure time for those in the workforce. Given this scenario, recreation and leisure would then become more important aspects of national life.

However, the decline in the workweek came to a halt at mid-century, and the average hours of work remained relatively stable in the period that followed. In the 1980s, reports began to indicate that a change was taking place in terms of work hours.

A *Wall Street Journal/NBC News* survey report in 1986 found that a substantial number of Americans claimed to have more work and less leisure than in the past.[30] In 1987 the Louis Harris polling organization found that the number of hours the average American worked each week had risen from 40.6 in 1973 to 48.4 in 1983. At the same time, leisure hours had declined from 26.2 to 17.7 hours a week, with the trend being most evident among the nation's most affluent sectors.[31]

In the early 1990s, *The Overworked American: The Unexpected Decline of Leisure,* a book by Harvard economics professor Juliet Schor, summed up these and other studies to conclude that Americans had lost as much as 160 hours of leisure a year—a full month—due to heightened work demands.[32] Various reasons were cited for this development, including the increased pressure placed on employees in companies that had downsized by reducing their work staffs without reducing the work load. Others suggested that, in an increasingly competitive environment, business executives in particular found that their lives had become one long, continuous work grind that squeezed out leisure time. The accelerated pace of business; the use of faxes, e-mail, pagers, cellular phones, and other electronic means of computer analysis and communication; and the globalization of the business world compelling round-the-clock decision making resulted in a significant increase in work-related stress.

Other Research Findings   Despite these widely circulated reports, other research studies suggested that work schedules had *not* increased for most Americans over the past three decades. Making use of systematic time diaries kept by a cross-section of working adults over the 1960s, 1970s, and 1980s, sociologist John Robinson of the University of Maryland concluded that leisure hours had actually risen by about 10 percent during this period.

His research also disclosed specific changes in the way that leisure hours were allocated to various activities. For example, he found that fitness participation had declined by 10 percent between 1985 and 1990. Among 22 physical recreation or fitness activities, only walking, bicycling, and basketball had gained in popularity during this period. Gardening and yard work, calisthenics and general exercise, jogging and running, and dancing, aerobics, and swimming as exercise had all declined.[33]

Robinson also suggested that certain groups of Americans actually do have less free time or feel greater work pressures. These include working women and single parents who must combine work with family responsibilities, parents who have unconventional work schedules, and individuals who have lost well-paying jobs and must now work at two or three different jobs to meet their responsibilities.

Supporting Robinson's general finding, a *New York Times* article in September 1995 reported that a three-year study of the daily activities of 3,000 adults throughout the United States showed that:

> Americans are working slightly less and playing more, on average. Although that contradicts the popular perception that people are continually working more, it appears to reflect job layoffs and the growing proportion of older people, who generally have more free time.[34]

Similarly, an earlier report of U.S. Labor Department statistics that were based on information taken from company payroll reports showed that there had been a steady decline in the number of hours worked from 1978 to 1988—a contradiction of the Harris Poll findings.[35]

Desire for More Free Time and Simpler Lifestyle

Among those groups that *are* experiencing increased work time and work pressures, there appears to be a trend toward achieving a simpler, less pressured, and more rewarding lifestyle. In many cases, this involves deliberately resisting job demands that require more work or that represent a threat to family life. Some individuals are even accepting part-time positions at lesser salaries. In a *Time*/CNN poll of representative adults, 61 percent agreed that earning a living today "requires so much effort that it is difficult to find time to enjoy life."

In a dramatic example of workers balancing work pressures against quality-of-life needs, several thousand workers at the General Motors plant in Janesville, Wisconsin, agreed in November 1994 to reject company demands that they work a 50-hour week to compensate for a sharply reduced workforce. Although they welcomed the overtime pay involved, these union employees felt that the increased hours and heightened pace of work would create stress and lead to accidents—and that they would rather have more free time than more money.[36]

The implications of this trend for the recreation field are clear. For those who seek to develop simpler and more relaxed lives, recreation, park, and leisure-service agencies must provide a rich array of challenging and satisfying experiences for their free-time enrichment. And for those who genuinely suffer from work overload and a shortage of leisure time, David Scott urges the recreation profession to use strategies that will help them to use their scarce free hours more productively. He writes:

> Leisure-service agencies must strive to insure convenience in program offerings [by scheduling] programs or services at times that are convenient for the clients [or by scheduling] some form of child care . . . or dual programming for children and adults.

[Another] strategy is to provide opportunities for shorter, more self-directed leisure experiences. Some ski areas, amusement parks, and golf courses do this now by providing half-day tickets or nine-hole rounds of golf at an adjusted rate. . . .

Another strategy is to provide complete information concerning time requirements in promotional literature. Many trail maps, for example, now include trail length in distance *and* approximate time.[37]

At the same time, such efforts to cram recreational experiences into smaller compartments of time illustrate the point that recreation itself can often be the cause of pressure and stress. Traditionally, leisure was thought of as unhurried, relaxed, and unstructured time. However, people today often commit themselves to schedules—for trips, sports sessions, club meetings, or lessons—that are as demanding as work.

Many individuals are striving to avoid such pressures and to allow free time that is casual, relaxed, private, and spontaneous in its possibilities. Recreation, park, and leisure-service programmers must be fully aware of this growing need as they seek to serve the public in the years that lie ahead.

Concern About Social and Family Values

A final major problem that has arisen in American society over the past several decades is the severe erosion in the civility and quality of everyday life. Social critics and political campaigners have stressed the need to strengthen family values, but the problem goes far beyond this. The increased reliance on drugs, gambling, and indiscriminate or commercialized sex, the shocking growth of random violence, the accelerating rate of imprisonment, and the presence of growing numbers of homeless persons on city streets are all indications of the breakdown of community life.

In addition to the kinds of privatization discussed earlier in this chapter, there is another kind of withdrawal today from experiences shared with others—a retreat of millions of Americans to secure existences behind the walls of private communities, or to the entertainment provided by television, CD-ROMs, and video games in one's own home rather than that provided in community social settings. What appears to be lacking is a shared sense of responsibility and communal values that would bring people together to build bridges between groups that are separated by gender, race, generation, or other differences.

What does this have to do with recreation and leisure? It is the leisure activities that are the key elements in current popular culture—namely, movies, television, music and video games—that are being blamed for many of the pathologies of community life today. However, recreation practitioners cannot simply condemn and seek to censor or control such forms of entertainment, but must provide alternatives in the form of active, positive, and challenging recreational opportunities and must effectively educate for the creative and constructive use of leisure by all age groups.

It is an ugly paradox that while middle-class or wealthy Americans are able to afford a huge range of positive and appealing forms of play, the poorest citizens with the greatest need for healthful and enriching leisure experiences are provided with only minimal recreation facilities and programs.

A critical challenge for all recreation, park, and leisure-service practitioners in the years ahead will be to gather evidence of the social value and outcomes of organized recreation beyond those already documented (see Chapter 6), and to make these known to the public.

Stronger advocacy of socially oriented recreation and park services that reach all elements in the community will do much to counter the negative family and social trends that trouble Americans today.

SUMMARY

The years following World War II represented a period of immense change in the lives of Americans. From 1945 to the early 1970s, it was a time of prosperity and optimism for most families. As great numbers of young people—generally white and working- or middle-class—moved into suburban areas, recreation and park programs flourished and leisure was seen as part of the good life.

Recognizing that a substantial part of the population continued to live in urban slums, with limited economic and social opportunities, the federal government launched a "War on Poverty," in which recreation played a significant role. Under pressure from the civil rights movement, many recreation and park agencies began to give a higher level of priority to serving minorities. With the inner-city riots of the mid- and late 1960s, this effort was expanded throughout the country. At the same time, the counterculture movement which saw young people rebelling against traditional authority and establishment values transformed the society, with its resistance to the work ethic and its acceptance of drugs.

The late 1960s and 1970s were also a time when minority groups—including women, the elderly, persons with disabilities, or those with alternative sexual lifestyles—began to demand greater social, economic, political, and leisure opportunities. For them, recreation represented a means of gaining independence and achieving their fullest potential.

Beginning in the 1970s and intensifying during the decade that followed, recessions, inflation, rising costs of welfare and crime, and declining tax bases, created an era of austerity that affected many government agencies. With sharp cutbacks in their budgets, many recreation and park agencies imposed severe staffing and maintenance cuts and relied more fully on fees and privatization to maintain their programs. The entrepreneurial marketing strategy that prevailed widely at this time meant that many public departments were forced to give less emphasis to socially oriented programming.

Toward the end of the 1980s, surveys indicated that many Americans were working longer hours and had less leisure. While this appeared to affect professionals, business managers, and other successful individuals more than others, it emphasized the need of all Americans for leisure as a means of balancing work pressures and enriching the quality of life.

Questions for Class Discussion or Essay Examinations

1. During the 1950s and 1960s, Americans became sharply aware of environmental problems, and the federal government took action to curb pollution and protect open spaces. What were some of the key events in this process, and how did it affect the recreation and park movement? Describe the changes that occurred with respect to federal environmental policy in the 1980s and 1990s.

2. Poverty, racial unrest, and the youth counterculture movement were important trends or concerns during the 1960s and 1970s. What actions did government take with respect to these problem areas, and how did they affect public values and behavior with respect to recreation? Some critics suggest that the breakdown in family values and social stability

of the last two decades had its roots in this earlier period. Could you make a case for this argument?

3. Immediately after World War II, social forecasters predicted that free time would increase greatly by the turn of the 21st century, and that society would adopt humanistic leisure interests and lifestyles, largely replacing the work ethic. From the perspective of the mid-and late-1990s, what has actually happened?

Endnotes

2   Herman Kahn and staff of the Hudson Institute, *The Year 2000: A Framework for Speculation on the Next 33 Years* (New York: Macmillan, 1967): 195. See also Peter Henle, "The Quiet Revolution in Leisure Time," *Occupational Outlook Quarterly* (U.S. Department of Labor, May 1965): 5–9.

3   David Gray and Seymour Greben, "Future Perspectives," *Parks and Recreation* (July 1974): 53.

4   Richard Kraus, *Leisure in a Changing America: Multicultural Perspectives* (New York: Macmillan College Publishing, 1994); 61.

5   John Daniel, "Toward Wild Heartlands," *Audubon* (September–October 1994): 38.

6   Leo McAvoy, "An Environmental Ethic for Parks and Recreation," *Parks and Recreation* (September 1990): 89–92.

7   Edward Rothstein, "Playing to Tomorrow's Audience," *New York Times* (24 December 1995): 2–1, 2–26.

8   Michael Harrington, *The Other America* (Baltimore: Penguin Books, 1962).

9   For eyewitness accounts of riots in major cities, see *New York Times* (15 July 1967, 10; 26 July 1967, 18, 29; 7 April 1968, 62.)

10   John Kelly, *Leisure* (Boston: Allyn and Bacon, 1996): 270.

11   Daniel Yankelovich, "The Work Ethic Is Under-Employed," *Psychology Today* (May 1982): 6.

12   Fred Best, "Preferences in Worklife Scheduling and Work-Leisure Tradeoffs," *Monthly Labor Review* (June 1978): 31–37.

13   See Kraus, *op. cit.,* 100–104.

14   Diana Dunn, "Women in Recreation," *Parks and Recreation* (July 1977): 24.

15   William Theobald, *The Female in Public Recreation: A Study of Participation in Public Recreation* (Waterloo, Ontario: University of Waterloo and Ontario Ministry of Culture and Recreation, 1976): 33.

16   Michael Heit and Don Malpass, *Do Women Have Equal Pay?* (Ontario, Canada: Ministry of Culture and Recreation, 1975).

17   "Homosexuals Hold Festival in Theme Park: Disney World Event Draws Some Protests," *New York Times* (5 June 1994): 27.

18   See for example Janet Sable and Jill Gravink, "Partners: Promoting Accessible Recreation," *Parks and Recreation* (May 1995): 34–38.

19   John Crompton and Brian McGregor, "Trends in the Financing and Staffing of Local Government Park and Recreation Services, 1964/65—1990/91," *Journal of Park and Recreation Administration* (Vol. 21 No. 1 1994): 19.

20   *Ibid.,* 22.

21   "Recreation Industry Strong," *AALR/AAHPERD Reporter* (August 1986): 1.

22   J. Zenger, "Leadership: Management's Better Half," *Trends* (Vol. 4 No. 3 1987).

23   Gary Cohen, "On God's Green Earth," *U.S. News & World Report* (24 April 1995): 31.

[24] Richard Kraus, *New Directions in Urban Parks and Recreation: A Trends Analysis Report* (Department of Recreation and Leisure Studies, Temple University, and Heritage Conservation and Recreation Service, 1980): 6.

[25] Crompton and McGregor, *op. cit.*, 25.

[26] Ellen Weissinger and William Murphy, "A Survey of Fiscal Conditions in Small-Town Public Recreation Departments from 1987 to 1991, "*Journal of Park and Recreation Administration* (Vol. 11 No. 3 1993): 61–71.

[27] Jack Foley and Veda Ward, "Recreation, the Riots and a Healthy L.A.," *Parks and Recreation* (March 1993): 68.

[28] *Statistical Abstract of the United States 1995* (Washington, D.C.: U.S. Department of Commerce, 1995): 253.

[29] Thomas Blaine and Golam Muhammad, "An Empirical Assessment of U.S. Consumer Expenditures on Recreation-Related Goods and Services 1946–1988." *Leisure Sciences* (Vol. 13 1991): 111–122.

[30] Jolie Solomon, "Working at Relaxation," *The Wall Street Journal* (21 April 1986): 1–2.

[31] Louis Harris, *Inside America* (New York: Random House, Vintage, 1987).

[32] Juliet Schor, *The Overworked American: The Unexpected Decline of Leisure* (New York: Basic Books, 1991).

[33] John Robinson and Geoffrey Godbey, "Has Fitness Declined?" *American Demographics* (September 1993): 38.

[34] Suzanne Hamlin, "Time Flies, But Where Does It Go?" *New York Times* (6 September 1995): C–1.

[35] Ann Kolson, "A Question of Time," *Philadelphia Inquirer* (26 October 1989): 9–C.

[36] Peter Kilborn, "Overtime Is Money, but G.M. Assembly Workers Say They've Had Enough," *New York Times* (22 November 1994): A–16.

[37] David Scott, "Time Scarcity and Its Implications for Leisure Behavior and Leisure Delivery," *Journal of Park and Recreation Administration* (Vol. 11 No. 3 1993): 51–60.

The Leisure-Service System: Government's Role

I n this era of reinventing government, many park and recreation managers are turning to partnerships to stretch limited tax dollars while attempting to meet the expanding public demand for quality recreation opportunities. Managers entering the murky world of cooperative agreements, corporate sponsorship, and joint ventures usually navigate by instinct and gut feelings. But help is on the way. An emerging body of literature in the recreation field, as well as in other social service disciplines, is beginning to establish some general principles and guidelines for initiating and sustaining effective partnerships.[1]

INTRODUCTION

Having examined the concepts, personal and social values, and history of recreation and leisure, we now turn to an analysis of organized recreation and park services.

This chapter first describes the leisure-service system and its component parts. It then focuses on government's role in providing recreation and park opportunities and facilitating the work of other community organizations. It discusses leisure-service agencies at the federal, state, and local levels, outlining not only their missions and programming strategies but

---

[1] Steve Selin and Nancy Myers, "Current Research in Parks and Recreation," *Parks and Recreation* (November 1994): 12.

also the ways in which they have adapted to changing social and economic conditions. The chapter concludes with an examination of the concept of partnership, or synergy, through which various types of recreation and park organizations share their resources to maximize the public's leisure-service opportunities.

THE LEISURE-SERVICE SYSTEM

Today, one might describe the recreation, park, and leisure-service field by listing its different kinds of organizations and major facilities at random. However, this type of presentation would not lend itself to a clear understanding of the field and its varied sponsorship patterns. Instead, it is more appropriate to group the different agencies under several distinct headings or categories that are characterized by shared purposes and program elements. These categories can be perceived as components within a national leisure-service system. The word "system" is generally used to identify components that are directly or indirectly related to each other over a period of time.[2] One might refer to the health-care or educational system of a nation or, at a less complex level, the operational system of a riding stable or ice-skating rink—in describing all of the functions, agents, and processes within each enterprise.

In its most advanced sense, the term *system* implies that all component parts, or subsystems, are fully interrelated, with each having carefully designed tasks and sequences of action. Arthur Laufer writes:

> Any group of things which are interrelated and combined so as to form an integrated whole can be called a system. It is not the individual parts that are important, but it is the connecting together or the interrelationships of these parts which is important to the making of a system.[3]

When the leisure-service field is examined as a system, it is clear that its parts or subsystems are *not* fully interdependent. That is, the parts do not have clearly assigned functions that are designed and coordinated to promote the most efficient and effective recreation opportunities. Instead, different components often have little contact with each other and community planning among leisure-service agencies is rare. However, the field clearly operates as a system in two respects : (1) different recreation organizations compete with, assist, or influence each other; and (2) instances of purposeful networking or developing partnerships are steadily growing among all kinds of program sponsors.

The System's Structure

In a 1991 text, James Murphy, E. William Niepoth, Lynn Jamieson and John Williams designated three overlapping subsystems that, in their view, constituted the community recreation system. (See Table 10.1.)

While this structure is a helpful way of categorizing elements in the system, it represents an oversimplification. Under public subsystems, for example, the designation is incomplete in that cities and schools are not the only kinds of public, tax-supported agencies providing or assisting leisure programs. Other such agencies include county, special-district, or township recreation and park departments, as well as municipally supported libraries, museums, and housing, welfare, and youth-service offices. Similarly, the designation of tennis or golf clubs as necessarily being commercial centers, or of country clubs as being a private nonprofit

TABLE 10.1   Community Recreation and Leisure-Service System[4]

PUBLIC SUBSYSTEM	PRIVATE NONPROFIT SUBSYSTEM	COMMERCIAL SUBSYSTEM
City recreation and parks departments City recreation commissions School-sponsored recreation	Youth-serving agencies (YMCA, Girls Clubs, Boy Scouts) Church-sponsored recreation Social and fraternal organizations (country clubs, Kiwanis)	Amusement parks Theaters Tennis, golf, sailing centers Hotels Resorts

subsystem may be inaccurate; many public departments have extensive sports facilities, and some country clubs are sponsored by major corporations on behalf of their employees, while others are commercially operated.

It is therefore better to ignore specific types of facilities in describing the leisure-service system and to focus instead on the eight major types of recreation sponsors.

This chapter outlines the role of government in providing recreation facilities and programs on three levels: federal, state, and local. Chapters 11 and 12 describe the seven other categories of agencies within the leisure-service system.

GOVERNMENT'S RESPONSIBILITY IN RECREATION AND PARKS

As recreation sponsors, government agencies have the following characteristics: (1) they were the first type of agency to be formally recognized as responsible for serving the public's recreation needs and, as such, have constituted the core of the recreation movement; (2) the primary means of support for most government recreation and park agencies has been tax funding, although in recent years other revenue sources have begun to be used; (3) government recreation and park agencies operate on three levels of government (federal, state, and local) and have a major responsibility for the management of natural resources; and (4) they are obligated to serve the public at large, rather than special segments of it, and to provide socially useful or constructive programs because of their tax-supported status.

Federal Government's Role

The federal government's responsibility for managing parks and providing or assisting other leisure services evolved gradually. Reynold Carlson and his co-authors have summarized the process as follows:

> In the more than two hundred years of our history as a nation, the attitudes and services of the federal government regarding responsibility for leisure have undergone dramatic changes. In the early years of the republic, the official attitude was one of indifference, even though public lands were used for recreation, particularly fishing and hunting. Later, as public lands were reserved for parks and forests, recreation gained status as one of their important uses. Even though recreation was permitted, however, the federal government held—and still holds—these lands primarily for the protection of natural resources.[5]

Overall, the federal government has developed a multitude of programs related to recreation—more than 90 separate departments, bureaus, commissions, or councils and 300 different operations—without having a systematic plan to determine priorities or allocation responsibilities. For the most part, federal agency functions in recreation evolved as secondary functions of other projects. For example, the initial purpose of the Tennessee Valley Authority lakes and reservoirs was to provide flood control and rural electrification; only over time did the outdoor recreation function become apparent.

There are no constitutional provisions that identify recreation as a function of the federal government. However, judicial interpretations of the constitutional provision that permits the federal government to tax and spend for the general welfare have permitted it to play a role in almost all significant areas of public and private activity. Its primary area of concern has been the management of the vast park and recreation areas that have been made available for public use, and a number of its agencies have played a key role in this field.

The specific functions of the federal government in recreation and parks may be grouped under the following headings:

Direct Management of Outdoor Recreation Resources   The federal government, through such agencies as the National Park Service and the Bureau of Land Management, owns and operates a vast network of parks, forests, lakes, reservoirs, seashores, and other facilities used extensively for outdoor recreation.

Conservation and Resource Reclamation   Closely related to the preceding function is the government's role in reclaiming natural resources that have been destroyed, damaged, or threatened and in promoting programs related to conservation, wildlife, and anti-pollution controls.

Assistance to Open-Space and Park Development Programs   Chiefly with funding authorized under the 1965 Land and Water Fund Conservation Act, the federal government has provided hundreds of millions of dollars in matching grants to states and localities to promote open-space development. Also, through direct aid to municipalities carrying out housing and urban development projects, the federal government has subsidized the development of local parks, playgrounds, and centers.

Direct Programs of Recreation Participation   The federal government operates a number of direct programs of recreation service in Veterans Administration hospitals and other federal institutions, and in the armed forces on bases throughout the world.

Advisory and Financial Assistance   The federal government provides varied forms of assistance to states, localities, and other public or voluntary community agencies. For example, many community programs serving economically and socially disadvantaged populations have been assisted by the (then) Departments of Health, Education and Welfare, Housing and Urban Development, Labor, and others.

Aid to Professional Education   Federal agencies concerned with education and the needs of special populations have provided training grants for professional education in colleges and universities throughout the United States.

Promotion of Recreation as an Economic Function   The federal government has been active in promoting tourism, providing aid to rural residents in developing recreation enterprises, and assisting Indian tribes in establishing recreational and tourist facilities on their reservations. Such agencies as the Bureau of the Census and the Coast Guard also provide needed information for those interested in travel, boating, and similar pastimes.

Research and Technical Assistance   The federal government has supported a broad spectrum of research on topics ranging from outdoor recreation trends and needs and the current status of urban recreation and parks to specific studies of wildlife conservation, forest recreation, or the needs of special populations.

Regulation and Standards   The federal government has developed regulatory policies with respect to pollution control, watershed production, and environmental quality. It has also established standards with respect to rehabilitative service for the ill and disabled and architectural standards to guarantee access to facilities for the disabled.

The first two areas of responsibility are carried out by seven major federal agencies that are either service units or bureaus in cabinet departments or separate authorities. They are the National Park Service, the Forest Service, the Bureau of Land Management, the Bureau of Reclamation, the U.S. Fish and Wildlife Service, the Tennessee Valley Authority, and the U.S. Army Corps of Engineers. Altogether, over 16 billion visitor-hours were recorded at facilities operated by these seven agencies in 1992.[6]

The National Park Service

One of the leading federal agencies with respect to outdoor recreation is the National Park Service, housed in the Department of the Interior. Its original mission, as defined in the National Park Service Organic Act of August 1916 was to

promote and regulate use of the Federal areas known as National parks, monuments, and reservations . . . to conserve the scenery and the natural and historic objects and the wild life therein and to provide for the enjoyment of the same . . . [and to] leave them unimpaired for the enjoyment of future generations.

Most of the property administered by the Park Service in its early years was west of the Mississippi, but in recent decades it has added major seashore parks and other areas both in the country and closer to urban centers. For example, East Coast sites now include the Fire Island National Seashore on Long Island, Acadia National Park in Maine, Assateague National Seashore on the Maryland coast, Cape Hatteras National Seashore in North Carolina, and Gateway East, in the New York–New Jersey harbor area.

The increase in recreational uses, linked with severe problems of maintenance caused by overcrowding, increasing thefts, and vandalism have led to renewed dialogue concerning the Park Service's appropriate mission. At the beginning of the Reagan administration, Secretary of the Interior James Watt sought to reverse the trend of developing national recreation areas close to large urban centers. In his view, these playground parks were inappropriate to the historical mission of the agency, which should have been to give top priority to the "crown jewels"—the internationally known and unique natural parks in the West. In the mid- and late 1980s, however, it was made clear that the National Park Service would not retreat to the narrow mission of preserving only the unique national parks. Instead, it has continued to develop and maintain close-to-home seashores, recreation areas, and historic sites.

The national park system generates a huge volume of tourism, with appeal for domestic travelers and foreign visitors and with major benefits for the nation's economy and the balance of trade payments with other countries. Thousands of businesses in and around the parks are direct recipients of this benefit. Priscilla Baker writes:

Our own park concessions, hotels, motels, gift shops and service stations in gateway communities, tour operators, automobile and recreational vehicle rental companies, and suppliers of recreation equipment are but a few of the types of travel industry organizations that depend on the . . . movement of outdoor enthusiasts for their survival.[7]

In 1986, the role of the National Park Service was expressed in the following terms:

The Service and the parks it manages offer stunning diversity. Remote and rugged landscapes, lively, populous cityscapes, dramatic vistas, soaring monuments, quiet, gentle trails, and humble homes of ordinary people can all be found within the national park system. . . . This system of parks represents the colorful, varied history of the United States and the continent where it was born and grew into worldwide influence. The cultural heritage is reflected in Indian archaeological sites, black history sites, battlegrounds, bleak prisons, homes of the wealthy and influential and the poor and struggling. An incredible array of natural features, from the mighty canyon we call Grand to the delicate wildflowers above the Arctic Circle, are protected for future generations as well as our own.[8]

The concept of providing outdoor recreation resources has become so strongly accepted within the Park Service that it now provides tent, cabin, and hotel accommodations, bridle and hiking trails, marinas and boat docks, museums, and picnic facilities for public use. In many parks, it offers an interpretive nature program through conducted walks, tours, museums and other displays, lectures, and campfire programs. The Park Service does not allow hunting or commercial fishing, cutting of timber, or exploitation of other resources; its emphasis is strongly conservationist.

In recent years, the National Park Service has continued to be troubled by overcrowding, shrinking or frozen budgets, and Congress's appetite for "pork"—the determination of legislators to have the federal government establish new sites in their states. *U.S. News & World Report* commented in 1995:

While tight budgets are forcing the park service to defer maintenance, cut staff and programs, and allow environmental problems to fester at many units, Congress has pushed through some 83 new national parks [or other recreational or historic units] in the past 20 years. In the decade ending in 1993, lawmakers ordered almost $1.4 billion worth of projects the park service didn't want but could not refuse. Once they were established, Congress starved them of operating and maintenance funds.[9]

Today, the National Park Service manages 368 areas, including national parks, monuments, historic areas, recreation areas, seashores, and other miscellaneous sites. In 1994, its budget was over $1.4 billion, and it recovered almost $100 million from its operations, with 267 million visitors a year.[10]

The Forest Service

A second federal agency that administers extensive wilderness preserves for public recreation use is the Forest Service within the Department of Agriculture. In contrast to the National Park Service, the Forest Service is responsible not for scenic monuments and historical or geological treasures, but for huge areas of forests and grasslands. Rather than following the National Park Service's single-use concept of preservation and public enjoyment of natural areas, the Forest Service accepts the multiple-use concept of federally owned land under its control; mining, grazing, lumbering, and hunting are all permitted in the national forests.

A related function of the Forest Service has been human resource development. Its annual report in the early 1980s stated:

> Ever since the Civilian Conservation Corps of the 1930's, National Forests have provided work and training for the nation's underemployed. Today, the Forest Service participates in many Federal human resource and community programs aimed at putting people to work, training disadvantaged youth, and improving living conditions in rural areas.[11]

The recreation function of the Forest Service has continued to grow steadily. In 1994, it encompassed a total forest system of 191.6 million acres, which included 35 million acres of wilderness as well as major elements of the National Scenic Byways and National Wild and Scenic Rivers Systems, wildlife and fish habitats, and numerous other special-use areas. In the same year, the Forest Service recorded 330.3 million visitor-days and served over 120,000 persons in its human resource programs, as well as permitting extensive commercial uses with respect to timber harvesting, grazing, and mining operations.[12] Its major recreational uses in 1994 were for mechanized travel and viewing scenery; camping, picnicking, and swimming; hiking, horseback riding, and water travel; winter sports; and hunting and fishing.

At the same time, the Forest Service has been forced to carefully review its basic mission, as its extensive logging programs have come under attack by environmentalists. Making use of strategic planning tools such as market surveys, focus groups, and similar methods, it is redefining its goals to provide greater protection for wildlife systems and to meet people-related needs.[13] As part of this process, it is assuming a more active role in promoting rural tourism in order to assist those regions that have experienced declines in natural resource-related employment, such as mining or timber industry jobs.[14]

The Bureau of Land Management

The Bureau of Land Management was formally established in 1946 with the merger of the U.S. Grazing Service and the General Land Office within the Department of the Interior. The BLM administers over 270 million acres, chiefly in the western states and Alaska. Its properties are used for a variety of resource-based outdoor recreation activities, as well as for mining, grazing, and lumbering activities that yield over $800 million a year in revenue—with much of it being returned to state and local governments.[15]

The areas under Bureau management range from Alpine-like mountain lakes to canyons in southeast Utah, the Lost Coast of Northern California, and the Badlands of Montana. They are used extensively for typical outdoor recreation pursuits, such as camping, hiking, hunting, and fishing. The Bureau of Land Management also provides sites for high-risk recreation, such as hang-gliding, mountain climbing, and cycle racing over rough terrain. It sponsors a number of races, including dog-sled races, as well as model plane meets and other competitions. Approximately 70 million visitors a year use Bureau properties, and the use rate has been steadily increasing.

The Bureau of Reclamation

Housed in the Department of the Interior, the Bureau of Reclamation is responsible for water resource development, primarily in the western states. Although its original function was to promote irrigation and electric power, it has accepted recreation as a function since 1936.

The policy of the Bureau of Reclamation is to transfer reservoir areas wherever possible to other federal agencies; often these become classified as National Recreation Areas and are assigned to the National Park Service for operation. The emphasis is on active recreational use such as boating, camping, hiking, hunting, and fishing rather than sightseeing.

In 1980, annual recreation visitor-days totaled 66.5 million, compared to 19.5 million in 1958. However, by the late 1980s, the reported annual total was significantly lower, due in part to the transfer of a number of its recreation areas to other federal and nonfederal agencies, such as the National Park Service, for administrative purposes. Use of Bureau properties for outdoor recreation remained level through the early 1990s.

As in the case of the Forest Service, the Bureau of Reclamation has provided employment opportunities for thousands of young men and women through the Youth Conservation Corps (YCC) and Young Adult Conservation Corps (YACC), which have cooperated in rehabilitating or building campgrounds and boating facilities at recreation areas throughout the West. State and local government agencies may also develop or administer recreation sites on Bureau of Reclamation lands or water areas.

The U.S. Fish and Wildlife Service

The U.S. Fish and Wildlife Service originally consisted of two federal bureaus, one dealing with commercial fisheries (which was transferred to the Department of Commerce) and the other dealing with sports fisheries and wildlife (which remained in the Department of the Interior). Its functions include restoring the nation's fisheries, enforcing laws, managing wildlife populations, conducting research, and operating the National Wildlife Refuge System. This system includes 504 units comprising 92 million acres, of which 77 million are in Alaska. In addition to meeting the ongoing needs of hunters and fishermen, the Fish and Wildlife Service has been particularly active in helping to ensure the survival of endangered species, conserving migratory birds, administering federal aid programs that assist state wildlife programs, and contributing biological information with respect to energy and other development projects that may affect wildlife habitats.

Its refuges and fisheries are open to visitors; photography, picnicking, sightseeing, and other nonintrusive recreational uses are encouraged. The Service works closely with state game commissions and hunting and fishing federations, and it initiates new regulations when needed—such as a ban on lead shot, which has been shown to be toxic to waterfowl.[16]

Tennessee Valley Authority

Although the purpose of the Tennessee Valley Authority when created by Congress in 1933 was to develop the Tennessee River for flood control, navigation, and electric power, its reservoirs have become valuable as recreation resources in Kentucky, North Carolina, Tennessee, and other southern and border states. The TVA itself does not operate recreation facilities, but makes land available to other public agencies or private groups for development.

Visitor-days to TVA lakes within the Tennessee Valley region's more than 1,000 square miles of water surface and 11,000 miles of shoreline were reported to be approximately 80 million a year until 1987, when the TVA discontinued reporting visitation to nonfee-charging areas. Today the visitor-day total is reported to be approximately 14 million a year, but this includes those involved with the more than 30 universities and colleges that participate in resource management, environmental education, and campground operation programs through a consortium program at the Land Between the Lakes, an outstanding natural facility of more than 170,000 acres located in west Kentucky and Tennessee. TVA has also made over 192,000 acres of land and water available to state agencies and the U.S. Fish and Wildlife Service, and has numerous cooperative project agreements with other environmental agencies.[17]

The U.S. Army Corps of Engineers

The Corps of Engineers of the U.S. Department of the Army is responsible for the improvement and maintenance of rivers and other waterways to facilitate navigation and flood control. It constructs reservoirs, protects and improves beaches and harbors, and administers over 11 million acres of federally owned land and water impoundments. This includes 460 reservoirs and lakes; the majority of these are managed by the Corps, and the remainder are managed by state and local agencies under lease. Over two-thirds of the Corps' man-made lakes and reservoirs are located within 50 miles of Standard Metropolitan Statistical Areas (roughly defined as urban, or containing at least one city of 50,000 or more residents).

Army Corps of Engineers recreation sites are heavily used by the public for boating, camping, hunting, and fishing. Under the Water Project Recreation Act of 1965, recreation and fish and wildlife development are regarded as equal in priority to other uses for which federal water resource projects may be initiated. Visitor-days at Army Corps of Engineer sites increased dramatically from 63 million in 1955 to 350 million in the mid-1970s to more than 500 million a year in the late 1980s.[18] The Corps often leases shoreline sites along its reservoirs to commercial concessionaires or makes them available to private citizens and organizations for building camps and summer homes.

Other Federal Outdoor Recreation Functions

In addition to the agencies just described, other federal offices and bureaus play an important role in outdoor recreation, particularly through funding and technical assistance efforts. Several such agencies are part of the Department of Agriculture.

The Agricultural Stabilization and Conservation Service has assisted farmers in developing ponds and reservoirs on private land and stocking them with fish. The Farmers Home Administration gives credit and management advice to rural organizations and farmers in developing recreation facilities. The Soil Conservation Service has aided landowners in establishing income-producing recreation areas. Extension Service aids community recreation planning in rural areas and advises states on outdoor recreation development, working in many states through extension agents at land-grant agricultural colleges.

The Bureau of Indian Affairs exists primarily to provide service to American Indian tribes in such areas as health, education, economic development, and land management. However, it also operates (under civilian control in the Department of the Interior) Indian-owned properties of about 56 million acres with more than 5,500 lakes, which are used heavily for recreational purposes, including camping, museum visits, hunting, and fishing (see page 149). It should be noted that the Bureau of Indian Affairs has recently come under searching scrutiny and severe Congressional criticism for its bureaucratic management of housing, education, and other social services for the one million Indians who live on reservations today, chiefly in the Southwest.[19]

In the Department of Commerce, the Bureau of the Census furnishes the population statistics and projections needed for effective recreation planning, including trends in recreation demand and participation. The Economic Development Administration researches the economic effects of recreation development on businesses in local communities and provides grants and loans for public works. The Coast and Geodetic Survey Nautical Charting program provides charts and related information about tides, currents, and weather for safe navigation by boating enthusiasts.

Given the number and variety of federal agencies with outdoor recreation functions—many of which are also linked to state and local government programs—there has obviously been a long-standing need for coordination of federal outdoor recreation activities. Two agencies that played an important role in this effort during the 1960s and 1970s were the Bureau of Outdoor Recreation and the Heritage Conservation and Recreation Service (HCRS).

Bureau of Outdoor Recreation

Bureau of Outdoor Recreation   This agency was established in the Department of the Interior in 1962 to help unify and promote federal programs concerned with open space, natural resources, and outdoor recreation. It was made responsible for administering the Land and Water Conservation Fund, which gathered revenue from entrance admissions or user fees at federal recreation areas, receipts from the sale of federal properties and offshore oil-drilling leases, and taxes from the sale of motorboat fuel. Under the Land and Water Conservation Fund (LWCF) program, hundreds of millions of dollars were awarded each year to states and communities to acquire outdoor recreation sites under matching grants programs.

Another function of the Bureau was to coordinate the activities of the National Wild and Scenic Rivers System and the National Trails System. In addition, it conducted studies of national outdoor recreation trends and needs, carried out inventories, and assisted in the coordination of federal outdoor recreation programs by reviewing budgets and evaluating and monitoring the work of 16 different agencies.

Heritage Conservation and Recreation Service

Heritage Conservation and Recreation Service   During the late 1970s, the Bureau of Outdoor Recreation assumed fuller responsibility for protecting historic and archaeological sites and promoting cultural heritage activities. It also became responsible for administering the Urban Park and Recreation Recovery (UPARR) program, a funding program that assisted state and local recreation and park agencies in rehabilitating outdoor areas and historic sites. With these new responsibilities came a change in the agency's name to the Heritage Conservation and Recreation Service in 1978. It continued to administer the LWCF grants program and to provide technical assistance in recreation and park planning to states and communities.

In 1981, the Reagan administration discontinued HCRS, assigning its functions to other agencies within the Department of the Interior, chiefly to the National Park Service. In addition, the UPARR and LWCF funding programs were both sharply cut as federal policy with respect to open-space and parks preservation shifted in the direction of a multi-use, business-oriented approach. Throughout the 1980s, a struggle continued on the part of Congress and a number of environmental organizations to restore the vigorous efforts to reclaim and protect the environment—with acid rain and pollution of the ocean two of the most important concerns at the end of the decade.

Current Proposal for Federal Action

In the mid-1990s, following a decade and a half of neglect and efforts to eliminate the Land and Water Conservation Fund and the Urban Park and Recreation Recovery program, a citizen-based advisory board set up at the request of the National Park Service Director, Roger Kennedy, issued a report that called for the two programs to be combined. This combined program was to be funded with one billion dollars annually, with 30 percent distributed equally to federal, state, and urban park systems and 10 percent to go to congressionally designated national priorities.

The report, entitled *An American Network of Parks and Open Space: Creating a Conservation and Recreation Legacy*, concluded:

> the failure to reinvest in parks, preserves, and recreation programs adequately is to jeopardize America's heritage of scenic, natural, cultural and recreation places. It hampers economic growth and diminishes opportunities for our children and future generations to enjoy decent and productive lives . . . .[20]

OTHER FEDERAL FUNCTIONS

In addition to its responsibilities in outdoor recreation and parks, the federal government sponsors a number of functions relating to recreation programs in the armed forces and in institutional settings. It provides an extensive network of recreation facilities and programs designed to serve servicemen and women and their families in the major branches of the armed forces. Within each service, such as the Air Force, the programs are administratively structured somewhat differently, have a different emphasis, and seek to meet different goals. Armed forces recreation programs are described in full detail in Chapter 12. In addition, therapeutic recreation programs are provided in Veterans Administration hospitals and in treatment and research centers operated by the National Institutes for Health.

Further, the federal government promotes and assists state and local efforts in such areas as the development of commerce, programming for disadvantaged and disabled persons, physical fitness, and the arts.

Programs in Health and Human Services, Education, and Housing

A number of federal agencies related to health and human services, education, and housing and urban development have provided funding, technical assistance, and other forms of aid to recreation programs designed to meet various social needs in American communities. Within the federal Department of Health and Human Services, such units as the Administration on Aging, the Children's Bureau, and the Public Health Service have been active in this area. For example, the Administration on Aging, authorized by the Older Americans Act of 1965, promotes comprehensive programs for elderly persons and supports training programs and demonstration projects intended to prepare professional personnel to work with older people. It also gathers information on new or expanded programs and services for the aging and supports research projects in this field.

The Children's Bureau, created in 1912, is concerned with the welfare of children and youth—especially those in migrant families and those with physical or mental disabilities or in institutional care. It publishes guides and handbooks related to recreation, and has worked through states and a variety of national organizations to improve services for young people.

Through the Bureau of State Services, the Public Health Service provides technical assistance for improvement of the environmental, sanitation, and safety aspects of recreation facilities and programs. The Public Health Service has also awarded grants to the National Recreation and Park Association for the training of leaders to work with persons with disabilities in community settings. The National Institute of Mental Health, a branch of the Public Health Service, assists research into the cause, prevention, and treatment of mental illness, including recreation-related projects. The Public Health Service also sponsors a number of direct recreation programs at institutions such as St. Elizabeth's Hospital in Washington, D.C.

The Rehabilitation Services Administration administers the federal law authorizing vocational rehabilitation programs designed to help persons with physical or mental disabilities gain employment and lead fuller lives, and it has been responsible for special projects in the areas of research, demonstration, and training. During the 1960s, several college departments training therapeutic recreation specialists received curriculum development and scholarship grants from the Vocational Services Administration, which is now part of the Rehabilitation Services Administration.

In February 1975, the *Federal Register* published guidelines and regulations in which the U.S. Office of Education stressed the need to recognize physical education and recreation as essential needs for children with disabilities. And, in legislation such as the Education for All Handicapped Children Act of 1975, the federal government upheld its recognition of recreation as a significant area of service for special populations.

Other federal legislation, such as Section 504 of the Rehabilitation Act of 1975 (often called the "nondiscrimination clause) and the Americans with Disabilities Act of 1990, has been instrumental in pressuring school systems, units of local government, and other agencies to provide equal opportunity for people with disabilities in a wide range of community opportunity fields.

The work of educational agencies in promoting community-oriented programs, adult education programs, and informal social education programs has also been supported by the federal government. Several pieces of legislation in this area have had implications for the support of recreation as a school-connected service. For example, the Elementary and Secondary Education Act of 1965 provided grants for supplemental educational centers and services, in-service training programs, and institutions providing camping, cultural, physical education, recreation, and other special programs to serve those with disabilities. The Supplemental Education Centers and Services provisions of this act authorized outdoor education and recreation projects such as nature centers, teacher training, museums, and field trips. The Community Schools Act of 1975 authorized several million dollars a year to support varied community education projects, including recreation.

Functions Related to Housing and Urban Development

The federal government has also had a broad record of promoting slum clearance and assisting housing programs in America's cities, with the provision of recreation areas and facilities in housing projects being one of the components.

The Federal Department of Housing and Urban Development was established in 1965, with responsibility for a range of federally assisted programs, including urban renewal and planning, public housing, mass transit, and open space. With funding of $7.5 billion for a four-year period, HUD was empowered to provide up to 50 percent of the cost of land acquisition, development, and beautification. Section 705 of the act, known as "the small parks program," authorized grants for extensive planning and development in depressed urban areas. Federal programs under the Model Cities Program, Metropolitan Development Act, and Neighborhood Facilities Program provided matching funds to help local governments develop parks, playgrounds, and other facilities, particularly in disadvantaged urban areas. During the mid-1970s, a number of such programs merged into the Community Development Block Grants program.

Although most of the programs aiding the disadvantaged that were initiated during the 1960s were cut back sharply or terminated during the decade and a half that followed, a number of federal departments, including Labor, Agriculture and Transportation, continued to provide assistance to community programs serving inner-city and at-risk youth.

Support of the Arts

Another important area of federal involvement in recreation and leisure in the United States has reflected the growing public interest in the arts and a wide range of cultural activities. Created as an independent federal agency in 1965, the National Foundation on the Arts and the Humanities supports and encourages programs in the arts (including dance, music, drama, folk art, creative writing, and the visual media) and humanities (including literature, history, philosophy, and the study of language).

In the 1980s, the National Endowment for the Arts and its advisory Federal Council provided grants of over $180 million a year to help individuals and nonprofit, tax-exempt organizations in the arts, dance, literature, music, and theater. Aid has been given not only to established arts organizations, but also to unconventional and innovative arts programs in communities throughout the United States. A special "expansion arts" category of funding has assisted coordinated arts programs and other unique community efforts, including programs for inner-city areas, prisons, and similar special settings.

In recent years, as Chapter 9 has shown, conservative religious leaders and legislators have joined together in a determined effort to end federal funding of the arts and humanities. Although their pressure has resulted in a more cautious approach to funding controversial projects and in a severe cutback in the amount of money granted, the National Endowment for the Arts has continued to function through the mid-1990s. Strikingly, an impressive majority of the public, when polled, indicated their support for federal assistance to the arts.[21]

Physical Fitness and Sports Promotion

Another recreation-related effort of the federal government has been the President's Council on Physical Fitness and Sports. Created in 1956 to help upgrade the fitness of the nation's youth, and broadened in 1968 to include the promotion of sports participation, the Council has operated to encourage public awareness of fitness needs and to stimulate school- and community-based sports and fitness programs. It has conducted nationwide promotional campaigns through the media, and has sponsored many regional physical fitness clinics.

This effort has continued through the 1990s, with a President's Challenge Physical Fitness Program providing for state and federal goals and guidelines, school "championships," and participant fitness awards. Along with community school systems, many local recreation and park agencies and professional groups have assisted in such fitness programs.

OVERVIEW OF FEDERAL RECREATION PROGRAMS

As this chapter has demonstrated, the federal government has been involved in a wide variety of recreation and park programs and services—related to parks and the management of outdoor recreation resources, but also concerned with other aspects of community life.

The criticisms of the federal role have been: (a) it has tended to focus primarily on rural areas or western regions far from the great urban centers and the mass of population in the nation; (b) it has given relatively generous support to the acquisition of land and the development of facilities, but little support to program development or other operational needs; and (c) it has tended to provide too many programs sponsored by different agencies, without any attempt to define a coherent policy or develop meaningful coordination.

Many who are concerned with the development of recreation and leisure in the United States suggest the creation of a federal agency, preferably on the cabinet level, with jurisdiction over *all* recreation programs and governmental operations (including those related to health, education, and welfare, housing and urban development, and other social concerns). Such a department would provide needed national leadership and direction, and would lead to federal recognition of the growing importance of leisure as a national concern and to stronger support for professional development in this field.

RECREATION-RELATED FUNCTIONS OF STATE GOVERNMENTS

The role of state governments in recreation and parks has generally rested upon the Tenth Amendment to the Constitution, which states, "The powers not delegated to the United States by the Constitution, nor prohibited by it to the States, are reserved to the States respectively, or to the people." This amendment, commonly referred to as the "states' rights amendment," is regarded as the source of state powers in such areas as public education, welfare, and health services.

Sources of Power

The power to establish public recreation and park programs is generally given to municipal governments by constitutional, statutory, or charter provisions granted by the state legislature. Although local governing bodies have certain assumed powers in this areas under the principle of "police powers," specific legal authority is needed for them to acquire properties, employ personnel, or impose taxes to support recreation.

In almost all states today, county, municipal, and sometimes school authorities are authorized to operate facilities and provide programs. Enabling legislation may range from rather simple authorizations to fully detailed codes that specify such elements as the method of acquiring and developing properties, financing recreation and park programs, and establishing public boards, commissions, and special districts.

Outdoor Recreation Resources and Programs

Each state government today operates a network of parks and other outdoor recreation resources. The programs may vary in nature, but generally include the following types of facilities and areas:

wilderness areas, which may be left nearly untouched in order to retain their primitive character;

state reserves or *natural preserves,* which are usually set aside for their specific cultural, natural, or scientific value and sometimes because they contain unique natural specimens or topographical features;

historical monuments or *cultural preserves,* which may include locations of important historical significance or of special archaeological or other cultural interest;

recreation areas, which are intended for active recreational use and which may include camping areas attached to larger preserves, smaller wayside campgrounds and wayside rests, and beaches, lakes, ski areas, vehicular recreation areas, underwater recreation areas, forests, and other locations for backpacking and various leisure uses.

During the 1960s and early 1970s, most state governments expanded their recreation and park holdings, primarily with funding assistance from the Land and Water Conservation Fund—but also through major bond issues totalling hundreds of millions of dollars in many cases. Open space and natural beauty were widely supported catchwords and the public enthusiastically supported programs of land acquisition and water cleanup.

In the late 1970s, however, economic conditions forced many states to cut back on their recreation and park expenditures. Budgets were frozen or reduced, and extreme shortages of personnel and equipment were responsible for the deterioration of many state park sites. At the same time, the energy shortage and rising gas prices compelled many families to change their vacation plans. Instead of traveling long distances to federal parks, they tended to camp and enjoy outdoor recreation much closer to home—and, as a consequence, many state campgrounds became unbearably crowded. Today, state parks have weathered this storm and are functioning effectively, despite lean workforces and a continuing period of austerity. Different states have come up with a variety of techniques to pay for their parks, including new bond issues, lotteries, and revenue from cigarette taxes, as well as partnership with private business.

Even with the economic constraints of the last two decades, a number of state governments have continued to upgrade their park and recreation operations. For example, in Pennsylvania in 1993 the state legislature approved a funding plan based on a $50 million bond issue and revenues to be derived from the state's real estate transfer tax. Supported by over 60 environmental, cultural and recreational organizations, the plan was designed to provide a permanent source of funding for maintenance needs and capital improvements at states and local parks, libraries, public zoos, historic sites, and museums.

In addition, a number of states have developed new facilities in or close to crowded urban centers—as opposed to past policies of having state parks only in remote, heavily wooded or mountainous areas. An outstanding example of a new state park constructed in a city is White River State Park in Indianapolis, which combines state, municipal, private, and commercial funding in the construction and operation of an outstanding zoo, family theme park, museums, sports facilities, and other outdoor recreation attractions. Some states have even initiated busing programs to transport low-income urban residents to state parks and recreation areas.

In general, while the federal bureaucracy has been shrinking steadily over the past three decades, the functions of state and local government have remained the same or even increased. With federal functions having been reduced, state and local governments now administer some programs and services that are funded but no longer directly managed by Washington agencies—with the strong trend apparently being to downsize the federal role even more in the years ahead.[22]

Assistance to Local Governments   State park and recreation agencies assist local authorities in a variety of ways: they provide consultants, do research studies, call conferences, and promote the work of recreation agencies on the local level. Particularly in terms of statewide planning and the coordination of grant applications for federal funding assistance, many state agencies work closely with local government units. For example, they aid municipalities by coordinating and reviewing their applications for grants under the Land and Water Conservation Fund programs and by providing matching funds.

Direct Recreation Involvement in Other Settings

Another important function of state governments is to provide direct recreation services within the institutions or agencies it sponsors, such as mental hospitals or mental health centers, special schools for mentally retarded persons, and penal or correctional facilities. Many of the largest networks of facilities that employ therapeutic recreation specialists are tax-supported state mental health systems or similar organizations.

Promotion of Professional Advancement   While states promote effective leadership and administrative practices in recreation and parks by developing personnel standards and providing conferences and research support, their major contribution lies in the professional preparation of recreation practitioners in state colleges and universities. Of the colleges and universities in the United States with professional recreation and park curricula, a substantial majority are part of state university systems.

Many state agencies also assist professional development by conducting annual surveys of municipal and county recreation and parks departments and publishing their findings on facilities, fiscal practices, and personnel. In some cases, several states have joined together to provide such services, along with technical assistance. W. Tom Martin and Carl Hust write:

> The Southern Consortium now conducts joint cooperative projects, regularly exchanges publications, studies, reports, and job vacancy referrals; involves . . . the National Park Service, the U.S. Forest Service, educational institutions, and therapeutic services on a regular basis; and has been instrumental in initiating technical/advisory services, both within the region and beyond it.[23]

Development and Enforcement of Standards   States also have the function of screening personnel by establishing standards and hiring procedures, or by requiring Civil Service examinations, certification, or personnel registration programs in recreation and parks.

Many states also have developed standards relating to health and safety practices in camping and similar settings. State departments enforce safety codes, promote facilities standards, ensure that recreation resources can accommodate persons with disabilities, regulate or prohibit certain types of commercial amusements, and in some cases carry out regular inspections of camps, swimming pools, resorts, or proprietary institutions that provide leisure services, such as nursing homes or long-term care facilities. All states have camp licensing requirements, and many have camp safety laws that specify requirements for camps within their jurisdictions.

> **M**any states have authorized various forms of gambling as a source of revenue. Legalized gambling in New Jersey, for example, generated more than $4 billion in state funds in the years prior to 1988. By 1995, 37 states had initiated state lotteries, with the intention of providing funds for education, the aging, or other state programs. At the same time, such programs have contributed to the growing number of gambling addicts in the United States, which is estimated to have risen to 12 million nationwide. And, contrary to public perception, with the exception of several of the larger states, income from lotteries contributes a relatively small amount of income to state budgets. Many economists regard them as a regressive form of tax—despite their voluntary nature—which is levied on the poor, who spend the largest portion of their incomes on the lottery.

Promotion of Recreation as Economic Asset

Another important function of state governments is to promote all aspects of leisure involvement that support economic development. At a 1983 state conference of the Pennsylvania Recreation and Park Society, a state senator commented that one of his colleagues had traditionally been concerned only with promoting "real jobs"—in the steel industry or in housing, for example. This legislator was surprised to learn from a recent publication of the Pennsylvania Department of Environmental Resources that state residents had spent approximately $11.8 billion (12.6 percent of their total personal consumption dollars) on leisure pursuits in the previous year, and that recreation represented the state's second largest industry.

In a growing number of cases, large mills, factories, and other heavy industrial plants that have gone out of operation are being transformed into tourist attractions that provide an understanding of the region's past and help to rebuild local economies. John Brant points out that "heritage" projects are now taking shape in 80 areas around the United States:

> A project in rural Iowa tells of the rise and fall of the family farm; a project in West Virginia traces the waxing and waning of the coal industry, and another in Butte, Montana, does the same for the city's mammoth open-pit copper mine . . . .[24]

Since 1988, the Southwestern Pennsylvania Heritage Preservation Commission, operating with Department of the Interior grants, has created a "Path of Progress" (including two popular Johnstown flood museums) that attracted 580,000 visitors in 1994—contributing a direct economic impact of $40 million to the region. During the past two decades, other states have initiated similar efforts. In the late 1980s, Andrew Malcolm wrote that all 50 states were spending several hundred million dollars a year to promote tourism. For example:

> Nevada urges gamblers to stay an extra day to see the desert; New Jersey, too, has persuaded its casino operators to push the state's other entertainment possibilities. Connecticut has divided itself into 19 tourism districts, each with its own appeal. Wisconsin offers free coffee and racks of tourist literature at booths along the interstates. New England has toll-free telephone numbers where prospective leaf gawkers may learn of the advance of autumn colors. States advertise in newspapers and magazines, on radio and television; New York, which more or less started the whole thing with its "I Love New York" TV ad campaign a decade ago, now spends $15 million a year to promote itself.[25]

Traditions

Many cities emphasize their historic traditions or local color to attract tourists. In Santa Fe, New Mexico, pueblo Indians dance and display their crafts in the city's plaza (top left and below). Bronco riders perform in the famous Calgary Stampede rodeo events (top right).

Role of State Fairs   A unique aspect of state-sponsored or assisted recreation is the state fair. This term covers a wide variety of fairs and expositions held each year throughout the United States and Canada and includes carnivals and midways, displays and competitions of livestock and produce, farm equipment shows, and a host of special presentations by corporations of every type. The majority of such fairs are run by nonprofit organizations that are publicly owned and operated—including a number of bona fide state agencies. Attended by about 160 million persons each year, they promote civic and state boosterism, offer a showcase for agricultural and other regional industries or attractions, and provide varied forms of entertainment.

While at one point state fairs were heavily subsidized by government, many states mandated several years ago that their fairs become self-sufficient. This has been accomplished through increasing corporate sponsorship and providing more revenue-yielding attractions.[26]

Other State Functions

Many state governments have offices or sponsor arts councils that distribute funds to nonprofit organizations and performing groups or institutions in various areas of cultural and creative activity.

In addition to operating numerous facilities such as hospitals, special schools for the retarded, or correctional centers where recreation is part of overall rehabilitation service, many states also have youth bureaus or aging offices that assist local governments in providing services for these special populations.

An important function of state government is to assist and work with local governments in environmental efforts. Just as no single municipality can clean up a polluted stream that flows through a state, so in the broad field of urban planning, recreation resource development, and conservation problems *must* be approached on a statewide or even a regional basis. In such planning—as in many other aspects of federal relationships with local communities—the state acts as a catalyst for action and as a vital link between the national and local governments.

Need for Coordination of Federal and State Efforts

One of the critical issues affecting state recreation involvement has to do with the relationship of state governments with various federal programs. For example, in 1981, the House Intergovernmental Relations Subcommittee of the U.S. Congress held a series of meetings to examine the federalist system. During the hearings, representatives from the National Conference of State Legislatures and the National Governors' Association presented a joint statement on federalism to the subcommittee. Expressing the conviction that many federal programs are "unmanageable, ineffective, costly, confusing, and unaccountable to the public," both groups called on Congress and the President to

> sort out roles and responsibilities among the three levels of government. The division of labor should recognize the primary federal responsibility for national defense, income security, and a sound economy, and the primacy of state and local governments in such areas as education, law enforcement and transportation. . . . the sorting out process must clarify the responsibilities of each level of government and the tax sources required to meet those responsibilities.[27]

THE ROLE OF COUNTY AND LOCAL GOVERNMENTS

While federal and state governments provide major forms of recreation service in the United States, the responsibility for meeting year-round leisure needs belongs to agencies of local government. These range from counties, special park districts, and townships (which embrace larger geographical areas) to cities, villages, and other political subdivisions.

For recreation and parks in the United States, all powers that are not vested in the federal government belong to the states. In turn, local governments must get their authority through enabling laws passed by state legislatures or through other special charter or home-rule arrangements.

Of all branches of government, the local government is closest to the people and therefore most able to meet the widest range of recreation needs.

County and Special Park District Programs

As an intermediate stage between state and incorporated local government agencies, county or special district park and recreation units provide large parks and other outdoor recreation resources as a primary function. They may also sponsor services for special populations—that is, programs for the aging or disabled—as well as services for all residents of the county, such as programs in the fine and performing arts.

During the early decades of the century, county governments had relatively limited functions. However, since World War II, the rapid growth of suburban populations around large cities has given many county governments new influence and power. Counties have become a base for coordinating and funneling numerous federal grants-in-aid programs. As a result, county park and recreation departments expanded rapidly, particularly in the 1960s.

Since that period, county recreation and park systems have continued to expand, but at a slower rate. Charles Nelson and Lawrence Leroy summarized the findings of a study of 250 county park agencies carried out by Michigan State University in 1980 which noted that two groups of counties stand out as providing the widest range of facilities—those with populations greater than 500,000 and those with between 50,000 and 100,000 residents.

Nelson and Leroy point out that there is typically great diversity among county government recreation and park systems:

> While some counties may have thousands of acres of recreational lands, a large staff, and a handsome operating budget, neighboring counties may not have one county park. Another county may be heavily involved in resource-based recreation while another is heavily committed to athletic field provision.[28]

Dade County, Florida   The Metropolitan Dade County Park and Recreation Department operates an outstanding network of sixteen parks, beaches, gardens, auditoriums, and camping areas, as well as five golf courses and three large tennis centers. It offers four miles of sandy ocean beaches, atoll pools in Biscayne Bay, and five marinas offering wet and dry docks. In all, Dade County has 8,000 acres of carefully planned and developed park and recreation facilities serving more than 18 million visitors and residents each year. Vizcaya, a 70-room Italian villa built by a prominent industrialist and now owned by the county, serves as a magnificent museum and garden attraction. The Crandon Park Zoo, Dade County Auditorium, and other facilities are important elements in this recreation-oriented metropolitan area, which depends heavily on its tourists. In addition, the Dade County department promotes numerous other privately owned or nonprofit attractions and leisure facilities—such as an impressive array of art museums, galleries, and collections in the metropolitan area that are sponsored by universities, individuals, and civic groups.

King County, Washington   The King County Parks Division (a unit of the County Department of Planning and Community Development) is an example of how county recreation and park departments have expanded to meet growing urban and suburban needs during the past three decades. This impressive system, which includes the city of Seattle, was established in 1949, at which time it included 20 parks on 236 acres.

Thanks to the passage of a large park-bond issue in 1968, King County embarked on an extensive land acquisition and park development program that resulted in the expenditure of $48 million by 1976. Today, it operates 5,070 acres of land, including neighborhood, community, urban, saltwater, freshwater, and regional parks and nature areas ranging in size from one-quarter acre to nearly 500 acres. King County now has sixteen pools, twelve beaches, six large community centers, two stadiums, and extensive sport, equestrian, biking, picnic, and boating facilities.

Montgomery County, Maryland   The Montgomery County Department of Recreation, which serves an area close to Washington, D.C., has a remarkable range of facilities and programs. In addition to managing 13 regional and special parks that include major athletic complexes and conservation areas, it operates campgrounds, conference centers, public display gardens, ice skating rinks, boat rental facilities, golf courses, riding stables, tennis facilities, and miniature trains, carousels, and children's farms.

The Department of Recreation also schedules varied events—leagues, classes, tournaments, and special-interest activities for all ages—in sports, the arts, social activities, fitness and aerobics, aquatics, and hobbies in 16 community schools, including outstanding programs for individuals with disabilities.

Regional and Special Park Districts

Several states, including California, Illinois, Oregon, and North Dakota, have enabling legislation that permits the establishment of special park and recreation districts. Illinois has 345 such districts, including forest preserve and conservation districts. North Dakota has 225 park districts and California 118, while Oregon has 17 park and recreation districts.

Many special recreation and park districts are in heavily populated areas; in some cases, they may encompass a number of independent, separate counties and municipalities in a single structure. Frequently, special park districts and counties are able to carry out vigorous programs of land acquisition in a combined effort or to impose other means of protecting open space. Many counties have enacted laws requiring home developers to set aside community recreation areas. One such example is Anne Arundel County, Maryland, which since 1957 has required all developers to allocate five percent of the land to be developed as park areas. Some county governments are establishing permanently protected green belts to halt the tide of construction. Strengthened zoning policies and more flexible building codes that permit cluster zoning of homes with larger and more concentrated open spaces are also helpful.

East Bay Regional Park District   The East Bay Regional Park District offers an outstanding system of parks, public trails, and lakes in Alameda and Contra Costa Counties in California. Founded in 1934 by a group of public-spirited citizens, this park district today operates 50 parks and 20 regional trails, which offer fishing, swimming, hiking, picnicking, nature programs, and other active and nature-oriented pursuits.

Within its network of parks, the East Bay District offers numerous free opportunities for individuals and groups, along with an inexpensive permit system for group reservations or other special uses. Its proximity to San Francisco and other cities within the Bay area makes it an invaluable and readily accessible source of outdoor recreation for residents of all ages and backgrounds.

Other Such Districts   Richard Trudeau describes a number of other well-known special park districts in the United States and Canada, including: (1) the Huron-Clinton Metropolitan Authority, Brighton, Michigan, the largest regional park district in the United States, serving 4.5 million people in five counties; (2) the Cleveland Metroparks, Cleveland, Ohio, which covers all of Cuyahoga County and has land in five adjoining counties; and (3) the Greater Vancouver Regional District, Burnaby, British Columbia, Canada, a partnership of 18 municipalities and three electoral districts that serves half of the province's population.

Trudeau points out that special park and recreation districts have fared better than city and county park and recreation agencies in recent years:

> This is especially true of the independent special districts which have their own tax base, elected boards of directors, and considerable public involvement. . . . Over time, the districts have demonstrated they can deliver park and recreation services without paying the overhead costs incurred by other types of governing structures . . . with effective response to citizen needs [and they] are freer to act more boldly than the park and recreation departments in legislative matters.[29]

MUNICIPAL RECREATION AND PARK DEPARTMENTS

Municipal government is the term generally used to describe the local political unit of government such as the village, town, or city that is responsible for providing the bulk of direct community service such as street maintenance, police and fire protection, and education. Most areas depend on municipal government to provide many important recreation and park facilities and program opportunities, in addition to those provided by voluntary, private, and commercial agencies.

With the widespread recognition of this responsibility, municipal recreation and park agencies expanded rapidly in the United States during the period following World War II, with a steady increase in the number of departments, amount of acreage in park and recreation areas, number of full- and part-time or seasonal personnel, and total expenditures. A vivid example of how this growth took place in a single state is provided in an analysis of municipal recreation services in North Carolina over a 24-year period (1951–1974). Analyzing data gathered annually by the North Carolina Recreation Commission and its successor, the Department of Economic and Natural Resources, H. Douglas Sessoms and James Krug found that the operations budget for the 35 municipal park and recreation departments studied had increased by 1200 percent from $2.1 million in 1951 to $27.5 million in 1975. While comparable studies have not been carried out, it is likely that the findings in other states would be similar.[30]

Several decades ago, George Butler, a leading research authority for the National Recreation Association, offered the following arguments in support of municipally sponsored parks and recreation:

Municipal government offers many individuals their primary or only opportunity for wholesome recreational involvement, particularly among poorer people in large cities.

Only through government can adequate lands be acquired for playgrounds, parks, and other outdoor recreation areas.

Municipal recreation is "democratic and inclusive"; it serves all ages, races, and creeds, and places the burden of support upon the entire community.

Municipal recreation is relatively inexpensive, when compared with private expenditure for recreation; yet, by spreading the cost of development over the entire population, it can provide a full range of facilities and services.

Local government gives permanency to recreation, assuring both continuity and the ability to respond to changing population needs.

The job is too large for any private agency, whereas the city, with its powers of land acquisition and taxation, can provide inexpensive community-wide nonprofit services to meet total population needs.

Recreation plays an important role in the local economy, helping to stabilize property values and reduce social pathology, thus making communities more attractive for industries seeking new locations or families seeking new homes.

People demand public recreation and are willing to be taxed for it, as evidenced by the steady growth of programs, passage of referenda and bond issues, and overall support of recreation through the years.[31]

Functions and Structure of Municipal Agencies

Until World War II, many American communities had two or more leisure-service agencies existing side by side, such as a separate *park* department managing parks and other physical resources for outdoor recreation and a *recreation* department responsible for playgrounds and varied year-round programs. In the 1950s and 1960s, most such departments merged into single administrative entities, and new departments formed in other cities usually were structured as joint recreation and parks agencies.

Other municipal agencies may also sponsor special leisure services that are linked to their own missions. They may include: (1) police departments, which often operate youth-service centers or leagues; (2) welfare departments or social-service agencies, which may operate day-care centers or senior centers; (3) youth boards, which tend to focus on out-of-school youth or teen gangs; (4) health and hospital agencies, which sometimes operate community mental health centers or similar services; (5) public housing departments which sometimes have recreation centers in their projects; (6) cultural departments or boards, which frequently sponsor performing arts programs or civic celebrations; and (7) school systems and local community colleges.

Frequently, these other agencies assume recreation responsibilities in order to serve a particular population or meet a special need. For example, the Chicago Housing Authority instituted a widely publicized Midnight Basketball League in the late 1980s to help reduce crime in its projects. Similarly, the Minneapolis Park Police became actively involved in providing anti-gang services, which included various recreation elements, in an effort to prevent vandalism and delinquency in the city's park system.[32] In other communities, leisure services are connected with programs involving health and social services, streets and highways, or arena and stadium supervision.

Programs of Municipal Agencies

Municipal recreation and parks departments operate programs within several categories of activity: games and sports, aquatics, outdoor and nature-oriented programs, arts and crafts, performing arts, special services, social programs, hobby groups, and other playground and community center activities.

In addition, public recreation and parks departments often sponsor large-scale special events such as holiday celebrations, festival programs, art and hobby shows, and sports tournaments.

These departments also assist other community agencies to organize, publicize and schedule activities. Frequently, sports programs for children and youth, such as Little League or American Legion baseball, are cosponsored by public departments and associations of interested parents who undertake much of the actual management of the activity, including coaching, fund-raising, and scheduling. Similarly, many cultural programs, such as Civic Opera or Little Theater associations, are affiliated with and receive assistance from public recreation departments.

Varied Program Emphases

Cities tend to have different emphases in their recreation and park operations. Omaha, Nebraska, for example, has a well-established department that operates a major auditorium and stadium complex, extensive boating facilities, and other unusual physical facilities, including an outstanding indoor tennis complex and a trap-and-skeet shooting facility. With revenues from these sources, it is able to support a substantial portion of its overall recreation operations.

Vancouver, British Columbia, has given high priority to developing and maintaining an extensive network of parks, beaches, pools, golf courses, conservatories, ice rinks, community centers, and an outstanding zoo in famed Stanley Park. This landmark, established more than 100 years ago, has a remarkable seawall promenade, a zoo, an aquarium, outstanding sports facilities, and other sites for leisure participation. A section of Stanley Park was named a Heritage Park Site in 1980, and its meadows and forests are carefully preserved as magnificent examples of relatively untouched natural environments.

Indianapolis, Indiana, is an excellent example of a city that has combined vigorous expansion of its sports and cultural facilities and programs with a sound public recreation and parks program to enhance its appeal to new businesses, residents, and tourists. Once viewed as a less-than-lively midwestern town, Indianapolis is fast becoming known as the amateur sports capital of the nation. In addition to its famed Indianapolis 500 auto racing event, the city now has two major league sports teams, the Pacers and the Colts. It has spent over $130 million to build seven sports facilities, including the Hoosier Dome and other stadiums, velodromes, and natatoriums. Ten national sports associations have moved their headquarters to Indianapolis, including the Amateur Athletic Union, the U.S. Rowing Association, and the American College of Sports Medicine. In addition, the city boasts new art galleries, theaters, museums, and performing companies.

Fitness Programming

As a result of the growing concern about fitness, many cities have undertaken special programs to promote health, fitness, and sport. This effort has been assisted by the Fitness Coalition, a joint effort of the National Recreation and Park Association and the President's Council on Physical Fitness and Sports. The Coalition has sought to develop model community programs to enlist the wide-scale support of municipal recreation delivery systems. It has also called upon major corporations in the United States to help promote exercise, health, and nutrition—particularly asking for support from companies involved in manufacturing food, medicine, recreation and athletic equipment, and health products as well as companies selling life insurance programs.

Aquatic Facilities   Linked to this program emphasis is the recent trend by many city and county recreation departments to build outstanding new aquatic facilities that include extensive exercise and sport components. Prince William County, Virginia, for example, has constructed the outstanding Chinn Aquatics and Fitness Center, with such features as an 8-lane, 40-yard competitive swimming pool, a leisure pool, whirlpools, saunas, fitness rooms, a large gymnasium, racquetball courts, a youth center, and child-care facilities. Built at a cost of $10.4 million, this state-of-the-art facility is designed to be self-supporting financially and relies on charges of up to several hundreds of dollars for annual family memberships.

Other city and county recreation and park agencies have recently built water-play parks with such features as water-flume slides, wave pools, lap pools, leisure pools, diving wells, and facilities for hosting family parties. Costing several million dollars to build, such aquatic facilities average seasonal or annual attendance in the hundreds of thousands and, by including rental fees, instructional fees, and income from catering concessions, bring in substantial revenues in such locations as Kettering, Ohio, or North Clackamas, Oregon.[33]

Human-Service Programs

During the past two decades, many local recreation and park agencies have moved vigorously into the area of programming to meet human- and social-service needs. They provide activities for disabled persons, youth, the aging, drug abusers, or other special populations.

Many recreation and park administrators have initiated latchkey programs for children of working parents who would otherwise come home from school to empty houses or apartments. Such cities as Cincinnati, Ohio; Washington, D.C.; Austin, Texas; Richland, Washington; and Albuquerque, New Mexico, have developed extended-day programs to attract and serve such youngsters. The activities, which may or may not require special charges, often include tutoring and homework periods, field trips, a variety of typical play activities, and, in some cases, special transportation arrangements. A number of recreation departments and professional societies have taken the lead in mobilizing community groups to meet such needs. For example, the Connecticut Recreation and Parks Association has worked closely with the state's Commission on Children to extend and upgrade child-care programs.[34]

A trend of the last two decades has been to develop multiservice departments in which recreation and parks programs play a leading role. Thus, a merged department of community services might have responsibility for beaches, parking meters, special housing units, libraries, and other special public facilities or programs. Larger urban recreation and park departments may include management responsibilities for stadiums, convention centers, piers and marinas, or even municipal airports.

The Human Services Department of the city of Gardena, California, for example, offers the following services in addition to traditional recreation programs: (1) youth services, including individual, family and group counseling, tutoring workshops, and alcohol and drug abuse programs; (2) family services, including health-care and immunization clinics, emergency food and shelter programs, and child abuse or battered women's programs; (3) manpower and employment training, including youth job-readiness sessions, displaced homemaker workshops, and placement referral services; and (4) senior citizen activities, including health and welfare counseling, Social Security and Medicare assistance, daily lunch and Meals on Wheels programs, escort services, and homemaker referrals, along with tax and legal assistance.

Municipal recreation and park agencies have also been called upon to provide facilities, staff resources, and other forms of aid during emergencies—such as fires, tornadoes, hurricanes, and earthquakes. During the devastating southern California earthquake in January 1994, the Los Angeles City Department of Recreation and Parks provided public welfare and shelter services over a period of 34 days to more than 20,000 persons at 45 city parks, centers, public schools, and churches. Al Goldfarb writes:

> Support staff was assigned such tasks as moving equipment, trucking trash, cleaning chemical toilets, soliciting donations and coordinating activities with other involved public, nonprofit, and private agencies. . . . [Others managed camps and shelters and conducted] games and crafts for children at Federal Emergency Management Agency (FEMA) shelter sites.[35]

A number of cities have initiated vigorous gang-prevention programs that reflect a multiservice approach, if not a multiservice structure. In Long Beach, California, for example, the Department of Parks, Recreation and Marine has been an active participant in the city's Task Force on Gangs. Working with an urban population that has shifted from a primarily white, homogeneous community to one composed heavily of African-Americans, Latinos, and Asian-Americans or Pacific Islanders, the Task Force has developed a comprehensive approach that includes: (1) anti-gang instruction within the school district; (2) employment training and development; (3) strong linkages between the schools and the parks and recreation department, with extensive new leisure-service programs; (4) case management; (5) parent education; and (6) a resource directory of available community service.[36]

Mobile Recreation Units

Mobile Recreation Units Another approach used in many cities has involved mobile recreation units, consisting of traveling equipment or programs, such as skatemobiles, sportsmobiles, show wagons, mobile puppet theaters, libraries or film units, or other readily portable programs. Often, businesses are solicited to support such units. Mobile recreation received a major impetus in many larger cities during the 1960s, when it became apparent that residents of urban slums were inadequately served by existing recreation facilities and programs. Portable programs were devised to bring sports, cultural activities, science, hobbies, and other forms of entertainment into the neighborhoods, often on a schedule by which a given neighborhood might have a wide variety of special programs brought to its doorstep each week.

Mobile stages are being used for concerts and other large-scale special events, which are being featured by many cities, often with corporate sponsorship. New stage designs that incorporate built-in, state-of-the-art lighting and sound systems facilitate such events, as in Fort Lauderdale, Florida, which has adopted this concept to bring them to various community locations—rather than rely on fixed band shells in parks.[37]

Camping Programs

Another program area in which many large municipal and county recreation and park departments have diversified their offerings involves summer camping. The Montgomery County, Maryland, Department of Recreation schedules the following camps for children within specific age brackets, usually for two-week sessions: Summer Fun Day Camps, Sports Camps, Sailing Camps, Nature Camps, Arts Camps, Gymnastics Camps, Cheerleading Camps, Creative Theater Camps, Golf and Tennis Camps, Basketball Camps, and Therapeutic Recreation Camps designed for children in specific disability groups—with fees that are generally within a range of $140 to $180 per session. In addition, young teenagers are encouraged to enroll, for lesser fees, for volunteer and job-training experiences as mainstreaming companions, summer camp assistants, and playground and camp counselors-in-training.

Fee Based Programs

In response to the period of fiscal austerity described in Chapter 9, fee-based programs have gained popularity with recreation and park departments. Increasing numbers of public leisure-service agencies have expanded the use of such revenue sources where today few recreation opportunities are totally free of cost to the participant.

> **A** 1988 study of fees and charges in almost 500 municipal recreation and parks departments in eight Great Lakes region states by James Brademas and Julie Readnour found that 85 percent of all responding departments had increased fees in the 1986–1987 fiscal year, and that 73 percent anticipated doing so in the following year. The most widely found fees were charges for participating in program activities (97 percent), rentals (88 percent), user fees (72 percent), and sales (70 percent). The mean operating budgets of all responding departments was $1.78 million, and mean reported income from fees and charges was $542,947—almost one-third of the total budget of each agency. And, despite the possibility that increased fees might have reduced participation, 74 percent of the responding Great Lakes recreation and park directors found that the number of participants in their programs had increased.[38]

An excellent example of fees being used to achieve fiscal balance is found in the Cameron County, Texas, Park System. Aided by a considerable volume of tourist traffic in Isla Blanca and other county parks, the system's managers have been able to generate enough revenue to permit the parks to operate in the black and to reinvest substantial sums in renovating and developing the parks. While this park system is somewhat unusual in that it draws substantial revenue from motels, recreational vehicles, and mobile home permits, as well as user fees and other concessions—with a total income of $1.3 million as compared to operating costs of $1.0 million—it clearly illustrates the potential for recreation park agencies to become fiscally self-sufficient.[39]

In some cases, however, attempts to raise fees or to institute new fees have met organized opposition. A striking example occurred in 1986, when it was announced that the National Park Service would charge entry fees for the first time at the Independence and Valley Forge National Historical Parks as part of a national effort to boost Park Service revenues. In light of the forthcoming celebration of the bicentennial of the U.S. Constitution, which was to be centered in Philadelphia, the announcement aroused a storm of protest. This entry fee was called "slapping a price tag on the cradle of democracy" at a time when the nation's citizens—rich and poor alike—were being encouraged to visit Philadelphia for a patriotic celebration. Shortly, the plan to impose the new fees was rescinded.

ISSUES AFFECTING LOCAL PUBLIC AGENCIES IN THE 1990s

A comprehensive study of the trends and issues impacting local government recreation and park agencies during the 1990s was carried out with the assistance of members of the American Academy for Park and Recreation Administration and the Academy of Leisure Sciences. Using a Delphi forecasting technique to arrive at a consensus among these administrators and scholars, Digby Whyte identified 5 of 106 trends and 5 of 89 issues as having an extreme impact on local government recreation and park administration (see Table 10.2).

Other trends and issues that were ranked as having great impact included those having to do with neglect of children, growing cultural diversity, difficulty in providing equal opportunity to all people, building on the wellness movement, and improving the quality of life and the level of community trust and support.

Earlier Studies of Urban Recreation and Parks

The continuing concern over fiscal problems expressed in the Whyte study should be considered, however, in light of earlier studies. A number of studies of urban recreation and parks during the 1980s had revealed that a majority of public leisure-service agencies were weathering the fiscal crisis of that period with a reasonable degree of success. For example, a nationwide survey of 200 randomly selected park and recreation agencies in the mid-1980s—in districts or cities with populations of 50,000 or more—was carried out by the Leisure Research Institute at Indiana University. It examined selected aspects of agency operations from 1981 to 1985, including budget allocations, revenues, programs, maintenance, and the number of permanent, part-time, and volunteer personnel. In general, the survey findings were positive, with 77 percent of the responding departments reporting that they had increased their operating budgets over the four-year period.[40]

Losses in budget revenues from state and federal sources were largely offset by increases in fees, charges, local taxes, and gifts. A majority of agencies (82 percent of those responding) reported increases in the number of programs and facilities being provided, while a significant number (42 percent) reported that the quality of maintenance had either stayed the

TABLE 10.2   Ranking of Extreme Impact Trends and Issues[41]

TRENDS	OVERALL RANKING	RANKING BY ADMINISTRATORS	RANKING BY SCHOLARS
Deteriorating park and recreation infrastructures	1st	3rd	1st
Increasing crime (violence, drug use, vandalism, gangs) in communities and parks	3rd	4th	2nd
Declining park and recreation budgets relative to costs	3rd	1st	4th
Increasing competition for shrinking federal, state, and local tax resources	4th	2nd	6th
Massive public sector debts	5th	5th	2nd
ISSUES			
How to ensure adequate finance for capital development	1st	1st	2nd
How spending priorities should be set in face of budget cuts or when services are stretched too thin	1st	1st	2nd
How to make parks safe places from crime, etc., while maintaining visitor enjoyment	3rd	4th	1st
How public parks and recreation can strengthen its political position and shape future through affecting state and national policy	4th	1st	5th
How to compete successfully for funding against other community services (education, health, police)	5th	4th	4th

same or declined. In general, the number of full-time personnel had remained relatively stable, with two-thirds of the agencies also reporting increases in the use of volunteers.

Another major study of local public recreation services, carried out by a consortium of organizations (including the University of Georgia, the Forest Service, the American Park and Recreation Society, the National Park Service, and the National Society for Park Resources), surveyed more than 8,000 local parks and recreation departments nationwide. Conducted in 1986, it examined budgets, salaries, programs, and perceived needs and trends in parks and recreation. The study was particularly interesting for its comparison of large urban communities of more than 100,000 with much smaller communities of under 5,000. Strikingly, per capita expenditures for the smaller towns were almost four times higher ($36.60 annually) than they were for larger cities ($9.88 annually).[42]

Recreation in Rural Communities

Although attention has chiefly been focused on recreation programs in larger cities, increasing interest is being given today to the one-quarter of the nation's population (approximately 65 million) in smaller communities and rural areas. Lawrence Allen and his co-authors have documented the effect of recreation opportunities and services on rural residents' general satisfaction with community life. Examining 18 rural Colorado communities, they found that residents viewed medical services, economic stability and opportunities, and environmental

quality as the most important aspects of community life. The satisfaction ratings indicated that lack of adequate leisure opportunity would represent a major source of dissatisfaction—and that the leisure aspect of rural life was closely linked to overall assessment of community living.[43]

Problems in Larger Cities

As earlier chapters in this text have shown, problems related to inadequate budgets, increasing crime, and declining infrastructure and maintenance services tend to be most severe in older cities with limited public, nonprofit, and commercial leisure resources (see pages 235 and 236). Yet, even in these communities, recreation and park administrators are working to expand and improve leisure facilities, programs, and maintenance. New York City, which had experienced major cuts in recreation and park operations during the 1980s, has been able to mount aggressive campaigns to improve the care of its major parks such as Central Park and Prospect Park, through the contributions of thousands of businesses and individual residents who joined park foundations or conservancy organizations.

In August 1995, the city's mayor commented that in the previous year New York's Parks Commissioner, Henry Stern, had succeeded in acquiring 23 new properties and the city's Parks Foundation had raised over $7 million for program and playground improvements.[44] In addition, the Park and Recreation Department had initiated the largest work-fare and career-building program of its type in the country, with over 3,700 persons on public assistance now helping to maintain the parks and hundreds of others taking job-training classes and obtaining regular jobs.

New York has also successfully moved ahead with plans to develop its waterfront areas, as other cities like Baltimore have done, with mixed public, private, and commercial recreational uses. With the state's approval, four huge piers jutting into the Hudson River, which had been built in the early 1900s to accommodate a generation of giant ocean liners, are being converted into a huge sports and entertainment complex. While continuing to ensure public access to the waterfront, this $100 million project, known as the Chelsea Piers, has already constructed

> back-to-back ice rinks [where the city's youth and adult amateur hockey leagues, which had to travel to suburban rinks, can now practice and play], a golf-driving range, a huge gymnastics center, and two outdoor roller rinks. The rest of the project [will have] a sprawling fitness center with an indoor sand volleyball court, a rock-climbing wall and a quarter-mile running track that is billed as the world's longest indoor track, as well as restaurants . . . sound stages, a photography studio, and offices.[45]

While the Chelsea Piers project is primarily a huge commercial venture, it does represent: (1) an imaginative and productive use of abandoned facilities that had been an eyesore along New York's waterfront; (2) a way of meeting the diversified leisure interests of the city's residents and helping to maintain its attraction for business and industry; and (3) a recognition that public funding alone could not finance such a conversion—and that it was necessary to rely on private initiative and investments to carry it out.

TREND TOWARD PARTNERSHIPS IN GOVERNMENT

An important recent trend in municipal recreation and park programming has been the development of "synergetic" projects. This term describes the process of combining the resources of more than one agency to sponsor leisure services that could not be offered by agencies individually. Numerous examples may be provided of such synergetic programs.

A recent survey of more than 100 cities found that all but one municipal recreation and parks department conducted programs with other agencies and organizations; more than half of the respondents had ten or more synergetic programs during the year. They worked closely with voluntary agencies, schools and colleges, service clubs, and business and industry to promote sport, cultural, and other types of events and projects.

Today, the term that is used to describe such collaborative efforts is partnership. While all types of agencies make use of this approach, it is of special value to municipal recreation and park departments. Several years ago, John Crompton pointed out that the functions of public leisure-service managers had been transformed, due to the limitations imposed by the era of austerity in government funding. He wrote:

> The role of the public recreation and park manager has changed from that of being an administrator primarily concerned with the allocation of government funding to that of an entrepreneur who operates in the public sector with minimal tax support. He or she is charged with the responsibility of aggressively seeking out resources for the agency and exploiting them to ensure that client groups receive maximum possible satisfaction.[46]

Steve Selin and Nancy Myers agree, commenting that in this era of reinventing government, many recreation and park managers are turning to partnerships to maximize the use of limited tax dollars to meet expanding public demands for high-quality recreation experiences.[47] Typically, this is often done through coalitions of several different public agencies. Beverly Brandes writes:

> Many recreation and park programs interrelate with other public agencies, such as public housing authorities, school districts, court and probation agencies, city manager's offices, and the like. Some coalition projects even include the local departments of public works, transportation, human resources, and police or law enforcement agencies.[48]

Today, there are numerous examples of such linkages among government departments, as well as partnerships with private groups of citizens, corporations, and other types of educational or leisure-service agencies. Kathy Brown points out that in Durham, North Carolina, more than 40 public, nonprofit, and commercial organizations have joined together in a common effort to reduce juvenile delinquency.[49] Two historic parks in Connecticut— Hartford's Bushnell Park and New Haven's Green Park—have been fully restored and are being maintained through the efforts of well-organized public-private partnership groups— a pattern followed in hundreds of cities today.

Often, contractual relationships are established between public authorities and private or commercial businesses to operate major sectors of a community's recreation program. For example, in Dallas, Texas, the city's Park and recreation Department has contracted for 15 years with a private operator to manage five major tennis centers under an arrangement in which

> The park and recreation board approves court fees and policies.
> The [private] managers operate the facilities, keep them clean and are responsible for other expenses associated with the tennis business (labor, marketing, equipment, and office supplies fall in this category).
> The city is responsible for utilities, court, building and grounds repair, and maintenance costs, and site renovation or expansion expenditures.[50]

With this partnership agreement, the Department's revenues have increased annually and its expenditures have been reduced, while a high-quality tennis program has been maintained at the same time that other services have been cut back.

Numerous other examples of partnerships may be cited. John Crompton and Sarah Richardson point out that, for years, public recreation and park agencies have collaborated closely with private and commercial business in the promotion of tourism—to their mutual benefit.[51] In the province of Ontario, Canada, a number of municipalities have developed jointly constructed and operated school and community centers.[52] Public recreation and park departments frequently combine with corporations to jointly sponsor major tournaments, festivals, or other events—as is the case in Las Vegas, Nevada, where the Parks and Leisure Activities Department conducts a highly successful five-week event known as the Corporate Challenge. Patterned after the Olympic Games, this program was initiated in 1986 and has grown steadily. James Busser and David Kuiper point out that today the event involves more than 100 local corporations and 16,500 of their employees as participants.[53] The public relations value of such a program is immense.

> The governor of Nevada, mayor of Las Vegas, and representatives of each company generally participate in the torch relay, in which a torch is carried throughout the Las Vegas community and passed from person to person along the route. . . . Events are held at various recreational facilities throughout the community and require the support and cooperation of a number of different agencies, including the Clark County School District, National Park Service, Bureau of Land Management, Nellis Air Force Base, and the University of Nevada Las Vegas. Several activities, such as the fishing derby held at Lake Mead National Recreation Area and the running and bicycling events held at BLM's Red Rock Recreation Area, reflect the unique recreational opportunities available in the Las Vegas Valley.[54]

In many cases, colleges and universities also work closely with other agencies—such as government units, nearby communities, and nonprofit organizations—in partnership ventures. For example, the Recreation, Parks and Tourism Science Department of Texas A & M University, through the Sea Grant College Program and the Texas Cooperative Extension Service, assists small communities and rural areas in developing coastal tourism and recreation resources.[55] The University of Northern Iowa and University of Oregon have each conducted highly successful day and resident camping programs at U.S. Army Air Force bases in the United States and Korea, under contract with the Department of Defense.[56]

An additional example of partnership ventures is where a number of states and municipalities have joined together with commercial sponsors—under long-term funding and leasing arrangements—to build major sports stadiums to house professional teams. In other cases, public and private parties have been involved in "land-swapping" deals that have benefited both commercial and environmental interests. The most dramatic example of such cooperative efforts occurred in 1994 when the State of Washington and a privately held lumber corporation exchanged more than 100 separate parcels of forest and special-interest natural resource lands, totaling more than 20,000 acres, under an agreement enthusiastically supported by environmental groups.[57]

Collaborative arrangements of this type are growing in number and variety and are helping to build a climate of mutual assistance among the different elements that comprise the leisure-service system.

SUMMARY

Government's role with respect to organized leisure services is a diversified one. On the federal level, government is concerned with the management of outdoor recreation resources, either as a primary function or within a multiple-use concept, through such agencies as the

National Park Service, U.S. Forest Service, Bureau of Land Management, and TVA. The federal government also assists the states and local political units through funding and technical assistance for programs serving children and youth, those with disabilities, the elderly, and similar groups. Budget cutbacks in recent years have impacted federal land-management operations and, linked with conservative pressures, have reduced federal support for the arts and public media.

State governments operate major park systems and play an important role in promoting environmental conservation and outdoor recreation opportunities. They also set standards and pass enabling legislation that defines the role of local governments in the area of recreation and parks. In addition, states have traditionally maintained networks of state hospitals and special schools for those with disabilities, although this function has been reduced in recent years as a result of deinstitutionalization trends toward placing many such individuals in community settings.

This chief sponsors of government recreation and park programs are on the local level— city, town, county, and special district government agencies. They operate varied facilities and generally offer a wide range of classes, leagues, or special events in sports, the arts, social activities, and other leisure areas. They also provide or assist in many programs in the human-services area. While many municipal departments have expanded their revenue-source operations, departments in other larger and older cities suffer from depleted staff resources and have limited program and maintenance potential. In response to perceived needs, governmental recreation organizations on all levels have begun making fuller use of partnerships—coordinating their programs with or joining in shared operations with other government units, nonprofit or commercial organizations, and groups of private citizens.

Questions for Class Discussion or Essay Examinations

1. Review the major recreation and park functions of *either* the federal government *or* state governments, identifying key agencies and their leisure-related roles. Apart from managing resources for outdoor recreation, what are the other important activities of these two levels of government?

2. Municipal recreation and park departments, including city, town, or other types of local public agencies, provide a diverse range of leisure opportunities for community residents today. What are some of the major trends in municipal-recreation programming in recent years, and what problems have affected such departments as a result of fiscal austerity?

3. Discuss the concept of partnership arrangements among governmental and other types of nonpublic community organizations, in terms of recreation programming. What are the values and what are several examples of such partnership arrangements?

4. Based on the text and on your observation or experiences, what are some of the more positive aspects of local recreation and park government operations today? What are some of the problems or weaknesses affecting such agencies, and how would you as an administrator attempt to solve these difficulties?

Endnotes

2   James Murphy, E. William Niepoth, Lynn Jamieson, and John Williams, *Leisure Systems: Critical Concepts and Applications* (Champaign, Ill.: Sagamore Publishing, 1991): 31.

3   Arthur Laufer, *Operations Management* (Cincinnati: South-Western Publishing Co., 1975): 19.

4   Murphy et al., *op. cit.,* 101.

5   Reynold Carlson, Janet Maclean, Theodore Deppe, and James Peterson, *Recreation and Leisure: The Changing Scene* (Belmont, Cal.: Wadsworth, 1979): 117.

6   *Statistical Abstract of the United States 1995* (Washington, D.C.: U.S. Department of Commerce, 1995): 251.

7   Priscilla Baker, "Tourism and the National Parks," *Parks and Recreation* (October 1986): 51.

8   William Penn Mott, *Annual Report, National Park Service* (Washington, D.C.: National Park Foundation, 1986).

9   Michael Satchell, "Trouble in Paradise," *U.S. News & World Report* (19 June 1995): 25–26.

10   *Statistical Abstract, op. cit.*

11   *U.S. Department of Agriculture Report: U.S. Forest Service* (Washington, D.C.: Government Printing Office, 1982): 1, 49.

12   *Report of the Forest Service* (Washington, D.C.: U.S. Department of Agriculture, June 1995).

13   John Cushman, Jr., "Forest Service Rethinking Its Mission," *New York Times* (24 April 1994): 22.

14   Steve Selin and Franklin Lewis, "The USDA Forest Service and Rural Tourism Development," *Trends* (Vol. 31 No. 1 1994): 14–17.

15   *Annual Report, Bureau of Land Management* (Washington, D.C.: Department of the Interior, 1994).

16   Stephan Morgan, "U.S. Fish and Wildlife Service to Ask for Ban on Lead Shot," *Philadelphia Inquirer* (14 May 1995): C-16.

17   *Recreation on TVA Lakes* (Knoxville, Tenn.: Tennessee Valley Authority Brochure, 1991).

18   U.S. Army Corps of Engineers, *Lakeside Recreation in the Upper Mississippi Basin* (Washington, D.C.: Government Printing Office, July 1987).

19   "The Worst Federal Agency," *U.S. News & World Report* (25 November 1994): 61–64.

20   "Building on LWCF: A Call to Action," *Parks and Recreation* (November 1994): 19.

21   Louis Harris, "Support for the Arts Is on the Rise," *Philadelphia Inquirer* (28 April 1992): A-17.

22   Sylvia Nasar, "The Bureaucracy: What's Left to Shrink," *New York Times* (11 June 1995): 4–1.

23   W. Tom Martin and Carl Hust, "State Advisory Services," *Parks and Recreation* (July 1980): 61.

24   John Brant, "Unemployment: The Theme Park," *New York Times Magazine* (28 January 1996): 46–47.

25   Andrew Malcolm, "As Other Industries Fade, States Set Their Sights on Tourism," *New York Times* (6 September 1987): E-1.

26   Judith Berck, "When Broadway Meets the Midway, It's Big Business," *New York Times* (28 August 1994): F-5.

27   "Washington Scene: States Call for Federalism Reform; Some Implications for Recreation Grants," *Parks and Recreation* (August 1981): 11.

28   Charles Nelson and Lawrence Leroy, "County Parks: State of the Art Today," *Parks and Recreation* (January 1983): 84.

29   Richard Trudeau, "Special Park Districts," *Parks and Recreation* (January 1996): 63.

30   H. Douglas Sessoms and James Krug, "Municipal Recreation Services in North Carolina: A 24-Year Analysis," *Leisure Sciences* (Vol. 1 1977): 31–32.

31   George D. Butler, *Introduction to Community Recreation* (New York: McGraw–Hill, 1976): 58–62.

32   Loren Evenrud, "Facing the Reality of Gangs in Parks: An Inter-Agency Response," *Parks and Recreation* (March 1995): 44–50.

33 Denise Menke, "Waves of Excitement . . . Sounds of Success," *Parks and Recreation* (February 1995): 30–33.

34 "Park and Recreation Services Address the Child Care Crisis," *Parks and Recreation* (March 1992): 10.

35 Al Goldfarb, "Serving the Community in Times of Trouble," *Parks and Recreation* (October 1992): 58–63.

36 Steve Blancarte and Barbara Azeka, "A Pluralistic Approach to Gang Prevention: The Long Beach Model," *Journal of Physical Education, Recreation and Dance—Leisure Today* (April 1992): 31–33.

37 Terry Forsberg, "Mobile Stages and Special Events," *Parks and Recreation* (November 1995): 40–47.

38 James Brademas and Julie Readnour, research paper presented at the NRPA Congress, Indianapolis, Ind., October 1988.

39 Tressa Hawkins, "Parks for the People, By the People," *Parks and Recreation* (May 1988): 39–43.

40 Digby Whyte, "Key Trends and Issues Impacting Local Government Recreation and Park Administration in the 1990s: A Focus for Strategic Management and Research," *Journal of Park and Recreation Administration* (Vol. 10. No. 3 1992): 97–98.

41 "Changes in Park and Recreation Agency Operations Detailed in Survey," *NRPA Dateline* (March 1986): 6.

42 Barbara McD. Cordell, H. Ken Cordell, Daniel Hope III, and Donald English, "Local Government Park and Recreation Departments," *Journal of Physical Education, Recreation and Dance—Leisure Today* (April 1987): 12.

43 Lawrence Allen, Patrick Long, and Richard Perdue, "The Role of Leisure: Satisfaction in Rural Communities," *Journal of Physical Education, Recreation and Dance—Leisure Today* (April 1987): 5.

44 Douglas Martin, "The Greening of Gotham," *New York Times* (12 February 1995): 37.

45 Paul Goldberger, "Giving New Life to Abandoned Old Piers," *New York Times* (17 November 1995): C-1.

46 John Crompton, *Doing More With Less in the Delivery of Recreation and Park Services* (State College, Penn.: Venture Publishing, 1987): iv.

47 Selin and Myers, *op. cit.*

48 Beverly Brandes, "Build Success Through Coalitions," *Parks and Recreation* (June 1995): 2.

49 Kathy Brown, "Alternatives Through Interagency Collaboration," *Journal of Physical Education, Recreation and Dance—Leisure Today* (April 1995): 35–37.

50 Jere Mills, "Partnerships Providing Service," *Parks and Recreation* (May 1994): 32–34.

51 John Crompton and Sarah Richardson, "The Tourism Connection: Where Public and Private Leisure Services Merge," *Parks and Recreation* (October 1986): 38–44.

52 Ross Fair, "Strategic Alliances Ease the Pain of Recession in Ontario," *Recreation Canada* (Vol. 51 No. 3 1993): 30.

53 James Busser and David Kuiper, "Corporate Challenge: An Olympic Success," *Parks and Recreation* (November 1994): 39–43.

54 *Ibid.*, 42–43.

55 Ken Pagans, "Community Partnerships: A Creative Approach to Coastal Resource Development," *Trends* (Vol. 30 No. 2 1993): 18–22.

56 Christopher Edginton and Curtis Martin, "Camp Adventure: Promoting Cultural Diversity," *Journal of Physical Education, Recreation and Dance—Leisure Today* (April 1995): 31.

57 Ken Hertz, "Land Swapping: It Could Benefit Everyone," *Parks and Recreation* (May 1994): 53–57.

11
eleven

....

Voluntary Nonprofit, Commercial, and Private-Membership Organizations

....

An independent research study evaluated the effects of Boys and Girls Clubs on young people living in public housing as well as on the overall quality of life in housing developments. Focused on alcohol and other drug use, delinquency and vandalism, the study involved 15 different public housing developments over a three-year period.

The researchers found that Boys and Girls Clubs made a significant difference in the quality of life for residents in public housing. When compared to other public housing sites, those with Clubs experienced: (1) 23 percent less presence of crack cocaine; (2) 22 percent less overall drug activity; and (3) 13 percent reduction in juvenile crime. Preliminary school data suggest the potential impact of Boys and Girls Clubs on school performance: lower percentages of academic failure, and fewer behavior problems in schools attended by girls and boys from public housing sites with Clubs.[1]

The kaleidoscopic mix of leisure services offered by business and industry in North America is stunning. Capital investment in leisure services enterprises encompasses a wide range from small operations such as riverside campgrounds

----

[1] *Program Information Brochure* (Atlanta, GA: Boys and Girls Clubs of America, 1995): 1–2.

in which the investment is under $20,000 to spectacular theme parks such as Walt Disney World in which the capital investments exceed $300 million [in the mid-1980s]. Leisure-service organizations also are diverse in terms of the services they offer and include such ventures as video arcades, mountaineering schools, circuses, hotels, marinas, hunting clubs, dude ranches, billiard parlors, nature guide services, and raceways, to name just a few.[2]

INTRODUCTION

While government recreation and park agencies are responsible for providing a floor of basic leisure services for the public throughout the United States, the bulk of recreation opportunities today are offered by other types of organizations. This chapter describes three of these other types of leisure-service sponsors: (1) voluntary nonprofit organizations such as youth-serving groups or special-interest associations; (2) commercial recreation businesses; and (3) private-membership organizations that serve specialized segments of the population or focus on particular kinds of recreation on a limited-access basis.

VOLUNTARY NONPROFIT LEISURE-SERVICE AGENCIES

Organizations that are described as voluntary nonprofit leisure-service agencies (other descriptions for this category include public/private, quasi-public, and nonprofit community-service) have the following characteristics:

1. Usually established to meet significant social needs through organized citizen cooperation, community organizations represent the voluntary wishes and expressed needs of neighborhood residents. Thus, they are voluntary in origin.

2. Governing boards of directors or trustees are usually public-spirited citizens who accept such responsibilities as a form of social obligation. Thus, membership and administrative control are voluntary.

3. For funding, voluntary agencies usually rely on public contributions, either directly to the agency itself or to Community Chest, United Way, Red Feather Campaign, or similar shared fund-raising efforts. Contributed funds are usually supplemented by membership fees and charges for participation. In recent years, many voluntary organizations have also undertaken special projects for which they receive government funding.

4. Leadership of voluntary agencies is partly professional and partly voluntary. Management is usually by directors and supervisors professionally trained in social work, recreation, or education. At other levels, leadership is by nonprofessionals, part-time or seasonal personnel, and volunteers.

Voluntary agencies regard recreation as part of their total spectrum of services, rather than as their sole function. Typically, they recognize the importance of creative and constructive

---

[2] John Bullaro and Christopher Edginton, *Commercial Recreation: Managing for Profit, Service, and Personal Satisfaction* (New York: Macmillan, 1986): 39.

leisure and see recreation as a threshold activity that serves to attract participants to their agencies. In addition, they see it as a means of achieving significant social goals, such as building character among youth, reducing social pathology, enriching educational experience, strengthening community unity, and similar objectives. In general, even though voluntary agencies do not describe themselves as recreation agencies, this often tends to be the largest single component in their programs. However, recreation is not considered an end in itself, but a means through which to attain other agency objectives.

Nonprofit but Fee-Charging

Many voluntary organizations, while they are nonprofit and interested in meeting important social goals, may charge substantial fees. For example, YMCAs or YWCAs in suburban areas are likely to have fees that are as high as several hundred dollars a year for full family memberships, and to charge impressive sums for varied program activities. However, such fees are intended simply to help the organization maintain financial stability, *without* making a profit, and are frequently used to subsidize other services to disadvantaged or disabled populations who cannot afford to pay fees for membership or participation. The same type of organization in an inner-city environment will typically charge only nominal fees or none at all and will rely much more heavily on grants, contributions, and other forms of public support.

In the 1980s, many voluntary public-service organizations were forced to expand their fund-raising efforts and move into new, commercial-like ventures. Carlton Yoshioka summarizes the trend:

> . . . since the decline in the early 1980s of government support, nonprofit organizations have turned increasingly to fee revenue to finance their programs. . . . [However,] the development of the market economy approach appears to further intensify the competition between the commercial and nonprofit sectors, and weaken the traditional rationale for nonprofit tax-exempt status.[3]

Even though such enterprises are limited by Internal Revenue Service regulations that define the nature and limit the operations of charitable organizations, nonprofit groups have had a significant economic impact in the leisure-service field. Small business owners and the Small Business Administration have argued that nonprofit organizations have an unfair competitive advantage over commercial businesses providing similar services, due to their tax-exempt status, lower postal rates, and other factors that reduce their costs—such as the ability to recruit volunteers.

Because of the word "voluntary," some assume incorrectly that such agencies are staffed solely by volunteer workers. The reality is that, although some nonprofit organizations like the Boy Scouts and Girl Scouts rely heavily on volunteer leaders, all of them have full-time, paid professionals in their key management or supervisory posts.

It was estimated in 1986 that nonprofit organizations employed 7.2 million people—approximately one in 16 working Americans—and that the number would rise to 9.3 million in 1995. Salaries for professional employees of such bodies as Boy Scouts and Girl Scouts, the YMCA and YWCA, Junior Achievement, and Big Brothers/Big Sisters of America have all risen steadily in recent years. Indeed, during the early and mid-1990s, a wave of public criticism was directed at the executives of some major nonprofit, charitable organizations who had received exorbitant salaries and benefits.[4]

TYPES OF NONPROFIT YOUTH-SERVING AGENCIES

While voluntary nonprofit organizations fit under many headings—including the arts, education, health, and social service—the largest segment of such groups with strong recreational components is generally youth-oriented. Included in this segment are (1) nonsectarian youth-serving organizations; (2) religiously affiliated youth-serving or social agencies; (3) settlement houses and independent community centers; and (4) special-interest organizations in such fields as sports, outdoor recreation, and travel.

NonSectarian Youth-Serving Organizations

Nationally structured organizations that function directly through local branches, nonsectarian youth-serving groups have broad goals related to social development and good citizenship and operate extensive programs of recreational activity. There are hundreds of such organizations: many of them are junior affiliates of adult organizations, while others are independent. Sponsorship is by such varied bodies as civic and fraternal organizations, veterans' clubs, rural and farm organizations, and business clubs.

Boy Scouts of America   Founded in the United States in 1910, the Boy Scouts is a powerful and widespread organization. Table 11.1 depicts its levels of youth and adult membership, including a decline in membership that took place in the 1970s and 1980s as a result of the social changes described in Chapter 9. Close to 40 million people have been members of the Boy Scouts of America since its founding. In addition to its membership in the United States, the Boy Scouts is part of a worldwide scouting movement involving more than 100 other countries.

The primary purpose of scouting is the development of desirable traits of character and good citizenship, which is to be achieved through four levels of membership: Tiger Cubs, Cub Scouts, Boy Scouts, and Explorer Scouts. The program emphasizes mental and physical fitness, vocational and social development, and the enrichment of youth hobbies and prevocational interests, relying heavily on adventure and scouting skills and service activities.

About 50 percent of the local Scout units are sponsored by religious agencies, although membership is not usually restricted to a single denomination. The national organization firmly supports religious and spiritual values, however, and there have been cases of denial of membership to young applicants who objected to the religious emphasis. Although the Scouts employ thousands of professional Scout executives and regional staff members, the bulk of actual leadership is provided by parents and other interested adult volunteers.

The Boy Scouts have been regarded as a middle-class organization in American society, and as a small-town or suburban rather than a big-city phenomenon. However, beginning in the mid-1960s, the Scouts became more active in inner-city neighborhoods. In 1968 the Boy Scouts of America announced a nationwide campaign of expansion in city slums and impoverished rural areas in order to attract greater numbers of youth. The original focus on outdoor adventure and skills was broadened to include urban activities. Today, Scouts may earn badges in urban conservation and cleanup or block renewal.

Girl Scouts of the USA   The largest voluntary organization serving girls in the world, the Girl Scouts, is open to girls between the ages of 6 and 17 who subscribe to its ideals

TABLE 11.1   Boy Scout and Girl Scout Memberships: 1970 to 1993[5]

	1970	1980	1985	1990	1993
Boy Scouts of America					
Membership:	6,287	4,318	4,845	5,448	5,355
Boys:	4,683	3,207	3,755	4,293	4,165
Adults:	1,604	1,110	1,090	1,155	1,190
Total Units (packs, etc.)	157	129	134	130	129
Girl Scouts of the USA					
Membership:	3,922	2,784	2,802	3,269	3,440
Girls:	3,248	2,250	2,172	2,480	2,613
Adults:	674	534	630	788	827
Total Units (troops, etc.)	164	154	166	202	221

(In thousands. Includes Puerto Rico and outlying areas.)

as stated in the Girl Scout Promise and Law. It is part of a worldwide association of girls and adults in 104 countries through its membership in the World Association of Girl Guides and Girl Scouts. Its membership in the mid-1990s, as shown in Table 11.1, consists of 2.6 million members in five age categories (Daisies, Brownies, Juniors, Cadettes, and Seniors) and 827,000 adults, including volunteers, board members, and staff specialists. There are about 330 councils and 221,000 Girl Scout troops, including Troops on Foreign Soil (TOFS).

Founded in 1912, the Girl Scouts provides a sequential program of activities centered around the arts, the home, and the outdoors, with emphasis on character and citizenship development, community service, international understanding, health and safety. Senior Girl Scouts in particular may take on responsibilities in hospitals, museums, child care, or environmental programs. Like the Boy Scouts, the Girl Scouts today conducts special programs for the poor, those with physical, emotional, or other disabilities, and similar populations.

While continuing to support its original purpose of inspiring girls "with the highest ideals of character, conduct, patriotism and service," Girl Scouting has changed the basic laws that provide the ethical basis for its movement:

> Original laws that said, for example, "A Girl Scout is a friend to animals," and "A Girl Scout is thrifty," now say "I will do my best to use resources wisely" and "to protect and improve the world around me." A law that said, "A Girl Scout is clean in thought, word and deed," now says that a Scout will do her best "to show respect for myself and others through my words and actions."[6]

While the national Girl Scout organization has taken no stand on the women's liberation movement, self-worth and self-realization have become important goals, and proficiency badges today stress life skills for girls and young women. Where once the Girl Scout emphasis was on categories like "dressmaker" and "hostess," now badges are awarded for "aerospace" and "business."

Boys and Girls Clubs of America

The Boys and Girls Clubs movement is the fastest-growing youth-serving organization in the United States today. Originally composed of two separate organizations, the merged club movement holds a U.S. Congressional Charter and is endorsed by 21 leading service, fraternal, civic, veteran, labor, and business organizations.

Today, the Boys and Girls Clubs movement serves over two million young people in over 1,650 club facilities—buildings owned by the clubs themselves—around the United States.

Programs include sports and games, arts and crafts, social activities, and camping, as well as re-medial education, work training, and job placement and counseling. The national goals of the Boys and Girls Clubs of America include the following: citizenship education and leadership development; health, fitness, and preparation for leisure; educational-vocational motivation; intergroup understanding and value development; and enrichment of both family and community life. With the help of special funding from corporations, foundations, and government agencies, the organization has developed program curricula for several key projects in the social services area. While each club is an independent organization, with its own board and professional staff, the national headquarters and seven regional offices provide essential services to local clubs in such areas as personnel recruitment and management training, program research and devel-opment, fund-raising and public relations, and building design and construction assistance.

The movement is geared to serving disadvantaged and "at-risk" youth. In 1986, fewer than 40 Clubs operated in public housing settings. By the mid-1990s, some 270 Boys and Girls Clubs were located in low-income public housing projects, reaching more than 100,000 young people, with 53 percent of the organization's youth membership coming from single-parent families and 54 percent from minority families. Staffed by 5,600 professional leaders, 14,800 part-time employees, and 77,000 volunteers, the Boys and Girls Clubs movement has initiated a wide variety of community-service projects.

Police Athletic Leagues In hundreds of communities today, law enforcement agencies sponsor Police Athletic Leagues (PAL). Operating in poverty areas, the league programs rely primarily on civilian staffing and voluntary contributions for support, although they sometimes receive technical assistance from officers on special assignment from cooperative municipal police departments. In a few cities, men and women police officers provide the bulk of full-time professional leadership in PAL programs. Police Athletic Leagues typically provide extensive recreation programming, indoor centers, and summer play streets, with strong emphasis on sports and games, creative arts, drum and bugle corps, and remedial ed-ucation. Many leagues also maintain placement, counseling, and job-training programs, and assist youth who have dropped out of school.

The Police Athletic League is one of the few youth organizations that continue to resist juvenile delinquency as a primary thrust. One of its principal purposes has been to promote favorable relationships between young people and the police in urban settings, and it has been markedly successful in this effort. Like other voluntary agencies, Police Athletic Leagues rely on varied funding sources, including United Way, independent fund-raising campaigns, contracts with government, and often partial police department sponsorship.

Camp Fire Founded in 1910 under the name Camp Fire Girls, this organization has been concerned with character-building through a program of outdoor recreation, community service, and educational activities. Beginning in the 1970s, the membership of the Camp Fire Girls declined sharply from a high of more than 600,000 to approximately 325,000 in the early 1980s. The organization responded to this challenge by changing its name to Camp Fire Boys and Girls and embracing a coeducational membership diverse in racial, ethnic, religious, and economic terms.

With over 6,500 volunteer and paid leaders, the staff and board members work extensively in cooperation with local schools in conducting child-care programs. Many Camp Fire programs also sponsor day and resident camping programs for young people from kindergarten age to 21. Like other youth-serving organizations, Camp Fire seeks to be a strong advocate for young people:

> We work to influence public policies and legislation that affect young people. Child abuse, juvenile justice, child care, teen suicide, AIDS and crime prevention are among Camp Fire concerns. Other agencies often work with Camp Fire to achieve common goals.[7]

Numerous other national nonprofit and nonsectarian organizations—such as the Four-H Club and the Children's Aid Society—as well as independent local agencies, also sponsor combined recreational and social-service programs for children and youth.

Church and Synagogue Recreation Programs

Many religious organizations sponsor youth programs with recreational components today, including both activities sponsored by local churches or synagogues and activities sponsored by national federations that are affiliated with a particular denomination.

Recreation programs provided by local churches or synagogues tend to have two broad purposes: (1) to sponsor recreation for their own members or congregations in order to meet their leisure needs in ways that promote involvement with the institution; and (2) to provide leisure opportunities for the community at large or for a selected population group in ways that are compatible with their own religious beliefs. Typical activities offered by individual churches and synagogues may include the following:

Day camps, play schools, or summer Bible schools, which include recreation along with religious instruction.

Year-round recreation activities for families, including picnics, outings, bazaars, covered-dish suppers, carnivals, single adult clubs, dances, game nights, and similar events.

Programs in the fine and performing arts, including innovative worship programs involving dance and folk music.

Fellowship programs for various age levels, including discussion groups on religious and other themes.

Varied special-interest or social-service programs, including day-care centers for children, senior citizens clubs or golden age groups, and recreation programs for disabled persons.

Sports activities, including bowling and basketball leagues, or other forms of instructional or competitive participation.

In general, such programs are appealing, and parents can have confidence that they will be well-organized and wholesome. However, in some cases, when the sponsor is a church or denomination with an extreme fundamentalist position regarding "sin," the program is likely to be very narrowly conceived. For example, the Church of the Nazarene, a pentecostal, evangelical movement founded in 1886, denounces many forms of popularly accepted leisure activity, which it regards as subversive of the Christian ethic. Such activities would include not only much current literature, rock music, radio, and television—other than religious broadcasting—but also Scouting (because of its oaths, handshakes, and bonds of loyalty) and social or folk dancing, sports, field trips, and swimming if they involve immodest clothing or the risk of sexual misbehavior.

In contrast, other religious denominations that have a conservative moral code, such as the Church of Jesus Christ of Latter-Day Saints, do see wholesome recreation as an essential part of their faith. Better known as the Mormon Church, this powerful and successful sect maintains many centers throughout the world where regular programs of recreational activities are sponsored. Hundreds of thousands of Mormons participate regularly in sports leagues and tournaments and in

> marathon and mini-marathon runs, badminton, track and field meets, swimming outings, football, rugby, etc. Cultural activities such as choirs, theater productions, roadshows, dance festivals, and songfests provide wholesome avenues of expression and participation to additional multitudes of people.[8]

Family recreation, including camping and other outdoor pursuits, is particularly encouraged by Mormon elders as a means of strengthening family bonds and resisting negative forms of leisure involvement.

National Youth Organizations

On a broader level, such organizations as the Young Men's Christian Association (YMCA), Young Women's Christian Association (YWCA), the Catholic Youth Organization (CYO), and the Young Men's and Young Women's Hebrew Association (YM-YWHA) provide a network of facilities and programs with diversified recreation, education, and youth-service activities. Although their titles include the words "young" or "youth," they tend to serve a broad range of children, youth, adult, and aging members.

YMCA and YWCA   Voluntary organizations affiliated with Protestantism in general rather than with any single denomination, the Ys are devoted to the promotion of religious ideals of living and view themselves as worldwide fellowships "dedicated to the enrichment of life through the development of Christian character and a Christian society." However, the actual membership of the Ys is multireligious and multiracial. One out of four members of the YMCA is a girl or woman, and a 1960s study showed that the religious affiliation of Y members was 75.2 percent Protestant, 18.9 percent Roman Catholic, and 3.3 percent Jewish. In the United States, racial discrimination was formally banned by the National Council of YMCAs in the 1960s, and by the early 1970s almost all Ys, in both the North and the South, had integrated membership rolls and facilities.

The Y has assumed a major responsibility for meeting public recreation needs in many American and Canadian communities. In a number of Canadian communities, there has been a dramatic expansion of the YMCA in particular, with six centers built in the Toronto area alone during the early 1980s. In smaller cities and towns, it frequently provides the best facilities for indoor aquatics, sports and games, physical fitness, and social and cultural programs, and it often has the most effective organization and leadership.

Although both Y organizations have a strong commitment to urban needs, almost all of the more than 150 YMCAs developed in the early and mid-1970s were built in the suburbs. More recently, the YMCA has been successful in opening a greater number of inner-city branches. Both organizations have grown; the YMCA expanded from 5.5 million members in the mid-1960s to 8.8 million in the mid-1970s. The YWCA has a smaller membership; it serves over two million people in 374 community and student associations throughout the United States.

The YWCA has sought to change its image from a traditional, predominantly white, conservative organization to one more directly concerned with social needs and problems. This new attitude is illustrated by the list of courses, clinics, and workshops offered by many YWs today: Assertiveness Training for Women, Career Development, Personal Finance, Living Single, The Marriage Contract, Sexual Consciousness-Raising, Focus: Women Over Forty, Survival in the City, Women's Self-Expression Workshop, Know Your Body, and The Divorce Experience. Almost 200 YWCAs have initiated programs for battered women, and the National YWCA has initiated national conferences and workshops on domestic violence. Hundreds of YWCAs provide career-planning and employment programs; others focus on juvenile justice needs to reduce delinquency among "high-risk" young women, developmental day-care programs, and therapeutic services for disabled persons.

Many suburban Ys concentrate on recreational activities—including fitness facilities and programs for all ages, which are aggressively marketed and bring in substantial revenues. These may include various membership options for the use of pools, fitness centers, saunas, game courts, or classes and exercise sessions. They also may involve health and fitness seminars, physical fitness assessments, screenings, weight control programs, and similar offerings. Both organizations derive funding from varied sources: membership fees, corporate and private contributions to the United Way, fund-raising drives, and government and foundation grants. In some cases, private health club owners have gone to court to force YMCAs onto the tax rolls, claiming that they are actually functioning as businesses in competition with commercial operators and therefore do not deserve tax-exempt status.

Catholic Youth Organization   The leading Catholic organization concerned with providing spiritual, social, and recreational services for young people in the United States is the Catholic Youth Organization. CYO originated in the early 1930s, when a number of dioceses under the leadership of Bishop Sheil of Chicago began experimenting with varied forms of youth organizations. It was established as a national organization in 1951, as a component of the National Council of Catholic Youth. Today, the National CYO Federation has an office in Washington, D.C., as well as many citywide or diocesan offices. The parish, however, is the core of the Catholic Youth Organization, which depends heavily on the leadership of the parish priest and the services of adult volunteers from the neighborhood for direction and assistance.

Within its religious context, CYO is clearly recognized as a leisure program, meeting its goals through projects and activities operated through local clubs. The following official CYO statement illustrates its view of recreation as a means of rejecting negative or antisocial forms of leisure.

The most vulnerable period in the lives of our young people are the leisure-time hours when they are on their own, away from the positive influences of family, school and church. The values and standards of these significant institutions can then be challenged by the growing impulse for self-assertion and the natural instincts of pleasure-seeking and self-indulgence. This sensitive situation encompasses nearly half the lifetime of the pre-teen and teen-ager and it is the mission of the Catholic Youth Organization to "move in" on these idle hours to an extension of the family, church and school with recreation, spiritual, apostolic, social and cultural programming that will give the youngster attractive alternatives to the appealing excitement of the "offbeat" activities that are the root of delinquency.[9]

The goals of the CYO, like those of other religious organizations that work with youth, are directly related to spiritual values. Through participation in the CYO, Catholic youth become involved in retreats, workshops, religious education, and service programs that strengthen and enrich their faith. The social program also serves to attract and involve young people in center activities, thus helping the priest maintain contact with the young people in his parish. Sports are highly regarded not only as a means of attracting young people to CYO programs, but also as a way to impart desirable spiritual values. The coach is considered an important educator and transmitter of Catholic values.

Young Men's and Young Women's Hebrew Association   Today, there are 250 YM-YWHAs, Jewish Community Centers, and camps serving one million members throughout the United States and Canada. Like the YMCAs and YWCAs, the Jewish Ys do not regard themselves primarily as recreation agencies, but rather as community organizations devoted to social service but with a strong Jewish cultural component. Specifically, the YM-YWHA has defined its mission in the following way:

> To meet the leisure-time social, cultural, and recreational needs of its membership, embracing both sexes and all age groups.
>
> To stimulate individual growth and personality development by encouraging interest and capacity for group and community participation.
>
> To teach leadership responsibility and democratic process through group participation.
>
> To provide certain limited guidance services, including individual counseling, in preparation for referral to specialized services when indicated.
>
> To encourage citizenship education and responsibility among its members and, as a social welfare agency, to participate in community-wide programs of social betterment.

Customarily, leaders of the Jewish Community Center movement identify a set of priorities at five-year intervals, with specific implications for local community centers and for the Jewish Welfare Board, which serves to coordinate and assist both centers and Ys. Responding to changing demographic and social conditions, for example, the goals set for the 1990–1995 period included the providing of services that strengthen the Jewish family, provide outreach to community newcomers and immigrants, strengthen Jewish education, and develop new leadership for the Community Center movement.[10] In its leisure programs, the YM-YWHA has traditionally emphasized sports and physical fitness activities (with particular attention to populations with special needs) and cultural arts programs.

Settlement Houses and Community Centers

Another traditional type of nonprofit organization that provides extensive recreational programming is the settlement house or community center, which can be operated under either sectarian or nonsectarian auspices. Established in the United States in the late nineteenth and early twentieth centuries, settlement houses are usually regarded as social work agencies and draw their administrative personnel from that field. Their varied goals include education, counseling, health services, cultural enrichment, and recreation. .

There are about 1,000 such community centers today, usually in disadvantaged urban neighborhoods. In the past, settlement houses were run primarily by wealthy board members who did not live in the areas served, but who raised funds and determined agency policy. Today, board members or trustees of settlement houses tend to include more members from the surrounding neighborhoods to represent local views. Funding is now derived from both private and government sources, which tends to reduce the independence of voluntary agencies of this type in setting priorities and goals.

Special-Interest Organizations

Numerous other types of voluntary nonprofit organizations can best be classified as special-interest groups, concerned with promoting a particular area of activity or social concern. Their functions may include leadership training, public relations, lobbying and legislation, establishing national standards or operational policies, or the direct sponsorship of program activities.

Special-interest organizations may be free of commercial involvement, or may represent manufacturers of equipment, owners of facilities, schools, or other businesses that seek to stimulate public interest and support and, ultimately, improve their own business success.

Conservation and Outdoor Recreation

There are numerous organizations that seek to educate the public and influence governmental policies in the areas of conservation and outdoor recreation. In some cases, they lobby, conduct research, and sponsor conferences and publications. In others, their primary thrust is to mount projects and carry out direct action on state or local levels.

Sierra Club   Founded in 1892 and headed initially by the famous naturalist John Muir, the Sierra Club has sought to make Americans aware "of what we have lost and can lose during 200 years of continuing exploitation of our resources for commodity purposes and failure to realize their value for scenic, scientific and aesthetic purposes." In recent years, the Sierra Club has become known for its battles to protect major natural resources threatened by commercial exploitation. However, its activities are not restricted to conservation; it is also the nation's largest skiing and hiking club, operating a major network of ski lodges and "river runners," numerous wilderness outings, and ecological group projects. Since 1959, the Sierra Club has been a major publisher of books on conservation and natural resources.

Appalachian Mountain Club   This organization has a regional focus; its purpose when founded in 1876 was to "explore the mountains of New England and adjacent regions . . . for scientific and artistic purposes, and . . . to cultivate an interest in geographical studies." Since its inception, it has explored and mapped many of the wildest and most scenic areas in Massachusetts, New Hampshire, and Maine, in addition to promoting such sports as skiing, snowshoeing, mountain climbing, and canoeing.

Although practical conservation remains a primary concern of the club, it has also acquired various camp properties, published guides and maps, and maintained hundreds of miles of trails and a network of huts and shelters throughout the White Mountains for use by its members. It promotes programs of instruction and leadership training in such activities as snowshoeing, skiing, smooth and white-water canoeing, and rock climbing.

National Outdoor Leadership School   A number of other national nonprofit organizations teach outdoor leadership skills and promote sound environmental practices in the wilderness. The National Outdoor Leadership School sponsors a variety of courses in backpacking, mountaineering, rock climbing, sea kayaking and other outdoor adventure activities in settings throughout the western states, Alaska, and such foreign countries as Australia, Mexico, Patagonia, and Kenya. Other organizations offering programs concerned with environmental education, personal growth, and outdoor adventure recreation include the Wilderness Education Association, the Outward Bound National Office, and the Association for Experiential Education. Woodswomen, Inc., located in Minneapolis, Minnesota, is the oldest and largest women's adventure travel organization.

Organizations Promoting Youth Sports and Games

There are thousands of national, regional, and local organizations promoting and regulating sports of every kind. While many of these govern professional play or high-level intercollegiate competition, others are concerned with sports and games on a purely amateur basis. Several examples of such organizations follow.

Little League   Founded in Williamsport, Pennsylvania, in 1939, this is the largest youth sports program in the world today. In its various leagues, it serves more than three million players each year. As an example of its popularity, it fields 196,000 teams in 91 nations; 7,000 teams were in the tournament leading up to the 1995 Little League Baseball World Series, with 16,000 tournament games being played in six weeks.[11]

Little League operates an impressive headquarters complex and stadium in Williamsport, where camps, conferences, and the annual World Series are held. It has standardized rules of play, requirements for financial operation and fee structures, insurance coverage, approved equipment, and other arrangements for member leagues and teams. Little League also conducts research into youth sports and carries out a great variety of training programs for league officials, district administrators, umpires, managers, and coaches, as well as parent-education activities and publications. More than 750,000 adult volunteers are involved in running Little League.

Without question, this organization and its counterparts in other major team sports are responsible for a high volume of recreational participation that would probably not otherwise take place. Critics of Little League and similar organizations tend to question what they regard as an over-emphasis on high-pressure competition and winning, and an over-regimentation of youth in highly structured programs. However, Little League officials argue that it is not a win-at-all-costs program:

> There are no trophies to work toward. The program emphasizes team rather than individual achievements. As Little League President and Chief Executive Officer Dr. Creighton J. Hale explains. "If it's not fun, it's not Little League."[12]

To put youth sports in perspective, the most popular amateur team sports for Americans age 12 and under are: *basketball* (9.7 million participants); *soccer* (7.7 million); *softball* (5.3 million); *baseball* (5.1 million); and *volleyball* (5 million).[13] One or more national organizations help to organize instruction and competition in each of these sports. For example, the Amateur Softball Association sponsors leagues and tournaments for all ages, with a Women's World Championship that involves the United States and 27 foreign nations, including countries in Asia, Africa, and South America.

Youth sports in general are assisted by national organizations that set standards and promote effective, values-oriented coaching approaches, such as the National Youth Sports Coaches Association, the National Association of Youth Leagues, and the National Clearinghouse for Youth Sports Information. Examples of organizations that are particularly concerned with individual sports include Youth Basketball of America, the Young American Bowling Alliance, and the United States Tennis Association. The latter organization has mounted a vigorous campaign to promote tennis to children and youth through the schools and public recreation agencies—including a National Minority Participation Committee that seeks to increase participation by racial and ethnic minorities in tennis as a lifetime sport.

Arts Councils and Cultural Organizations

Another major area of activity for voluntary agencies is the arts. In addition to nonprofit schools and art centers that offer painting, drawing, sculpture, and similar programs, there are literally thousands of civic organizations that sponsor or present performing arts. These include symphony orchestras, bands of various types, choral societies, opera or operetta companies, little theater groups, ballet and modern dance companies, and similar bodies.

In many communities, special-interest organizations in the arts are coordinated or assisted by umbrella agencies that help to promote their joint efforts. For example, the varied community arts organizations in the Province of British Columbia are assisted by the Community Arts Council of Vancouver. Founded in 1946 as the first such organization in North America, this council's purpose has been to stimulate awareness and support of the various arts in community life. Working closely with universities, museums, performing groups, and other public and voluntary agencies, the Vancouver Arts Council has succeeded in achieving a favorable climate for all of the arts. Joanne Cram writes:

> Acting as an umbrella organization, the CAC collects, disseminates and publicizes arts information via newsletters, press releases, arts directories, and media contact, as well as dispensing advice on funding, employment in the arts, and a myriad of other concerns. Representing some 150 arts organizations and a large individual membership, the Arts Council is an important liaison between governments and the arts community. It adjudicates provincial monies to non-professional arts groups, makes recommendations on behalf of artists and organizations to all three levels of government, and acts as a spokesman on the arts in Vancouver in response to queries both locally and from further afield.[14]

Service and Fraternal Clubs

Another category of nonprofit organizations that provide recreation for their own membership and sponsor programs for other population groups is community service clubs and fraternal organizations.

These include service clubs, such as the Kiwanis, Lions, or Rotary clubs, which represent the business and professional groups in the community, and which have as their purpose the improvement of the business environment and contributing to social well-being. A number of organizations established specifically for women—such as the Association of Junior Leagues, the General Federation of Women's Clubs, and the Business and Professional Women's Club—have similar goals.

The goals of such groups may include publicizing environmental concerns or issues, promoting the arts and other cultural activities, helping disadvantaged children and youth, and providing programs for disabled persons. For example, many Kiwanis organizations are involved in providing camping programs for special populations.

Promotional and Coordinating Bodies

A final type of nonprofit organization in the recreation, parks, and leisure-service field consists of associations that serve to promote, publicize, or coordinate activities within a given recreational field. In bowling, for example, the American Bowling Congress is composed of thousands of individuals whose careers or livelihoods depend on bowling, and who therefore seek to promote and guide the sport as aggressively as possible—including setting standards and regulations and sponsoring a range of major tournaments each year.

There are hundreds of such nonprofit organizations in the fields of travel, tourism, entertainment, and hospitality, covering the range from associations of theme park or water-play park management to associations of tour directors or cruise ship operators. As an example, the Outdoor Amusement Business Association works to upgrade standards and services throughout the carnival and outdoor show industry. Its membership consists chiefly of manufacturers and distributors of trailers, tents and tarps, games supplies, and similar materials, as well as operators of many different kinds of travelling shows, concessions, and carnivals.

Within local communities, there are often several types of coordinating groups that serve to exchange information, conduct studies, identify priorities, develop planning reports, provide technical assistance, train leadership, and organize events related to recreation and leisure. In some cases, these include councils of social agencies, including religious, health care, youth-serving, and social work groups.

SIGNIFICANCE OF NONPROFIT ORGANIZATIONS

Without question, agencies in the nonprofit sector make a major contribution to recreation and leisure-service programming in the United States and Canada. They differ from government organizations in the recreation field in a number of respects.

First, their goals are broader in that voluntary and special-interest organizations tend to have a variety of social goals and purposes, rather than recreation alone. At the same time, they usually serve a membership group restricted by age level, religious or other demographic characteristics, or special-program interest.

Organizationally, they tend to be more flexible in determining goals and objectives and in changing priorities and programs as social conditions warrant. From a financial point of view, they are less secure than government agencies, which can usually count on continued support from year to year. Instead, voluntary agencies are heavily dependent on membership fees and dues and on community giving either through United Fund, Red Feather, Community Chest, or similar campaigns or through their own fund-raising efforts.

Those voluntary agencies that are part of national federations or associations must frequently conform to goals, standards, and policies established by the larger body. On the other hand, since they are usually governed by local boards or trustees and must work directly with advisory groups, volunteers, and other community representatives, they must also respond fully to local needs.

COMMERCIAL RECREATION

We now turn to the type of recreation sponsor that provides the largest variety of leisure opportunities in the United States and Canada today—commercial, profit-oriented businesses. Such organizations have proliferated in recent years, and they run the gamut from small "mom-and-pop" operations to franchised programs and services, large-scale networks of health and fitness clubs, theme parks, hotel and casino businesses, manufacturers of games, toys, and hobby equipment, and various other entertainment ventures.

The Nature of Commercial Recreation

Commercial recreation is easily defined. John Bullaro and Christopher Edginton write:

> A commercial leisure service organization can be thought of as a business, the primary purpose of which is to serve people while at the same time making a profit. [It] has two basic characteristics. First, it creates and distributes leisure services; second, it has as its primary goal, profit.[15]

The profit motive distinguishes a recreation business from any other type of leisure-service sponsor. While public or voluntary agencies may charge for their services and may seek to clear a profit on individual program elements—or at least to run them on a self-sustaining basis where possible—their overall purpose is to meet important community or social needs. But the commercial recreation organization has as a *primary* thrust the need to show a profit on the overall operation.

In the past, there was considerable concern about the extent to which profit-minded entrepreneurs were attracting the public in their programs. During the early decades of the century, commercial sponsors were viewed as unscrupulous, and their offerings were often seen as destructive to society. Today, it is taken for granted that, without commercial businesses that provide a host of important and high-quality leisure experiences, our recreational opportunities would be sharply diminished.

It is a mistake, however, to assume that commercial recreation managers are interested *only* in making a quick profit. Instead, such for-profit enterprises as summer camps, health spas, fitness centers, commercially owned clubs, and instructional centers recognize that they are dependent on public trust and goodwill—and that this can best be achieved by delivering high-quality leisure opportunities or products and by being responsible members of the community.

Categories of Service

Commercial recreation services may be classified under several major headings, including the following:

1. admission to facilities, either for self-directed participation (as in the use of a rented tennis court or admission to an ice-skating rink or billiard parlor) or for participation with some degree of supervision, instruction, or scheduling (as in admission to a ski center with use of a ski tow);

2. organized instruction in individual leisure activities or areas of personnel enrichment, such as classes in arts and crafts, music, dance, or other hobbies;

3. membership in a commercially operated club, such as a for-profit tennis, golf or boat club;

4. provision of hospitality or social contacts, ranging from hotels and resorts to bars, singles clubs, or dating services, which may use computers, videotaping, telephone contacts, or other means to help clients meet each other. At the socially less acceptable end of this spectrum of services are "escort services," "massage parlors," and sexually oriented telephone conversation operations;

5. arranged tours or cruises, domestic or foreign, which may consist solely of travel arrangements or which may also include a full package of travel, housing accommodations, meals, special events, side trips, or guide services;

6. commercial manufacture, sale, and service of recreation-related equipment, including sports supplies, electronic products, boats, off-road vehicles, toys, games, and hobby equipment;

7. entertainment and special events, such as theater, rock concerts, circuses, rodeos, and other such activities, when they are sponsored by a for-profit business, rather than a nonprofit, tax-exempt group.

Commercial and nonprofit recreation agencies frequently offer exactly the same kinds of programs and services and often work closely together. A local YMCA may plan a member outing to a commercially operated ski center, or a company recreation club may schedule an employee trip through a commercial travel agency. Thus, the for-profit sector must be viewed as an integral part of the leisure-service system.

Commercial recreation sponsors today have the following characteristics: (1) they must constantly seek to identify and capitalize on recreational interests that are on the rise in order to ensure a constant or growing level of participation; (2) they are flexible and independent in their programmatic decisions, and are not subject to the policy strictures of a city or town council or an agency board of trustees; (3) they constantly seek to promote and create a climate of desirability by packaging a product that will appeal to the public, by systematic marketing research, and by clever advertising and public relations; and (4) to be successful, they depend on effective entrepreneurship—a creative and aggressive approach to management that is willing to take risks in order to make gains.

TRAVEL AND TOURISM

One of the major types of commercially sponsored recreation is the field of travel and tourism. This typically involves vacation and weekend pleasure travel, including: (1) foreign travel; (2) travel to a specific domestic destination, such as a major amusement complex or national park; (3) short trips to vacation homes or camping areas; and (4) travel that mixes business with pleasure. It involves several separate areas of activity and expenditure including *transportation* arrangements (airplane, railroad, ship, motorcoach, bicycle, and limousine); *accommodations* (hotel, motel, resort, camp, ship, motor home, and inn); *activities* (conventions, festivals, business and trade meetings, visiting attractions such as theme parks, sports events, other recreational involvements, and studies); and *shopping* (gift and souvenir shops, arts and crafts shops, shopping malls, and indigenous markets).

Commercial Recreation

Riverboat casinos (top) are only one part of the larger gambling industry throughout the United States. Exciting forms of commercial recreation include the "Loch Ness Monster" roller-coaster (center) at Williamsburg, Virginia's Busch Gardens, and "Paintball in the Poconos," (below) a newly popular warlike game.

To indicate how such expenditures have typically been allocated, *The Wall Street Journal* reported the breakdown of consumer spending on recreational travel over a ten-year period from 1975 through 1985. (See Table 11.2). It should be noted that the "transportation" category does not include automobile travel, which is obviously a popular means of transportation for millions of domestic tourists. If it were included, the total would be substantially higher.

While not all travel is carried on for pleasure purposes, as Table 11.3 shows, the other major motivations include a degree of tourism as a rule. When one visits friends or relatives, the visit often includes socializing and visiting recreational events or places. Business conventions frequently include parties, golf tournaments, or other entertainment events, and are often held in large hotels or motels in typically attractive settings that appeal to tourists.

Over the past three decades, the growing prosperity of many Americans and Canadians has made it possible for many vacationers to indulge themselves with expensive, elaborate forms of travel. Luxury cruise ships are no longer simply a vehicle for getting from one place to another. Instead, they have evolved into floating amusement parks, health spas, classrooms, and nightclubs. The major cruise companies have also developed huge new vessels, and are catering to younger and less affluent individuals with relatively inexpensive short-term trips.

For those who want something more exciting than a cruise, there are more than 5,000 outfitters, guides, and select travel agents who now package specialty tours stressing adventure and exotic environments. Travelers seeking to trek the Himalayas or to do battle with the

TABLE 11.2   Travel Spending in the U.S. (In billions of dollars)

	1975	1980	1985
Transportation			
Air	$10.30	$23.32	$33.53
Bus	1.17	1.94	2.39
Rail	.21	.38	.52
Lodging	13.00	26.83	42.02
Eating and Drinking	51.07	89.92	131.63
Entertainment/Recreation	18.05	28.33	49.36
Annual Total:	$93.80	$170.72	$259.35

Source: U.S. Travel Data Center, 1986.

TABLE 11.3   Travel by U.S. Residents by Selected Trip Characteristics

CHARACTERISTICS OF TRIPS	*Annual Totals (in millions)*		
	1981	1986	1993
Total Trips Taken Annually	587.2	540.9	648.2
Purpose			
Visit friends	201.3	214.7	194.5
Other pleasure	187.4	200.3	226.9
Business or convention	113.6	140.0	207.4
Other	84.9	37.3	19.4

Source: *Statistical Abstract of the United States* (1995), p. 265.

white waters of the Zambezi River are readily accommodated. It is possible to travel by boat, rail, plane, horse, bicycle, or dogsled—and either experience extreme risk and discomfort or do it with relative luxury and safety, in every corner of the world.

Less expensive and challenging destinations frequently include the national and state parks and historic and scenic monuments. Recently, there has been a trend toward creating tourist attractions out of the sites of national disasters—such as Mt. St. Helens in Washington—and transforming famous prisons into museums, as was done with the federal penitentiary in San Quentin, California.

As an illustration of the extent to which tourism has prospered internationally, the Paris-based Club Méditerranée, which had operated 47 vacation villages in 1970, expanded its multimillion-dollar network of informal adult resorts in Europe, North Africa, the Near East, the South Pacific, and the Caribbean to over 90 by the mid-1980s. Responding to changing demographic trends, it began to develop clubs with more conservative approaches to appeal to the growing family market that was replacing the young, "swinging" adults who first thronged to Club Méditerranée.

Recognizing the economic importance of travel and tourism, the first White House Conference on Travel and Tourism was held in Washington in October 1995 and was attended by over 1,700 travel industry executives and government officials.

Marketing Advances in Travel and Tourism

Perhaps more than any other form of recreation, travel and tourism illustrate the increasing sophistication that is used to market leisure experiences today. Within this highly competitive but immensely lucrative field, as M. Uysal has pointed out, it is no longer possible to think of tourists as a large, homogeneous market. Instead, the planning and marketing of travel and tourist destinations must take into account the highly specialized interests of vacationers, their tastes in comfort and service, and their growing awareness of values and costs.[16]

Marketing segmentation studies, Uysal notes, must assess the socioeconomic and demographic variables of potential tourists, as well as product-related variables (having to do with transportation, length of stay, recreation activity, and similar factors), psychographic variables like personal lifestyle and personality traits, geographical variables, and cultural factors such as religion, ethnic origin, and national customs.

New Links Between Public and Commercial Sponsors

It is becoming apparent that both public and commercial agencies have an important stake in promoting successful tourist programs today. In the past, tourism has been regarded as a commercial economic phenomenon rooted in the private business sector. Today, with cities, states, and entire nations competing to attract large numbers of tourists because of their contribution to the overall economy, both government agencies and private entrepreneurs have joined forces in planning and promoting tourist attractions.

In some cases, local park and recreation departments have begun to sponsor packaged vacation trips as part of their overall programs. John Crompton and Sarah Richardson cite the example of the Jackson County, Missouri, Park and Recreation Department, which has been aggressively programming such tours:

> They . . . operate an expanding year-round travel program which consists of over 30 long-distance tours to destinations such as Europe, Hawaii, and Canada, 15 one-to-two-day trips, and a series of one-day

"look around the town trips." [Included are] five high adventure trips to Canada (with camping, lake fishing, canoeing, and a wilderness black bear hunt).[17]

THEME PARKS AND ENTERTAINMENT COMPLEXES

Closely linked to the growth of tourism as a form of recreation has been the expansion of theme parks like California's famous Disneyland. This major entertainment complex was built at a cost of over $50 million and covers 65 acres in Anaheim, California. Its success led to the construction of a second major Disney complex, Walt Disney World, at Lake Buena Vista, Florida.

John Crompton and Carlton Van Doren point out that Disney effectively resurrected a dying industry. The outdoor amusement park, once an important form of popular entertainment, had become a cultural anachronism. Disney's contribution, they note, was to emphasize cleanliness, courtesy, and safety, in marked contrast to the traditional amusement park. Furthermore, they write:

> The theology of pleasure is reinforced by promotional messages. The theme park creates an atmosphere in which the visitor is likely to experience fantasy, glamour, escapism, prestige, and excitement. . . . Once inside the gate, the visitor is completely shut off from the outside world and immersed in an enjoyable recreational experience. . . . The theme parks' primary market is the family; theme parks keep a family involved and entertained for a whole day.[18]

New Kinds of Theme Parks

Other entertainment entrepreneurs soon followed the Disney example, and by 1976 at least three dozen parks of similar scale had been built around the United States. Some parks concentrate on a single theme, such as Opryland, U.S.A. in Nashville and the Land of Oz in North Carolina. Others incorporate moving rides through settings based on literary, historical, or international themes; entertainment; and typical amusement park "thrill" rides like rollercoasters and parachute jumps.

A number of theme parks that were opened in the following years illustrate a trend toward developing novel programming approaches. Sesame Place, a child-oriented park, opened in 1980 in Langhorne, Pennsylvania, by the Busch Gardens Corporation in cooperation with the Children's Television Workshop, involves a relatively new concept of participatory play and the use of environments that stimulate creative discovery. It has more than 60 outdoor play activities for children and an indoor Science and Game Pavilion with over 60 computer-type games and science exhibits.

Another unusual facility opened in the early 1980s by Busch Gardens was Adventure Island in Tampa, Florida. This 22-acre water park provides vistas of white sand beaches, glistening waters, palm trees, and tropical plants. Built on varied levels with complex waterfalls, slides, pools, cliffs, and rocks, Adventure Island provides an all-inclusive water experience where visitors slide down twisting water chutes, ride the waves in the Endless Surf pool, dive from cliffs, and enjoy other forms of aquatic play.

Expansion of Disney Entertainment Empire

However, none of the other chains of theme parks or outdoor play centers could match the diversity and inventiveness of the Disney planners. In 1982, they opened EPCOT (an acronym for Experimental Prototype Community of Tomorrow), an $800-million, 260-acre development that was conceived of as being more than a theme park. Instead, EPCOT was intended to be a place that would offer an environment where people of many nations might meet and exchange ideas. It consists of two sections: (1) Future World, which contains corporate pavilions primarily concerned with technology; and (2) World Showcase, which has international pavilions designed to show the tourist attractions of various nations around the world.

Since then, Disney World has added a number of other spectacular and imaginative attractions, including Typhoon Lagoon, River Country, the Disney MGM Studios and, in 1995, Blizzard Beach, Florida's first "snow-capped" water park; it is patterned after an Alpine ski resort, with mountain slopes covered with toboggan slides, ski jumps, and slalom runs. In 1983, a new Disneyland opened in Japan, on 202 acres of landfill in Tokyo Bay and featuring the traditional Disney characters and popular rides and attractions. While the new attraction is owned by a Japanese corporation, Disney provided technology and guidance during the construction and operation of Tokyo Disneyland for a share of the gross ticket take. Then, with the opening of Disneyland Paris, otherwise known as Euro Disney, the company created the largest theme park in Europe. While it was initially resisted and had to revise its approach to suit French and European patrons, by 1995 Disneyland Paris began to return its first sizable profits.

However, Disney's influence on leisure goes far beyond the theme park ventures. Its highly successful film studios—with blockbuster successes like *The Lion King* and *Pocahontas*—and its record companies, television networks, sports teams, and publishing, video and other multimedia interests constitute an unprecedented entertainment giant. With its $19 billion merger with Capital Cities/ABC in 1995, the Walt Disney Company affirmed its status as the most powerful entertainment empire in the world—and a dominating force on leisure involvement everywhere.[19]

Other Fun Centers

In heavily populated metropolitan areas throughout the United States, other entrepreneurs have developed a variety of indoor fun centers, ranging from children's play, gymnastics, and exercise chains to family party centers, video game arcades, and huge restaurants with game areas. Typifying the latter, Dave and Buster's, an immensely successful chain of adult "fun-and-food" offerings in Dallas, Houston, Atlanta, Chicago, and Philadelphia, offers a host of simulated fun experiences: golf, motorcycling, race car driving, space combat, and virtual reality among others.

Similarly, the new children's and family play centers that have been established in thousands of suburban neighborhoods and shopping malls around the United States offer a combination of computer and video games, billiards and other table games, miniature golf, entertainment by clowns and magicians, music, and popular fast-food refreshments. Offering packaged birthday parties and other family play services, they illustrate commercial recreation's success in providing attractive play activities that have supplanted more traditional home-based and "do-it-yourself" kinds of recreation.

PARTICIPATION IN OUTDOOR RECREATION

Closely linked to travel and tourism is the broad field of outdoor recreation—defined as those leisure activities that depend on the outdoor environment for their special appeal or character.

Often, as Table 11.4 shows, surveys of outdoor recreation pursuits also include sports activities that are predominantly carried on outdoors. The peak age brackets for participation in most of these sports and outdoor recreation activities are the 25- to 34-year-old and 35- to 44-year-old age groups. Reflecting the fact that many of these activities are clearly part of commercial recreation—in terms of the purchase of equipment, travel, or access to recreational settings—the highest participation totals are found among those with incomes between $50,000 and $75,000 a year.

Typically, 37.9 million fishing licenses and 31.6 million hunting licenses were purchased annually in the mid-1990s. Overall, spending on all types of sports and outdoor recreation equipment rose from $16 billion a year in 1980 to $46 billion in the mid-1990s.[20]

Boating represents a major segment of the outdoor recreation commercial market, having had annual retail sales in the early 1990s in excess of $17 billion—with about $6 billion spent strictly on boats and another $2 billion spent on motors, trailers, and accessories. Dwayne Hollins writes:

The number of registered boats in the United States and U.S. territories is expected to grow to 14 million by the year 2000. Since more than one-half of the U.S. population lives within 50 miles of navigable

TABLE 11.4   Participation in Selected Sports and Outdoor Activities

ACTIVITY	ALL PARTICIPANTS	MALE	FEMALE
Aerobic exercising	24.8	3.5	21.3
Backpacking	9.2	6.2	3.0
Baseball	16.6	13.4	3.2
Basketball	29.6	21.3	8.3
Bicycle riding	47.9	24.5	23.4
Bowling	41.3	20.7	20.6
Calisthenics	10.8	4.5	6.2
Camping	42.6	23.1	19.5
Exercise walking	64.4	21.0	43.3
Exercising with equipment	34.9	16.9	17.9
Fishing—fresh water	45.3	30.4	14.9
Fishing—salt water	12.0	8.3	3.7
Football	14.7	12.9	1.8
Golf	22.6	17.2	5.4
Hiking	19.4	10.7	8.7
Hunting with firearms	18.4	16.3	2.1
Racquetball	5.4	4.1	1.2
Running/Jogging	20.3	11.4	8.8
Skiing—alpine/downhill	10.5	6.5	4.0
Skiing—cross-country	3.7	1.7	2.0
Soccer	10.2	6.5	3.7
Softball	17.9	10.4	7.5
Swimming	61.3	27.7	33.6
Target shooting	12.8	10.2	2.6
Tennis	14.2	8.3	5.9
Volleyball	20.5	9.8	10.7

Source: *Statistical Abstract of the United States* (1995), p. 260. Reports participation more than once, during preceding year, in millions.

waters, it is estimated that more than 73 million people participated [in a recent year] in at least one boating activity—canoeing, houseboating, waterskiing, fishing or cruising.[21]

Pursuits like backpacking and camping are carried on predominantly in publicly owned forests, parks, wilderness areas, lakes, or reservoirs, while other activities like skiing tend to be done chiefly in commercially operated areas.

Camping as a Form of Commercial Recreation

Residential camping is another important segment of the outdoor recreation market. Today, there are approximately 11,000 resident camps, of which about 2,500 are accredited by the American Camping Association, as well as many other short-term or nonresidential camps. Although these may be sponsored by various types of agencies, a substantial number are privately owned and operated on a commercial basis.

In addition to the typical summer camp programs for children and youth, which operate on a fixed site and offer a variety of outdoor recreation, sports, social, and cultural activities, there are a growing number of "specialty" camps. These include camps that concentrate on high-level sports skills, music, art, science, computer study, and similar interests; camps for the overweight; trip-and-travel camps that may involve extensive travel throughout the United States and Canada or even abroad; camps for disabled or elderly persons; and other year-round camping programs for varied age groups.

High-Risk Outdoor Recreation

In addition to traditional forms of outdoor recreation, the more exotic, high-risk forms of leisure activity have also been steadily gaining in popularity, often under commercial sponsorship. Diana Dunn and John Gulbis described this trend at an early stage:

> Parachuting, mountain climbing, motorcycling, auto racing, white water canoeing, hotdogging, snowmobiling, and spelunking are among the risk recreation activities which have gained devotees during recent years. Between 1971 and 1973, the Southern California Hang Glider Association increased from 25 to 4,000 members; by 1975, an estimated 25,000 hang gliding buffs nationwide were trusting their fates to the whims of cliff and mountainside air currents. Hot-air balloon pilots, registered by the Balloon Federation of America, increased from 5,000 to 15,000 between 1963 and 1973.[22]

This trend has continued through the 1980s and 1990s as outdoor recreation enthusiasts have sought out more extreme forms of exciting play—often with sophisticated and expensive equipment. Brad Wetzler writes:

> Bungee-jumping, speed rock-climbing and sky-surfing (leaping from a plane wearing a snowboard-like contraption while your partner videotapes your acrobatics in midair for earthbound judges) have big appeal for sports fans these days. . . .
>
> What has happened to the way we relate to the outdoors? Americans are in pursuit of new and bizarre ways to appreciate nature—or simply themselves. "Extreme" is the word that marketers in the booming outdoors industry like to use to describe the trend. We big-wall rock climb, big-wave surf, adventure snowboard and underwater hang glide.[23]

Technological Play   As examples of the use of high-tech equipment in outdoor recreation and sports, hunters today may rely on advanced "prey acquisition" systems, such as bird-calling flutes or cassettes, "bionic" earphones and infrared binoculars for night vision, sensors for trail monitoring of wildlife, and a host of new kinds of fishing gear for attracting and catching watery game. Some forms of outdoor play have military associations that reflect the historic linkage of hunting and warfare. Many outdoor hobbyists today enjoy enacting "combat" or "assassination" games, using "paintball" guns or other types of sophisticated weaponry and protective gear. Carried to an extreme, some military or war game buffs collect more exotic gear, as shown in a Christmas catalogue that offers the following:

> Viper rifle crossbows, medieval axes, Iroquois tomahawks, kung fu throwing knives, South African commando bayonets, [and other weapons or defensive equipment such as] a "Screaming Hot Venom" pepper gas guaranteed to drive off "grizzly bears, drunks, dope-heads and psychotics."[24]

At a less dramatic level, outdoor recreation also provides an excellent opportunity for enterprising individuals and businesses to develop new products and entrepreneurial services to meet leisure-consumer needs. Hunting and fishing, once carried on in public lands, or easily accessible farmlands, streams, and lakes, today often require special private preserves for high-quality sport. Thus, many landowners have developed unusual packages of hunting and fishing sites for commercial use by the public.

SPORTS AND GAMES

Without question, sports activities, in terms of both participation and spectator involvement, represent key leisure interests for most youth and adults today. Apart from amateur, school, and college play, there are professional sports, which have clearly become a form of big business. They are moneymakers, sponsored by powerful commercial interests and promoted by advertising, public relations, television, radio, magazines, and newspapers—and bolstered by the loyalty of millions of fans who identify closely with their favorite teams and star athletes.

In 1986, a new magazine of the sports business, *Sports Inc.*, reported that the sports industry had become the nation's twenty-fifth biggest form of enterprise. Among the key spending areas measured by Wharton Economic Forecasting Associates were

> leisure-and-participant sports, ranging from $4.3 million in Babe Ruth baseball team fees to $1.1 billion in ski-lift tickets, $3.9 billion in greens fees and $4.9 billion in health-and-fitness clubs. Equipment, clothing and footwear for players generated an additional $15 billion in revenues.[25]

Beyond these figures, gate receipts for college and professional sports brought in $3.1 billion, vendor sales amounted to $1.9 billion, sports-related advertising in print media cost $3.6 billion, and corporations sponsored $800 million worth of sports events. These figures attested to the tremendous popularity of sports in the United States and Canada, both as a form of active recreation for all ages and as spectator entertainment.

In the 1990s, the sports field has continued to grow, with the expansion of professional sports leagues, the emphasis on youth sports programs, and the spread of typically American sports, such as baseball, football, and basketball, to many other nations of the world. However, as sports have become more commercialized, with professional players receiving astronomical salaries and team franchises skipping from city to city, many fans have become disillusioned with the changing nature of sport.

Surveys of Participant Sports

While some sports, like bowling and racquetball, have gone through cycles of popularity and decline, most sports have increased steadily in public interest and participation over the past several decades. Traditional team sports, like baseball, basketball, and football, far outnumber lifetime sports, like golf or tennis, in school and college settings and in youth sports programs sponsored by nonprofit organizations.

Millions of boys and girls—as well as adults—take part in team sports through community-based organizations ranging from Little League and American Legion baseball to Biddy Basketball and Catholic Youth Organization leagues, public recreation department leagues, and even, in many cities, so-called bar leagues, in which players wear the uniform of their favorite saloon in sports such as soccer, rugby, flag football, and softball. Active participation statistics for several popular sports over the past two decades are summed up in Table 11.5.

Commercial Sponsorship   Commercial enterprises that offer specialized facilities for sports and games are becoming increasingly popular. Geoffrey Godbey writes that in some cases, such as bowling, the commercial sector is almost the sole provider of opportunity, although some colleges and Ys do operate bowling facilities.

> In others, such as tennis, the commercial sector sometimes overlaps the public and private non-profit sectors or may provide more specialized, elaborate facilities for the true tennis "nut" who is willing and able to pay for superior resources. Such operations may include swimming pools, tennis courts, fee fishing ponds and lakes, hunting preserves, golf courses, marinas, bowling lanes, skateboard centers, billiard parlors, ski centers, ice-skating rinks, racquetball centers, and many others.[26]

From the commercial investor's point of view, specialized facilities provide opportunities for great profit, but there are also decided risks involved. Numerous types of these facilities, such as indoor skating rinks, bowling centers, slot-car racing centers, video game arcades, and tennis centers, have enjoyed tremendous popularity and expansion—and then have rapidly lost their public following and attendance. Nonetheless, entrepreneurs keep seeking out new possibilities for participant sport facilities.

TABLE 11.5   Participation in Selected Sports: 1975 to 1993

ACTIVITY	UNIT	1975	1980	1985	1990	1993
Softball, amateur						
Total players	million	25	30	41	41	42
Adult teams	1,000	66	110	152	188	202
Youth teams	1,000	9	18	31	46	62
Golfers (one round						
or more)	million	13.0	15.1	17.5	27.8	24.6
Rounds played	million	308.5	367.7	454.7	502.0	498.6
Facilities	1,000	11.3	12.0	12.3	12.8	13.4
Tennis, amateur						
Total players	million	34.0	(NA)	33.0	31.0	22.0
Courts	1,000	130.0	(NA)	220.0	220.0	230.0
Tenpin bowling						
Total players	million	62.5	72.0	67.0	71.0	79.0
Establishments	1,000	8.5	8.5	8.2	7.5	7.1

Source: *Statistical Abstract of the United States* (1995), p. 259.
(NA means not available.)

Spectator Sports

Commercial and nonprofit sports overlap, as both professional and amateur leagues attract huge audiences today. Sports arenas and stadiums may be privately owned and operated or may be the property of universities, municipal governments, or stadium authorities. In some cases, they have been built on a cooperative basis, with city or county governments providing subsidies or long-term rentals to professional sports entrepreneurs.

Without question, viewing sports events in person or through television is a major leisure pursuit in the United States and Canada. Multimillion dollar contracts have become relatively commonplace for star athletes in such sports as baseball, basketball, football, and hockey, and even run-of-the-mill players in these sports earn hundreds of thousands of dollars a year. This has been made possible by television broadcasting of each of the major spectator sports during its own season, along with coverage of their championship playoffs and final events, such as the football Super Bowl, ice-hockey Stanley Cup, or baseball World Series. Despite television coverage, which may cut into attendance at "live" events, sports attendance has climbed dramatically over the past two decades.

New Arena Construction   With the immense growth of sports participation on amateur and professional levels, stadium facilities have become in part a measure of the success of a university's athletic teams—or the image of a city. As a university or civic gathering place, the stadium is expected to make an architectural statement or provide an image that the public will find appealing. In addition, new design features, such as club-level seating—which is usually merchandised to major corporations and wealthy individuals—provide substantial start-up revenue, with income from concessions and television also substantially increased.

In the dozens of new arenas and stadiums that are being built, commercial factors have influenced their design radically, both to increase their usage potential and to make them more attractive to fans and to the media. Contemporary facility designers are taking advantage of new construction possibilities offered by plasticized concrete, fabric roofing, and specialized steel products to provide maximum seating and visibility. New super arenas, such as the America West Arena in Phoenix, the Oregon Arena in Portland, the new Boston Garden, and Chicago's United Center, have been designed with extensive luxury boxes, sports bars and food courts, and shops with an endless variety of apparel and sports memorabilia—all geared to provide consumers with year-round access to major sports and entertainment events.

In city after city, major professional sports teams are moving—or threatening to move—to other locations where they can get more favorable deals in terms of state and local government assistance in building new stadiums or arenas with revenue-rich boxes and other commercial features. For example, in professional hockey:

> The National Hockey League is undergoing its own greed-fueled identity crisis. The Nordiques have abandoned their antiquated arena in Quebec City for a new one with lots of luxury suites in Denver, while the New Jersey Devils [who had played in Denver before they moved to the New York City area] are trying to clear the way for a move to a box-studded arena in the not particularly hockey-loving city of Nashville, Tennessee.[27]

Player-Management Conflicts   With immense revenues from television, preseason games, and the sale of team-related clothing and memorabilia, many professional team franchises have been on financial winning streaks, despite mounting payroll pressures.[28] Nonetheless, sustained strikes and failed negotiations between players and team owners in the mid-1990s resulted in the shutdown of both the professional baseball leagues and the professional hockey league—creating a crisis of professional sports that led many fans to regard the owners and players alike as greedy. *U.S. News & World Report* warned in February 1995 that the $1.9 billion baseball industry was in danger of suffering financial losses of debilitating proportions:

> Already, baseball's shutdown has exacted a huge price. The Players Association estimates that the strike has cost owners as much as $500 million. For their part, the players have forfeited $250 million in salaries. The collateral damage, ranging from lost income for cities to a drop in sales of baseball cards, has also been significant. According to a survey of mayors [in cities with professional teams] each of 669 missed games in the fall of 1994 cost host cities an average of $1.16 million [and] 1,249 full-and part-time jobs.[29]

Clearly, sports have become big business, on both the participant and the spectator levels. Television has been a key factor in making them so, and has influenced the nature of college and even secondary school sports. While they are nominally amateur, many college teams should no longer be seriously regarded as a form of cocurricular or recreational activity. Instead they are a kind of training ground, or minor league, for highly skilled performers, most of whom have been recruited into colleges because of their sports ability.

HEALTH AND FITNESS BUSINESSES

As Chapter 9 has shown, in the post–World War II era the pursuit of health and physical fitness became a major preoccupation of great numbers of Americans and Canadians. It provided the basis for much programming by public and voluntary recreation agencies and in employee recreation activities. It also had a major effect on commercial recreation trends in the form of health spas, privately operated racquetball centers, and related operations.

Two of the major appeals of jogging and running, swimming, the use of exercise machines, racquet sports, aerobic dancing, and "jazzercise" are that such activities can be carried on in a group setting and that they have a "fun" payoff. Unlike rigorous programs of conditioning or calisthenics, today many forms of fitness activity are programmed and presented to the public in an attractive social setting. In addition to offering the activities themselves—which often involve individualized exercise prescriptions, clinics, and special events or competitions—many fitness centers also provide indoor heated pools, lounges, small running tracks, saunas, weight rooms, whirlpool baths, and, in some cases, food and banquet facilities.

There is a new emphasis on co-recreational participation in many commercial health spas and fitness centers. Fitness centers have become a new and more popular "singles" meeting place—replacing singles bars as a place for young and middle-aged unmarried adults to meet.

So-called full-service clubs should be equipped to meet major fitness goals. The cardiovascular or aerobics component usually requires a pool for swimming laps, an indoor track, an aerobic exercise room, and treadmill or rowing machines. For strength and body toning, there should be free weights and variable-resistance equipment; in addition the club may sponsor special classes, including yoga. Qualified staff should be available to guide individualized exercise programs, and in some cases to supervise programs of rehabilitation based on medical or physical therapy prescriptions.

> ere is an illustration of how the fitness boom has expanded into new types of ventures. A number of major chains have moved into the "kiddie exercise" field. Regular workouts, in some cases for infants as young as six weeks, are offered at many community centers, health clubs, and local Ys. Viewed as a sort of "headstart" program for physical education, such classes promote motor skills, balance and flexibility and introduce children to varied equipment, such as giant balls, hoops, slides, mats, and trampolines. Their sponsors point to the high rate of failure of U.S. children in standardized physical fitness tests and have been successful in selling the American public on their value. During the 1980s, such children's exercise chains as Playorena and Gymboree expanded steadily through franchising—with hundreds of local centers and many thousands of young participants. The Gymboree chain has also been opening stores that sell expensive playsuits, exercise cassettes for children, and indoor exercise equipment.
>
> Child development experts have been critical of these kiddie exercise ventures, pointing out that they are not necessary for normal physical development, and that they illustrate the tendency—particularly among well-to-do, socially ambitious parents—to push children to achieve at too early an age. Recently, such criticisms have resulted in child fitness centers toning down their physical fitness theme, and instead stressing family togetherness and social interchange.

GROWTH OF ELECTRONIC ENTERTAINMENT

Without question, the most significant influence on the use of leisure has been television and the varied forms of electronic entertainment that followed it.

A Nielsen survey published in 1975 reported that 97 percent of American homes had TV sets, with 41 percent having two or more sets. By the late 1980s, television-watching had diversified with more than 45 million homes subscribing to cable television and 23 million to pay-television. Television-watching in American homes had reached a new high, averaging six hours and 48 minutes a day.

However, the most striking wave of popularity in the 1980s involved the home-viewing of rented films on videocassette recorders (VCRs). *U.S. News & World Report* pointed out in 1988 that 57 percent of all American households owned VCRs and that the number of videotape rentals had increased from 706 million in 1984 to 2.28 billion in 1987.

These trends, combined with others, such as personal computers combining the capability for business and home-management functions with instructional uses and video-game play, and sophisticated new forms of stereo equipment with laser-equipped turntables and tape-deck

TABLE 11.6   Nielsen Survey of Internet Users (1995)[30]

---

37 million, or 17 percent of the U.S. and Canadian population 16 and older, have access to the Internet.

24 million used the Internet in the past three months.

They spend an average of five hours and 28 minutes on the Internet per week.

34 percent are women.

66 percent reached the Internet from work.

25 percent of World Wide Web users have incomes of more than $80,000.

---

systems using digital recording methods, have revolutionized home entertainment. They have also radically influenced the nature of family life in millions of homes—and have cut sharply into other forms of leisure-time activity. For example, television watching displaced attendance at movie theaters, which dropped from about 3.4 billion admissions in 1948 (the year that major television networks got under way) to about 1.1 billion a year in the late 1960s. By the mid-1990s, annual movie attendance climbed slightly, to 1.24 billion a year. It is clear that participation in many other forms of recreation also dropped drastically because of television.

Where there is interaction, as in video games, too often it is between the watcher and the machine—as in "interactive" toys that can shoot at on-screen characters who electronically shoot back. For example, Mattel developed a new toy, the PowerJet XT-7 plane, which interacts with a children's television show, "Captain Power and the Soldiers of the Future." If Junior's too slow on the draw, "Lord Dread" fires back from the TV set and triggers the ejection of the pilot from the child's plane. Another manufacturer, SEGA Games Systems, developed a set of cartridges in which children may "play" at pro wrestling, football, road racing, and other contests, using a master video game system.

As a recent extension of such forms of play, CD-ROMs—the irridescent $4\frac{1}{2}$-inch discs that took over the music business and then invaded the home computer market—provide multimedia packages of words, images, and sound and permit users to tailor the communication experience to meet their individual needs or interests. In terms of interactive music CD-ROMs, for example, the listener may select various exotic instruments and blend them together, create videos by mixing clips from various sources, control the tempo, style, and sequence of performance, transcribe melodies, and add harmonies.

A major innovation of the 1990s was the Internet, a global network of computers linked to high-speed data lines and wireless systems. The World Wide Web is a hypermedia information storage system linking resources around the world, with more than 100,000 businesses and individuals having Web sites or home pages. Users can travel the world with little more than a local phone call and almost any computer and modem—using such online services as America Online, CompuServe, NETCOM, the Microsoft Network, or Prodigy.

Through the Internet, people can explore personal, business, or leisure interests and make friends around the world by "surfing" through a limitless variety of sources. The use of electronic bulletin boards has combined with traditional coffeehouse culture, in that cyberpunks today in a network of cafes in cities like San Francisco can meet electronically and share personal interests and ideas—often while maintaining their anonymity.

HOBBIES, GAMES, AND CRAFTS

Forty percent of all Americans are reported to take part in varied hobbies, ranging from ceramics, quilting, candle making, weaving, wood carving and similar crafts to gourmet cooking, writing poetry, and a host of other pursuits. For example, it has been estimated that close to 80 percent of U.S. households have gardens, and the *Statistical Abstract of the United States* reports that gardeners spend $22.4 billion annually on their horticultural activities.

Sixteen million Americans collect stamps, about six million regularly take part in dancing classes or clubs, and three million are active photographers. As of the early 1980s, more than half of the nation's households had pets, with the total care of dogs, cats, and other domestic animals (including food, cosmetic grooming centers, veterinarians' bills, and luxury pet accessories) amounting to an $8-billion industry. By the mid-1990s, annual spending on pets had risen to over $20 billion.

Children's games and toys represent $14 billion in annual retail sales, and hobby kits are a $2-billion industry today. It has been noted that, as more expensive forms of recreation are cut back during periods of economic recession or depression, home-based hobbies, games, and crafts appear to increase in sales, with people determined to create their own, less costly pleasure.

CULTURAL AND EDUCATIONAL PROGRAMS

Another area of commercially sponsored leisure activity today involves varied forms of cultural and entertainment programming, including both the performing arts and noncredit adult education and personal development workshops. The percentages of adult Americans who engaged in various forms of cultural activity—as either participants or audience members—during a recent year are shown in Table 11.7.

Performing arts programs in theater, music, and dance are often sponsored by nonprofit, community-based cultural organizations, including symphony and opera companies, university theater centers, and similar bodies. However, the most *popular* live entertainment programs, such as rock concerts, musical theater, and comedy shows, tend to be provided by commercial entrepreneurs on a for-profit basis.

Youth and adult education programs providing varied forms of cultural, self-development, and creative activities have also expanded greatly in recent years. Typically, many school systems, college adult education departments, and voluntary agencies like the YMCA and YWCA sponsor extensive lists of classes in hobby activities, arts and crafts, current events, life skills, foreign languages, investing and personal finance, and similar subjects.

In addition, there are many privately operated, for-profit dance schools, art and music classes, and similar programs that constitute a form of commercial recreation sponsorship. In some cases, such ventures are combined with resort, conference, or family camping programs to offer a cluster of educational and cultural vacation packages.

Another example of a commercially operated adult education program is The Learning Annex, an unusual presentation of short-term courses and workshops that evolved over a period of six years from a $5,000 investment to a multimillion dollar operation with over 300,000 people registering for classes in a recent year. With wholly owned subsidiary programs in a number of

TABLE 11.7   Participation/Attendance Rates for Cultural Arts and Related Activities (Adults 18 and older)

PERCENTAGE WHO ENGAGED IN ACTIVITY AT LEAST ONCE DURING PRECEDING YEAR		PERCENTAGE WHO ATTENDED EVENTS AT LEAST ONCE DURING PRECEDING YEAR	
Playing classical music	4	Jazz performance	11
Modern dancing	8	Classical music event	13
Pottery work	8	Opera	3
Needlework	25	Musical play	17
Photography	12	Non-musical play	14
Painting	10	Ballet	5
Creative writing	7	Art museum	27
Buying art work	22	Historic park	35

Source: U.S. National Endowment for the Arts and *Statistical Abstract of the United States* (1995), p. 263

major cities, including San Diego, New York, Chicago, Houston, Atlanta, Philadelphia, and Washington, D.C., The Learning Annex concentrates on the sometimes practical, sometimes fanciful interests of young and middle-aged urban adults. A recent Washington, D.C., catalogue of offerings, for example, included such subjects as : "Sushi and Sashimi," "Gourmet Cuisine in 15 Minutes," "Hair Loss: Getting All the Facts," "A Grammar Workshop," "How to Buy a House," "How to Marry Someone Stable," "Hot-Air Ballooning," "Catering for Fun and Profit," and "How to Land a Part in T.V. Commercials."

ECONOMIC IMPACT OF COMMERCIAL RECREATION

As Chapter 1 has pointed out, personal consumption expenditures on recreation in the early to mid-1990s amounted to over $300 billion a year—comparable to what is spent in the United States on public education and more than is spent on the nation's defense. However, this impressive figure, compiled by the U.S. Department of Commerce and published in the *Statistical Abstract of the United States,* does not give a complete picture of leisure spending today. For example, it does not include: (1) expenses related to forms of recreational participation in such areas as sports, travel and tourism, outdoor recreation, and varied illicit or marginal forms of play; or (2) the operational costs of many types of leisure-service organizations.

During the 1980s, *The Wall Street Journal* reported that Americans spend about $260 billion a year on travel—with surveys showing that two-thirds of domestic travel is carried out for pleasure or social purposes (to visit family and friends). Based on this analysis, tourism spending at the time amounted to about $175 billion a year, a sum that has risen dramatically over the past decade in terms of the expansion of cruise travel and overseas tourism. Yet, other than references to sightseeing guides and buses or the possible inclusion of tourism under a minor "miscellaneous" heading, pleasure travel is not counted at all in the *Statistical Abstract's* summary.

Vast amounts are spent by boating, hunting, fishing, and camping enthusiasts, but in the *Statistical Abstract* this area of participation is touched on only in terms of the purchase of sports equipment and boats and admission to "shooting places." Similarly, sports spending is analyzed with respect to the purchase of equipment and admissions to spectator sports events—but other costs of participation related to memberships, registration, training, travel to sports events, care of sports injuries, or even the purchase of sports memorabilia are not tallied.

Finally, the *Statistical Abstract* does not include spending on such marginal forms of leisure activity as gambling (other than parimutuel net receipts), drinking, use of illicit drugs, and commercialized sex. While accurate figures in a number of these areas are difficult to obtain, in the late 1980s various study groups or federal agencies reported the following estimates: spending on alcohol, $45 billion; purchase of narcotics, $100 billion; commercialized sex (including the pornography industry and varied forms of prostitution), $10 billion; and gambling, including racetrack betting, casino gambling, lotteries, and other forms of sports betting and games of chance, $150 billion. While some authorities might prefer not to regard such activities as recreation from a moral perspective, in the public's view they are clearly leisure activities undertaken for pleasure—and they amount to an estimated total of $305 billion annually.[31]

When all of these sums are combined with the *Statistical Abstract's* estimate of $304 billion, annual spending on leisure is probably closer to $750 billion. Indeed, an analysis published by the Academy of Leisure Sciences indicated that a *trillion* dollars a year is spent on recreation.[32] While it is possible that some spending categories were counted twice, the final sum is impressive—and the greatest portion of it reflects commercial recreation enterprises.

PRIVATE-MEMBERSHIP RECREATION ORGANIZATIONS

A significant portion of recreational opportunity today is provided by private-membership organizations. As distinguished from commercial recreation businesses—in which any individual may simply pay an admission fee to a theme park, for example—private-membership bodies usually restrict use of their facilities or programs to individual members and their families and guests.

Within the broad field of sport and outdoor recreation, there are many organizations that offer facilities, instruction, or other services for activities such as skiing, tennis, golf, boating, and hunting or fishing. Such organizations frequently exist as independent, incorporated clubs that own their own facilities, with policy being set by elected officers and boards and with the actual work of maintenance, instruction, and supervision being carried out by paid employees.

A major characteristics of many such organizations is their social exclusiveness; membership policies screen out certain prospective members for reasons relating to their expected compatibility with current members. Many country clubs, golf clubs, and tennis clubs discriminate against members of certain races or religions, although application of their policies is often arbitrary and contradictory.

It is important to recognize that although the ostensible function of such private organizations is to provide sociability as well as specific forms of leisure activity, the clubs also provide a setting in which the most powerful members of American communities meet regularly to discuss business or political matters and often reach informal decisions or plans for action. Those who are barred from membership in such clubs are thus excluded also from this behind-the-scenes, establishment-based process of influence and power.

In the late 1970s and early 1980s, such organizations received more public scrutiny, as the U.S. Senate Banking Committee initiated an investigation of the payment of employee membership dues to private clubs and social organizations by financial institutions. It was found that women as well as blacks and other ethnic minorities were frequently excluded from private clubs.

In a number of cases, national membership organizations have been compelled to open their membership rolls to minority-group members because of lawsuits that have threatened them with withdrawal of tax-exempt status. However, as recently as the late 1980s and early 1990s, some organizations, such as Rotary International, continued to do battle in the courts to maintain their sexually discriminatory policies, and have expelled member clubs that have yielded on the issue. In 1987, at a time when women made up 44 percent of the workforce and 37 percent of managers and executives, *U.S. News & World Report* commented that to exclude them from an organization designed for business promotion seemed "fusty" and old-fashioned. Yet,

> What surprises critics is not that some men's clubs are grudgingly cracking open their doors. It's that the issue continues to be debated at all—and with such ferocity.[33]

Residence-Connected Clubs

Other types of private membership recreation organizations continue to flourish—particularly in connection with new forms of home building and marketing. Many real estate developers have recognized that one of the key selling points in home development projects is the provision of attractive recreational facilities. Thus, tennis courts, golf courses, swimming pools, health spas, and similar recreation facilities are frequently provided for the residents of apartment buildings, condominiums, or one-family home developments whether the residents are families, "singles," or retired persons.

An important trend in American society has been the rapid growth of housing developments in the suburbs, with community associations that carry out such functions as street cleaning, grounds maintenance, security, and the provision of leisure facilities such as tennis courts, golf courses, and swimming pools. Once found chiefly in the Southwest, such developments and community association have now spread throughout the United States. In 1970, there were 10,000 such associations. But, writes Diana Schemo:

> In 1990 there were 130,000 associations housing 32 million Americans in arrangements as varied as co-op apartment buildings, condominiums and walled neighborhoods of free-standing houses. All these arrangements share a reliance on homeowner boards to provide services and govern residents. By 2000, the [estimate is that] the associations will number 225,000.[34]

Although such real estate developments tend to be expensive and thus intended chiefly for affluent tenants or homebuyers, there are exceptions. For example, a giant apartment development in Brooklyn, New York, known as Starrett City, was constructed in the mid-1970s to serve middle-income tenants drawn from varied ethnic populations—approximately half were of black, Hispanic, and Asian origin. Its thousands of residents enjoy a huge clubhouse with meeting rooms, hobby, craft, and dance classes, and an extensive pool program and tennis complex, as well as numerous classes, teams, and special events through the year.

Vacation Homes

A specialized form of such residence-connected recreation is often found in vacation home developments. During the 1960s and 1970s, direct ownership and time-sharing arrangements for such homes became more popular, often in large-scale developments situated close to a lake or other major recreational attraction. Godbey writes:

> Many large corporations are now getting involved in recreation real estate, not merely developing the land (for home sales) but also offering the leisure amenities which have become necessary to make a success of such complexes. Ski trails, tennis courts, golf courses, swimming pools, and riding stables must be developed, as well as boutiques, night clubs, hotels, lodges, and other amenities. The developer typically is not interested in offering these facilities himself. His object is to raise the value of the surrounding land so that houses or condominiums may be built and sold at a profit.[35]

The baby boom, with millions of couples reaching the age and financial status at which they are able to afford vacation homes, has led to a rapid rise in the number of such developments. According to demographic researchers, some 4.8 million U.S. households owned vacation homes or time-share condominiums in 1994, with the expectation that the population group most likely to buy—35- to 54-year-olds with no kids at home—could double by the year 2,000.[36]

Typically, time-sharing apartments or condominiums in attractive vacation areas today cost as much as $15,000 to $20,000 for the right to use the facility one week each year. While this may seem expensive, it is minimal compared to the cost in vacation areas where the "jet set"—the wealthy elite of American society—enjoy their vacations. Illustrating the tendency to seek privacy in exclusive surroundings, a number of millionaires and billionaires who formerly enjoyed their vacations in Aspen, Colorado, left that area when it became too well known and popular. Today they fly their own jets to a stunningly beautiful mountain hamlet in Wyoming known as Saratoga. Members of the Old Baldy Club live in "cottages" that would be considered mansions anywhere else and enjoy privacy on an elegant golf course, at a well-stocked trout fishing stream, and in the festivities of a club known as Conquistadors del Cielo. When asked how much it cost to join the Old Baldy Club, a well-heeled local resident received the reply, "If you have to ask, you can't afford it."

Retirement Communities

Similarly, large retirement villages offer recreation and social programs for their residents; often they are actually called "leisure villages." A vivid example may be found in Sun City, Arizona (see page 110). Established in 1960, this community has about 45,000 residents, with an additional 25,000 living in nearby Sun City West. Marla Dial writes:

> At the Sundial—one of seven multimillion-dollar recreation centers here—residents can participate in everything from swimming and weight training to sewing, ceramics or art classes. The building also houses a mineral museum, photo lab and shuffleboard facilities. Eleven golf courses have been built over the years, and designers are making each one tougher, as they find that retirees are better golfers than they first thought.
>
> "You can do as little as you want to, you can do as much as you want to," said [one long-term resident]. "That's the life here. It keeps us moving, keeps us young." [37]

DIFFERENCES AND SIMILARITIES AMONG AGENCIES

This chapter has described the provision of organized recreation service today by three types of agencies: nonprofit, commercial, and private-membership. Clearly, each of these types of leisure-service organizations plays a different role in the overall recreational system, while at the same time interacting with and supplementing the other types.

Nonprofit voluntary agencies are generally most concerned with social values and with achieving constructive outcomes either for the community or for specific population groups. They see recreation both as an end in itself and as a means to an end, and are generally respectful of the environment and sensitive to gender- and race-related issues.

Private-membership organizations tend to center around more narrowly defined groups of participants—either in terms of socioeconomic class and lifestyle attributes or with respect to specific recreation interests. While they serve many millions of individuals, they are not generally concerned with promoting constructive social outcomes and, until recently, have often been identified with patterns of ethnic or gender discrimination. At the same time, they meet important leisure needs of many groups—such as the elderly, for example, in retirement communities.

Of the three types of sponsors, commercial recreation sponsors provide by far the greatest range of recreational services and opportunities today, and they represent a steadily growing sphere of organized leisure programming. In some ways, profit-oriented businesses are similar to public and nonprofit recreation and park agencies in terms of their offerings and the leisure needs they satisfy. What distinguishes them is their ability to commit substantial sums to developing facilities and programs that will attract the public. Huge corporations that are able to design and build theme parks, aquatic complexes, stadiums, health and fitness clubs, and other types of specialized equipment or programs obviously have a tremendous advantage in appealing to those who are able to pay the necessary fees and charges. Commercial recreation sponsors have harnessed technology and industry in creating spectacular environments for play and have used the most subtle and sophisticated public relations and advertising techniques to market their products successfully.

Recognizing these strengths, it is also necessary to point out that commercial recreation sponsors are motivated chiefly by the profit drive and therefore in *some* cases they create and stimulate public demand for leisure products that are morally or physically harmful. Commercial recreation sponsors also contribute to passive, overly spectator-oriented forms of leisure. However, Reynold Carlson and his co-authors stress both the positive and negative aspects of profit-oriented leisure enterprises in pointing out that television (as a prime example of commercially sponsored recreation)

> both shapes and is shaped by our culture, and . . . can be influence for the best as well as for the worst. The same statement applies to all types of commercial operations. Many commercial operators are aware of their social influence and attempt to contribute to the well-being of participants.[38]

FACTORS INFLUENCING COMMERCIAL RECREATION

It would be wrong to assume that recreation businesses are entirely free to provide any sort of leisure service they wish. Obviously, health clubs, camps, theaters, dance halls, gambling casinos, taverns, and a host of other facilities are subject to regulation under state, county, and municipal laws. These may include provisions regarding the sale of liquor, sanitary conditions, service to minors, safety practices, hours of operation, and similar restrictions. Many enterprises that require licenses may have these withdrawn if the operators do not conform to approved practices. Similarly, trade associations often influence practices, even though they may not have the legal power to enforce their rulings.

Public attitudes—as expressed in the press; through the statements of leading citizens, civic officials, or religious organizations—or, through consumer pressures—are often able to influence the operators in desired directions. For example, when Time–Warner was sharply criticized in the press for its promotion of violent, racist, and sexist "rap" music products, it divested itself of the involved recording label.

The competition of other organizations and products is another key factor in the management of commercial recreation agencies. Often, better products and services within a branch of the industry will serve to drive out inferior competitors. The entire field of recreation service and participation may be viewed as a marketing system in which the economic forces of supply and demand work so that, as a new product or service appears, existing products and services are threatened. Within this framework, there is a constant pruning and reshuffling of recreation enterprises as competing sponsors seek to maintain public interest and attendance.

INFLUENCE OF LEISURE-SERVICE PROFESSION

A final and as yet unmeasured influence on commercial recreation involves the recreation and park profession. In general, commercial recreation managers have not traditionally been identified with the leisure-service profession or the recreation movement as such. Yet, as it has become evident that this area represents a major source of potential employment for recreation graduates, more and more colleges and universities have instituted courses and specialized curricula in commercial recreation.

Similarly, the major professional organizations have begun to include commercial recreation elements in their publications and conferences. Separate segments of commercial recreation now have their own professional or trade associations, which are beginning to develop standards and strategies for successful practice. It seems probable that many commercial recreation operators will eventually be drawn more fully into the mainstream of the professional leisure-service field.

Many planners, researchers, and managerial personnel who have taken degrees in recreation, parks, and leisure studies have already found their way into the commercial recreation field. Undoubtedly, greater numbers of them will do so in the years ahead. As this occurs, it seems likely that profit-oriented leisure-service operators will become increasingly aware of the importance of their field to the community and will assume more social and civic responsibility. This would represent a major step toward complete coordination and integration of all organizations and professionals who seek to meet public recreational needs.

SUMMARY

As a logical extension of Chapter 10's description of the government's role in leisure-service programming, this chapter describes three other key players in the leisure field: (1) voluntary nonprofit organizations; (2) commercial recreation businesses; and (3) private-membership associations.

Voluntary agencies place their greatest emphasis on using leisure to achieve positive social goals. Several types of youth-serving organizations are described, including both sectarian and nonsectarian groups. Such agencies rarely consider themselves to be primarily recreation organizations; instead, they generally prefer to be regarded as educational, character-building, or youth-serving organizations. However, recreation usually does constitute a sector of their program activities.

A second type of nonprofit leisure-service agency consists of special-interest groups, which usually promote a particular area of activity in outdoor recreation, sports, the arts, or hobbies. Such groups, while they may include many enthusiasts as members, are often formed to promote business interests within the particular leisure specialization.

Commercial recreation businesses offer an immense amount of public recreational opportunities today in such areas as travel and tourism, outdoor recreation, sports, popular entertainment and the mass media of communication, hobbies, and crafts and toys. Their primary goal is to make a consistent profit, and in many cases they are huge, and highly diversified operations, such as the Walt Disney organization with its theme parks, resorts, and television, movie, and popular music components. From a social perspective, while many for-profit businesses offer constructive, high-quality programs, in some cases—as in sectors of the entertainment industry—they are believed to contribute to youth violence, sexism, and racial hostility.

The third type of organization described in this chapter, the private-membership association, includes a wide range of country clubs, golf clubs, yacht clubs, and other social or business membership groups that often tend to be socially exclusive. They represent a growing trend in the United States today, with millions of families now living in residential developments that have their own community associations to provide services, including recreation. This tends to limit their interest in, or dependence on, public, tax-supported recreation services.

Questions for Class Discussion or Essay Examinations

1. What are the major differences between voluntary nonprofit agencies and government departments providing recreation facilities and programs? Compare goals and objectives, funding, individuals or groups served, and program elements.

2. Define commercial recreation agencies and indicate several of the major categories of leisure services provided by such businesses. Select one major area of commercial recreation, such as outdoor recreation or travel and tourism, and describe trends in this field, the nature of service offered, and problems or issues connected to that particular recreation.

3. What is the unique role of private-membership organizations and what are some of the examples of this type of leisure-service sponsor? How do they differ from governmental, voluntary nonprofit, and commercial recreation agencies? Indicate some of the social issues that center around such private organizations.

Endnotes

[3] Carlton Yoshioka, "Organizational Motives of Public, Nonprofit, and Commercial Leisure Service Agencies," *Journal of Applied Recreation Research* (Vol. 15 No. 2 1990): 60.

[4] Adam Zagorin, "Remember the Greedy: Exploiting Their Tax-Exempt Status, a Number of Nonprofits Put Themselves Before the Poor," *Time* (16 August 1993): 36.

[5] *Statistical Abstract of the United States* (Washington, D.C.: U.S. Department of Commerce, 1995).

[6] "Girl Scouting, 64 Years Old, Is Changing," *New York Times* (8 March 1976): 29.

[7] *The First Fire We Light Is the Fire Within* (Brochure of Camp Fire Boys and Girls, 1995).

[8] *Report of Activities Committee* (Salt Lake City, Utah: Church of Jesus Christ of Latter-Day Saints, 1993).

[9] *Youth . . . Apostles to Youth* (New York: Catholic Youth Organization, Annual Report, 1967).

[10] *Agenda for Action: Priorities 1990–1995* (New York: Jewish Welfare Board, 1990).

[11] "Data Base: Little League," *U.S. News & World Report* (21 August 1995): 8.

[12] *Little League Baseball: Today's Youth, Tomorrow's Leaders* (Williamsport, Penn.: Little League Brochure, 1988): 3.

[13] "Data Base: Youth Sports," *U.S. News & World Report* (21 August 1995): 8.

[14] Joanne Cram, "People Power Works—The Arts Council Movement in British Columbia," *Recreation Canada* (July 1981): 7.

[15] Bullaro and Edginton, *op. cit.*, 17.

[16] M. Uysal, "Marketing for Tourism, A Growing Field," *Parks and Recreation* (October 1986): 61.

[17] John Crompton and Sarah Richardson, "The Tourism Connection: Where Public and Private Leisure Services Merge," *Parks and Recreation* (October 1986): 44.

[18] John Crompton and Carlton Van Doren, "Amusement Parks, Theme Parks and Municipal Leisure Services: Contrasts in Adaptation to Cultural Change," *Journal of Physical Education, Recreation and Dance—Leisure Today* (October 1976): 45.

[19] Geraldine Fabricant, "Walt Disney Acquiring ABC in Deal Worth $19 Billion: Entertainment Giant Born," *New York Times* (1 August 1995): 1.

[20] John Skow, "Business: Geared to the Max," *Time* (6 September 1993): 48.

[21] Dwayne Hollins, "Marinas are Big Business in Texas," *Parks and Recreation* (November 1992): 42.

22   Diana Dunn and John Gulbis, "The Risk Revolution," *Parks and Recreation* (August 1976): 12.

23   Brad Wetzler, "The New Extremists," *New York Times* (16 July 1995): 15.

24   Maureen Dowd, "Antlers, Boleros and Crossbows," *New York Times* (23 November 1991): 27.

25   "Sport Your Economy," *U.S. News & World Report* (7 December 1987): 59.

26   Geoffrey Godbey, *Leisure in Your Life: An Exploration* (Philadelphia: Saunders College Publishing, 1981): 80–81.

27   Steve Wulf, "How Suite It Isn't," *Time* (10 July 1995): 52.

28   "Playing the Money Game," *U.S. News & World Report* (15 May 1995): 59.

29   Jim Impoco, "Down to the Last Out?" *U.S. News & World Report* (13 February 1995): 66.

30   Julian Dibbell, "Nielsen Rates the Net," *Time* (13 November 1995): 121.

31   These figures are drawn from various trade journals, industry reports, and other publications issued between 1986 and 1990. As an example of how they may underestimate such leisure spending, recent reports on gambling indicate that it involves between $330 billion and half-a-trillion dollars. See William Safire, "Gambling Fever," *New York Times* (10 April 1995): A-15, and Gerri Hirshey, "Gambling Nation," *New York Times Magazine* (17 July 1994): 34.

32   Daniel Stynes, "Leisure—The New Center of the Economy?" in Geoffrey Godbey, Ed., *Issue Papers, 1993* (University Park, Penn.: Pennsylvania State University and Academy of Leisure Sciences, 1993): 11–17.

33   "Tap, Tap, Tap on the Clubhouse Door," *U.S. News & World Report* (11 May 1987): 72.

34   Diana Schemo, "Community Associations Thrive . . . ," *New York Times* (3 May 1994): B-6.

35   Godbey, *op. cit.*, 81.

36   "The New Vacation Home Bonanza," *U.S. News & World Report* (10 April 1995): 65.

37   Marla Dial, "At 35, A Model Retirement Community Finds Life Still Golden," Associated Press (8 January 1995).

38   Reynold Carlson, Janet MacLean, Theodore Deppe, and James Peterson, *Recreation and Leisure: The Changing Scene* (Belmont, Cal.: Wadsworth, 1979): 197.

twelve

12

Specialized Agencies: Armed Forces, Employee, Campus, and Therapeutic Recreation Service

[The purpose of military recreation is] to provide facilities and programs to enhance the physical and mental well-being of service men and women and their families. . . . To better support the armed forces mission of readiness, the primary objectives of MWR are tied to fitness, unit and community cohesion, family well-being, quality of life, and recreation awareness and outreach.[1]

As a profession committed to advocating an enhanced quality of life for individuals with disability, how can we impact on these attitudes and belief systems as we move toward full inclusion? . . . What particular contribution can the modality of leisure activities make to altering these attitudes of acceptance? Certified Therapeutic Recreation Specialists (CTRS) can serve a critical consultation role by helping to create environments which are supportive of clients currently based in the community or transitioning to community.[2]

---

[1] Sam Lankford and Don DeGraaf, "Strengths, Weaknesses, Opportunities and Threats in Morale, Welfare and Recreation Organizations: Challenges of the 1990s," *Journal of Park and Recreation Administration* (Vol. 10 No. 1 1992): 31–32.

[2] Janet Sable, "Efficacy of Physical Integration, Disability Awareness, and Adventure Programming on Adolescents' Acceptance of Individuals with Disabilities," *Therapeutic Recreation Journal* (3rd Quarter 1995): 207.

INTRODUCTION

We now examine four specialized types of recreation-delivery systems: *armed forces, employee, campus,* and *therapeutic recreation service* agencies. Recreation is not the primary function of these four categories of leisure-service agencies. The essential purpose of the armed forces is to defend the nation. The purpose of business concerns such as manufacturing, airline, or insurance companies is to meet public needs for a commodity or service and, in so doing, make a profit. The purpose of colleges, universities, and school systems is obviously to educate. Therapeutic recreation programs are usually part of larger institutions or agencies designed to provide medical treatment or rehabilitation services for individuals who are ill or have continuing physical or mental disabilities.

Yet, recreation has become a significant element within each of these types of organizations for reasons that are described in this chapter. In each case, its practitioners typically develop a philosophical framework and a set of programmatic strategies and techniques that will help their sponsoring organization to achieve its fundamental goals.

ARMED FORCES RECREATION SERVICE

For the past several decades, a major recreation-related function of the federal government has been the provision of facilities and programs for the armed forces, both in the continental United States and abroad. While these programs are government-sponsored and might therefore have been described in Chapter 10, they constitute a highly specialized type of leisure service and are therefore included in this chapter.

For many years it has been the official policy of the military establishment to provide a well-rounded "morale, welfare, and recreational program" for the physical, social, and mental well-being of its personnel. During World War I, Special Services Divisions were established to provide social and recreational programs that would sustain favorable morale, curb homesickness and boredom, minimize fatigue, and reduce AWOL (absent without leave) and venereal disease rates.

Today, each branch of the armed forces has its own pattern of recreation sponsorship, although they are all under the same Morale, Welfare and Recreation Program (MWR), which is administratively responsible to the Office of the Assistant Secretary of Defense for Manpower, Reserve Affairs and Logistics. They serve several million individuals, including active duty, reserve, and retired military personnel and their dependents; civilian employees; and surviving spouses of military personnel who died in active duty.

Goals and Scope of Armed Forces Recreation Today

Francis Kinsman presents the rationale underlying armed forces recreation's role, and the justification for its receiving fiscal support in a period of budgetary restraints:

[Military recreation programs] contribute to the readiness of the armed forces by enhancing physical fitness, leadership, military skills, unit cohesiveness and high morale.

During mobilizations such as Desert Shield/Desert Storm they provide our deployed military personnel with essential morale and recreational activities.

They assist in recruiting outstanding young soldiers, sailors, airmen and marines by portraying individual service members in a positive light and the military community as an attractive place to serve and live [and they support retention of personnel] by providing a high quality of life for both the military member and his or her family.[3]

Sam Lankford and Don DeGraaf summarize the scope of armed forces recreation today by pointing out that it serves more than 2.1 million active military personnel; more than 2.7 million family members ranging from infants to retirees; and more than 1.4 million National Guard and Reserve members who are eligible for recreation programs. They conclude that the military recreation system involves more employees, facilities, and expenditures than any other single federal, state, or local recreation delivery system.[4]

Program Elements

MWR programs include an extensive range of sports, fitness, social, creative, outdoor recreation, travel, entertainment, and hobby leisure pursuits. In the Air Force, for example, an extensive program of sports activities has typically included six major elements: (1) *instruction* in basic sports skills; (2) a *self-directed* phase of informal participation in sports under minimum supervision or direction; (3) an *intramural* program, in which personnel assigned to a particular base compete with others at the same base; (4) an *extramural* program, which includes competition with teams from different Air Force bases or with teams from neighboring communities; (5) a *varsity* program, which involves high-level competition with players selected for their advanced skills, who compete on a broader national or international scale; and (6) a program for *women* in the Air Force.

In addition to such programs attached to individual services, the armed forces promote an extensive range of competitive sports programs. Through interservice competition in such sports as basketball, boxing, wrestling, track and field, and softball, all-service teams are selected; armed forces teams are then chosen to represent the United States in international competition.

Fitness Programs   Health and wellness has become a major focus of armed forces recreation. To improve fitness levels of personnel, the Air Force has installed Health and Wellness Centers (HAWC) on each base; these centers are well-equipped and are staffed with leaders qualified to provide the following services: fitness and health risk assessments, exercise programming and weight counseling, stress management and smoking cessation assistance, and similar activities.

On some military bases, fitness is promoted through well-publicized and challenging special events. At the Marine Corps Base at Camp Lejeune, North Carolina, the Le Jeune Grand Prix Series features a number of competitive events that involve hundreds of service personnel in a European Cross Country race over natural terrain; a Tour d'Pain, a grueling endurance cycling race; a Masters Swim Meet; a Davy Jones Open Ocean Swim; a Toughman Triathlon, and other types of races.

Outdoor Recreation   Often outdoor program activities are keyed to the location of a base. For example, Fort Carson, Colorado, sponsors an extensive ski program that features an annual Ski Expo, with over 150 vendors and representatives of ski areas and average attendance of more than 5,000 skiing enthusiasts. Responding to widespread interest in mountain climbing and rock climbing, this Army base has constructed a 17,400-square-foot outdoor recreation center that features a 32-foot-high indoor climbing wall with the look and feel of natural rock, and climbing routes geared to different skill levels.

Recreation planners at Fort Hood, Texas, have developed a major outdoor recreation facility at Belton Lake that includes the following areas and services:

Sierra Beach, a sandy beach for swimming with 45 family picnic shelters, 10 large picnic pavilions, and facilities for jet skiing, wind surfing, fishing, water skiing, and party boating, as well as an enclosed fishing marina, a floating facility that accommodates 100 fishermen on the inside or 150 on outside decks.

Ten fully equipped cottages, several areas for tent camping and 53 recreational vehicle (RV) sites with full hookups, and extensive additional picnic facilities.[5]

Family Recreation   The Department of Defense has become increasingly aware of the need to provide varied family-focused programs to counter the special problems that may affect the spouses and children of military personnel. Particular emphasis is given to the need to serve military youth. Steven Waller and Asuncion Suren write:

Adolescents residing in military installations are confronted with the same range of social problems that occur within society as a whole. Crime, violence, substance abuse, the social environment and the unproductive use of leisure time are critical issues that confront military youth.[6]

As one response to this challenge, MWR planners have developed a Drug Demand Reduction Task Force, a program designed to combat substance abuse affecting at-risk youth on military bases and in communities where the bases are located. This program employs structured recreation activities including athletics and high-risk outdoor pursuits, day and residential camps, and other counseling and educational programs designed to build self-esteem, self-discipline, and leadership among youth—particularly in Marine and Navy base settings.

In order to meet family needs more effectively, many U.S. Army bases have developed Community Activity Centers (CACs). These facilities are based on a one-stop recreational shopping approach that has three key objectives: (1) to provide patrons with a wide range of recreational options; (2) to serve various age groups and skill levels; and (3) to maximize the use of facilities. McKeta describes programming based on the CAC concept at Fort Sam Houston, Texas:

In just one facility, a patron can buy a shirt, sign up for a tour, register for a class, buy a concert ticket, grab a snack, obtain information, rent a video, receive Army Community Service (ACS) counseling, and much more.[7]

In Wildflecken, Germany, military personnel and their dependents can play bingo, take art classes, join a computer users group, use the fitness center, record vocals with professional accompaniment, learn an instrument, attend dinner theater, check out recent bestsellers, or enjoy Mexican food while watching an NFL game on television.

On many bases, centers have been developed with an emphasis on providing lively social entertainment comparable to the offerings in civilian recreation settings. At the Naval Air Station at Lemoore, California, for example, the base's enlisted club, Squigglee's Nightclub and Cafe, was redesigned in 1994 to include a Rock and Roll Cafe, a 40-game high energy video arcade, a double 360-degree waterslide, a new sand volleyball area, and other attractions.

Community Relations   Many military bases in the United States and overseas place a high priority on establishing positive relationships between armed forces personnel and nearby communities.

Civilian MWR personnel working around the globe in such settings as Europe, Korea, and Central America, and even Saudi Arabia, Turkey, and Africa, seek to provide a wealth of outdoor recreational experiences and positive intercultural experiences with local residents.

> Activities for family members [overseas] may include living aboard a tall ship for a few days and learning how to work together and sail the coast of Holland or backpacking in the Swiss Alps. Soldiers and airmen learn teamwork, leadership, communication skills and technical skills . . . from a ropes course, playing paintball, rock climbing, kayaking, or rafting down an Austrian river . . . . [Our mission is also to] bridge the cultural gap and introduce the Americans to their new—albeit temporary—homeland by integrating activities and resources with those of the host nation.[8]

Recreation Facilities

MWR facilities on military bases may include an extensive range of structures and outdoor areas, as shown in Table 12.1.

Fiscal Support of Armed Forces Recreation

Military recreation has traditionally depended on two types of funding: *appropriated funds,* which are tax funds approved by Congress, and *nonappropriated funds,* which are generated on the military base through a combination of Post Exchange profits and other revenue from fees, rentals, and other recreation charges.

The Bureau of Naval Personnel in the Department of the Navy defines the different types of recreation funds generated by Navy personnel and their dependents to help provide financial support for their recreation activities. Specifically, these are

> monies received from Navy exchange profits, fees and charges placed on the use of recreation facilities and services or other authorized sources for the support of Navy recreation programs. Unit Recreation

TABLE 12.1   Typical Recreation Facilities on Military Bases[9]

SPORT AND FITNESS	RECREATION	LODGING	FOOD, BEVERAGE, ENTERTAINMENT	CHILD AND YOUTH CARE
Fitness center	Bowling center	Short-term	Club	Child development
Gymnasium	Marina	Hotel/Motel	Fast food	center
Racquetball/Squash	Golf course	Residential hotel	Bars/Pub	Teen center
court	Equipment rental	Recreational lodging	Night club	Youth center
Swimming pool	Arts and crafts center		Snack bar	
Outdoor track	Auto hobby center			
Playing field	Outdoor parks			
	RV park			
	Campground			
	Riding stable			
	Trap and skeet range			
	Archery range			

Funds are those which serve the recreation needs of individual ships, shore stations and other Navy activities. Composite Recreation Funds are those which serve two or more activities which share the same recreation facilities. Consolidated Recreation Funds are those which serve the recreation needs of several separate installations within a geographical area.[10]

Since such funds operate outside of the normal sphere of tax-appropriated monies, thorough control procedures have had to be instituted to ensure that they are not misused. In addition, a sophisticated approach to marketing programs and services has been developed. Under a policy introduced in the late 1970s—that programs be made as self-sufficient as possible with specific percentages of income to be derived from fees and charges for various program elements—new techniques for pricing, promoting, and placing recreation programs were developed.

In the late 1980s, the Department of Defense classified all MWR activities as either *mission-sustaining activities,* such as overseas entertainment, physical fitness centers, or temporary lodging facilities, or *business activities,* such as amusement machine centers, bingo, golf courses, marinas, and rod-and-gun clubs. Guidelines suggested that there be higher levels of fiscal support for more critical services, and lower support levels for purely recreational activities that have the potential for being self-sustaining.

New Fiscal Strategies

In the early and mid-1990s, growing numbers of base closures and budgetary cuts have compelled military recreation professionals to adopt new and even more business-oriented approaches to facilities development and program operations. Pat Harden, director of Navy recreation training at Patuxent River, Maryland, has pointed out recently that two prevailing orientations have generally guided armed forces recreation: (1) the quality of life approach that sees MWR recreation and club services essentially as an amenity, although deserving of Department of Defense support; and (2) the businesslike marketing approach that urges that all recreation services be viewed primarily as a commodity to be merchandised, with a minimum of social and mission support goals or constraints.

Instead, Harden argues, it is essential to define the important mission of MWR programs within the overall Department of Defense structure and to work effectively to achieve the goals related to this mission. He quotes a Defense Department official as follows:

Readiness is the cornerstone of this administration. A ready-to-fight force is linked intrinsically to the morale, sense of well-being, commitment and pride in the mission of each Service and family member. Our Morale, Welfare and Recreation programs play a direct role in developing and maintaining these characteristics within our force and are more important than ever during this time of transition, when profound changes are taking place that are having a powerful impact on Service members and their families.[11]

Increasingly, systematic research is being used within the military to evaluate the effectiveness of current operations, to identify new trends and needs within the armed forces, and to formulate effective strategies for the years ahead. For example, Lankford and DeGraaf have described the use of workshops—involving middle and top-level professionals working in Armed Forces recreation programs in Okinawa and Korea—to gather this kind of information (see Table 12.2).

TABLE 12.2 Emerging Leisure Trends in Okinawa Marine Corps MWR That Influence Recreation-Service Delivery in the 1990s[12]

TRENDS	YOUTH SERVICES	SPORTS	BOWLING/ GOLF	ARTS & CRAFTS	ADMIN.	TOTALS*
Emphasis on wellness	19	9	—	—	31	59
Need for new facilities	13	14	16	4	—	47
Emphasis on quality programs	17	—	12	3	—	32
Need for staff training	—	—	—	—	23	23
Family-oriented activities	—	—	—	—	17	17
The ability to manage resources	—	10	—	5	—	15
More sophisticated customer	—	7	—	—	8	15
Lifelong participation	—	4	10	—	—	14
Reduced funding	10	—	—	—	—	10
Increased interest in computers	—	—	—	10	—	10
More interagency cooperation	—	—	8	—	—	8
Need for arts and crafts day camps	—	—	—	8	—	8
Expanded college credit opportunities	—	—	—	—	8	8

Note: The numbers indicate the importance assigned by personnel within each of the five service specializations (Youth Services, Sports, etc.) to each of these trends, based on a weighting system.

Professionals on all levels within the four major branches of the Department of Defense are using sophisticated planning and evaluation methods similar to these workshops to respond positively to the challenges facing MWR military units during this period of rapid change.

EMPLOYEE RECREATION PROGRAMS

A second important category of specialized recreation delivery systems involves the role of business and industry in providing programs of recreation and related personnel services.

Background of Company-Sponsored Programs

Employee recreation (formerly called "industrial recreation") began in the nineteenth century, but did not expand rapidly until after World War II. In 1975, *The New York Times* reported that 50,000 companies were spending $2 billion a year on recreation-related programs. Recent reports indicate that 4,000 businesses and other types of institutions are affiliated with the National Employee Services and Recreation Association (NESRA), with a substantial number belonging as well to the Association for Worksite Health Promotion.

While the providers of employee services and recreation originally were manufacturing companies and other industrial concerns, today many different types of organizations also sponsor employee activities. They include such diverse groups as food market chains, airline companies, insurance concerns, hospitals, and government agencies.

Goals of Employee Recreation

The major goals of the institutions providing such programs and services include the following.

Improvement of Employer-Employee Relations   Earlier in America's industrial development, there was considerable friction between management and labor that often resulted in extended and violent strikes. A major purpose of industrial recreation programs at this time was to create favorable employer-employee relationships and instill a sense of loyalty among workers. Today, with relative peace in most industries, this remains a significant goal of employee recreation. It is believed that such programs tend to create a feeling of belonging and identification among employees, and that group participation by workers at various job levels contributes to improved worker morale, increased harmony, and an attitude of mutual cooperation.

In the intense competition that characterizes business in the 1990s and with the declining morale of many employees in a period of downsizing, these goals have become particularly important. A survey of the nation's senior executives drawn from 1,000 of America's largest corporations has concluded that building the morale and productivity of employees should be given a high degree of priority and that effective employee service and recreation programs represent a useful means of accomplishing this task. Jerry Junkins, Chairman and Chief Executive Officer of Texas Instruments Inc. in Dallas, Texas, expresses this view:

> We see employee services and recreation as one part of a total package that includes competitive salaries, benefits and health promotion services and activities. All of these are designed to let our people know we value them, and we view them as the key contributors to our company's success. . . . We've tried to design our ES & R programs to address the total well-being of our employees and their families by providing them with programs that can enhance their physical, mental and emotional health.[13]

Directly Promoting Employee Fitness and Efficiency   Corporations large and small today have become concerned about maintaining the health of their employees. One reason may be the skyrocketing costs of health insurance. It was reported in 1988 that General Motors alone was spending some $2 billion annually on medical care coverage for its 2.3 million employees and retirees and their dependents. Beyond this, it costs huge sums for companies to replace middle- and upper-level managers who suffer heart attacks or other fatal illnesses that could be avoided by appropriate programs.

Numerous reports from varied company sources document the effectiveness of recreation and fitness programs in achieving health and productivity-related goals:

> At General Electric in Cincinnati, exercisers [in company-sponsored fitness programs] were absent from work 45 percent fewer days than nonparticipants.
>
> General Mills found that participants in its employee fitness program had a 19 percent reduction in absenteeism compared to a 69 percent increase in nonparticipants.
>
> Toronto Life Assurance found that employee turnover during a 10-month period was substantially lower for program participants than for nonparticipants—1.5 percent versus 15 percent.[14]

Recruitment/Retention Appeal and Company Image   Another purpose of employee recreation programs is to assist firms in their efforts to recruit or retain employees. An attractive program of recreation that can meet the needs of both the employee and his or her family can be a persuasive inducement. When an industry is a considerable distance from communities with adequate public recreation and park facilities and programs, it becomes virtually necessary for the company itself to provide leisure opportunities.

Linked to this is the company's goal of building a desirable image for itself by sponsoring or co-sponsoring community-based programs in the arts and other cultural activities, sports, or service to the disabled. Such community-service projects help to promote the company's identity as a public-spirited, responsible business.

Jill Decker has summed up the trend as follows:

> In less than a decade, event marketing and sponsorship has gone from infancy to a billion dollar industry. Sports, arts, cause-related events, and fairs and festivals are the primary beneficiaries of corporate sponsorships. Virtually every major special event held today requires at least some financial support from commercial sponsors.[15]

Administrative Arrangements

There are various approaches to the management of employee service and recreation programs. In some, the company itself provides the facilities and leadership and maintains complete control of the operation. In other organizations, the company provides the facilities, but an employee recreation association takes actual responsibility for running the program. Other companies use combinations of these approaches. Frequently, profits from canteens or plant vending machines provide financial support for the program, as does revenue from moderate fees for participation or membership. Many activities—such as charter vacation flights—are completely self-supporting; others are fully or partly subsidized by the company.

Some companies restrict participation in recreation programs to employees and their families, while others make them available to the surrounding community. For example, the Flick-Reedy Corporation designed its main building for the recreational use of the entire community, with thousands of children and adults using its gymnasium, auditorium, or dining room for special banquets and events each year.

Frequently, the director of the employee services and recreation program is also given responsibility for numerous community-relations activities of the company. The employee services coordinator for the M. D. Anderson Cancer Center at the University of Texas in Houston, Texas, recruits

> employees for community events such as the Houston/Tenneco Marathon and the University of Texas Health Science Center Sportathon. We sponsor health fairs and guest lectures during the Texas Medical Center Wellness Week. We promote cultural events in Houston throughout the workplace with the Council for the Visual and Performing Arts.
>
> We maintain seasonal special events, such as our Employee Christmas Dinner, Christmas decorating contest, National Hospital Week, Savings Bond drive, United Way, etc. . . . We handle discount programs for employees dealing with sporting and cultural events and various coupon books. We maintain our institutional bulletin board which publicizes our programs and those from other departments. We are also in charge of the monthly Outstanding Employee Award program.[16]

Activities and Services

In the past, company recreation programs tended to be limited to a narrow range of functions. Today, they include a great variety of activities, as shown in a mid–1980s NESRA membership survey (see Table 12.3).

TABLE 12.3   Characteristics of Company Services and Recreation Programs[17]

PHYSICAL PROGRAMS	% RESPONSE	SERVICE PROGRAMS	% RESPONSE
Softball	64.5	Discount service/tickets	73.5
Bowling	57.8	United Way drive	63.4
Golf	48.4	Blood drives	59.2
Basketball	42.9	Award/recognition program	58.9
Volleyball	35.5	Discount service/products	54.4
Tennis	30.3	First aid/CPR training	50.2
Fitness program	30.0	Employee assistance program	28.6
SOCIAL/CULTURAL PROGRAMS		**FACILITIES OPERATED**	
Picnics	64.5	Ball diamond	19.9
Christmas parties	60.0	Fitness facility	18.8
Dinner/theater outings	28.6	Basketball court	16.0
Travel program	24.0	Activities field	15.3
Adult education (non-job-related)	20.9	Activities building	13.2
Drama/theater	19.2	Employee park	9.4
		Fitness trail	9.4

In a recent survey of expenditures of NESRA member companies on various program elements, the total sums spent annually were as follows: company service awards, $35 million; recreation leagues and fitness equipment, $30 million; social programs, $25 million; employee store merchandise, $18 million; service programs, $15 million; employee travel, $11 million; discount buying programs, $9 million; cultural programs, $7 million; and child-care services, $6 million.[18]

Wellness Programs and Fitness Centers   The largest single thrust in employee service and recreation programs is toward providing health and wellness activities. Beyond simply offering exercise equipment or classes, wellness programs may include activities that promote physical, emotional, social, environmental, and even spiritual health. Jack Kondrasuk and Christy Carl have listed the varied components that are typically found in many company sponsored wellness programs today:

> Screenings, health risk appraisals (HRA): Blood pressure, weight, body fat, pulse, diabetes, AIDS, cardiovascular diseases, cancer and mammography, lifestyle and environmental questionnaires.
> Exercise programs: Endurance/cardiovascular/aerobics, strength training, flexibility.
> Education/awareness and possible interventions: Stress reduction, smoking cessation, obesity/weight control, lipid control, back pain, blood pressure/hypertension reduction, retirement and pre-retirement counseling, pre- and post-natal education, employee/family counseling on emotional issues, relaxation programs/meditation, producing healthier environments (like health food in vending machines).
> Developing healthful skills, behaviors: First aid, CPR use, back injury prevention, increasing seat belt use.[19]

Many companies have established extensive and well-equipped recreation and fitness centers and staffed them with qualified personnel. The new Texins Activity Center in Dallas, serving employees of Texas Instruments, contains a multi-use gymnasium, strength and cardiovascular exercise areas, conference rooms, child-care rooms, club rooms, and a Natatorium with a six-lane, 25-lap pool, two aerobic studios, an indoor running track, and varied outdoor facilities.

In terms of services, some NESRA members offer a full range of assistance and staff resources along the entire spectrum from illness to wellness. For example, SmithKline Beecham, a leading pharmaceutical company, operates a Life Management Center at its Philadelphia location that provides professional and personalized exercise programs and guidance to all employees within its Wellness Rx Facility. Lisa Kurzeja writes:

> The Facility is open 13 hours a day, Monday through Friday. It is staffed at all times with degreed exercise physiologists who assess employees' initial levels of fitness, discuss their goals, [and] then develop individualized exercise programs. These programs are regularly checked and updated. Formal re-evaluations and reviews are scheduled every six months. . . . Regular exercising at the Wellness Rx Facility has helped many of our members improve their health. For example, several members with hypertension lowered their blood pressure so much that their doctors have lowered the dosage on their medication.[20]

Administrative Flexibility: Off-Shift Programming   Employee service and recreation managers must adapt to the special circumstances of their organizations and the changing needs of the employees they serve. Often this may involve providing a wide range of special courses designed for vocational or career development, cultural interest, or personal enrichment. Some large corporations seek to meet the needs of their employees who work second and third shifts by scheduling facilities like health clubs or weight rooms to be available at odd hours of the day and night. For example, Phillips Petroleum and Pratt and Whitney schedule morning and midnight softball and bowling leagues for off-shift workers, and make gyms, tennis courts, and other facilities, as well as discount ticket operations, available to them at convenient times.

Innovation and Entrepreneurship

Just as in other sectors of the leisure-service field, employee service and recreation practitioners have experienced the need to become more fiscally independent by generating a fuller level of revenues through their offerings and by demonstrating their value in convincing terms. Joe Hauglie points out that this area of professional service grew rapidly during the 1970s and early 1980s as a consequence of the rapid growth and financial success of American businesses. However, he continues:

> Now, many global economic factors and a slowdown in the U.S. economy are resulting in dramatic reductions, or in some cases, elimination of ES&R funding and programs. To counteract this trend, ES&R managers must adopt an entrepreneurial attitude about their job and their departments.[21]

The purposes of adopting businesslike values and strategies are: (1) to enable employee programs to become less dependent on company financial support; and (2) to ensure that funds allocated to them by management yield significant, quantifiable benefits. A number of employee service and recreation directors in major corporations have been quite innovative in developing revenue sources based on businesslike ventures. Hauglie cites two examples of such ventures:

> *Employee Stores.* At Control Data Corporation in Minneapolis, Minnesota, a business plan was developed for an employee store, including a needs assessment, marketing strategy, profit-and-loss

projections, and start-up funding requirements. Following approval, which included a business loan from the company, the project was set in motion. By the early 1990s, three employee stores were operating successfully, and Control Data's initial investment was paid back within the first year of the program's operation.

Employee Association. Following an investigation of similar groups at Lockheed, 3M, General Dynamics and other companies, the employee services and recreation manager at Honeywell, Inc. in Minneapolis organized the Honeywell Employee Club, incorporated as a separately chartered entity. Operating with a receivables account so the Employee Club can reimburse Honeywell for expenses, and strengthening its self-generation of resources, this venture resulted in the program's becoming more financially independent, and the company's contributing considerably less to ES&R than in the past.[22]

In an example of systematic documentation of the benefits of employee services and recreation, the outcomes of the wellness program of the Coors Brewing Company in Golden, Colorado, were analyzed by researchers from the University of Oregon's Graduate School of Management. On the basis of the program's comprehensive approach to promoting wellness through health-risk assessments, nutritional counseling, stress management, smoking cessation, orthopedic rehabilitation, and other services, they concluded that it would save Coors at least $19 million during the next ten years through decreased medical costs, reduced sick leave, and improved productivity—a projected return of $6.15 for every $1 spent on the program.[23]

CAMPUS RECREATION

The nation's colleges and universities provide a major setting for organized programs of leisure services involving millions of participants each year in a wide range of recreational activities. While their primary purpose is to serve students, on many campuses, faculty and staff members may also be involved in such programs.

All institutions of higher education today sponsor some forms of leisure activity for their resident and commuter populations. Many of the larger colleges and universities have campus unions, departments of student life, or student centers that house a wide range of such activities. Frequently, a dean of student life is responsible for overseeing these programs, although intramural and recreational sports may often be administratively attached to a department or college of physical education and recreation or to a department of intercollegiate athletics.

The diversified leisure-service function may include operating performing arts centers (sometimes in cooperation with academic departments or schools in these fileds), planning arts series, film programs and forums with guest speakers, and similar cultural events. Student union buildings may include such specialized facilities as bowling alleys, coffee houses, game rooms, restaurants, bookstores, and other activity areas.

Rationale for Campus Programs

Several logical reasons for sponsoring college and university recreation programs may be cited.

Leisure as Co-Curricular Enrichment   Not all of the learning that takes place in higher education is provided in the classroom or laboratory. Many special interests of students can be explored to the fullest only by co-curricular (non-class) experiences, ranging from the journalism major who works on the staff of the campus newspaper or literary magazine to the botany major who becomes involved in wilderness backpacking or camping. Often such programs are carried on with the express cooperation of the campus department most directly involved with the leisure interest.

Maintaining Campus Control and Morale   Historically, American and Canadian colleges acted *in loco parentis;* that is, they were obligated to maintain a degree of control over the private lives of their students in areas such as drinking, gambling, sexual behavior, or the general domain of health and safety. For centuries, they therefore maintained codes of behavior, rules for on-campus living, curfews, and numerous other restrictions that controlled various forms of leisure behavior.

During the 1960s and 1970s, many campuses relinquished their responsibility for supervising students' private lives, particularly in areas related to personal morality. They did so at a time when students were forcibly demanding fuller rights of participation in campus governance, freedom from restrictive campus rules, and less structured academic curricula. However, during the 1980s, many institutions not only reintroduced curriculum requirements, but also became aware of the necessity to maintain fuller control over the social lives of their students.

The need for such supervision became evident in the mid- and late 1980s. In a series of feature articles, the *Chronicle of Higher Education* documented the striking growth in student drinking and drug abuse, including deaths stemming from forced drinking in hazing, increased incidents of drunken driving, and wild, mob-like behavior during spring breaks in Florida and on the Texas Gulf Coast.[24]

If anything, many of these problems have become even more severe in the 1990s. In 1993, the *New York Times* pointed out that many colleges and universities were reporting growing numbers of violent assaults, hate crimes, alcohol violations, and sexual assaults—carried out both by outsiders and by students themselves.[25]

In general, it is now believed by many that colleges must play a larger role in guiding the lives of students outside of the classroom. While few administrators are seeking a return to the days of single-sex dormitories, dress codes, curfews, and other rigid rules, a consensus has grown that many of today's college students lack the responsibility to handle their new-found freedom sensibly and that it is necessary to establish and enforce some guidelines for students' social behavior.

Beyond being part of the effort to control negative kinds of behavior, campus recreation promotes positive student growth throughout the college experience. At a number of eastern colleges, students are drawn into outdoor recreation or community-service projects beginning with their freshman orientation period. At Lehigh University and Lafayette College, for example, new students are drawn into overnight canoe and backpacking trips and begin to make new friends immediately. Similarly, entering students at Bryn Mawr College are assigned one day service projects with the Philadelphia Zoo, the Children's Hospital of Philadelphia, and Habitat for Humanity.

Enhancing the University's Image   Particularly in an era in which colleges and universities must compete for the enrollment of high-quality students, maintaining an appealing and impressive institutional image is critical. Probably the best-known vehicle for doing this is by fielding teams that play glamorous schedules in such popular sports as football or basketball. However, there are many other ways of building a positive image—through academic distinction, by winning prizes and awards, by having outstanding orchestras or theater companies, by having a distinguished university press, and through the accomplishments of alumni.

Certainly, having attractive recreational facilities and campus leisure programs also helps to build a positive image—particularly for potential students who visit a campus and are considering whether they want to live there for the next four years. Higher education appeals to a number of values and needs: not the least of these is the student's desire for an exciting and interesting social life.

This function of campus recreation is especially important in view of the great numbers of students who transfer from their initial choice of a college or university—often within the first eight weeks of the semester. In the words of one director of student activities, recreation programs and the overall orientation process provide a "window of opportunity" to help students begin to make connections with each other and feel comfortable in the campus setting.

Contributing to Student Development   Beyond enriching a student's formal academic experience, involvement in noncurricular experiences contributes significantly to his or her overall personal growth. In their article on academic productivity, Judith Bryant and James Bradley cite a Harvard University report, *Teaching, Learning, and Student Life*, which stresses that out-of-classroom activities relate directly to higher grades and to social integration.[26] Furthermore, a study of recent alumni of the University of Tennessee found that participation in intramural sports was an important factor in the following areas of growth:

> Working cooperatively in a group; ability to lead and guide others; getting along with people of different racial or ethnic backgrounds.
>
> Understanding and applying principles and methods; defining and solving problems; understanding graphic information; understanding written information.
>
> Ability to grow and learn as a person; self-confidence in expressing ideas; ability to adjust to new job demands; practical skills for employment.[27]

Range of Campus Recreation Experiences

Campus recreation programs today are becoming more diversified, including a wide range of recreational sports, outdoor activities, entertainment and social events, cultural programs, activities for persons with disabilities, and various other services.

Recreational Sports   During the 1970s and 1980s, both intramural leagues and sports clubs expanded rapidly in many institutions, with a growing emphasis on lifetime sports and on coeducational participation. Due in part to changed sex-role expectations and the effect of Title IX, many more girls and women are involved in sports today than in the past. More and more colleges and universities are providing varied facilities for sports and games, including aquatic facilities, boxing/martial arts and exercise rooms, saunas and locker rooms, extensive outdoor areas with night-lighting for evening play, and other special facilities for outdoor hobbies and instruction.

As an example of the variety of physical recreation activities offered on college campuses, the Recreation and Intramural Sports Programs (RIM) at the University of Oregon include the following elements: intramural athletics (14 competitive sports in men's, women's, and coed divisions); mini-leagues; one-to-three-day events/special events; open recreation;

recreation classes; court reservations; maps/fitness trail information; athletic training services; and an employee health enhancement program.

Outdoor Recreation   Outdoor recreation, which includes clinics, clubs, and outings, may involve hiking, backpacking, camping, mountain climbing, scuba diving, sailing, skiing, and numerous other nature-based programs. These are often sponsored by campus outing clubs, which may in turn be affiliated with national organizations or federations. Gary Nussbaum points out that a well-developed outdoor recreation program may yield positive benefits in student achievement and satisfaction, and suggests that such programs should be used to enrich the intramural programs at many colleges and universities. In addition to actual sponsorship of such activities, campus recreation directors may provide varied support and information services. Examples might include

> the inexpensive rental of backpacking and camping gear . . . the provision of information including resource data, the location of clothing/equipment outfitters, and a directory of other clubs, organizations and commercial enterprises offering outdoor recreation services. . . . [and] Outdoor literature (e.g.,"how-to" books, periodical works), may be a joint provision of the intramural office and the university library.[28]

A specialized type of outdoor activity that is becoming increasingly popular on many college campuses is the challenge course. This is a type of adventure program that offers groups and individuals the opportunity to participate in varied activities involving emotional and physical challenges. Often they are designed to simulate the challenges found while hiking or mountain climbing. Wayne Fett writes that the purpose of a ropes course, for example:

> is to identify and develop the participants' behaviors and attitudes which optimize the group's collective force. Group cooperation and problem solving are important learned assets. The safety of each participant is carefully guarded by the group, the individual and the facilitators involved in each course.[29]

Special Events: Entertainment and Cultural Programs   Many campuses sponsor large scale entertainment events and cultural series. Typically, singers, rock bands, and comedians are booked to entertain students in stadiums, field houses, and campus centers. The college or university's own departments of music, theatre, and dance may provide performing companies that present concerts or other stage presentations, along with other kinds of specialized programs.

Large-scale special events that students plan and carry out themselves—such as sports carnivals or other major competitions—are highlights of campus social programs. They involve both intimacy of interaction among leaders and participants and an intense outpouring of energy as people share fun in a crowded school or college setting. Similar excitement may be noted at major musical events like rock concerts, although such programs often require supervision to assure adherence to campus policies regarding alcohol and drugs.

Services for Special Populations   Students with disabilities are being encouraged and assisted to participate in general campus recreation programs, whenever possible. However, for those students whose disability is too severe to permit this, or who have not yet developed the needed degree of confidence and independence, it has been necessary to design special programs using modified facilities and adapted instructional techniques or rules of play.

Outstanding examples of such programs are those offered by the University of Illinois, which provides special teams in the areas of football, softball, basketball, swimming, and track and field for physically disabled students. Other activities, such as archery, judo, swimming, bowling, and softball, have been adapted for such special groups as the visually impaired.

Community Service Projects   Many students also become involved in volunteer community projects such as repairing facilities, working with the elderly, or providing "big brother" or tax assistance services. Such efforts are important for two reasons: (1) they illustrate how student-life activities may include a broad range of involvements beyond those that are clearly recognizable as recreational "fun" events; and (2) they serve to blend academic and extracurricular student experiences, increasing the individual's exposure to life, and enhancing his or her leadership capability. Findings of the Cooperative Institutional Research Program at the University of California at Los Angeles show that the more students are involved in their education, the more likely they are to remain at an institution: "The most successful students . . . are those who live and work on their campuses, participate in college activities and academic programs outside of their classes, and interact with faculty and staff members."[30]

OVERVIEW OF CAMPUS RECREATION

In general, campus recreation provides students with the opportunity to gain practical experience within a wide range of functions that supplement and enrich their academic programs. For example, many students may gain administrative or business skills, often on an advanced level. The Associated Students' Organization of San Diego State University in California provides a setting for such learning experiences. This multi-million-dollar corporation, funded by student fees, operates the Aztec Center, the college's student union building. Among its services are a successful travel agency, intramurals and sports clubs, special events, leisure classes, lectures, movies, concerts, an open-air theater, an aquatics center, campus radio station, child-care center, general store, campus information booth, and other programs. The bulk of its recreational activities are operated directly by the Recreation Activities Board, a unit within the overall Associated Students' Organization.

At the same time, many aspects of college and university life are becoming more commercialized as greater numbers of services are supplied within a market-oriented framework. Typically, instead of continuing to maintain university-run dining rooms or campus cafeterias, more and more institutions today have contracted out eating services to fast-food franchise chains such as Taco Bell or Pizza Hut. Increasingly, college bookstores are being operated by commercial entrepreneurs that provide a broad range of consumer goods, and a number of universities have even introduced commercially run shopping malls in their student centers.

In general, advertising in college stadiums and arenas has begun to pop up everywhere:

on scoreboards and video monitors, on ramps, plaques, marquees, directional signs, above shot clocks, on hockey helmets and even in rest rooms [above men's urinals and on the back doors of women's toilet stalls]. All this is done to cut back on creeping ticket prices, pay for skyrocketing overhead costs and ease tightening budgets.[31]

What are the implications of this trend toward commercializing varied aspects of campus life? First, it illustrates the drive toward generating expanded revenues through various entrepreneurial strategies that is found throughout the leisure-service system today. Second, and more subtly, it tends to change the atmosphere within which students live: they recognize that now even the halls of higher learning are part of the business-driven culture.

OTHER SETTINGS FOR CAMPUS RECREATION

While the term "campus recreation" is generally applied to programs offered on college and university campuses for students, faculty, and staff, it should be recognized that many educational institutions on the lower levels—such as elementary and secondary school systems—also provide recreation facilities and programs.

School District Programs

Throughout the twentieth century, many school districts established extensive programs of extra- and co-curricular activities for students, including clubs, sports, music and drama groups, and similar types of leisure involvement. While budget restraints of the 1980s and 1990s have compelled many districts to reduce such offerings, they still provide an opportunity for school-centered recreation in many communities. Beyond this, a growing number of school systems now provide impressive adult education classes on a fee basis; these may include both remedial or diploma-oriented options and offerings relating to varied hobby interests, such as language, arts and crafts, sports skills, literary and musical topics, investment planning, fitness, and other similar self-enrichment subjects.

Another aspect of school-centered recreation involves the direct responsibility of school districts for providing community recreation programs. This practice was widespread during the 1920s and 1930s; after World War II, however, schools tended to give up the community recreation function as municipal recreation and park agencies merged into single departments. Now, there has been a resurgence of interest in this function in some school districts. H. Douglas Sessoms and Karla Henderson write:

> The degree to which school systems are a provider of recreation services varies from community to community. In some states, school law and codes are liberal in their support of recreation services through the public school system. This is especially true in Pennsylvania, Wisconsin, and California. In other states, such as North Carolina, the laws limit the schools in providing public recreation service. Although not all school systems are sensitive to their role in education for leisure, growing interest exists in the cooperation between local public recreation systems and boards of education and school authorities.[32]

In other settings, this cooperation may take the form of shared responsibility for constructing and maintaining facilities that are used jointly by schools and municipal authorities. Frequently, such facilities become multiservice community centers that blend educational, recreational, and social services. For example, in New Brighton, Minnesota:

> the Mounds View School District owns 12,500 square feet of the parks and recreation department's 70,000-square-foot Family Service Center, which the district uses for its early childhood and family education program. The park department also is renting an additional 1,000 square feet to the school district

for the adult education component of its program and 1,000 square feet to the nonprofit Northwest Youth and Family Service, a teen counseling group.[33]

Similarly, in Sunnyvale, California, the City of Sunnyvale, in cooperation with the elementary school district, constructed a $3.5-million addition to its Columbia Middle School in the mid-1990s. The AMD Sports and Service Center (named after Advanced Micro Devices, a local company that contributed $1 million to the project) includes a gymnasium, counseling rooms, and a health center. The gymnasium is used by the school during the day and by the city during nonschool hours.

THERAPEUTIC RECREATION SERVICE

Over the past 50 years, there has been increased recognition of the need to provide special or adapted recreation programs for those persons with disabilities who function in community life, and the need to use recreation as a means of treatment or rehabilitation for those individuals with more serious illnesses or impairments.

Early Development of Therapeutic Recreation

The history of past centuries provides a number of examples of the use of recreation in the treatment of psychiatric patients, in both Europe and America. The fullest impetus for therapeutic recreation, however, came in the twentieth century in three types of institutions: (1) hospitals and rehabilitation centers for those with physical disabilities; (2) hospitals for mentally ill persons; and (3) special schools for those with developmental disabilities.

After both World War I and World War II, there was a wave of concern about the need to rehabilitate veterans who had sustained major physical injuries or psychological trauma while in service. As a consequence, Veterans Administration and military hospitals developed comprehensive programs of rehabilitative services, including physical and occupational therapy, psychotherapy, social service, vocational training, guidance—and recreation. In such settings, recreation was perceived as being one of several techniques that contributed to patient recovery.

A significant reason for the growth of support for therapeutic and special recreation services for persons with disabilities stemmed from the fact that many such individuals had been encouraged by World War II to seek new levels of independent functioning. Many men with mental retardation, for example, had been recruited into the military straight out of institutions; after having served successfully in the war, many refused to go back into custodial care and entered community life.

Other disabled men and women—including blind, deaf, and orthopedically disabled individuals—found varied forms of war work or other defense-related assignments. After V-J Day, most of these disabled persons were fired—many never to work again—and their jobs were given to the returning veterans. However, just as the war had created higher expectations for women and racial minority group members, so it did for disabled people. Then, the period of the counterculture revolution of the late 1960s and 1970s, described in Chapter 9, raised these expectations even higher.

Supported by the demands of families of persons with disabilities and other advocate groups, there was steadily increasing pressure to provide fuller opportunities for disabled persons in many spheres of daily life. Leisure-service educators, practitioners, and professional societies issued strong philosophical statements confirming the rights of all individuals—including those with disabilities—to fulfilling leisure experiences as an essential part of human existence.[34]

Federal legislation promoting the rights of special populations, particularly with respect to education, included recreation as a form of related or supportive service. For example, in 1976 Congress enacted the Education for All Handicapped Children Act, which resulted in dramatically increased programs for children with disabilities, including physical and occupational therapy and recreation (identified as important "related services" for the disabled). Section 504 of the Rehabilitation Act of 1973, often called the "non-discrimination clause," made it illegal to bar otherwise qualified individuals who were disabled from any program or activity receiving federal funding. Numerous federal agencies, such as the Bureau of Education for the Handicapped of the Office of Education, the Division of Mental Retardation of the Rehabilitation Services Administration, and the Administration on Aging, have funded training and research programs, as well as ongoing services, within different categories of disability.

Awareness of Leisure Needs of Persons with Disabilities

For the first time, there was widespread public awareness of the special needs of persons with disabilities with respect to leisure and recreation. It was recognized that while all people need diversified recreational outlets, those who have a significant degree of disability frequently find it especially difficult to meet their needs in constructive and convenient ways. In part this is because serious physical impairments, emotional difficulties, or cognitive limitations may legitimately constrict the potential range of participation by persons with disabilities.

Much of the recreational deprivation of disabled individuals, however, is caused by society's failure to assist them, or even *permit* them, to engage in activity to the full extent of their potential. Many communities and organizations in the past did not make the design adaptations that would permit disabled persons to use their facilities. In some cases, recreation and park departments have barred disabled persons from their programs, arguing that they did not have staff members who were skilled in working with special populations or that serving the disabled would impose the risk of accident lawsuits and increased insurance costs. In other cases, administrators have felt that the presence of blind, retarded, or orthopedically disabled participants would be distasteful to the public at large, which might then cease to use the facilities. Sometimes parents or relatives have tended to shelter them excessively, and often their lack of skill or fear of rejection by others has caused persons with disabilities to limit their recreational participation.

This picture has been rapidly changing. Increasingly, recreation professionals and others concerned with the needs of the disabled in modern society have fought to improve the opportunities open to them in both institutional and community settings. This trend has not been unique to the United States; similar developments have taken place in other industrialized nations. In regard to Canada, for example, Mark Searle and Russell Brayley have commented that:

A significant turning point for individuals with special needs in Canada was the amendment of the Human Rights Act in 1974 which prohibits discrimination against persons for a position of employment for reasons of physical or mental disability. Though this did not specifically relate to recreation and leisure, it served notice to the Canadian public that persons with disabilities "have rights."

.... from 1975 to 1979 seven provinces and the Northwest Territories acquired financial support from Recreation Canada to assist in the establishment and operation of councils on recreation for special groups. During this same time period the Canadian National Institute for the Blind (CNIB), the Canadian Mental Health Association (CMHA), the Canadian Rehabilitation Council for the Disabled (CRCD), and the Canadian Association for the Mentally Retarded (CAMR) received federal funding to promote interagency recreation programming for persons with disabilities.[35]

Shift to Community Focus

Growing awareness of the leisure needs of persons with disabilities meant that it would no longer be appropriate to think of recreation programs for ill and disabled persons as being the concern only of residential institutions such as hospitals, special schools for the retarded, or other treatment settings. It was recognized that far greater numbers of disabled perons lived in the community than in residential treatment centers, and that they had equally strong needs for recreation. Municipal recreation and park agencies began to assume a higher degree of responsibility for providing special programs for the disabled—usually rather limited activities for groups with a particular type of impairment, such as blind, physically disabled, or mentally retarded persons. Voluntary agencies also gave fuller emphasis to programming social activities, adapted sports, or camping for special populations. For the first time, the term *therapeutic recreation service* began to be widely used, in *both* treatment and community settings. It was defined in the following terms:

> Therapeutic recreation service is the specific use of recreational activity in the care, treatment and rehabilitation of handicapped and aging persons with a directed program.[36]

Mainstreaming as a Goal

While the primary thrust of therapeutic recreation as a professional specialization continued to be on formal treatment and institutional programs, there was a pronounced growth of concern about persons with disabilities in community settings. This shift was in part a response to the deinstitutionalization of hundreds of thousands of mentally retarded and mentally ill individuals that took place very widely in the 1960s and 1970s. For the first time, great numbers of such individuals were no longer shut up in long-term care in isolated custodial institutions, but lived in the community, receiving services in local mental health centers and residing in independent or semi-independent environments.

Mainstreaming became a popular slogan, with its avowed goal of integrating disabled persons and serving them in the least-restricted environment. Realistically, however, it became apparent that, even with the best intentions, it was not possible to serve those at *all* levels of disability in completely integrated community settings.

In recognition of this, a number of different patterns of service have been developed for disabled persons in community settings. In some cases, severely impaired individuals may be served in entirely separate agencies or facilities. In others, less severely disabled persons may be partially integrated with the nondisabled, taking part in certain joint activities with them and enjoying adapted programs on a separate basis. In still other cases, a high level of integrated participation for disabled persons has been achieved.

Recreation Programming for Persons with Disabilities

San Francisco's RCH, Inc. has an outstanding swimming pool (top) with ramps and other equipment to serve all age groups. Center, orthopedically disabled persons use modified cycles (center) in New England's Northeast Passage outdoor recreation program. Below, individuals with and without disabilities enjoy mass game activities in Westchester County's Southeast Consortium day.

At this time too, many of the terms that had traditionally been used to describe persons with disabilities were carefully reviewed by persons in the fields of rehabilitation, special education, and therapeutic recreation. Negative terms that were used to classify categories of persons with developmental disability are no longer regarded as acceptable because of the image they convey of disability and its impacts. Gradually, they have been excised from the professional literature and the titles of agencies serving persons with disabilities.

Today, varied forms of therapeutic recreation services are sponsored by a wide variety of institutions and agencies, including:

1. Hospitals of all types, serving those with every form of illness or disability in active treatment programs.
2. Nursing homes and long-term or intensive care facilities, serving chiefly the infirm or disoriented aging person but also persons in other age categories who have had major trauma (strokes or disabling injuries) and cannot live independently.
3. Schools or residential centers for those with developmental disability, severe learning disability, or emotional disturbance.
4. Special schools, treatment centers, or penal institutions for those with social deviancy.
5. Residential centers for aging persons who, while not requiring full-time nursing care, cannot safely live independently.
6. Centers for physical medicine and rehabilitation, which provide programs of physical, psychological, and vocational rehabilitation.
7. Programs provided by public recreation and park agencies.
8. Programs provided by voluntary agencies, including both organizations concerned with a particular disability and its varied service needs and organizations designed to provide recreation and related social services to those with different categories of disability; and
9. Aftercare and other sheltered environments or workshop programs that assist persons with disability living in the community.

Models of Therapeutic Recreation

A number of different approaches to therapeutic recreation have been employed over time, ranging from a purely diversional approach to more serious rehabilitative efforts. In the mid-1970s, Gerald O'Morrow identified five such models of service:

Custodial Model: Recreation programs are provided in long-term care settings in which little effort is made to provide rehabilitation or meaningful educational or other needed services. Recreation is primarily employed to lighten the atmosphere and improve the morale of the institution; it may also be part of the reward-and-punishment system, or may be a useful means of creating a favorable public relations image for the outside world.

Medical-Clinical-Model: In most treatment settings, this has been the dominant pattern. Recreation is viewed as an important element in the treatment plan, and is designed to help treat illness, under medical direction. It has been most widely found in psychiatric institutions or physical rehabilitation settings.

Therapeutic Milieu Model: Also found predominantly in programs for the mentally ill or socially deviant, this approach stresses the need to create a healthy environment, or therapeutic community in which all staff members and patients or clients themselves act as therapeutic agents. Recreation becomes a useful medium for group living, planning and carrying out projects, and the development of daily living skills.

✗ Education and Training Model: This is a goal-oriented approach, often used with the mentally retarded; it places heavy emphasis on occupational therapy, remedial education, vocational training, and similar modalities. Recreation is used to teach basic cognitive or social skills, and may also be used as part of behavior modification programs with the disturbed or socially deviant.

✗ Community Model: This describes the type of therapeutic recreation service that is provided in the community at large. Often, it has been the goal of institutional personnel to help equip their patients or clients to return to community life and function successfully; in many cases, beginning contacts and involvements have been made while they are still under care in the treatment setting.[37]

In an effort to clarify the appropriate focus and philosophy of therapeutic recreation service, in the early 1980s the National Therapeutic Recreation Society (NTRS), a branch of the National Recreation and Parks Association, developed a comprehensive definition of the field. NTRS identified three services that should be offered as part of a comprehensive approach to therapeutic recreation. These are: (1) *therapy,* (2) *leisure education,* and (3) *recreational participation.* In any given situation, the therapeutic recreation specialist should be ready to provide any or all of these services.

> The decision as to where and when each of these services would be provided would be based on the assessment of client need. Different individuals have a variety of different needs related to leisure utilization. For some clients, improvement of a functional behavior or problem (physical, mental, social or emotional) is a necessary prerequisite to meaningful leisure experiences. For others, acquiring leisure skills, knowledge, and ability is a priority need. For others, special recreation participation opportunities are necessary, based on place of residence or because assistance or adapted activities are required.[38]

The NTRS statement is based on a principle known as "progressive patient care." It implies that at each stage of a patient's illness and recovery (or a client's involvement over a period of time with a service agency), program experiences are provided that are geared to achieving maximum benefit for the subject appropriate to that stage, and helping the individual move along constructively to the next stage.

CONTRASTING EMPHASES IN THE FIELD

While the NTRS statement presents an idealized picture of what the field of therapeutic recreation seeks to accomplish, it does not realistically describe *all* present-day practices. Many recreation specialists in treatment centers continue to provide essentially diversional programs, while others who work in the community simply provide modified recreation programs for groups of disabled individuals, without clearly rehabilitative purposes.

In light of these practices, it would appear that two distinctly different approaches to serving disabled persons in modern society with recreation may be identified. The first of these may be called the *clinical approach,* and the second *special recreation.*

Clinical Approach

This model of service is clearly designed to carry out significant goals of rehabilitation within the overall treatment program. It is found in most therapeutic recreation textbooks and curricula today, and is the basis for national and regional workshops dealing with hospital or rehabilitation-centered programs.

It includes the following elements: (1) a clear definition of program goals and philosophy; (2) individualized assessment of patient or client status, functional capability, needs, and interests; (3) individualized treatment plans, prepared under medical or other authoritative supervision with input from other members of the treatment team; (4) activity analysis, adaptation of facilities and leadership methods, and other modifications intended to facilitate successful performance of the activity; (5) regular observation and evaluation of patient or client progress, with detailed progress notes; and (6) continued consultation with other members of the treatment team, and modification of the treatment plan as necessary to ensure its success in achieving stated goals.

How did the concept of using recreation as a form of treatment gain acceptance? As stated earlier, it initially was viewed primarily as a diversional service, designed to improve patient morale and help make patients more amenable to other types of treatment. In the early years of the therapeutic recreation movement, there was considerable disagreement as to whether recreation should actually be considered a therapy as such. Some argued that it was a form of experience that was therapeutic for all participants—but not a medically proven service comparable to surgical care or drug-based therapies. Others cited the supportive statements of medical authorities who agreed that recreation indeed could be prescribed to support overall treatment goals.

Roxanne Howe-Murphy and Becky Charboneau define "rehabilitation" and "habilitation" as the broad areas of professional service within which clinical recreation service functions. Rehabilitation is defined as a "dynamic process with the purpose of restoring an individual to maximum physical, mental, [and] emotional functioning and to a valued status and role in society." It is usually carried out after a severe disease or traumatic accident has left a previously nondisabled person with severe impairment.

Rehabilitation is a holistic process that encompasses the following:

(1) physical rehabilitation (medication, surgery, exercises, prostheses, and survival technology, such as dialysis machines); (2) vocational rehabilitation (work adjustment, job placement); (3) social rehabilitation (social-skill development, sex therapy, activities of daily living, leisure development); and (4) psychological rehabilitation (counseling, psychotherapy, emotional support). As an individual-oriented process, it addresses the whole person by recognizing that disability can affect every aspect of life.[39]

Habilitation, as these theorists note, is similar but is directed at individuals who were congenitally impaired or became disabled in the early developmental years. Within this spectrum of services, therapeutic recreation may obviously be used to promote social and psychological rehabilitation directly, and may also be used to contribute to physical rehabilitation.

Howe-Murphy and Charboneau point out that the clinical model, which they refer to as the "therapy/medical model," is dominated by the medical profession. It is the doctor who prescribes all care; other health professionals serve in supportive roles and deliver services only as directed or approved, and the patient typically assumes a passive role. However,

patients in rehabilitation settings also need relaxation, freedom to choose, and opportunities for non-goal-oriented experiences. These opportunities may well occur during evening and weekend hours.[40]

In contrast to this approach is the effort to serve special populations in community life with recreation that is adapted to meet their needs but is not regarded specifically as therapeutic or rehabilitative—and that is not necessarily directed by a professionally qualified leader.

Special Recreation

Dan Kennedy and his co-authors explain the concept of special recreation as follows:

> The term *special recreation* has recently emerged to describe recreation and leisure provisions that accommodate recreation participation by members of special population groups, and particularly by persons with disabilities. . . . [They] allow participation by individuals who have disabilities that necessitate special accommodations (modifications of activities, altered environments, personal assistance, etc.) above and beyond the kinds of accommodations generally provided.[41]

While they do not deliberately gear programs to achieving specific treatment or rehabilitative goals within a clinical framework, those providing special recreation do have important purposes. They value recreation as an important life experience for persons with disabilities and seek to achieve positive physical, social, and emotional outcomes, making whatever adaptations in programming, facilities, equipment, or leadership methods are appropriate.

In an attempt to gain an overview of community-based special recreation programs, the Prince George's County, Maryland, Department of Parks and Recreation carried out a survey of 18 county or municipal programs serving persons with disabilities throughout the United States. It revealed a wide range of program trends and positive developments in the field of special recreation, but also uncovered problems in such areas as competition for funding, recruitment and placement of volunteers, changing community attitudes, and educating both persons with disabilities and their families as to the importance of recreation and their basic rights.

Numerous local agencies participating in the survey provided detailed descriptions of their services, such as the following summary from San Jose, California:

> *Office of Therapeutic Services* offers a continuum of services which include: therapy, leisure education, and recreation participation in segregated, integrated and mainstreamed settings. We also provide services that are highly specialized in the community such as Stroke Support Groups, Parkinson's Exercise programs, Arthritis Exercise and Support Groups, Head Injury Recreation Services and Wheelchair Sports. We also provide cooperative programs for the deaf, blind and sight impaired. Our integrated programs include Saturday Kinder-Fun, summer day camps, creative crafts for kids and creative movement and dance. The aquatics programs include specialized exercises for individuals with stroke and arthritis, child swim lessons and family swim. The Special Olympics programs provide year-round training for individuals with developmental disabilities in twelve Olympic-type sports. The mental health programs provide leisure education and recreational activities for individuals with mental illness and developmental disabilities.[42]

TRENDS AND ISSUES IN THERAPEUTIC RECREATION

In the closing years of the twentieth century, a number of distinct trends and issues in the overall field of therapeutic recreation service may be noted. The following section briefly discusses these trends and issues.

Expansion of Sports and Outdoor Recreation Participation

At every level, people of all ages with physical or mental disabilities who had been unable in the past to engage in active forms of play are now taking part in varied forms of sports, camping, and outdoor recreation pursuits. Many of these activities are promoted by

Wheelchair Sports, USA (formerly the National Wheelchair Athletic Association), a multisport organization for disabled athletes who compete annually in regional, national, and international games. Included among the competitive events for both men and women are archery, athletics (track and field, pentathlon, road racing), basketball, quad rugby, shooting, swimming, table tennis, tennis, and weight-lifting. Thousands of young athletes also participate in Special Olympics events, while many others compete in marathons, bowling leagues, and other individual or team sports.

In terms of outdoor recreation, since the 1950s camping and outdoor adventure programs have become increasingly geared for individuals with disabilities. Michael Kelley points out that numerous research studies have confirmed the positive effects of outdoor adventure activities, such as wilderness backpacking, canoeing, mountaineering, whitewater rafting, and other Outward Bound–type programs for emotionally disturbed or chronically mentally ill individuals.[43]

Disabled persons are also beginning to engage in other forms of outdoor play. David Hewitt and Larry Crump point out that people with disabilities are taking part in fishing, hunting, and similar forms of outdoor recreation at fish and wildlife habitats managed by the U.S. Army Corps of Engineers, and that help is provided by park rangers and volunteer leaders. They describe an event held at the Corps' Omaha District, associated with

"Fishing Has No Boundaries," an organization that holds a fishing day at Lake Oahe each year for 130-plus individuals with disabilities ranging from mental retardation to paraplegia. Each angler is accompanied by a friend or family member, and several hundred volunteers provide boats, prepare the picnic site, cook and serve meals, clean and package fish and clean up afterwards. They also use a lift to get wheelchairs into boats.

Their reward comes when they witness a severely disabled man in his 40s say, "This is the best day of my life," after his boat captain brings him to the dock, or after a child with cerebral palsy catches an especially large salmon and can barely contain his excitement long enough for a photo.[44]

Use of Technology and Assistive Devices

Sophisticated technology is also being brought into play to permit persons with disabilities to participate successfully in different leisure activities. For several decades, various modified instruments or pieces of equipment have been used to help disabled individuals take part in card and table games, arts and crafts, team and individual sports, and other pursuits. For example, the kinds of equipment used for blind persons in sports and games include:

(1) guide ropes that enable blind individuals to run at top speed without fear, holding a short rope attached to a ring that slides along a wire without interference; (2) audible goal detectors (consisting of a motor-driven noisemaker that makes clicking sounds at a constant rate); (3) audible balls for modified ball games, such as kickball, that have either a battery-operated beeper or bell placed inside; and (4) a portable aluminum rail for use in bowling that is movable from lane to lane and orients the blind bowler.[45]

Aerodynamic wheelchairs are now being used by disabled racers, and carbon-fiber prosthetic feet enable amputee athletes to run almost as fast as able-bodied athletes. Research into the use of electrodes to jolt the leg muscles of persons with spinal cord injuries promises ultimately to help them "walk," while numerous other devices are being invented each year to facilitate independent functioning for disabled persons. Electronic devices such as "aura interactor" strap-on vests enable deaf people to dance, without straining to hear the music, and help blind videogame players to feel laser beams "bouncing" off the screen.

Ladd Colston has noted that persons with disabilities are among the fastest growing market segments in the United States. He writes:

> It has been estimated that a significant percentage of America's 43 million disabled citizens spend billions of dollars each year on technology products ranging from wheelchairs to braille versions of Monopoly and Scrabble. According to ABLEDATA, a database on assistive technology, there are more than 16,000 [such] devices commercially manufactured by over 2,200 companies nationwide.[46]

Also, for many severely disabled persons who are unable to leave their otherwise isolated worlds, the Internet and other forms of interactive games and electronic communication help them to make extended forays into cyberspace—and engage in exciting forms of play there and often make new friends.[47]

Mainstreaming and Leisure Integration

One of the primary goals of clinical practice in therapeutic recreation has always been to use the process of progressive patient care to help patients or clients achieve the highest possible level of independent functioning and involvement in community life.

In the field of education, terms like "total inclusion" and "least restrictive environment" have dominated the discussion since federal legislation in the mid-1970s ensured the mainstreaming of disabled children into the public schools. While the principle of mainstreaming in educational settings is widely supported, many school systems are chafing at the very high costs of the special arrangements it requires. Also, in many cases the parents of disabled children are opposed to having their children placed in regular classes where, as in the case of deaf children, they often have great difficulty in functioning.

Within the field of recreation, many agencies that formerly operated segregated programs have shifted their emphasis to stress integration of disabled participants—either simply by encouraging them to enter, with assistance, into general programs or by structuring activities to include both disabled and nondisabled individuals. The integration issue was dramatized in the late 1980s in a critical analysis of Special Olympics, an outstanding sports program for mentally retarded children and youth. Jack Hourcade pointed out that Special Olympics had begun at a time when children with mental retardation either were completely excluded from the public schools (and thus physical education) or were given only minimal access to such instruction. At that time, the program filled an important need. However, he continued:

> The principle of normalization has become an inherent guiding philosophy in program development for individuals with developmental disabilities [with administrative arrangements] such that meaningful integration of persons with disabilities into the societal mainstream is achieved. Special Olympics, by its very nature a "special" or segregated activity characterized by "extremely homogeneous grouping arrangements," has been frequently criticized on the basis of its lack of adherence to normalization philosophy.[48]

In the years that followed, many community recreation organizations serving persons with disabilities adopted policies designed to promote the inclusion of their clients in programs serving the general public or in programs serving "mixed" populations. While many such agencies have reported favorable outcomes, there is also evidence that mentally retarded children placed in integrated camp settings may experience failure, rejection, or a weakening of self-concepts, as compared to children in segregated camp programs. In addition, Linda Heyne and Frederick Green have summarized research suggesting that the friendships that develop between developmentally disabled and nondisabled individuals as a consequence of mainstreamed recreation tend to be relatively superficial and lacking in real intimacy and empathy. Often, they find:

> these "friendship" relationships do not pass the test of endurance and are discontinued because the non-disabled child's "friend" with a developmental disability does not fit into their extended social network.[49]

However, in another report of a recreation program involving children with and without developmental disabilities over a two-year period, Heyne, Stuart Schleien, and Leo McAvoy found that very positive friendship outcomes occurred—with subjects reporting many more "likes" than "dislikes" about each other, and with substantial benefits for the disabled participants in terms of self-esteem, friendship skills, communication, and a sense of well-being.[50]

Leandra Bedini points out that social skills training and the support of families and related social networks are essential if integrated environments are to have positive outcomes.[51] Beyond this, it seems clear that no single mainstreaming model is likely to be effective in all areas of activity or with all populations. Recognizing this, the Easter Seal Society of North Carolina closed its segregated camp for children and adults with physical and multiple disabilities and expanded its service system to provide a year-round program with a more complex set of program options. Charles Bullock, Michael Mahon, and Luanne Welch write:

> This change in the service delivery system, called the Progressive Mainstreaming Model, guarantees camping and other community leisure services to individuals previously served in segregated settings, and enables Easter Seals to serve *more* children and adults with disabilities in *better* ways at a *lower* cost.
>
> The Progressive Mainstreaming Model offers three basic options: segregated, modified mainstream, and mainstream. The initial evaluation shows that the model encourages the *maximum participation* of campers in the least restrictive environment, and offers an *expanded* range of experiences in a larger number of geographic locations.[52]

Cooperative Networks of Agencies

Because many community and nonprofit organizations lacked the staff resources or special facilities required to provide comprehensive leisure-service programs for disabled persons, the 1980s and 1990s saw a trend toward developing cooperative networks of such agencies.

In such structures, two or more public or nonprofit human-service organizations—or a combination of both types—share their funding and facilities to provide needed recreation programs in a number of locations. For example, there are over 20 independent Special Recreation Associations (SRAs) in northern Illinois, with budgets ranging from $50,000 to $1.5 million annually, based on revenue generated from special direct property taxes. All SRAs are coordinated by boards representing the cooperating communities. They interface with municipal recreation and park departments and offer programming for persons with all types of disabling conditions in both integrated and segregated groupings.

In another example of jointly operated programs, the Southeast Consortium for Special Services has been established in Westchester County, New York, to serve nine towns, cities, and villages with a wide range of special recreation activities and services. Since the bulk of its funding (apart from contributed facilities and staff resources) is received from the State Office of Mental Retardation and Developmental Disabilities, it focuses on individuals with autism, cerebral palsy, epilepsy, mental retardation, and neurological impairment or multiple disabilities and provides services in a variety of integrated and separate groupings.

Professional Standards of Practice

The practice of therapeutic recreation service has become increasingly sophisticated—particularly within the domain of clinical service. Consequently, in February 1994, the National Therapeutic Recreation Society approved the following revised definition of therapeutic recreation:

> Practiced in clinical, residential, and community settings, the profession of therapeutic recreation uses treatment, education, and recreation services to help people with illnesses, disabilities, and other conditions to develop and use their leisure in ways that enhance their health, independence, and well-being.[53]

Following this statement, the NTRS Standards of Practice Committee published a detailed set of standards, criteria, and operational guidelines for practitioners in this field, covering the following elements of service: (1) scope of service; (2) mission and purpose, goals and objectives; (3) individual treatment and program plan; (4) documentation; (5) plan of operation; (6) personnel qualifications; (7) ethical responsibilities; and (8) evaluation and research.

The detailed nature of these Standards of Practice is indicated by the criteria used to support the guidelines for development and implementation of recreation services under *Standard I, Scope of Service.* These are as follows:

a. There is a plan for assessing and identifying goals and objectives, client leisure needs, interests, competencies, and capabilities. This is sometimes referred to as a needs assessment or benefit-based management.

b. Opportunities are available for clients to provide input into the development of their recreation experiences.

c. Barriers to client participation are identified, considered and accommodated for in the planning and implementation of recreation activities. These can include architectural, financial, transportation, communication, and/or attitudinal barriers.

d. Plans are developed for each client to participate at his/her optimal level of ability and to progress according to interests, competencies, and capabilities.

e. Planned activities are age and developmentally appropriate, and modified through the use of accommodations, including adaptive equipment and techniques.

f. Recreation services are planned and implemented to accommodate the client's cultural, social, educational, and economic background.

g. Recreation services are plannd to encompass the normal rhythm of life, and attempt to align with normalization principles and the promotion of integration and inclusion.

---

h. Persons who deliver recreation services are qualified by holding a current certificate as Certified Therapeutic Recreation Specialist (CTRS), Certified Leisure Professional (CLP), and/or Certified Leisure Associate (CLA).

i. Recreation services are planned and integrated within the agency to achieve maximum use of available resources.

j. Program plans, protocols (procedures), and risk management policies exist, and risks and potentials for risk are identified for the client prior to recreation participation.

k. Essential eligibility criteria are established for all activities.

l. There is an initial client orientation, with assistance provided to the available recreation programs, facilities, and resources to achieve maximum mobility and independence.

m. There is a plan for homebound/bedside activities, when needed.

n. There is a plan for client feedback regarding program effectiveness.

o. There is periodic evaluation of the recreation services program plan.[54]

Emphasis on Outcomes: Efficacy Research

A key element in the maturing of therapeutic recreation as a field of professional service linked to the medical and other health- or social-service fields has been the increased emphasis given by educators and practitioners to the evaluation of therapeutic recreation program outcomes. The most comprehensive compilation of efficacy study findings was carried out by Catherine Coyle, W.B. Kinney, Bob Riley, and John Shank as part of a study at Temple University. Supported by the National Institute on Disability and Rehabilitation Research of the federal Department of Education, this report compiled the positive findings of hundreds of research studies on therapeutic recreation's impact from a medical perspective.[55] As this chapter has shown, therapeutic recreation may be provided by many different kinds of sponsors, including public, nonprofit, and other groups. Even commercial recreation plays a role in providing services for persons with disabilities, as is indicated by the numerous tourism and travel businesses that now package tours and resort opportunities for such groups.

SUMMARY

The four specialized areas of leisure-service delivery described in this chapter illustrate the diversity of agencies that provide organized recreation opportunities today. In each case, they have their own goals and objectives, populations served, and program emphases. Yet they are important elements within the overall leisure-service system and represent attractive fields of career opportunity for recreation, park, and leisure-service students today.

Armed forces recreation professionals serve a distinct population, composed both of large numbers of relatively young service men and women—often single and away from home— and of families and dependents with special needs prompted by the military setting. Morale, fitness, and mission accomplishment are important armed forces recreation goals, and these

are reflected in an increasingly businesslike approach to planning, marketing, and evaluating programs. With reduced budgets caused by downsizing and a greater emphasis on fiscal self-sufficiency, military recreation has undergone major transformations in recent years; yet it continues to offer a wide range of attractive program opportunities and often has excellent facilities, both stateside and abroad.

Employee recreation and services today have gone far beyond their original emphasis on providing a narrow range of social and sports activities designed to promote company-worker relationships. They are carried on in many different kinds of organizations and include varied health and fitness-related program elements, as well as such other personnel services as discount programs, company stores, community relationships, and other benefits-driven functions—all necessarily provided within a business-oriented framework that demands productivity and demonstrated outcomes.

Campus recreation is probably the least professionalized of these services, in terms of its being carried on within an educational setting with relatively little interaction with the overall recreation and parks field. At the same time, it has important responsibilities in terms of promoting the overall well-being of students, helping to reduce negative or destructive forms of play, extending and enriching academic learnings, and contributing to other college and university goals.

Finally, therapeutic recreation service, in its two areas of professional emphasis—clinical or treatment service and community-based special recreation—is probably the most highly professionalized of all the separate disciplines in the leisure-service field. It has a long history of professional development, with separate sections of state and national societies, early emphasis on registration and certification (as Chapter 13 will show more fully), numerous specialized curricula, and a rich literature and background of research. With the possibility of lessened support being given to clinical therapeutic recreation in an era of cost-cutting, hospital retrenchment, managed patient care, and deinstitutionalization, it is probable that community-based special recreation, with its emphasis on mainstreaming, will constitute an increasingly important element in therapeutic recreation.

Questions for Class Discussion or Essay Examinations

1. What are the major goals of recreation in the armed forces? Describe some of the key programming areas and indicate how military recreation planners have adapted to problems posed by cutbacks in military bases and personnel and fiscal restraints.

2. One of the chief emphases in employee services and recreation programs involves health and fitness. Using examples taken from the chapter, what forms of services are provided and what documented evidence is there to support their value?

3. Campus recreation has a number of important values for colleges and universities today. Identify and describe these and then focus in detail on the *in loco parentis* function of institutions of higher education. What does this principle involve and why is it particularly important today? Applied to your own institution, how does the administration provide a degree of control over students' lives and what part does campus recreation play in this effort?

4. Describe the two major thrusts in therapeutic recreation service today. In terms of special recreation, explain the current thinking with respect to mainstreaming individuals

with disabilities. What limitations, if any, should be applied to the integration of persons with disabilities in all ongoing community recreation programs?

Endnotes

[3]   Francis Kinsman, "Military Recreation and Mission Accomplishment," *Parks and Recreation* (October 1991): 42–43.

[4]   Lankford and DeGraaf, *op. cit.*, 32.

[5]   Bob McKeta, "Army Outdoor Recreation: Building for Year 2000 and Beyond," *Parks and Recreation* (December 1994): 33–34.

[6]   Steven Waller and Asuncion Suren, "Recreation and Military Youth," *Journal of Physical Education, Recreation and Dance—Leisure Today* (April 1995): 22.

[7]   Bob McKeta, "Bringing Recreation to the Whole (Army) Family," *Athletic Business* (September 1988): 38–40.

[8]   Gail Howerton, "American Armed Forces Overseas: The Few, the Proud, the Creative," *Parks and Recreation* (December 1994): 57.

[9]   John Kelly, Curt Cornelssen, and Margaret Bailey, "Military Base Closures Can Change: Lands to Parks," *Parks and Recreation* (January 1996): 71.

[10] Richard Kraus and Joseph Curtis, *Creative Management in Recreation and Parks* (St. Louis: Mosby, 1982): 206–207.

[11] Carolyn Becraft, Deputy Assistant Secretary of Defense, quoted by Pat Harden, "Armed Forces Recreation Services Our Hallowed Ground Raison D'Etre," *Parks and Recreation* (December 1994): 24.

[12] Lankford and DeGraaf, *op. cit.*, 40.

[13] "NESRA's Employer of the Year," *Employee Services Management* (May/June 1991): 17.

[14] Steven Blair, "Worksite Health Promotion "Bottom-Line" Facts and Figures," *Employee Services Management* (May/June 1995): 31–33.

[15] Jill Decker, "Seven Steps to Sponsorship," *Parks and Recreation* (December 1991): 44.

[16] "Member Success Profile," *Employee Services Management* (September 1991): 13.

[17] "Tracking Trends in Employee Services and Recreation: NESRA's 1984 Biannual Survey," *Employee Recreation* (December/January 1984/1985): 12–16.

[18] "You're Part of the $160 Million Employee Services Market," *Employee Services Management* (January 1995): 23.

[19] Jack Kondrasuk and Christy Carl, "Wellness Programs, Present and Future," *Employee Services Management* (December/January 1991/1992): 9.

[20] Lisa Kurzeja, "SmithKline Beecham Wellness Rx Facility," *Employee Services Management* (May/June 1995): 16.

[21] Joe Hauglie, "Adopting an Entrepreneurial Attitude," *Employee Services Management* (May/June 1991): 14.

[22] *Ibid.*, 15.

[23] *Ibid.*, 16.

[24] "Alcohol Seen as No. 1 Campus Abuse Problem," *Chronicle of Higher Education* (25 March 1987): 32.

[25] Anne Matthews, "The Campus Crime Wave," *New York Times* (7 March 1993): 38.

[26] Judith Bryant and James Bradley, "Enhancing Academic Productivity: Student Development and Employment Potential," *NIRSA Journal* (Fall 1993): 42.

[27] *Ibid.*, 43.

[28] Gary Nussbaum, "Adventures in Intramural Outdoor Recreation Programming," *Journal of Physical Education, Recreation and Dance* (February 1987): 58.

[29] Wayne Fett, Challenge Courses on University and College Campuses," *NIRSA Journal* (Fall 1993): 52.

[30] There is evidence of this at the secondary school level as well. See "Link Found Between High School Activities and Good Grades," Associated Press (20 December 1980).

[31] "Bathroom Reading," *Athletic Business* (October 1994): 46–47.

[32] H. Douglas Sessoms and Karla Henderson, *Introduction to Leisure Services* (State College, Penn.: Venture Publishing, 1994): 205.

[33] "Family Service," *Athletic Business* (October 1995): 32.

[34] Charles Sylvester, "Therapeutic Recreation and the Right to Leisure," *Therapeutic Recreation Journal* (2nd Quarter 1992): 9–20.

[35] Mark Searle and Russell Brayley, *Leisure Services in Canada: An Introduction* (State College, Penn.: Venture Publishing, 1993): 144–145.

[36] Public Health Service, *Health Resource Statistics—1968* (Washington, D.C.: U.S. Public Health Service, 1968): 185.

[37] Adapted from Gerald O'Morrow, *Therapeutic Recreation: A Helping Profession* (Reston, Va.: Reston Publishing, 1976): Chapter 7.

[38] See *Statement of Philosophy of Therapeutic Recreation Service* (Arlington, Va.: National Therapeutic Recreation Society, 1982).

[39] Roxanne Howe-Murphy and Becky Charboneau, *Therapeutic Recreation Intervention: An Ecological Perspective* (Englewood Cliffs, N.J.: Prentice-Hall, 1987): 220.

[40] *Ibid.*

[41] Dan Kennedy, David Austin, and Ralph Smith, *Special Recreation: Opportunities for Persons with Disability* (Philadelphia: Saunders College Publishing, 1987): 31.

[42] *Survey on Community-Based Therapeutic Recreation Programs and Services* (Prince George's County, Md.: Maryland–National Capital Parks and Planning Commission, Department of Parks and Recreation, 1993): 24.

[43] Michael Kelley, "The Therapeutic Potential of Outdoor Adventure: A Review with Focus on Adults with Mental Illness," *Therapeutic Recreation Journal* (2nd Quarter 1993): 110–121.

[44] David Hewitt and Larry Crump, "Outdoor Recreation for Persons with Disabilities," *Trends* (Vol. 29 No. 4 1992): 4.

[45] Richard Kraus and John Shank, *Therapeutic Recreation Service: Principles and Practices* (Dubuque, Iowa: Wm. C. Brown, 1992): 208.

[46] Ladd Colston, "The Expanding Role of Assistive Technology in Therapeutic Recreation," *Journal of Physical Education, Recreation and Dance—Leisure Today* (April 1991): 15.

[47] Anita Srikameswaran, "Children in Hospital Get On-Line Fun," *Philadelphia Inquirer* (13 August 1995): A-5.

[48] Jack Hourcade, "Special Olympics: A Review and Critical Analysis," *Therapeutic Recreation Journal* (1st Quarter 1989): 58–65.

[49] Linda Heyne and Frederick Greene, "Friendship Between Adults With and Without Developmental Disabilities," *Parks and Recreation* (October 1994): 14, 16–18.

[50] Linda Heyne, Stuart Schleien, and Leo McAvoy, "Friendship Development Between Children With and Without Developmental Disabilities in Recreation Activities," *Abstracts of NRPA Leisure Research Symposium* (1993): 20.

51   Leandra Bedini, "Transition and Integration in Leisure for People with Disabilities," *Parks and Recreation* (November 1993): 20.

52   Charles Bullock, Michael Mahon, and LuAnne Welch, "Easter Seals' Progressive Mainstreaming Model: Options and Choices in Camping and Leisure Services for Children and Adults with Disabilities," *Therapeutic Recreation Journal* (4th Quarter 1992): 61–62.

53   *Standards of Practice in Therapeutic Recreation Service* (Arlington, Va.: National Therapeutic Recreation Society, 1994): i.

54   *Ibid.*, 1.

55   Catherine Coyle, W. B. Kinney, Bob Riley, and John Shank, *Benefits of Therapeutic Recreation: A Consensus View* (Philadelphia, Penn.: Temple University and National Institute on Disability and Rehabilitation Research, 1994).

thirteen 13

Career Opportunities and Professionalism in Recreation, Parks, and Leisure Services

[**A**n] important milestone has been reached in recreation, parks, and leisure services education. COPA, the Council on Postsecondary Accreditation, the "accrediting body of accrediting bodies," has recognized the NRPA-AALR Council on Accreditation for recreation, park resources and leisure services education. This recognition, granted on October 3, 1986, in Chicago, Illinois, includes membership in the Assembly of Specialized Accrediting Bodies. We join such prestigious COPA-recognized disciplines as medicine, law, journalism, architecture, social work, and teacher education. Our field, for the first time, is recognized as a unique discipline by the authoritative recognition-body of American higher education.[1]

INTRODUCTION

As earlier chapters have shown, recreation, parks, and leisure services have expanded rapidly over the last several decades as a diversified area of employment. Today, several million men and women work in different sectors of the leisure-service field, including amateur

---

[1] Donald Henkel and Tony Mobley, "The Quest for COPA Recognition," *Parks and Recreation* (November 1986): 50.

and professional sports, entertainment and amusement services, travel and tourism, recreation-related businesses, and government and nonprofit community organizations.

As a distinct part of this larger group, several hundred thousand men and women are directly involved as recreation leaders, supervisors, managers, therapists, planners, and consultants in public, voluntary, commercial, therapeutic, and other types of agencies. These individuals, with a primary concern for the provision of recreation services, are generally regarded as *professionals* on the basis of their job responsibilities, specialized training, and affiliations with professional societies.

How did this come about, and what are the present characteristics of recreation, parks, and leisure services as a career field? This chapter examines the changing identity of the leisure-service field, using several criteria that are commonly used to measure the degree of professionalism of occupational fields.

RECREATION AS A CAREER

People have worked in recreation for many centuries in the sense that there have been professional athletes and entertainers throughout history. Musicians, tumblers, dancers, huntsmen, park designers, and gardeners were all recreation specialists attending to the leisure needs first of royalty, and ultimately the public at large. However, the idea of recreation itself as a career field did not surface until the late 1800s, when public parks and playgrounds, along with voluntary social-service and youth-serving organizations, were established.

After the turn of the century, courses in play leadership were developed by the Playground Association of America and were taken by many teachers. In the middle 1920s, the National Recreation Association provided a graduate training program for professional recreation and park administrators, and leisure as a distinct area of public service came to be recognized. This recognition increased during the great Depression of the 1930s as many thousands of individuals were assigned by the federal government to emergency posts providing community recreation programs and developing new parks and other facilities. But it was not until the development of separate degree programs in a handful of colleges that higher education in recreation and parks as a distinct career field came into being.

H. Douglas Sessoms has described the background of this development with emphasis on the emerging role of leisure-service leaders:

> Parks and recreation is an amalgamated field of service. It did not result from one social movement, but is the product of several. One component—recreation services—resulted from the playground and scientific charity movements which occurred at the beginning of the 20th century. Leaders of those movements were concerned about the quality of life for youth and the importance of play for all children. They believed in the inherent value of play, and the responsibility of society to create and sustain organizations (privately and publicly), especially comprehensive community centers which would promote and/or provide play opportunities. They were against social injustices and thought that proper play behavior would help the child grow into a healthy adult, a good citizen.[2]

By the second half of the twentieth century, careers in recreation and parks were seen as a growth area. A nationwide study of workforce requirements in the 1960s concluded that there would be a need for hundreds of thousands of new recreation and park professionals in the years ahead. The U.S. Department of Labor reported widespread shortages of leisure-service personnel in local government, hospitals, and youth-serving organizations. Several factors, such as the federal government's expanded activity in outdoor recreation and open space and the establishment of the National Recreation and Park Association, stimulated interest in this field. In the 1970s, as employment grew, curricula in recreation and leisure service gained increased acceptance in higher education.

With the expansion of recreation and park programs, different leisure-service agencies began to define the functions of their employees on different hierarchical levels and in terms of the types of responsibilities they had. In part, such analyses were influenced by the essential missions of each type of agency. For example, James Murphy and Dennis Howard outlined the functions of practitioners in local public recreation and park organizations on a continuum from a centralized management role to a decentralized advocacy role.[3] Numerous other texts described the roles of recreation practitioners in leadership, supervisory, and administrative positions and in such specialized fields as therapeutic, armed forces, and commercial recreation.

Scope of Employment Today

Today, as previous chapters have shown, the kinds of organizations that employ recreation and park personnel are highly diversified. In a comprehensive analysis of the managed recreation system, *Recreation, Sports and Leisure* points out that the director of a hotel/spa complex grossing $30 million is a managed recreation professional:

> So is a student athletic director, and a stadium manager. Also included are health club owners, Jewish community center directors, county fair operators, tennis pros and dozens of others. Some have MBA's and practically live in vested suits; others couldn't survive without a pair of sneakers.[4]

The report goes on to point out that in every category—from educational background to salary levels or job responsibilities—recreation professionals are a diverse group. Many feel no special professional or emotional kinship with their peers. The element that they share in common is that they are all in the same business—the business of providing recreation and leisure programs in large, competitive environments.

A report on the growing recreation field, published in 1965 by the U.S. Department of Labor, pointed out that it was difficult to determine the exact number of people employed in the recreation field, because so many occupations—such as those connected with travel—are only *partly* based on leisure motivations. Nonetheless, through the years numerous reports on employment in recreation, parks, and leisure services have been issued.

In 1995, the *Statistical Abstract of the United States* reported that employment totals in various leisure-related fields were as follows: hotels and other lodging jobs: 1.5 million; motion picture industry: 404,000; amusement and recreation services: 1.1 million; and social services (museums, zoos, and membership organizations): 1.9 million.[5]

In separate tables, it reported that positions as amusement and recreation attendants were projected to grow from 121,000 in 1992 to 303,000 in 2005, and that jobs as sports and fitness coaches and instructors were estimated to increase from 260,000 to 355,000 over the same period.[6]

In 1995 government recreation and park employees on all levels (federal, state, and local) totaled 345,000, while those concerned with natural resources numbered 436,000.[7]

PROFESSIONAL IDENTIFICATION IN RECREATION

At this point, it is appropriate to focus more sharply on the recreation, park, or leisure-service *professional* as such. This term is commonly applied to persons employed in such major categories of recreation services as public recreation and park departments, voluntary agencies, therapeutic programs, the armed forces, campus recreation, commercial recreation, and employee programs.

What does being a professional mean? At the simplest level, it indicates that one is paid for one's work—as opposed to an amateur, who is not paid for it. Thus, an athlete who receives pay for playing for a team is classified as a professional. (Professional may also imply being very good at one's work; thus, the phrase he—or she—is a real pro!)

But this obviously is not a sufficient definition of the term in that many forms of paid work are *not* considered to be professional. A more complete definition of the term would suggest that a professional is one who has a high degree of status and specialized training and provides a significant form of public or social service. A position paper of the Society of Park and Recreation Educators defined *profession* as follows:

> A profession is a vocation whose practice is founded upon an understanding of the theoretical structure of some department of learning or science and upon the abilities accompanying such understanding. This understanding and these abilities are applied to the vital practical affairs of man. . . . The profession, serving the vital needs of man, considers its first ethical imperative to be altruistic service to the client.[8]

In his review of the recreation and park field's advancement between 1955 and 1985, Donald Henkel pointed out that generally accepted indicators of professionalism include: (1) a defined body of knowledge; (2) formal academic preparation prior to practice; (3) standards of practice that are restrictive and require continuation of education; (4) professional organizations; (5) a code of ethics; and (6) public acceptance.[9]

With these criteria as guidelines, this chapter now proceeds to examine the recreation, park, and leisure-service field to measure its current standing as a profession. It begins by asking whether those working in this field perform services that are of real value to society.

CRITERION 1: SOCIAL VALUE AND PURPOSE

As earlier chapters in this text have shown, the public has demanded recreation facilities and programs with increasing urgency through the years and has been generally supportive of leisure-service agencies. The actual purposes of such facilities and programs may vary greatly—from providing fun and relaxation to promoting physical fitness and the improvement of personal health, or inculcating desirable social values and helping to reduce or prevent delinquency or other social pathologies.

The specific social goals of public and nonprofit community leisure-service agencies are described in detail in Chapter 6. As a single example of how a national nonprofit organization has committed itself to a set of significant social goals, the YWCA is dedicated to the empowerment of women and girls and the elimination of racism. The oldest American organization owned and managed by women, its 374 member organizations provide safety, shelter, day care, physical fitness and recreation programs, counseling, and other social, health, educational, and job-related services to millions of women and girls and their communities each year. In 1994:

> Local YWCAs provided one million women and girls with rape and domestic violence counseling, 350,000 children participated in day care programs, 90,000 women enrolled in job training services, and more than

300,000 homeless women and children, many of whom were escaping violence, sought safety in transitional housing. A leader in violence prevention, some YWCAs offer 24-hour hotlines, emergency transportation, family and children's counseling, and programs for men who batter. Many associations offer bilingual services to reach culturally, racially and economically diverse members of the communities they serve.[10]

While many of these services are obviously *not* forms of recreation, sports, crafts, hobbies, the arts, and social activities represent a major element in overall YWCA programming and serve to attract many members of all ages and backgrounds. Similarly, in many other community-based leisure-service agencies, recreation offerings are closely integrated with other social services or serve to accomplish important social outcomes in their own right.

CRITERION 2: PUBLIC RECOGNITION

The rapid expansion of the leisure-service field over the past several decades does not necessarily mean that the public at large understands and respects it fully or that they regard it as a distinct area of professional service. To illustrate, most individuals today know what recreation is, and many regard it as an important part of their lives. Most are prepared to pay substantial portions of their income for recreation goods or services, such as memberships in health clubs, vacations, sports equipment, television sets, and other leisure-related fees and charges. However, they are often less willing to pay taxes in support of public recreation and park facilities and programs than they are to spend privately for their own leisure needs. While this may simply be due to a generalized reluctance to pay taxes, it may also suggest that people are often not convinced that recreation is a critical area of government responsibility.

However, in a detailed analysis of the public's perception of local public recreation and park agencies, Geoffrey Godbey, Alan Graefe, and Stephen James surveyed a broadly representative sample of 1,305 households throughout the United States. A substantial member of those queried had visited parks and playgrounds during the preceding year and had participated in such activities as sports leagues, educational classes, and artistic or cultural events in their communities. The majority of respondents reported significant individual, household, and community benefits provided by their local recreation and park agencies.[11]

Even though the value of organized recreation service may be acknowledged, how aware is the public at large of the leisure-service field *as a profession*? The likelihood is that most individuals recognize the roles of recreation professionals within specific areas of service. For example, they are likely to be familiar with the function of a recreation therapist in a mental hospital or nursing home, or the function of a community center director, a park ranger, or a sports specialist in an armed forces recreation program.

What they tend not to understand is that recreation represents a unified profession that requires special expertise and educational preparation in a college or university. At issue is the image of the recreation professional.

Image of the Professional

The public's perception of those working in the recreation field tends to be unclear. Often, the recreation professional is confused with the physical educator, because of the strong emphasis on sports in many recreation programs and the close connection between the two fields in early professional preparation.

Recreation professionals themselves have assumed such a wide variety of roles that no single image stands out. Sessoms commented a number of years ago that "we would like to be all things to all people: entertainers, promoters, counselors, psychiatric aides, and social analysts," concluding:

> I am afraid the public sees us either as ex-athletes, or gregarious, fun-and-game leaders wearing short pants, knee socks, and an Alpine hat, calling for all to join in.[12]

He later suggested that one of the problems was that recreation was not perceived as an occupational field that required special preparation and long-term training, and that it was ranked only "average" in remuneration. In part, the question of identity is one that workers in this field must settle for themselves. For example, a study of therapeutic recreation employees in Michigan showed that many respondents did not hold degrees in the field or belong to state or national professional organizations, and were not professionally registered. It would seem clear that, if recreation and leisure-service employees are to sharpen their identity and support, they must enrich their own competence through specialized professional study and by joining organizations that strengthen their field.

On the positive side, a number of outstanding recreation and park professionals in communities throughout the United States have enhanced the image of the field through their dedicated leadership. As a single example, Robert Crawford, a veteran recreation and park administrator, was widely known and admired for his success as Commissioner of Recreation in Philadelphia, Pennsylvania. When Crawford came to Philadelphia in 1952

> the city had 95 recreational areas. By the time he left, it had 815, including parks, playgrounds, swimming pools and community centers. He also helped to transform the way cities and residents viewed parks.
>
> In the 1930s, when he began in recreation, parks were considered ornamentation. But in positions on the East and West Coasts, Mr. Crawford was among the first to advocate transforming them into recreational areas for a community with diverse interests and needs.
>
> Under his leadership in Philadelphia, parks added trails for hikers, basketball courts for people who used wheelchairs, and exercise programs based in community centers for the elderly. He also set up advisory groups to identify the recreational needs in specific neighborhoods.[13]

Professionals like Robert Crawford are often able to gain the wholehearted support of the business community, to encourage widespread citizen involvement and advocacy, and to strengthen the public's awareness and support for the recreation, park, and leisure-service field.

CRITERION 3: SPECIALIZED PROFESSIONAL PREPARATION

A measure of the professional authority of any given field is the degree of specialized preparation that people must have to function in it. Typically, the most highly regarded professions in modern society, such as medicine or law, have rigorous requirements with respect to professional education. These have evolved through the years and involve higher education curricula on the graduate level, supported in some cases by required internships or periods of professional practice and by comprehensive examinations prepared or administered by professional societies.

Professional Preparation in Recreation and Parks

The early period of the development of higher education in recreation, parks, and leisure services was described earlier in this text. Over the past five decades, college and university curricula in recreation and parks have been developed on three levels: two-year, four-year, and graduate (master's degree and doctorate).

Two-Year Curricula   During the late 1960s, and early 1970s, many community colleges began to offer associate degree programs in recreation and parks. Typically, these sought to prepare individuals on para- or sub-professional levels, rather than for supervisory or administrative roles. Most community colleges offered recreation majors a choice of two types of programs: terminal and transfer. Terminal programs were intended to equip students immediately for employment, and gave heavy emphasis to developing basic, useful recreation leadership skills, often within a specific field of practice. Transfer programs were intended for students who hoped to transfer to four-year degree programs.

During the late 1970s and early 1980s, many community college programs in recreation and parks suffered enrollment declines and were cut back or discontinued. However, a number of excellent curricula continue to offer two-year associate degrees, with graduates who either go directly into the field or transfer to baccalaureate programs.

Four-Year Programs   The most widely found degree program in recreation and parks has been the four-year bachelor's degree curriculum. Initially, most such programs consisted of specialized degree options in college departments of health, physical education, and recreation—although some were located in departments or schools of landscape architecture, agriculture, forestry, or social work. Today, although many departments are still situated administratively in schools or colleges of health, physical education, and recreation, they have achieved a high level of curricular independence—with their own objectives, courses, degree requirements, and faculty.

Four-year programs typically have established degree options in areas such as recreation programming, recreation and park management, resource management, therapeutic recreation, and commercial recreation. The normal pattern has been to require all department majors to take certain *core* courses representing the generic needs of all pre-professionals, including basic courses in recreation history and philosophy, programming, management, and evaluation and/or research—and then to have a separate cluster of specialized courses for each different option.

At the same time that baccalaureate study in the leisure-service field has become more highly specialized and sophisticated, concern has been expressed about the need to have it include a strong liberal arts component. Ronald Riggins, Charles Sylvester, and James Moore describe liberal education that enables persons to live fully, freely, and responsibly. Focusing heavily on the humanities and on values before preparing competent professionals, liberal education seeks to cultivate virtuous persons—intelligent, broadminded, humane, and ethical. They continue:

"Know how," or technical skills, constitute the brick and mortar of our profession and are necessary for the creation and delivery of services. By themselves, however, these skills do not assist professionals in determining the ends to which they should be directed and the

> conditions of their use. This is the difference between the technician and the professional. Technicians know "how." Liberally educated professionals not only understand "how," they also know "why," "whether," and "when." Consequently, they can apply technical skills in a broader framework of aims and values.[14]

During the 1980s and early 1990s, there was considerable flux in four-year recreation and park curricula in the United States and Canada. M. Deborah Bialeschki points out that in the early 1980s, there appeared to be a significant decline in the number of undergraduate students entering this field—but that this trend was reversed by the end of the decade. In a number of colleges and universities, established curricula were either eliminated or cut back sharply, or were transferred to new departmental settings and given new titles. Bialeschki comments that such changes must be understood within the context of conditions that affected institutions of higher learning at this time:

> The idea of the collegiate environment as "home" or "family" [or as an academic setting focused primarily on scholarship] has been replaced by a notion of the campus as an efficient machine designed to motivate performance and enable financial success in the post-college world.
>
> The economic conditions of the federal and state governments also have affected college campuses. The first signs of economic limits began to appear in the late 1970s. And over the years, the impact on some campuses has been dramatic: academic cutbacks, increased student tuitions, elimination and downsizing of departments, and increased pressure on faculty to generate revenue.[15]

With the onset of the era of economic austerity, many public recreation and park agencies had either frozen their staffs or cut back on them; as a result, there was little demand for new graduates in the governmental leisure-service agencies. However, there was growing academic awareness of the job opportunities in other recreation areas. As a result, a number of college and university programs changed their titles and departmental affiliations to reflect the new interest in commercial recreation, travel and tourism, sports management, hotel and resort management, and similar specializations. In many cases, curriculum revision was based on the requirements or recommendations of professional societies, such as the Resort and Commercial Recreation Association (RCRA), the North American Society for Sport Management (NASSM), the National Association for Sport and Physical Education (NASPE), and the National Employee Services and Recreation Association (NESRA).

SPRE and other professional societies or branches of the National Recreation and Park Association have sponsored numerous conferences, institutes, and workshops designed to promote more effective higher education in the leisure-service field. At the same time, it is clear that conflict exists between those educators who seek to promote a conceptually oriented approach to curriculum design that is focused heavily on philosophical, historical, or sociological examination of leisure and those who—bolstered by market pressures—emphasize the need to recruit students through an entrepreneurial approach that emphasizes effective career preparation and job placement.

Master's Degree and Doctoral Programs   Although it is generally agreed that the four-year curriculum should provide a broad base of general or liberal arts education along with the core of essential knowledge underlying recreation service, the specific function of graduate education in this field is not as clearly defined.

Some authorities have suggested that graduate curricula should accept only those students who have already taken a degree in recreation and should focus on providing advanced professional education within a specialized area of service. However, there tends to be little support for this position, and many graduate programs accept students from other undergraduate disciplines as well as those holding undergraduate degrees in recreation.

In general, authorities agree that master's degree work should involve advanced study in recreation and park administration or in some other specialized area of service, such as therapeutic recreation. The assumption is that individuals on this level are preparing for supervisory or managerial positions, or in some cases roles as researchers, evaluators, planners, or consultants.

Specialized Body of Knowledge

At the outset, many recreation and park degree programs were established as "minor" specializations in other areas of study. As such, they tended to lack theoretically based courses within the field of study. Over the past four decades, this deficiency has been largely corrected.

However, there continues to be some concern about whether the degree programs in this field are based on a legitimate field of academic study. Typically, critics argue that it is simply an area of practical management or, from a theoretical point of view, a field with a hodge-podge of ideas drawn from other disciplines—but lacking a unique body of knowledge. What *is* a professional body of knowledge? Thomas Yukic writes that it is

> an aggregate of theories, facts, principles, understandings and skills, formally and systematically organized as academic courses of study. It must be agreed upon by a teaching faculty, and approved by field professionals as providing a framework of vocational and educational concepts indispensable to proficiency in a recreation service job at a particular level.[16]

The knowledge itself must be both conceptual and practical or applied. Conceptual knowledge consists of information about the historical and philosophical roots of leisure and recreation, the social and economic significance of leisure and recreation in the community and nation, the role of play as a phenomenon of human development, and other specific theoretical concepts about environmental issues and processes, the interaction of government and other agencies, and the needs of special populations.

Practical or applied knowledge relates to the specific skills needed by recreation practitioners. Depending on the agency and population served, these may include skills of direct leadership and program development or managerial functions such as personnel management, fiscal operations, facilities planning and maintenance, public relations, research and evaluation, and similar tasks.

On undergraduate levels, a major element in the process of imparting practical knowledge and skills to students consists of required field work and internship experiences. While these vary from institution to institution, in general they require at least a semester of full-time commitment to work in an agency of high quality within the student's expressed field of professional interest. Such placements should extend far beyond an agency's using field work or internship students in routine or mechanical roles as a source of cheap labor. Instead, they are meant to involve a full range of realistic job assignments and exposures, as well as conscientious counseling and supervision by professional staff members.

As an example, Bob McKeta describes the value of placing student interns in U.S. Army Morale, Welfare and Recreation (MWR) settings, particularly those in outdoor recreation, sports and sports management, youth activities, and community recreation.

Placement opportunities include a substantial number of summer interships, with about half of them in overseas areas such as Okinawa, Korea, Japan, and Germany. This experience involves many functions in military recreation relating to management, administration, marketing, and programming, which, as McKeta points out, easily transfer to other organizational settings in the corporate, municipal, and private recreation fields.[17]

The knowledge and skills components of higher education in recreation, parks, and leisure studies—while they may involve content taken from other scholarly disciplines or fields of practice—are formulated in terms that are specifically applicable to the recreation field.

Given the recent impressive growth in both research studies and publication of findings, it seems clear that the field does have a legitimate body of knowledge that must be possessed by professionals. Indeed, within some areas of practice, there has been systematic study of the competencies and knowledge that entry-level practitioners should possess, so as to provide a basis for curriculum development. David Austin, for example, has reported on the competencies needed for special recreation leaders, and Norma Stumbo has defined the entry-level knowledge essential for therapeutic recreation practice.[18]

Philosophical Orientation   An important component of specialized study in the leisure-service field involves the transmission of a positive philosophical orientation regarding the role of recreation and leisure in the modern community. This orientation, which is described more fully in Chapter 14, includes both a full appreciation of the importance of recreation in contemporary life and a set of principles to govern policies with respect to agency priorities and program strategies.

Accreditation in Higher Education

The most significant effort that has been made to upgrade curricular standards and practices in recreation, parks, and leisure studies has come in the accreditation process. The first attempt to develop a separate accreditation review process in recreation and parks was undertaken by the Federation of National Professional Organizations for Recreation in 1963, with a threefold purpose: (1) to develop for the National Commission on Accrediting a statement supporting recreation as a significant field of public service and as a profession; (2) to develop standards and evaluative criteria for recreation education at both undergraduate and graduate levels; and (3) to raise funds to carry out the actual process of accreditation.[19]

In 1965, the Recreation Education Accreditation Committee identified several appropriate areas of degree specialization, and proposed guides for approved practices as well as specific criteria by which college departments might be judged. This document was revised in light of several pilot accreditations, and was published again in 1972 by the National Recreation and Park Association Board on Professional Education.

In order to ensure broader representation in the process, a new Council on Accreditation was formed with representation from both the National Recreation and Park Association and the American Association for Leisure and Recreation. By 1980, approximately 30 college departments had applied for and received accreditation for all or part of their programs. In the course of this process, clearly defined standards and procedural guidelines for departments seeking accreditation had been developed, including guidelines regarding courses, administrative support, student selection and services, faculty resources, and other curriculum components.

In 1982, the Council on Postsecondary Accreditation agreed to consider the NRPA/AALR Council's application, an important first step in the process. In addition, steps were taken to streamline the accreditation operation by limiting its application only to baccalaureate programs and simplifying review procedures. After an arduous series of hearings and a review of the documents supporting the legitimacy of recreation, parks, and leisure studies as an area of significant scholarly concern, the Council on Postsecondary Accreditation finally granted recognition to it as a field of study and to the Council as the accrediting body.[20]

This served as a strong stimulus to the accreditation process, with the number of approved curricula increasing steadily from approximately 50 in the mid-1980s to 92 in 1993. It is widely recognized that accreditation has both internal and external benefits: (1) internal in that it requires a focused effort to upgrade curriculum content and program standards and tends to create a higher level of respect for approved departments within overall institutions; and (2) external in that it improves the level of instruction throughout the field and results in more highly qualified graduates entering the field.

CRITERION 4: EXISTENCE OF A PROFESSIONAL CULTURE

Another important characteristic of professions in modern society is that they have strong organizations, shared values, and traditions. How does the recreation and park field measure up to this criterion?

In both the United States and Canada, professional recreation societies have been in existence for a number of years. Like their counterparts in other professions, recreation and park associations have the following functions: they (1) regulate and set standards for professional development; (2) promote legislation for the advancement of the field; (3) develop programs of public information to improve understanding and support of the field; (4) sponsor conferences, publications, and field services to improve practices; and (5) press for higher standards of training, accreditation, and certification.

National Recreation and Park Association

Because of the varied nature of professional service in recreation and parks and the strong role played by citizens' groups and nonprofessional organizations, many different associations were established through the years to serve the field. Five of these (the National Recreation Association, American Institute of Park Executives, National Conference on State Parks, American Association of Zoological Parks and Aquariums, and American Recreation Society) merged into a single body in 1965, with Laurance S. Rockefeller as president. Within a year or two, other groups, such as the National Association of Recreation Therapists and the Armed Forces Section of the American Recreation Society, had merged their interests with the newly formed organization.

This national body, the National Recreation and Park Association, is an independent, nonprofit organization intended to promote the development of the recreation and park movement and the conservation of natural and human resources in the United States. It is directed by a Board of Trustees which meets several times each year to guide its major policies. Several separate branches carry out the work and serve to coalesce the special interests of members; these include the American Park and Recreation Society; the National Society for Park Resources; the Ethnic Minority Society; the Armed Forces Recreation Society; the National Therapeutic Recreation Society, the Society of Park and Recreation Educators; and the National Student Recreation and Park Society. The American Association of Zoological Parks and Aquariums was initially a branch of NRPA, but it withdrew in 1972.

Throughout the 1980s and early 1990s, NRPA played a vigorous role in helping to bring about a fuller national consciousness of the value of recreation and leisure through varied public information campaigns, publications, research efforts, and legislative presentations.

NRPA provides extensive services with respect to general and professionally oriented information through the NRPA/SCHOLE Network with links to Delphi and the Internet, the global database of communication that helps information flow through the government, business, education, research, and computer worlds.

Network features include: (1) electronic mail that facilitates instant teleconferencing among colleagues worldwide; (2) an information forum with an interactive on-line bulletin board; (3) timely updates of federal legislative action and initiatives; (4) a national employment bulletin with listings for numerous job and internship opportunities; (5) the NRPA Marketplace and Bookstore; (6) professional announcements; (7) an ongoing calendar of conferences and workshops; and (8) reports on research in progress, including abstracts from numerous scholarly and professional publications.[21]

The National Recreation and Park Association also sponsors the *Trends Action Group* (TAG), which monitors trends related to the field, shares information with professionals and agencies, implements proactive programs and services, and forecasts future developments.

NRPA publishes *Dateline,* a newsletter that focuses primarily on national issues related to recreation and parks. Through its Resource Development Division, it responds to thousands of inquiries and requests for technical assistance from practitioners. NRPA representatives regularly testify before Congressional subcommittees in support of legislation and funding proposals dealing with the environment, social needs, and similar national problems.[22]

In cooperation with various universities and other professional organizations or through its separate branches or state societies, NRPA sponsors numerous important workshops, management schools, and seminars each year. These deal with such functions as sports and aquatic management, facilities maintenance, revenue sources, programming for special populations, executive development for recreation and park professionals, computer technology, legal issues symposiums, and safety management.

Role of NRPA Branches and State Societies

Each of NRPA's branches carries on vigorous programs related to its specialized area of interest. For example, the National Therapeutic Recreation Society is active in developing professional standards and an effective certification process for therapeutic recreation personnel. It also promotes research and publication, sponsors conferences and workshops, helps shape higher education curricula, and carries out legislative and lobbying campaigns to block federal cutbacks in social services and achieve a higher level of support for therapeutic recreation services.

Despite this record of accomplishment, some of NTRS's members were discontented with the support given them by the national organization and complained that it failed to recognize their authority with respect to therapeutic recreation service and programming for special populations. As a result, a number of leading therapeutic recreation specialists formed a new national organization, the American Therapeutic Recreation Association, in the mid-1980s to focus more sharply on the concerns of this specialized field. Many professionals maintain membership in both groups; others, because of limited time and money, have been forced to choose one or the other. The ATRA/NTRS example demonstrates the difficulty faced by the National Recreation and Park Association in attempting to represent and serve the entire leisure-service field today.

The NRPA branch directly concerned with professional education and development is the Society of Park and Recreation Educators (SPRE), which defines its mission as that of an association of scholars who believe that leisure makes a valuable contribution to society:

> The Society facilitates for its members, the park and recreation profession, and society at large, the continuing investigation of leisure, and the development and dissemination of a body of knowledge that verifies its contributions . . . .
>
> Furthermore, the Society supports the development of techniques to improve professional practice and serves as a conduit for demonstrating the impact leisure has on society, including communities, the economy, and the development of individuals.[23]

Like NTRS, SPRE sponsors numerous conferences and workshops, promotes research efforts, and plays a leading role in processes concerned with certification, research, and the various functions that link recreation and leisure with other elements in the academic world and community life. Other NRPA branches, like the American Park and Recreation Society, and divisions, like the Recreation Programmers Division, carry out the functions related to their special emphases as professional bodies.

Even more influential than the branches are state recreation and park societies, which serve to meet local or regional needs directly and which command a large overall membership and level of active participation.

Other Professional Organizations

Many other organizations sponsor programs supporting the recreation and park field or one of its specialized components. For example, the American Alliance for Health, Physical Education, Recreation and Dance (AAHPERD) has several thousand members who have a specialized interest in education for leisure, school-sponsored recreation, the promotion of school camping and outdoor education, and adapted physical education and recreation programs for the disabled.

The branch of AAHPERD that has been most directly concerned with these functions has been the American Association for Leisure and Recreation (AALR), which has (1) worked closely on the accreditation process with NRPA through the Joint Accreditation Steering Committee and later the National Council on Accreditation; (2) played a key role in promoting community education and leisure education projects; (3) published *Leisure Today,* an outstanding series of special-theme inserts in the *Journal of Physical Education, Recreation and Dance;* and (4) assisted in job placement of recreation personnel and similar functions.

Other important organizations that have made important contributions to this field include: (1) the American Camping Association, the national professional organization of the organized camping movement; (2) the American College Personnel Association, which includes many people working in student residence halls and campus unions; (3) the American Association of College Unions, which has a similar function; (4) the Amateur Athletic Union, which promotes and sets standards for a wide range of participant sports in the United States; (5) the National Intramural-Recreational Sports Association, which promotes intramural sports competition in colleges and universities; (6) the National Employee Services and Recreation Association, which serves personnel directors and other professionals providing recreation, fitness, and related personnel services; and (7) the World Leisure and Recreation Association, which deals with the international recreation and leisure movement, has helped build several regional associations and has promoted a number of exchange programs among recreation and leisure students and professionals around the globe.

It is clear that no one organization can possibly speak for or represent the entire leisure-service field today. As each specialized area of recreation has become more active and successful, it has tended to form its own professional society to deal with its unique needs and interests.

Canadian Professional Societies The major Canadian organization in this field is the Canadian Parks/Recreation Association (CPRA), which has its national office in Ottawa, Ontario. Its major objectives are:

To acquaint Canadians with the significance of leisure in a changing society;

To assist in the development, organization, and promotion of the parks and recreation service delivery system in Canada;

To involve the membership in the development of national policies of significance to the parks and recreation movement in Canada; and

To promote effective planning, design, and development of parks and recreation facilities in Canada.

The CPRA receives substantial support from the Canadian federal government. It has approximately 3,000 members, publishes a monthly magazine, *Recreation Canada,* and, like NRPA, sponsors an annual conference, provides consultation and technical assistance to both government and nongovernment agencies concerned with recreation, parks, and leisure, and generally promotes this field throughout Canada and internationally. In addition, each of the Canadian provinces has its own recreation and park professional society, and there are specialized organizations related to camping, industrial/employee recreation, and similar functions.

CRITERION 5: CREDENTIALING, STANDARDS FOR SCREENING PERSONNEL

Credentials are qualifications that must be satisfied through a formal review process before an individual is permitted to engage in professional practice in a given field. Obviously, this is a very important criterion of professionalism. If anyone can call himself or herself a qualified practitioner in a given field—without appropriate training or experience—that field has very low standards and is not likely to gain or hold the public's respect.

Because the recreation and park field has been so diversified, no single standard or selection process has been devised for those who seek employment in it. However, within the field of recreation and parks, a number of special screening procedures have been developed, including: (1) registration; (2) certification and licensing; (3) Civil Service position requirements; and (4) other job specifications or qualification systems, such as those established by national voluntary organizations, which outline personnel qualifications and guidelines for their local branches to follow.

Registration

This procedure represented an early effort to rely on professional societies to screen and identify those who are considered to be qualified in their respective fields. North Carolina in 1954 became the first state to establish a registration plan for recreation administrators in local communities. During the 1950s, a number of recreation and park societies in such other

states as California, New York, Wisconsin, Washington, Colorado, and Texas also initiated registration plans.

Typically, the registration boards of state societies identified a set of requirements, including both educational and on-the-job experience qualifications, that applicants had to meet in order to become registered at given levels of service. Usually, several levels of responsibility (such as leader, supervisor, or commissioner) were identified in such state plans, with the requirements being established according to the position level and the size of the community being served. State registration plans usually defined personnel standards for each job level, including the duties and distinguishing features of the position, the knowledge and abilities required to carry it out effectively, and the minimum education and experience required for eligibility.

Because of the difficulty of maintaining standards through 50 different state plans, the National Recreation and Park Association developed and implemented a process of national registration. Following guidelines set forth in a model registration plan approved by the NRPA Board of Trustees in 1973, it reviewed and approved the plans of a number of state societies, encouraging a standardized approach to registration and reciprocity agreements among these states.

Registration in Therapeutic Recreation   Registration programs for therapeutic recreation specialists were available as early as 1956. The Council for Advancement of Hospital Recreation (CAHR) registered practitioners who met the qualifications established by the Hospital Section of the American Recreation Society, the Recreational Therapy Section of the American Association for Health, Physical Education and Recreation, and the National Association of Recreational Therapists at that time.

In 1970, the National Therapeutic Recreation Society developed its own registration plan. This plan, with carefully defined combinations of education and professional experience as criteria for registration, was well received professionally, with about 3,000 practitioners being registered by the early 1980s.

In 1981, the NTRS Registration Board was formally disbanded, and its functions were transferred to the National Council for Therapeutic Recreation Certification, an independently administered body of the National Recreation and Park Association. It was agreed that the existing levels of service would be grouped under a new two-level system: professional (therapeutic recreation specialist) and paraprofessional (therapeutic recreation assistant). It should be noted that at this point the term "registration" was changed to "certification."

Certification and Licensing

These two terms refer to the process of examining the credentials of persons in given occupational or professional fields and, if they meet stated qualifications, giving them permission to practice. *Licensing* governs the scope of professional practice, defining the specific services that may be provided, the populations to be served, and other conditions. Licensing applies not only to health-related-fields, but also to such areas of employment as driving taxis or operating barber shops or beauty parlors. Stumbo cites the U.S. Department of Health, Education and Welfare's definition of licensing as the process by which an agency of government

grants permission to persons meeting predetermined qualifications to engage in a given occupation upon finding that the applicant had attained the minimal degree of competency necessary to ensure that the public health [and] safety will be reasonably well-protected.[24]

She goes on to point out that licensing is the most restrictive form of credentialing, since it requires state governments to enact legislation defining the scope of professional practice and makes it illegal for those not licensed to perform services within this scope. Customarily, licensing programs are overseen by state regulatory agencies, which screen applicants, set practice standards and codes of conduct, and investigate charges of incompetence or impropriety against licensees, taking necessary disciplinary action where justified.

In contrast, *certification* refers to the process through which a nongovernmental organization grants recognition—usually in the form of the right to use a professional title—to an individual who has met predetermined qualifications specified by that organization. Certification is usually a voluntary process and is not always required to practice in the profession, although states, voluntary or therapeutic agencies, and other hiring bodies may choose to require a given certification title of candidates for employment.

Certification in Therapeutic Recreation   As indicated earlier, therapeutic recreation was one of the first professional specializations in recreation to initiate a strong national registration plan. Its revised certification standards, instituted in 1981, specified that, to become a qualified therapeutic recreation specialist on the professional level, a person needed to meet one of four optional criteria. These ranged from holding a baccalaureate or higher degree from an accredited curriculum with a major or option in therapeutic recreation to an "equivalency" combination of five years of full-time paid experience in an approved therapeutic recreation setting and a degree in a recreation-related field including upper-division therapeutic recreation credits. On the paraprofessional level, candidates for certification as therapeutic recreation assistants were given five similar but less stringent options.

Over time, these requirements have been redefined to take into account changing standards for professional practice, the credentialing processes enacted by other organizations in the hospital and health-care fields, and the accreditation standards applied to college and university professional preparation curricula.

National Certification in Recreation, Parks, and Leisure Services

In the early 1980s, the NRPA Board of Trustees set in motion a two-to-five-year plan that sought to link the three elements of certification, accreditation, and continuing education in a certification procedure that would apply broadly to the overall recreation, parks, and leisure-service field.

T he new Model Certification Plan for Recreation, Park Resources, and Leisure Services Personnel was designed to provide a national means of attesting to the educational and experiential qualifications of people receiving compensation in public, quasi-public, and private employment in the recreation field. Its purpose was to

establish standards for certification in recreation, park resources, and leisure services professions; provide recognition of individuals who have qualified; and afford a guarantee to employers that certified personnel have attained stated education and experience qualifications.[25]

Among the unique elements of the plan was the stipulation that everyone seeking certification after November 1, 1986, would be required to hold a degree from a college or university with a curriculum accredited by NRPA. Other stipulations were that recertification would be mandatory every two years, beginning in 1983, and that individuals would be required to earn a minimum of two Continuing Education Units (CEUs) or equivalent college course work within each 24-month period from the date of certification. Implied in the plan was that many of the professional development programs offered or sponsored by NRPA would be approved for CEU credit.

This ambitious plan, however, was largely unenforced in government or voluntary agencies that chose not to comply with it. A number of professionals were outspoken in their opposition to a strong certification requirement because of its effect on thousands of practitioners and hundreds of institutions not meeting NRPA's criteria.

After a lengthy process of development, a Certified Leisure Professional (CLP) Examination was administered for the first time in October 1990. Testing three ability areas of applicants (knowledge, application to professional concerns, and analysis of program solutions), the examination dealt with four major content areas: (1) leisure service management, including budget and finance, staff development and supervision, and policy formulation; (2) leisure/recreation program delivery, including assessment, planning, implementation, and evaluation; (3) natural resource facilities management; and (4) therapeutic recreation service.[26]

Under the NRPA plan, three levels of certification are provided: Certified Leisure Professional (CLP), Certified Leisure Provisional Professional (CLPP), and Certified Leisure Technician (CLT).

In reviewing the positive and negative aspects of professional certification, Nancy Gladwell and Cheryl Beeler have pointed out that this process helps to confer a higher degree of status on qualified individuals and helps the profession itself to clarify its functions and achieve a higher level of quality performance and recognition. On the other hand, they point out several weaknesses of certification as a viable credentialing tool:

Many employers do not require or encourage certification as a criterion of employment, and many educators do not support or encourage student interest in applying for certification, thus weakening it as a process.

In several states, city and local governments are not permitted to legally require certification of job applications, on the basis that setting such a standard would require a higher range of personnel expenditures. . . .

Many of the continuing education programs offered for CEU credit as part of the certification requirement are not relevant to job performance, and certification is not generally recognized in the leisure-service field, other than in recreation and park agencies.[27]

Despite these areas of difficulty, it is expected that certification within the broader recreation and park field will become more widely used and recognized. In a recent year, for example, the CLP examination was presented in October and November at the NRPA National Congress and at 30 different sites across the United States.

Continuing Education   A key element in the certification process is the requirement for continuing education participation by professionals. Continuing education represents a noncredit program of study planned and organized around learning experiences

designed to meet specific professional objectives. One of the requirements to remain certified is the attainment of two Continuing Education Units (CEUs), requiring 20 contact
hours in organized learning activities over a two-year period. Michael Huffman and Mel
Humphreys point out that the CEU is a uniform unit of measurement adopted by most regional college and school accreditation associations that

> [may be based on] an individual's participation in formal classes [although it does not constitute acade-
> mic credit], courses, programs and informal or non-traditional modes of non-credit education, including
> various forms of independent study.[28]

Many of the sessions offered at professional conferences, as well as various institutes, workshops, and symposiums sponsored by regional or state associations and other professional societies, are designed to provide CEU credits. When questioned in a survey as to their motives
for engaging in continuing education, therapeutic recreation professionals emphasized the
need to improve their on-the-job competence, keep abreast of new developments in the field,
interact with other professionals, strengthen their professional identity, and contribute to personal productivity and job security.

Problems with Enforcement   Requirements were established that by 1990 all states
have their own professional certification plans based on NRPA's national guidelines—including the stipulation for maintaining certification through continuing education participation—
and that the job specifications of all administrative employees in public recreation and park
departments include such certification as a requirement. By the late 1980s, it was apparent
that such requirements could not be widely enforced in light of the inability of professional
societies to impose their standards on legally independent government bodies without formal
legislation to support them.

Civil Service in Recreation and Parks

Across a wide range of public, tax-supported departments—including not only local government agencies but also federal, state, provincial, and armed forces recreation programs—the
most common means of screening applicants for government employment is through Civil
Service procedures. Civil Service is a general descriptive term that applies to many different
agencies, boards, and personnel systems that attempt to provide a politically neutral method
of employment under which individuals are hired because they meet formal qualifications
rather than because they have political contacts or influence. Often referred to as the "merit
system," Civil Service involves a complicated job classification system with promotional steps
and salary ranges under many job titles. It also includes detailed procedures for eligibility,
examinations, appointment, probationary periods, promotion, separation, and personnel
rights and benefits.

On the federal level, full-time professional employees in such agencies as the National
Park Service or the Veterans Administration are normally part of the federal Civil Service
system. Similarly, most state employees (with the exception of upper-level administrators
and part-time or seasonal workers) in hospitals, penal institutions, recreation and park
departments, and other agencies fall under Civil Service.

However, it appears that Civil Service standards for public recreation and park personnel have been minimal and loosely enforced. A 1976 study by Godbey and Henkel found

that substantial numbers of superintendents, directors, division heads, and district supervisors of recreation and parks lacked bachelor's degrees in recreation or related fields. Among recreation supervisors and center directors in five major categories, 42 percent had less than a bachelor's degree. Similarly, in Canada, despite efforts to promote certification of personnel, a study in the early 1970s showed a low level of specialized academic training among employees in public recreation and park agencies and in voluntary, nonprofit agencies and institutions.[29]

The reluctance of local government officials or Civil Service boards to apply higher hiring standards does not apply only to the recreation and park field. Local officials resist higher standards in many fields simply because they would limit their flexibility in being able to reward loyal partisans or their families and friends with jobs as political payoffs. Recreation in particular offers the opportunity to hire many part-time and seasonal employees in expanded summer programs and has often been manipulated for this purpose.

Despite such resistance, efforts to upgrade Civil Service selection standards should continue to be made, in tandem with the efforts being made nationally and on the state level to gain compliance with the NRPA certification plan. The fact that Civil Service is *in place* and actually governs current hiring and personnel practices means that it has the potential for being strengthened and being used more effectively to improve professional performance. In a number of states, approved standards for therapeutic recreation personnel—not only in state agencies but also in private or voluntary institutions such as nursing homes, which come under the jurisdiction of state health departments—have been modeled on the personnel standards of the National Therapeutic Recreation Society.

In addition to such efforts, many local recreation and park agencies have made strenuous efforts to upgrade the professionalism of their staff members through extensive in-service education programs. In the City of Oakland, California, for example, literally dozens of courses and special workshops were offered for recreation and park employees in a recent year, covering such subjects as supervisory skills, conflict resolution, responding to the Americans With Disabilities Act, computer skills and languages, customer-focused management approaches, first aid, working with gangs, maintenance methods, and varied recreation activity skills.[30]

STANDARDS IN NONPUBLIC LEISURE-SERVICE AGENCIES

Both the National Recreation and Park Association and the American Association for Leisure and Recreation, which have been the prime movers in the attempt to strengthen professionalism in leisure-service agencies, have had as their main targets either public recreation and park departments or schools and colleges. In general, the employees of voluntary agencies, such as nonprofit, commercial, private, or employer sponsors, have not been identified as key elements in the recreation movement. Hiring in such agencies has therefore not been influenced by the NRPA/AALR accreditation efforts or the certification plan just described.

However, national organizations like the Ys, Scouts, and Boys' and Girls' Clubs are obviously concerned with helping their local councils, branches, or other direct-service units maintain a high level of staff competence. Their national offices therefore typically prepare job descriptions or recommended standards for employment within given categories of professional positions.

Personnel Policies of YMCA and Boys' and Girls' Clubs of America

Several thousand professional staff members are employed by the approximately 1,800 YMCAs in the United States, with about 500 persons entering YMCA service each year as professional workers. The Y policy has been to have entry-level personnel begin as staff associates or directors for a two-year period during which they and the employing agency test their aptitude for YMCA work. Positions are usually classified according to job titles.

The National Council of the YMCA recommends that YMCA staff members have the following qualifications: (1) commitment to YMCA purposes and goals; (2) integrity of character and interest in working with young people for their personal and social growth; (3) sound health; and (4) an undergraduate degree or equivalent, preferably in one of the social or behavioral sciences, such as psychology, economics, sociology, government, or education, or in liberal arts generally. In addition, professional training of YMCA staff directors should cover such areas as leadership of informal groups; counseling and guidance; administration of social and religious agencies; leadership supervision and training; and understanding of the history, objectives, programs, and methods of the YMCA.

Similarly, the Boys' and Girls' Clubs of America has a recommended personnel hiring policy for professional staff workers. To be certified as a full-time administrator in a Club, one must meet the following criteria: (1) a degree from an accredited four-year college; (2) satisfactory performance in two years of program leadership or administrative work in a Club or as a member of the National Staff; and (3) a total of ten training credits in conferences and training sessions sponsored by the Regional or National Manpower Development Committees of the Boys' and Girls' Clubs of America or other authorized training institution.

Independent Credentialing Efforts

A final approach to credentialing personnel may be found in specialized recreation activity areas, particularly those relating to outdoor recreation or aquatics. For example, the Wilderness Education Association and affiliated universities and colleges have developed a National Standard Program for Outdoor Leadership Certification for the United States and Canada. Three- and five-week programs are offered year-round, with emphasis on safety in trip and adventure programs and on sound environmental practices.

Pool and beach safety supervision has long been an area in which the need for properly qualified personnel has been widely recognized by public recreation and park authorities, camp directors, and other agency managers. While there are a number of organizations that have sponsored certification programs in aquatics, the Red Cross sequence is the best known and most widely used. Typical qualifications for waterfront directors or lifeguards today include: (1) American Red Cross Advanced Lifesaving Certification (renewed every three years); (2) American National Red Cross Lifeguard Certification (renewed every two years); (3) American National Red Cross Advanced First Aid Certification; and (4) current CPR Certification.

Other leisure-related areas where certification is offered by professional societies or councils representing trade associations include: (1) Certified Travel Counselor (CTC), through the Institute of Certified Travel Agents; (2) volunteer youth sports coaching certification through the National Youth Sports Coaches Association; and (3) certification of employee recreation directors through the National Employee Services and Recreation Association.

CRITERION 6: CODE OF ETHICAL PRACTICE

A final important measure of any profession is that it typically outlines the public responsibilities of practitioners and sets up a code of ethical behavior. In fields such as medicine or law, where the possibility of malpractice is great and the stakes are high, strict codes of ethics prevail—although they tend to be enforced rather inconsistently.

In the field of leisure services, it might appear that any issues related to ethical practice are not as critical as in these other professions. However, in specialized areas such as therapeutic recreation service, where patients or clients are likely to be physically, emotionally, or economically vulnerable, the opportunities for harmful, negligent, or unprofessional behavior are great. In other areas of leisure service as well, professionals should have a strong sense of obligation to those they serve, to their communities, and to the profession itself.

For these reasons, in the early 1980s the National Recreation and Park Association prepared a recommended code of ethics, which included general principles that applied to state recreation and park societies and affiliated professional organizations, and a set of special principles that related to such NRPA branches as the Society of Park and Recreation Educators and the American Park and Recreation Society. The general principles presented in this document were broad, including such statements as the need for the professional to be "of high moral character in fulfilling obligations to and protective of the public's trust." Gerald Fain, however, argued that ethical codes should more directly

> reflect the ongoing business of the practitioner, the felt need within the society, and the critical issues identified by the profession. Commitment to the study, promotion, and regulation of ethical practices has a beginning but it has no end. When people actively work to enhance the lives of others, they accept a responsibility that is greater than themselves.[31]

To make ethical codes more relevant, Fain suggested that codes for college or university faculty members might address such issues as the sexual harassment of students, responsibilities when conducting research with human subjects, roles and functions on dissertation or thesis committees, and similar matters. Ethics codes for therapeutic recreation specialists might deal with such important issues as the confidentiality of the patient/client relationship and the relative rights of the patient/client, the treatment team, or the institution when these are in conflict.

In a 1986 survey of state recreation and park societies Ira Shapiro found that societies in only 17 states and the District of Columbia reported having a written code of ethics, while even fewer reported having a state code of ethics committee.[32]

Nevertheless, NRPA continued to address the ethics issue, forming a new task force in 1991 to formulate a concise code of ethics that would apply to all organization members. It was initially agreed that this code should be short, concise, and backed up by a plan for enforcement. However, in a series of hearings, considerable resistance was expressed to the enforcement concept and to any punitive procedures, and the enforcement element was therefore eliminated from the code. As approved by the NRPA Board of Trustees at the 1994 Congress in Minneapolis, the adopted code contained the following statements:

> Membership in NRPA carries with it special responsibilities to the public at large, and to the specific communities and agencies in which recreation and park services are offered. As a member of the National Recreation and Park Association, I accept and agree to abide by this Code of Ethics and pledge myself to:
>
> > Adhere to the highest standards of integrity and honesty in all public and personal activities to inspire public confidence and trust.

Strive for personal and professional excellence and encourage the professional development of associates and students.

Strive for the highest standards of professional competence, fairness, impartiality, efficiency, effectiveness, and fiscal responsibility.

Avoid any interest or activity that is in conflict with the performance of job responsibilities.

Promote the public interest and avoid personal gain or profit from the performance of job duties and responsibilities.

Support equal employment opportunities.[33]

In a much more extensive statement, the National Therapeutic Recreation Society approved a Code of Ethics in 1990 and a set of Interpretive Guidelines in 1994. This organization's overall code contained an explanatory preamble followed by six detailed sections on the obligations of professionals and the profession itself to individuals served, to other individuals and society, to colleagues, to the profession—and to "professional virtue." One of the specific guidelines in the NTRS Code presents the following statements under the heading of *The Obligation of the Professional to the Individual.*

A. Well-Being: *Professionals' foremost concern is the well-being of the people they serve. They do everything reasonable in their power and within the scope of professional practice to benefit them. Above all, professionals cause no harm.*

Therapeutic recreation professionals enter into or continue professional relationships based on their ability to meet the needs of clients appropriately. Similarly, they terminate service and professional relationships which are no longer required or which cease to serve the client's best interests. Recognizing that the private and personal nature of the therapeutic relationship may unrealistically intensify clients' feelings toward them, they take special efforts to maintain professional objectivity. They are careful to avoid, and do not initiate, personal relationships or dual roles with clients.

Appropriate settings are chosen for one-on-one interactions, in order to protect both the client and the professional from actual or imputed physical or mental harm.

When the client's condition indicates that there is clear and imminent danger to the client or others, the therapeutic recreation professional must take reasonable personal action or inform responsible authorities. Consultation with other professionals must be used where possible. The assumption of responsibility for the client's behavior must be taken only after careful deliberation.

A professional who knows that he or she has an infectious disease, which if contracted by another would pose a significant risk, should not engage in any activity which creates a risk of transmission of that disease to any others with whom he or she would come in contact. The precautions taken to prevent the transmission of a contagious disease to others should be appropriate to the seriousness of the disease and must be particularly stringent in the case of a disease that is potentially fatal.[34]

CURRENT LEVEL OF PROFESSIONAL STATUS

When the six accepted criteria of professionalism reviewed above are used as the basis for judgment, it is apparent that the recreation, parks, and leisure-service field has made considerable progress toward becoming a recognized profession.

Some elements are already securely in place, such as the development of a unique body of knowledge and the establishment of a network of college and university programs of professional preparation. As for the professional organization element, the National Recreation and Park Association and other national associations or societies do represent a significant force for upgrading and monitoring performance in the recreation field, but their attempts to serve the interests of a wide variety of leisure-service agencies also illustrate the field's continuing fragmentation. Realistically, many practitioners in such specialized disciplines as therapeutic recreation service, employee services and recreation, and varied aspects of commercial recreation tend to identify more closely with their separate fields than they do with the overall leisure-service field. Even in the more difficult areas of certification and the development of ethical codes, some considerable progress has been made although the concept of enforcement continues to be a problem in both areas.

Nonetheless, professionalism in recreation, parks, and leisure services has increased greatly over the past five decades, along with the growing recognition of the field's value in modern society. Because of the immense scope of the diversified recreation field in terms of employment, it has the potential for becoming even more influential in contributing to community well-being in the years ahead. To fulfill this potential, leisure-service professionals will have to confront a number of significant issues and problems. Among the most pressing internal problems facing them today are: (1) efforts being made to separate higher education into practical and theoretical elements; (2) the roles of women and other minority groups within the profession; (3) the need to have professionals become more fully involved in political and public policy activities; and (4) the resistance of some factions within the field to fuller professionalization.

These concerns are discussed more fully in the final chapter of this text, which explores the conceptual base of the field, outlines a number of areas of relevant philosophical inquiry, and suggests principles that leisure-service practitioners and agencies should consider as a basis for policy-making and program development.

SUMMARY

Recreation, parks, and leisure services have grown immensely as a career field, with several million men and women now employed in different areas of organized recreation programming, facilities management, or other leisure-related functions. Of this overall group, it is estimated that several hundred thousand individuals should be regarded as professionals due to their academic training, job functions, and organizational affiliations.

This chapter describes several important criteria of professionalism, including the following:

1. Having a significant degree of social value, in terms of providing benefits to individual participants and/or to community life;

2. Being recognized by the public as a meaningful area of social service or as a legitimate occupational field;

3. Requiring specialized professional preparation on the college or university level, based on a distinct body of theoretical and practical knowledge;

4. Possessing a professional culture that involves national and regional organizations that sponsor conferences, research, publications, and other efforts to upgrade practice, and that promote collegiality and a sense of commitment among the practitioners;

5. Having a credentialing system to ensure that only qualified individuals—usually identified through a system of certification or licensing—are permitted to undertake professional-level tasks; and

6. Having a code of ethics to ensure that responsible and effective service is provided to the public.

While the recreation, parks, and leisure-services field has not as yet met all of these criteria of professionalism fully, it has made substantial progress on most of them. As recreation and leisure become increasingly important aspects of life in the years ahead, the challenge to the leisure-service field will be to become even more highly professionalized by building on the foundation that has already been laid.

Questions for Class Discussion or Essay Examinations

1. Before reading this chapter, what was your understanding of the meaning of the term "profession?" Since reading the chapter, has your understanding of this word changed? How important do you believe it is for any occupational field to be regarded as a profession?

2. There are several criteria that are generally accepted as hallmarks of professionalism, such as having a social mandate or set of important social values, or having a body of specialized knowledge. Select any four of these, and discuss the extent to which you believe the recreation, park, and leisure-service field meets these criteria of professionalism.

3. Some educators believe that the field of professional preparation in recreation and parks has two contrasting sets of priorities: (1) the need to provide practical skills in personnel management, budgeting, marketing, programming, and similar functions; and (2) the need to focus on the theoretical (philosophical, historical, etc.) study of recreation and leisure. Do you believe this is a significant concern? Present an argument for either of these two positions.

4. The leisure-service field has developed into at least eight different specialized areas, such as public, nonprofit, commercial and therapeutic recreation—with some of these having a number of distinct sub-specializations. Do you believe that it is possible for this fragmented field to develop and maintain a single, common identity in order to gain fuller public support and understanding? How could this be done?

Endnotes

2   H. Douglas Sessoms, in Thomas Goodale and Peter Witt, eds., *Recreation and Leisure: Issues in an Era of Change* (State College, Penn.: Venture Publishing, 1980): 250.

3   James Murphy and Dennis Howard, cited in James Murphy, N. William Niepoth, Lynn Jamieson, and John Williams, *Leisure Systems: Critical Concepts and Applications* (Champaign, Ill.: Sagamore Publishing, 1991): 117.

4   "Professionals in Managed Recreation," *Recreation, Sports, and Leisure* (August 1985): 49.

5   *Statistical Abstract of the United States* (Washington, D.C.: U.S. Department of Commerce, 1995): 416.

6   *Ibid.*, 414.

7   *Ibid.*, 322.

8   *Education for Leisure*, Position Paper of Society of Park and Recreation Educators, 1975.

9   Donald Henkel, "Professionalization: The Saga Continues, 1965–1985," *Parks and Recreation* (August 1985): 50–54.

10   *YWCA Fact Sheet* (New York: Young Women's Christian Association, March 1995).

11   Geoffrey Godbey, Alan Graefe, and Stephen James, "Reality and Perception: Where Do We Fit In?" *Parks and Recreation* (January 1993): 76–83.

12 H. Douglas Sessoms, "A Critical Look at the Recreation Movement," *Recreation for the Ill and Handicapped* (Washington, D.C.: National Association of Recreation Therapists, July 1965): 11, 14.

13 J. Michael Elliott, "Robert W. Crawford, 89, Father of Philadelphia's Park System," *Philadelphia Inquirer* (15 April 1995): A-20. See also "Tribute to Robert Crawford," *Parks and Recreation* (August 1985): 28–37.

14 Ronald Riggins, Charles Sylvester, and James Moore, "Liberal Education: The Foundation for Prepared Professionals," *Parks and Recreation* (November 1985): 52.

15 M. Deborah Bialeschki, "What's Happening to Our Curricula in Recreation, Park Resources and Leisure Services?" *Parks and Recreation* (May 1994): 24.

16 Thomas Yukic, "Advancing a Professional Body of Knowledge," *California Parks and Recreation* (December 1980/January 1981): 6.

17 Bob McKeta, "Be an Intern with the Army," *Parks and Recreation* (October 1993): 30–35.

18 See David Austin, "Professional Leadership: Competencies Required for Special Recreation Programs," *Journal of Physical Education, Recreation and Dance—Leisure Today* (May–June 1985): 4; and Norma Stumbo, "A Definition of Entry-Level Knowledge for Therapeutic Recreation Practice," *Therapeutic Recreation Journal* (4th Quarter 1986): 15–30.

19 See Tony Mobley, "Accreditation Becomes of Age," *Trends* (Vol. 3 No. 3 1993): 21–25.

20 Henkel and Mobley, *op. cit.*

21 Britt Davis, "Coming Online with the NRPA/SCHOLE Network," *Parks and Recreation* (June 1993): 50–54.

22 For example, see *Dateline: NRPA* (April 1994) for article on NRPA Congressional testimony on recreation and crime prevention.

23 "Development of a Vision Statement for the Year 2000," *Society of Park and Recreation Educators* (Fall 1995/1996): 3.

24 Norma Stumbo, "Overview of State Credentialing Concerns: A Focus on Licensure," *Therapeutic Recreation Journal* (2nd Quarter 1990): 40–59.

25 See "New Certification Plan Gives Profession a Boost," *Parks and Recreation* (January 1982): 6–7.

26 H. Douglas Sessoms, "Anatomy of the Leisure Service Professional Certification Examination," *Parks and Recreation* (December 1991): 54–58.

27 Nancy Gladwell and Cheryl Beeler, "Professional Certification: Its Benefits and Problems," *Trends* (Vol. 30 No. 3 1993): 17–20.

28 Michael Huffman and Mel Humphrys, "Continuing Education in Parks and Recreation: Trends, Issues and Potential Solutions," *Trends* (Vol. 30 No. 3 1993): 4–6.

29 For a fuller description of recreation and park personnel hiring practices, see Richard Kraus and Joseph Curtis, *Creative Management in Recreation, Parks, and Leisure Services* (St. Louis: Times Mirror/Mosby, 1990): 147–152.

30 *Training Calendar,* City of Oakland, California, Department of Parks and Recreation, 1992–1993.

31 Gerald Fain, "To Protect the Public: A Matter of Ethics," *Parks and Recreation* (December 1983): 53.

32 Ira Shapiro, "The Existence of Ethical Codes and Ethics Code Committees in State Recreation and Park Societies," *Pennsylvania Recreation and Park Society Magazine* (Summer 1987): 3.

33 David Clark, "A New Code of Ethics for NRPA," *Parks and Recreation* (August 1995): 40.

34 "National Therapeutic Recreation Society Code of Ethics," in *NTRS Report* (Vol. 19 No. 2 1994): 5.

fourteen 14

Philosophy of Recreation and Leisure: Future Perspectives

Definitions of Philosophy

... the science which investigates the most general facts and principles of reality and of human nature and conduct; specifically ... the science which comprises logic, ethics, aesthetics, metaphysics and the history of knowledge.

The body of principles or general conceptions underlying a given branch of learning, or major discipline, a religious system, a human activity, or the like, and the application of it.

An integrated and consistent personal attitude toward life or reality, or toward certain phases of it, especially if this attitude is expressed in beliefs or principles of conduct.[1]

INTRODUCTION

The remarkable growth of organized recreation, park, and leisure services throughout the United States and Canada has been documented throughout this text. Despite the impressive recent history of this social movement and field of professional activity, a number of serious questions still exist in regard to the appropriate role of recreation in community and national life as we approach the twenty-first century.

---

[1] Webster's *New International Dictionary*, 1954 edition, s. v. "philosophy."

For example, how can recreation contribute more effectively to the battle against such social ills as poverty, racial or ethnic hostility, crime and delinquency, and economic deprivation? What solutions can be found for the overcrowding and vandalism that affect many urban, state, and federal parks and recreation facilities?

How should the major priorities of organized recreation service in the United States and Canada be determined? In what ways can government provide more effective and efficient services in this field? What are the special responsibilities of organized recreation toward the physically and mentally disabled, toward the aging, or toward those who may have had inadequate opportunities in the past because of their gender or other demographic factors?

Should recreation sponsors simply seek to meet the expressed wishes of the public for enjoyable play—or do they have a moral responsibility to present only socially constructive and desirable leisure programs? With regard to violence, overemphasis on winning in sport, and policies governing drinking, drugs, gambling, or sexually oriented play, what should the role of recreation professionals be?

How will the changing social and economic conditions in the decades ahead affect the public's leisure values and patterns of participation—and how can recreation, park, and leisure-service professionals and organizations respond effectively to the challenges of the future?

NEED FOR A SOUND PHILOSOPHICAL BASIS

Obviously, such issues should be resolved within the context of a coherent set of values, moral beliefs, and social priorities. What is needed is a sound philosophy of recreation and leisure that can serve the leisure-service field in ongoing policy formulation and program development.

Meaning of Philosophy

The term "philosophy" often conveys an image of ivory tower abstraction, divorced from practical or realistic concerns. Understandably, many practitioners are likely to be suspicious of any approach that appears to be overly theoretical, rather than pragmatic and action-based.

How then is philosophy to be defined? Of the possible examples presented on page 376, the second one, stating that philosophy consists of the body of principles underlying a major discipline or human activity, as expressed in guidelines for conduct, is the most useful for our purpose. In this chapter, we are concerned with presenting an analysis of the fundamental beliefs and values that underlie and provide a base for planning, organizing, and carrying out recreation programs.

This chapter will *not* present a single philosophy of recreation and leisure and argue that it represents the only acceptable system of goals and values. Instead, it will: (1) briefly review a number of approaches taken by philosophers and other scholars to the analysis of recreation and leisure in the past; (2) identify seven prevailing approaches to providing organized recreation services in the present; (3) discuss various changes that are occurring today in terms of work and leisure availability, demographic influences on leisure, and prevailing social values as they affect recreational participation; (4) present a number of forecasts of future trends; and (5) suggest some guiding principles for the organization of community recreation services in the years ahead.

Overview of Past Views of Recreation and Leisure

As earlier chapters have shown, recreation, play, and leisure have been examined by numerous philosophers throughout history. Obviously, the views expressed reflected not only the personal beliefs of the individual writers, but also the dominant religious and social ideals of each period, ranging from the early Greek and Roman era through the Industrial Revolution.

Greek philosophers like Aristotle and Plato described the significant role of leisure and play in Athenian life and childhood upbringing, and authors during the Renaissance and Reformation periods supported the value of play in early education. During the nineteenth century, fears about the danger of illicit uses of leisure were widely expressed, and a system of "rational" recreation that would support the Protestant work ethic and the expanding capitalist system gained support in the industrialized West.

Early Twentieth-Century Views

In the beginning decades of the twentieth century, as the recreation and park movement gained momentum, pioneer recreation leaders like Joseph Lee, Jane Addams, and Luther Halsey Gulick developed a philosophy of play and recreation that stressed their importance as vital aspects of community life, important forms of education, and essential ways of combating juvenile delinquency and other problems afflicting urban industrial life. Play was widely viewed as an instrument for spiritual development, and leisure and recreation were praised as a means of achieving the happy life through promoting moral values and engaging in the "best" activities of which one was capable. Other writers at this time preached that national prosperity and welfare would be assisted by the fuller availability of leisure because it would enrich democratic culture and strengthen community and family life.

Two sharply contrasting views of leisure emerged during the 1920s and 1930s: (1) leisure seen as a social danger, with poorly used free time providing the opportunity for vice, drunkenness, and other negative forms of play; and (2) leisure seen as an idealized form of human expression that promoted artistic and cultural growth. Eloquent spokesman like J. B. Nash and L. P. Jacks argued that it was necessary at this time to educate for the fullest and most creative use of leisure.

Recreation and Leisure as Social Instruments

During the Great Depression of the 1930s, recreation was used to provide an alternative to the civic despair stemming from unemployment and widespread poverty. The federal government spent huge sums on parks and other leisure facilities, and employed thousands of recreation leaders, as well as artists, writers, and performers, to enrich popular culture. In the 1960s, recreation was used as a social instrument during the so-called war on poverty. During the late 1960s and early 1970s, as rebellious youth protested against traditional establishment values, leisure came to be perceived as a means of achieving holistic life values. Recreation, with its implied freedom and emphasis on self-discovery and self-actualization, was also perceived as an ideal vehicle for achieving the goals of the "counterculture."

It was at this time that writers like James Murphy, David Gray, and Seymour Greben urged the organized recreation system to respond forcefully to the critical social challenges of disadvantaged urban populations, minority groups, women, the disabled, and environmental population. They sought the fullest possible mobilization of the recreation and park movement to respond in a dynamic way to such needs, to form an effective political force, and to collaborate with other citizen groups and environmental organizations to make recreation and parks a vital force in national life.[2]

This philosophy—inspiring as it was—did not really express the views of most recreation and park professionals and educators, who generally were more conservative in their outlook. Most practitioners in public agencies tended to regard themselves as civil servants who provided an important but relatively low-priority community service. Beyond this, they were pressured by fiscal constraints and prevailing social values in their communities, and were more concerned with professional survival than they were with the ambitious social agenda presented by Gray, Greben, and others.

Trends in the 1980s

The prevailing trend in many public and voluntary recreation and park agencies during the 1980s essentially reflected a cautious philosophy that sought to maintain support by offering programs and services that met important human needs but were noncontroversial and did not break new ground. As the fiscal crisis lessened, many recreation and park agencies began to recover, rehabilitating major parks and developing new facilities and programs as part of their cities' efforts to improve their image and popular appeal.

National values changed sharply in the late 1970s and 1980s, resulting in new attitudes toward recreation, leisure, and work. Building successful careers and making impressive incomes became the primary goals of many young people, as evidenced by annual surveys of beginning college students. Social goals and values were no longer in fashion, and a new work ethic seemed to have captured the national consciousness.

PHILOSOPHICAL ANALYSES OF RECREATION AND LEISURE

Given this historical background, what formal analyses were made of recreation and leisure from a philosophical perspective during the middle decades of the twentieth century? Some textbook authors examined the field making use of widely accepted philosophical systems. Earle Ziegler, for example, examined the field of health, physical education, and recreation in light of several such philosophical systems—including naturalism, realism, idealism, and experimentalism. However, because his primary emphasis was on recreation education rather than recreation and leisure in national culture, his analysis is somewhat remote from the concerns of leisure in modern society.[3]

Later authors carried out similar analyses, but with a sharper focus on recreation and leisure. They showed how many practitioners and educators were influenced by an idealist philosophy, seeing leisure as a means of working for societal improvement and human perfection. Others, holding a realist position, were concerned with the quantification of leisure services and the application of formal standards to recreation and park management. Professionals with a pragmatist orientation were flexible in their approaches to responding to community needs. Those influenced by contemporary existentialist thinking tended to believe that there are no absolute values, and that all practices and policies are subject to change. Finally, the humanist philosophy was action-oriented and stressed purposeful programming that meets important social goals within a holistic framework.[4] All of these philosophies continue to have adherents today—either in their pure form or in some variation or combination of them.

Apart from such generalized analyses, a number of writers examined specific components of leisure behavior in terms of accepted philosophical criteria.

Sport as a Focus of Inquiry

For example, the immense growth of popular interest in sports led a number of writers to examine amateur and professional athletics from a philosophical perspective. Carolyn Thomas studied sports in light of the major branches of philosophical inquiry, including: (1) metaphysics, the branch that explores the nature of being and mankind's relationship to God and nature; (2) epistemology, concerned with the origin and acquisition of knowledge; (3) axiology, which examines human ethics and moral conduct; and (4) aesthetics, which is concerned with the nature and form of beauty and art.

Each of these forms of inquiry may be used to study and understand sport in society. Thomas writes, for example, that

> Many ethical questions are directly related to sport. . . . The nature and intensity of competition, which is part of sport, often leads to ethical questions related to the appropriate emphasis on ends versus means. Sportsmanship, winning, gambling, player and owner rights, and coaching techniques all fall to ethical scrutiny in the sport setting.[5]

In *Sport: A Philosophic Inquiry,* Paul Weiss argues that play and games must be defined within the larger context of work and leisure time. Of all forms of experience, he writes, sport constitutes our greatest opportunity for achieving and witnessing human excellence.[6] Joseph Mihalich points out that leading philosophers, including Kierkegaard, Nietzsche, Camus, and Sartre, have explored the meaning of sport and play in human existence. In the writings of Sartre, an existentialist, a central theme has been absolute freedom—"to be human is to be free, and to be free is to be human." Mihalich elaborates:

> This is the theme he perceives clearly in play and games and sports and athletics, and this is the measure of the play world's reality and authenticity. Mankind committed to the serious work world is not free—only man at play is free to be creative and to establish rules and principles for authentic human existence.[7]

Moral Values and Leisure

In another analysis of the philosophy of leisure, Charles Sylvester contrasts the traditional moral view of leisure (as exemplified in the writings of Aristotle and applied in the twentieth century by J. B. Nash) with an existentialist approach based on Sartre, Ortega, and Jaspers. In the older view, Aristotle argued that happiness was the greatest good in human life and that it was the result of having lived one's life virtuously, chiefly through contemplation and exercise of one's intellect in leisure. Following this line of thought, Nash presented a twentieth-century theory of leisure-time morality in which human beings have the freedom to choose between "good," "bad," and "best" uses of leisure. Sylvester points out that Nash's model of leisure ranged from delinquent and destructive acts against oneself and society at the base to creative participation at the pinnacle:

> it also reflected his belief in the moral separation between mind and body. Essentially spiritual, the mind was connected with the highest forms of leisure expression. The body, on the other hand, was linked with appetites, weaknesses, and occasional debauchery. Intellectual and spiritual pursuits were superior to purely physical activities.[8]

In contrast, the existential view of human life rejects any *a priori* laws as to good or bad behavior. Sartre wrote, "Man is nothing else but what he makes of himself," and Ortega argued that man "is the novelist of himself." An existentialist would return to the Latin root, *licentia,* or its English descendant, *license,* as providing an appropriate framework for understanding leisure. Sylvester concludes:

> *Licentia* first means freedom to act as one pleases . . . . if leisure is intended to enable us to be what we want to be, unfettered by moral prescriptions pronouncing what we ought to be then license is fundamental to leisure rather than antithetical.[9]

That such analyses are not ivory tower abstractions is shown by the continuing conflicts or contradictions in society's approach to controlling varied forms of morally marginal leisure pursuits. For example, while it is widely recognized that gambling, substance abuse, and commercialized or indiscriminate sexual activity have destructive consequences for society, we are ambivalent with respect to public policy and laws regarding them. At the same time that we regulate and prosecute—often inconsistently—private enterprises engaged in providing these forms of play, government condones and promotes the same activities through state liquor stores, through lotteries, legal casinos, and racetracks with parimutuel betting, and through ignoring the open operation of massage parlors and escort services.

Shift in Professional Orientations

As a third example of philosophical analyses in recreation and leisure studies, a number of authors have examined the changing approaches found within the recreation and park profession. To illustrate, Wayne Stormann points out that there has been a pronounced shift from the early decades of the twentieth century—when the field was dominated by progressive reformers who sought to improve community life through organized play—to today, where recreation has become an area of professional service that has been, in his words, "bureaucratized, commercialized, and centralized."[10] The popular idea of the professional as an expert technician who markets leisure "products" or prescribes social services and solutions is in sharp contrast to the idea of leisure as a domain in which participatory democracy can flourish and community residents can gain valuable experience in managing their own lives.

OPERATIONAL PHILOSOPHIES OF RECREATION AND LEISURE

Such analyses may have only limited application for those who are directly concerned with the recreation movement today. For them, it is more helpful to examine the philosophical views of those who *direct* this movement—the boards, administrators, and leaders of recreation and park agencies, voluntary organizations, commercial businesses, and other specialized leisure services. These views are generally expressed in mission statements, membership brochures, or other materials that describe the goals of such organizations.

It is possible to identify several approaches or orientations found in leisure-service agencies today that may be called *operational philosophies.* These include the following: (1) the *quality-of-life* approach; (2) the *marketing* approach (3) the *human-services* approach; (4) the *prescriptive* approach; (5) the *environmental/aesthetic/preservationist* approach; (6) the *hedonist/individualist* approach; and (7) the *benefits-based* approach.

Quality-of-Life Approach

This approach has been the dominant one in the field of organized recreation service for several decades. It sees recreation as an experience that contributes to human development and to community well-being in various ways: improving physical and mental health, enriching cultural life, reducing antisocial uses of leisure, and strengthening community ties.

The quality-of-life orientation stresses the unique nature of recreation as a vital form of human experience—one that is engaged in for its own sake, rather than for any extrinsic purpose or conscious social goal. For example, George Butler wrote in 1959:

> Recreation is . . . a vital force influencing the lives of people. It is essential to happiness and satisfaction in living. Through recreation the individual grows and develops his powers and personality. . . .The man who plants his garden or plays his violin or swings lustily over the hills . . . [is] even though in small degree, investing life with the qualities that transform it into the delightful and adventurous experience it ought to be.[11]

Generally, proponents of this view have agreed that recreation satisfies a universal human need that has been made even more pressing by the tensions of modern urban society, the changed nature of work, and other social conditions. In an early text, Harold Meyer, Charles Brightbill, and H. Douglas Sessoms commented that community recreation led to the development of democratic citizenship and sound moral character, and to the reduction of social pathology. They concluded that the choices people make regarding their leisure are highly individual and stem from a basic need for creative self-expression:

> Recreation provides the opportunity for free expression and thus gives the best chance for creative living, which is its own reward. . . . If recreation has any purpose, it is the enjoyment it can produce and the happiness it can help achieve.[12]

Those holding this view argue that the pleasure, freedom, and self-choice inherent in recreation and leisure are their most vital contributions to the lives of participants. Quality-of-life advocates have tended to assume that public recreation should be supported for its own sake as an important area of civic responsibility, and that adequate tax funds should be provided for this purpose.

Marketing Approach

This business-oriented approach to providing organized recreation and park programs and services evolved rapidly during the late 1970s and 1980s as a direct response to the fiscal pressures placed on public and voluntary leisure-service agencies. As noted in earlier chapters, steadily mounting operational costs and a declining tax base during that time forced many recreation and park departments to take drastic measures in order to survive, adopting what has come to be known as the marketing approach to agency management. This approach is based on the idea that public, voluntary, or other leisure-service providers will flourish best if they adopt the methods used by commercial recreation businesses. It argues that they must become more aggressive and efficient in developing and promoting recreation facilities and programs that will reach the broadest possible audience and gain the maximum possible income.

John Crompton, one of the leading exponents of this position, has commented on the growing interest in adapting marketing concepts and techniques (ranging from needs-assessments and target marketing to sophisticated pricing methods) to the needs of nonprofit recreation organizations:

> This interest reflects a growing recognition that marketing is the essential core discipline upon which the success or survival of any agency depends. For a park and recreation agency to carry out its mission, it requires resources and support from citizens. It seeks to obtain these ingredients by delivering services which provide benefits sought by client groups. In *exchange* for services delivered, the agency receives resources in the form of tax dollars and/or direct user charges. Thus, marketing may be defined as a set of activities aimed at facilitating and expediting exchanges with target markets.[13]

Proponents of the marketing approach take the position that recreation and park professionals should not have to plead for tax-based support solely on the basis of the social value of their programs, but should seek to become relatively independent as a viable, self-sufficient form of community service. In a discussion of the direct benefits of a comprehensive revenue-generating program, Crompton points out that such a program makes it possible to offer a broader range of services without increasing taxes, stimulates staff members by offering a new challenge, enhances an agency's political strength, and gives the program's administrator a reputation for being an innovator in municipal government.

It should be recognized that the marketing trend has influenced far more than public recreation and park agencies alone. Many large nonprofit youth-serving organizations, such as the YMCA, YWCA, and YM-YWHA, have been forced to increase their reliance on self-generated revenues and to move into more aggressive marketing of a wide range of leisure programs, including their fitness services. In employee recreation programs, many companies that had formerly provided substantial subsidies for recreation and fitness programs have reduced their level of support and have required self-generated funding support from employee groups. In the area of culture and the arts, growing numbers of museums, libraries, and similar institutions have expanded their services to increase sales and fee-based programs.

While the marketing approach has been enthusiastically received by many recreation and park managers, it raises a number of issues with respect to the essential purpose of public and voluntary leisure-service agencies. The argument has been made that increased fees and charges—whether imposed by the agencies themselves or by concessionaires or contractors working under privatization plans—tend to exclude the people in greatest need of inexpensive public recreation opportunities, such as children, persons with disabilities, or the economically disadvantaged. Beyond this concern, it is believed that agencies that become dependent on fees and charges are likely to develop a profit-oriented set of values and ignore their traditional mission, making policy decisions chiefly on the basis of maintaining an impressive revenue flow.

Some authorities in the field have questioned the appropriateness of public recreation and park professionals embracing business philosophies drawn from the commercial field. In reply, Mark Havitz argues that contemporary marketing methods are neutral tools that can be used to assist any agency—whether a humanistic social-service organization or a capitalist, commercial business—in achieving its objectives. Cautioning against "crass commercialism, excessive profit taking, and environmental degradation," he makes the case that effective marketing can help any recreation and park organization function more effectively in serving a broad range of community residents.[14]

Human-Services Approach

In direct contrast to the marketing approach is the human-services approach to organized recreation service. This approach regards recreation as an important form of social service that must be provided in a way that contributes directly to a wide range of desired social values and goals. The human-services approach received a strong impetus during the 1960s, when recreation programs were generously funded by the federal government as part of the war on poverty, and recreation was used to offer job training and employment opportunities for economically disadvantaged youth and adults in America's ghettos.

F. William Niepoth summarizes this approach as follows:

1. The human services are a collection of agencies, with some characteristics held in common, whose primary functions are to maintain or enhance the well-being of individuals within the framework of societal norms.

2. Human service agencies adhere largely to a philosophy that focuses on the whole person, on the totality and interrelatedness of an individual's needs and desires.

3. The type of delivery system used by human service organizations is based on linkages between agencies to provide a broader base of services than any one agency could supply.[15]

The human-services approach is similar to the quality-of-life approach in its recognition of the social value of recreation service. However, it does not subscribe to the latter's idealization of recreation as an inherently ennobling kind of experience, carried on for its own sake. Instead, within the human-services framework, recreation must be designed to achieve significant community change and to use a variety of appropriate modalities. Niepoth points out that this does not mean that recreation personnel should seek to *be* health educators, employment counselors, nutritionists, correctional officers, legal advisors, or housing experts. Rather, he writes, they must recognize the holistic nature of the human condition, provide such services when able to do so effectively, and cooperate fully with other practitioners in the various human services fields when appropriate.

Operating under this approach, many public recreation departments have sponsored youth or adult classes in a wide range of educational, vocational, or self-improvement areas, and have also provided day-care programs, special services for persons with disabilities, roving leader programs for juvenile gangs, environmental projects, and numerous other functions of this type. The human-services approach is not limited to public agencies. In the field of employee recreation services, for example, many personnel managers today operate extensive fitness and stress-reduction programs, counseling assistance, and preretirement workshops as services for employees.

In its forceful emphasis on the need to meet social problems head on and achieve beneficial human goals, the human-services approach to recreation and park programming may at times be at odds with the marketing approach to service. In the marketing approach, efficient management and maximum revenue are often the primary aims. In the human-services orientation, social values and human benefits are emphasized.

This does not mean that human services cannot employ efficient and cost-effective management. To fulfil their goals, human-services managers must be highly practical and down-to-earth in identifying and meeting needs, developing interagency cooperation, and obtaining needed funding. They should make the fullest possible use of available community resources and, indeed, should coordinate and co-sponsor their programs with other agencies wherever possible.

Prescriptive Approach

Of the orientations described here, the prescriptive is the most purposeful in the way it defines the goals and functions of the recreational experience. The idea that recreation should bring about constructive change in participants has been stressed in a number of textbooks on programming. For example, Ruth Russell describes "programmed recreation" chiefly as a form of organized and purposeful activity designed in an orderly and deliberate way to achieve desirable individual and group results.[16] Similarly, Christopher Edginton, David Compton, and Carole Hanson define a recreation program as:

> a purposeful plan of intervention, which is deliberately designed and constructed in order to produce certain behavioral outcomes in an individual and/or group.[17]

The clearest cases of prescriptive recreation programs are found in therapeutic recreation. For example, Paul Wehman and Stuart Schleien describe the curriculum design sequence in therapeutic recreation as it is used to develop either an individualized education program or an individualized habilitation plan. In order to help patients or clients master important motor skills, improve social behavior, or achieve other goals of treatment, members of the treatment team review the individual's level of illness or disability, past recreation, education, other experiences and skills, and current level of functioning. On the basis of this review, a curriculum is devised to include the following program components: (1) a program goal; (2) an instructional objective (short-term); (3) a task analysis of each skill; (4) the verbal cue required for instruction in the skill; (5) materials that are required for instruction; and (6) teaching procedures and special adaptations for each skill.[18]

The prescriptive approach can also be used in nontherapeutic settings. One example would be armed forces recreation programs, where personnel may be required to take part in physical fitness and sports activities—both to maintain physical vigor and endurance and to keep morale and competitive intensity at a high pitch.

While it is similar to the human-services approach in its emphasis on deliberately achieving significant social goals, the prescriptive approach differs in its reliance on the practitioner's expertise and authority. In contrast, a recreation professional working within a human-services framework would be much more likely to value the input of community residents and to involve them in decision making.

Environmental/Aesthetic/Preservationist Approach

This unwieldy title is used as a catch-all model to lump together three elements that are not synonymous but that do exhibit a high degree of similarity.

The *environmentalist* obviously is concerned with protecting the outdoor environment and preserving it in as natural and healthy a state as possible. The *aesthetic* position is one that values the appearance of the environment, both natural and artificial, and stresses the inclusion of cultural arts and other creative experiences within a recreation program. The *preservationist* seeks to maintain the physical environment—not simply out of a respect for nature, but to preserve evidence of an historical past and a cultural tradition.

This approach to recreation planning is more likely to be evident in agencies that operate extensive parks, forests, waterfront areas, or other natural or scenic resources. Thus, one might assume that it would chiefly be found in such government agencies as federal, state, or provincial park departments that administer major parks and outdoor recreation facilities.

However, this is not the full picture. Many urban recreation and park planners are responsible for large, older parks. Often they may help to rehabilitate or redesign rundown waterfront areas, industrial sites, or gutted slum areas. In many cases, their purpose is to preserve or rebuild historic areas of cultural interest that will maintain or increase the appeal of cities for tourism and cultural programming.

Environmental Awareness   A key element in this approach is the deep reverence that many individuals have today for nature in its various forms. Daniel Dustin has described the experience of being interconnected with the natural world, and the spiritual value that human beings derive from their varied experiences with wilderness.[19] Douglas Knudson points out that love for nature and acceptance of responsibility for it is

> more than watching birds with binoculars or identifying spring wildflowers. It is the perceiving—the understanding—of the ways in which nature operates. The relatedness of all elements of the environment provides the key to perception. The rhythm of natural changes provides the beat. When man perceives the processes, he understands better the Creation and feels the refreshment of recreation in its deepest sense.[20]

However, environmental programming approaches cannot be carried out simply through a poetic evocation of the beauty of nature. Instead, Knudson points out that economic and social analyses of visitors, the roles of public and private investment in outdoor recreation, and knowledge of how to deal effectively with different segments of the public are all critical elements in the programming and decision making carried on by modern recreation and park professionals. Scientific expertise is also essential to ensure that outdoor recreation sites are managed within their natural parameters, with concern for biological interactions and carrying capacity.

Political and economic realities also come into play when environmental decisions must be made. For example, a continuing controversy over opening up redwood forest areas in the west has involved the argument that the lumbering industry provides year-round employment to thousands of workers in states such as California and Oregon—and that this fact outweighs the need to preserve these historic areas.

The last two decades have seen a concerted effort to reverse the progress made in the 1960s and 1970s in protecting and restoring the environment. *New York Times* columnist Anthony Lewis has described the recent efforts of a determined faction of Congressional conservatives to cripple the United States Environmental Protection Agency, gut environmental laws, and set up a virtual environmental "exemption bazaar" with bills that would:

> Open the Arctic National Wildlife Refuge in Alaska, which may be America's greatest unspoiled ecosystem, to oil and gas drilling;
>
> Prevent the EPA from keeping possibly toxic fill out of lakes and harbors;
>
> Deprive the EPA of funds to keep raw sewage out of rivers and away from beaches;
>
> Prohibit for a year the listing of new endangered species for protection and kill most of the funding to carry out the Endangered Species Act;
>
> Cut by two-thirds, from 300,000 to 100,000 acres, the wetlands to be bought from farmers by the Agriculture Department for a reserve; and
>
> Increase logging in the Tongass National Forest, a remarkable rain forest in Alaska.[21]

Other proposals that threatened the national parks in the mid-1990s involved shrinking the boundaries of Shenandoah National Park in Virginia; opening up designated wilderness areas within Voyageurs National Park in Minnesota to motorized vehicles and boats; and limiting funding of the National Park Service for maintenance of the new Mojave National Preserve in California to $1.

Such legislative assaults, plus other pitched battles over the use of public lands for lumbering, mining, grazing, and oil drilling, represent a continuing threat to the environmental ethic today. In addition, there is a growing realization that recreation itself poses a continuing threat to the wilderness, and that abrasive conflict exists between different groups of outdoor recreation enthusiasts, such as the tensions between snowmobilers and cross-country skiers, canoers and motorboat owners, and hikers and mountain bikers.

These concerns call not only for a carefully defined philosophy to promote the appropriate uses of national and state parks and forests, but also for adequate financial support to permit park management of environmental programs to function effectively. This overall issue is not of concern to the United States alone. In Canada, for example, a Task Force on Park Establishment created by the national Minister of Environment issued a report, "Our Parks—Vision for the 21st Century." This report urged that a plan be enacted to ensure protection of the nation's natural resources. It concluded:

> Unprecedented public support exists for natural heritage preservation.... Even though we have entered an era of shrinking budgets, jurisdictional conflicts, and a quest for local autonomy, the Task Force believes that Canadians want action to protect out natural treasures, not retrenchment; vision, not resignation. With proposals for more than 500 new parks arising from the recent parks centennial . . . the objective of representing each natural region with at least one park remains a realistic minimum objective.[22]

Hedonist/Individualist Approach

This approach to recreational programming is concerned chiefly with providing fun and pleasure. It regards recreation as a highly individualistic activity that should be free of social constraints or moral purposes. The term "hedonist" is used to mean one who seeks personal pleasure—often with the implication that it is of a sensual, bodily nature. The term "individualist" is attached because this philosophical approach stresses the idea that each individual should be free to seek his or her own fulfillment and pleasure untrammeled by group pressures or social expectations.

The hedonist appeal is most vividly illustrated by the worldwide chain of exotic vacation places operated by Club Med, where guests are promised an environment free from the restraints and demands of the everyday, conventional world. Indeed, an independent Caribbean resort on the island of Jamaica has chosen the name "Hedonism II." In its promotional brochure, it defines "hedonism" as a pleasure-seeking way of life and states:

> We believe that pleasure—the feeling of pleasure—the most normal and natural of all states and that it is great deal more natural than its opposite alternative! We believe, too, that pleasure comes in many forms and that it is most gratifying when it involves all your parts—mind, body, spirit, soul. . . . Hedonism II is a tropical village by the sea where adults share the pleasures of mind, body, spirit, soul. There are no children. No formality. No need for money of any kind. . . . You simply enjoy everything we have to offer without a second thought. . . . Please consider this to be your passport to the best holiday of your life. Above all, enjoy, enjoy.[23]

Obviously, certain forms of leisure activity that have gained increased popularity in American life fit this description. The accelerated use and generally freer acceptance of drugs, alcohol, gambling, sex as a commercialized recreational pursuit, and other forms of sensation-seeking entertainment and play all illustrate the hedonist approach to leisure.

These forms of play may best be described as morally marginal, in the sense that they are legal in some contexts or localities and illegal in others, regarded as acceptable leisure experiences by some population groups and condemned by others. In each case, it is clear that they have persisted throughout human history and that they have become increasingly widespread in recent years.

Drug and Alcohol Abuse   The use of mind-altering or mood-changing substances as a form of pleasure-seeking or socializing experience has been found in many cultures and human societies, both past and present. Alcohol may be legally sold and consumed by adults throughout most of the United States and Canada, and is generally considered to be a useful social lubricant—consumed at weddings and family parties, business luncheons, neighborhood taverns, and a host of other kinds of recreation settings. In contrast, the use of narcotic drugs is illegal, unless medically prescribed, and provides the basis for an immense underworld industry.

Drugs are generally regarded as a far greater threat to health and safety than alcohol. Yet, each year, while cocaine, crack, and heroin take about 7,000 American lives, alcohol claims about 100,000. Someone is killed by a drunk driver every 24 minutes, and over 500,000 people are injured in alcohol-related traffic accidents each year.

Reports by major study groups indicate that the use of marijuana by American teens almost doubled between 1991 and 1995, in contradiction to earlier reports that such use had been declining among the young. Other reports by the Federal Substance Abuse and Mental Health Services Administration confirm that visits to hospitals for heroin-related emergencies rose by 44 percent in the early 1990s. The scope of the problem was indicated at a 1994 United Nations–sponsored conference on organized international crime, where it was reported that drug trafficking worldwide involved annual profits of $500 billion, with the United States representing the major user of illegal narcotics.[24]

Organized Gambling   Over the past three decades, organized legal gambling in the form of casinos, lotteries, racetrack betting, and numerous other commercially sponsored games has proliferated at breakneck speed in the United States. *The New York Times* reports that no American industry in the present decade, with the possible exception of computer software and on-line technology, has grown as rapidly and pervaded society as thoroughly as legalized gambling:

> In 1988 casino gambling was legal in only two states—Nevada and New Jersey. Today [November 1995] casinos, including those on Indian reservations, operate or are authorized in 23 states. In 1994 gamblers armed with lottery tickets, chips and slot machines wagered a whopping $482 billion in this country, which is more than the gross national product of China and represents a 22 percent increase over the previous year.[25]

Throughout the United States, city after city has fallen for the economic lures of legalizing varied forms of gambling, authorizing riverboat casinos that never leave the shore (except when they travel to a more attractive setting financially) and approving off-track betting parlors and varied slot-machine gaming operations. While the argument is made that tax revenues, gaming-related jobs, and visitor spending help to sustain local economies, there is growing evidence that the social costs of gambling make it an unprofitable enterprise for most localities.

What is most significant about the tremendous growth of the gaming industry is that it illustrates a basic transformation in America's prevailing value system. While some still reject legalized gambling as not only destructive of the lives of millions of compulsive bettors but also as a cynical exploitation of the public trust, the majority of citizens today tend to accept it as an appropriate kind of leisure experience.

Commercialized Sex   A third form of morally marginal play that is a key component of the hedonist approach to recreation and leisure is the use of sex as a form of play or entertainment. Commercialized sex has expanded dramatically over the three decades following the counterculture movement of the 1960s.

It takes many forms, including legalized houses of prostitution in Nevada, call-girl rings, and the escort services and massage parlors that represent thinly disguised forms of prostitution in many cities; sex films, books, and magazines that may now be legally purchased; the widespread rental of X-rated videocassettes for home viewing; and the increased showing of sexual images and themes on network television programs and of "soft porn" on cable television.

A recent manifestation of commercialized sex as an element in popular culture involves its broader exploitation within the mass media of entertainment and communication. Increasingly, the phenomenon of "cyberporn"—the transmission of varied types of erotica on the Internet—has prompted national concern. Awareness that children have easy access to such materials and that the Internet is being used for recruitment of sexual partners led to an effort in the mid-1990s to curb such abuses.[26]

While public, nonprofit, and other types of community-based leisure-service organizations generally do not sponsor substance abuse, gambling, or sex-oriented types of entertainment, such activities are widely available through commercial sponsorship and, in many cases, have governmental approval or tacit acceptance. They represent a major sphere of recreational involvement for the public at large and a distinct approach to leisure programming.

Benefits-Based Management Approach

This final philosophical approach to the design and implementation of recreation, park, and leisure-service programs is relatively new. It has been the subject of a number of presentations of NRPA Congresses in the early and mid-1990s, and has been discussed in numerous publications.[27] Essentially, this approach holds that it is not enough to verbalize a set of desirable goals or mission statements or to carry out head-counts of participation and tally the number of events sponsored by a leisure-service agency.

Instead, governmental, nonprofit, therapeutic, armed forces, and other types of managed recreation agencies should more clearly define their roles and purposes in terms of community and participant benefits. Geoffrey Godbey has argued that services provided in the public sector differ from similar efforts in the commercial sector in a fundamental way:

> The public sector must market for more than economic profit. A case must be made that the welfare of the public is improved and such a case must start with an understandable concept. If no such case is established for its existence, the public service in question may cease to exist other than as an extremely limited "proprietary" function of government.[28]

As Chapter 6 has shown, community-based leisure services provide major social benefits within a number of important outcome areas. Christopher Jarvi has summarized recreation's role in community life as follows:

> We provide community pride; crime prevention and deterrence; opportunities to develop and maintain family unity; economic development and tourism enhancement; community unity and a sense of

belonging; environmental protection/education/stewardship; community culture in the form of heroes, celebrations, sacred places, mythology, rites of passage and rituals; community involvement; shared management and leadership development; and ethnic and cultural understanding.[29]

In practice, the benefits-based approach is based on a three-step implementation process: (1) *benefits and opportunity identification:* determine a core group of benefits that users seek and agencies can realistically provide, along with the management changes needed for benefits achievement; (2) *program implementation:* make facility or staff modifications needed to achieve desired benefits, and carry out systematic monitoring procedures during programs; and (3) *evaluation and documentation:* analyze data, determine if program benefits were achieved, develop reports, and disseminate findings to appropriate audiences.[30]

Within this process, it is essential that target goals be defined in terms of concrete and measurable benefits. Bill Exham, manager of the Community Services Department in Scottsdale, Arizona, stresses that this should be done in terms of *outcomes* that measure change or effect, rather than *outputs* that simply describe a program (see table below).

Differences Between Outcomes and Outputs[31]

OUTPUTS	OUTCOMES
115 participant-hours in substance-abuse seminar	20 percent reduction in alcohol use
400 registrants for learn-to-swim program	98% (392 out of 400) passed basic swimming skills test
75 meals served in senior center per day	65% of senior participants made new friends at congregate meals program
52 participants in agency rafting program	85% reported feeling a sense of adventure on rafting trip

Lawrence Allen points out that a number of studies are under way to develop a realistic set of significant target benefits for use by public and other community-based leisure-service agencies in implementing a benefits-based management approach. When this has been accomplished and when the recreation, park, and leisure-service profession moves purposefully to accomplish, document, and publicize its important contributions to community life, the field itself should benefit from heightened public awareness and support.[32]

Philosophical Approaches: No Pure Models

It should be stressed that, while these seven approaches to the definition and management of organized leisure services are separate and distinct philosophical positions, it is unlikely that any single agency or government department would follow one approach exclusively.

Many organizations combine two or more positions in defining their own missions. This blending of emphases was illustrated in the opening statement of the 1987 report of the President's Commission on Americans Outdoors. Entitled *Americans and the Outdoors,* the report begins:

It enriches us in many ways . . .

The great outdoors is a great health machine, toning up our minds and bodies. The engineer kayaking through a cataract and the assembly-line worker hunting in quiet woods are both recharging themselves for more productive work.

Our economic health benefits more directly. Recreation products and services are a 300-billion-dollar industry, and the economic web does not stop there. The clothes we wear, the automobile that takes us to recreation areas, and the photographic equipment that records the highlights all derive in part from the outdoor use of leisure time.

Open space is a silent social worker as well, in its ability to reduce crime and delinquency. A drop in vandalism accompanied the building of a small park in Trenton, New Jersey, prompting Mayor Arthur Holland to tell the commission, "You don't throw stones when you've got a basketball to throw around."[33]

This message contains clearly identifiable elements of the quality-of-life, marketing, and human-services approaches, with a strong environmentalist thrust as well.

KEY PRINCIPLES GUIDING LEISURE-SERVICE DELIVERY TODAY

For recreation, parks, and leisure-service practitioners, it is possible to identify a number of key principles that should be used to guide their professional operations today. First, it is assumed that such individuals—no matter what their fields of specialization—regard recreation and leisure as important to human growth and community development

A contemporary philosophy of organized recreation service should therefore deal with such important issues as the place of recreation and leisure in modern life, the role of government, the development of programming based on significant social needs, and the place of leisure education. The following examination of these issues provides a basis for developing principles or guidelines for operating leisure-service programs.

Place of Recreation in the Modern Community

In American and Canadian society, our view of recreation as a social phenomenon and area of community involvement is influenced by our governmental systems. In our Constitution and in court decisions that have influenced government policy and practice through the years, we have accepted the view that, on various levels, government has the responsibility for providing certain major services to citizens. These include functions related to safety and protection, education, health, and other services that contribute to maintaining the quality of life of all citizens.

Linked to this system of governmental responsibility is our general acceptance of the Judeo-Christian concepts of the worth and dignity of all human beings, and the need to help each person become the most fully realized individual that he or she is capable of being. Through government and through many voluntary community associations, we have accepted the responsibility for providing needed services and opportunities for people at each stage of life, and for those who because of disability have been deprived in significant ways.

Needs of Individual Citizens

Recreation and leisure are important aspects of personal experience in modern life for the physical, social, emotional, intellectual, and spiritual benefits they provide. Positive leisure experiences enhance the quality of a person's life, and help each person develop to the fullest potential. To make this possible, government and other responsible social agencies should provide recreation resources, programs, and, where appropriate, leisure education to help people to understand the value of free time, when constructively and creatively used.

Government's Responsibility

In addition to providing these personal benefits, recreation helps a community to meet health needs, gain economic benefits, and maintain community morale. On each level (local, state or provincial, and federal), appropriate government agencies should therefore be assigned the responsibility for maintaining a network of physical resources for leisure participation—including parks, playgrounds, centers, sports facilities, and other special recreation facilities. Government should be responsible for planning, organizing, and carrying out programs, under proper leadership, for all age levels.

Government cannot and should not seek to meet *all* of the leisure needs of the community. It must recognize that other types of community organizations—including voluntary, private, commercial, therapeutic, industrial, and educational groups—sponsor effective recreation programs, which are often designed to meet specialized needs or more advanced interests. Therefore, its unique role should be to provide a basic floor of recreational opportunity, to fill the gaps that are not covered by other organizations, and to provide coordination and overall direction to community leisure-service programs.

There has been a growing body of opinion that local government recreation and park agencies should take less responsibility for the direct provision of program activities—particularly when limited by fiscal constraints—and should move instead into the role of serving as an advocate for recreation and leisure in community life and providing coordinating or facilitating assistance to other agencies.

A major concern should be to ensure an equitable distribution of recreational opportunities for the public at large. This would not guarantee that all residents will have totally equal programs and services, but would represent a pledge that, within the realities of community needs and economic capabilities, facilities and programs will be distributed so as to bring about a reasonable balance of such opportunities for different neighborhoods and community groups.

Goals of Other Organizations

Each type of organization that makes a contribution to this field should determine its own specialized goals for recreation service, depending on its overall purposes, the nature of its membership, and its available resources.

Armed forces recreation should give its highest priority to helping develop and maintain a high level of physical fitness and positive morale; building an esprit de corps; reducing problems related to alcohol or drug abuse, or the taking of unauthorized leave; and providing needed leisure programs for the families of service personnel.

In employee recreation programs, the goal generally is to improve the productivity of workers by enhancing their physical and mental fitness and morale, improving relationships between management and line personnel, assisting in recruitment and retention of skilled employees, and reducing problems related to boredom and monotony on the job.

In therapeutic recreation service, the specific goals of treatment or rehabilitation, as developed by an interdisciplinary team of professionals working in collaboration with clients or patients themselves, serve to direct the course of programming.

A prevailing principle today is that all forms of organized recreation service provided by government or nonprofit community-service organizations should be goal-oriented and purposeful. While recreation may certainly be carried on by individuals without any clear sense of purpose, if leisure-service programs are to justify the support of taxpayers or those who contribute to the funding of community agencies, they *must* be designed to bring results of significant value to the community.

Programming Directed to Community Needs

As the preceding principle suggests, organized recreation service today should meet significant community needs. Leisure-service practitioners and educators should be alert to emerging trends and problems in society, and should seek to provide programs that deal with them in innovative, constructive ways.

Examples of such trends might include: (1) the continuing fragmentation of family life and the need for leisure programming, day-care, and other services designed to assist either families as a whole or specific age groups, such as children, at-risk youth, or the aging; (2) the battle to protect the outdoor environment (including national and state parks, forests, waterways, and beach areas) from pollution, uncurbed industrial or commercial uses, and the damaging effects of certain forms of outdoor recreation; (3) the accelerating rate of violence in community life, and the specific problems attached to conflict and hostility among different racial and ethnic groups; (4) continuing efforts to provide integrated, mainstreaming programs for persons with disability; and (5) building on the progress that has been made in achieving gender equity in recreation and leisure, as well as recognizing the need to provide fuller opportunities and services for those with alternative sexual lifestyles.

OTHER GUIDELINES

In addition to these general guidelines, there are a number of others that are of particular relevance to the role of leisure-service professionals. They relate to such areas of concern as the lack of coordination among recreation sponsors, the role of participants in determining recreation programs, and the need to balance the various approaches to recreation management and to educate the public as to recreation's proper role.

Coordination Among Agencies

American society today has many organizations of various types that provide leisure services, but they often do so with marked duplication and in unnecessary competition with each other. At the same time, there are continuing gaps in service that result in unmet needs.

It is therefore essential that public, private, voluntary, commercial, and other types of leisure-service organizations cooperate fully in determining community needs and accepting appropriate functions and roles for themselves in providing recreational opportunities. This will help to prevent unnecessary competition among agencies, and help to identify and fill gaps in community leisure services. Similarly, the various types of sponsors could share resources and know-how, and even develop joint programming that will be more effective than the work of any single agency could be.

Participant Input

A sound contemporary philosophy of recreation dictates that participants themselves should be as fully involved as possible in the determination of program emphases and needs. This can be accomplished through the use of neighborhood committees or advisory councils, recreation and park boards, task forces, or volunteers. Such participation has a dual benefit: (1) community residents are able to provide leadership, advice, assistance, and other resources to the program; and (2) they are engaged supporters of the program and represent an active constituency for it in political and other strategic terms.

While this principle is most obviously of use in government-sponsored recreation and park programs, it also applies to other types of membership organizations or specialized services. Particularly in such fields as campus, employee, and voluntary-agency recreation, volunteer participation in planning groups and in the actual operation of programs is essential.

Balance of Marketing and Human-Services Approaches

These two approaches to leisure-service management appear to represent sharply opposed philosophical orientations. Can they be reconciled? As earlier chapters have shown, economic and other factors have compelled a much more aggressive and fiscally hardheaded thrust in the marketing of leisure services, among nonprofit as well as profit-oriented agencies. Yet, a number of authors have emphasized that organizations in the public sector—while they may adopt an entrepreneurial approach—must also be concerned with social and economic priorities that benefit the overall community. Ronald Riggins writes:

> In a profession increasingly dependent on commercial profitable enterprise, it is not difficult to foresee an emphasis on targeting for service those groups and individuals supplying profits. Carried too far, this action will reverse longstanding commitments to uphold the principle of a society where individual well-being is bound to the welfare of the whole.[34]

Riggins argues that increasing privatization of public leisure-service agencies, with a strong commercial emphasis, could seriously limit open access to needed recreation facilities and programs. Yet, from a pragmatic point of view, it is necessary to link the marketing and human-services approaches through appropriate objectives, policies, and management techniques. This means that while every effort should be made to plan and market recreation programs and services as efficiently and economically as possible—with the intention of maximizing revenues for support of the department—it is also necessary to establish certain social priorities and to meet these critical needs despite their costs or the inability of recipients of special services to pay their way.

Within this context, the benefits-based management approach described earlier in this chapter provides a potentially useful means of reconciling the marketing and human-services models. Agency targets may incorporate both fiscal and social elements and, when achieved, should result in a higher level of financial support overall for recreation and park budgets.

Need for Effective Leisure Education

Finally, there is a need to promote effective leisure education among the various sectors of the public and among professionals in other areas of community service or in special disciplines.

The heritage of our Puritan forebears and our centuries-long dependence on the Protestant work ethic have combined to make many Americans and Canadians suspicious of recreation and to keep them unaware of its potential value in human society and in the day-to-day lives of individuals and families. Not only do people misunderstand the value of leisure experiences, but also they are often willing to be satisfied by the most limited, superficial, or even self-destructive kinds of recreational involvement. Thus, recreation and park practitioners must strive to promote awareness of the scope, values, and specific contributions of recreation in the modern community, and must fight vigorously for its support.

The effort to encourage a fuller understanding and appreciation of creative and constructive forms of leisure involvement is particularly critical today, in light of the changes that have occurred over the past two decades. As described in earlier chapters, many of the most popular forms of entertainment in sports, the mass media, tourism, and similar leisure domains are now dominated by a few huge conglomerates—multibillion dollar businesses that determine the kinds of free-time attractions to be presented to the public. Their primary concern is profitability, and often their products and services include negative or self-destructive forms of play that are designed and marketed in highly sophisticated and efficient ways.

In the mid-1990s, it became clear that the nation was greatly concerned about the breakdown of traditional family values and social structures and that the mass media of entertainment were increasingly being seen as a leading cause of major social problems. This development provides an important opportunity for recreation, park, and leisure-service professionals to make their voices heard and to promote a positive and constructive set of leisure values among Americans and Canadians of all ages.

FACING THE CHALLENGE OF THE FUTURE

The principles and guidelines that have been presented above deal essentially with the *present*. However, those who read this book—primarily college and university students in recreation, park, and leisure-studies curricula—are looking ahead to careers in the *future*. What will the twenty-first century bring us in terms of demographic, social, and economic changes that can radically affect our uses of leisure?

Patricia Farrell and Richard Trudeau argue that we are in the midst of a "social upheaval" that will continue through the next decade and beyond. If professionals in the park and recreation field miss the import of what is occurring today, the danger of their being left behind is all too real. Instead, they must be a part of the nation's development of a new social ethic:

> These times will require an "ethic of commitment" which will demonstrate evidence of growing concern with community and a sensitivity to human relationships. Strategic management of the human climate will be of paramount importance in the decades to come.[35]

Supporting these views, Frank Benest, Jack Foley, and George Welton comment that we live in a time of great concern, uncertainty, and change. However, such conditions bring both crisis *and* opportunity, and make possible reforms that could never be accomplished in times of stability. Within the recreation, park, and leisure-service field, they argue, all organizations must review their own roles and programs to ensure that they serve community needs.[36]

Many contemporary authorities in the leisure-service field emphasize that bringing about such changes will require a new wave of entrepreneurship. Recreation and park professionals in all spheres of service need to think more imaginatively and innovatively, need to be more goal-oriented and flexible, and need to be more willing to take risks in order to achieve outstanding results. They need to cultivate an organizational and professional climate that is interactive, with everyone sharing common purposes and working to achieve them. Above all, they need to be optimistic both about the future of society and about the role of recreation, park, and leisure-services professionals in helping to achieve a fuller, richer, and more productive life for all citizens.

Elements of Oncoming Change

What are the elements of change that directly impact on recreation, park, and leisure-service agencies and programs in the last decade of the twentieth century and that promise to become more intense and critical in the early decades of the twenty-first century?

New patterns of urban and suburban living, work structures and opportunities, and family values and lifestyles are likely to be accompanied by growing concerns about children and youth who are at risk and about the social pathologies linked to poverty and violence that often express themselves in leisure behaviors.

In the early and mid-1990s, the United States witnessed a massive wave of corporate downsizing, with major companies like AT&T, IBM, Xerox, and Chase Manhattan Bank eliminating millions of white-collar workers and managerial personnel, or entering mergers or engaging in restructuring with similar results.[37] This trend has created a widespread sense of economic insecurity and stress, and has helped to create a growing gap between the wealthy and the poor—greater in the United States than in any other industrialized nation.[38]

In terms of intergroup relations, as the number of racial and ethnic minorities continues to swell, it is predicted that Hispanic and Asian population growth in particular will result in the United States no longer being a predominantly white society by the mid-twenty-first century.[39] With growing evidence of racial hostility and a wave of social conservatism that seeks to reduce health and welfare benefits and other social-service government programs and to substitute an increasingly harsh penal system for efforts at crime prevention and rehabilitation, the potential for widespread social unrest seems great.[40]

The increased use of technology in creating new leisure products and services, linked to the commodification of recreation and its control by huge, multinational conglomerates, makes it likely that commercial recreation will dominate major portions of the free time of Americans in the years ahead. In terms of government policy, the move toward privatization through subcontracting with commercial or private organizations to carry out major public functions seems likely to grow. However, in a number of cases, evidence in the mid-1990s has suggested that privatization of prisons and public school systems has not been a success—and some of these arrangements have been terminated.[41]

Recognizing a variation of privatization, a number of social critics have documented the growth of new "edge cities," communities at the fringe of major metropolitan areas that not only contain huge new business complexes but also provide luxurious housing, mall shopping, and other services for the well-to-do. Increasingly, successful professionals, business executives, and other upper-class individuals live in such areas, which are often managed by quasi-nongovernmental associations that act as "shadow governments" in serving their residents. This trend is linked to the current tendency of wealthy and influential families to withdraw from reliance on public services. Instead, writes Robert Reich:

As public parks and playgrounds deteriorate, there is a proliferation of private health clubs, golf clubs, tennis clubs, skating clubs, and every other type of recreational association in which costs are shared among members. Condominiums and the omnipresent residential communities dun their members to undertake work that financially strapped local governments can no longer afford to do well—maintaining roads, mending sidewalks, pruning trees, repairing street lights, cleaning swimming pools, paying for lifeguards and, notably, hiring security guards to protect life and property.[42]

As a single vivid example of this trend, there now are chains of commercial indoor playgrounds and fun or fitness centers for children that provide play experiences in carefully guarded surroundings for a relatively modest fee. Such ventures have been encouraged by consumer group studies that indicate that more than 90 percent of the country's public playgrounds are now unsafe, leading to many thousands of injuries each year.[43]

Symbolically, playgrounds have represented the beginning impetus and one of the key contributions of the overall recreation and park movement to the leisure needs of community residents. Their commercial privatization and the withdrawal of economically capable and influential families from the use of public playgrounds represents a serious threat to the future support of government-sponsored leisure-service programs. This trend suggests a move toward further social exclusivity and away from the role of recreation as a force that brings people of different backgrounds together in shared communal experiences.

On a broader scale, a number of social critics have commented on the widespread trend away from varied forms of organized group social activity or membership in such civic associations as the PTA, labor unions, the Elks Club, the League of Women Voters, and the Red Cross. Adult involvement in such organizations has declined steadily over the past three decades, as television watching has increased.[44] While varied types of support groups—such as Alcoholics Anonymous or town watch groups—have grown, shared forms of neighborhood sociability have declined sharply—a trend with serious implications for leisure-service professionals.

EFFORTS TO PREDICT THE FUTURE

A number of major study groups in the United Stables and Canada have attempted to develop systematic predictions of social changes that will accelerate as we enter the twenty-first century. For example, a collaborative study by the Canadian Park and Recreation Association and the Rethink Group, a leading-edge research and planning organization, has identified a number of "macro" trends that are expected to characterize Canadian society in the decades ahead. These include:

"Adultism": The Altered Family
This will involve a shift from a youth-oriented to an adult-oriented society, with an increasingly older population. By the year 2016, we will see a fixed working-age cohort at about 60 percent of the population, with the percentage of children declining as the percentage of elderly persons increases.

Single-person households will expand to 30 percent by 2011, with projections that the percentage of working women will rise to 75 percent by the early 2000s. Need for day-care programs and services for latch-key children will continue to rise, and households not related by birth or marriage are expected to increase at three times the rate of family households.

Structural Economic Change
We are witnessing a shift from one complex of production technologies to another, with the combination of computer and telecommunications advances speeding the transition from an industrial to a post-industrial economy. Society will become increasingly divided into "technocrats" and "technopeasants." For

many, there will be temporary dislocation and unemployment; older "technopeasants" will face early forced retirement.

Educational systems will employ the most sophisticated computer and telecommunications learning tools. The "work-at-home" phenomenon will expand rapidly through electronic "cottage" industry.

Greening: The Environmental Imperative

With growing awareness that the industrial age has polluted our air, water and food, and increasing sensitivity to problems associated with waste management and the life-threatening consequences of global warming, there will be a shift from the present energy economy to other fuel sources. Increasing concern for habitats and at-risk species will influence national politics and business policies.

Electronic Entertainment "Cocoons"

Homes are steadily evolving into the information age, with television, VCRs, computers and word-processors, video games and CD-ROMs offering communication and entertainment. Electronic systems will link the home with the community, in terms of shopping, banks and other businesses, and entertainment options. Families will increasingly rely on the safety and comfort of their homes for recreation, and virtual reality will make it possible to explore a host of new experiences.[45]

Other major trends cited in this Canadian futurist report include: increasing globalization; mounting intercultural concerns; budget cutbacks and the shrinking leisure dollar; the use of recreation as a form of prevention and therapy; the growth of women's influence in leisure; and the decline of institutions, with an emphasis on moving away from centralized, authoritarian structures toward community-based leadership.

U.S. Views: Agenda for the Twenty-first Century

Many of the same trends described in the Canadian *Leisure Watch* report have been noted by leisure-service professionals and scholars in the United States as well.

For example, in the early 1990s two national conferences were held to identify the critical needs in the field, with the sponsorship of the National Symposium Committee and with the findings published by the National Recreation and Park Association. Somewhat more sharply focused on the direct concerns and priorities of the recreation and park field than was the Canadian report, these conferences led to a substantial number of conclusions, including the following:

Park and recreation professionals must be able and willing to identify, analyze, promote and respond to change in society.

There is a strong trend toward greater participation in the decision-making process by citizens and employees. New leadership techniques will be required of park and recreation professionals to facilitate consensus building.

Multicultural diversity will continue to grow rapidly. Parks and recreation must find ways to celebrate the variety of cultures within the community.

The wellness movement will continue to grow, and parks, recreation and leisure services must facilitate and identify directly with the growing wellness movement.

Success will depend on an organization's ability to build cooperative relationships and establish networks and coalitions with other organizations.

It is essential to improve the image of the profession, both externally and internally, so that the relationship between recreation and park programs and values and contemporary issues is clearly apparent.

Tourism has emerged as one of the world's growth industries and an increasingly important part of leisure expression. Parks and recreation must be involved in mutually beneficial partnerships with tourism.

Environment will increasingly become a focus of international concern. The park and recreation profession must take its rightful place as a leader in shaping environmental policy.

The park and recreation profession must develop and articulate clearly defined mission statements, goals and objectives of the field.[46]

STRATEGIES AND VISIONS FOR THE FUTURE

In light of all of the trends for the future that have been outlined in this chapter, numerous professional societies and government agencies have sought to outline appropriate strategies for the decades to come.

For example, the Bureau of Land Management in the U.S. Department of the Interior developed a major report, *Recreation 2000,* which identified the specific challenges facing it in the years ahead and suggested strategies to deal with these concerns. Overall, it outlined 14 specific policy statements dealing with such issues as resource monitoring and protection, visitor services, partnership, use limits and allocation of resources, fees for the use of public lands, tourism, and professionalism and career development for BLM resource management specialists.[47]

From a broader perspective, a number of other groups in the United States have sought to define their role for the years ahead. For example, the Illinois Park and Recreation Society held a "Gateway to the Future" Conference in 1993, which summed up its vision for the future in "Visions 2003". A number of its predictions follow:

By the year 2003, parks and recreation agencies will be recognized by all as essential to "quality of life":

the champion of the wellness imperative for our citizens and communities—recognized as the key preventive services in the health field

a catalyst and advocate for the environmental movements—stewards of our natural environments, leaders in environmental education, committed to ecologically sound operations and services

programming and facilities that are accessible to all—increasingly responding to challenged, disadvantaged and "at risk" individuals, "families" and neighborhoods—providing the cultural and social connections that build harmony

excellence in government management—demonstrating responsiveness, optimal use of all available resources, generating creative revenue alternatives to invest in quality services

leaders in the public sector movement toward partnerships and strategic alliances that help achieve the full potential of our leisure, learning, health, police and social service enterprises[48]

Obviously, the kinds of roles and changing professional priorities outlined in these reports do not happen automatically. They occur when they are consciously worked toward by leisure-service professionals who see their programs not as end products in themselves, but rather as means to an end—with the ultimate end being the development of better human beings and the furtherance of community wellness. In this important sense, the future planning and implementation of recreation programs in the United States and Canada must be consciously benefits-driven if they are to survive and flourish.

SUMMARY

Philosophy, seen as a set of carefully evolved principles that express the fundamental values and goals of any field of professional service, is a critical element in professional practice. This chapter presents a brief review of some earlier approaches to defining the meaning of recreation, play, and leisure and their roles in community life, followed by a discussion of recent efforts in this area.

It then identifies seven distinct operational philosophies that influence the provision of organized recreation services today. These range from the quality-of-life and marketing orientations to a more recent model of service, the benefits-based management approach. While the chapter notes that most leisure-service organizations employ a blend of two or more orientations in their policy-making and program planning, it suggests that the benefits-based model would appear to be particularly useful in an era of dramatic social change and economic challenge.

The concluding section of the chapter discusses a number of these changes, particularly relating to such areas of concern as population growth, shifts in employment patterns, environmental challenges, the impact of technology and commodification on leisure, privatization of government functions, and the withdrawal of the elite from many areas of community life. Several examples of studies that predict future trends in both Canadian and American society are summarized, with an emphasis on the need to anticipate and deal with change in a proactive way, rather than through passive or reluctant responses. Ultimately, this chapter serves to illustrate the blending of theoretical and practical concerns that must characterize all fields of public service if they are to be successful.

Questions for Class Discussion and Essay Examinations

1. Define the term "philosophy." Why is it an important element in recreation, park, and leisure-service planning, policy-making, and administrative practice? Give one or more examples of the kinds of issues facing practitioners in this field that involve philosophical issues or require the application of management principles based on a sound set of agency values and goals.

2. What is your personal philosophy with respect to the meaning of recreation and leisure in contemporary society? This may be answered in terms of the functions it fulfills in community life or in terms of the overall mission of a particular type of leisure-service sponsor.

3. Chapter 14 presents seven different approaches to recreation, park, and leisure-service management today (examples: quality-of-life or marketing models of service). Select any three of these orientations and show how their influence is reflected in the practices of recreation agencies with which you are familiar. Which of the seven approaches do you find most compatible with your own views?

4. The chapter presents a number of predictions for the future with respect to demographic, social, economic, and other changes. Which of these do you believe present the most important challenge for the recreation, park, and leisure-service field? In what ways should leisure-service professionals seek to meet them constructively as we approach the twenty-first century?

Endnotes

2   See David Gray and Seymour Greben, "Future Perspectives," *Parks and Recreation* (July 1974): 53.

3   Earle Zeigler, *Philosophical Foundations for Physical, Health and Recreation Education* (Englewood Cliffs, N.J.: Prentice-Hall, 1964).

4   H. Douglas Sessoms and Karla Henderson, *Introduction to Leisure Services* (State College, Penn.: Venture Publishing, 1994): 89–92.

5 Carolyn Thomas, *Sport in a Philosophical Context* (Philadelphia, Penn.: Lea and Febiger, 1983): 21–22.

6 Paul Weiss, *Sport: A Philosophical Inquiry* (Carbondale, Ill.: Southern Illinois University Press, 1969).

7 Joseph Mihalich, *Sports and Athletics: Philosophy in Action* (Totowa, N.J.: Littlefield, Adams and Co., 1982): 10.

8 Charles Sylvester, "The Freedom to Be What We Want to Be: A Philosophical Comparison of Traditional and Existential Approaches to the Ethics of Leisure" (Presentation at the Leisure Research Symposium, NRPA Congress, Anaheim, Cal., 1986): 2–3.

9 *Ibid.*, 5.

10 Wayne Stormann, "The Recreation Profession, Capital and Democracy," *Leisure Sciences* (Vol. 15 1993): 49–66; and "The Ideology of the American Urban Parks and Recreation Movement: Past and Future," *Leisure Sciences* (Vol. 13 1991): 137–151.

11 George Butler, *Introduction to Community Recreation* (New York: McGraw–Hill and the National Recreation Association, 1959): 10.

12 Harold Meyer, Charles Brightbill, and H. Douglas Sessoms, *Community Recreation: A Guide to Its Organization* (Englewood Cliffs, N.J.: Prentice-Hall, 1969).

13 John Crompton, "Selecting Target Markets—A Key to Effective Marketing," *Journal of Park and Recreation Administration* (January 1983): 8.

14 Mark Havitz, "Marketing Is Not Synonymous with Commercialization," *Parks and Recreation* (May 1988): 34–35.

15 F. William Niepoth, *Leisure Leadership* (Englewood Cliffs, N.J.: Prentice-Hall, 1983): 3.

16 Ruth Russell, *Planning Programs in Recreation* (St. Louis, Mo.: C. V. Mosby, 1982): Chapter 2.

17 Christopher Edginton, David Compton, and Carole Hanson, *Recreation and Leisure Programming: A Guide for the Professional* (Philadelphia, Penn.: W. B. Saunders, 1980): Chapter 2.

18 Paul Wehman and Stuart Schleien, *Leisure Programs for Handicapped Persons* (Baltimore, Md.: University Park Press, 1981): 89.

19 Daniel Dustin, "Managing Public Lands for the Human Spirit," *Parks and Recreation* (September 1994): 92–96.

20 Douglas Knudson, *Outdoor Recreation* (New York: Macmillan, 1980): 31.

21 Anthony Lewis, "On Another Planet?" *New York Times* (29 September 1995): A-3.

22 *Our Parks—Vision for the 21st Century,* Report of the Minister of Environment and the Task Force on Park Establishment (Ottawa, Canada, December 1986): vii–viii.

23 *Hedonism II: The Pleasure Comes in Many Forms* (Resort Brochure, Negril, Jamaica,) 2–3.

24 See "Drugs and Alcohol Use Rising Among Teenagers: A Study Finds," Associated Press (17 December 1995); and "Outlook Database: Global Gangsters," *U.S. News & World Report* (28 November 1994): 33.

25 Kevin Sack, "There Are Two Sides to Every Game in Town," *New York Times* (5 November 1995): 4-E.

26 Philip Elmer-Dewitt, "On a Screen Near You: Cyberporn," *Time* (3 July 1995): 38–45.

27 See Lawrence Allen, "Time to Measure Outcomes," (Presentation at NRPA Congress, Minneapolis, Minn., October 1994).

28 Geoffrey Godbey, "Redefining Public Parks and Recreation," *Parks and Recreation* (October 1991): 57.

29 Christopher Jarvi, "Leaders Who Meet Changing Needs Today," *Parks and Recreation* (March 1995): 86–93.

30 Allen, *op. cit.*

31 Bill Exham, "Time to Measure Outcomes," (Presentation at NRPA Congress, Minneapolis, Minn., October 1994).

32   Lawrence Allen, "Benefits-Based Management of Recreation Services," *Parks and Recreation* (March 1996): 65–76.

33   *Americans and the Outdoors,* Summary Report of President's Commission on Americans Outdoors (Washington, D.C.: U. S. Government Printing Office, January 1987): 5.

34   Ronald Riggins, "Social Responsibility and the Public Sector Entrepreneur," *Journal of Physical Education, Recreation and Dance—Leisure Today* (October 1988): 27–28.

35   Patricia Farrell and Richard Trudeau, "Strategic Management for the Coming Decade," *Journal of Park and Recreation Administration* (July 1984): 1.

36   Frank Benest, Jack Foley, and George Welton, "Managing Our Way to a Preferred Future," *Parks and Recreation* (November 1985): 49.

37   Abigail McCarthy, "Has Anyone Thought of Jobs?" *Commonweal* (24 February 1995): 7; and George Church, "Disconnected," *Time* (15 January 1996): 44–45.

38   Keith Bradsher, "Widest Gap in Incomes? Research Points to U.S.," *New York Times* (27 October 1995): D-3.

39   "Ahead: A Very Different Nation," *U.S. News & World Report* (25 March 1996): 16.

40   See Ted Gest, "Crime and Punishment," *U.S. News & World Report* (3 July 1995): 24–26; and Brent Staples, "The Chain Gang Show," *New York Times Magazine* (17 September 1995): 62–63.

41   "Privatized Lives," *Time* (13 November 1995): 88; and Jim Impoco, "Do Firms Run Schools Well?" *U.S. News & World Report* (8 January 1996): 46–49.

42   Robert Reich, "Secession of the Sucessful," *New York Times Magazine* (20 January 1991): 44.

43   "Most Playgrounds Are Unsafe, Report Says," *New York Times* (29 May 1994): 16.

44   Anthony Lewis, "An Atomized America," *New York Times* (18 December 1995): A-17; and Sam Roberts, "Alone in the Wasteland," *New York Times* (24 December 1995); E-3.

45   "Macro Trends Prescribe Canada's New National Vision for Recreation and Parks," *Leisure Watch* (Vol. 2 No. 3 1993): 1–4.

46   Tony Mobley and Robert Toalson, eds., *Parks and Recreation in the 21st Century* (Arlington, Va.: National Symposium Committee and NRPA, 1992). See also "Vision 2000: A Strategic Plan for the Future," *Parks and Recreation* (April 1995, n.p.).

47   *Recreation 2000: Executive Summary* (Washington, D.C., U.S. Department of the Interior, Bureau of Land Management, n.d.).

48   "From the Leading Edge: Innovative View of the Future" (Presentation at NRPA Congress, San Jose, Cal., October 1993).

Bibliography

Apter, Michael. *The Dangerous Edge: The Psychology of Excitement.* New York: Free Press/Macmillan, 1992.

Arian, Edward. *The Unfulfilled Promise: Public Subsidy of the Arts in America.* Philadelphia, PA: Temple University Press, 1989.

Austin, David. *Therapeutic Recreation: Processes and Techniques.* Champaign, IL: Sagamore Publishing, 1996.

Bammel, Gene and Lei Lane Burrus-Bammel. *Leisure and Human Behavior.* Dubuque, IA: Wm. C. Brown, 1982.

Barnett, Lynn. *Research About Leisure: Past, Present, and Future.* Champaign, IL: Sagamore Publishing, 1995.

Bullaro, John and Christopher Edginton. *Commercial Leisure Services: Managing for Profit, Service, and Personal Satisfaction* New York: Macmillan, 1986.

Bullock, Charles and Michael Mahon. *An Introduction to Recreation and Therapeutic Recreation Services for Persons with Disabilities.* Champaign, IL: Sagamore Publishing, 1996.

Busser, James. *Programming for Employee Services and Recreation.* Champaign, IL: Sagamore Publishing, 1990.

Caillois, Roger. *Man, Play and Games.* London: Thames and Hudson, 1961.

Coakley, Jay. *Sport in Society: Issues and Controversies.* St. Louis, MO: Mosby, 1994.

Compton, David, ed., *Issues in Therapeutic Recreation: A Profession in Transition.* Champaign, IL: Sagamore Publishing, 1996.

Cordes, Kathleen and Hilmi Ibrahim. *Applications in Recreation and Leisure: For Today and the Future.* St. Louis, MO: Mosby, 1996.

Cross, Gary. *A Social History of Leisure Since 1600.* State College, PA: Venture Publishing, 1990.

Crossley, John and Lynn Jamieson. *Introduction to Commercial and Therapeutic Recreation.* Champaign, IL: Sagamore Publishing, 1993.

Dulles, Foster. *A History of Recreation: America Learns to Play.* New York: Appleton-Century-Crofts, 1965.

Dumazedier, Joffre. *Sociology of Leisure.* Amsterdam: Elsevier, 1974.

Dustin, Daniel, Leo MacAvoy, and John Schultz. *Stewards of Access, Custodians of Choice.* Champaign, IL: Sagamore Publishing, 1995.

Fain, Gerald, ed., *Leisure and Ethics: Reflections on the Philosophy of Leisure.* Reston, VA: American Alliance for Health, Physical Education, Recreation and Dance, 1991.

Farrell, Patricia and Herberta Lundegren. *The Process of Recreation Programming: Theory and Technique.* State College, PA: Venture Publishing, 1991.

Godbey, Geoffrey. *Leisure in Your Life: An Exploration.* State College, PA: Venture Publishing, 1994.

Godbey, Geoffrey. *The Future of Leisure Services: Thriving on Change.* State College, PA: Venture Publishing, 1989.

Goodale, Thomas and Peter Witt, eds., *Recreation and Leisure: Issues in an Era of Change.* State College, PA: Venture Publishing, 1991.

Goodale, Thomas and Geoffrey Godbey. *The Evolution of Leisure: Historical and Philosophical Perspectives.* State College, PA: Venture Publishing, 1988.

Guttmann, Allen. *Women's Sport: A History.* New York: Columbia University Press, 1991.

Henderson, Karla, M. Deborah Bialeschki, Susan Shaw, and Valeria Freysinger. *Both Gains and Gaps: Feminist Perspectives on Women's Leisure.* State College, PA: Venture Publishing, 1996.

Howard, Dennis and John Crompton. *Financing, Managing and Marketing Recreation and Parks Resources.* Dubuque, IA: Wm. C. Brown, 1985.

Huizinga, Johan. *Homo Ludens: A Study of the Play Element in Culture.* Boston, MA: Beacon Press, 1950.

Hunnicutt, Benjamin. *Work Without End: Abandoning Shorter Hours for the Right To Work.* Philadelphia, PA: Temple University Press, 1988.

Iso-Ahola, Seppo. *The Social Psychology of Leisure and Recreation.* Dubuque, IA: Wm. C. Brown, 1980.

Jackson, Edgar and Thomas Burton, eds., *Understanding Leisure and Recreation: Mapping the Past, Charting the Future.* State College, PA: Venture Publishing, 1989.

Kelly, John. *Leisure.* Boston: Allyn & Bacon, 1996.

Kelly, John and Geoffrey Godbey. *The Sociology of Leisure.* State College, PA: Venture Publishing, 1992.

Kelly, John and Rod Warnick. *Recreation Markets: Trends Toward the Year 2000.* Champaign, IL: Sagamore Publishing, 1996.

Knapp, Richard and Charles Hartsoe. *Play for America: The History of the National Recreation and Park Association.* Arlington, VA: National Recreation and Park Association, 1980.

Kraus, Richard. *Leisure in a Changing America: Multicultural Perspectives.* New York: Macmillan College Publishing, 1994.

Kraus, Richard. *Recreation Programming: A Benefits-Driven Approach.* Needham Heights, MA: Allyn & Bacon, 1997.

Kraus, Richard and Lawrence Allen. *Research and Evaluation in Recreation, Parks and Leisure Studies* (Scottsdale, AZ: Gorsuch Scarisbrick Publishers, 1997).

Kraus, Richard and John Shank. *Therapeutic Recreation Service: Principles and Practices.* Dubuque, IA: Wm. C. Brown, 1992.

Larrabee, Eric and Rolf Meyersohn. *Mass Leisure.* Glencoe, IL: The Free Press, 1958.

McFarland, Elsie. *The Development of Public Recreation in Canada.* Vanier City, Ontario, Canada: Canadian Parks/Recreation Association, 1970.

McGuire, Francis, Rosangela Boyd, and Raymond Tedrick. *Leisure and Aging: Ulyssean Living in Later Life.* Champaign, IL: Sagamore Publishing, 1996.

Mobley, Tony and Robert Toalson, eds., *Parks and Recreation in the 21st Century, Chapters I and II.* Arlington, VA: National Recreation and Park Association, 1992, 1993.

Mundy, Jean and Debby Smith. *Leisure Education: Theory and Practice.* Champaign, IL: Sagamore Publishing, 1996.

Murphy, James, E. William Niepoth, Jynn Jamieson, and John Williams. *Leisure Systems: Critical Concepts and Applications.* Champaign, IL: Sagamore Publishing, 1991.

Nash, Jay B. *Philosophy of Recreation and Leisure.* Dubuque, IA: Wm. C. Brown, 1960.

Pieper, Josef. *Leisure: The Basis of Culture.* New York: Mentor-Omega, 1963.

Rossman, J. Robert. *Recreation Programming: Designing Leisure Experiences.* Champaign, IL: Sagamore Publishing, 1994.

Schleien, Stuart, M. Tipton Ray, and Frederick Green. *Community Recreation and People with Disabilities: Strategies for Inclusion.* Baltimore, MD: Paul Brookes Publishing, 1996.

Searle, Mark and Russell Brayley. *Leisure Services in Canada: An Introduction.* State College, PA: Venture Publishing, 1993.

Sessoms, H. Douglas and Karla Henderson. *Introduction to Leisure Services.* State College, PA: Venture Publishing, 1994.

Torkildsen, George. *Leisure and Recreation Management.* London: E. and F. N. Spon, 1992.

Index